The RAGE of PARTY

The RAGE *of* PARTY

HOW WHIG VERSUS TORY MADE MODERN BRITAIN

GEORGE OWERS

C

CONSTABLE

CONSTABLE

First published in Great Britain in 2025 by Constable

5 7 9 10 8 6 4

Copyright © George Owers, 2025

The moral right of the author has been asserted.

A CIP catalogue record for this book
is available from the British Library.

ISBN: 978-1-40871-909-1 (hardback)

Typeset in Perpetua by SX Composing DTP, Rayleigh, Essex
Printed and bound in Great Britain by Clays Ltd, Elcograf S.p.A.

Papers used by Constable are from well-managed forests
and other responsible sources.

FSC
www.fsc.org

MIX
Paper | Supporting
responsible forestry
FSC® C104740

Constable
An imprint of
Little, Brown Book Group
Carmelite House
50 Victoria Embankment
London EC4Y 0DZ

The authorised representative
in the EEA is
Hachette Ireland
8 Castlecourt Centre, Dublin 15,
D15 XTP3, Ireland
(email: info@hbgi.ie)

An Hachette UK Company
www.hachette.co.uk

www.littlebrown.co.uk

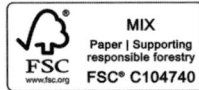

To Clare, the best wife a man could have.

To my beloved sons Charles and James.

Contents

Introduction

On the day that the 2017 general election was called, a lady called Brenda, hailing from Bristol, clearly summed up the feelings of many poll-weary voters when she exclaimed: 'You're joking! Not another one! For God's sake, I can't honestly, I can't stand this . . . there's too much politics going on at the moment.'[1]

Brenda should be very glad that she did not live during the reigns of William III and Queen Anne. Between 1695 and 1715, there were ten general elections, and political partisanship gripped England to an extent seldom known before or since. Two political parties – Tory and Whig – engaged in a ferocious and all-consuming political battle royale over issues of religion, monarchical succession, foreign policy, finance and much more besides.

In retrospect, we can see that this was in some – but by no means all – respects the last gasp of the devastating political conflict that had gripped the country since the 1640s, arguably even before. All the antipathies of the Civil War, between Cavalier and Roundhead, the Church of England and the Puritans, were revived and transformed into a new era of partisan strife. The battle, although rambunctious, polarising and sporadically violent, allowed the nation to negotiate its way through a tumultuous period without another civil war or major bloodshed.

This political conflict – usually known as the 'Rage of Party' – was extraordinary in intensity and duration. At the level of high politics, it was a tale of peculation, betrayal, attempted assassination, whoring, outrageously cynical parliamentary scheming and even sensational accusations of lesbianism. It crept into every aspect of British public life, from the Queen's bedchamber and the House of Commons down to the crevices of everyday life, from which doctor or astrologer one patronised to which coffee-house one supped in. This book aims to tell this story.

During the summer of 1709, thousands of exhausted, traumatised refugees arrived in London. They were from the Palatinate, a region of Germany that had been devastated by the aggression of the French army of Louis XIV and the general upheaval created by years of European conflict. Famine and illness had reduced their war-weary homeland to near desperate straits. By the time they arrived in England, they were in an appalling condition. Several Lutheran ministers who attended to them reported that they had found 'often 20 to 30 men and women together with their Children in one room'.[2] Many of them were 'very sikly and that severall of 'em are dead here already'.[3] They hoped that their flight to England – and perhaps thereafter to the American colonies – would be their salvation.

Luckily for them, the British government of the day was dominated by the Whigs, who were sympathetic to the plight of the refugees. Not only did the general Christian duty to welcome the stranger apply but they also saw the Palatines as plucky Protestant heroes owed help and assistance by their European co-religionists. The Whigs also hoped that these refugees would prove an economic boon, in the same way that previous waves of Protestant immigration – most notably the Huguenots some decades earlier – had. Many of the Huguenots had been skilled artisans who had bought new skills and expertise, in areas such as silk weaving and banking, to England and bolstered their new country's economic prospects. The assumption was that the Palatines would be similar. In any case, as one pamphlet put it, 'Wealth increases in an equal Proportion to the additional Number of Inhabitants': immigration would make Britain richer almost by definition.[4] So, in order to allow the Palatine incomers to settle in England, the Whigs passed the Foreign Protestants Naturalisation Act in early 1709.

Not everyone was as welcoming as the Whigs. England itself was suffering badly. Years of economic strain created by continual, eye-wateringly expensive warfare had been tipped into outright crisis by the winter of 1708–9, which was the worst anyone could remember. Bread prices rocketed up due to a poor harvest. Many of London's own poor had been reduced to outright destitution, and the British state had few mechanisms to assist them. Having to compete for what private charity existed with thousands of foreigners was not popular.

As such, the Whigs' great rivals – the Tories – had much popular support in their outright opposition to allowing the Palatines into England. Far from being an economic boon, they argued, the Palatines would prove a massive drain on an already stretched country. 'Poor industrious' English families would be ruined by competition for scarce jobs. In any case, the influx of foreigners would be resented by people hostile to rapid social change, which could cause civil disorder: one Tory complained of the 'universal Disgust and Jealousy throughout the Nation' occasioned by the arrival of the Palatines, leading to many 'Complaints and Commotions in London, and elsewhere, on occasion of Foreigners'.[5]

One such 'commotion', witnessed near Harrow on the Hill, is recorded by Thomas Hearne, an ultra-Tory Oxford scholar, who gave an account of it in his diary:

> 3 or four honest Englishmen being got together, and being drinking a Pot or two of Ale, they happened to see the said Palatines go by, and of course they made some Reflections upon the Receiving of these People into the Kingdom; which being heard by one of the Palatines, he gave a hint to his Companions, & they all immediately came into the Room, beat the Persons in a very rude and inhumane manner, and were about to have cut their Throats, but the Constable being call'd in and a number rais'd they were over-power'd in their Attempt; but instead of receiving condign Punishment when they were had before a Justice of Peace they were dismiss'd with a soft Reprimand, & the answer given for this Easy Penaltie was that being Forreigners they were ignorant of our English Laws, & 'twould be a piece of Barbarity to make them subject to it as yet.[6]

Hearne's view was clear: not only was the English working man being swamped by foreigners, he could also expect to face two-tier justice if he stood up to them.

The influx of Palatines to England turned into a disaster. They were not skilled silk weavers or adroit financiers but mostly vineyard workers. Expertise in wine production was of little use in England. Their only real economic option was to compete for unskilled jobs with the native poor, and such jobs were scarce indeed in 1709. Most could not speak English and so integration was difficult. The government found it impossible to work out what to do with them: it tried to pay parishes across the country to take them in, but there was almost no take up. Eventually, the government dumped most of them in Ireland, where they had few prospects and little assistance. They found conditions there little better than their ravaged homeland, and before long many ended up returning to Germany. A Tory-dominated government repealed the Foreign Protestants Naturalisation Act a few years later.

The 'Poor Palatines' debate, as it became known, neatly touches on almost every single one of the major controversies that made the political conflict known as the 'Rage of Party' consequential then, and resonant today. This struggle, the first major bout of party-political polarisation in English history, reached its climax between 1689 and 1714. It emerged partly as a function of the tumultuous conflicts that had roiled England in the seventeenth century, and partly as a response to the huge new challenges that arose at the dawn of the eighteenth century. It was a momentous political conflict that would determine the fate of a country which, by the end of the century, would be one of the world's great superpowers.

It is usual to see the enormous upheavals of seventeenth-century England – most dramatically the Civil War between Charles I and Parliament in the 1640s – as a process whereby England was transformed from a country that was in some respects still a late medieval state, in which the monarchy and the Church remained the most fundamental sources of authority, to a country transformed by the dynamic forces of liberal modernity, on the cusp of capitalism, representative government, religious pluralism and empire.

The path to this outcome was not straightforward. The attempt to rule England as a republic in the 1650s, after the execution of Charles I, eventually collapsed under the weight of its own chaotic contradictions, notwithstanding Oliver Cromwell's temporarily successful attempt to weld it together under his leadership, and an exhausted country, unsure what else to do, brought back the monarchy. The Restoration of Charles II in 1660 seemed, at least superficially, like the triumph of the old forces, as the monarchy and the Church of England reasserted their power.

However, the disastrous attempt by Charles II's successor, Catholic King James II, to rule in increasingly arbitrary and authoritarian fashion led to a revolution – the 'Glorious Revolution' of 1688–9 – which established a qualified though crucial victory for the forces of modernity. Although monarchy remained and the constitution was not dramatically transformed, Parliament's authority was finally confirmed, basic liberties confirmed by the passing of the Bill of Rights, and a degree of religious toleration introduced under a new king, Dutchman William III. The country had reached the political settlement that would underpin its eighteenth-century rise to the status of economic and military powerhouse, great European power, and imperial top dog.

Although there is much truth in this broad-brush picture of the conflicts of the seventeenth century, it is incomplete. The Glorious Revolution itself may have been a precondition of Britain's rise to either liberty-loving greatness, or self-interested oligarchy and imperialist hubris (according to taste), but it was by no means conclusive. The final and definitive battle over the sort of country Britain should be was fought in the twenty-five-year period after the Glorious Revolution, during the reigns of William III and Queen Anne, in which one party (the Whigs) fought to defend and expand the logic of 1688–9, and another (the Tories) fought a rearguard action against it. The Whigs ultimately won, a victory marked by the unleashing of the political power of finance and banking in the form of the creation and growing importance of the Bank of England and the national debt, the enormously expanded power of the military-fiscal state, and the acceptance of an important, albeit incomplete, measure of religious toleration and pluralism.

* * *

To understand this process, we need to grasp the central importance of three things, all ultimately connected: religion, war and money.

The Reformation of the sixteenth century had made England into an overwhelmingly Protestant country. However, during the reigns of Elizabeth I and James I, and then even more spectacularly under Charles I, it became clear that English Protestantism was chronically divided. Crudely put, the crux of this division was between a more conservative vision of Protestantism, which retained the medieval Catholic idea of the church as a divine and authoritative body with considerable social and political power, and a more radical and individualist one influenced heavily by continental movements such as Calvinism. This divide – between defenders of the established Church of England, and especially its 'High Church' faction, and the movement that became known as Puritanism – was one of the chief factors behind the Civil War.

After the Restoration, this cleavage became crystallised permanently in the form of the division between the Church of England and the heirs to the Puritans, the 'Dissenters', the more thoroughgoing Protestants who 'dissented' from the Church. Between 1660 and 1689, a battle ensued whereby the establishment churchmen – the early basis of the Tory Party – tried to completely suppress Dissent, and the Dissenters, supported in due course by their Whig political allies, attempted to establish their right to freedom of worship. In 1689, the Dissenters won a real but partial victory when the Toleration Act was passed, which essentially made their worship and existence legal, although it did not give them full political rights. This was the extent of the religious toleration won by the Glorious Revolution.

For the Tories, the political party that represented the authoritative claims of the Church of England to be the one and only legitimate Christian, protestant Church, this development was a baleful one. To them, the Dissenters were rebels who undermined the religious basis of order and stability – the Church of England – and who had been responsible for the 'Great Rebellion' (the Civil War). The Tories feared that the increased status and legal rights of the Dissenters could only lead to new threats to political order and social stability.

These threats, also enmeshed in such religious questions, increasingly came from outside too. The mid-to-late seventeenth century was characterised by the rise of France to the position of Europe's premier superpower, the result of the aggressively expansionist foreign policy of Louis XIV, the 'Sun King'. His continuous wars of expansion were inevitably seen by many in Europe in religious terms. Louis had pursued an aggressively Catholic policy internally, revoking the edict of Nantes, which gave toleration to French Protestants, and then persecuting them. Externally, he had also spent much time and effort attempting to annex the Dutch Republic, one of the most important Protestant (specifically Calvinist) powers in Europe. Although he also fought against the Habsburg Empire, a fellow Catholic power, many in western Europe saw Louis XIV as conducting a religious war to crush Protestantism and establish a 'universal Catholic monarchy' in Europe.

The actions of Louis XIV drove the Whig view of foreign policy. The Whigs defined themselves most fundamentally by opposition to the Tories' support for the total religious and political monopoly of the Church of England. They were sympathetic to the Dissenters and emphasised the importance of uniting Protestants, domestic and foreign, against the real enemy, Catholic France. This was turbocharged by the fact that, during the Glorious Revolution, the Whigs had supported replacing a Catholic monarch – James II – with a Dutch Calvinist, William III. However, James and his supporters – the 'Jacobites' – did not give up on the idea of regaining the throne for him and his heirs, and to do this they sought the help of Louis XIV. Supporting war in Europe against the French, to defend Protestant comrades in Europe like the Dutch and prevent any chance of Louis XIV reimposing James or his son on the English (and Scottish) thrones, was the crux of Whig policy.

The Tories had a very different view. Although no friends to Roman Catholicism, they saw the disputes of Europe as being someone else's problem. They were generally hostile, or at best indifferent, to most European expressions of Protestantism. They saw Calvinists such as the Dutch as equivalent to English Dissenters, kindred spirits to the rebels and traitors that their Cavalier forebears had fought during the Civil War. As such, they were instinctively sceptical towards any English involvement in

7

European wars: why should English money and blood be wasted on helping Dutch Calvinists?

Their scepticism towards war was also rooted in their misgivings about how such a war was to be funded and fought. England had not fought a significant land war on continental Europe since the Hundred Years' War in the medieval period. War had got only more complex and expensive since then: paying for it would require an enormously increased load of taxes, vastly expanded state borrowing and a much bigger, more modern state apparatus. The Tories' core supporters were disproportionately drawn from the lower and middle ranks of the landed gentry, the 'squirearchy', who would bear the brunt of increased taxes (as land taxes were the chief fiscal instrument of the state at that point). Worse, those taxes would in part be used to pay the interest on a burgeoning national debt, facilitated by new and vastly more sophisticated financial institutions, most obviously the Bank of England, founded under Whig auspices in 1694.

Who were the bankers and financiers who profited from these innovations? To a disproportionate extent, they were Dissenters, who – partly because they were legally excluded from various aspects of social and political life – tended to gravitate towards occupations like finance. This meant that war would effectively suck wealth away from the Tory squires towards the Whigs and the Dissenting moneylenders. The dependence of the state on financiers who were either Dissenters or sympathetic to Dissent would make it ever more impossible to reimpose the Church's sole authority on English society, as Dissenters would hardly fund a state that was religiously hostile to them – the forces of religious pluralism and financial innovation were intertwined. Furthermore, the whole process of transforming the small and rackety English state into a machine capable of funding and fighting a massive European war would, many Tories feared, create a vast new body of bureaucrats, hangers-on and toadies, all of whom would have a financial interest in perpetuating war and supporting the Whig policy.

In short, the Tories' great fear was that the intertangled tentacles of war, taxes, debt and Dissenters, represented by their Whig enemies, would drag the Old England they knew into the murky depths of chaos and instability. New dynamics – of religious pluralism, impersonal financial transactions and growing state power – would undermine the stability and morality of an agrarian country governed by the authority of squire and parson and create an uprooted, uncertain commercial society in which all that was solid would melt into air, all that was holy would be profaned. Their discontent was made more intense and confused by the fact that the accession of William III as king had meant that their traditional (if often deeply ambiguous or unhelpful) ally in upholding the status quo – the monarchy – was no longer necessarily, or even usually, on their side.

The simple reality was that a Dutchman becoming king had made it practically impossible for England to keep out of continental war. William III had a claim to the English throne by virtue of being Charles I's grandson, and when he exploited the unpopularity of James II and made that claim into a reality during the Glorious Revolution, his main objective was to bring England into the Dutch Republic's war with France, which he duly did in 1689. England would remain the great ally of the Dutch in its bloody conflict against France throughout the course of the Nine Years War (1689–97) and then the War of the Spanish Succession (1702–12). The process of fighting these wars was to make the Tory vision of peace, low taxes and securing the privileges of the Church ever more difficult to implement. Their battle to do so against their Whig opponents – a truly epic and lively struggle that aggressively polarised England along cultural, religious and economic lines for a generation – is the subject of this book.

It is perhaps clearer now how the debate over the Poor Palatines, with which this chapter started, is such a perfect microcosm of the wider 'Rage of Party' between Whig and Tory, and the basic issues of religion, war and money that fuelled it.

For the Whigs, it was completely natural to support continental Protestants who were the victims of Louis XIV's wars of aggression. In their eyes, pan-Protestant solidarity across Europe was crucial to secure triumph in the great military struggle against the papist menace posed by Catholic France (and possibly the Jacobites too). Furthermore, the Whigs hoped that the refugees consisted of a new wave of dynamic financiers and entrepreneurs who could help forge the modernised Britain of Whig dreams. Immigration expressed their cosmopolitanism and their support for vibrant commercial dynamism.

The Tories, on the other hand, were aghast at an influx of European Protestants, mostly Calvinists and Lutherans. Such newcomers were unlikely to be in communion with the Church of England: most likely they would help swell the ranks of the Dissenters further and undermine the Tories' vision of national cohesion and stability, which was based predominantly on the religious monopoly of the Church of England. For them, the Palatines were just another burden produced by the never-ending, ruinous European war that was pauperising them and enriching their religious enemies. Furthermore, the newcomers would either prove to be as the Whigs claimed – i.e. a new wave of treacherous financiers and bankers helping to sell England to the highest bidder – or would simply add to the travails of the native poor.

The contemporary echoes of the debate over the Poor Palatines are obvious, and it is not an isolated case. The origins of numerous political cleavages that persist today litter this book. Although the forms taken by such debates have naturally changed over the previous 300 years and are noticeably less driven by openly religious considerations, the 'family resemblances' between them and modern political divisions are only too glaring. Perhaps most obviously, the contrast between one view of English politics that stresses the importance of cosmopolitan openness to the world and the importance of engaging with Europe on questions of economics and security, and another which is sceptical of involving Britain in foreign entanglements, alliances and 'forever wars', and places greater weight on the importance of maintaining a cohesive sense of common national identity and culture, is clearly still with us, even if it doesn't map very neatly onto twenty-first-century party politics.

This shouldn't be surprising, as we still live in a society shaped, more or less directly, by many of the institutions, changes and attitudes produced by the era of the 'Rage of Party'. The new fiscal-military state created by the gradual victory of the Whigs was the basis of Britain's rise to imperial greatness throughout the rest of the eighteenth century, culminating in Britain's triumphs in both the Seven Years War and the Napoleonic Wars.

The British Empire in anything like the form it ended up taking, for good or ill, is unthinkable without the innovations that took place during these years. The Bank of England and the City of London are still the great decision-making centres of much of our economy, which is now far more financialised than even the most sophisticated Whig of the 1690s could have ever dreamed of. The Union between England and Scotland was, as we shall see, a product of wrangling for party advantage between Whigs and Tories as much as anything else.

The Whig victory during the 'Rage of Party' helped to unleash all manner of structural forces, economic and political, that continue to shape us and our politics. But whatever else it was, Whig versus Tory was also a culture war, and one fought in terms as vitriolic, and rooted as much in conflicting senses of identity, as any social media spat in the twenty-first century. This legacy still shapes us, not least because the divide upon which it was based most fundamentally, between the Church of England and Dissent, continued to form one of the most fundamental cultural and social dividing lines in British politics until the early twentieth century. Although that divide has now faded with secularisation and the precipitous decline of all Christian denominations, culture is 'sticky': its imprints endure for centuries. The fading of its original religious framework doesn't mean that the attitudes this divide produced have disappeared. Anyone who listened to both Remainers and Leavers express their astonishment that anyone would even have considered voting for the other side during the Brexit referendum – a classic conflict between Tory nationalism and Whig cosmopolitanism – was hearing an audible echo of that historical culture war play itself out 300 years later.

Although the Church–Dissent cultural divide had origins earlier than Whig versus Tory – most notably in Cavalier versus Roundhead during the Civil War – it was the 'Rage of Party' that embedded it in its enduring form in British life and made it the centre of a stable pattern of more-or-less peaceful party-inflected politics. This relates to its other enormous contribution to politics as we understand it today. In an important sense, the 'Rage of Party' was the means by which the unsettled business of the Civil War was regularised and then (more-or-less) resolved. In the process, the bitter hatreds and religious polarisation of that upheaval were subsumed into conflict between two political parties who gradually gave up the use of violence as the central means of resolving their conflicts.

Battles and executions gave way to election hustings and fierce parliamentary disputes. Whig versus Tory domesticated the conflict that emerged in the 1640s. This process was not without its untidy edges: as we shall see, partisan mobs beat each other senseless at election time, leading politicians killed each other in duels and politicians found themselves in the Tower of London. The threat of Jacobitism meant that civil war remained a real possibility. However, broadly speaking, Englishmen learned to settle their intractable political divisions without killing each other.

That is perhaps the most positive enduring legacy of the 'Rage of Party', but to contemporaries it was the heat of the battle that was most striking. It is to the story of how this battle took shape and played itself out that we now turn, beginning with the origins of Whig and Tory in the reign of Charles II.

Note: I have often used the language of the time in this book. For example, I often use the term 'papist' or similar to refer to Roman Catholics. This is meant as no slur on Roman Catholics: it simply makes sense to use the language that was so widely current at the time. In general, I am not in favour of editing the language used by historical figures to cater to contemporary fashion and moral tastes. It was what it was.

Please also bear in mind that 'Britain' does not come into existence until 1707: England and Scotland shared the same monarch, through a union of the crowns, but were separate polities. Before 1707, except when referring to events in the future, I accordingly refer to England, which, to prevent this book becoming even longer than it already is, is the overwhelming focus of the book, except insofar as I examine Scotland in the context of the Union of 1707.

1

The Birth of Whig and Tory

In 1678, a foul-mouthed ex-Anabaptist pederast with a chin the size and shape of a small ironing board threw a grenade into the already-none-too-placid world of English politics. His name was Titus Oates.[1]

On 28th September, Oates and his associate Israel Tonge, a mentally disturbed Protestant fanatic, appeared before the Privy Council, a body composed of the King's chief ministers and advisers. By the time Oates was called to address them, the King, Charles II, and his brother James, Duke of York, had just left for Newmarket for a spot of racing. Their cousin, Prince Rupert of the Rhine – the heroic Royalist cavalry commander of the Civil War who was by now a confused geriatric riddled with syphilis – was left in the chair as the King's senior advisers and ministers settled down to listen. One imagines that Oates's discourse was lively enough to penetrate even the muddled brain of the old Cavalier hero.

Without notes, Oates fluently launched into a summary of a hair-raising deposition, containing eighty-one articles, that he had recently sworn to before a justice of the peace, Sir Edmund Godfrey.

The deposition claimed that Oates had, courtesy of his time spent among Roman Catholic priests, stumbled across evidence of an intricate plot to kill King Charles II, foment a massive armed uprising in Scotland and forcibly convert England back to Rome at the point of the sword. Oates accused an unholy alliance of Jesuit priests, Benedictines, Dominicans and even 'people in high places' of a monstrous conspiracy that, if real, threatened to plunge the country back into outright civil war.

The Popish Plot was born.

One might wonder why anyone would listen to Oates, and still less Tonge, with anything other than disdain and disbelief.

Tonge was a well-known lunatic who had spent some time trying to convince anyone who would listen that the Jesuits were responsible for pretty much every single major modern disaster, ranging from the Great Fire of London to the execution of Charles I.

Titus Oates was perhaps less obviously insane, but he was no one's idea of trustworthy. Notoriously coarse and mendacious, he had developed a reputation for his 'Canting Fanatical way' as early as his undergraduate days at St John's College, Cambridge.[2] The son of an Anabaptist who had been a chaplain in the New Model Army during the Civil War, Oates managed to find a benefice in the Church of England in 1673 despite this extreme puritan background and the fact that he was, according to his Cambridge tutor, 'a great dunce'.[3] Stupid as he may have been, he was to prove to have one pre-eminent talent: being a tremendously prolific and inventive fantasist.

He quickly fell out with his Church of England congregation, who accused him of being a drunkard prone to 'use some very indecent expressions concerning the mysteries of the Christian religion'.[4] He returned home to Hastings, where he disgraced himself by making wild accusations of sodomy and treason against a local rival family. He was promptly found guilty of perjury and fled to become the chaplain of the frigate HMS *Adventure*. Swiftly kicked out of the navy for, ironically enough, 'homosexual practices' (he became notorious for his predilection for sex with young boys), he soon found himself on his uppers. His solution to his poverty was to convert to Rome (almost certainly insincerely) and sponge off various priests and Jesuits.[5]

In December 1677, one of his much put-upon Roman Catholic allies, Father Richard Strange, decided that it was a good idea to allow Oates to attend the Jesuit seminary in St Omer. Heartily hated and derided by his fellow students, one of whom allegedly 'broke a pan about his head for recreation', he was, despite his professed desire to be admitted into Jesuit orders, expelled from the seminary in July 1678.[6] He returned to England penniless and without a friend in the world, except one: Israel Tonge.

Tonge, having listened to Oates's lurid 'testimony' of a Jesuit plot, had managed to make contact with the King via a friend, Christopher Kirkby, who had met Charles due to their mutual interest in amateur chemistry. Tonge and Oates managed to contrive a personal meeting with the King to inform him of the threat to his life by hanging around Whitehall and waiting for him to make his habitual early morning walk in St James's Park. Charles II himself was sceptical, but any threat to his life could not simply be dismissed out of hand. His chief minister, the Earl of Danby, was inclined to give Tonge and Oates a hearing.

The specific details of Oates's testimony were shocking. Oates claimed to have recently attended 'a secret conclave of the Jesuits held at the White Horse tavern in London on 24th April 1678' in which they plotted open treason and a papist military uprising.[7] Even more sensationally, he accused Edward Coleman, a clerk who worked in the household of the Duke and Duchess of York, of having had secret correspondence with Louis XIV's confessor concerning the plot. The implication was clear: James, Duke of York, the King's brother and heir (and himself a Roman Catholic convert), was uncomfortably close to the plot, possibly involved.

People listened to Oates – despite the fact that he was a convicted perjurer – for several reasons. His deposition – a bizarre mish-mash of gossip, mad digressions and very specific allegations – contained the name of many real Jesuit priests and a number of meetings that had actually taken place. Oates gave a very convincing performance to the Privy Council: his fluent oral testimony coincided almost perfectly with the written deposition in terms of the details of names and dates. He larded it with plenty of apparently plausible circumstantial details. The council began to take it seriously.

The plot was, however, a gigantic tissue of lies, the invention of Oates's fertile, fevered imagination. He almost certainly saw it as an opportunity to trade off his insider knowledge of English Jesuits, to save himself from total penury, and whitewash his reputation.

15

None of this prevented his astounding accusations quickly becoming a public sensation. In fact, they were soon to trigger a series of events that led to the birth of party politics in England.

Oates's lurid tale had the explosive impact that it did because it fed directly into a rich seam of bigotry that had a long history.[8]

English political and religious culture by the late seventeenth century had few more stubbornly engrained prejudices than fear and hatred of Roman Catholicism. Papists were the perennial bogeymen always lurking in the shadows. Burning effigies of the Pope was one of the period's great pastimes, both as carnivalesque entertainment and political statement.

By the 1670s, generations of Englishmen had been brought up within the culture of anti-Catholicism. Politically, Protestantism was almost universally seen as synonymous with liberty and national independence; Roman Catholicism with slavery and bondage to hostile foreign powers (traditionally the Spanish Empire but, as it declined, increasingly France). Spiritually, in this view, the corruption of the Church during the Middle Ages had led to the true essence of Christianity being buried under a 'welter of vain and irrelevant ceremonies'.[9] The priesthood and papacy had arrogated to itself an unconscionable and financially corrupt degree of spiritual (and indeed political) authority.

This was presented within a popular Protestant historical narrative which painted Catholics as bloody fanatics who wished to snuff out the light of the Gospel by murder and collaboration with tyrannical regimes abroad. This story highlighted the execution of Protestant martyrs under Queen ('Bloody') Mary; the plots against Elizabeth (usually portrayed as sainted Protestant heroine 'Gloriana') and attempted invasion by the Spanish Armada in 1588; the Gunpowder Plot; the military despotism of Louis XIV; and various other alleged or real plots and bloodbaths. John Foxe's *Acts and Monuments*, commonly known as Foxe's Book of Martyrs, was a colossally influential book, read avidly by generations of Englishmen, which inculcated this view with its lurid tales of brave Protestant martyrs being persecuted and incinerated by unhinged papist princes, priests, prelates and popes during the Reformation.

Almost all depravities and vices were attributed to papists. By definition they could never be real patriots, as their first loyalties were always to the Pope, foreign Catholic regimes and, generally speaking, the Roman Catholic Church, seen as a sort of quasi-criminal international conspiracy. Their untrustworthiness was a byword: it was widely believed that they were under no obligation, by papal dispensation, to tell the truth to 'heretics' (that is, Protestants). Papists were even blamed for the Great Fire of London in 1666; indeed, just about any fire or act of arson was habitually blamed on Catholics. They were widely seen as sexual deviants too, particularly Catholic priests, whose clerical celibacy was seen as a cover for innumerable unspeakable vices. The Jesuits came in for particular scorn as the most malignant of all, secretive, sinister agents of the papist Antichrist.

There was, of course, an element of truth to this picture: Mary had burnt a lot of Protestants and Protestant England had had to fight hard to maintain its religion and independence during the Elizabethan years. By the mid-to-late seventeenth century, however, Roman Catholics in England were a tiny minority: around 60,000 adults in the reign of Charles II in total, which amounted to around 1.2 per cent of the overall population.[10] The majority of Catholics in the country wished for little more than the right to be left alone to worship in private. True, the Old Faith was more common among the social and political elite, particularly in the courts of Charles II and James II, where a small number could hope to exercise genuine political influence, at least for a time. The aggressive actions of Louis XIV against French Protestants had also caused an understandably anguished and fearful reaction among their co-religionists across Europe, including in England. However, the idea that there were hordes of bloodthirsty English papists waiting to inflict mass murder upon their Protestant countrymen at the drop of a papal tiara was utterly farfetched. It was nonetheless widely believed.

It is not hard, therefore, to understand why the Popish Plot landed on fertile ground.

It was not, however, simply the longstanding history of anti-papist feeling that explains why Oates's accusations were so potent. During the 1670s, the actions of Charles II and his brother and heir James, Duke of York, had provoked more 'respectable' political figures into suspecting that a popish plot of less outlandish proportions was already afoot at the highest levels of English politics.[11]

When the monarchy had been restored in 1660, it had been an act of political exhaustion. Endless constitutional permutations had failed and only the military dictatorship of Cromwell had prevented total disorder. In the period of confusion following Cromwell's death even some of the more moderate Puritans, including many Presbyterians, supported the return of Charles II as king. They hoped that it would represent a return to stability, and that Charles would give them a degree of religious toleration in exchange for their support.

They were disappointed. There were two sides to Charles II's religious policy. Firstly, a sneaking regard for Roman Catholicism, which would end in deathbed conversion to the Old Faith. Secondly, and far more importantly, a ruthless pragmatism driven almost solely by his desire to consolidate his own power. In general, this led him to use the Church of England as the main religious support for his rule, but he always saw to it that he had other options open.

The chief of these was an alliance with France, which had the potential to ease the purse strings of Louis XIV, the absolute monarch of the most powerful Catholic power in Europe, and thereby allow Charles to rule without the tiresome necessity of calling the parliaments he otherwise needed to keep him in funds. One price of this alliance, sealed in the secret provisions of the 1670 Treaty of Dover, was a promise by Charles to Louis to himself convert to Roman Catholicism, and, in time, to bring his kingdom itself back into the papist fold.

Although Charles had no intention of publicly avowing Roman Catholicism, as he knew that Protestant England would not wear it, he was quite happy to make sufficient gestures in that direction to satisfy the French and procure him funds. Accordingly, in 1672 he had issued a Declaration of Indulgence, which suspended all penal laws in England against both Roman Catholics (and Dissenters). It came at the same time as he had agreed to give the French military support in their war against the Protestant Dutch Republic. The suspicions of many stout Protestant MPs began to rise, and the political reaction was swift.

Parliament not only forced Charles to withdraw his Declaration but also, in a determination to stamp out any hint of pro-Catholic sentiment and assert themselves, in March 1673 they passed the Test Act, which made taking communion within the Church of England – as well as a declaration against the Roman doctrine of transubstantiation – a prerequisite of holding public office.

Soon after, anti-papist fervour reached new heights when long-standing rumours that the King's brother, James, Duke of York, the next in line to the throne, had himself converted to popery were confirmed. In response to the Test Act, he resigned as Lord High Admiral and refused to take communion within the Church of England. It was tantamount to an admission of his being a Roman Catholic and made entirely plausible rumours that the court and government were riddled with papism. It heralded the possibility of a Catholic King, an idea that was utterly taboo in the minds of most Englishmen.

Events boiled over further with the revelation a few months later that James had married a Roman Catholic princess, Mary of Modena. As James had had only female children (both brought up Protestant) with his previous wife, Anne Hyde, this reignited the chances of James producing a male heir to the throne, and almost certainly a Roman Catholic one. The prospect loomed of a Catholic royal dynasty.

The reaction was far from measured. A wave of anti-Catholic hysteria swept the nation. Crowds in London gathered to burn effigies of the Pope. One pamphlet wrote that 'the certain consequences of a Popish government' were 'bloody massacres and inhuman Smithfield butcheries'.[12] One of the leading parliamentary scaremongers, Lord Shaftesbury, 'told the Lords that there were sixteen thousand papists in London ready to try desperate measures and that nobody's life was safe'.[13] In response Charles ordered all Roman Catholics to leave London and remain at least ten miles away.

The behaviour of Charles and James had, in short, poured fuel on the fire of engrained English anti-papism. A significant opposition group in parliament seriously saw Charles's alliance with the French, combined with the prospect of the heir to the throne becoming and then marrying a papist, as the prelude to the institution of absolutist Roman Catholic rule on the model of Louis XIV. The situation threatened to spiral out of control, and Charles realised that he had no choice but to backtrack and change policy.

The mainstay of this new approach was to return to his most solid basis of domestic political strength: the old 'Church and King' party, rooted in the authority of the Church of England. To this end, in 1673, he appointed a new chief minister, Thomas Osborne, soon to become the Earl of Danby. A man of solid old Cavalier family and unimpeachable Anglican credentials, Danby was a doughty and dependable, albeit bombastic and rarely popular, Yorkshire squire. Even his friend John Evelyn noted that, although 'a man of excellent natural parts', he had 'nothing generous or gratefull in him'.[14]

Danby was, however, an often brutally effective political manager who devised a clever agenda to negotiate this new, febrile political atmosphere. Danby wished to simultaneously reverse the King's unpopular pro-French foreign policy and dampen down fears of papist influence, while reconstructing a solid basis of support for the government by returning to a policy of strict Anglican supremacy against the Dissenters. He thus began to systemically build up a bloc of dependable court MPs by liberal use of patronage and doling out pensions and other financial douceurs. He tried to tempt the King away from the lure of French gold by reconstituting his finances on a more solid footing, appealing to a hopefully pliant Commons to provide more generous supplies.

Why was it, then, that Charles, to shore up his reign, chose at this point to turn back to the 'Church interest', and in the process return from his short-lived policy of religious indulgence to once again renewing persecution of Dissenters? Who were the Dissenters anyway, and what role did they play in the politics of the era? To answer these questions, we need to briefly examine the recent religious and political history that formed the mental backdrop of men like Danby.

By the 1670s England was a country that had, within living memory, been torn apart by intra-Protestant religious hatreds which had immense political implications. Understanding the history of these divisions is crucial to understanding the rise of Tory and Whig.

By the reign of Charles I, the ambiguous Protestant religious settlement imposed by Elizabeth I had been destabilised by considerable polarisation within the Church of England.

On the one hand stood the Puritans. At first Puritanism predominantly took the form of a movement known as Presbyterianism, which was based upon Calvinist theology and a rigid determination to conform the Church to what its proponents saw as a pure, biblical model. This increasingly came to mean opposition to rule by bishops and a strong emphasis on strict spiritual, moral and social discipline instituted by the godly 'saints' who were predestined to eternal life by the unsearchable sovereignty of God. It emphasised the primacy of scripture and the importance of preaching (*lots* of preaching). Puritans were deeply suspicious of elements of the Elizabethan religious settlement, and wished to further reform and 'purify' the Church's doctrines and liturgy (as epitomised particularly by the Book of Common Prayer).

The Puritans were opposed by the High Church movement, which advocated a more (small 'c') catholic conception of the church as the 'mystical body' of Christ, in which sacraments and ritual played a crucial role in conveying God's grace. The High Churchmen increasingly came to see both episcopacy and monarchy as divinely ordained orders, based on the idea that Church and State were really two sides of the same coin, part of a single, unified Christian commonwealth. In this vision, both the spiritual authorities (bishops) and the secular authority (the king) were God-given and mutually supporting parts of one organic and hierarchical social and political body.

The High Churchmen were a minority, but in the 1630s they gained control of the church leadership under William Laud, Archbishop of Canterbury, and attempted to impose their more ritualistic form of Protestantism on the Church. Laud was not popular. He was seen as high-handed and his attempt to rethink the nature of the post-Reformation church was perceived by some as crypto-papism. Even many moderates thought that Laud was straying too far from the mainstream of English Reformation Protestantism and enforcing his views with too much vigour.

21

The religious policy of Laud, which was vigorously supported by Charles I, was – along with Puritan extremism – one of the chief causes of the Civil War, which was, ultimately, an intra-Protestant religious conflict. As the country descended into chaos and strife in the 1640s, gradually the Presbyterians, who dominated in parliament, gained ascendancy. They abolished bishops, banned the Book of Common Prayer, which they saw as an 'imperfect book culled and picked out of that popish dunghill, the Masse', and purged the clergy of men not loyal to their vision of Church government, which they imposed in the high-handed fashion of Laud.

However, their period of dominance was short, and their system of church governance was never properly implemented, for the chaos of the Civil War had conjured up new forces that they could not control. Puritan radicalism was not confined to the Presbyterians. A whole range of new, more extreme Protestant sects emerged in the years of war. They dominated Cromwell's New Model Army, and most of the leading Presbyterians were expelled from parliament during Pride's Purge in 1648.

During the political and religious chaos that ensued during the Commonwealth period, one constant endured: persecution of royalists and Anglicans, albeit at varying levels of intensity. Cromwell waxed and waned in terms of his attacks on the besieged Anglicans, but nonetheless all bar a minority of Churchmen who 'adapted' to the times were expelled from their livings. They were forced to meet and worship in secret to avoid arrest and prosecution.

The ironic result of these years was that Laudian High Churchmanship, previously a minority position within the Church of England (albeit one espoused by its leaders in the 1630s), began to become the Anglican mainstream. Persecution and the tireless efforts of the younger Laudians drove Churchmen increasingly towards a High Church position. By the time of the Restoration in 1660, to be a loyal royalist was increasingly to be a High Churchman.[15]

The Restoration in 1660 did not solve the country's religious tensions, despite promises by Charles II that he would allow 'liberty for tender consciences' and hints that he would accommodate the Presbyterians, if not the wilder sects. Instead, the High Churchmen gained the ascendancy, and, with the help of the new parliament, which was dominated by old Cavaliers, they passed a body of laws – known as the 'Clarendon Code' – that, in theory at least, outlawed Protestant Dissent. Dissenting religious meetings – 'conventicles' – were made illegal, and all holders of public office had to be communicants of the Church of England.

The men who rejected this vision – the heirs of the Puritans – were ejected from the Church of England in 1662. They formed what became known as Dissent, or Non-conformity: a significant and permanent body of Protestant Christians outside of the Church of England. Although the extent to which the Clarendon Code was enforced varied, and there were long periods where Dissenters were largely allowed to worship in peace, the divisions of English Protestantism were now formally entrenched.

Most Dissenters saw the High Churchmen as ritualistic quasi-papists whose emphasis on divine right episcopacy and monarchy led to absolutism. The High Churchmen saw the Dissenters as fanatical enthusiasts whose presumptuous rejection of all traditional authority, including bishops, led to rebellion and chaos. They rejected ideas of religious pluralism and wished to enforce the Church of England's spiritual and political monopoly.

In the middle were the Low Churchmen, who, although within the Church of England, sympathised with the Dissenters politically, were more sceptical about 'high' claims to divine episcopal authority, and advocated a less dogmatic approach to religion that tried to reconcile divisions through an emphasis on the 'essentials' of belief that united all Protestants.

As the High Churchmen had come to dominate the Church of England by the 1670s, the simple reality was that they were the most loyal prop of the Stuart monarchy. They were both zealous supporters of the authority of the King but also had the politically invaluable advantage of not being papists. Hence why Charles II turned, in the mid-1670s, to a 'Church and King' man from a solid Cavalier background: Danby.

Danby's task – re-establishing Charles II's authority in face of the growing fears of papist influence at court – was about to be made a lot more difficult by the dramatic revelations of Titus Oates.[16]

Oates's story did not stand up well to scrutiny. Early on in the proceedings, the King had torn holes in his testimony, which was riddled with inconsistencies and errors. Luckily for him, however, one of his accusations turned out to be more-or-less true by accident. The papers of Edward Coleman, the secretary of James's wife Mary, turned out to indeed contain treasonable correspondence with France, including wild talk of converting England to Roman Catholicism and 'the utter subduing of a pestilent heresy' (that is, Protestantism).[17]

Soon after, the magistrate who had taken down Oates's deposition, Sir Edmund Godfrey, was found murdered in a ditch on Primrose Hill, strangled and run through with his own sword. This mysterious death (which has never been satisfactorily explained) was widely taken as evidence of the reality of the plot.

The result, in 1678, was a particularly virulent example of one of England's periodic outbursts of mad anti-Catholic paranoia. In London, a young Catholic called William Staley was rapidly hanged, drawn and quartered for the crimes of speaking in French and accusing the King of being a heretic; in the provinces, stories of 'night-riders', armed bands of would-be Catholic assassins, proliferated. All fires were attributed to roving bands of papist arsonists. Wild rumours abounded. Put simply, in the autumn of 1678, many Englishmen and women went to bed every evening convinced that they would have their throats cut in the night by marauding parties of bloodthirsty papist murderers.

The opponents of Charles II were quick to seize on this hysterical atmosphere in order to attack both papist elements at court and the 'Church and King' policies of Anglican loyalists such as Danby. These men – who were initially known as the 'Country Party' but were soon to be called 'Whigs' – had been coalescing into an increasingly coherent parliamentary opposition for some time.

Lead by Anthony Ashley Cooper, Earl of Shaftesbury, they combined concerns about popery and the King's foreign policy with a general suspicion of the waste and corruption of Charles's court and fear that the independence and power of parliament were being undermined. Many started to worry that Danby's Royalist-Anglican regime, which had proven adept at managing parliament using patronage and preferment, was itself an agent of absolutist government.

Joined by more radical opponents of Charles – including out-and-out republican radicals who had opposed Cromwell's military dictatorship from the 'left' in the 1650s, many of them former Levellers – the Country Party believed that Protestant unity against the evil machinations of papists at home and abroad was paramount, and that it required a measure of toleration for Dissenters. They all saw the court as a hotbed of French vice and moral corruption (not, it has to be said, entirely inaccurately). They feared a king determined to rule without parliament, potentially using French gold to pay for a 'standing army' that could be used to establish outright military tyranny and papist domination.

What they feared most of all was the prospect of a papist king. When the accusations against Edward Coleman appeared to indirectly implicate James, the opposition realised that they had been gifted a loaded political gun. They would use the hysterical atmosphere created by Oates to demand that James, Duke of York, be excluded from the throne. This was by no means their only grievance – they continued to plug away at wider fears of papist influence and the growth of arbitrary government – but Exclusion gradually became their central focus.

They were a loose and multi-faceted group, little more than the bare kernel of anything that we would recognise as a 'political party'. Many of them were members of various political clubs that provided a degree of co-ordination when it came to propaganda and political tactics. The most famous of these was the Green Ribbon Club, formed as early as 1674, which met in the King's Head Tavern in Chancery Lane and sported the old colours of the Levellers.[18] It mixed together hot-headed republican extremists – mostly lawyers – and radical politicians, including many Exclusionist parliamentarians.

In the eyes of their opponents, the Green Ribbon Club was the shadowy nucleus of a powerful and disreputable cabal determined to destroy all sentiments of loyalty and undermine the Church. This latter view was given trenchant expression by staunch royalist Roger North, who described the club's members as:

> Carriers up and down, or Dispersers of seditious Talk, at proper Times, as Blood from the Heart, to nourish Sedition all over the Town, to the Exchange, Westminster, Coffee-Houses, and Sub-Coffee Houses.[19]

In reality, this view overestimates the centrality of the club: the Green Ribbon Club was only one example of a number of similar clubs, both in London and the provinces, organising a loosely co-ordinated, often ad hoc, campaign against the court; it was perhaps the most important, but by no means some centralised proto-Whig organisational nerve centre.

Nonetheless, the Exclusion campaign undoubtedly did have an important degree of national coherence. This can be seen particularly in terms of some of its important leaders, of whom the most significant was Anthony Ashley Cooper, the first Earl of Shaftesbury.

Shaftesbury was, depending on one's point of view, a shuffling opportunist chiefly notable for the fact that he betrayed nearly every single political leader in seventeenth-century English history from Charles I onwards, or a prudent man of principle who adapted with great facility to many vicissitudes in troubled political times. By the early 1670s, he had, in the space of thirty years, gone from royalist supporter of Charles I to Roundhead to servant of the Commonwealth to opponent of Cromwell to supporter of the Restoration to servant of Charles II – he was nicknamed the 'Dorsetshire Eel . . . because he could wriggle out of anyone's grasp'.[20] Nonetheless, a case can be made that underlying these many volte-faces lay a genuine, if somewhat shop-soiled, dedication to the cause of Protestantism and constitutional liberty.

What is not in doubt was that, despite appalling health and a notably diminutive stature – he possessed a 'pygmy body', as poet John Dryden described it – he was a natural-born leader.[21] When a student at Oxford, he had, altogether characteristically, led an undergraduate revolt against a plan by the authorities of Exeter College to water down the beer, a fact that must have inspired a soupçon of sympathy for the man in the breast of even his most determined opponent. He was charming and popular, brilliant at the softer arts of political organisation, and constantly tormented by the conflict between his raging ambition and high principles.

Nonchalantly casting aside the fact that, in the early 1670s, Shaftesbury had in fact been one of Charles II's leading ministers, by the mid-1670s he had adopted the role of anti-Catholic populist with energetic cynicism, and soon thereafter he became the chief assailant of the Danbyite 'Church and King' policy. In 1675 he had written (probably with some assistance from his political dogsbody and occasional personal doctor, John Locke) a pamphlet entitled *A Letter from a Person of Quality to his Friend in the Country*. This incendiary pamphlet was a brutal assault on 'the high Episcopal Man, and of the old Cavaliers' – that is, Danby and his supporters – whom he accused of wanting to institute a quasi-theocratic form of Anglican-monarchical absolutism:

> they design to have the Government of the Church Sworne to as Unalterable, and so Tacitely owned to be of Divine Right . . . Then in requital to the Crown, they declare the Government absolute and Arbitrary, and allow Monarchy as well as Episcopacy to be Jure Divino, and not to be bounded, or limited by human Laws.[22]

As this pamphlet shows, Shaftesbury and his Country supporters, had, by the time the Popish Plot set alight English politics, made it abundantly clear that they would stop at nothing to halt not only the creeping menace of court popery but also the iron fist of the Anglican Cavalier men.

In October 1678, parliament met for the first time since the Popish Plot had been 'uncovered', and Shaftesbury and his allies lost no time in exploiting the plot ruthlessly.

They soon whipped up the Commons into a state of hysteria, easily passing a motion stating that a 'damnable and hellish plot' was afoot to kill the King and destroy Protestantism.[23] Parliamentary committees to investigate the plot and bring prosecutions were quickly established. Oates soon made new, dramatic accusations, this time against five Catholic lords, who were quickly arrested. Before long, a rag-tag band of booze-sodden criminals, nuisance accusers and terrified simpletons had come forward to the authorities with new stories of alleged Catholic malfeasance to supplement Oates's story.

Shaftesbury and his allies gave every encouragement and support (including financial) to Oates and these new informers. A grim procession of trials, many of them travesties of justice, began, which resulted in the execution first of Coleman, and soon numerous innocent Catholic priests (who represented the final cohort of the more than 300 Catholics put to death for their religion in England since the first in 1535).

Danby's hope that he could exploit the situation himself by rallying loyalists to a king who had allegedly been the subject of an assassination plot soon proved illusory. Despite the fact that Danby had in fact been scheming for a war *against* France and was regarded by Louis XIV as an enemy – to the extent that French agents had begun to intrigue with, and bribe, leading opposition figures to dampen down pro-war, anti-French sentiment in parliament – the opposition soon moved to impeach him on the basis of his (reluctantly) obeying Charles II's direct orders to attempt to negotiate a further subsidy from France.

Although the Exclusionists dominated the Commons, the Lords, which was packed with Court supporters and bishops, would prove a tougher nut to crack. Shaftsbury and his allies began to realise that openly breaching the question of excluding James from the succession in this parliament would not succeed, but this was soon rendered a moot point by Charles's decision to dissolve parliament and call the first general election in nearly twenty years.

It was an understandable decision – the plight of Danby had reduced the court organisation within parliament into utter disarray, and Charles could see little basis for cohesive government under those circumstances – but it was a total miscalculation. The new parliament, elected in March 1679, gave the Exclusionist leaders a considerable majority, which they quickly used to intensify their investigations into the Popish Plot and push on with the impeachment of Danby.

Realising that Danby had to be sacrificed to prevent a total parliamentary gridlock, Charles dismissed him and switched tactics. He attempted to ease the logjam by reconstituting the Privy Council. He expanded it and incorporated within it some of the government's chief critics, including Shaftesbury (who was made Lord President of the Council) and one of his chief lieutenants in the Commons, Lord William Russell. It also included witty, urbane opportunist George Savile, the Marquess of Halifax, an old rival of Shaftesbury who was now jostling for the leadership of the opposition. The more radical Exclusionists started to suspect a sell-out by their leaders, and were determined to push on to the main issue: the succession.

The King did indeed hope to defang the Exclusionist leaders by persuading them to accept a less radical solution to the problem of James than outright exclusion. This was the idea of introducing limitations on James's power when he became king. These 'limitations' generally consisted of enshrining parliament's absolute right to sit under a popish king; transferring certain prerogative powers, such as the appointment of government officials, judges, naval and army officers and others to parliament; and limiting the King's power over the Church of England. Other solutions – such as legitimising the Protestant Duke of Monmouth, Charles' eldest illegitimate son, and making him heir to the throne – seemed non-starters.

Although some of the opposition leaders – including Halifax – were aware of how radical it was for parliament to dare to attempt to dictate who should become king and supported the King's compromise proposal of limitations, Shaftesbury stuck to the more radical course of supporting Exclusion. This was partly because he wished to outmanoeuvre his hated rival Halifax, but also because Exclusion had the virtue of simplicity and thoroughness relative to the alternative: would the guarantees of a limitations statute prove to be worth the vellum they were written on once James came to the throne?

It is likely that Shaftesbury was also to some extent a leader determined to follow his own troops. Exclusion was the position that many opposition MPs began to coalesce around in spring 1679, and Shaftesbury realised that he had to go along with the proposal to retain his prominent role within the parliamentary leadership of the opposition. A series of hot-headed younger MPs made incendiary anti-James speeches in the debates on the Exclusion Bill and it passed its second reading in the Commons on 21st May by a majority of seventy-nine.

The King was livid. Outright support for Exclusion was tantamount to a declaration of war. By attempting to alter the line of succession to the throne, in his view they were trying to affect a constitutional revolution that would make the Crown effectively elective. To a Stuart like Charles, who believed fervently in divine hereditary right, this was sacrilege as well as rebellion. Many supporters of the court began to rally as they realised that the King was prepared to stand and fight over Exclusion, and more moderate MPs began to fear that the Exclusionists were troublemakers out to foment a second civil war.

Almost immediately, the King dissolved parliament in preparation for another election, and a major step towards irreversible polarisation into two camps – Exclusionist (Whig) and Loyalist (Tory) – had taken place.

Although the fresh election – held across August and September 1679 – produced an even more pro-Exclusion parliament, it was irrelevant, as Charles quickly adopted a much harsher policy. He dismissed Shaftesbury from his Privy Council and prorogued parliament before it could meet. His plan was to prevent parliament from sitting indefinitely and thereby buy time in which the Popish Plot agitation could cool down. He hoped that this, accompanied by signals from him that he was by no means 'lax on popery' – such as sending James into exile and enforcing recusancy laws against Catholics – would take the wind out of the Exclusionists' sails.

In response, the Exclusionists sought, by propaganda and rallying public opinion, to force Charles to allow parliament to sit. The Exclusionists assumed that, eventually, the King would have to give in: he could not operate without supply from parliament, and he had backed down when faced with a recalcitrant parliament many times before. It seemed by no means an unreasonable gambit.

One of the chief means by which the Exclusionists hoped to force the King's hand was by a mass petitioning campaign, beginning in December 1679, which called on the King to allow the prorogued parliament to sit. Extraordinarily for the time, the Exclusionists took some pains to gather the signatures of all social classes, even the relatively poor. They printed ready-prepared blank petitions in their hundreds, which, in London, they gave to house-to-house canvassers who collected signatures. They even left copies, with pens and ink, in inns and taverns.

In the provinces, according to Roger North, the blank petitions 'were put into the hands of agitants and sub-agitants in the counties about, branching forth so nice as into hundreds of towns and villages . . . and these agitators, being choice party men, and well-instructed, went to every free voter' to ask for his signature, often focusing on county fairs and markets.[24] The biggest petition, from the inhabitants of London, Westminster and Southwark, attracted 50–60,000 signatures.

The King was furious at what he saw as an implicitly seditious appeal to the mob. He contemptuously rejected the petitions and announced a further, longer prorogation. Divisions increased, but not noticeably in the King's favour, for Shaftesbury and his allies proved very adept at maintaining popular anger and an atmosphere of heightened political tension as the prorogations dragged on.

A continual stream of lurid 'revelations' about the Popish Plot helped but needed to be supplemented by further 'fake news' concerning papist outrages. A contrived rumour about an Irish uprising in April 1680, playing on longstanding English fears about the Catholic threat from 'uncivilised' Ireland, helped fan the flames. A shambolic attempt by papists, masterminded by a disreputable midwife called Elizabeth Celier, to stage their own equivalent of the Popish Plot – the so-called 'Meal Tub Plot', based on the fact that sham papers suggesting an Exclusionist plot to murder James and take power were found in her meal tub – miserably failed, and indeed played into the hands of the Exclusionists, as did a whole range of similar tactics (Mrs Celier was also involved in an unsuccessful attempt to get another Exclusionist leader, the Duke of Buckingham, indicted for sodomy).[25]

In short, the King's hope that pro-Exclusionist sentiment would die down was proving a vain one, and by the summer of 1680 Shaftesbury even felt bold enough to attempt to indict, via the pro-Exclusion grand jury of Middlesex, the Duke of York as a papist, and the King's mistress, fellow Roman Catholic the Duchess of Portsmouth ('Squintabella') as a 'common nuisance' (which meant, bluntly, 'whore').

That summer also saw rising support for the Duke of Monmouth as a potential alternative heir to James. The other options were problematic: Mary, James's eldest daughter and the actual second in line to the throne, was not widely favoured on account of being a woman. In any case, many assumed she would be under the thumb of her husband, Dutch leader William of Orange. William himself, another candidate, was not popular and some Exclusionists feared that he himself might well prove as authoritarian as Charles.

Monmouth had gained massive popularity a few years earlier by putting down a rebellion of wild Scottish Presbyterians, angry at the government's repressive religious policies, with efficiency, all while showing great clemency to the defeated Protestant rebels. Charming and popular – albeit also reckless and vain – Monmouth gradually became a formidable popular hero: the 'Protestant Duke'.

Although Shaftesbury was sceptical of Monmouth's desire to become king, he saw that the Protestant Duke might be a useful focal point for popular support for Exclusion. This came spectacularly to fruition in the summer of 1680 when Monmouth conducted an extraordinary unofficial 'Royal Progress' of the West Country to great popular applause, and even touched for the king's evil (scrofula), believed to be an ability given only to God's anointed monarch. Support for him as a possible Protestant heir grew.

The Whigs were on the march.

The failure of the King's policy of prorogation was becoming clearer, and many of his advisers – most notably Robert Spencer, Earl of Sunderland, one of the court's most shadowy and self-interested 'fixers', who exercised great influence in the King's inner closets and counsels – began to advise capitulation. Charles was not willing to abandon his brother, but did reluctantly decide to allow parliament to sit: he could see no alternative.

Although Exclusion predictably passed the Commons with a big majority, the King decided to focus on defeating it in the Lords. Galvanised by the rhetorical fireworks of wily Lord Halifax, Shaftesbury's old rival, and the King's own presence in the chamber – to intimidate peers he 'put on a virtuoso performance of nods, smiles, grimaces and scowls at each speech' – this tactic worked.[26] Warnings of the danger of a civil war if the Exclusionists persisted in their behaviour also made a deep impression on the peers, and Exclusion fell by sixty-three votes to thirty.

The Exclusionists did nothing to relieve fears of looming civil war by their response. They advocated the formation of a Protestant association composed of bishops, judges, MPs and others, which would take up arms on the death of the King to defend the country from papist outrages and ensure that parliament met, by force if necessary. Irritated in the extreme, Charles soon lost patience and once again dissolved parliament. The ensuing election resulted in yet another hefty Exclusionist majority.

When this parliament met in March 1681, Charles had several trump cards up his sleeve. After lengthy and complex negotiations with Louis XIV and his ministers, he had secured a fresh French subsidy. He had actually managed to retrench and manage his customs income sufficiently well to not need it in strictly financial terms, but it gave him the confidence not even to ask for supply, and undoubtedly gave him room for manoeuvre.

He then confounded the Exclusionists by summoning parliament, not to its traditional Westminster home, but to Oxford, the epicentre of loyal pro-monarchical sentiment. He was on home ground. Royalist mobs shouting, 'Let the King live and the Devil hang the roundheads', gathered; a welcome change, so far as Charles was concerned, from the demonstrations and processions of the ultra-Protestant mobs of London in favour of Exclusion.[27] The King called up a regiment of troops in case of disturbances, leading many Whigs to come armed, something that pro-Charles propagandists presented as evidence of their rebellious intent.

Charles was highly successful in making the Oxford Parliament into an exercise in intimidation and highly effective propaganda. He opened the parliament by contrasting his own supposed willingness to consider compromise and obey the law with the Exclusionists' intransigent and monomaniacal obsession with the extreme policy of Exclusion. The Exclusionists stuck to their guns, and the King quickly lost patience, especially when Shaftesbury, determined to try to exploit the popularity of Monmouth, openly proposed the Protestant Duke as heir to the throne for the first time.

To totally humiliate the Exclusionists, Charles decided to dissolve parliament in the most sudden and perfunctory way, interrupting the first reading of the new Exclusion Bill, in his full regalia, without warning and announcing the dissolution with one, curt sentence.

33

Parliament would never sit again under Charles II.

The Exclusionists had assumed that, under an incessant barrage of propaganda and with a majority in parliament, the King would have to give way. They had miscalculated. The absolute resolution of Charles against Exclusion, his newfound (relative) financial freedom, and a more united court galvanised by the abilities of Halifax meant that the opposition, who fancied themselves an unstoppable force, increasingly had to recognise that they faced a monarchy determined to prove itself an immovable object.

The tide was about to turn.

During the course of this titanic struggle, the political nation gradually polarised into two hostile camps. So far, this narrative has largely referred to 'the Exclusionists' or 'the Country opposition' versus 'the Court', but by early 1681 these two irreconcilable parties began to be referred to using new labels: 'Whig' (to denote Country oppositionists/Exclusionists) and 'Tory' (to denote anti-Exclusion supporters of the King).[28]

At a simplistic level, the demands of the Whigs are very easy to define. They were in favour of a Protestant succession and the exclusion of the Duke of York from the throne; frequent free parliaments; hard persecution of Roman Catholicism and the elimination of all papist influence at every level of English society and government; and toleration for Protestant Dissenters. The clearest scarlet thread that ran through all the Whigs was a religious one: they were the party of anti-papism, sympathy to Dissent, and 'Protestant Unity'. This aspect of their politics would endure and remain their most foundational commitment.

These broad commonalities papered over, however, important constitutional differences, which become rather clearer if we consider the political thinking of the leading Whigs.

The Whig heritage was that of the Country opposition of the 1670s, which was, in essence, rooted in suspicion of central government, and in particular the supposedly crypto-papist 'Church and King' authoritarians who ran it. They decried how it subverted the independence of parliament and ruled, via corruption and bribery, to further its own interests, sucking the country dry through taxes. Those taxes were then, they argued, used to perpetuate the cycle of corruption and suborning parliament that was destroying England's liberties. Although most believed that this could be corrected by returning to England's historic 'mixed' constitution, composed of king, Lords and Commons, others, the radical fringe of 'True Whigs', were out and out republicans who would abolish monarchy altogether.

Other Whig theorists may not strictly have been republicans, but they did see attempts to appeal to historical precedent as a waste of time. They realised precedents could be adduced, much more accurately, in favour of Tory principles than Whiggish ones, and in any case, such appeals to musty old documents failed to get to the real moral and political heart of the matter.

Much better, argued some, to see government as a matter of contract between rulers and ruled based on popular sovereignty. These thinkers argued that the laws of nature, given by God, prescribed that government be instituted to protect, as Whig political thinker James Tyrrell put it, 'the common good and preservation of mankind', particularly the protection of their property, life and liberties.[29] Some Whig thinkers even defended an out-and-out right on behalf of the community – which, in the view of that most radical Whig and associate of Shaftesbury, John Locke, included in extremis even the 'rabble' of the great mass of ordinary people – to forcefully resist any king who broke the terms of the contract.

Locke's *Two Treatises of Government*, his programmatic statement of contract theory and the right of resistance, was written during the Exclusion Crisis, and before long Locke and his friend and ally Shaftesbury were to conclude that Charles had indeed broken that contract and their obligation of obedience to the King had therefore been dissolved. By the end of the Exclusion struggle, many leading Whigs were, by any definition of the term, out-and-out revolutionaries.

At the street level of political argument, away from the rarefied distinctions of theorists like Locke, Whiggery was rather more brutal and straightforward. The most consistent purpose of Whig propaganda was to fan anti-Catholic bigotry. The message was clear: support the great Exclusionist cause or see Protestantism and liberty extirpated by hordes of crazed papist psychopaths.

Consider, for example, a Whig pamphlet published in 1681 entitled *A scheme of Popish cruelties*. It is a lurid collection of often semi-pornographic images of unspeakable acts of Catholic barbarism, which are described in some detail. In one, 'Ruffians and Hectors, Popish Priests, Jesuites, Monks, and the rest of the Black Guard to the Prince of Darkness' are 'endeavouring to Ravish your Wives, your Daughters, your Sisters, and your Mothers', before 'beating out the Brains of Infants, and snatching them out of their tender Mothers Arms'.[30] The average Protestant reader was left in no doubt about the fate that awaited him in the event of the Duke of York's succession to the crown.

Although the Whigs were not, at this point, a 'political party' in a modern sense, they had a fairly well-organised network by which they distributed their propaganda, particularly via their clubs, of which the Green Ribbon Club was perhaps the most important. They also had a number of 'party papers', the most prominent of which was Henry Care's subtly entitled *The Weekly Pacquet of Advice from Rome*. The epicentre of this network was London, the great Whiggish stronghold throughout the Exclusion Crisis. Lord Guildford, a disapproving Tory, claimed that in twenty-four hours the Green Ribbon Club 'could entirely possess the City with which reports they pleased and in less than a week spread it over the entire country'.[31]

The Whigs by no means confined themselves to pamphlets and broad-sheets, or their other famous tactic, mass petitioning, which came to a head in the great campaign of 1679. Men were hired to walk from coffee shop to tavern back to coffee shop to spread the Whig message by word of mouth (which occasionally caused pub brawls with angry Tories). Tunes and broadsides were written and sometimes political ballads sung on the streets. Plays, such as *Rome's Folly: Or, the Amorous Fryar* (no doubt a sensitive depiction of Roman Catholicism), were written and performed to spread the message. Whigs even appealed to London's gamblers by producing sets of playing cards depicting scenes of papist outrage.

By far the most famous and prominent means of Whig political communication were their massive Pope-burning processions. They had begun in earnest back in 1674, but during the Exclusion Crisis they became bigger and more elaborate. The most spectacular examples took place on

17th November, Queen Elizabeth's accession day, or on Bonfire Night. Typically, they would consist of a lurid parody of a papal coronation: an effigy of the Pope would be carried through the City of London accompanied by a train of enthusiastic Whig activists dressed up as Catholic priests. The Pope – and perhaps effigies of cardinals or unpopular Tories suspected of being papists – would then be cast onto a pyre, along with various other papist devotional items, such as rosary beads and vestments.[32]

These carnivalesque processions attracted huge crowds: 200,000 people were alleged to have witnessed the Pope-burning ceremony carried out at Temple Bar on 17th November 1679. Sometimes the assembled crowds could be used for a bit of old-fashioned political intimidation, but often they were made into 'merry' occasions: many people in the crowd would come in fancy dress, dressing up as Catholic priests or devils, while they sang anti-papist songs and drank toasts to Lord Shaftesbury and Protestant liberty. Fun, no doubt, for all the family.

It wasn't only the Catholics that came under fire. Cautiously at first, and then more brazenly, Whig propaganda found another target: the Church of England. Many Whigs were themselves Churchmen, and attacking the 'Protestant religion as by law established' was risky. However, Dissent, particularly in London, was the mainstay of the Whig activist base, and many Whig politicians came from a Dissenting background. In any case, the Church Whigs, overwhelmingly Low Churchmen, were not averse to bashing their High Church opponents. Accordingly, during the Exclusion Crisis, the political fault-line increasingly reflected the old Civil War division: Puritans versus Anglicans, Dissent versus the Church of England, Low versus High Churchmen.

From the Whig perspective, the High Churchmen who dominated the Church's leadership, with their suspicious penchant for ceremonial worship, were almost as much the enemy as the actual papists. The fact that most senior churchmen opposed the Exclusion campaign confirmed all of their deeply held suspicions. They nicknamed anti-Exclusionist churchmen 'Tantivies', 'tantivy' meaning gallop or ride, the implication being that they were preparing to 'gallop off' to Rome and the Pope. At election time, Whig mobs were not above abusing parsons: in one Essex constituency in the second

1679 election they called their clerical opponents 'Dumb Dogs, Jesuitical Dogs, Dark Lanthorns, Baal's Priests, Damned Rogues, Jacks and Villains, the Black Guard, the black Regiment of Hell'.[33]

For old Puritan radicals like Roger Morrice, whose diary is one of the best sources we have for the period, the struggle over Exclusion was really a battle between what he called 'the true Hierarchicall interest', that is, the High Churchmen, 'that were for the Persecution Tyrany and Debauchery of the Church of England' by reducing it to a state of near-popery, and 'the Dissenters Wiggs, and sober Church of England men, who have asserted Liberty and Property, and . . . would have a good understanding with . . . the Protestant Dissenters'.[34] He was not alone.

The Tories were initially nowhere near as well organised or well defined as the Whigs, and a specific 'Tory' message tended to emerge in reaction to the Whig campaign throughout the Exclusion Crisis. They had few obvious stand-out parliamentary leaders; their real political leader was the King, if anyone.[35]

Outside of parliament, their most effective and important propagandist and figurehead was a man called Roger L'Estrange. Journalist, sometime press censor, courtier and all-round rogue, L'Estrange is perhaps best described as the id of Cavalier England, a man who had actually got in trouble just after the Restoration for being *too* gung ho in favour of the royalist cause: he had opposed Charles II's policy of forgive and forget towards former rebels, and was nearly jailed for his trouble.

Vehement, sweary and outrageous, albeit 'courtly and full of compliment' according to Samuel Pepys, L'Estrange devoted his entire career to defaming, attacking and mocking all he suspected of Puritanism, republicanism, Presbyterianism, sedition, Dissent or any other trace of rebellion.[36] His propaganda during the Exclusion Crisis against the Whigs was vicious: they were 'nonconformists, factious, king killers, mob rousers, tyrants, and hostile to the Church of England'.[37]

It is fair to say that L'Estrange was not well loved by his opponents either, who routinely depicted him as a fat papist dog named 'Towzer' and nicknamed him 'the Devil's Bloodhound', 'Mr Filth' and 'Crackfart', the last for his alleged flatulence.[38] One Whig, Lord Lucas, described him in parliament as 'one of the greatest villains upon earth – the bugbear of the Protestant religion . . . a dangerous rank Papist, who deserves of all men to be hanged'.[39] The sentiment was very much returned.

It was L'Estrange who co-ordinated the Tory propaganda response to the Whig onslaught, and indeed wrote much of it himself in various pamphlets and his own newspaper, *The Observator*. Although they couldn't rival the Whigs in terms of press co-ordination and campaigning infrastructure, the Tories did possess their own clubs, notably L'Estrange's favoured Sam's Coffee-House, and L'Estrange organised and assisted a group of publishers and printing houses who churned out Tory propaganda.[40] To emphasise their message, they copied many Whig tactics, using plays, playing cards, songs and even politically tinged astrology almanacks to get their message across. They even had their own equivalent of Pope-burning processions, in which they burnt effigies of 'Jack Presbyter', a symbol of Dissenting sedition.

What, then, was the Tory message?

At the less highfalutin level, L'Estrange's aim was twofold: to undermine the credibility of the accusations made as part of the Popish Plot (often with much justice), and, more substantially, to paint the Exclusionists as the heirs to the parliamentary rebels who had plunged the country into civil war in the 1640s. In place of the papist conspiracy central to Whig propaganda, he substituted his own. The Whig cause and Exclusion campaign was, he argued, merely a political cover for a Dissenting plot to overthrow the monarchy and plunge the country back into the chaos of the 1640s. The events of 1641, when John Pym and the parliamentary side made a mass appeal, through pamphlets and propaganda, to resist Charles I and the supposed threat of popery, seemed to be echoed in the tactics of the Whigs: and look, argued the Tories, where that had ended. '41 has come again' became perhaps the most consistent Tory battle cry.

The end result of this, L'Estrange argued, would be another arbitrary military dictatorship, just as had occurred in the 1650s under Cromwell and the Major-Generals. Then, the rebels had, argued Tory propagandist Nalson, 'Taxed, Assessed, Decimated, Fined, Imprisoned, Sequestered, Plundred, Banished' the people, and so they would again.[41] Not only that, growled L'Estrange, but they would promote the joyless moral policing that had resulted in the Commonwealth banning such pastimes as 'Comedies, Interludes, Wrastlings, Foot-Ball Play, May-Games, Whitson-Ales, Morrice-Dances, Bear-Batings'.[42] In short, Whig victory would result not in the saviour of the rights and liberties of Protestant Englishmen but their subversion.

As time went on, elements of the Tory case began to resonate louder with the public. The Whig use of mass petitioning campaigns and popular demonstrations gave some credence to the idea that they were the party of 'mob rule', and a number of counter-petitions were organised 'abhorring' the seditious tumult of the Whigs (this gave rise to one of the early nicknames for the Tories, 'abhorrers'). At first, these efforts were rather half-hearted, but as time passed and Whig leaders, including Shaftesbury, became increasingly vehement in their advocacy of the formation of an armed Protestant Association to defend the rights of Englishmen, the idea that the Whigs were Puritan revolutionaries became more plausible.

The Tory case, however, was broader than these (often shrewd) propaganda hits by L'Estrange and his allies. They were, put simply, the party of traditional subordination in Church and State on the basis of notions of divine right, as well as legal precedent. The source of all authority for the Tories was God, not the people. The King was, as one Tory poet put it, 'God's servant, not the People's slave'.[43]

The tracts of Sir Robert Filmer, written some thirty years prior but republished during the Exclusion Crisis, summed up the case well. He maintained that the King's power emanated directly from God. Governments had been divinely ordained since the time of Adam, and Adam's absolute authority descended down the male line by hereditary succession, ultimately to contemporary monarchs. Even Filmer was prepared to admit that the Stuarts could not claim a direct lineage to Adam, but he still maintained, by analogy, that 'since political authority always rested on God's will, and since this authority was absolute and irresistible, then the Stuarts ruled by God's will and the kings of England possessed absolute power'.[44]

In general terms, the Tories saw the social and political order as analogous to a family, in which the King stood at the top as the father, accountable only to God. He would pass on his divinely ordained authority and office to his heir. Relations within society more generally – between master and servant, between local office holder and ordinary people, between actual father and children – reflected the divinely ordained relationship of legitimate, benevolent authority and loyal obedience that also characterised, at the political level, relations between the King and his people. All were obliged – as the Book of Common Prayer put it – 'to do my duty in that state of life, unto which it shall please God to call me'.

This was, indeed, the view inculcated by the Church of England, the political faith of which was rooted in the idea that subjects were obliged by God to obey their anointed monarch, and that any resistance or rebellion was sinful. This doctrine of non-resistance was softened somewhat by the fact that there were two types of obedience. 'Active' was to be paid 'in the case of all lawful commands', but if a monarch 'enjoins anything contrary to what God hath commanded', then only passive obedience was required.[45] This meant refusing to be actively complicit in the sovereign's unrighteous commands, while 'patiently suffer[ing] what the ruler inflicts on us for such a refusal'.[46]

The Tory view militated strongly against any contractual view of government or society. Government could hardly be a contract between rulers and ruled, subject to the vagaries of human convenience and therefore alterable, if ordained by God and necessitating almost complete obedience to the ruling powers. Man's spiritual existence was governed by the Church and civil matters were ordered by the King within one overarching, unified organic Christian commonwealth.

The Tories' veneration for both obedience to the monarchy and the authority of the Church of England, causes deeply intertwined in their worldview, was perhaps best symbolised by the cult of Charles King and Martyr. For Tories, the execution of Charles I in 1649 was the ultimate symbol of the chaos and impiety that Dissent and disobedience entailed. He had been the anointed King and therefore the *fons* and *origo* of legitimate political authority, but his refusal to compromise over the true apostolic constitution of the Catholic Church – that is, his refusal to agree to the abolition of bishops – also made him an explicitly religious martyr, the closest thing that the Church of England had to a saint. The day of his execution, 30th January, was enshrined in the Book of Common Prayer as a day of solemn repentance, and became the characteristic Tory date of commemoration; a time for mournful national repentance for the sin of treason when all good Tories would retire to peruse the *Eikon Basilike* (the book of pious autobiographical reflection widely thought to have been written by the King as he awaited his execution).

Does this imply that the Tories all believed in absolutism? Although that sometimes appeared to be the case, in practice many Tories adopted a more moderate constitutional royalism which stressed the importance of a king working within the customary framework of established constitutional principles. This included an important role for parliament, as advisers and counsellors representing the interests of the most substantial elements of the community.

This view held that, even if the monarch was above the law in extremis, he should, as a matter of prudence, exercise his power in accordance with the constitutional practices that had developed over the centuries, particularly co-operation with Lords and Commons and respect for the rule of law. Such Tories would usually stress that Charles II had, in fact, done nothing illegal, and it was the Whigs, pushing as they were for an unprecedented policy without the support of the House of Lords, who were attempting to subvert the constitution.

It should be emphasised, however, that, whatever the importance of constitutional questions, the most consistent and important basis of the Tory cause was loyalty to the Church of England. Indeed, for many decades after 1679–81 the terms 'Tory Party' and 'Church Party' would be used interchangeably. Whether the Church was valued for political reasons, as the indispensable bulwark to state authority and therefore order and peace – summarised by James I's old adage 'No Bishop, no King' – or for more rarefied reasons, as the true, Catholic Church which combined Protestant doctrinal purity with apostolic authority – or, more usually, a bit of both – it was central to the men who, mostly, lived lives defined and given meaning by their Christian faith. For them – as for most of the Whigs – 'politics' and 'religion' were never really separate categories.

* * *

What is striking is that, whether in the press or on the hustings, even by the unedifying standards of twenty-first-century political partisanship, the first Whigs and Tories abused each other with extraordinary bitterness and vigour. One Whig pamphlet published during the Exclusion Crisis, *The Character of a Tory*, began by claiming that 'A Tory is a Monster with an English Face, a French Heart, and an Irish Conscience', composed of four elements: 'noise and debauchery, oaths and beggary'.[47] Whig firebrand Morrice littered his diaries with abuse of the Tories: they were the 'cankared mercenary Tories', 'the debauched party', 'Hierarchists' and knaves one and all, who had sold their soul to the devil.[48] Not only did Whig propagandists supply Roger L'Estrange with a whole range of abusive nicknames, they even burnt effigies of him on pyres along with popes, priests, rosaries and relics.

The Tories were scarcely less vituperative. The Whigs were king killers; republicans; murderers; atheists; possibly in league with Satan, or at the very least fanatical Genevan Calvinists or Scottish Covenanters. One arch-Tory pamphleteer described them as 'demure, conscientious prick-eared vermin'.[49] Another described Henry Care, the publisher of a leading Whig newspaper, as 'Monkey Care', suggesting that he was 'so unlike Mankind, that an Indictment is preferred against his Wife at the Old-Baily for Bestiality, where he is to prove what species he is of'.[50]

L'Estrange's views on 'how to be a Whig' were fairly fruity stuff:

> To be a Right Whig , you must never Remember Benefits, nor Forget Injuries, you must never Repent of any Wickedness that you were the better for, you must learn to lift up your Eyes, and Pick your Neighbors Pocket, all in a motion, you must gape, and constantly carry Liberty of Consciences and Religion upon the Tip of your Tongue; but if you swallow either of them, if ye are a Right Whig, 'twill Choak ye.[51]

A particular target for Tory abuse was Shaftesbury. They delighted in the fact that he had a rather unfortunate medical condition, a sort of bodily abscess on his breast (probably a hydatid cyst), which necessitated the insertion of a permanent tube into his body to help drain it. Tory propagandists leapt on the idea that this made him a bit like a barrel of beer with a tap, and nicknamed him, for the rest of his life, 'Tapski' (the 'ski' at the end of his name was a reference to his supposed preference for an elected king, of the sort they had in Poland).[52]

Not only this, but it became a staple of Tory propaganda to suggest that the abscess was somehow a result of Shaftesbury's fornication, which, in Tory eyes at least, was of quite startling proportions. Jacobite Tory Roger North alleged years later (somewhat dubiously) that Shaftesbury rivalled Charles II in the sexual promiscuity stakes, and would get his groom to give refreshment to his whores in Hyde Park in preparation for their lengthy sessions of sexual gymnastics (specifically 'Rhenish wine and sugar, and not seldom a bait of cheese cakes').[53]

One poem written on his death encapsulates the general Tory attitude to him:

> Ye Mortal Whigs for Death prepare,
> For Mighty Tapski's Guts lie here
> Will his great name keep sweet, d'y' think?
> For certainly his entrails stink.[54]

Contemporary poet John Dryden summed up the state of the party battle aptly when he remarked that, 'He who draws his pen for one party must expect to make enemies of the other, for wit and fool are consequents of Whig and Tory, and every man is a knave or an ass to the contrary side.'[55]

Dryden, however, was being self-consciously disingenuous, for he was responsible for perhaps one of the most famous pieces of literary partisanship of all. In November 1681 he published *Absalom and Achitophel*, a vicious piece of anti-Whig propaganda. The poem plays on the biblical story of Absalom's rebellion against King David. The Duke of Monmouth is portrayed as Absalom, the rebellious son of King David (Charles II), who is tricked into rebellion and attempted patricide by scheming adviser Achitophel (Shaftesbury). Dryden's portrayal of Shaftesbury as a hypocritical, opportunistic rebel pulled few punches:

> A Name to all succeeding Ages curst.
>
> For close Designs, and crooked Counsels fit;
>
> Sagacious, Bold, and Turbulent of wit:
>
> Restless, unfixt in Principles and Place;
>
> In Pow'r unpleased, impatient of Disgrace.[56]

Referring to the fact that Shaftesbury had previously been one of the King's chief ministers, he continued:

> In Friendship false, implacable in Hate:
>
> Resolv'd to Ruine or to Rule the State.
>
> To Compass this, the Triple Bond he broke;
>
> The Pillars of the Publick Safety shook:
>
> And fitted Israel for a Foreign Yoke.
>
> Then, seiz'd with Fear, yet still affecting Fame,
>
> Usurp'd a Patriot's All-atoning Name.[57]

Much of this rancour and hatred was a product of the fact that men on both sides saw the rising tensions of 1679–81 in terms indelibly marked by the memory of the Civil War. Many of them were old enough to remember or even have participated in the bloodshed and polarisation of the 1640s. These feelings ran deep and provoked passionate emotions of hatred, fear and bitterness. The idea that the Whigs were the latest face of the Parliamentarians and Roundheads, and the Tories the newest incarnation of the Cavaliers, was common currency.

One last question about the birth of Whig and Tory should be asked. How did they get their names?[58]

It is striking how much variation there was in the terms used to describe the two sides initially. In the early stages, Tories generally described themselves as 'the Loyall Party', and were castigated by their opponents as, variously, 'Yorkists', 'Abhorrers', 'Tantivies', 'Sham Plotters', 'Masqueraders', 'Church Papists', 'Protestants in Masquerade', 'Pensioners' and 'God-damnees'.[59]

The Whigs also attracted various names, such as 'the adverse party', 'the malignant party', the 'fanatics', the 'patriots' and 'the mutineers'.[60]

For a while it seemed that the Exclusionists would be known as 'Bromidghams' or 'Bromigems'. This came from the fact that Birmingham ('Bromidgham' as it was often called) was associated with the forging of false coins. The Tories accused the Whigs accordingly of being 'True Bromidgham Protestants' – i.e. counterfeit or false Protestants. This was duly shortened to 'Bromigem'. One of the country's greatest historical political parties was only a hair's breadth away from being known as, essentially, 'The Brummies'.

The two terms that were eventually chosen were essentially insults based on prejudice against respectively the Scottish and the Irish.

The 'Tories' were a group of Roman Catholic brigands, many of them victims of Cromwell's confiscations of Catholic land, who menaced the Anglo-Irish gentry. They were led by the notorious chieftain Redmond O'Hanlon. 'Tory' was, however, an obscure term. It only gained temporary political currency in 1680–1 as a result of the Irish dimension of the Popish Plot, when the Whigs claimed that the Tory Lord Lieutenant of Ireland, the Duke of Ormonde, had been employing the 'Tory' brigands to assist a (non-existent) Catholic plot to facilitate a French invasion. This lie was soon exposed, but the term 'Tory' was briefly used to refer to the anti-Exclusionists by Whig propagandists.

'Whig' came to relative prominence as a result of the Presbyterian uprising of 1679. Scotland was a hotbed of radical Presbyterians (usually referred to as Covenanters), but its majority Presbyterian religion had been largely suppressed since the Restoration, when the Episcopal Church of Scotland (essentially the Scottish Anglican Church) had been re-established. The hardline Presbyterians – who attracted a range of labels, including, as a term of abuse, 'Whiggamaire' or 'Whig' – had continued holding illegal outdoor meetings. In 1679 there was an uprising of Presbyterians in the western Lowlands, which was put down by the Duke of Monmouth at the Battle of Bothwell Brig.

Daniel Defoe's account of this, written years later, suggested that Charles II's chief Scottish minister Lauderdale reported that 'the Duke [of Monmouth] had been so Civil to Whigs, because he was a Whig himself in his Heart'.[61] This was then, supposedly, taken up at Court, and soon entered common usage as an insulting term for the Exclusionists. There is, however, no evidence at all that this is true. Indeed, 'Whig' was not taken up as a general term until 1681.

The real impetus for the widespread adoption and longevity of both terms, was, in fact, the writings of Roger L'Estrange. In spring 1681, L'Estrange began, in his *Observator* newspaper, to semi-ironically refer to himself and his political allies as 'Tories', largely to illustrate the dishonesty of his opponents over the fake Irish plot. Casting around for an equally obscure (and unflattering) term for his opponents, he started to couple 'Tory' with the term 'Whig'. This combination was first used in the *Observator* of 2nd July, when he started a famous, long-running dialogue between 'Whigs' and 'Tories', the point of which was to paint the Exclusionists as murderous fanatics ('Whigs') who regarded the King, his heir and their defenders as no better than renegades and outlaws ('Tories'). In any case, soon other writers began to use the distinction and it took on a life of its own.

So the terms came to prominence in essence because of the scurrilous propagandising of that most disreputable and brilliant of Tory writers, Roger L'Estrange.

By the time L'Estrange was popularising the terms 'Whig' and 'Tory', the tide was turning against the Whigs. With Charles in a stronger position, he had no need or desire to call any more parliaments, and without parliaments as a focus for the pro-exclusion campaign, the Whig cause lost steam. Interest waned in the lurid details of the Popish Plot. The view that the Whigs had pushed things too far, and risked civil war, gradually began to gain wider currency, a view adroitly encouraged by the King, who knew how little stomach the country had for another civil conflict.[62]

Charles smelt blood, and began to make slow, steady preparations for his revenge. The Whigs had had their turn at abusing the legal system for political reasons: over the course of the Popish Plot, they had helped ensure that scores of innocent Catholics were judicially murdered. Now Charles was determined to return the favour and use the full force of the legal system — seen more as a sort of political weapon than an instrument of justice on both sides — against the Whigs.

In order to do this, and consolidate his grip on all levels of the state apparatus, Charles began to institute legal proceedings to purge Whigs and Dissenters from local office. 'Quo warranto' proceedings – which asked 'by which warrant do you possess your current charter?' – began to be used to remove Whigs and Dissenters from corporations and impose new charters and personnel. Loyal churchmen, prepared to do the will of their king, were installed instead. Many corporations had, in fact, long since acted against the law by not removing Dissenters from their ranks, and there was little about these proceedings that was, strictly speaking, illegal.

These proceedings allowed legal actions against Whigs to progress successfully, as juries were generally impanelled by local office holders such as sheriffs. Until now, sympathetic sheriffs had often been able to give leading Whigs effective legal immunity, which Charles was determined to reverse. In addition, as most parliamentary constituencies were borough constituencies, and borough corporations often controlled the local parliamentary seat, these actions meant that any future general election would likely produce a more Tory parliament.

In summer 1681, the prosecutions began, with the hapless Stephen College, 'the Protestant Joiner', who was eventually found guilty by a blatantly packed jury and executed soon thereafter, becoming the first Whig martyr. This was quicky followed up by a purging of the corporation of the City of London and remodelling of its charter, which opened up the way for mass prosecutions of key Whigs in London, previously a Whig stronghold. Gradually, leading Whigs began to be charged with treason or sedition as the full force of the legal system rebounded on them.

The obvious symbolic target was Shaftesbury. The first victim had been a joiner: an ominous Tory pamphlet soon asked *'Have you any work for a COOPER?'* (Cooper being Shaftesbury's surname).[63] The first attempt to prosecute him, undertaken before the Tories' takeover of the City of London corporation, was bungled. The Whigs used all of their legal wiles to save Shaftesbury, and were successful, giving rise to wild Whig celebration: the 'hollowing and shouting' in court went on for half an hour.[64] Crowds toasted Shaftesbury and lit bonfires in celebration; bands of Whigs paraded in the streets shouting 'No Popish Successor, No York, A Monmouth, A Buckingham, and God bless the Earl of Shaftesbury!'[65]

Although the Whigs fought hard against the rising Tory tide, as this victory attests, they were on an increasingly sticky wicket. They continued with intense propaganda efforts, and fought desperate rearguard actions against quo warranto proceedings: in Rye, rival mayoral candidates both claimed to have been elected and John Turney, the Whig candidate, ended up taking possession by breaking into the town hall with the help of 'a rabble of near three hundred'.[66]

It was, however, to no avail. Loyalist street demonstrations became more raucous and frequent, ringing to cheers of 'Remember Forty One!' and 'No Bill of Exclusion, No Whig'.[67] Tories staged rambunctious celebrations, complete with bonfires and toasts, to mark their frequent victories in battles to wrest control of local corporations. The Tory onslaught got so intense that at one point the King, worried that a loyalist plan to burn Cromwell in effigy in London might provoke street fighting and riots, had to ban 'tumultuous assemblies'.[68]

The reality began to dawn on the Whigs: the King was wresting back complete control. A trickle of prosecutions for treason or sedition became a flood. The laws against Dissenters were enforced with increasing fervour, and thousands of them were hit with ruinous fines or thrown into jail. Even if a parliament were to be called, the remodelling of corporations meant that it might well be packed with Tories. Increasingly, Whig hopes turned in more desperate directions.

Plans to rebel by force of arms had been mooted by leading Whigs since the meeting of the Oxford Parliament, mostly focussed on schemes to prevent James becoming king when Charles died. When, in July 1682, it became clear that Tory control over the City of London had been secured totally, and therefore it was simply a matter of time before senior Whigs were prosecuted with almost no chance of acquittal, rebellion became a more urgent matter.

Shaftesbury began to meet with senior Whigs in his London residence, Thanet House, to plan a nationwide uprising. Monmouth was tasked with making another one of his 'progresses', this time to Cheshire, to rouse the north-west; Shaftesbury would organise a rebellion in London, Russell the west country, and so on. From September, Shaftesbury, wide open to a second prosecution, became a wanted man, hiding in the London houses of various sympathisers. He sounded out various underground radicals about a separate plot, to kill the King and the Duke of York on their way to the races at Newmarket. But the plots were delayed. A very jittery Shaftesbury knew that he could be arrested at any moment and his nerve faltered. In late November, he finally fled to the Netherlands. Followed by Charles's spies, he soon fell desperately ill, unable to take any nourishment. He died, surrounded by loyal political cronies in a garret in Amsterdam, on 21st January 1683.

Those who stayed in England soon regretted it. Plans to assassinate the King and James continued: they would soon be known as the 'Rye House Plot', so-named because the murder was planned to take place on the Rye farm near Hoddesdon in Hertfordshire, which belonged to one of the leading conspirators.

This plot fell apart very quickly. The assassination was bungled when the royal brothers postponed their visit to Newmarket due to a fire, and then the whole plan was betrayed to the government by one of the conspirators in June 1683. The prosecution of those involved followed, and several, including leading Whigs such as Lord Russell and Algernon Sidney, were executed. The convictions contained their dubious legal points, but there is no doubt that the plotting was real and the indictments substantially true. Certainly, the Whig 'martyrs' of 1683 received fairer trials and a good deal more justice than the many Roman Catholics executed as part of the Popish Plot. This did not prevent them becoming, in the pantheon of Whig history, glorious patriotic heroes who died to secure the country's freedom, bearing witness, as Algernon Sidney's speech on the scaffold put it, to 'that old cause in which I was from my youth engaged', the cause of Protestantism and liberty.[69]

The King was ruthless and determined to destroy the rebels and plotters who had pitilessly assailed his authority and the succession of his brother since 1679. He wanted vengeance for his many Catholic friends whom he knew had been wrongly convicted. The Whigs had prospered by means of packed juries and perjured convictions for three heady years. They now suffered by exactly the same means.

The Tory revenge was, for now, unstoppable.

2

Revolution and the Whig Comeback

In the early hours of 11th December 1688, a tall, gaunt man, wearing a (none-too-thorough) disguise of 'a short black wig [and] a patch on his upper lip on the left side' galloped through the Kent countryside in a desperate hurry, accompanied by two nervous-looking companions.[1] He avoided the main roads for fear of discovery. He was bound for a ferry station near Feversham in Kent, where he hoped to find passage across the channel to France.[2]

He seemed lucky at first. A suitable vessel was hired and the three men clambered aboard. Unfortunately, the ship's master insisted that they halt to take on more ballast at Sheerness. By 11 p.m., they were minutes away from being ready – but as they prepared to set sail, they were accosted by a group of sixty armed men who boarded the ship from three fishing boats. They were looking for Catholic priests and other 'suspect persons' to take before the mayor of Feversham. Although they recognised one of the men – a local nobleman named Edward Hales – they had no idea who his bewigged, lanky companion was. They assumed he was a Jesuit priest, and roundly abused him, calling him an 'ugly, lean-jawed hatchet-faced Jesuite' and a 'popish dog'.[3]

This Jesuit's possessions were confiscated by the leader of the armed band, but soon the gang suspected that something was being held back. A rougher search of the three strangers was conducted. They 'fell a Searching their pockets and opening their breeches'.[4] They 'felt all about in a very rude manner, and the more' on the Jesuit's person, finding a diamond bodkin

51

which contained pieces of jewellery that he had hidden in his underwear.[5] Luckily, the incompetent searcher only found a toothpick case and some keys in the bodkin, and missed the jewellery.

Both the three men and their captors spent an uncomfortable night in the ship, waiting for the tide to turn to take them to Feversham. Once they arrived there the next day, the three prisoners were taken to an inn.

It soon became very clear that the man whose breeches they had rifled through was no Jesuit priest. Several people at the inn recognised him through his half-hearted disguise.

The man was His Majesty James II, King of England, Scotland and Ireland.

It had all been very different little less than four years previously. Despite the tumults of the Exclusion Crisis, a papist king was welcomed with surprisingly little fuss.[6] Indeed, the reaction to James's accession in February 1685 was generally positive, even joyous. An Anglican priest claimed that his proclamation as king met with 'the universal joy, contentment and applause of all good people'.[7] This might have been something of an exaggeration – no doubt many were wary – but overall the response was better than anyone could have expected. Four-hundred-and-thirty-nine loyal addresses congratulating the King on his accession poured in from throughout the country. There was a general upsurge of loyal sentiment.

How did it come to pass, then, that by December 1688 the King was attempting to flee his own kingdom in such disorganised haste that he ended up having his underwear manhandled by a bunch of rowdy Kentish fishermen? Why, in late 1688, were roving bands of volunteers scouting the coasts for Catholics and Jesuit priests?

The orgy of baby roasting and murderous papist rapine predicted by Whig pamphleteers did not come to pass on James's accession. Nonetheless, it was ultimately James's religion and his attempts to promote it to his unenthusiastic subjects that were to prove his undoing.

When James became king, the monarchy was in its strongest position for decades. His brother had been ruthlessly effective at suppressing the

Crown's enemies and had purged the political structure of England at every level to replace rowdy Whigs with loyal Tory Anglicans. Furthermore, the financial position of the Crown was strong: no parliament had met since the Oxford Parliament because Charles could afford not to call one. It looked entirely possible that the English monarchy might come to match its French equivalent in power and authority.

But James had one overweening objective that he was absolutely determined to pursue. The problem was that, with the vast majority of his subjects, it was about as popular as the periodic outbreaks of plague that still bedevilled late seventeenth-century England. It was to demolish every prop of his regime with astonishing speed.

James wanted full toleration for Roman Catholics, and he would use any means within his power to achieve it. More than that, he wanted to make it legal – and even give some degree of state support – for Roman Catholics to proselytise.

James had a streak of sincerity to his personality that was so naive that it might have been charming had it not been so catastrophic. His conversion to the Roman church had been entirely sincere, and his faith was unbending and serious (some would say to the point of sectarian bigotry). The souls of men – specifically, his own subjects – were at stake, and he seemed to genuinely believe that if the penal laws against Roman Catholicism were lifted, the bluff Protestant citizenry of England would soon be converted.

Charles had the realism to see that this was utterly delusional, but James had little of his brother's pragmatism (or brains). Indeed, Charles was alleged to have predicted that James, who was as licentious as himself, though apparently with less taste, would 'lose his kingdom by his bigotry and his soul for a lot of ugly trollops'.[8]

The problem for James was not the hostility of Whiggery. The Whigs had been cowed during the Tory reaction – indeed, many of their leaders had been executed or forced to flee aboard. Their aversion to James was therefore irrelevant. So long as he retained the thoroughgoing support of the Church of England and the stout Tory gentlemen, who now controlled the enormous web of local office-holders in the counties and corporations that enforced the law, he looked unassailable.

The problem, of course, was that the Tory, Anglican hierarchy, although they could stomach a Roman Catholic monarch so long as he protected their power, would not tolerate anything like what James had in mind. For all of the Whigs' jibes about them being 'Tantivies', most Tories were no keener on popery than the Whigs, and had no intention of tamely accepting James's agenda, whatever their own doctrines of non-resistance or passive obedience might say.

It was on this massive iceberg that the good ship James would soon run aground.

Once the loyalist revellers had slept off their hangovers, James's reign began propitiously. Protestant nerves were settled by his promise to 'preserve this Government both in Church and State as by Law Establish'd'.[9] He explicitly denied that he was a 'Man for Arbitrary Power' and promised to be a model of constitutional moderation.[10]

He soon strengthened his hand further. Helped by the active use of government patronage and the political impact of Charles II's quo warranto proceedings against recalcitrant Whiggish corporations, the election of spring 1685 saw a mere fifty-seven Whigs elected in a parliament of 513 seats; it was not so much a Tory landslide as a Tory tsunami. The result was a parliament stuffed with Tories, who soon voted him a generous supply for life.

The first major challenge to James's regime came with the news that Charles II's rebellious illegitimate son, the Duke of Monmouth, who had fled into exile during the Tory reaction with the more notorious Whig rebels, had landed in Lyme Regis on 11th June with the intention of fomenting an uprising against the King. It was part of a co-ordinated assault in conjunction with the Earl of Argyll, who led a similar landing in Scotland. Both assaults began with tiny numbers – Monmouth landed with just eighty-three men, Argyll with just under 300 – and stymied themselves by making no attempt to appeal outside of their obvious political 'base', which consisted of convinced Whigs and radicals. Both issued declarations suffused with the ideology of radical Whig contractarianism. Monmouth presented rather more of a threat, as he managed to raise some 3,000–4,000 troops and put up a surprisingly stiff fight, but was soon overwhelmed by the army, led ably by a thrusting young officer, Brigadier John Churchill.

However, it didn't take long for cracks to show. In response to the Monmouth Rebellion, James quickly bolstered the size of the army, never a popular move in a country traditionally sceptical of permanent, standing armies. Even more explosively, he had appointed a number of Roman Catholic officers, which was illegal under the Test Act; he got around it by granting dispensations to the officers in question, arguing that it was within the King's power to suspend the operation of specific laws in individual cases ('the dispensing power').

This created an uproar even within his loyalist parliament: John Evelyn noted in his diary that the King's Speech demanding MPs' approval of his controversial actions was 'very unexpected and unpleasing to the Commons'.[11] Many of his harshest critics were Tories of impeccable Anglican-Cavalier pedigree, such as Sir Thomas Clarges, who moved in the Commons that a 'standing army is destructive to the country'.[12] Fellow Tory Sir Edward Seymour pointedly remarked that 'it is treason for any man to be reconciled to the Church of Rome'.[13] Parliament grumbled and offered a considerably lower sum in supply than he wanted. In the end, tired by their complaints, James prorogued parliament before even that was granted.

James's court quickly divided into factions. On one side, Henry Hyde, the Earl of Clarendon and his brother Laurence, the Earl of Rochester (the sons of Charles I and II's great ally and statesman, Edward Hyde) – the living embodiments and figureheads of the old Cavalier cause and staunch High Churchmen – attempted to rein in the King. On the other, Robert Spencer, the Earl of Sunderland – the famously opportunistic and ethically flexible veteran from Charles's reign who was soon to convert to Roman Catholicism himself to ingratiate himself with the King – led a pro-Catholic faction that saw its role as implementing the King's agenda as efficiently as possible.

The Sunderland faction quickly carried all before it. A test case on the issue of the dispensing power, Godden versus Hales, concluded in summer 1686 that the King had every right to dispense with the laws in individual cases. Although he purged the judicial bench to ensure he got the verdict he wanted, it was at least a legally plausible position and emboldened James not only to allow Roman Catholics to hold fellowships at Oxford and Cambridge (bastions of Anglicanism and Toryism) but also to appoint Roman Catholics to the Privy Council, which bolstered the Sunderland faction's numbers within the King's counsels.

More shocking still to the Protestant conscience was James's unabashed encouragement of Catholic worship and proselytising. He effectively halted prosecution for recusancy and provided funds for the establishment of Catholic schools and chapels. By spring 1686, cities such as London, Worcester and Bristol had opened Catholic chapels. Catholic apologetics began to pour from the presses. The Mass, for the first time since the death of Queen Mary I, was being celebrated openly in England.

The hierarchy of the Church of England and its Tory allies were aghast. The response was immediate and co-ordinated. Books and sermons attacking the Roman Church began to appear in earnest. The King forbade the clergy from preaching on any matter of sectarian controversy, but many Anglican priests merrily ignored him, including one John Sharp, rector of St Giles-in-the-Fields, London. James ordered the Bishop of London, Henry Compton, to suspend Sharp. Compton refused.

In response James set up an Ecclesiastical Commission to 'inspect' Church affairs. Although it included representatives of the Rochester-Anglican faction, including Rochester himself, it promptly suspended Compton. Rochester protested feebly, but it was to no avail. By this point, James had no intention of paying any lip service to the Tory-Anglican interest. In January 1687, he dismissed Rochester and Clarendon and began to personally interview all office holders and MPs to see if they would agree to go along with the agenda of Catholic toleration. He promptly sacked anyone in the direct employment of the Crown who refused, which was many.

By this point it was clear that there was no prospect of achieving his aim by persuading MPs, so he decided to use more direct methods. In April 1687, he prorogued parliament again and issued a Declaration of Indulgence, which suspended all of the penal laws against both Roman Catholics and Dissenters.

This marked his final break with the Tory-Anglican interest, and the rise of a completely new strategy. If his old friends wouldn't co-operate, then there was an alternative possibility: court the Dissenters. A Catholic-Dissenting alliance against the Church of England was the ultimate nightmare of the Church establishment. It could, James reasoned, lead to England becoming a bastion of religious toleration in Europe, attracting traders and investment from all over the continent on the model of the Dutch Republic. Why, after all, would the Dissenters have any sentimental qualms about the Church of England, an institution that had connived in their persecution for decades?

James had been cultivating the Dissenting interest since early 1686, pardoning and granting dispensations from the Clarendon Code to many Baptists and Quakers. He even recruited William Penn as his chief Quaker cheerleader for toleration. Following the Declaration of Indulgence, he used the services of a motley crew of propagandists to sell his agenda to the public. He managed to recruit not only Roger L'Estrange, who was consistent enough to uphold the absolute authority of James II in all circumstances, and his former arch-enemy, Whig propagandist Henry Care, who had been L'Estrange's chief journalistic opponent during the Exclusion Crisis. Care, an unlikely hired pen for a papist king, was prepared to co-operate with James in order to promote religious toleration. The political world went topsy-turvy: a Stuart monarch abandoned his Tory Anglican base, old Exclusionists joined hands with extreme Tories, and some of the hottest Protestants in the land went in to bat for a papist king.

Such an odd set of political bedfellows had a tough task on its hands. Although Dissenters naturally supported toleration, many of them, especially the Presbyterians, were uneasy. They might approve the Declaration in substance, but they disapproved of the method of enacting it (royal prerogative) and they distrusted the man responsible.

As for the Tory-Anglicans, James had made a fatal misjudgement. It was true that the situation placed Tories in a terrible situation. There had always been a potential tension between the two lodestars of their political universe: Church and king. There was an enormous irony in men who had preached non-resistance and passive obedience opposing the King's will, a point made in pungent terms by one Whig in conversation with a couple of bishops: 'You have made a turd pye, Seasoned it with passive obedience, and now you must eat it your Selves'.[14]

57

However, James had chosen the one issue that trumped the Tory-Anglican high view of royal power: the security of the Church of England. If pushed to choose, the vast majority of Tories would plump for the Church over the absolute authority of the King, no matter how conflicted or uncomfortable they might feel about it. It was a truth that James was to realise too late.

Meanwhile, James had decided that merely suspending the penal laws was not enough. He wanted to engineer a new parliament that would agree to change the law and purge the entire superstructure of recalcitrant Tory-Anglican office-holders throughout the land. He dissolved the 1685 parliament and, in an ironic twist of fate, set about purging the corporations of all those loyal Tories who Charles II had placed there largely because of their support for his own accession. He replaced them with a ragtag band of Roman Catholics and co-operative Dissenters. He decided on a general election for November 1688, and reissued the Declaration of Indulgence.

He then made the fateful step of reigniting direct confrontation with the Church of England by ordering the clergy to read the reissued Declaration to their congregations during Sunday services. In response, seven bishops, including the staunchly Tory Archbishop of Canterbury, William Sancroft, petitioned the King to request that he withdraw his order. He responded with cold fury to the bishops: 'Here are strange words. I did not expect this from you. This is a standard of rebellion.'[15] It was a 'standard of rebellion' hoisted aloft with alacrity by the vast majority of Anglican priests, who overwhelmingly refused to obey the King's command.

James responded by indicting the bishops on a charge of seditious libel merely for the act of petitioning him. It was an enormous miscalculation. The trial essentially boiled down to whether the bishops were merely requesting that the King obey the law, or whether their petition was a calculated attempt to 'disturb the government, or make mischief and a stir among the people'.[16]

At 10 a.m. on 30th June, the jury returned a verdict of 'not guilty', and the reaction was joyous. The bishops were widely seen by the whole of Protestant England, Dissenters as well as Anglicans, as brave bulwarks against the onwards march of popery. The London crowds went wild with triumph.

The fact that many Dissenters saw Archbishop Sancroft and his colleagues as heroes was significant. In response to the King's attempt to win over Dissenting 'hearts and minds' to his unlikely new alliance, various leading Anglicans had launched their own charm offensive. Leading Anglican politicians like Halifax, who had been alienated by James's policy, wrote pamphlets appealing directly to the Dissenters not to allow a papist king to play divide and rule and split the Protestant interest. Although the irony of Anglicans appealing to pan-Protestant unity was not lost on the Dissenters, neither was the even greater irony of a papist king courting them when convenient.

Most Dissenters, however, found Halifax's claim – that they were to be 'hugged now' only that they might 'be the better squeezed at another time' – to be persuasive.[17] Could they really stomach an alliance with a king whose faith was, in their view, inherently prone to absolutism? Was a toleration won by illegal methods not poisoned by the very means of its implementation? The fact that the Anglican propagandists also showed some contrition for past wrongs and promised to make amends in more propitious times also told. The leading Dissenters refused to side with James; having abandoned his most secure prop, the Tory-Anglican interest, he had failed to acquire a new one.

By spring 1688, James was in trouble, but his cause was by no means desperate. He had no male heirs, and next in line to the throne was a staunch churchwoman, his eldest daughter Mary. James was widely rumoured to be in poor health; few thought he had long to live. His wife, Mary of Modena, had had a series of miscarriages and it seemed unlikely that she would ever bear him a son. The easiest course for his opponents was to wait until he died, when all his work to promote popery would be undone overnight.[18]

This calculation was torpedoed in June 1688 by the birth of a living male heir, James Francis Edward Stuart, just a few weeks before the verdict in the trial of the Seven Bishops. The King would obviously bring his son up as a devout Catholic, and there was every chance of the perpetuation of a long line of papist kings of England. The 'wait until all this blows over' approach became unviable overnight, despite widespread (and false) attempts to claim that the baby boy was 'suppositious', an imposter snuck into the birthing chamber in a warming pan.

This was not, however, enough of itself to threaten James's rule. Tory Anglicans might be acutely unhappy with the King, but they still retained enough of their old principles to make active rebellion on their part vanishingly unlikely. As for the Whigs and Dissenters, only a fiery minority would go as far as insurrection, and they had failed miserably in a not dissimilar situation, after the dissolution of the Oxford Parliament in 1681. The Monmouth and Argyll rebellions had similarly failed. The bonfire had been well supplied with tinder by James, but it would take an external flame to light it.

Luckily for James's opponents, there was a prime candidate for that role: Willem Hendrik van Oranje, Stadtholder of the Dutch Republic (the United Provinces), better known to us as William of Orange. Charles I's grandson (by his daughter Mary), William was both the nephew and son-in-law of James, married as he was to James's eldest daughter and heir to the throne, Mary. He was himself therefore a Stuart on one side, and, prior to the birth of James's son, third in line to the throne. He had been seen as one of the likeliest candidates for the English throne back during the Exclusion Crisis.

A staunch Calvinist, William was widely seen as the standard bearer of the Protestant cause in Europe against the aggression of Catholic wannabe 'Universal Monarch' Louis XIV, against whom he had been fighting (on and off) for over fifteen years. He had come to power as a twenty-one-year-old in 1672 in the midst of a near-disastrous French invasion, which had been staved off only with great difficulty, partly through the expedient of opening the Dutch dykes and flooding swathes of his own country to prevent the French advance. The peace subsequently secured was precarious, and William had spent much of the period since in furious diplomatic activity to stave off geopolitical isolation and prepare for a likely resumption of hostilities.

By 1688, the Revocation of the Edict of Nantes, which reversed toleration for French Protestants, had raised Protestant–Catholic tensions across Europe. The French launched a trade war which hit the Dutch merchants hard. In response, William, convinced that the French were planning another invasion, made extensive military preparations, building up his fleet and fortifying his land border. Matters quickly escalated, with Louis encouraging James to build up his own fleet, implying that the Dutch might intervene in English affairs.

He was dead right. William was convinced that war with France was imminent. The Dutch Republic, a small country unable to match the great French monarchy in power and resources, had only staved off defeat before with the greatest difficulty, making him very twitchy. Ironically, at this point Louis had no plans for a major war and was essentially focusing on defensive manoeuvres, but William was convinced otherwise. His eyes turned towards James II's crown, the possession of which would enable him to mobilise England's considerable resources against Louis XIV.

Back channels between some of the most discontented among the English elite and William had been open for some time, and assurances were received that, in the event of a Dutch invasion, widespread disaffection in the army and navy would lead to desertions. On 30th June 1688 – the day of the acquittal of the Seven Bishops – the so-called 'Immortal Seven' (seven senior figures from the English political elite) – sent a formal invitation to William to intervene militarily to save them from James's 'tyranny'. Composed of two Tories and five Whigs, the figures represented some of the chief landed magnates (Danby and the Earl of Devonshire), the church (Bishop Compton of London), the army (the Earl of Shrewsbury and Lord Lumley) and the navy (Edward Russell and Henry Sidney).

William's interests in preserving English liberties were secondary, although maintaining that they were his central objective was politically essential. To justify his intervention in the eyes of his allies and English public opinion, he issued a Declaration shortly before the invasion, which was widely circulated in England. It strenuously insisted that his intention was merely to help his Protestant brothers in England defend their religion and liberties, and his invasion force was 'intended for no other design, but to have a free and lawful parliament assembled as soon as possible'.[19] The reality was quite otherwise: although at first he may have contemplated trying to secure his objectives more indirectly, before long he realised that the only sure way to bring England into the war against France was to obtain the throne. However, claiming that his intention was limited to helping his co-religionists secure a free parliament was less likely to frighten the horses, especially Tory ones.

James was very slow to believe that his 'nephew and son-in-law could be capable of so ill an undertaking', even when made aware of William's extensive military preparations.[20] By September, William was ready, but James was convinced until very late that William wouldn't commit his army to England and open himself up to possible French invasion. In any case, it seemed unlikely that Louis XIV would allow such a move to go unopposed: William gaining the resources and power of the English throne was hardly in his interests.

Louis, however, had various other considerations to weigh, his forces committed elsewhere. Although late in the year, which made the weather more unpredictable, a window was opened for William to take the initiative. His invasion force – made up of around 15,000 troops (many of them, ironically, Roman Catholic mercenaries) – was ready by October.

His first attempt at invasion was quickly abandoned in mid-October in the face of fierce storms. Gales blowing from the west pinned his fleet into port for weeks. Then, in late October, the weather changed, confining the English fleet to the Thames Estuary and allowing the Dutch to sail.

The 'Protestant Wind' had blown.

Once James began to realise that the reports from his agents about a massive Dutch invasion force destined for England were true, he immediately took steps to bolster his defences, calling in reinforcements from Scotland and Ireland. He was steeling himself to fight.

Nonetheless, the Anglican-Tory hierarchy seized on the uncertainty and attempted to force upon James a return to the 'old ways' of Stuart–Church alliance. On 3rd October, a deposition of bishops met James and demanded a reversal of his entire religious and political platform and a genuinely free parliament. James havered at first, but then began a halting compliance with some of their wishes. It was a classic case of a desperate U-turn made far too late.

However, when William landed at Brixham in Devon (his ships anchored in nearby Torbay), James did not appear, necessarily, to be a defeated man. The Prince of Orange received a mixed reception. At the first major city he entered, Exeter, all of the aldermen of the city except one remained loyal to James, and the clergy refused point blank to read his Declaration in their churches. Defections from the army were no more than a slow trickle, and few major country magnates or peers declared for him at first.

However, soon momentum began to build behind the invader. A spate of Whig nobles, including a young rakehell called Thomas Wharton, joined William in mid-November. More ominously for James, Sir Edward Seymour, a haughty Tory grandee who exerted huge control over the politics of the west country, also deserted James. The fall of the garrison at Plymouth cleared William's way for a march on London. Meanwhile, a series of uprisings in the North and Midlands, one led by that bulwark of the High Tory interest, the Earl of Danby, multiplied James's problems. Riots and anti-Catholic looting broke out throughout the country, most severely in London.

James's strategy was, initially, to try to contain William in the west country. He dispatched his forces to Salisbury Plain, where he joined them personally on 19th November. Not long after, he received a bitter blow: some of his most important army officers, including John Churchill and even the Duke of Ormonde, grandson of the truest of the Cavaliers, had gone over to the enemy. Morale in the army collapsed as the suspicion that any officer could be a traitor took hold. James's own morale – and health – was scarcely much better. According to Gilbert Burnet – William's Whig chaplain and soon-to-be bishop whose *History of His Own Time* is one of our key sources for the period – 'his spirits sunk extremely' and 'his blood was in such fermentation, that he was bleeding much at the nose, which returned oft upon him every day'.[21] James called a council of war, which advised retreat: the army was in no state to fight. William was left to advance at a leisurely pace towards London.

James had no option but to look for a political solution to his desperate straits. Fleeing back to London, he called a meeting of peers and bishops, who advised calling a free parliament and negotiating with William. James duly issued the writs for a parliament to be held in January. He sent three agents – lords Halifax, Nottingham and Godolphin – to visit William and seek for some sort of settlement.

William set out his terms: the dismissal of all papists from office, pardons for all in rebellion, financial provision for his army, and the placing of key military garrisons in 'neutral' hands. He wanted to be present at the new parliament, with both armies forty miles away. These mild-sounding terms seemed consistent with his professed aim of merely seeking a free parliament. He had little choice, as many of the men who had supported him, especially Tories, had taken his promises at face value.

At this point, James spectacularly played into William's hands. Panicking, badly hurt by the defection of his daughter Anne, he made the fateful decision that would end up in some most unregal manhandling by the fishermen of Kent. He chose to flee.

In many ways, James's decision seems incomprehensible. However desperate his situation in a military sense, he still had major political and moral cards to play. While he remained in the thick of the action, William was in a real bind. Claiming the throne while the lawful king was still very much around was not easy, particularly considering the limited pledges outlined in his Declaration.

Although many Whigs found little to trouble their consciences in deposing the King, for the Tories it was a different matter. Even the more gung-ho Tories, like Danby, who had signed the invitation to William, did not necessarily endorse overthrowing the King – they merely wanted to force him to stick to his original promises. The Tories did not give up their scruples easily, and in many cases not at all; some simply sat on their hands, many actively disapproved of the whole affair and would only come to reluctantly accept it later. A few never accepted it and became Jacobites. William faced a massive falling out with the Tory elements of his ragtag anti-James coalition if he wasn't seen to keep his promises.

However, when we consider the wider context of December 1688, James's actions appear more understandable, if still perhaps unwise. The Revolution of 1688 was often presented by its subsequent Whiggish eulogisers as a 'bloodless', tame, even genteel affair, but this was far from true.

The crisis of James's regime had lit the fuse of anti-Catholic sentiment. London erupted into rioting and vandalism against Catholic chapels from September onwards. The risings against James in the Midlands and North saw an orgy of anti-Catholic violence: the houses of known papists were ransacked, chapels burnt and individual Catholics humiliated. In Cambridge, a priest avoided a lynching only by hiding 'in a bogg house' and a crowd made one unfortunate individual 'dance naked in a ditch until he promised to change his religion'.[22]

This atmosphere was heightened by various circumstances and cynical ploys. James had called up Irish (and therefore mainly Catholic) reinforcements when William's invasion became certain. Many were quick to exploit this. A fanatical Whig, Hugh Speke, published a fake Declaration, purporting to be from William himself, claiming that a hoard of papist villains was heading to London to loot, rape and murder, and probably burn down the city. Danby himself cynically played on this fear during the rising he led in Yorkshire, using an imaginary papist incursion to justify his seizure of York.[23]

A frenzy of rumour and panic broke out nationwide: phantom papist armies 'roamed' the countryside of England, and a Chinese whispers-effect set in, whipping up men all over the country to volunteer to defend their homes and hearths against dark Romish outrages. In this frenzied situation, it's not hard to see why James might have lost his nerve. It was in this atmosphere that the fishermen of Kent prowled the coast, searching for Jesuit priests and papist troublemakers.

Aptly, given the sort of luck he had had so far that year, even James's attempt at escape didn't work. The temporary government that had been cobbled together in London gave orders for him to be escorted back to London from Faversham. On his return, he was actually given a hearty welcome from the crowds, and Tory hopes for a compromise settlement with William rose.

James's mind, however, was still set on escape. The idea of sitting watching a parliament decide his fate, with William and his army looming in the background, sickened his proud Stuart heart. He had no intention of becoming a nominal puppet king, or being conveniently bumped off. If he could get away to France, his friend Louis XIV might help restore him to his full authority by force.

James's return was a profound irritation to William, who wanted to see the back of him as quickly as possible. He decided that the best course was to give James every opportunity to escape again. He left him very slackly guarded. It worked. On a desolate and bitter Christmas Eve, James slipped out of his glorified makeshift prison. He arrived in France on Christmas morning.

He would never see England again.

James left a scene of complete political confusion behind him, in part deliberately. Just before he fled, he had countermanded the election writs that he had reluctantly agreed to earlier in December and dropped the Great Seal – the means by which the King gave his approval to major decisions, including royal assent to laws – into the Thames. He hoped thereby to make the conduct of any new government legally impossible.[24]

William had entered London on 18th December to cheering crowds of supporters, many of whom wore orange ribbons or waved oranges impaled on sticks to signal their support for him. He considered simply declaring himself king, but he knew that this would sit ill with the Tories. So he improvised. He hashed together a sort of makeshift 'parliament' which rapidly approved of William taking up the practical reins of government. He called elections, to be held in January 1689, to choose a 'convention' (a 'parliament' that isn't technically a parliament, as a parliament can only be called by a sitting monarch, which William was not – yet).

The election seems to have been more tranquil than might have been expected. The issue of what to do about the throne was not a central issue in many places: the fact that many pro-church Tories signalled their support for William took the heat out of that most pressing of issues. Some constituencies (all of which elected two MPs) sent one Whig and one Tory without a contest; the Revolution had been a joint Tory–Whig venture after all. Nonetheless, Roger Morrice recorded that the election 'was contended fervently in very many places, but with great regularity and faireness'.[25] The key issue underpinning the election – whether always consciously aired or not – was whether the new political settlement was to be a return to the status quo ex ante, underpinned by the Tory-Anglican alliance, or whether the opportunity for a more radical alteration was to be taken.

The result was a fairly balanced parliament. It seems clear that there were 174 known Whigs and 156 known Tories, along with a large contingent of MPs of less obvious commitments. The Tories held the balance in the Lords.

Once the convention met, it had essentially five options. First, attempt to call back James and allow him continue as king, under conditions. Second, act as if James were a madman or a child and hand effective power over to William as regent, with James remaining (nominally) king. Third, declare Mary, James's eldest daughter, sole monarch. Fourth, declare William and Mary as joint monarchs. Fifth, declare William as king.

Calling back the King was completely impractical and declaring William sole monarch politically impossible unless no concession was to be paid to Tory scruples at all. The more viable solutions, however, still involved fundamental issues, especially on the Tory side. Indeed, the Tories encountered head-on a series of agonising dilemmas, related to two closely connected issues: disobeying the King in the first place and the succession.

Legions of High Tory Anglican clerics had spent years declaiming the necessity of complete obedience to the anointed king. Were the men who preached fiery annual sermons on the anniversary of Charles I's execution denouncing rebellion to suddenly admit that their principles were wrong? Had they not claimed that disobedience led ineluctably to civil war and regicide?

By the time the convention met, however, the question of rebellion was a moot point: what was done was done. The live issue was what to do about the Crown. Even many Whigs were chary about outright declaring that James's breaking of the 'original contract' gave parliament the right to depose the King, and the Tories would never consent to it. However, the fact that the King had fled gave MPs, whether more moderate Whig or Tory, something of a basis for getting round this.

James's desertion of his post could be construed, if one squinted very hard and didn't think too much about it, to be an implied 'abdication'. John Maynard, a Whig, claimed that 'it is not the question whether subjects can depose their king, but whether the King can depose himself'.[26] As this sort of fudge, when allied to the simple fact that James had left the country, was something most Whigs and some Tories could live with, it formed the crucial basis of the Commons' famous resolution, that:

> King James the Second, having endeavoured to subvert the Constitution
> of the Kingdom, by breaking the original Contract between king and

people, and, by the advice of Jesuits, and other wicked persons, having violated the fundamental Laws, and having withdrawn himself out of this Kingdom, has abdicated the Government, and that the Throne is thereby become vacant.[27]

The simple fact was that this statement was a polite fiction. James had fled the country because he feared he might be killed or coerced, not because he wished to communicate, in some convoluted way, a desire to abdicate.

The Tories in the Lords were not prepared to countenance this. One in particular stepped forward to destroy the logic of this 'argument'.

Daniel Finch, the Earl of Nottingham, was the austere conscience of the Tory Party. Tall, dark, angular, he was a man of complete honesty and sincerity, but also the driest of dry sticks. A devout and unflinching High Churchman, indeed the leading lay Anglican of his generation, Morrice called him (contemptuously) 'Patron of the Hierarchists'.[28] Most knew him as 'Dismal', on account of his gloomy temper, prickly nature and unusually swarthy complexion. Unable to tell a convenient lie or accept a politic fiction, his grim rigidity often inspired grudging respect but rarely popularity.

He had no truck with the Commons' convenient untruth. He argued that for parliament to unilaterally claim the right of judging a king to have voluntarily forfeited his own crown was unknown in English law, and would make them the sole supreme power in the land, which was contrary to all ideas of the 'mixed' English constitution. Put simply, there was no legal basis for the interpretation the Commons wished to put on the King's flight.

However, even Nottingham had to admit realities. Recalling James was simply not practical politics, not least because there was no chance of him returning to face the same indignities he had just escaped from. The next best option from Nottingham's point of view was a regency, which would retain James as king, at least formally, while transferring the real powers of state to William.

The Tories, however, were not united. Another faction, led by Danby, favoured declaring Mary queen. If one admitted that James had 'deserted', and maintained the dubious notion, which was lent nominal credence by the 'warming pan' story, that James had no living son, then she was next in line to the throne. It thereby allowed the Tories to salve their consciences over hereditary succession, albeit tenuously. Danby argued that a regency was impractical, and, in an acrimonious debate sided with the Whigs to defeat the proposal by three votes.

The Lords did, however, reject the Commons' resolution that the Crown was vacant, and that the King had abdicated. A back and forth now ensued between the Commons and Lords, ending in complete deadlock. The Lords might have rejected the Commons' resolutions, but they were incapable of uniting behind any alternative. They also refused to accept the Commons' delusory, albeit grimly pragmatic, solution. Lord Wharton, the brutally frank Whig lord, summed up, with a great deal more honesty than most MPs or peers, the simple reality:

> whether he may be deposed, or deposes himself, he is not our King. 'Tis not for mine, nor the interest of most here, that he should come again. Abdication and Direliction are hard words to me, but I would have no loop-hole to let in the King; for I believe not myself nor any Protestant in England safe, if you admit him.[29]

Reality quickly dawned. The deadlock was soon rendered moot. Ultimately, with James gone, William was in a strong position: everyone knew that, one way or another, he had to be given effective control of the government, and by simply refusing to countenance any option other than being made king, it became clear that the Lords had to give way. He declared that if he was not offered the throne, he would pack up and go home: he would not, he claimed, be his wife's 'gentleman usher'. He was, however, prepared to appease Tory scruples by agreeing to be crowned jointly with his wife, making her (technically) co-monarch, if the administration of the government were given to him for his lifetime. He would also agree to allow Anne's heirs to be preferred in the succession to any he might have with Mary.

When the crunch vote came in the Lords, the issue was already decided. William held all the cards. Enough Tories diplomatically stayed away to allow the Commons' original resolution to pass. Even Nottingham knew that the game was up: he spoke to some of his allies and 'prevailed with [them] to stay away, that the other side might carry the question; for fear of a civil war, if they had lost it'.[30] The throne was declared vacant. William and Mary were to be crowned king and queen.

First blood had gone to the Whigs.

The next task was to decide upon what terms William would rule. Would parliament use the situation to impose a new constitutional settlement on the incoming king, one that gave themselves more power? Or would it merely restore the constitutional status quo ante?

To determine this, the Commons appointed a committee 'to bring in general Heads of such things' as were 'absolutely necessary . . . for the better securing our Religion, Laws and Liberties'.[31] This was a cross-party initiative: it wasn't only the Whigs who had objected to the King's arbitrary use of his power. Particularly on issues such as the security of the Church, most Tories had similar concerns.

The debates over what was to become the Bill of Rights gave some sense of the first stirrings of the ideological change that the Revolution was to produce within both the Whig and Tory parties.

The reign of James II had shown the inconveniences to the Tories of absolutism, of course, but the fact that the new king was not, in the view of most Tories, king de jure, only king de facto, inevitably changed their attitude as well. Although they had reluctantly agreed to William's accession, they could hardly hope for him to be 'their' king in the way that Stuart monarchs usually were. Many of the men who came across with William, who had fled England after the Exclusion Crisis, were Whigs. The Tories in the Lords had just expended much effort in trying to prevent William becoming king in any straightforward sense. They sensed he would be a 'Whig king', and this made them rather more amenable to the idea of restricting monarchical power. The Whig attitude was the mirror image. If William was 'their' monarch, then was it really necessary to go too far in constraining his power?

In short, both sides became rather more suspicious or supportive of royal power according to whether they judged the monarch was 'their king' or not. Some stuck more stubbornly to their old party prejudices – ideological baggage is a hard to shed – and the process by which the parties did an about turn on their attitude to royal power was a slow one, but it is detectable from this early stage.

The result was a document that was rather conservative and incorporated a lot of concerns that were as much Tory as Whig. It condemned various 'cross-party' grievances against James: the royal dispensing and suspending powers, the use of ecclesiastical commissions to interfere with the Church (anathema particularly to the Tories), and the keeping of a standing army in times of peace.

The Whigs moved that the document be split into two sections, the first being merely declarative of existing laws (or so it was claimed), the second consisting of demands requiring new legislation (which the Convention, not yet technically being a legal parliament, could not enact). To this second list were banished reforms, such as securing frequent meetings of parliament, that might prove inconvenient to the Whig leaders in due course, or were opposed by William himself, who had no desire to be a toothless monarch. Battles over these issues would be left to the future.

With the questions of the royal succession and the Bill of Rights settled, the King declared the Convention to be an official parliament.

External events had meanwhile become pressing. The main purpose of William's mission to England was to secure resources and support for his major objective: war against France. He wanted to take the initiative. Citing France's trade war and the need to protect Dutch nationals in France, the Dutch declared war in early 1689; England officially followed suit in May.[32]

Before battle could be taken to the French on the continent, it had to be waged nearer to home first. Most of Ireland supported James, and the government in Dublin was still presided over by Richard Talbot, Earl of Tyrconnell, James's appointee, who girded himself for war to retain Ireland for King James. James needed to act quickly if he wanted to take back his throne, and Ireland was his obvious entry point. His only hope was a military expedition backed by France. Louis XIV was only too willing to oblige, and on 12th March 1689, James arrived in Ireland to take command of his armies personally, backed by 6,000 French troops. Consolidating his hold over the whole of Ireland was the first step – the intention was then to use his armies to reclaim England.

William needed to move quickly and mobilise the English state for war. The year 1689 would be touch-and-go for him, with military matters in Ireland in the balance and his own regime far from secure. Gaining supply, building up England's armed forces and mobilising against James in Ireland became his overwhelming priority. To do this successfully, he needed to negotiate the febrile internal politics of the Convention parliament.

This would not be easy. William was a difficult man: brusque, cold and high-handed. It is easy to forget that he was in many ways a Stuart himself; some Whigs during the Exclusion Crisis had been sceptical of backing his claim to the throne should James be discarded on the basis that he may well prove to be a Stuart 'tyrant' like his grandfather (Charles I) or uncle (Charles II). They weren't altogether wide of the mark.

His personality did him no favours. He was not 'clubbable' and refused even to attempt to ingratiate himself with the English political elite. He shunned the social round, the parties and feasting, which had greased the wheels of the Stuart court. His character had been indelibly shaped by adversity and the loneliness of command: he had been grimly fighting for the independence of his country since he was a young man. The vicious internal battles of Dutch politics had made him morose, distrustful and secretive. Burnet observed that 'he hears things with a dry silence that shows too much of distrust of those to whom he speaks'.[33] Those few he did trust were all Dutchmen, his long-standing retainers who had campaigned with him for years. A consummate military man, he found the English to be nowhere near martial enough in their outlook for his taste. He kept them at arm's length. As he himself remarked, 'I see that I am not made for this people, nor they for me.'[34]

He looked upon the partisan passions of English politics with weary distaste. All he wanted from parliament was co-operation with his military objectives. He cared not a jot who served him, Tory or Whig, so long as they could supply him what he wanted: chiefly, taxes. Given that the Glorious Revolution had been something of a compromise between Whig and Tory, and a mixture of Tory support and acquiescence had been a *sine qua non* of the Revolution's success, he no doubt hoped that party politics might wither away, or at least die down. The reality, however, was summed up well by one of his irritated courtiers, who remarked:

> How was my wonder and indignation increased when as a proper means to attain authority and power the buried names of Whig and Tory were revived in parliament, and from thence dispersed through the nation.[35]

While religious passions continued to animate English politics, and while the wounds of the immediate partisan past still smarted, this was inevitable, so William had to find a way of coping with the two parties.

He was conscious of his debt to the Whigs, but he never really trusted them: he suspected that, at heart, the Whigs – or at least their wilder elements – were republicans who could not be trusted to protect his prerogative power and really wanted to make him a mere toothless 'Doge of Venice'.[36] On the other hand, he didn't trust the Tories either: though their historic prejudice in favour of the monarchy might be useful, he suspected their loyalty. Given that the genesis of the Tory Party was the battle to protect the right of a Stuart monarch to accede to the throne, based on ideas of divine right and non-resistance, could he really trust them to support him rather than James? This suspicion was well summed up by a man who was to become one of his chief advisers, the shameless Earl of Sunderland, who commented: 'it was very true that the Tories were better friends to monarchy than the Whigs were, but then his majesty was to consider that he was not their monarch'.[37]

Whatever the truth of Sunderland's statement, there was no doubt that the claims of James would cast a long shadow over post-revolutionary politics, and by extension over the battle between Whig and Tory.[38]

The cause of those committed to the restoration of the deposed Stuart king and his successors – the 'Jacobites' – was destined to fail, but this was by no means obvious at the time. The Stuart line had been dethroned and restored before, and it was perfectly possible that the new Williamite regime would fall apart as the Cromwellian one had in the late 1650s. James had the backing of the most powerful military force in Europe, the French, as well as a disaffected majority of one of the constituent nations of the British Isles, Ireland; neither was he bereft of loyal supporters in Scotland, or, to a lesser extent, in England.

William's regime lived from hand to mouth in the confused circumstances immediately following the Revolution, and his success was by no means assured. William may have defeated James and his Jacobite forces at the Battle of the Boyne in mid-1690, but the same month saw naval defeat at the Battle of Beachy Head, which left England wide open to French invasion. Although his regime survived that challenge, the military situation remained finely poised throughout the rest of the war. Jacobite plots swirled around the confused atmosphere of the decade, Jacobite propaganda was pumped out by a small band of doughty loyalists, and minor outbreaks of Jacobite rioting, particularly as William became more unpopular in the mid-1690s, could be relied upon to occasionally set Whig nerves a-jangling.

The spectre of Jacobitism interacted with party politics in subtle ways.

If one had taken the Tories' previous absolutist rhetoric about total obedience to the anointed monarch seriously, one might have expected them to have been Jacobites almost by definition. In fact, despite some foot-dragging, very few Tories refused to accept William as king, and many Tory thinkers were soon adapting their ideology to the new realities.

There had always been a brand of more moderate Toryism – pioneered by Charles I's chief adviser, the Earl of Clarendon, earlier in the seventeenth century – which held that the constitution was a 'mixed monarchy' in which the King ruled as one of three estates (alongside the Lords and Commons). In this view, the King possessed vital prerogative powers and a crucial co-ordinating role within the overall balance of the constitution, but his power was constrained by law and he was not permitted to usurp the due rights and privileges of parliament.

Post-revolutionary Toryism quickly revived this ideological framework. Tory thinkers argued that the idea of a 'mixed monarchy' could accommodate the old doctrines of passive obedience and non-resistance: these duties were owed, in this view, not simply to the person of the king, but to the supreme legislative power exercised by the 'King-in-Parliament'. James II, by attempting to unlawfully usurp the rightful powers of parliament, had disrupted this traditional constitution and forfeited his legitimacy: resisting him had not been the people resisting the sovereign power, but rather elements *of* the sovereign power preventing the illegitimate dominance of the other element of that power.

The accession of William III was certainly more of a problem for them, but Tory thinkers came up with various ways of justifying their acquiescence. Some invoked God's providence to show it must have been His will; others professed themselves satisfied with the dubious notion that James had 'abdicated' and so forfeited his crown. Some were even prepared to countenance the idea that, in extreme cases, of which the Revolution was one, resistance could be justified as an act of national self-preservation.

These ideological manoeuvres meant that many Tories were able to oppose Jacobitism, accept William, and claim the mantle of the post-revolutionary constitution for themselves. Even the more extreme among them, who theoretically still saw James as the true king and were therefore committed to some abstract form of Jacobitism, were in fact hardly ever Jacobites in any practical sense: they mostly argued for peaceful submission to William as the de facto ruler and rarely lifted a finger to assist Jacobite scheming.

However, the Tories did not dodge the Jacobite issue as simply as this. Many Tory politicians were, for some time, reluctant to formally renounce James's theoretical de jure claim to the throne or officially 'abjure' their allegiance to him. Many unreconstructed High Church Tories *were* at least theoretically Jacobites. When combined with a lingering Whig suspicion that their opponents still really harboured their old 'absolutist' principles, the Tories found it hard to shake off the taint of crypto-Jacobitism.

The fact that there was almost always a small Jacobite wing of the Tory Party (albeit one that usually left such thoughts unspoken) did not help matters. Many Whigs also suspected that at least residual sentiments of romantic loyalty to the House of Stuart fluttered in the breasts of many Tories who had apparently reconciled themselves to William, with what truth it is hard to say. At the very least, it seems probable that a considerable chunk of the Tory Party always felt a creeping sense of unease about deposing James and a distinct lack of adulatory loyalty towards William.

The Whigs, in contrast, were – with the exception of a tiny number of eccentrics who became wholly disillusioned with the Williamite regime – completely unified on the issue: they supported William as legitimate de jure King and their whole existence depended on extirpating the Jacobite threat. The contrast with the Tories' less straightforward position was one that both they and William were well aware of, and the Whigs accordingly exploited the Jacobite issue against the Tories whenever they could. When genuine Jacobite plots did emerge, the heightened sense of fear and paranoia created tended to cast doubt on the Tories, bolster the Whigs, and give the latter excellent opportunities to embarrass the latter.

The irony was that many politicians in the 1690s – including many senior Whigs – hedged their bets and put out feelers to the Jacobite court in exile at Saint Germain. Knowing that a Jacobite restoration was a possibility, they sought 're-insurance' in case the worst happened. Even such a convinced Whig as Shrewsbury had friendly communications with Saint Germain. In the topsy-turvy world of this era of politics, where regimes could change and heads roll, men were acutely attentive to the cold, hard politics of survival and adaptation.

The Whigs would soon attempt to turn the Jacobite question against the Tories, but the first outbreak of party hostilities, beginning even before William was crowned king, related to the most profound source of party animosity: the Church.[39]

Practically all of the major political players, Whig and Tory, agreed that something had to be done for the Dissenters. Most of them had shown enormous restraint in not playing ball with James's charm offensive, and in 1687–8 senior churchmen had given them assurances that they would be rewarded for this pan-Protestant solidarity later. Most – including senior Tories – agreed that some form of legal toleration for Dissenting worship was therefore necessary. The precise way in which that would be implemented, however, and the broader issue of the legal position of Dissenters and the Church, attracted no such consensus.

The reign of James II had been a perilous time for the Church of England. The Declaration of Indulgence had undermined the Church's authority immediately and dramatically, whatever its legality. How could Church of England attendance be compulsory if the King had declared Dissent and papism legal? Church attendance fell and its discipline faltered. In response, many of the more pragmatic senior churchmen decided that they had to try to combine the need for toleration with maximum restoration of the Church's overall social and moral authority.

The solution favoured by many High Churchmen was toleration allied to 'comprehension'. The idea was that by relaxing some elements of the church's liturgy and doctrines to take account of the scruples of the Dissenters, it would allow the vast bulk of them – especially the Presbyterians – to rejoin (be 'comprehended' within) the Church of England. This would mean that the Church could realistically retain a near-religious monopoly, and the authority and discipline that came with it. Toleration would only apply, on strict and limited terms, to the extreme fringes of Dissent. This was the scheme favoured by Nottingham, who was entrusted with the settlement of the Church by William, and one he introduced into parliament on 27th February.

The fundamental problem was that this scheme was too generous to Dissenters for some Tories, and nowhere near enough for many Whigs. The terms of Nottingham's Comprehension Bill were seen as too harsh even by many moderate Presbyterians, but Tory MPs tried to make them harsher still. The radical Whig Richard Hampden, in response, introduced a completely different version of the bill that would have changed the practices of the Church of England to the extent that 'it made the Church of England more Dissenters and not the Dissenters Church of Englandmen'.[40] Tory outrage was palpable: Sir Edward Chisnall, a staunch Church Tory, moved a motion that the bill be adjourned 'till Doomsday'.[41] Not for the first or last time, the Tories raised the cry of the 'Church in Danger'.

The debate was made far more heated due to the intervention of the King. William, himself a Calvinist, was a strong supporter of the Dissenters. On 16th March, in an address to both houses of parliament, he announced his hope that parliament would 'leave room for the Admission of all Protestants that are willing and able to serve'.[42] This outraged the Tories: it would fatally undermine the political ballast that gave security to Anglican supremacy, the Test Act. One-hundred-and-fifty Tory churchmen met at the rather inappropriately named Devil's Tavern to agree their strategy for defying William and protecting the Church.

These Tories were generally lukewarm, or outright hostile, to even the idea of Comprehension. In their view, the concessions needed to entice considerable numbers of Dissenters to conform to the Church risked watering down its doctrines unacceptably; it would 'introduce a Schism into the very bowels of the Church', admitting all of the errors of Dissent into the Church of England.[43]

In the end, with Hampden's bill having failed and the chances of success for Nottingham's amended bill unclear, a compromise was tacitly agreed. The issue of comprehension would be referred to convocation, the Church's own 'parliament'. There, it would almost certainly fall, given the attitudes of most churchmen. Realising that repeal of the Test Act would not fly either, not least because a sizeable minority of Whigs would not consent to it, the Whig leaders and William let the issue die. In exchange, the Toleration Act would be allowed to pass, but the clergy would be required to take an oath of loyalty to the new king.

The 'Toleration Act' – actually entitled 'An Act for Exempting their Majestyes Protestant Subjects dissenting from the Church of England from the Penalties of certaine Lawes' – was, however, a minimal affair. It did not repeal the penal laws against Dissent, but merely exempted from their penalties some of those who were prepared to take oaths pledging allegiance to the regime. It specifically excluded from its terms Dissenters who did not believe in the doctrine of the Trinity. It only allowed people to recuse themselves from church services if they went to a Dissenting one instead: irreligion was not to be 'tolerated'.

It was, nonetheless, momentous. Protestant Dissent was finally to be legal, its adherents free to worship in public. The Church of England's monopoly was broken. The Tories exulted, as they had seen off the threat of Test Act repeal. Over time, their exultation would fade and the broader implications of toleration would become clear. Their growing discontent would underpin much of the party war of the next twenty-five years.

* * *

The religious issue settled, William turned to the realities of governing his new realm. His initial strategy was to rule via a mixed ministry, made up of the configuration of Whigs and Tories whom he supposed were best able to manage his business. The logic was inescapable: he needed to pay his debt to the Whigs, especially those who had loyally served him during the Revolution, but he also needed the experience of leading Tory veterans, given that no Whig had served in government for decades. In any case, he did not want to become the puppet of either party, and supposed he could balance them against each other.[44]

Accordingly, key posts were given to various Whig grandees who had supported his ascent to power, such as the Earl of Shrewsbury and Thomas Wharton, as well as Tory old lags like Danby (now promoted in the peerage to become the Marquis of Carmarthen) and Nottingham. The comprehensiveness, if not the cohesion, of the government was expanded by even accommodating a host of radical Whigs – former 'Commonwealth men' like John Wildman and Richard Hampden – in minor offices.

This arrangement satisfied nobody. The Tories were alarmed at the presence of radicals like Hampden; John Evelyn, an old Royalist and Tory, remarked that the new administration had 'a Republican Spirit' which boded ill for the 'prosperity of the Church of England'.[45] The Whigs were aghast at the appointment of the Tory hatchet men of the bad old days of Charles II and James II, and were convinced that the King had lost his senses by appointing crypto-Jacobites of doubtful loyalty. They had supposed that William's accession would lead to their dominance and were bitterly disappointed. William had let them down.

Whig bitterness soon spilled over into a petty refusal to assist the King in pursuing his immediate objectives, chief of which was securing generous supply to fund his war. Mindful of the disastrous consequences of their generosity to James II, parliament, spurred on by factious Whig backbenchers, ensured that William received only short-term and often inadequate grants of supply. The Commons knew that granting taxes for only short periods guaranteed that parliament must meet regularly, and was determined to keep the King short if it secured parliament's constitutional position. It was, indeed, this fact, more than any formal constitutional reform, that secured the increasing power and regularity of parliament in the post-revolutionary period.

William's other major priority was to dampen down political instability, which could only help the Jacobites, by seeking peace between the parties. This the Whigs were determined to prevent: they wanted revenge for the actions of the Tories during the latter years of Charles II – for the men sacked or exiled, the corporations purged, the Whigs tried for their life – not to mention punishment for those who had acquiesced in James's measures. The fact that the men who had supported these sickening crimes were now in the employ of William drove them wild with outrage. If he wouldn't sack them, they would destroy them.

Accordingly, they frustrated William's desire for an indemnity bill that would pardon misdemeanours committed under previous regimes. The King was strongly of the view that punishing past offenders harshly would alienate many from his regime and frustrate his attempts to cement his position; best to leave these things to oblivion, except for a few notorious offenders.

The Whigs first blocked this move, and then tried to ambush parliament into passing legislative vengeance on the Tories. This was the 'Sacheverell Clause', named after Whig MP William Sacheverell, which stipulated that any officials who had connived in the quo warranto proceedings under Charles II and James II should be banned from public office for seven years. The effect would have been a mass purge of Tories across the country from local offices, kneecapping the Tory's political base across England.

Sprung on a half-empty house on 2nd January 1690, with most notoriously lazy Tory backwoodsmen still sleeping off their Christmas hangovers, the clause was initially passed. William was furious. The legislation was delayed to allow the Tories to return, and eventually defeated after a spectacular partisan shouting match in the Commons (one excitable Tory exclaimed, 'We routed Jack Presbyter horse and foot!').[46] The Whigs had achieved nothing other than alienating the King.

The Whigs had not finished annoying him yet. With military matters not going to plan, in January 1690 the King decided to leave for Ireland to take control of his forces personally. The Whigs violently objected to this, arguing that anything that could put William's life in danger could jeopardise the entire revolution. According to Roger Morrice, Whigs thought it 'a most unaccountable resolution, and many fear it was suggested and cherished by [William's] enemies'.[47] The implication was clear: only Tory Jacobite traitors could have advised such a dangerous course.

The King was by now convinced that the Whigs were practically republicans, determined to defy him and make him nothing more than a figurehead king. Having once again delayed indemnity, the Whigs then had the effrontery to bring a motion before the Lords requesting him not to go to Ireland. The King's thoughts began to turn to governing through the Tories.

This was made easier by the fact that William became increasingly satisfied of Tory loyalty. The major issue here was the oaths. In order to secure his regime, William had made an oath of allegiance to him as monarch compulsory for all civil and military office holders and all Anglican clergymen. The oath had been designed to be as broad as possible: it was couched in de facto rather than de jure terms, thanks to the intervention of Nottingham and Danby. Still, for many, particularly conscientious Anglicans, it presented a crisis of conscience. The Earl of Clarendon, who refused the oath and therefore cast himself into political outer darkness, summed up the view of many scrupulous Tories well:

> I was fully satisfied, that I could not be absolved from the oaths I had taken [to James]; to which these new ones were contradictory; that, having already taken the former oaths, my allegiance was due to King James, and not in my power to dispose of . . .[48]

God had appointed James as king, and solemn oaths could not be lightly cast away. No amount of Jesuitical tergiversation could get round this.

To the clergy this was a particularly acute dilemma, and some refused to take the oaths, which meant ejection from their livings and ecclesiastical positions. Known as the nonjurors, they included many of the Church's greatest minds and prominent men: most notably, William Sancroft, the Archbishop of Canterbury, and six other bishops, but also 400 ordinary clergymen.

Although this split was significant, it had become clear over the course of 1689 that it was not as damaging as many had feared. Most Tories and Churchmen had taken the oaths, and William was impressed by the loyalty of senior Tories like Nottingham. William began to countenance a dissolution and a general election in which the Tories would strengthen their position, followed by a clear shift to a predominantly Tory ministry.[49]

This was precisely what happened. In the bitterly contested general election of February–March 1690, the Whigs sought to use the fact that many Tories voted in favour of the Lord's rejection of James's 'abdication' and against the vacancy of the throne to claim they were Jacobites who would bring back the tyrannical King James in a heartbeat. The Tories responded by arguing that the Sacheverell Clause was a factious attempt to purge loyal churchmen and install a monopoly of Whigs and Dissenters. One Tory argued that the purpose of the clause had been to exclude 'the Church of England Party out of parliaments for seven years, until the Nation shall be settled upon new, and, as some fancy, better principles'.[50] The none-too-subtle implication was that it was a plot to force republican and anti-Church measures on the King. The whiff of '41 was on the breeze.

These issues made the election a particularly bitter one. One noblewoman wrote to a relative expressing her weariness over the heat of the battle: 'Never was greater animosities and divisions than there is at this day, Whig and Tory more than ever.'[51] In Suffolk, a 'fanatic rabble', according to a Tory source, smeared anyone 'with the face of a gentleman' as a 'papist'.[52] On the other side, the clergy rallied decisively in favour of the Tories. In Middlesex, the men of the cloth piled in so decisively – 'not above four parsons' voting for Whig grandee Sir John Maynard – that it swung the election for the Church Party candidates.[53]

The basic drift of the election had been made almost certain by the fact that when he had dissolved parliament, William had made clear that he favoured the return of 'moderate men of the Church Party'.[54] The voters obliged, the Tories made considerable gains and William quickly made more changes to his ministry to favour the Tories. Nottingham in particular increasingly became the King's chief agent in naval and Church affairs, and although it remained a mixed ministry, with many Whigs retained, it was clear that the King leaned ever more on the Church Party.

The Whigs were bruised, but they had no intention of giving up their long-term project of making William see sense and forcing their way into power. The man who would mastermind this strategy was one of the most controversial and influential political figures of the next twenty-five years of party struggle and state policy: Thomas Wharton.[55]

Wharton had been one of those most guilty of alienating William within the upper echelons of his party. At the height of Whigs' anger at William's refusal to allow them to monopolise government office, he had written an extraordinarily intemperate letter to the King. He told him, in no uncertain terms, that the Tories were disloyal, his inherent enemies, and that his only hope for success was to dismiss them and perhaps proscribe them. The tone of Whig entitlement and frustrated rage was palpable:

> We have made you King, as the greatest return we could make for so great a blessing, taking this to be your design; and if you intend to govern like an honest man, what occasion can you have for knaves to serve you? Can the same men who contrived and wrought our ruin, be fit instruments for our salvation? Or with what honour can you employ those against whom you drew your sword?[56]

He continued:

> Your coldness and slowness in business hath made your enemies think you are afraid of them, & your trimming between Parties is beneath both you & your cause.[57]

Whether or not he sent the letter is unclear, but Wharton's aggression did the Whigs no favour as William turned against them. So far as Wharton was concerned, this was nothing more than a temporary setback.

Wharton was a colossal figure bestriding the territory of post-revolutionary English politics, the 'tutelary God of the Whigs'.[58]

He was a veteran of the old battles, having been a young protégé of Shaftesbury. He was suspected – but never proven – to be implicated in the Rye House Plot. During the Revolution, he wrote a famous anti-Irish song – 'Lillibullero' – that became the theme for the anti-James forces, rallying their spirits; he claimed that he had 'sung a deluded Prince out of three kingdoms'.

He was the consummate 'party man', dedicating his entire life to advancing the good old cause of Whiggery and the Protestant interest. So far as he was concerned, what was good for the Whig party was good for the country; the Tories were crawling servants of papism and tyranny who would betray the Revolution and bring back James. He wanted nothing less than their complete and utter destruction, and would spare no pains to try to make it happen.

His efforts were, however, often hamstrung by his notoriously dissolute private life. Although he was from one of the leading Presbyterian political families, and his father was a stern, moralistic Puritan, his passion for wine and women was nearly as strong as his love for Whiggery. One of the finest swordsmen of his age, young Whigs looked up to him as a dashing hero, drinking and duelling his way through late Stuart England with brio and exuberance. He fought four duels, mostly against Tory political enemies, and never lost. He was one of the greatest figures of the Turf of his age, owning the best stable of horses in England. His pride and joy, the aptly named 'Careless', only ever lost one race.

He was infamous for his infidelity to his wives. Handsome and charming, he was rarely without a mistress or two in tow (at one point, one of Sir Robert Walpole's sisters). He also notoriously built a house on the edge of his enormous Winchendon estate as a residence for his long-term mistress. The small, turreted abode commanded excellent views of Quainton racecourse, leading wags to remark that it allowed him to indulge his two favourite pleasures at the same time.

When in his cups, however, his antics could take a distinctly less amusing turn. Back in 1679, he and some of his exuberant young Whig cronies disrupted a genteel party held by a Mrs Willis, smashing up the house and breaking the windows; he had to make a hasty exit to escape the attentions of a local constable. He ran riot at a theatre a few months later, 'throwing candles . . . calling my lord Sunderland a traitor, the Duke of York a rascal' and 'toasting the Duke of Monmouth'.[59] On one occasion, he even attacked a local Tory earl with a whip.[60]

All of this paled in comparison with his most notorious escapade. In 1682, Wharton, his brother Goodwin and some other drinking companions committed an outrage at a church in Great Barrington, Gloucester:

> In a drunken fit early in the morning [they] broke open the doors of a church . . . and comitted many horrible acts there . . . which shall have no name . . . [they] tare good part of the bible out, pull down or defaced the pulpit and some other ornaments and goods of the church . . .[61]

The 'horrible acts' were, years later, named by Jonathan Swift, who recounted how Wharton had 'mounted upon the Altar, and there did that which in cleanly Phrase is called "disburthening of nature"'.[62] Rumour held that as well as pissing on the altar, he had also defecated in the pulpit.

The sacrilegious nature of such an act in the eyes of the Church Party can well be imagined. It was seen as indicative of his general irreligiosity: despite presenting himself as a proud upholder of the Dissenting Protestant interest (though he had to nominally conform to the Church of England to hold office), he was in fact a deist, possibly an outright freethinker: the most apt description is probably 'an atheist grafted on a Presbyterian'.[63] In the eyes of sober Tories, when combined with his aggressive Whiggery, this made him the Satan of English politics, a determined enemy of God, the Church and everything good, true and holy. It is no coincidence that he was the particular personal enemy of sober, pious Nottingham.

It wasn't only his debased personal life and religious apostasy that told against him in the eyes of the Tories: they also hated him because he was the most effective and determined master of the art of electioneering, riding across the country with unstinting zeal to bribe, cajole and charm voters into casting their vote for whichever Whig puppet he was supporting at the time. He was able to use his influence on elections all over the country, including in Cumberland, Oxfordshire, Westmorland, Wiltshire and Yorkshire, but most particularly in his native Buckinghamshire. At the height of his power he controlled at least fifteen seats in the Commons, but had an indirect influence far wider than that. He was prepared to spend extraordinary amounts of money on the Whig cause: he once paid £600 (a small fortune) for the votes of three men in Brackley (a small corporation borough which only had a handful of voters). In 1689, he spent the extraordinary sum of £2,200 to win the seat of Appleby.

He was also an expert in using his personal charm to win over the voters. On a canvass in Wycombe in 1695, he went to the local shoemaker's shop to visit a voter called Dick:

> [He] asked where Dick was? The good woman said, her husband was gone two or three miles off with some shoes, but his Lordship need not fear him, she would keep him tight. I know that, says my Lord, but I want to see Dick, and drink a glass with him. The wife was very sorry Dick was out of the way. Well, says his Lordship, how does all thy children. Molly is a brave girl I warrant by this time. Yes, and thank you my Lord, says the woman, and his Lordship continued, Is not Jemmy breeched yet? The gentleman crossed over to his friend on the other side of the way and cried, Even take your horse and be gone. Whoever has my Lord Wharton on his side has enough for his election.[64]

He would remember and pay court to even the humblest man if he thought it would win him a few precious votes.

Ultimately, Wharton was a gambler, always ready to roll the dice and take a chance, whether on the horses (he once bet £1,900 on a single race) or by embarking on some high-stakes gambit in parliament. He was about to find out how effective this 'all-or-nothing' approach would prove in his endeavour to win the King's favour and force the Whigs into office.

Wharton's strategy was to demonstrate to William that the only reliable means of achieving his objectives – particularly funding for his war – was to oblige the Whigs in their desire for office. The basis of this strategy was 'assistance and resistance'.[65] On an issue-by-issue basis, the Whigs would sometimes support the court, to show to the King that the Whigs could 'deliver the goods', and sometimes block its measures, to underline to the King the weakness of any government that did not possess Whig backing. The hope was that the King would gradually realise that giving in to the Whigs represented the path of least resistance.

This strategy was made possible by a mixture of Whig discipline combined with the otherwise increasingly fractured and unpredictable nature of parliament. William faced a situation where he desperately needed fresh taxes every parliamentary session, but a large swathe of MPs were not inclined to oblige him without concessions on various controversial issues.

The MPs that presented the King and his government with their biggest difficulty were those of the 'Country interest'. These were MPs who still cleaved to many of the old ideals of the pre-revolutionary Whig Party: chiefly, suspicion of the overweening power of the monarchy and central government, which they saw as a threat to the independence of parliament and the nation's basic liberties (especially the liberties of the landed gentlemen who made up the backbone of the Country interest).

The 'Country' MPs feared that the court may subvert the independence of the Commons in many ways. One way was high taxes (largely land taxes), which were not only used to fund bribes and douceurs handy for keeping MPs quiet (who would become 'pensioners'), but also depressed the fortunes, and therefore political independence, of the landed country gentlemen. Country members also feared more direct corruption, in the form of fixing elections to ensure that government stooges were elected, or by giving out crown employments to members of parliament, who would then be expected to vote the way the court wanted ('placemen'). A government could even simply refuse to call regular parliaments altogether, or only call elections infrequently, allowing parliaments to become unaccountable and corrupt.

It could also fund its expenditure by contracting large amounts of debt, which would ultimately have to be paid back by ever heavier taxes on the landed gentlemen. Debt also created a whole new financial interest – the 'monied men'– who enriched themselves from the interest paid on the debt. These men had no fixed or permanent stake in the country, their profits weren't taxed (unlike land) and they could reliably be expected to brown-nose the executive and use their money to buy their way into parliament, thus turning parliament into a compliant instrument of courtly tyranny.

The Country members were hugely sceptical about war. Wars were expensive, and expense meant taxes and debt. Wars required large standing armies, which *in extremis* could be used as an instrument of repression against the country's liberties, but also gave government ever greater means of patronage. Profiteers and moneylenders loved wars and would support prolonging them unnecessarily in order to maximise their ill-gotten gains.

In short, they believed that an interconnected web of war, finance and Crown patronage would gradually subvert the nation's liberties. To counter this threat, they advocated a programme of minimising wasteful or corrupt government spending; lower taxes; expelling pensioners and placemen from parliament by the means of 'place bills'; more frequent (usually triennial) parliaments; replacement of the standing army with citizen militias; and paying off the national debt.

Although this was traditionally a Whig platform, the accession of William III changed everything. The Whigs were heavily invested in supporting William in his struggle against the French and their Jacobite hangers on, but that required war, taxes and debt. Many Whigs – 'Court Whigs' – of whom Wharton was a leading example – were prepared to gradually and quietly abandon many of their 'Country' commitments accordingly, but the more principled among them were not. These 'Country Whigs' seemed, at first sight, to cause Whig party managers like Wharton a big headache.

In due course they would indeed do so, but in the short term this was counterbalanced by other factors. Firstly, the 'Country' platform became increasingly attractive to many Tory backbenchers. Tories saw no reason to be obsequiously loyal to William, whom they supported as a matter of pragmatism rather than divine right. Their support was heavily concentrated among the landed squirearchy, who suffered most from the taxes and debt required to fund King William's wars. In addition, they increasingly noticed that taxes and douceurs tended to flow into the pockets of either foreigners, William's Dutch favourites, which piqued their patriotic ire; or financiers, who were disproportionately likely to be Dissenters, their religious enemies.

The Country Whigs, on the other hand, were often willing to be more pragmatic, as they balanced their Country views with their Whig desire to see William win his war against the French and keep out the Jacobites. The biggest grouping among them – soon to be known as the 'New Country Party' – was led by morose, earnest Paul Foley (nicknamed 'Heavy Paul' for his grave disposition and high-minded notions) and increasingly a young man called Robert Harley. They largely drew their ranks from MPs hailing from the Welsh Marches in Herefordshire, Worcestershire and adjoining counties.[66] Many of them were related (Harley was Foley's nephew), and they came from a predominantly conservative Presbyterian background.

Wharton and his court Whigs could threaten the King by holding out the prospect of supporting the Country MPs, especially the Country Whigs, to pass measures that he hated (such as Place Bills or the Triennial Bill, which required elections every three years). This was the stick. The carrot was to work to ensure that parliament would provide him generous supply to fight his war.

Meanwhile, Wharton could batter the Tories in three ways. Firstly, by using the same 'Country' measures to divide the Tories between their Court and Country factions, and thereby make the Tories ever more ineffectual and unable to support the King's agenda in a unified and effective fashion. Secondly, by bringing various bits of legislation – most usually 'abjuration bills', which required anyone holding public office, including MPs, to abjure King James's de jure claim to the throne and acknowledge William's 'lawful and rightful title' – that exploited Tory ambiguities over the succession and allowed the Whigs to paint them as Jacobites. Such measures tended to unite the Whig Party. Thirdly, by attacking the military failures of the largely Tory-run government: whenever the war started to go badly, Wharton would imply that this was because the Tories were Jacobite saboteurs.

Wharton's strategy depended upon the Whigs maintaining more unity and discipline than the Tories, splits between Court and Country Whigs notwithstanding. If the Whigs became too factious and divided, then they would be unable to persuade the King that governing via them would be the more stable and effective option.

Wharton's strategy gradually proved more and more successful, and began to gather momentum in 1692. Lacklustre military performance, including William's loss of the important fortress of Namur in the Spanish Netherlands, led Nottingham, Tory naval supremo, to argue for a bold new strategy: a lightning seaborne attack on the French mainland, at St Malo, which could inflict major blows on the enemy's soft underbelly at much less cost than the land war strategy. This 'descent' into France proved far more logistically difficult and militarily risky than Nottingham realised. By late summer, the plan had been abandoned in a welter of bitterness and recriminations.

When parliament met in November, the Whigs pounced. They vigorously supported proposals for giving William ample supply, but were quite willing to also withhold their support on certain matters to demonstrate the weakness of the ministry without the votes they could muster in the Commons. They skilfully exploited William's frustrations over attempts by xenophobic backbench Country Tories to ensure that all future appointments in foot regiments would be of Englishmen (and not Dutch foreigners), stressing the extent to which Tories clearly distrusted William's army officers. Tory splits were increasingly alienating the King, for all his distrust of the Whig leaders.

On debates over the mismanagement of naval affairs, they implied that the shambolic failure of plans for the 'descent' was rooted in the disloyalty of Nottingham, who was impugned by Wharton as a quasi-Jacobite. In a fiery speech in the Commons, he thundered:

> Your chief men that manage matters are such as submit to this King upon wrong principles, because he has the governing power, but will be as ready to join another [James] when he prevails.[67]

Such an accusation was unfounded, but it dented Nottingham's reputation and weakened the government.

Wharton and his allies followed this up in early 1693 by playing chicken with the King over two classic 'Country' measures, a Triennial Bill and a Place Bill. Brought forward by the Country Whigs, these proposals were anathema to the King. The Place Bill would ban all crown office-holders from sitting in the Commons, thus preserving parliament's independence. The Triennial Act would ensure that the maximum period between general elections would be three years. William saw both measures as unacceptable incursions on his prerogative powers that would make the Commons even more difficult to manage that it already was.

Wharton and the Whig leaders decided to sit on their hands and let the ineffectual court managers twist in the breeze, powerless to stop the measures from advancing. So the Country Whigs combined with the backbench Tories to pass the Place Bill through the Commons: only a desperate rearguard action in the Lords managed to defeat it, by a mere two votes. The exact same tactics were applied to the Triennial Bill, which actually passed both houses and forced William to exercise his veto.

The message conveyed to the King was clear. Ally with the Whigs, and all of these problems would disappear. The Whigs had the power to advance the King's agenda, if given the rewards and patronage they craved for, whereas the divided, raggedy Tories did not.

William realised he had no choice but to oblige the Whigs, and this drift was accelerated by events. In July 1693, naval disaster struck. A valuable merchant fleet fell into the hands of the French while travelling to the Turkish port of Smyrna due to a naval blunder. Nottingham was not in any way responsible, but it didn't matter: the Whigs were determined to 'lay all miscarriages at [Nottingham's] door', and it was easily spun as his fault in a febrile House of Commons.[68]

Another factor also bubbled away under the surface. In despair at the turbulence of domestic affairs, William had been casting around for impartial advice and assistance for some time. From mid-1692 he had found it in a rather murky place: Althorp, the residence of the reviled Robert Spencer, Earl of Sunderland. The man who had turned his coat more times than a winterwear model, who had converted to Roman Catholicism in a bid to win the confidence of James, who was widely seen by everyone, Tory or Whig, as a cross between Judas Iscariot and the Devil himself, was back. William was a complete pragmatist and was prepared to employ anyone who could advance his business; and much as Sunderland was a hectoring thug, and as popular as a papist in a conventicle, he *was* a brilliant operator and gifted tactician.

Sunderland's analysis was simple:

> the great mistake that has been made . . . has been to think that [the two parties] were equal in relation to this government, since the whole of one may be made for it, and not a quarter of the other ever can. Whenever the government has leaned to the Whigs it has been strong; whenever the other has prevailed it has been despised.[69]

The Whigs were more united and decisive, and that was the key to managing parliament. It was hard for William to disagree with his disreputable adviser.

So in November 1693 William took the plunge. He told the Queen that he thought 'his case so bad that he was forced to part with Lord Nottingham, and to please a party he cannot trust'.[70] Sacking Nottingham was widely seen as the prelude to more changes in favour of the Whigs. Wharton signalled his willingness to throw the Court Whigs' influence behind the Crown.

Initially, William's move seemed to work as well as Sunderland had predicted. The Whigs obliged their master on financial matters: they managed to persuade the Commons to increase the number of soldiers in William's army by 20,000, and by the time Christmas 1693 came around, they had secured Commons approval for big increases in military spending. Furthermore, Wharton and his allies had rallied against a wave of Country legislation that was distasteful to the King: although another Place Bill was approved by both houses and had to be vetoed, the Whigs quashed a revival of the Treason Trials Bill and allowed two new attempts at a Triennial Bill to die.

William had to grudgingly concede that the Whigs had revived the government's parliamentary position markedly. So he rewarded them by sacking a number of Tories, most notably old Tory diehards Sir Edward Seymour and Lord Rochester, and promoting Whig financial expert Charles Montagu to be Chancellor of the Exchequer. He was also obliged to agree to let a Triennial Bill pass to woo Shrewsbury back to his old position as Secretary of State, thus giving a fillip to one of the Whig's old principled causes and taking some of the heat out of the Country Whig opposition. It was to have a profound effect on English politics over the next twenty or so years, which would see ten elections, an average of one every two years; it spelled a new era of ever more intense political warfare in the country and instability in the Commons.

However irritating the Whigs might be to the King, and however much a concession like the Triennial Act stuck in his craw, the simple fact was that the Whigs were better able to oblige him on the subject that trumped all others: money. Throughout 1694 William continued to enjoy the boost that the accession of the leading Whigs to his parliamentary phalanx had given him. Tory courtiers were slow to go into anything like outright opposition, making the parliamentary situation as easy as it was likely to get. Ample financing gave William the funds to properly resource his armies, meaning that the war was waged more successfully: the French advance in Flanders was halted by William's capture of the Flemish town of Huy, and the next year would see even greater success as William won an important victory at Namur.

For now, the Whig advance seemed unstoppable. They had finally won the favour and rewards they had expected all along from 'their' king, and so long as the war continued, it was hard to see how William could do without Wharton and his allies.

Under the surface, however, dangerous political currents were swirling furiously. The Whigs were about to find out how dangerous.

3

The Realignment

One of the more bizarre bits of parliamentary mischief that occurred as party tensions rose in the mid-to-late 1690s was made possible by the sort of cruelty to animals that was widely seen as entertainment in the late seventeenth century. In a debate over the rights of trading companies, it was alleged that some Whig whips had conspired with the court managers to try to swing a close Commons vote by luring some younger MPs, who were minded to defy the government, to 'see the baiting of a tiger by a pack of mastiffs'.[1] The distraction worked.

Whether that story is apocryphal or not, many of the leading Court Whigs who, by 1694, were increasingly ruling the roost saw politics as very much modelled on the behaviour of cage-fighting beasts. The most significant of these men, who provided the Whig Party with cohesive, effective and often brutal leadership, were increasingly being referred to as 'the Junto'. Wharton was joined at the head of affairs by wily John Somers, one of the greatest lawyers of his generation who had served William as both Solicitor General and Lord Keeper; Charles Montagu, who focussed mainly on financial matters; and the party's naval expert Admiral Edward Russell. Whereas Russell was the least important of the four, mainly lending them military prestige, and Somers was a cautious, patient man – the Junto man most trusted by William – Wharton and Montagu became increasingly high-handed and were detested by the Country Whigs.

Wharton was blunt, aggressive and always mistrusted by Country back-benchers on account of his devious partisan manoeuvring, but he did, at least, have a certain charisma and charm. Montagu, however, was a crude, nasty political thug, mean and supercilious, loved by no one outside of the Junto (and often not even within it). Ambitious, self-promoting and thrusting, one of his own allies described him as 'like the fly upon the wheel, that would always thrust himself upon people and fancy he did great matters, when in truth he only made himself ridiculous' – though his political acumen could not be denied.[2] Wharton and Montagu took to meeting with their allies at the Rose Tavern to scheme and plot their parliamentary strategy. They revelled in tactics such as springing measures on members unexpectedly or in a thin House in order to win by surprise – or if all else failed, a bit of bullying usually sufficed.

Crude at times they may have been, but so far the Junto men had pursued a very successful strategy. They had managed the increasingly wayward antics of their Country Whig colleagues to impressive effect, ensuring that the Whigs, marshalled by their ruthless leadership, were a more unified and cohesive force than their Tory opponents.

However, over the previous few years there had been signs that the Country Whigs were beginning to cool towards the Junto. The leaders of the largest bloc of Country Whigs, the 'New Country Party' – veteran Paul Foley and young gun Robert Harley – had started to tire of the cynicism of the Junto. They began to suspect that Wharton and his allies were almost entirely concerned with advancing their own interests with little regard to the national interest. The Junto would often hijack non-partisan Country measures and use them to try to embarrass the Tory ministers, before dropping them when convenient. In mid-1692, Harley and Foley had even gone to the length of siding with the Tories to oppose one of Wharton's abjuration bills, on the basis that it was a purely cynical exercise designed to undermine the unity of Country Tories and Whigs.

Indeed, Country Whigs and Tories had been working together for some time on a backbench committee, the Commission of Accounts, that had been set up in 1691 to scrutinise the nation's finances. It was to be a fateful alliance, for as they investigated government mismanagement and waste together, they began to realise that they held many of the same grievances.

The complaints of the Country members were not without foundation. The consequence of the war that loomed largest in their minds was a simple one: expenditure and levels of taxation had ballooned. Average annual government expenditure under James II had been around £1.7 million per year – during the reign of William, it settled at somewhere between £5 million and £6 million per year. The tax burden essentially doubled in total during the war years. The bulk of this was levied by the land tax, which hit the independent country gentlemen hard (they were often paying something like a fifth of their income towards it), and customs duties on imported goods such as beer, salt, leather and other goods (which tended to disproportionately wallop the poorest).[3]

Despite the heavy taxation, it was never enough to cover the government's needs, and so it became increasingly necessary to borrow money to cover the difference. Historically, and in the early years of William's reign, public borrowing had tended to be chaotic, short term and expensive. High interest rates and quick repayment were expected from creditors, which made financing a long-term commitment like a land war in Europe difficult and expensive.

Gradually, moves were made to rectify this situation, based upon the idea of long-term lending to the state by private investors, who were to receive a dependable return, all guaranteed by future state taxation (a 'funded debt'). At first, this was done in the form of one-off loans and state lotteries, but in 1694 Charles Montagu, newly promoted Whig financial guru, approved the foundation of the major instrument of this 'Financial Revolution': the Bank of England. The bank was established in mid-1694, raising £1.2 million in investment in the form of a stock subscription. That money was then lent to the government for an indefinite period in return for an annual payment of 8 per cent interest. The bank also helped the situation by using its cash reserves to buy up the previous, short-term debts contracted by the crown, which eased the pressure on the government. The national debt was born.

The foundation of the Bank of England by no means solved all of the state's financial problems overnight – rates of interest were still higher than the general market rate and long-term borrowing was, initially, tentative and relatively small scale. However, it was a sign of things to come and was, over the course of the next century, to underpin Britain's rise to greatness – fundamentally, a sustainable way of tapping the great wealth of Britain for the purposes of the state had been found. Military success and the acquisition of empire would come to depend on the great engine of taxation, debt and war that emerged in the 1690s.

Perhaps more important in the short run were its political implications. Those who bought bank stock were in a sense investing in the post-revolutionary regime. Their investment was predicated on the rising importance of parliament and its role in approving taxation. Those taxes funded the war which defended that new political settlement. Many suspected, as one Tory was to put it, that the post-revolutionary settlement 'could not be so effectually secured any way, as it would be if the private fortunes of great numbers were made to depend on the preservation of it'.[4] Prominent among those lending their 'private fortunes' were the merchants and money men of the City of London, a disproportionate number of whom were Dissenters (around 40 per cent of the Bank of England's directors and a quarter of the substantial stockholders of the bank were Dissenters in this period).[5]

The fear on the part of the Tories, and many Country Whigs, was not only that they were loading future generations with crippling debt but also that the financial revolution would herald the increased wealth and influence of the 'monied men' and beggar the landed interest, who were the ones chiefly being taxed to pay back the interest on the loans. The investors, in contrast, paid no tax on their returns. In short, the country gentlemen feared that the monied men would become dominant and be able to buy their way into parliament and engross all the political power for themselves.

Fears of increased taxation and rising debt may seem quaint to us now, who are used to a large national debt and levels of taxation that make the fiscal burden of the 1690s seem miniscule by comparison. It must be remembered, however, that these things were unprecedented, novel innovations that seemed to be the handmaidens of war, beggary and a frightening new world in which bankers, bondholders and speculators held the upper hand. Many country gentleman referred to the national debt as 'the Great Mortgage', and few of them had positive experiences of mortgages.

The new techniques of debt and credit had already been used in the Dutch Republic for some time and accordingly came to be impugned as 'Dutch Finance'. But it wasn't just the importation of Dutch financial methods that rankled: in general, it also came to be increasingly feared that William's regime was more focussed on Dutch than English interests. William gave estates and preferment within the British Isles to Dutchmen, most notably his close ally Willem Bentinck (created Earl of Portland). He gave commands and promotions in the army chiefly to his countrymen. The expensive land war was being fought mainly to defend the Dutch Republic from the encroachment of Louis XIV's armies, despite the fact that English gentlemen paid for the bulk of it.

This sentiment was common among both Country Whigs and Tories. Country stalwart Robert Price summed up the feelings of many in an extraordinary rant in the Commons in 1695, in response to Portland being granted extensive lands around the Welsh border by the King:

> We see most places of power and profit given to foreigners . . . How can we hope for happy days in England, when this great man [Portland], and the other . . . are in the English, and also in the Dutch councils? . . . I foresee, when we are reduced to extreme poverty, as now we are very near it, we are to be supplanted by our neighbours and become a colony to the Dutch.[6]

It's easy to dismiss this sentiment as xenophobia, but is it any wonder that MPs were unimpressed? England and the Dutch Republic may have shared William as national leader, but they remained separate countries whose interests by no means necessarily coincided. They had frequently been rivals in trade and war over the past thirty years. Why should the fortunes of this national rival concern Englishmen? After all the war was, ultimately, part of a long-term confrontation in Europe between two major Roman Catholic powers, neither of whom were obvious allies to England: Louis

XIV's France and the Habsburg Empire. To many Englishmen, it seemed far from obvious that their own country had much of a dog in that fight: not, certainly, enough to justify the expenditure of so much treasure and blood.

Some of the last cords attaching leading Tories to the court were cut by the death of Queen Mary in December 1694. A devout and pious Anglican, she had become increasingly friendly with many of the leading churchmen, particularly Nottingham, bound together by their common concern for the health of the Church of England. She was seen as something of a moderating influence on William. Although many leading Tories had been bred to see opposition to the Crown as akin to disloyalty, they now became increasingly critical of the government and ready to attack some of William's measures more robustly.

Meanwhile, the Junto's strong-arm tactics were alienating the New Country Party ever more. In March 1695, Wharton tried to bully the Commons into choosing a court patsy, Sir Thomas Littleton, as Speaker of the Commons over Foley. This was a big mistake. The Commons was jealous of its right to elect its own Speaker, and resented Wharton's high-handedness. Country members went ballistic as Wharton read out Littleton's name. Members started to bawl, 'No! No! No!'[7] In the end, Foley won easily, 179–146.

Montagu had already provoked Foley by advocating an excise on leather, which threatened the livelihood of his Hereford constituents. After the Speaker election, Foley claimed that Montagu had 'played a trick or two' on him after a 'solemn promise passed between them'; it seems likely that Montagu and Wharton had promised to support him for Speaker, then reneged on it.[8] Foley was furious and declared it would 'never be forgotten'.[9]

Sunderland made attempts to soothe the ruffled feathers of the Country Whigs and reconcile them with the Junto, but to no avail: Foley refused point-blank to work under Wharton and Montagu. Indeed, the Foley-Harley grouping began to see themselves as potential rival Whig leaders; an agent of Sunderland reported that Foley was increasingly 'positive that by a little pains [the Whig party] will finally leave [Mr Wharton] and [Mr Montagu]'.[10] Sunderland was sceptical of this, but it was clear that Junto supremacy in the

Commons was less than secure. After all, the principles of the Junto and the Country Whigs had been clearly drifting apart for some time. Perhaps these troubles presaged a more permanent split in the Whig Party?

Matters were hardly helped by Wharton, in response, drawing up a list of members that the government, by Treasury influence, would try to turf out in the next election, which was looming. Among the names on it was Foley's leading ally, Robert Harley.

Wharton was overconfident and unwise. When the election was called, for November 1695, he was to get something of a shock. In general, the campaign was rather less heated than the last, many of the usual Whig-Tory partisan issues having been relatively dampened down: Church affairs had been quiet, bickering over the revolution settlement and 'de facto vs. de jure' had diminished, and fewer constituencies were contested at the poll. Ostensibly, the Whigs appeared to make gains from the Tories, but the question on everyone's mind as parliament assembled in late November was: which sort of Whigs?

It soon became clear that many of the gains had accrued to what Burnet called 'the sourer sort of Whigs', i.e. the Country Whigs (others sometimes nicknamed them the 'Grumbletonians').[11] Harley was returned, and in total 179 new members were elected, many of whom were Country Whigs not easily amenable to Wharton's ways. It left the position of the House more rather than less uncertain and allowed Harley and Foley to seriously stake themselves out as alternative parliamentary leaders to the Junto.

The members that they sought to rally were not just 'Grumbletonian' Whigs but also many of the Tories. Some of the older Country Tories were ailing or dead: Clarges had gone, but the ones that remained, such as Sir Christopher Musgrave and Sir Edward Seymour, realised that the Harley-Foley group was their best hope for a coherent alliance to challenge the Junto, and were happy to co-ordinate with them. Harley was increasingly becoming the leading man in the Harley-Foley partnership, and backbench Tories were increasingly content to rally to him. In effect – and rather paradoxically – Harley was becoming the nearest thing the Country Tories had to a parliamentary leader.

Who was this young man called Robert Harley?

* * *

Robert Harley must rank as one of the enigmas of the age. His approach was conspicuous for its paradoxes, contortions and incongruities even within an era of tumultuous and ever-shifting politics. Harley was a product of a line of notoriously prickly Presbyterians who nonetheless became the leader of the gentlemen of the Church of England; the violent Country Whig who ended up a Tory; the famously slippery political operator, nicknamed 'Robin the Trickster', who was nonetheless among the most honest politicians of an era in which corruption was routine.[12]

His grandfather, also called Robert Harley, was a zealous Puritan who had, during the Civil War, chaired the Commons committee charged with smashing up pictures and stained-glass windows within churches throughout the country. His father, Edward Harley, although he attended Church of England services, was a stern crypto-Dissenter who insisted on the young Robert attending morning prayer at 6 a.m. sharp.

So it was no surprise that the young Robert inherited a strong streak of Puritan sensibility. He was a grave young man of impeccable piety and upstanding morals. After attending a Dissenting academy, his father bridled at sending him to Oxford, centre of crypto-papist and Jacobite intrigue, and sent him instead to a French Protestant academy in London, Foubert's Academy, which he soon left 'in disgust at the licentiousness of his companions' there.[13] His strict upbringing gave him an almost fatalistic belief in the unalterable and awesome nature of God's divine providence, and the importance of submitting to its unsearchable dispensation, that was to never leave him.

Like most Dissenters, the Harleys were staunch Whigs. They had loyally backed the Parliamentary side in the Civil War and were under such suspicion for being sympathetic to Monmouth's rebellion that they were put under house arrest. During the 1690 general election, both the young Robert and his father were on a list of the most violent Whig candidates circulated to good Tories to indicate who *not* to vote for.

It was therefore truly curious to find Harley increasingly in league with the Tories. The truth is that Harley was a reluctant servant of any party. His ideal political outcome was always, in fact, the honest gentlemen of England, of any party and, ideally, none, uniting to serve Crown and country and advance the common good. He hated the arrogance and presumption of the emergent phenomenon of the violent 'party man', determined to force single-party government on the monarch and rule by bullying, coercion and bribery (Wharton being the pre-eminent example). He had, however, little choice but to dirty his hands and embroil himself in party intrigue: his towering contempt for the Junto, and determination to keep them out at almost all costs, meant alliance with the Tories. He was, however, never to be a clear-cut Tory – he felt distaste for the vehement High Churchmen as well as the Junto and would often work to rein them in as well. For now, the best option was to try to cement a motley crew of Country Whigs and backbench Tories into something like a coherent opposition.

It was during these years of opposition that he began to learn the arts of parliamentary management and intrigue that he was later to perfect. He was to become famous for what his enemies called his slipperiness, and his supporters his subtlety. There were always wheels-within-wheels-within-wheels with Harley. He was a master of the arts of delay, misdirection and parliamentary feint. He seemed dissatisfied with any political manoeuvre that involved only two or three acts of subterfuge or skullduggery when it could encompass two or three dozen. He preferred to manage men by playing with their expectations for office, by procrastination, dark hints and ambiguous obfuscations. Directness was never his way: he much preferred the shadowy backstairs negotiation, the nod and the wink, the secret parley away from the baying parliamentary crowds. One Whig commentator dubbed him 'an exquisite juggler'; he was, depending on one's point of view, either a loathsome liar, a master of 'artifice and dissimulation', or a brilliantly subtle operator.[14]

He could certainly be incredibly effective, more often than not triumphing against the more direct, not to say ruthless, tactics of the Junto men or the bluff no-nonsense plain-speaking of the High Church Tories. His mastery of the shady arts of politics was usually directed to finding a calm, moderate path through a thicket of bone-headed partisanship and apparently intractable practical difficulties, but he was also prepared to be forceful and persuasive when needed. Indeed, he was one of the first English politicians to truly understand the power of the press, and was adept at persuading (or cajoling) the best journalists and writers to promote his political agenda; as we shall see, he persuaded literary figures of the calibre of Jonathan Swift and Daniel Defoe to write for him.

His slipperiness was, in fact, almost certainly a product of his gentleness. He was allergic to self-assertion or aggrandisement, hated direct exertions of power, despised tyrants, and couldn't bear to say no to anyone. His moral character was a great weapon in his political armoury; whereas the Junto was infested with amoral libertines and atheists, and the man who was later to become his chief Tory rival, Henry St John, would have been invited to the London prostitutes' Christmas parties had such events occurred, Harley was a loyal, uxorious family man, a doting father and a gentleman famous for his probity in an era not renowned for its high moral standards. His modesty was renowned. Although Harley did have a weakness for drink that was to worsen as the pressures of high office mounted, he detested gambling and was unusually financially honest at a time when backhanders, peculation and the 'perquisites' of the job were seen as standard for most office-holders. He must be one of the few, perhaps the only, statesman of the era who left public employment poorer than when he entered it. The contrast to the Junto men was striking.

He was also famous for his learning and wit. He possessed a formidable reputation as a scholar, and was one of the great bibliophiles of his age: his extraordinary collections of books and manuscripts formed the basis of the British Museum's manuscript collection. He was undoubtedly popular among some of the liveliest literary man of his ages. Swift, a close friend, was very impressed by 'the Goodness of his Humour, and agreeable Conversation in a private capacity'.[15] He would later become intimate with Alexander Pope, John Gay and John Arbuthnot, some of the most polished wits and poets of their age. But in the heat and fury of party battle, he was a formidable opponent. He would be the thorn in the side of the Junto for the next twenty years.

The growing unity and strength of the Country interest appeared to be causing the Junto more and more problems in late 1695, but the dynamic was soon to be dramatically – if temporarily – altered.

On 24th February 1696, both houses were summoned to the Lords unexpectedly and at short notice. The King announced, to a hushed House, the dramatic news:

> I have received several concurring informations of a design to assassinate me; and that our enemies at the same time are very forward, in their preparations for an invasion of this kingdom.[16]

In 1694–5, as the war had started to go better for William, the French were becoming frustrated. Louis XIV became increasingly desperate to knock England out of the war. He communicated to the Jacobite court his willingness to provide an army of 12,000 men to invade England in the spring of 1696, but only in concert with an uprising in England itself. James dispatched his agents to England to prepare the ground, including one George Barclay. Barclay soon realised that it was far too risky to attempt an uprising in England, so he improvised a plot of his own. Along with a secret underground Jacobite cell, he decided that he would try to assassinate William while the King was riding his carriage in Richmond Park.

The plot was betrayed, and the government acted to round up hundreds of suspected Jacobites and bolster internal security. A flood of pro-William sentiment gushed forth and his growing unpopularity received a major check. Whigs and Dissenters attributed the failure of the plot to the wonderful providence of God, while Harley and his Tory allies in the Commons were soon lamenting the political fallout.

Wharton's constant warnings about foul Jacobite plots suddenly looked a lot more prescient, and he soon moved to capitalise on the situation. His mentally unstable brother Goodwin (in a break from his usual pastimes of visiting his personal fairy kingdom on Hounslow Heath and receiving messages from angels telling him to seduce his stepmother) proposed the formation of an association to protect and uphold William. It required taking an oath affirming that William was 'rightful and lawful king' and promising 'to stand by and assist each other to the utmost of our power, in the support and defence of his majesty's most sacred person and government' against the Jacobites.[17]

The oath of association was drawn up in a way likely to be the least acceptable to any Tories who still had doubts about William's de jure title to the throne. It was designed to discredit the Tories and it worked: around ninety Tories in the Commons and twenty peers in the Lords refused to append their name to it (they became known as the 'non-associators'). Soon, the Whigs successfully moved to make it compulsory for all office-holders to take the oath, including members of all subsequent parliaments.

This was a blow to Harley: it marked out many of his new allies as maligned men, arguably enemies to the King. His frantic attempts to persuade the Tories to take the association oath were only partially successful. In the febrile atmosphere of the post-assassination plot period, the heart was taken out of the opposition and initiative flowed back to the Junto.

Such was the political advantage gained by the Junto from the assassination plot that they managed to ride out the storm created by a major financial crisis in summer 1696.

Since the beginning of the war, the English coinage had been compromised by an epidemic of 'clipping' – shearing the edges off silver coins and selling the clippings to goldsmiths. This was accelerated by the demand for silver bullion to pay for army supplies in Europe. By the mid-1690s, this had become unsustainable: the currency was being debased rapidly, and confidence in it began to collapse. By 1696 it was obvious that a new coinage must be minted.

It was terribly botched. There was a fatal gap between the point at which the old clipped coins were no longer accepted as payment for tax, and the minting of the new coinage. The old clipped coins were no longer accepted as a means of payment, and unclipped coins were being hoarded. There was simply a lack of money and the usual operations of the economy ground to a halt; many were unable to buy basic provisions. It also had a disastrous effect on England's war effort. Sterling collapsed, the Bank of England was plunged into dire straits, confidence in the English credit to pay for the war effort diminished and the army could barely feed its own troops. Although the newly minted currency gradually began to circulate and ease the situation, the coinage crisis had one important effect. The economic instability it created killed off a nascent financial scheme championed by Country Whig and Tory MPs, the Land Bank (designed to raise money on land as a rival to the Bank of England), before it could even start operation.

The financial crisis over, the Whigs continued in the good offices of the King. Greedy to secure all government offices for themselves, they were rewarded with more promotions, with Montagu (despite his mishandling of the coinage crisis) becoming First Lord of the Treasury and peerages for Russell and Somers. However, this was not enough for the Whigs, who were determined to impose complete single-party government on the King. Wharton, who coveted the highest offices but was persistently blocked by Sunderland and the King, and had to make do with his relatively lowly official role as Comptroller of the Household, was especially frustrated. Wharton's importunity and hostility to Sunderland would, over the course of 1697, help to gradually alienate William at a time when a complete change in the mentality of the Commons presented ample other problems for the Junto.

The assassination attempt on the King had been a tremendous piece of luck for the Junto. For a while, the entire atmosphere of politics had taken the wind out of the sails of Harley and his Country allies. What was round the corner, however, was another sea-change, this time in the opposite direction.

The time had come for William to turn his mind to the matter of peace. The strains of war had been showing for some time, and the coinage crisis began to incline the King to think about moving towards a peace settlement; England simply couldn't economically sustain the war for much longer. The French had their own even worse financial problems, and accordingly negotiations were opened in early 1697. The Peace of Ryswick was finally signed in September.

The basis of the Whigs' ascendancy had been their willingness to back William over supply and be 'the War Party'. Peace posed obvious political problems for them. Although the Country MPs and Tories had been troublesome for some time, while there was a war on they were rarely deaf to the need for constructive proposals. They often huffed and puffed at what they saw as mismanagement and corruption, but the Foley-Harley group were generally responsible enough not to outright block supply, and indeed they saw their role as trying to provide more efficient, less wasteful means of administering the war.

Peace meant they no longer felt any need to do this. The Whigs and the King suspected that peace would be short-lived, given the vaunting ambition of Louis XIV, and were keen to retain as much of the military establishment as possible as a precaution. In contrast, for Country Whigs – and most Tories – it was time to retrench and relieve the country from the crushing burden of war taxation. The King realised that some reduction was inevitable, but was absolutely determined to retain a substantial peacetime army of 30,000 men.

To almost everyone in the political nation other than the King, courtiers and the Junto Whigs, this was an outrage. Hadn't the Bill of Rights outlawed standing armies in peacetime? Weren't standing armies the tools of tyrants? Would the torrent of taxes, debt and corruption never end?

A flurry of pamphlets and propaganda vociferously attacking standing armies followed, mostly written by 'True Whigs', the most radical fringe of Whiggery which had never quite gone away. One of the most outspoken, John Trenchard, argued that other countries in Europe had succumbed to arbitrary and absolute government in contrast to England's happy state of liberty, and the reason was clear: 'we shall find their Miseries and our Happiness proceed from this, That their Necessities or Indiscretion have permitted a standing Army to be kept amongst them'.[18] The only fit form of army for a free people was, he argued, a militia, in which the sturdy independent gentlemen would arm and defend their country themselves.

Although few elite Whigs were as radical as these men, their jeremiads voiced sentiments to which every stout Country Whig bosom could return an echo. Harley sensed the atmosphere, observing that 'the argument against a standing army has raised a great heat in the town. There is very little prospect of moderate councils'.[19] He was right. In December 1697, an alliance of disgruntled Tories, Country Whigs and even some normally loyal court supporters, marshalled by Harley, humiliated the King over the army issue, agreeing to pay for the upkeep of a (to William's mind) measly 10,000 troops. The King bitterly commented that the House of Commons had done more in a day than Louis XIV had managed in eight years.

The Junto's response to this situation was hamstrung by constant bickering between them and Sunderland, who blocked Wharton's promotion and intrigued with other members of the Junto, disrupting their usual unity. In disarray, the Junto were ill-equipped to counter Harley's manoeuvres in favour of disbanding most of the army. Wharton even unleashed his own followers on Sunderland in the Commons, opening a floodgate of attacks from the whole House, many of whom nursed old resentments against the major-general of corruption. Sunderland, old and ill, was hounded into retirement.

The whole incident left William in despair. To the Junto, the ousting of Sunderland was a prelude to their utter domination of the ministry, but the King did not share their view. When he had most needed the Junto to close ranks and work with his advisers, they had descended into self-interested politicking. They existed, the King increasingly thought, purely to 'carry . . . on their own interest, to which the concerns of the public must give way'.[20]

Still the Whigs pressed themselves on William. At the Newmarket 1698 spring meeting (a common place to conduct political business, in between raillery and races) the chief Whigs importuned the King: 'the Whigs maintain that they will not be satisfied, nor will my business by concluded to my satisfaction, if I do not please Wharton'.[21] On the one hand, William hated Wharton and would not be driven by anyone. On the other hand, the Junto and their allies still seemed like the only force likely to push vigorously for supplies and a bigger army, whatever their recent bickering and blunders. For the moment, the ministry stumbled on, too strong to fall and too weak to do much of what the King wanted.

A general election was due in the summer of 1698, and it did Whig fortunes no favours. The Junto were increasingly hated in the country: in Wharton's home turf, Buckinghamshire, his candidates were shouted down and angry constituents held banners reading 'No Courtier, No Pensioner, No Judas'.[22] Most of them lost. Defenders of the court and the Junto attempted to smear 'the New Country party so-called' as Jacobites, working for the restoration of King James in alliance with their Tory cronies 'under pretence of easing the people of taxes'.[23] Tories who had refused to subscribe to the association did badly, but there was an injection of new strength into the ranks of the High Church Tories. Nottingham believed the new House to be 'much better than the last'; it seemed that only Tory-Country Whig splits could save the Junto's bacon.[24]

It was not to be. Harley — now the leading man of the New Country Party as Foley's health declined — worked furiously in the new parliament to weld together the Tories and Country Whigs into a more unified opposition. It worked: on 17th December they combined to reduce the army even further, to a mere 7,000 men. Ministerialist efforts to reverse the decision in January 1699 failed miserably.

Not only were fewer troops to be maintained but the House insisted that they be Englishmen: one MP noted in his diary that 'the ill humoured part of the house were much against the forreigners and would not have so much a naturall born Scot to have been capable of being any part of the 7000 that were to be kept'.[25] Funding even for William's own Dutch Guards was withdrawn. The King was furious at the feeble efforts of the Junto to hold back the Country tide, and threatened to leave the country and never return. No one believed him.

Harley and his forces smelt blood. Their next target was Irish land sales. MPs had assumed that the land confiscated from Jacobites who had fought against the King in the war of 1690–1 would be sold to pay for the cost of the war. William had instead gifted them to some of his cronies, including the Countess of Orkney (his mistress), Portland and his new Dutch favourite the Earl of Albemarle. Disgruntled in the extreme, in April 1699 parliament appointed a commission to investigate the land issue. When the commission reported in December, the scale of the King's land grants became clear. Led by fiery Jack Howe, an old Country Whig who was drifting closer and closer to the Tories, the Commons resolved that the gifting of the land 'had been the Occasion of contracting great Debts upon the Nation, and laying heavy Taxes on the People', which was 'highly reflecting on the King's Honour'.[26] It was a stinging rebuke, but William wasn't going to tamely consent to confiscating the land from his factotums.

In April, Tories in the Commons took the drastic step of tacking their 'Resumptions' Bill (which would have set up a commission of enquiry with a view towards returning the lands to government ownership) to the bill for the Land Tax: this meant that if the Lords threw it out, they would also have to reject a bill approving the government's single biggest source of income. There was a constitutional stand-off. Wharton in the Lords passed wrecking amendments and sent the bill back to the Commons.

The Commons reacted angrily, not only over the issue itself but over the Lords daring to meddle with a money bill. Harley rose and gave a stirring speech in which he urged the House to 'think of England' and show that MPs were not 'insensible' to the insults piled upon them by such corrupt proceedings.[27] Those who were thought to have advised the King on the legitimacy of the land grants – predominantly Somers and Portland – were threatened with impeachment. One member went further, asking ominously, in response to objections to the use of the 'tack': 'How would they like to have bills of supply with bills of attainder tacked to them?'[28] This was essentially a threat to execute Somers. In another audacious move against the King, a motion was passed calling the King to remove all foreigners (referring mainly to Portland) from his counsels.

The Junto was now tottering. Over the course of 1699, Harley and his motley crew of Country Whigs and Tories had essentially been running the King's affairs from the backbenches. One court manager observed in January 1700 that 'Mr Harley now manages the whole business of supply, and the House hath hitherto entirely approved of his scheme'.[29] Attempts by the King's managers to draw him into an official agreement with the court had foundered in mid-1699 over his refusal to work with the Junto.

The first signs of the crumbling Junto hold on government came with the resignation of Orford (Russell) in May. Montagu, despairing at events, had taken the novel approach of simply retiring to the country and refusing to do any work, before eventually resigning. The outpouring of bile against Somers after the Irish Resumptions hoo-hah forced William to dismiss him. The Junto was being picked off one by one.

By late 1700, after endless, fruitless negotiations to try to avert it, the King had no choice: a change of ministers was inevitable. Harley had been coming to an agreement with senior Tories, including Rochester and Godolphin, a mildly Tory-leaning financial technocrat essential to the credibility of a non-Junto-led government. Gradually, the King began to appoint senior Tories to government. He brought in Rochester as Lord Lieutenant of Ireland and Godolphin as head of a new treasury board. Harley was to become Speaker and manage the new government's business in the Commons.

The Tories were back.

Unfortunately for the new ministry, they came to power in a difficult and dangerous European context.

It all hinged on the fate of the Habsburg king of Spain, Carlos II. Sickly and mentally underendowed, he had failed to produce any issue, and on his death there would be terrible uncertainty over who would succeed to his throne and inherit the still considerable Spanish Empire and its imperial possessions and resources. One of his sisters, the eldest, had married Louis XIV. The other had married Leopold, the Austrian Habsburg emperor. This led to there being two major candidates for the Spanish throne: initially on the Habsburg side Joseph Ferdinand, grandson of Leopold, but then, after his death, Leopold's younger son Archduke Charles; on the French side, the elder son of Louis XIV, Louis, the Grand Dauphin.

If the Habsburg candidate were to accede, Louis XIV could claim with some justice that it would leave France surrounded by Habsburg possessions. If the French candidate were to accede, France's power would be augmented to such a great extent that Louis's kingdom would become, in the eyes of many, the overmighty master of Europe. Either outcome was likely to result in the resumption of European hostilities. France had no great desire for war at this point, so it turned to William, the power broker of north-western Europe, to help engineer some sort of compromise, whereby the Spanish possessions would be carved up between the French and the Austrian Habsburgs (naturally, without consulting Leopold himself), in the form of a partition treaty.

In the event, two partition treaties were needed, as the death of Joseph Ferdinand rendered the first one obsolete almost immediately. The Second Partition Treaty, signed in late 1700, gave Spain, its American empire and the Spanish Netherlands to Archduke Charles, and Spain's Italian lands to the dauphin. Unfortunately, Carlos II's will left the entire Spanish inheritance to another candidate altogether, Philip of Anjou, the second son of the French dauphin. Shortly after making this will, Carlos rather inconsiderately died.

Louis XIV promptly accepted this will and the claims of his grandson Philip, totally ignoring the terms of the Second Partition Treaty. It was unlikely that Leopold was going to accede to this fait accompli without a fight. Initially, however, an eery calm descended and England cautiously accepted the accession of Philip of Anjou. The hope was that Philip would be his 'own man', not simply an appendage of the French king, and respect English trading interests with the Spanish empire. The fact that Philip, as the younger son of the dauphin, would not inherit the French Crown (which risked uniting the French and Spanish lands into one western European superpower) eased fears. Nonetheless, Europe teetered on the edge of full-scale continental war.

This wasn't the only important issue facing the new ministers. On 30th July 1700, Prince William, Duke of Gloucester, the heir but one to the English throne, died aged eleven. Gloucester was the son of the current heir, Princess Anne, James's youngest Protestant daughter and Mary's sister. The only one of Anne's sons to have lived past early infancy, despite many pregnancies, he was, crucially, a Protestant; an heir who was both a Stuart and a Protestant was the political golden ticket in the future succession stakes, as he would satisfy both Whigs and Tories. His death plunged the whole question of who would succeed to the throne after Anne into uncertainty. It seemed highly unlikely that Anne would produce another son after so many miscarriages, and William and Mary had had no children. So who was to succeed Anne?

The next Protestant in line to the throne after Anne was a German princess, Sophia, Electress of Hanover, a granddaughter of James I. By any normal standards, her claim to the throne was tenuous: there were fifty-six Roman Catholics before her in the line of succession. Furthermore, as well as being a foreigner (not an ideal qualification in the eyes of those who had become so bitter towards William and his unloved foreign advisers) she was seventy years old when Gloucester died, meaning that in practice it was likely that her son, George, Elector of Hanover, would become king.

Nonetheless, there were no alternatives except one: a Jacobite restoration. Most Tories were distinctly unenthusiastic about either option; neither a Roman Catholic in league with France nor some minor German princeling were altogether attractive choices. Whatever romantic pro-Jacobite sentiments some Tories may have retained, their heads told them that, unless the Stuart heir could, by some miracle, be tempted back to the fold of the Church of England, his accession unviable. A papist king would never be accepted again after the debacle of James II. The bulk of the Tory Party were therefore prepared, with varying degrees of grudging reluctance, to back a Hanoverian succession. The Whigs, on the other hand, had no compunction: they were gung ho for the Hanoverian succession and totally united on the issue; this was to be a great source of strength in the years to come.

With Gloucester dead, some legislative provision had to be made for the succession. Harley piloted an Act of Settlement, which entrenched the Hanoverian claim in law, through the Commons. It prompted remarkably little disagreement: only one recalcitrant High Tory openly supported a Jacobite claim, and the bill passed all its readings without the need for a single division. Tory acquiescence may have been unenthusiastic, but it was real.

However, there was a massive sting in the tail. The Tories only agreed to support the bill on the condition that a whole series of incredibly stringent conditions be placed on a future Hanoverian monarchy. No foreigners were to be allowed to advise the future monarch, hold any public office or be gifted English land. No Hanoverian king was to be allowed to involve the realm in wars to defend their foreign possessions, and holders of Crown Office or pensions were to be banished from the Commons.

In short, large swathes of the Country agenda were shoehorned into the Act of Settlement. Although these provisions could only be applied to future monarchs, the implied rebuke to William could hardly be clearer. Never again, said the Tories, would a damned foreigner be able to bleed England dry and drag her into a lot of distant wars and entanglements.

Meanwhile, Westminster had been plunged into a maelstrom of furious Whig-on-Tory partisan action.[30]

William had called an election for early 1701, partly under Tory pressure for a dissolution to allow them to try to force gains and consolidate their position, partly because he believed that the impending issues of the foreign situation and the succession were too large to be addressed at the fag end of a parliament. The election was split largely on the basis of Whig pro-war sabre rattling and a Tory desire for a peace. The result were minor Tory gains, which allowed Harley to be elected as Speaker by a landslide.

The new Tory ministry was torn. On the one hand, a war was the last thing they wanted, and their fiery backbench supporters were absolutely opposed to more debt and taxes. They didn't care who the king of Spain was, hoped Philip would not be Louis XIV's puppet anyway, and wished that the whole thing would blow over. The feelings of the Tories, and much of the nation, was summed up by Dryden's verses:

> Enough for Europe has our Albion fought
> Let us enjoy the peace our blood has bought[31]

On the other hand, William was keen to make preparations for war, and the Tory ministers needed to propitiate him in order to maintain office.

In February 1701, events began to make the Tory position difficult to sustain. The French were 'invited' by Philip to enter Flanders (part of the Spanish Netherlands) and seized the Dutch garrisons there. Concessions for French traders were promptly granted by the Spanish. The idea that Spain under Philip wouldn't be a French client looked increasingly unlikely. It was a major step to war.

The Tories hesitated. In response to the King's Speech of 11th February, which called on parliament to increase military preparations, many leading Tories voted against a strongly worded address implying support for intensified war preparation. There was a clear reluctance to allow the country to drift to war if anything could be done to prevent it.

The Whigs leapt on this reluctance as proof that the Tories were not really serious about supporting the Protestant succession and were really pro-French, pro-papist and pro-Jacobite. Whig propagandists poured out warmongering propaganda, insisting that the Tories, by failing to assist the

Dutch, 'would introduce the Design of enslaving our Bodies under a French Yoke'.[32] They went on the offensive by organising petitions and addresses from around the country demanding a harsher anti-French line.

One petition in particular, from the grand jury of Kent, gained particular publicity. It urged the Commons to supply the King with the money he needed to 'powerfully assist his allies before it is too late', and implied that the Tories were guilty of 'blackest ingratitude' to their sovereign.[33] The Tories responded angrily, condemning the petition as 'scandalous, insolent, and seditious' and imprisoning the men who had presented it to the Commons.[34]

The outraged Whig response was given vehement expression by a political journalist called Daniel Defoe (better known today as the author of *Robinson Crusoe* and *Moll Flanders*). He attacked the House's 'illegal and unwarrantable practices', accusing them of being 'very negligent of the safety of England, and of our protestant neighbours' by not assisting the Dutch.[35] The Tories, he suggested, had inflicted 'saucy and indecent reproaches' upon the King.[36] An extraordinarily violent attack on parliament, not only did it imply that the people would be justified in 'proceed[ing] against them as traitors and betrayers of their country', by force if necessary, but it signed off in terms amounting to a threat:

> if you continue to neglect [your duty], you may expect to be treated according to the resentments of an injured nation; for Englishmen are no more to be slaves to parliaments, than to a king.
>
> Our name is Legion, and we are many.[37]

Tempers boiled over, and the Commons seethed in this febrile atmosphere. Outraged by the aspersions cast on their loyalty by the Whig propaganda campaign, the Tories decided to strike back by attempting to politically assassinate the Junto leaders. They brought impeachment proceedings against Somers, Orford and Montagu (now raised to the peerage as Baron Halifax; henceforth 'Halifax' refers to Montagu). The main attack was mounted on Somers, who was accused of having given official sanction to the partition treaties without informing parliament.

The impeachments were detailed and occasioned lengthy responses from the Junto lords, but in reality the specifics were neither here nor there; they were an outpouring of pent-up Tory anger towards the imperious behaviour of the Junto during their ascendancy, assailing in a scattergun manner many of their alleged misdemeanours. The Tories wanted their heads; it was purely a partisan manoeuvre. Somers, the consummate lawyer, defended himself ably, but Tories didn't have the votes in the Lords to carry the impeachment anyway. The Junto men were acquitted in June.

The impeachments sent a clear signal to the King that the Tories resented the bellicose and high-handed nature of his approach to foreign policy. None-theless, as the Whig out-of-doors campaign against the regime's more pacific policy raged – more than a hundred constituencies had written to their MPs urging a harsher anti-French line by early June – the Tories began to realise not only the political danger of being seen to obstruct war preparations but also the reality that Spanish policy was being dictated by Louis XIV.

So they became more amenable to William's frantic attempts to persuade them of the necessity of preparing for war. In April the Commons voted to assist the Dutch in accordance with their treaty obligations, and a small English army was sent to the Dutch Republic, commanded by John Churchill, Earl of Marlborough. By June, the Commons resolved to support William's attempts to reunite the military alliance of the Nine Years' War, between England, France and the Austrian Habsburgs, 'for the preservation of the liberties of Europe, the prosperity and peace of England, and for reducing the exorbitant power of France'.[38]

When James II died in September, Louis XIV's raised the temperature by recognising the deposed king's son, James Francis Edward Stuart, as the legitimate king of England, Scotland and Ireland ('James III' or 'the Pre-tender', according to taste). Buoyed by the wave of patriotic anger produced by this, the Whigs scented their chance. They began to put pressure on the King for a dissolution and fresh election on the basis that he could only hope to satisfactorily prepare for war with a fresh infusion of Whig blood into the Commons. The Tories, they argued, were disloyal Jacobites who would never wholeheartedly back his war. William made overtures to the Junto, then agreed to go to the country.

The election was a heated one, with an outpouring of invective and mud-throwing. The Whigs were quick to exploit the embarrassment of three prominent Tories, including leading economist and pamphleteer Charles Davenant, who had been found carousing with the French chargé d'affaires Poussin on the day that orders for his expulsion had been given by the government. It gave the colour of truth to their accusations that the Tories were treacherous Jacobites.

The election resulted in Whig gains, but nothing like the landslide that the Junto had been hoping for. When parliament convened in December, Whig efforts to unseat Harley as Speaker were to no avail: Harley scraped home by four votes. The parties had reached almost complete parity, and the next few months saw parliamentary trench warfare break out with undiminished ferocity.

With war looking increasingly inevitable and the parties at loggerheads, the future looked uncertain. The King's mind turned to a rapprochement with the Junto and ministerial changes in their favour.

Mortality was to intervene before any such changes could be made. On Friday 21st February, the King went out riding in Richmond Park, trying out a new horse. His inexperienced mount started to gallop but quickly stumbled and fell. The King was thrown off and landed heavily. In Jacobite mythology, he was dismounted by tripping over a molehill, which gave rise to many subsequent toasts among the Pretender's supporters to 'the gentleman in black velvet'.

At first, this seemed nothing more serious than a broken collar bone. After eight days, he was able to dress properly and be seen in public; he was even reported to be 'very merry'.[39]

Then everything happened very suddenly. The King began to feel weary and fell asleep in a chair. When he awoke he felt feverish. The next day he took a turn for the worse and began to feel and look much weaker. The pain became unbearable, and attempts to ease his fever with quinine didn't work. His old ally Portland sought desperately to be admitted to his chamber; by the time he was, the King could no longer speak. He had just enough strength to grasp his old retainer's hand and place it on his heart.

Between eight and nine o'clock on Wednesday 8th March 1702, William, King of England, Ireland and Scotland and stadtholder of the United Provinces, died.

The politics of the age of William can seem confused and chaotic, but considerable insight on how the dynamics of Whig and Tory stood as the era of the irascible Dutchman drew to a close can be gained from examining the party propaganda pumped out during the final election of his reign.

The Whig case was put by Somers in a blistering pamphlet attacking the Tories and their Harleyite allies, *Jura Populi Anglicani*. In it, he pointed out the incongruence of old Presbyterians who until recently were out-and-out Whigs – Harley being the most obvious target – allying themselves with true-blue old Cavalier Tories. He comments ironically on the incongruity of Tories, supposedly defenders of the power and rights of kings, attacking William:

> Formerly, the Tory Doctrine was, that the King was the Breath of our Nostrils, that we fail'd in our Allegiance to him, and deserv'd not the name of Loyal Subjects unless we valued his Life more than our own, and would do all that lay in our power to preserve him and his Government . . . Is this the Temper and Spirit of our Present Tories?[40]

The answer, in short, was no. Many of them had shown their indifference to the King's life by 'refus[ing] the voluntary Association' in the aftermath of the assassination plot.[41] It was the *Tories*, of all people, who had vehemently protested against the King retaining a serviceable army, against his grants of lands and his right to conduct his foreign policy as he wished. What a curious reverse!

Two implications flowed from this. Firstly, it was the Whigs who have 'born a constant Affection to the King, and endeavoured to continue him in Possession of all his Rights and Prerogatives' and proven that their 'Loyalty is greater than the Tories'.[42] Secondly, if the Tories had loyalty to any king, it was not William, but rather the one dwelling at Saint-Germain (or perhaps the one at Versailles):

> To this loyal Tory-Party . . . we find all those atttach'd, whose Principles
> . . . make them firmly adhere to the Interest of King James . . . In this
> Party are all those likewise whom either the Love of Money, or of the St.
> German Family, or Popery, has reconcil'd to the French Interest.[43]

Only Jacobite loyalties could explain such strange alliances and odd alterations of principle.

The problem for Somers was that this argument cut both ways. How could it be that the Whigs had become the party of overweening monarchical power, standing armies and an enormous load of taxes? It was a point that Charles Davenant, a Tory financial expert and political polemicist, was quick to throw back in the Whigs' faces in his contribution to the election paper war. He paints a caustic picture of the new breed of corrupt, self-interested Whig, summed up in the person of 'Tom Double', a personification of the Junto's principles. Tom asks:

> What have we in us that resembles the Old Whigs? They hated arbitrary
> government, we have been all along for a standing army: they desired
> triennial parliaments, and that trials for treason might be better regulated,
> and it is notorious that we opposed both those bills. They were for
> calling corrupt ministers to an account; we have ever countenanced and
> protected corruption to the utmost of our power. They were frugal for
> the nation and careful how they loaded the people with taxes; we have
> squandered away their money as if there could be no end of England's
> treasure.[44]

Many old Whigs who had stayed true to their principles made much the same point. John Toland, a fiery radical, wrote in the same year that the Whigs had grown 'by degrees the most pliant gentlemen imaginable'.[45] They

> could think no revenue too great for the king, nor would suffer his pre-
> rogative to be lessened, they were on frivolous pretensions for keeping
> up a standing army to our further peril and charge, they filled all the
> places in their disposal with their own creatures.[46]

* * *

Both Somers and Davenant had a point. Although his accusation that the Tories were all Jacobites was unfair, Somers was correct to say that the Tories had drifted into increasingly overt opposition to the Crown as the decade had gone on. They were no longer the straightforward allies of monarchy. The old Country interest, many of whom had formerly been Whigs, increasingly united around the Tory banner. A 'New Tory Party', noticeably different from the old Cavalier-Court Party, had been born.

There was still, however, a very strong line of continuity. They remained fundamentally the Church Party. In the middle years of William's reign, Church matters had fallen considerably down the political agenda in parliament, and the Church Party increasingly found itself concentrating on the Country issues. This made it rather easier for the Tories to make common cause with the Harley-Foley faction and other Country Whigs who drifted into the 'New Tory Party'. By the end of William's reign, however, the Church had started to drift back onto the agenda: William's last parliaments saw sporadic attempts by Tory high-fliers to attack attempts by Dissenters to evade the Test Act. Time would tell whether rising tensions on Church versus Dissent matters would make the adhesion of the Tories to their ambiguous new leader Harley hard to maintain.

The Whigs had, in the final years of William, reunified. The irreconcilables of the Harley faction had (mostly) broken away, but those who remained rallied around the Junto, who provided clear, ruthless leadership. Although unrecognisable in many respects from the old libertarian party of the Shaftesbury era, strands of continuity remained. Religious toleration and backing for the Dissenters was still the scarlet thread connecting the Old Whigs to the new Juntoised party. That, combined with the cause of the Protestant succession, and, by extension, the need to wage war against the Jacobites' only real chance for a restoration – Louis XIV's France – formed the bedrock of the new Whiggery.

As the age of Queen Anne dawned, these oddly realigned parties limbered up for the most violent Whig-on-Tory action yet seen.

The 'Rage of Party' was only just warming up.

4

The Promised Land

Queen Anne's coronation was a magnificent affair. Arrayed in glorious robes 'of Gold tissue, very Rich Embroydery of jewelry about it, her peticoate the same of Gold tissue with gold and silver lace, between Rowes of Diamonds', Anne was carried into Westminster Abbey on a sumptuous sedan chair, made specially at a cost of £250.[1] She wore a brand new crown, bearing jewels worth an eye-watering £79,000. The galleries and scaffolds from which the cheering crowds welcomed their new monarch were planned by Sir Christopher Wren; the lavish commemorative medals were designed by Isaac Newton. The whole ceremony cost, in modern day money, around £8–12 million. It was, said one onlooker, 'more magnificent than any in England till that time'.[2]

Aside from a few rumblings from discontented Jacobites, the new queen was panegyrised and lauded to the skies by her subjects. The Archbishop of Canterbury's coronation sermon, based on the classic text Isaiah 49:23 ('Kings shall be thy Nursing Fathers, and their Queens thy Nursing Mothers'), heralded her as a pious upholder of the Church and Protestant faith – a new Elizabeth I. Indeed, Anne herself liked to project the image of being a second Gloriana: during her accession speech to parliament she had deliberately modelled her dress on a famous portrait of Elizabeth, and quickly adopted the Virgin Queen's motto, *Semper Eadem* ('Always the Same'), as her own.

121

It was a comparison beloved of the host of panegyrists who rushed to praise their new monarch:

> Since once the nation has so happy been,
> Beneath the conduct of a maiden queen,
> What present hopes must then possess our isle,
> When beauty so divinely sweet,
> Virtue and piety so great,
> Wisdom so clear, and temper serene
> Do in one sacred princess meet,
> And on our kingdom smile.[3]

The personal truth behind this glittering façade of crowns, jewels and grand rhetoric was, however, a bitter and sorrowful one. The Queen bore a heavy load of grief and pain under her gold-tissued robes.

Anne was carried into her coronation in a specially made sedan chair, not primarily as a symbol of her majesty and superiority, but rather because years of rheumatism and illness had rendered her unable to walk. Her health had been poor from childhood: in her early years, she had suffered from 'defluxion' of the eyes (acute eye-watering) and her sight never fully recovered. As she entered middle age, she became increasingly afflicted by agonising bouts of gout.

She was certainly no 'Virgin Queen': her health had been broken by scores of miscarriages, stillbirths and other ill-fated pregnancies. Between 1684 and 1700, she conceived seventeen times. Out of these pregnancies, only five living children were born: two died well short of their second birthday having contracted smallpox; one survived a few hours; another a few minutes. Only one survived longer than early infancy: Prince William, Duke of Gloucester, in whom many hopes were invested as a Stuart heir to the throne. His death of smallpox aged eleven was perhaps the most bitter of all Anne's numerous griefs; she had doted on the boy, and she never entirely escaped the melancholy induced by his sudden demise.

Her sorrow had political causes too. For years, she had been snubbed, bullied and browbeaten by William III, whom she nicknamed 'Mr Caliban'.

William, aware that her claim to the throne was better than his, had sought to keep her financially dependent on him and to control whom she employed as her personal servants. These conflicts led to a dramatic estrangement from her sister, Queen Mary, which was only reconciled on Mary's deathbed. Anne intensely resented William and Mary's treatment of her, and she pointedly drew a contrast to her foreign-born predecessor in her first speech to parliament as queen, when she declared: 'I know my own heart to be entirely English'.[4] Although inserted for political reasons by her High Tory uncle Lord Rochester, it's hard to believe that she didn't voice this resonant statement with a degree of grim satisfaction.

Her sorrows had deeper roots than that. During the Glorious Revolution, she had faced an agonising conflict between her staunchness for the Church of England and her loyalty to her father James II. Ultimately, she had chosen her faith over filial fealty. Shortly after her husband, Prince George, and close political associate, John Churchill, had abandoned James and thrown their weight behind William, she narrowly managed to make a dramatic escape down the backstairs of her apartment in Whitehall in the middle of the night, fleeing London a mere three hours before James gave the order to place her under military guard. Although she accepted the revolution, her enforced betrayal of her father, necessary as it may have been, never sat entirely easy with her. The treatment subsequently meted out to her by the beneficiary of this filial perfidy, William III, made her feelings all the more bitter.

So if the death of William seemed to many across Europe – from the English Whigs to his fearful Dutch countrymen – to be a shattering blow presaging an uncertain and potentially disastrous future, the loss of the great Protestant warrior-bulwark against French designs of domination, then to Anne it was the long-looked-for day of jubilation and triumph. 'Caliban' was finally gone. After years of gloom, the 'SunShine Day' of her accession was here at last.[5]

On her accession, her first thought was to reward those who had sustained her during the dark years of melancholy and humiliation.[6]

First was her husband Prince George of Denmark – a dithering, if amiable, man, of whom Charles II famously said, 'I have tried him drunk, and

I have tried him sober and there is nothing in him' – whom she adored with a fervour that many of her contemporaries found somewhat baffling.[7] She provoked hearty amusement when she tried to insist on his appointment as captain-general of the Dutch Republic after the death of William (the request was diplomatically ignored, but he was nominally made generalissimo of the English forces and Admiral of the Fleet). However bumbling and indolent he was, he was nonetheless a brave and loyal soul who amply returned his wife's simple affection; they seem to have been a genuinely devoted couple who sustained each other through the almost unimaginable heartbreak of losing child after child.

Most politically significant among the Queen's inner circle were a married couple who were to be elevated to the first ranks of English honour during her reign: John and Sarah Churchill, the soon-to-be Duke and Duchess of Marlborough.

John Churchill was a dashing, dishy courtier who had made his name in the service of James II. Coming from a depressed branch of the minor gentry who had suffered for their loyalty to Charles I, he had managed, through dint of his father Winston Churchill's social connections, to gain a place as a page in the household of James, Duke of York. Seeking out military experience as a means to further his ambition, he briefly served under Louis XIV in his war against the Dutch, before returning in 1675 to continue his military career and take up a new role as James's gentleman of the bedchamber.

The bedchamber proved an early source of profit – and infamy – for the young John Churchill. From around 1771, he had conducted a steamy affair with Barbara Villiers, the Duchess of Cleveland, the man-eating mistress of Charles II. Described by one contemporary as 'a woman of great beauty, but most enormously vitious and ravenous', the tempestuous Barbara began her affair with John when he was twenty and she twenty-nine.[8] Separating out truth from rumour in the accounts of their amours is close to impossible, but a contemporary account has it that, on one occasion, when the King walked in on his young rival in flagrante with Barbara in her bedroom, John 'saved her honour – or what remained of it – by jumping from the window, a considerable height, into the courtyard below'.[9] Another rumour held that John managed to buy his way out of Louis XIV's service by means of money that Barbara acquired by pimping herself out for a night to a wealthy eccentric. Shortly after, Churchill extricated himself from this lascivious entanglement, only to fall in love with the similarly tempestuous, albeit less scandalous, Sarah Jennings, a fifteen-year-old maid of honour also in the service of the York household.

In the mid-1680s, the Churchills attached themselves to the household of Princess Anne (as she was then), although John maintained his key role as military officer, diplomatic agent and political advisor in the service of James. His role was that of loyal lieutenant of secondary status rather than top dog, although his loyalty was (for a while at least) much valued; he backed James throughout the Exclusion Crisis and supported the new king during the early years of his reign, masterminding the crushing of the Duke of Monmouth at Sedgemoor. As James's reign wore on, however, his stout Protestantism chafed at James's religious policies, and his defection to William in December 1688 was one of the key incidents in destroying the King's grip on power.

Life under William proved to be little more joyous for Churchill than for Anne, with whom he and Sarah became increasingly identified under the new regime. Frustrated by William's unwillingness to give him military promotion, despite his competent performance in Ireland in 1690 against the Irish Jacobites – William would only appoint his Dutch cronies to key commissions – Churchill soon dabbled with the Jacobites, agitated with his wife on behalf of Anne in her quarrels with the monarchs, and fell under suspicion of disloyalty. Some highly disputed evidence even suggests that he may have been implicated in leaking English military secrets to the French, giving details of a projected English attack on Brest in 1694. Stripped of his positions and even arrested and briefly detained in the Tower of London, Marlborough's political career hung by a thread.

However, gradually there was a rapprochement. The more lurid accusations against Churchill proved false, and William came to realise, as his own health dwindled, that Churchill, as one of the most talented English military officers as well as a key political figure sharing his anti-isolationist views on European foreign policy, would be key to continuing his own crusade against French domination in Europe after his death. Shortly before William's demise, as war became increasingly inevitable in 1701, he appointed Churchill as commander-in-chief of the English and Scottish forces assembling in the Dutch republic, and as his ambassador extraordinary in the negotiations with the French and Spanish. He was, effectively, William's anointed military and diplomatic successor.

Churchill was, as Lord Chesterfield later put it, a man who 'possessed the graces in the highest degree, not to say engrossed them'.[10] He was famously handsome – a slight, delicate man, 'his features without fault, [with] fine sparkling eyes, good teeth, and his complexion such a mixture of white and red as the fairer sex might envy' – and a great charmer: smooth, calm and unruffled, able to persuade anyone of (almost) anything.[11] In short, he was the consummate courtly operator, and his deferential manners (at least in early years) and chivalric gentleness made him a great favourite with Anne. Indeed, his good nature did not just apply to his monarch and social equals: like Wellington, he was always ready to share the hardships of the men he commanded and his personal bravery was never questioned, even by his most bitter opponents.

His Achilles heel was his extraordinary avarice, his insatiable appetite for monetary gain and social advancement for him and his family. Even by the standards of a mercenary age in which enriching oneself from public service was not so much frowned upon as seen as practically compulsory, he was greedy for lucre, and he became notorious for it. Having been born into a desperately financially insecure family, he was determined to gain security, regard and wealth for his family, but he simply did not know when to call it a day. It was a vice that also manifested itself in his notorious niggardliness: he was obsessed with economy and pedantic to a fault on all pecuniary matters. Sufficient to say that he was not the sort of person who would simply agree to split a tavern bill equally: he would have his abacus out to determine his precise share of the balance before one could say 'Blenheim'.

Politically, Churchill had another massive problem to contend with: his wife. Sarah Churchill was a dazzling woman: ravishingly beautiful with her magnificent tresses of reddish-gold hair and delicate, pale prettiness, she was also a woman of sharp wit, intellectual vitality and extraordinary energy. One of her friends remarked that it looked 'as if the maker had designed [her body and mind to be] immortal, had he not been engaged to the contrary'.[12]

The problem was that her almost hyperactive energy, when roused by perceived slights or error, often manifested itself as a ceaseless, destructive zeal for confrontation. A contemporary (unfriendly) commentator nicknamed her 'Mount Aetna'; she hated and loved passionately, and was utterly incapable of anything other than total, and often completely counterproductive, frankness, which often became utter tactlessness.[13] She was incapable of calm diplomacy or discretion, which she inevitably saw as craven dishonesty: 'Dissembling is so great a force to my nature that I could never bring myself to it', she observed.[14] Her fits of vituperative rage were ungovernable, and were to ultimately prove her (and to some extent her husband's) downfall.

Something of this is illustrated by an extraordinary incident that occurred when the Tories, led by Rochester, had returned to high office in 1700 under William. At the time, John was a tactical supporter of Rochester, and invited him to dinner one evening to discuss the political situation. Sarah, always a violent Whig, despised Rochester, and so Marlborough refrained from informing her that he was due at their table until the last moment, when she was combing her hair at her dressing table. She reacted with utter fury, which John tried to placate by admiring her famously beautiful hair. Incensed by this flattery, Sarah grabbed a pair of scissors and furiously sheared off her tresses, purely to spite him. Many years later, after his death, she found these locks of hers among his most precious keepsakes. Whatever their faults, there is no doubt of the mutual love between them.

For many years, she was an asset to her husband. Princess Anne adored her, even before she officially became her lady of the bedchamber in 1683. Whereas Anne was dull, depressive and insecure, her friend was (when in the mood) warm, ebullient and witty, and Anne soon became emotionally dependent on the one person able to lighten the darkness of her years of grief and humiliation. As Anne became estranged from her sister, and in need of succour and advice in the face of her maternal tragedies, she craved a companion to confide in on terms of equality, or at least on the basis of a fiction of equality: Sarah filled the role perfectly. Their deepening intimacy was sealed by their adoption of 'pet' names: Anne became Mrs Morley and Sarah Mrs Freeman. In those times of adversity, when Anne and the Churchills forged a close political and personal bond based partly on hostility to the common enemy of 'Mr Caliban', Sarah and her magnificent truculence was ranged on Anne's side, and caused few difficulties between them. Indeed, Sarah's close personal relationship with Anne helped cement John's pre-eminence in her counsels, and later her government.

This was, slowly but surely, to change once Anne became queen. The common enemy of William gone, gradually a fundamental tension between the two became more and more obvious. The Queen was a devout and doughty churchwoman who distrusted the hauteur, suspected theological unsoundness and general disreputable nature of the Whig Junto men. Although she had no wish to be dominated by either party, in her heart she leaned towards the Tories. Sarah, on the other hand, was an unabashed and zealous partisan of the Whig cause, who saw all Tories as truckling crypto-papist Jacobites. She had no compunctions about advising Anne to abandon the Tories and embrace Whig hegemony in increasingly heavy-handed and tone-deaf ways. Infuriated at Sarah's impudence, in disagreement with Sarah's political analysis, Anne became increasingly exasperated with her old friend, who before long poisoned not only the two women's relationship, but also Anne's with John.

Anne was certainly no intellectual, and incapable of the sort of witty pyrotechnics that were second nature to Sarah. Quiet and shy, prone to burrowing herself away with a small coterie of long-established, trusted advisers, her court was no whirlwind of social brilliance or haunt of entertaining debauchees. Her main occupation, outside of a tenacious commitment to her official duties, was regular attendance at church services.

The assumption of most politicians as she came to the throne was that she was a nonentity, a poor weak woman incapable of governing in her own right, sure to be a mere puppet of the Churchills – or perhaps the High Tories.

This was to prove a very inaccurate prophecy.

She may not have been a dazzling wit, but Queen Anne was in possession of some considerable virtues, many of which were to prove to be of far more use to her country than any amount of book learning or superficial repartee. Foremost among these was her profound sense of duty and determination to place the national interest above any other consideration, including the scheming and partisanship of both major political parties – 'I have no thought but what is for ye good of England', as she put it herself in a letter to Marlborough.[15] She was quite prepared to bitterly resist the humours of both High Church Tories and Junto Whigs when necessary. A pushover she was not: her obstinacy, particularly when party men attempted to force government appointments that she disapproved of, was immense. Even when the whole political world was against her, she would hold out if she thought that the demands of her religion, her country and her common sense demanded it.

Anne was no fool, either. She had an excellent memory, and her lack of interest in abstract intellectual matters was the flip side of her doughty common sense and pragmatism. Having spent years embroiled in court intrigue against William, she had mastered the art of cloaking her feelings when necessary, of subtle manoeuvring and backstairs manipulation.

Everyone underestimated her, and many were to end up regretting it.

Although Anne leaned towards the High Church Tories on ecclesiastical matters, she was not naive about the designs of Louis XIV. She was quite convinced that, vile as William may have been, his assessment of the fortunes of Europe in the year of his death was generally correct: the war against France – which was quickly declared shortly after her accession – must be waged vigorously. She also agreed with her predecessor that the man for the job was John Churchill, soon to be the Duke of Marlborough, who was on the verge of being appointed as captain-general of the English forces, and given overall command of the Anglo-Dutch armies on the continent.[16]

To fight an expensive war on the scale required, however, needed sound administration, particularly on the financial side, and the backing of parliament. Marlborough, away on the continent fighting, was of little direct use in either department. The last war had stretched the country's means to its limit, despite enormous financial innovations, and many MPs in a House of Commons that was usually tilted more towards the Tories were heartily sceptical about what they saw as throwing away enormous quantities of English lives and money on what might well prove to be another wearisome and inconclusive war. How was the war, and parliament, to be managed?

Politics in this era worked quite differently than today, because the idea of government by party was not widely accepted. One did not simply appoint the leader of the party with a majority as chief minister and let him get on with it. The Glorious Revolution had not formally clipped the constitutional powers of the monarch very much at all: the Queen was still sovereign, and appointed ministers to serve her as she saw fit, as more-or-less personal servants. Anne would have been only too happy to appoint her ministers purely on the basis of her estimation of their abilities and character, and willingness to serve her agenda, with little input from parties at all.

Since the Glorious Revolution, this vision had become impracticable. Whatever the (considerable) remaining prerogatives of the monarch, they were very much bound by parliament and statute law. The financial pressure of funding William's war, and the reluctance of parliament to award generous lifetime supply after its experience with James II, had made parliament, and specifically the House of Commons, into a permanent institution that held annual sessions, and one increasingly powerful in fiscal matters. So the Commons had to be carefully managed to ensure supply, and it was filled overwhelmingly with party men, meaning that the leadership of those parties had to enter heavily into any monarch's calculations. Anne, like William, could only try to manage parliament in these conditions with the assistance of a group of political intermediaries, 'managers' whose job 'served the dual purpose of buffers, protecting the monarch as far as possible from the importunities and encroachments of the partisans, and of brokers, negotiating with the party politicians on the Crown's behalf'.[17]

The court and its managers did have some parliamentary resources that were to a greater or lesser degree separate from the whims of party. Firstly, there were the out-and-out 'government members', men who held offices ('places') within the gift of the Crown and were not party aligned; since they were liable to lose their place if they opposed the Queen's will and had no party ties, they were very reliable. They usually amounted at this time to around forty to sixty MPs. In addition, there were another sixty or so MPs who also held places, but, being aligned with Whig or Tory (albeit loosely), were liable to defect, especially on party political matters, and were therefore far less reliable – although the threat of being sacked could often discipline them. This group, of around 100–120 MPs, was a reasonable core of support for the government, but far from sufficient.

The task of the managers was, therefore, to plot some way to win over sufficient numbers of the more clearly party aligned MPs to get government business passed, without, ideally, falling entirely into their power. The Queen was desperate to avoid a situation where she would be completely dictated to by the party leaders.

There were two essential strategies for doing this. The first was a 'mixed' or coalition ministry, a bipartisan scheme which would ally the court interest with the moderate men from both parties. As parties in parliament had nowhere near the hold that modern parties have over their MPs, being looser coalitions with only crude methods of discipline, this was possible, particularly when the parties in parliament were evenly balanced and the general political temperature on highly emotive partisan issues could be kept as low as possible. The second was a scheme whereby one party would be more favoured than the other in terms of ministerial positions, but only on the condition that the leaders of that party should be content to play subordinate roles. It was also essential that the other party should not be shut out of favour completely, and wise for special attention to be paid to courting the more independent 'country' members of both sides.

Either of these schemes could be bolstered by very intricate deal-making with individuals, often on the basis of patronage or family or local 'interests', attempts to intervene in specific elections and the exploitation of personal loyalties or friendships.

There was, of course, a third possible outcome: that one party should become so dominant and united that it would be in a position to 'force the chamber' – in others words, give the Queen no choice but to appoint party leaders to leading offices, and more or less dictate policy to the Crown.

In reality, things were messier than these neat options imply: actual governments plodded through with all sorts of improvisations and schemes that combined some elements of various of these outcomes, to varying degrees. What was certain was that the Queen desperately needed skilful managers to help her negotiate through the thickets of this forbidding political forest and avoid the nightmare of 'party government'.

The Queen's natural choice for her chief minister was her loyal old friend Sidney Godolphin. Godolphin was a political survivor, who had managed to negotiate his way through the tumult of the Glorious Revolution and the 1690s largely through discretion, dependability and competence – as Charles II had quipped many years before, he was 'never in the way and never out of the way'.[18] Godolphin hated conflict and was naturally a small 'c' conservative who saw loyalty to the Crown as the highest good: he had stayed loyal to James II, whom he served as Treasury financial expert, until the bitter end. As a result, he had usually been counted as a Tory; the Whigs heartily distrusted him and often tried to remove him from office during William's reign. William, however, saw that Godolphin was a hard-working and useful servant and employed him sporadically at the Treasury throughout the 1690s. Godolphin's diplomatic interventions on behalf of Anne during her disputes with Caliban endeared him to her – it was to turn out to be an astute move.[19]

Painfully shy and sensitive to criticism, Godolphin dreaded the limelight and usually had to be carefully cajoled into returning to office; when there, he infinitely preferred poring over Treasury figures to engaging in the hustle and bustle of partisan speechmaking. Years of experience had given him a command over government finance matched by very few, and his dedication to the details of public business was remarkable. He was scrupulously honest, hated sycophancy and brown-nosing, and performed Herculean feats in his attempts to balance the country's books and supply Marlborough's armies, relieved only by indulging his towering passion for horse racing and a hearty gamble (he would conduct a non-trivial amount of political business at Newmarket).

Godolphin was more than simply an austere bureaucrat, but he was not a natural politician, being insufficiently gregarious, a poor public speaker and impatient with the hustling and huckstering of Westminster. Marlborough, while perhaps more astute, and able to exert huge influence on domestic politics – partly through his personal adherents and family but mainly through the prestige of his military success – had similarly high levels of distaste for the dirty side of party politics. In any case, he clearly could not manage everything while abroad fighting for much of the year, and both he and Godolphin were in the House of Lords, not the Commons. While Marlborough would fight the war and Godolphin would fund it, the 'duumvirs' (as they became known) needed a man capable of managing an increasingly tumultuous situation in the Commons.

In some ways one might think that Robert Harley was an unlikely candidate: he had, after all, spent much of the 1690s making the lives of government ministers very difficult indeed. He was the consummate 'Country' man, agitating for the rights of the honest independent gentlemen against the depredations of the court. However, by nature a man who erred towards moderation, in 1701 his attitude towards the Tories that had become his allies in the later 1690s cooled. As religious tensions over Dissent and the Church mounted, Harley, not a natural ally of the high-flying churchmen, was not inclined to side with them, and despaired at their lack of political nous. More importantly, he took the view that the threat of Louis XIV was now too obvious and urgent to ignore. The times required a responsible attitude. Always possessed of a strong sense of vocation and duty, inherited from his serious Presbyterian background, the call to serve proved too difficult to resist.

From the point of view of the duumvirs, Harley was the perfect man. Already Speaker of the House of Commons, he had proved his ability to practically manage the government's programme already under William III. He excelled at every political art they looked at with distaste: the everyday game of manipulation, dissimulation and tricks that was necessary for managing the unruly backbenchers, proud party chieftains and unscrupulous hacks that made up the Commons.

These three men were to have their work cut out. Their chief challenge, as they surveyed the political scene in 1702, was to manage the newly resurgent Tories.

The accession of Anne had raised Tory morale hugely. She had a far better hereditary claim to the throne than William, and was a Stuart. If one could convince oneself that James II's son was an imposter smuggled into the bedchamber in a warming pan, then she was the legitimate heir. In any case, the accession of James II's daughter eased the consciences of Tories who acquiesced in handing the crown to William in 1689.

Everyone also knew that the Queen was a staunch churchwoman, and she was associated strongly with the High Church element. This led many Tories to think that she was 'their queen' (much in the way that many Whigs assumed that William would be a 'Whig monarch' in 1689). She deliberately encouraged this impression in a speech she made dissolving parliament and heralding the 1702 election when she remarked that 'my own principles must always keep me entirely firm to the interests and religion of the Church of England and will incline me to countenance those who have the truest zeal to support it'.[20] This, along with her pointed description of herself as 'entirely English', was taken as a none-too-subtle indication that she favoured the election of Tories.

The Church Party's spirits soared: the 'Promised Land' of Tory domination was, they thought, here. They could finally dish the Dissenters, restore the Church to its proper place of supremacy, and get rid of the stink left by the grim old Dutchman. Tory propagandist James Drake summed up the note of bullish Tory optimism:

> God has been graciously pleased to give us a queen as truly English by inclination as by birth who . . . has given us undoubted demonstration of her sincere affection and zeal for our church and constitution. If, therefore, we do not make use of this blessing to second her pious intentions, and establish both for ever, we should guilty of a great neglect of providence.[21]

The Queen's early ministerial changes had already given encouragement to the Tories. Before he died, William had been on the brink of sacking the Earl of Rochester as Lord Lieutenant of Ireland, but Anne retained his services. Nottingham returned to his old post as Secretary of State, alongside the staunch Tory Sir Charles Hedges. Other key Tories, such as truculent old warhorse Sir Edward Seymour – nicknamed 'Sir Chuffer' by the younger Tories, many of whom saw him as a ridiculous old relic – and the Earl of Jersey, were also brought into the ministry.[22]

This was certainly a predominantly Tory administration, but it was by no means a clean sweep for the high-fliers. Admittedly, the Queen very pointedly sacked Wharton and dramatically struck his name off the list of privy counsellors, which was seen as a particularly forceful way of expressing her disapproval of the Junto in general, and dissolute old atheist Wharton in particular. However, many Whig ministers at the lower level were retained, and the fact remained that the really key figures – the duumvirs and Harley – were all Tories of the most moderate stamp, if at all. Much to his chagrin, High Tory Rochester was *not* to be the leading minister. In addition, Anne made absolutely clear her commitment both to maintaining the Toleration Act and the continuation of William's anti-French policy in the same speeches that were taken as barely veiled declarations of Tory allegiance, which might have given the more unrestrained Tories pause for thought.

The main figurehead of this supposed new Tory millennium was Laurence Hyde, the Earl of Rochester, uncle to the Queen and the long-serving standard bearer of the high-fliers. A veteran of the struggles of the reign of James II, when he had led Anglican resistance to the King's catholicising policy, Rochester was an almost comically vehement, presuming and self-important figure – known, according to Thomas Macauley, for his 'boundless arrogance, for extreme violence of temper, and for manners almost brutal'.[23] He saw himself as the living embodiment of the High Church tradition, the unstinting champion of the country squire and the lower clergy. To be fair to him, the fact that he had held firm against James II's intense efforts to convert him to Rome, preferring to be sacked rather than forsake his principles, suggests that he certainly was not entirely unscrupulous; nor was he without industry and competence, especially on financial matters, of which he had some experience.

His zeal for the Church and Crown did not, however, curb his rather ungodly infirmities – namely, according to one contemporary, 'his passion, in which he would swear like a cutter, and the indulging himself in wine' – which became notorious.[24] His intense loyalism and hard drinking is well summed up by one notorious incident in 1686 when he and Lord Chancellor

Jeffrey became so intoxicated that 'they stripped into their shirts, and had not an accident prevented had gott upon a sign-post to drinke the King's health'.[25] Whigs still suspected this old servant of James II of being an old Jacobite, although, in justice to him, there is no evidence of this: James's actions against his beloved Church of England made him wary of any Stuart restoration.

A general election was traditionally called on the accession of a new monarch, and Rochester sought to exploit the pro-Tory mood in the country by the publication, a few weeks after the dissolution was announced, of the first volume of his father the Earl of Clarendon's *History of the Rebellion*. The very subject of this monumental work – the descent of the three kingdoms into civil war in the 1640s – was of propaganda value, recounting as it did how the 'fanaticks' (i.e. the Puritans) had plunged the country into anarchy and republican chaos. The implicit message was clear: their descendants, the Dissenters (and by extension the Whigs), were inherently politically rebellious, and only by giving the Tories a clean sweep could they be put in their place.

Rochester compounded this by writing an extraordinary preface to the work, which, as well as underlining his own immense sense of self-regard, implicitly set out the Tory agenda for the new reign.[26] He used the historical events explored in his father's book to underline the importance of redeeming the Church of England from 'oppressions' and of monarchs not 'throwing away their best and ablest ministers' (such as, it was heavily hinted, himself).[27] He also gave a fairly clear idea of his views on military strategy in the war with France, complaining that:

> When we have to do with an enemy whom we so far excel in strength at sea, that, with a little more than ordinary application, we might hope to restrain his exorbitant power by our naval expeditions, we have employed our greatest industry, and a vast expense, to attack him by land in that part, where, by the strength of his numerous garrisons, he must be, for many years at least, invulnerable.[28]

These two key themes – the status and strength of the Church and the best military strategy to pursue in the war – were to quickly become the key battle lines in the political struggle of the next few years, and in the election.

In the immediate term, the Tory tide was unstoppable. The favour shown to the Tories by a popular new queen inevitably had its effect among the electorate – as Gilbert Burnet, Whig bishop and acute political observer, put it, 'her inclination to the tories appearing plainly, all people took it for granted, that she wished they might be the majority', which is what duly occurred.[29] Contemporaries estimated that the Tories had prevailed over the Whigs by three or two to one – modern calculations suggest a slightly more modest majority of eighty-three overall.[30]

Although by the beginning of Anne's reign the Tories had – mostly – accepted the need for England to play some role in waging war against Louis XIV, divisions immediately opened on the issue of how to fight the war.[31]

The High Tories were heavily influenced in their attitude by memories of the last war in the 1690s. That conflict had become a largely inconclusive war of attrition in which the armies of William III and those of Louis XIV had become bogged down in endless sieges. Enormous amounts of money had been spent merely to maintain a stalemate, which had led to a peace settlement representing something of a score draw. The best that could be hoped for in a large continental land war against the French – who had the largest and best army in Europe – was, in their view, the same again.

Why not, argued the Earl of Rochester, leave the Dutch to fight to an inevitable standstill against the French – making some small contribution of troops – and concentrate English forces on a naval war against France, making 'descents' (amphibious attacks) on France, Spain and in the colonies to weaken her and bring Louis to the negotiating table? This would be cheaper, play to England's strengths and avoid the futility of an unwinnable land war. England could play the role of mere 'auxiliaries'. Other leading High Tories did not take as forceful a view as Rochester: Nottingham was prepared to countenance a greater commitment to land war in Europe, albeit with more emphasis on supporting and opening up campaigns on the Iberian Peninsula and in Central Europe rather than getting bogged down in Flanders. However, even he and most of the other High Tories wanted an approach based far more on a naval – what became known as a 'blue-water' – strategy.

This was by no means a contemptible view. It was not unreasonable to assume that the war just beginning was likely to be an uninspiring replay of King William's efforts in the previous decade. Tories reasoned that, since the Dutch bore the greatest risk of French invasion, it was hardly unreasonable that they should bear the vast bulk of the cost and trouble in waging the land war. Why shouldn't England play to its strengths anyway? The blue-water strategy held out the promise of England being able to acquire new colonies and improve its trading privileges relative to its imperial rivals. It was, indeed, a strategy that would succeed spectacularly sixty years later under Pitt the Elder.

The problems with the Tory argument were to some degree unforeseeable. Firstly, they could not have predicted that Marlborough would turn out to be one of the nation's greatest ever military geniuses; under any other general, the Tories' assessment of the likelihood of success in a continental land war would probably have been borne out. Secondly, as they were soon to find out, naval warfare based on amphibious assault, over very long distances, was, with the technology and knowhow available at the time, extremely difficult to conduct successfully.

The other problem was political. Although the Tory view of the war was rationally defensible, there was no doubt that much of it was rooted in a hearty hatred for the Dutch, who were, after all, one of the greatest maritime commercial powers in Europe, and therefore natural trading competitors and rivals. Worse than this, in Tory eyes, was the fact that the Dutch had bled England dry at the behest of William III in the last war, purely to serve their own interests.

This wasn't in itself necessarily a problem – anti-Dutch sentiment was not unpopular in the country. The problem was that indifference to the fate of the Dutch could easily be framed as disguised sympathy for the French, who were the greatest supporters of the pretensions of the Pretender. This allowed the Whigs to present the Tory attitude as merely window dressing for their Jacobite sympathies: they really wanted Louis XIV to win the war so that the Stuarts could be restored and absolute monarchy on the French model to be installed. This was the stuff of Whig propaganda at every election for many years. Ironically, it was probably never less true than in 1702, given that a

Tory dominated administration had recently been responsible for securing the Hanoverian succession in law; an Abjuration Act had just been finally been passed and the oath taken by almost all Tories; and the enthusiasm for Queen Anne made Jacobitism an ever-less-attractive prospect for the Church Party. This didn't stop the Whigs from tarring the Tories with the brush of Jacobitism, however.

More broadly, divisions over the war reflected a wider contrast between the Tories and the Whigs. The Whigs favoured an essentially Europe-centric policy, seeing England's fate as inextricably linked with the fortunes of the continent. For them, pan-European Protestant solidarity was crucial to constrain the power of France and ensure that there was absolutely no chance of a Stuart restoration: England's place in the world was, one might say, at the heart of Europe.

The Tories were far more sceptical, seeing entanglement in the affairs of the continent as being more likely to damage national prosperity and drag the country into disputes that were of little more than peripheral relevance to England's interests. The war was not, after all, so much between Protestant Europe and Catholic France, but rather a conflict between two Catholic superpowers: the Habsburg Empire and France.

From a modern-day perspective, one might say that the Whigs cast the Tories as, if not actually treacherous due to their perceived Jacobitism, then at the very least insular, xenophobic and isolationist, whereas the Tories claimed that the Whigs wished to embroil England in a bloody and expensive 'forever war' at an enormous cost in life and lucre, largely to serve the interests of the Dutch, and, indeed, the disproportionately Dissenting (and Whig) financiers who made a huge profit from lending the government the money needed to pay for the conflict.

Whatever the vagaries of the big picture, the immediate reality was that Rochester's strategy was (aptly enough) dead in the water almost instantly. His attempt to persuade the government to enter the war only as auxiliaries failed in early May 1702. Military policy was really being dictated by Marlborough and Godolphin, who were thoroughly committed to the essentially Whiggish policy of waging the most vigorous continental war possible by harnessing every ounce of England's financial, economic and military might. This did not stop intense efforts by High Tory ministers over the next two years to force the government into a more naval-centric and Dutch-sceptical war policy, with occasional moderate success, but ultimately they were hamstrung by the simple fact that, whatever the Queen's sympathies on Church politics, on military matters she was a firm supporter of the duumvirs.

It was, however, the question of Church politics that was immediately to come to fore as the new parliament met in October 1702. To understand this, we need to examine the broader context of the fortunes of the Church since the Glorious Revolution.[32]

Although at the time most High Tories saw passing the Toleration Act in 1689 as a small price to pay to avoid comprehension, the legislation had subsequently had a severe impact on religious attendance and discipline. Although technically the Act stipulated that Sunday worship, whether in church or conventicle, was still compulsory, in practical terms it was impossible to enforce: anyone not attending church could claim to have been to a Dissenting place of worship instead, and vice versa, and there was no co-ordination to check. As a result, churches in many parts of the country saw the number of people taking communion decline precipitously.

As unwelcome to churchmen was the mushrooming of now legal Dissenting meeting houses and chapels. Far more licences for Dissenting worship were issued than anyone had predicted: 939 alone in the first year, and that number continued to grow. Throughout the country, parsons suddenly found themselves in competition with new, legal nonconformist congregations. A new wave of 'Dissenting academies', which were essentially nonconformist universities-cum-seminaries, and even schools, which threatened the Church's monopoly of education, were set up. In reality, Dissent was plateauing and becoming rather more respectable, but Dissenters were prominent in many urban and mercantile communities, and many churchmen feared that their numbers and power would only grow and grow.

There were broader problems. Clergymen were being hit by increased land taxes, as many lived off profits from the land through tithes. Many benefices were not lucrative anyway, and it was not uncommon for vicars to be unable to 'buy books, distribute charity or keep his family above servile labour'; as Tory pamphleteer Charles Davenant remarked, 'the scandalous poverty of the clergy has very ill effects'.[33]

To add insult to injury – in the eyes of the majority of the clergy – was the spiritual temper of the times. The 1690s saw a burst of heterodox and anti-clerical writings that deeply shocked loyal churchmen. A group of writers began to attack traditional Christian ideas of revelation and church authority. Thinkers such as John Toland and John Locke argued for a pared down Christianity rooted in natural reason. Traditional doctrines such as the Trinity were dismissed as absurd impositions on man's rational capacities. God was cast as a little more than a dim and distant first mover, Jesus little more than a talented ethical teacher. The spiritual power of the church, rooted as it was in ideas about Christ's divinity and the Church's status as the 'body of Christ', was dismissed as a barbarous system of superstition that gave altogether unjustified influence to priests, who abused their dominance to keep men in a state of credulous intellectual infancy and 'bring the world into a blind submission to them'.[34] Such ideas were openly advocated in books and pamphlets – although how many actually took any notice of them was another question.

All of these tendencies provoked loathing and often panic in rectories throughout the country: the infernal forces of Dissent, and worse, had been unleashed on the Church and threated to completely undermine its authority and doctrines. It was, however, the internal dynamics and response of the Church itself that really drove the High Churchmen and Tories into paroxysms of fury: rather than fight back hard against these baleful developments, the Church's leadership – that is, the bishops – had, in the eyes of the majority of the lower clergy, done little or nothing, or, even worse, been complicit in advancing them.

The context for this was the impact of the nonjuring schism of the early 1690s. After the Revolution, all in ecclesiastical authority had been compelled to take the oath of allegiance to William and Mary, or be deprived of office. Overall, a large majority, with varying degrees of sincerity, pledged their allegiance to the new regime. However, among those who refused were a disproportionate number of bishops, including the Archbishop of

Canterbury himself (William Sancroft) and other key figures, who were duly deprived of their office.

This outraged majority clerical opinion for several reasons. Firstly, it gave William and his ecclesiastical advisers an opportunity to appoint a tranche of senior bishops who were very much at odds with High Church opinion. These men – usually called 'Low Church' or 'latitudinarian' – had a far 'lower' view of the authority of the Church, seeing it more as a voluntary society of individual Christians justified by faith and nourished by an individual relationship with God. They were far more tolerant of Dissent, stressing what Protestants had in common. They were pretty much all Whigs.

Secondly, it heralded what many High Churchmen saw as a scandalous Erastianism – that is, the view that the Church is subordinate to the civil state and can be ordered and governed by it. The deprived bishops had effectively been dismissed from their spiritual role by the secular state authority: their episcopal ministry had been made conditional on taking a political oath. Most High Churchmen saw the Church as having its own authority – over its doctrines, liturgy and priesthood – that could or at least should not be abrogated by the civil authorities. William had no right to dismiss bishops and appoint new ones. Nonjurors tended to openly make these arguments and claim that the bishops appointed by William were invalid – indeed, some nonjurors (most of whom were Jacobites) established their own episcopal succession – but many who took the oaths of allegiance sympathised with this view.

This dividing line – between High Churchmen and Low Church latitudinarians – had two aspects: one a question of ecclesiastical politics, the other a question of civil politics. With regards to the former, the High Churchmen argued that the Church's right to govern itself needed to be reasserted. In practice, this took the form of demanding a revival of convocation. Convocation was effectively the Church's own 'parliament' (the nearest modern equivalent would be the General Synod). It had fallen into disuse in the 1660s, but as the 1690s wore on and the weaknesses of the Church became more obvious, some High Churchmen started to argue that convocation needed to be revived so that the Church could take the actions needed to revive itself and combat the rise in heterodoxy.

In 1696, a fiery high-flier, Francis Atterbury, wrote a book that started the 'convocation controversy', and heralded the beginning of a dramatic revival of the High Church movement in the country. Entitled *Letter to a Convocation Man*, it argued that not only did the church desperately need convocation to be recalled to put in train a programme of revival, but it had an established constitutional right to sit regularly. It had largely been assumed hitherto that, since the Reformation, convocation could only meet if given permission to do so by the King. Atterbury embarked on a forensic account of ecclesiastical and constitutional history, which purported to show that convocation was an essential part of parliament – 'as one was the King's highest temporal court, so [convocation] was the highest spiritual court'.[35] The implication was that convocation had as much right to sit regularly as parliament did, quite independently of the whims of any monarch.

Replies followed from Whiggish clerical opponents which disputed Atterbury's historical account, and largely bested him on the detail, but it didn't matter. Atterbury was a scintillating polemical writer and his arguments galvanised the High Church clergy brilliantly, making the meeting of convocation one of the central demands of their newly energised movement – and, indeed, of Tory lay politicians like Rochester.

The more expressly political element of the High Church revival came into focus shortly after, in around 1697. High Churchmen saw the role of the state as to uphold the exclusive rights and privileges of one true holy and apostolic Church – that is, the Church of England – and ensure that civil government was rooted in its teachings. Most High Churchmen claimed to support the limited toleration offered by 1689, but mere suspension of legal penalties against Dissenters did not mean that the state should not be assertively and exclusively Anglican. The lynchpin of this was the Test and Corporation Acts, which made political and state office a Church of England monopoly.

The problem with this theory was thrown into sharp relief in 1697. One Sunday, the Lord Mayor of London, Sir Humphrey Edwin, processed, in full mayoral regalia and riding his mayoral coach, from morning prayer under the auspices of the Church of England at St Paul's Cathedral to an afternoon worship meeting at Mead's meeting house, a Presbyterian conventicle.[36] It was a deliberately defiant act that illustrated the phenomenon of 'occasional conformity': when Dissenters took Communion the minimum number of legally prescribed times in an Anglican church purely in order to qualify to hold public office.

Occasional conformity was an obvious evasion of the Test and Corporation Acts, but not one that was easy to combat unless a priest was prepared to refuse communion to someone who attempted to take it, which was legally troublesome. High Churchmen saw it as a cynical act designed to undermine the legal monopoly of churchmen on public office: they reacted with white fury to Edwin's provocation. Low Churchmen tended to downplay the issue, stressing the need for Protestant unity. Dissenters were divided on it. Some saw the law as unjust and therefore were happy to flout it. Some attempted to justify it as an act of charity and solidarity between Protestants. Others argued that whatever the justice of the Test Act, it was a profane act that reduced the holy sacrament to a mere act of political cynicism: Daniel Defoe, himself a Dissenter, called it 'playing Bo-peep with God almighty'.[37]

High Church anger built during the final years of William III's reign. When the Tories came back into office in 1700, one of Rochester's main conditions for agreeing to join the ministry had been the calling of convocation, which duly occurred in February 1701. It was a chaotic mess. Despite High Church support for episcopal authority in theory, in practice there was no love lost between the High Church lower clergy and the Low Church, Whiggish bishops. Thomas Tenison, the latitudinarian Archbishop of Canterbury, prorogued the meeting almost immediately, terrified that the predominantly High Church lower clergy, egged on by the vehement Dr Atterbury, would attempt to force convocation to act beyond what he saw as its remit.

Atterbury and his allies ignored the prorogation, openly defied Tenison's authority, and proceeded to draw up a programme of suppressing heresy and asserting the constitutional rights of convocation. An unseemly stand-off ensued, which only ended when the King himself prorogued convocation. The lower clergy were furious at Tenison's high-handed behaviour; the Whiggish bishops were appalled at the violence of the High Church assault and became ever more blatantly pro-Junto in their politics. Once again, the Church was riven by politics, politics by the Church.

Between 1697 and 1702, High Church anger had grown but little had come of it in parliament. The accession of Anne, known to be in sympathy with the high-fliers, was therefore seen as heralding a new dawn of High Church dominance.

The high-fliers soon went on the assault. In June, a then little-known Oxford cleric, Dr Henry Sacheverell, delivered an incendiary sermon entitled 'The Political Union'. His general theme was the natural dependence of the state on the Church and the alliance between Dissenters in religion and the agents of 'Rebellion and Usurpation' in the state. The usual heated comparisons between the present day and the Puritan rebellion of the 1640s were drawn. He warned that a 'Confus'd Swarm of Sectarists [Dissenters]' had gathered about the Church, 'not to partake of its Communion, but to disturb its Peace' and to 'Undermine and Destroy it'.[38] Worse still were the 'False and Perfidious Members' of the Church itself, who were allowing the Dissenters 'to Debauch Its Doctrines, Over-run its Discipline, and to Subvert the very Being of That Constitution'.[39]

The message was clear: the Low Church bishops would allow the Church to be subverted by their indifference to, among other issues, occasional conformity. Sacheverell's message was essentially that which would become the standard Tory battle cry of the next decade or so: 'the Church in Danger'. The only sane response to this was, he argued, to defy both Dissenters and mealy-mouthed bishops and instead 'hang out the bloody flag and banner of defiance'.[40] Sacheverell, with his compelling, if blood-curdling, oratorial style and reactionary zeal, soon became a High Church standard bearer: Defoe called him 'the bloody flag-officer'.[41]

The impending conflict between high-flying Tories and the Whigs and their episcopal allies was symbolised neatly in the 1702 election by the conflict in Worcestershire between staunch High Churchman Sir John Pakington and the Whig Bishop of Worcester, William Lloyd.

Lloyd, as partisan as any of his High Church opponents despite being well into his seventies, nursed a vehement hatred for Sir John, the Tory

MP for the county. He proceeded to conduct a vicious campaign to unseat Pakington. 'He charges his Clergy . . . every where, upon their canonicall obedience, not to give theyr votes for Sr J Pak', wrote one observer.[42] Lloyd did everything he could to bully and cajole local rectors and tenants of church land not to vote for Sir John. He summoned legions of unimpressed local parsons in order to character assassinate Pakington, whom he accused of libel, Jacobitism and even 'Drunkenness, Swearing and Whoredom'.[43] To one unfortunate would-be Pakington supporter, the bishop said that 'if he voted for Sir John Pakington, he should think him led by Wicked and Carnal Principles'.[44]

Sir John had the last laugh. Not only did he enlist newly prominent High Church bad-boy Henry Sacheverell to write a vicious attack on Lloyd in response – entitled 'The Character of a Low-Church Man' – but he scraped home in the election, and then got the newly Tory-dominated House of Commons to pass a motion condemning Lloyd as 'malicious, unchristian and arbitrary' and demanding that the Queen sack him from his role as Lord Almoner, which she duly did.[45]

This symbolic little skirmish was a mere entrée, whetting Tory appetites for the main meal: a full-blown legislative assault on occasional conformity.

5

The Tories and the Tack

All the omens seemed good for the High Tories. Their victory in the 1702 election gave them a huge majority for occasional conformity legislation. The Queen was known to support it. Nottingham quickly authored a bill to that effect, received the Queen's blessing for introducing it, and persuaded the MP for Oxford University, William Bromley, to propose it.

Bromley, as the member for the spiritual home of High Church politics, entered the fray as one of the newer generation of high-flying Tories. A man of genuine integrity – not to say rigidity – of purpose, upstanding morality and no-nonsense directness, he was already highly respected among the Tory ranks, and soon to become one of the few able to impose some order on the fissiparous material that was the Tory squirearchy. His motives were, no doubt, largely inspired by his disgust at the desecration of the sacrament implied by taking Communion dishonestly for purely political purposes: he described it in one letter as 'that abominable hypocrisy, that inexcusable immorality' (although his opponents argued that the fault lay with making the partaking of Holy Communion a political test in the first place).[1]

It is fair to say, however, that for many Tories, political considerations were at least as much in their mind as spiritual ones when it came to occasional conformity. It was, in fact, rare for Dissenters to get anywhere near the upper echelons of public office, and there were very few Dissenting MPs. The real impact was felt in the corporations, where occasional conformity was increasingly common, and because many parliamentary seats were elected by members of the corporation, it effectively enfranchised a lot of overwhelmingly Whig-voting Dissenters in around seventy or eighty tightly contested seats. In short, outlawing occasional conformity might well swing a considerable number of constituencies in the Tories' favour: this was as much a matter of hard politics as religious scruple.

The bill introduced by Bromley – and seconded by a young Tory who was quickly to make a name for himself, Henry St John (the future Viscount Bolingbroke) – imposed a £100 fine on any civil or military office-holder who qualified for their post by taking Communion the requisite number of times in the Church of England but then subsequently 'resorted to conventicles'.[2] If they continued thereafter to hold their office, they would be fined £5 per day they remained in post. Once found guilty of this offence, any offender would subsequently be barred from holding public office unless they conformed for one year to the Church without visiting a Dissenting place of worship. These were stiff penalties. The bill passed in the Commons with a huge majority, and a confident group of Tories, in a show of strength, carried it up to the Lords in person.

The duumvirs were not enthusiastic about the bill. They wished to avoid major partisan strife in the Commons, as such division was liable to infect other parliamentary business and hold up the crucial voting of supply for the war. They also had no wish to provoke the Dissenters, given their disproportionate presence among the ranks of the financiers upon whom public credit depended – a point made by Somers in the Lords debate when he asked, 'My lords, if ye do not preserve them [the Dissenters], how can ye expect to reap the fruits of their Labours?'[3]

With the Commons and the Queen against them, the Whigs had a hard job blocking the legislation. However, with a House of Lords in which the Whigs were much stronger than in the Commons, they had a chance. Their strategy was to load the bill with amendments in the Lords, which would make them unacceptable to the Commons and cause a stalemate between the two houses, which would eventually cause the bill to fall.

Outside parliament, a fierce controversy raged in pamphlets and news-papers. Whig opponents of the bill painted it as a measure of persecution which would undermine the Toleration Act, discomfit England's Protestant allies and threaten national unity at a time of war. Only the French and Jacobites could welcome such a bill. As one propagandist put it:

> it will weaken and divide us at Home; it will discourage our Allies abroad, especially the Dutch . . . nor can a more likely step be taken, to defeat our hopes of a Protestant Succession, and to render us at last but a Province of France.[4]

These sentiments were expanded upon in parliament by the Whig Lords who contended that, since 'a vote for representative in parliament is the essential privilege whereby every Englishman preserves his property; and . . . whatsoever deprives him of such vote, deprives him of his birth-right', the bill essentially made good Protestant Dissenters political second-class citizens unable to claim due security for their property.[5]

In one sense, the Tories had the better of the debate. As they pointed out, the bill had no effect on the Toleration Act: to confound the issue of freedom of worship with the issue of the political rights of the subject was incorrect. The bill was simply intended to provide proper enforcement of laws already on the statute book, the Test and Corporation Acts (the preservation of which was, some Tories rather mischievously pointed out, one of William's stated aims when he invaded in 1688). As they put it, 'it enacts nothing new . . . it is intended to make the laws in being more effectual'.[6]

Logically, one could quite rationally argue that the only two consistent options were to enforce the Test and Corporation Acts properly, or repeal them altogether. The Whig opposition to the bill was really rooted in the political impact of disenfranchising many of their most loyal supporters, and the suspicion that this was the thin end of the wedge. They thought – probably not wrongly in some cases – that this was merely the first step for the High Tories, whose ultimate aim was to repeal the Toleration Act altogether and return to the pre-1689 days of outright persecution of the Dissenters. Strictly speaking, however, their claims that occasional conformity bills were 'persecution' that would destroy toleration were untrue.

The most explosive contribution to the debate came in the form of an anonymous pamphlet entitled *The Shortest Way with the Dissenters*. It was fiery stuff, making even Sacheverell look like a bit of a milksop. Unless firm action was taken against the Dissenters, the author suggested, churchmen would witness 'our Church . . . suppressed and persecuted, our religion trampled underfoot, our estates plundered, our persons imprisoned and dragged to jails, gibbets and scaffolds'.[7] It would be better for churchmen to 'summon our own to a general massacre' so as not to 'betray them to destruction by our supine negligence'.[8] The only solution, the pamphlet argued – the 'shortest way' of the title – was simply to murder the Dissenters:

> 'Tis Cruelty to kill a Snake or a Toad in cold Blood, but the Poyson of their Nature makes it a Charity to our Neighbours, to destroy those Creatures, not for any personal Injury receiv'd, but for prevention; not for the Evil they have done, but the Evil they may do.[9]

If this sounds too hyperbolic to be meant seriously, even for the firebrands of the High Church, then that's because it was. Although the 'they won't rest until we're all murdered in our beds!' quality of this pamphlet only slightly exaggerated the hysteria of many of the High Tories, it was, in fact, a parody, written by Daniel Defoe, designed to mock the bloodthirsty tone of the clerical Tories. Contemporaries claimed that some actually believed it to be genuine and was even read with approbation at the firesides of various Oxford colleges.[10]

Whether that is true or not, the High Churchman soon realised that it was a savage joke at their expense, and reacted in their usual way: by going ballistic. Nottingham – not a man renowned for his sense of humour at the best of times – made it his personal mission to uncover the author and punish him. Betrayed by a middleman, Defoe was tried by a set of men he had only a few months before brutally lampooned in an extraordinarily imprudent (albeit ballsy) series of satirical poems. Unsurprisingly, they were not sympathetic: he was put in the pillory and given a stretch in Newgate for his trouble (although Defoe turned this into a triumph, as the crowd refused to throw anything at him worse than flowers, and he published a defiant poem about the incident).

The fury provoked by Defoe was nothing to the apoplexy of the massed ranks of the Church Party in response to the course of events in parliament. The Whig wrecking tactics worked. Wharton's superior organisation paid off: by minute majorities, a series of amendments were passed in the Lords, which rendered the bill unacceptable in Tory eyes.

The fact that the Queen ordered her husband – ironically himself a Lutheran – to vote for the bill, despite the fact that in its original form it would have disbarred him from his role as head of the Admiralty (he was alleged to have remarked to Lord Wharton, in his heavy Danish accent, shortly before voting for it, 'my heart is vid you'), did not save the bill.[11] To Tory fury, most of the bishops supported the Whig line, confirming every high-flying fear about the cravenness of the latitudinarian episcopal bench. Godolphin and Marlborough voted for the bill in deference to the Queen's wishes, but made no effort to rally support in the Lords for it. The bill got bogged down in fruitless conferences between the houses. Neither side would budge, and, in early 1703, the legislation fell.

The occasional conformity battle had raised partisan rancour in parliament to new heights, which was precisely what the duumvirs and Harley had wanted to avoid. Irritated Tories, led by Edward 'Sir Chuffer' Seymour, who appeared to become more cantankerous as he got older (and iller: he seemed to be perpetually on the cusp of dying of diabetes, but somehow always soldiered on), had attempted to delay the passage of the Malt Tax. Talk was abroad of refusing crucial war supplies in order to force the Occasional Conformity Bill through, although even Seymour wasn't prepared to go that far yet. Harley ducked and weaved and attempted to divert the Tories by allowing them to investigate the financial malpractices of William's reign: he got the supplies through, but it wasn't as easy as he would have liked. An exasperated Godolphin complained in a letter to Harley:

> Does anybody think England will be persuaded that this Queen won't take care to preserve the Church of England? And do they forget that not only the fate of England but of all Europe depends upon the appearance of our concord in the dispatch of our supplies?[12]

Meanwhile, divisions over war policy between the High Tory ministers and the court grew behind the scenes.

At one level, this was a personal vendetta. Rochester, who had presumed that Anne would appoint him, not Godolphin, to the role of Lord Treasurer, was suffering from a bad case of injured pride. He heartily despised the duumvirs and had a particular personal animus against Marlborough: he was convinced that he, not they, should be dictating policy, in the context of an out-and-out Tory regime.

He proceeded to do everything he could to harry and harass his rivals in alliance with awkward-squad allies like Seymour. He called for a complete purge of all Whigs still in place, from the ministry right down to the lord lieutenancies, contrary to the duumvirs' desire to keep as many moderate Whigs on board as possible. He used all his parliamentary influence to (successfully) vote down a proposal, urged by the Queen, to give Marlborough a permanent parliamentary grant of £5,000 year, to support his newly acquired dukedom and as a token of Anne's confidence in him. He worked to undermine Marlborough's military strategy at every turn. Marlborough was close to the end of his tether.

By February 1703, with the parliamentary session at an end, the Queen had had enough. Rochester was meant to be Lord Lieutenant of Ireland, but had stayed in London to foment trouble (but not, apparently, attend cabinet meetings). She ordered him to attend to his duties in Dublin. He outright refused, so she simply sacked him. He went off in a sulk, going into outright opposition to the ministry (not that this involved much change in his behaviour).

This was by no means an end to the duumvirs' troubles, however. Their entire approach was to seek national unity and go for broke in the war, but throughout the campaigning season of 1703 military success eluded them. Marlborough was continually frustrated by the caution of the Dutch, who thwarted his bold plans to take the initiative in Flanders. A plan by Nottingham to wage war against France in the colonies was sunk by the failure of the Dutch to make good on their promise to support a proposed naval expedition to the West Indies. MPs were outraged that the Dutch continued to trade with France despite being at war with them; the suspicion that everyone was making money out of the war except the Tory squires, who were paying ever more in taxation, stirred their every prejudice. Harley reported to Godolphin in September 1703 that even some Whigs were beginning to ponder the 'uselessness of an offensive war in Flanders'.[13]

Tensions between Nottingham – now the leader of the High Tory faction within the government – and the duumvirs continued to bubble away under the surface over the course of spring and summer 1703. Nottingham was not an intransigent wrecker like Rochester. He was certainly sceptical of Marlborough's strategy, complaining that a land war based in Flanders was 'still more useless and ruinous than it was even in the last war'.[14] Nonetheless, he was genuinely committed to winning the war, and had his own positive strategy to advocate – of changing the emphasis of the war away from Flanders towards supporting the Habsburgs in Central Europe and waging war in Spain itself – which at certain points overlapped with the duumvirs.

He and the envoy to Portugal, John Methuen, achieved a sensational success when they managed to persuade Portugal to enter the war on the allies' side, thus opening up a potential new front against the French on the Iberian Peninsula (although the commitment in the treaty, that no peace should be made until the French claimant to the throne of Spain, Philip V, was dislodged from Spain, was to have massive later repercussions). Marlborough continually worried, however, that Nottingham's favoured strategy would weaken his forces in Flanders by diverting them to Spain or the colonies, and thereby stymie his preferred plan of taking the war to the French closer to home.

Harley and the duumvirs were under no illusions about the likely temper of parliament when it met in October 1703. Tory fury had not abated: they hoped, by a further heave, to convince the Queen to throw her weight behind them and govern as their cipher.

Robert Harley, however, had a plan. He and Godolphin needed to defeat the High Tories, secure crucial supplies for the war, and unite the government under the banner of moderation, but a frontal assault was likely to be futile. The Tories were still dominant in the Commons and the gates of hell itself would not deter them from bringing forward another Occasional Conformity Bill in the new parliamentary session. However, by utilising all his political wiles he began to implement a strategy to divide, disarm and divert his opponents.

Firstly, he would work on the more reasonable and ambitious parts of the Tory leadership in the Commons. William Bromley, although intractable on religious matters, was a genuine patriot and was not wont to make unnecessary trouble on other matters. So Harley made a deal: he would raise no obstacles in the Commons to a fresh Occasional Conformity Bill in exchange for Bromley's acquiescence in securing war supplies. Since Harley knew that the Lords would be the key battleground for defeating such a bill anyway, it lost him nothing but made his job on the financial side much easier.

Harley also sensed something of a generational divide within the ranks of the High Tories. Much of the trouble was being caused by old stagers like Rochester, Nottingham and Seymour. What if he could convince some of the more promising younger ones – men like Henry St John, the rising star of the Church Party – to be patient and adopt a more moderate course that could bear fruit in the medium term, and gain them the emoluments of government office in the short term? The 'yesterday's men' who were throwing their weight around would then be reduced to irrelevant opposition.

Secondly, Harley recognised that the government needed some reliable means to put its case across in the press and refute the partisan scribbles and squibs emanating in bulk from both sides of the partisan divide.

In 1695, the Licensing Act had expired and not been renewed, which meant that pre-print government censorship of newspapers, books and periodicals ceased. This coincided almost exactly with the passing of the Triennial Act, which meant an increasing frequency of elections. The combination of these two events had resulted in an enormous growth in printed political propaganda in the late 1690s and early 1700, and since literacy rates had continued to increase, more and more people could actually read it. 'Public opinion' became an increasingly important factor in the calculations of politicians wishing to ensure favourable election results. Although many in the political class were ambivalent about such a development, fearing the impact of pandering to irrational and sometimes poor voters easily swayed by tricksome rhetoric, the savvy ones realised that it was a reality that could not be wished away. Harley grasped this point earlier than any other political figure of the era. He realised that it was essential to persuade the public that the Tories were overplaying their hand and becoming a threat to national unity in a time of war.[15]

What he needed in particular was a skilled polemical writer who would do his bidding. Luckily, he had just the right man to hand. Daniel Defoe was still languishing in Newgate, unable to pay his fine. He had recently been declared bankrupt and his business had gone bust. He had no way of supporting his family, and was in utter despair. Harley knew that he was a brilliant writer, direct and forceful, and that a poor, unemployed man is in no position to quibble about employment. So Harley arranged for his fine to be paid, and gave him a job, both as his chief hired pen and all-round intelligence gatherer. Harley had already begun to develop a system of informers and political agents throughout the country – it was key to his political approach to be the best-informed man in the country, as knowing who was who and who wanted what was key to his machinations – and Defoe could help with that too.[16]

Not only that, Harley had also managed to win over another invaluable propagandist: Tory Charles Davenant. Deeply in debt, Davenant could no longer afford his principles. Godolphin and Harley, with whom he had a long association, rated his abilities, and he was desperate for a job to ease his financial worries, so they procured a government post for him. His gratitude appeared to mellow his politics: he agreed to write for the ministry *against* the Occasional Conformity Bill.

Events were turning in Harley and Godolphin's favour in any case. Queen Anne was becoming ever more ambivalent about the bill, worried that the party heats it was provoking were disturbing the national unity and parliamentary efficiency needed to raise funds for and prosecute the war; its reintroduction was, she worried, a 'pretence . . . for quarrelling'.[17] She did not object to it in principle; in response to hectoring about it from Sarah Churchill she made it clear that she still believed that it was necessary to protect the Church and saw 'nothing like persecution in the bill'.[18] This, however, was not the right time for it. She made this very clear in her opening speech to the new session of parliament:

> I want words to express to you my earnest desire of seeing all my subjects
> in perfect peace and union among themselves . . . Let me therefore
> desire you all that you would carefully avoid any heats or divisions that
> may disappoint me of that satisfaction, and give encouragement to the
> common enemies of our church and state.[19]

The Queen was very quickly to be a disappointed woman.

As universally predicted, on 25th November Bromley introduced the
second Occasional Conformity Bill. It was somewhat toned down – the fines
were reduced – but in essence it was the same bill. Sir John Pakington
gave a rousing, if rather overwrought, speech in its favour, predicting dire
consequences if the scandal of occasional conformity were to be suffered
to continue:

> Mr. Speaker, I take this practice of Occasional Conformity, to elude the
> force of one of the best laws made in the church of England's defence,
> that it is scandalous and knavish in itself, and I will pretend to foretel
> this; that, by the benefit of this Occasional Conformity, the dissenters
> will come to be the majority of this house; and then I will venture to
> pronounce the days of the church of England few.[20]

It easily passed the Commons by a majority of 223 to 140. Its reception
in the Lords, however, would be quite another matter.

Pakington's speech made much of the fact that the Queen had signalled
her support for the last bill by sending her husband to vote for it. It was perhaps not the wisest emphasis to take, for Anne had made a crunch decision:
she would allow Prince George to be tactfully absent from the Lords when
it came to its crucial second reading there.

Marlborough and Godolphin were desperate to kill the bill but were also
desperate not to provide ammunition to Rochester and his cronies, who
would love to cast them as opponents of the Church. They were therefore
inclined to vote for it while doing everything they could to ensure it didn't
pass. Sarah was furious and put increasing pressure on her husband to vote
against it. Marlborough replied that he 'must be careful not to doe the thing

in the world which my Lord Rochister would most desire to have mee doe, which is to give my vote against this bill' — but he did 'promis sollemly' that he would 'speak to nobody living to be for itt'.[21]

Luckily for the duumvirs, the Whigs, sensing that the mood at court was shifting, decided to put all of their considerable parliamentary skills into outright opposition to the bill in the Lords. Charles Spencer, Earl of Sunderland (son of the notorious turncoat from the reign of James II and William III, now dead), a rising star in the Whig firmament and the newest addition to the ranks of the Junto, was detailed with managing the assault on the bill in conjunction with Wharton. They turned every screw and ruthlessly manipulated the system of proxy votes (whereby absent lords could nominate someone to cast a vote on their behalf) in order to rally opposition.

Meanwhile, Harley's propaganda operation began to go into effect. Daniel Defoe published an effective attack on the Occasional Conformity Bill, *The Challenge of Peace*, and in November Davenant published his *Essays upon peace at home, and war abroad*. This was a sensational turnaround from the old Tory warhorse. The book preached the benefits of burying faction in the face of mortal danger to the Protestant interest from France. He argued that it was crucial to avoid 'Heats . . . if we would preserve that Union, which alone can make us powerful Abroad, and strong at Home'.[22] Given Davenant's previous record of being a vicious partisan, and of hobnobbing with French Jacobites, one could forgive the Tory squires for choking over their ale on reading such words from his pen. Edward Seymour called him a 'profligate scribbler' and Tory propagandists savaged his treachery, but his defection was a blow to the Tory cause.[23]

The dispute spilled over into everything. Jonathan Swift, who was visiting London at the time, gave a sense of the factious mood abroad in London that autumn in a letter to a friend:

> I wish you had been here for ten days, during the highest and warmest reign of party and faction, that I ever knew or read of, upon the bill against occasional conformity . . . It was so universal, that I observed the dogs in the streets much more contumelious and quarrelsome than usual; and the very night before the bill went up, a committee of Whig and Tory

cats, had a very warm and loud debate, upon the roof of our house. But why should we wonder at that, when the very ladies are split asunder into high church and low, and out of zeal for religion, have hardly time to say their prayers?[24]

One day after Bromley introduced the new Occasional Conformity Bill into the Commons, England was ravaged by one of the greatest storms in its history. The fleet was only narrowly saved from destruction; Admiral Cloudesley Shovel's ship HMS *Association* was blown from Harwich in Essex to Gothenburg in Sweden.[25] Overall, somewhere between 8,000–15,000 people died. Trevelyan describes the devastation:

> Starting from Cornwall, the Great Storm traversed England in an eastern direction with a touch of north. Trees went down in battalions; the lead roofs on cathedrals and parish churches were all rolled up like carpets; in many places scarce a chimney remained standing, not a roof uninjured.[26]

The Bishop of Bath and Wells was killed in his bed by a collapsing chimney stack. Defoe summed it up: 'No Pen can describe it, no Tongue can express it, no Thought conceive it, unless some of those who were in the Extremity of it'.[27]

The symbolism of the storm happening at the height of the controversy over the bill was not lost on anyone. An official response from the Queen was published in the government newspaper the *London Gazette*, calling it a calamity:

> so Dreadful and Astonishing that the like hath not been seen or Felt, in the Memory of any Person Living in this Our Kingdom, and which Loudly Calls for the Deepest and most Solemn Humiliation of Our People.[28]

Although the implication was partly that the declining morals of the country had brought God's wrath down against a sinning nation, the political subtext was also clear: England was being punished for its endless factious quarrelling and should repent and turn to more responsible courses. Tories however, might have put a different complexion on it: a portent of doom if the government refused to give proper protections to the Church.

The dispute soon came to a head in parliament. The Tories in the Lords – never the most disciplined bunch – had no chance. In the end it wasn't even that close: the bill fell on its second reading by fifty-nine votes to seventy-one. The absence of the Queen's husband from the debate gave tacit permission to five waverers to vote against it. Godolphin and Marlborough voted for it, and even had the effrontery to enter their parliamentary protest at its rejection into the record, but they had got exactly what they wanted: the defeat of the bill without their fingerprints all over its demise. Meanwhile, supplies were agreed easily. The government had managed the situation adroitly.

The fury and frustration of the Church Party rose to a new pitch. Their triumphant expectations on the accession of Anne seemed to have turned to ashes: even the Queen had abandoned them. She was hardly any better than Dutch William. As Burnet put it, 'The clergy over England, who were generally inflamed with this matter, could hardly forgive the queen and the prince the coldness that they expressed on this occasion'.[29] A popular Tory doggerel exclaimed:

> And yet the Whigs vote for the Queen
> More heartily than we do;
> And is not this as sad a thing
> As any man can see to?[30]

Blinded by anger, the Tories in parliament looked for new ways to vent their spleen.

They soon found one. During the general elections of 1698 and January 1701, a poor cobbler named Matthew Ashby was prevented from casting his vote in the Aylesbury constituency by the mayor, William White, on the grounds that he was not a settled inhabitant of the borough, a decision that was upheld by the House of Commons on an election petition. Ashby subsequently won a legal action against the mayor, and the assize court ordered him to be restored to the electoral register. White appealed to the

Queen's Bench, on the basis that only the House of Commons had a right to make decisions on electoral questions, and won. The case was then taken to the House of Lords as the highest court of appeal.[31]

The whole business might sound like small beer, but it was being manipulated for political purposes. Ashby was a Whig, Mayor White was a Tory, and the borough of Aylesbury was a hot election battleground between Lord Wharton and Sir John Pakington. Wharton saw an opportunity: he decided to pay Ashby's legal fees and make the case a cause célèbre. It was all part of his wider parliamentary strategy. Conscious of the Whigs' weakness in the Commons, Wharton knew that the best way to maximise Whig strength was to make as many issues as possible into a trial of strength between the House of Lords – in which the Whigs had the edge – and the Commons. He knew that by taking the case to the Lords, the Commons would be incensed at perceived encroachment by the upper house on the prerogatives of the lower. So long as everything could be manipulated into a battle between Lords and Commons, the Tory majority in the Commons could be neutralised, much chaos created (which would feed the Tory reputation for bunging up parliamentary business with factional squabbles), and he might even be able to force a general election.

On 14th January 1704, the Lords, with much assistance from Wharton, decided the case in favour of Ashby. The Commons came within an inch of staging a riot. It was effectively a case of the Lords using its judicial role to interfere in the Commons' ability to determine their own elections, a privilege jealously guarded by the House. The fact that the Commons in this case had determined the case in favour of the Tory mayor gave the whole thing an obvious partisan edge. The Tories (rightly) suspected that Wharton's influence was behind the whole escapade – Edward Seymour mordantly observed that 'I do not think there was virtue enough in the cobbler of Aylesbury, nor had he purse enough, if a lord had not acted that part'.[32] Everyone knew which lord he meant.

In response to the Lords' decision, an outraged Commons voted through a defensive and over-the-top resolution that 'any attorneys, solicitors, coun-sellors or serjeants at arm who acted on any suits on the same grounds as Ashby v. White would be guilty of a high breach of the privilege of the

House'.[33] The problem for MPs was that, however manipulative the tactics of Wharton may have been, the notoriously unfair and partisan nature of the Commons in its adjudication of disputed elections was well known. Losing candidates could petition the House to reverse an election result, and almost all MPs voted on partisan lines, with no regard to the truth of the case. Both Whigs and Tories did so, but as the Tories were in the majority at the time they were the worst offenders. The Lords responded justifying its decision, and the Whigs had every intention of using the abuses of the Tory Commons as an election issue. The whole incident made the Lords look like an impartial judicial arbiter and the Commons as a corrupt den of Tory vituperation (though Wharton was hardly a model of impartial probity either).

As court frustration with the Tories' obstreperous tactics rose, the position of Nottingham seemed ever more insecure. The Whigs soon scented an opportunity to undermine him even further when, in December 1703, news of a botched Jacobite scheme – the so-called 'Scotch Plot' – started to leak out. It gradually emerged that, in the course of this plot, Nottingham, acting on poor advice from the Duke of Queensbury, the Queen's chief minister in Scotland, had accidentally allowed a double-turned-triple agent working for the Jacobites to escape the country. The Whigs in the Lords used this to attempt to smear Nottingham as a Jacobite. He was vindicated by the evidence, but some of the mud stuck, and once again the issue became a political football between Lords and Commons that gummed up parliamentary time.

By the end of the parliamentary session, the patience of the duumvirs – and indeed the Queen – had snapped. Harassed by the Tories at every turn, their attitude hardened markedly. In response to the usual mischief-making from Sir Edward Seymour, Marlborough had written to Sarah:

> We are bound not to wish for anybody's death, but if Sir Edward Seymour should die, I am convinced it would be no great loss to the Queen, nor the nation.[34]

Nottingham had further irritated Godolphin by placing a printed edition of the Occasional Conformity Bill in the *London Gazette* without notifying him, which Nottingham intended to signify official government support for the measure. It was impossible to act with a single voice with High Tories still in high office. Everyone could see that the current situation was unsustainable.

At this point, Nottingham made a stunning political miscalculation. Angered by the Whigs' attacks on him over the Scotch Plot and the course of the Occasional Conformity Bill, he decided to demand the sacking of various remaining Whig ministers; as he put it to Godolphin, 'the Queen could not govern but by one party of the other', and it had to be the Tories.[35] It was a spectacularly naïve move in the context of the court's growing hostility to the Tories. It backfired: a deeply unimpressed queen dismissed Nottingham's plea, he promptly resigned, and Anne decided to move in the exact opposite direction. She quickly moved to sack the other prominent High Tories still in office, Edward Seymour and the Earl of Jersey.

By presumption, poor parliamentary tactics and overplaying their hand, the Tory ministers who had swept into office in 1702 had thoroughly alienated their sovereign.

Purging the government of almost all the leading Tory leaders was one thing, but the government had to find alternative supports, given that it seemed increasingly likely that many Tory MPs would, in fury at the last parliamentary session, go into open and unrestrained opposition.

The Whigs, who had helped the ministry out on occasional conformity, expected to be rewarded. No matter how much the High Tories had annoyed the duumvirs, Harley and the Queen, they had no appetite for that. The Queen heartily hated the Junto and had no intention of turning to them. Godolphin saw the Whigs as 'an angry party who breath nothing but violence and confusion when the whole power of the government is not entirely in the hands of their own creatures'.[36] Marlborough had long been wearied by both sides – he remarked to his wife during the summer of 1703 that 'I think the two partys are soe angry, that to ruin etch other, thay will make noe scrupel of venturing the whole'.[37] He disdained the 'detested nams of Wigg and Torry', and had no illusions that the Whigs would be any less presumptuous than the Tories had proven.[38]

The danger was, however, that by not obliging the Whigs, they would provoke them into opposing the ministry in an attempt to extract ministerial appointments. With the High Tories in revolt, the managers might alienate all sides and end up with no majority for their measures. As Defoe put it:

> all the Whigs of King William's reign expected to have come into play again, and had fair words given them, but they see it was but wording them into a fools' paradise, and now the two ends will be reconciled and overturn the middle way.[39]

Harley, however, had been working on his plan to divide the Tories and provide a solution to this problem throughout the parliamentary session.

As Harley's propagandists poured out their odes to moderation and unity, and the political atmosphere began to change, the Tories began to look irresponsible. Younger Tory thrusters realised that there was no chance of their party forcing themselves into office and compelling the Queen to pass their measures. Harley's more subtle approach – moderation now in order to build up credit for (allegedly) a more thoroughgoing Tory policy in due course – began to appear more sensible. Harley, therefore, upped his efforts to buy off and placate some of the more ambitious Tory partisans.

The chief of his recruits was Henry St John (better known to posterity as Viscount Bolingbroke, a title he would not receive for some years to come). St John had cut a real dash among the Tory backbenchers since first being elected in 1701 aged just twenty-three, making his name as one of the most energetic young members and one of the Commons' most witty and polished speakers. He sought to court favour among the Tory ranks by acting as an eloquent mouthpiece for the squirearchical battalions of the backbenches. His efforts on behalf of the first Occasional Conformity Bill marked him out as 'one to watch'. He was in many ways an unlikely mouthpiece for the Church Party: the evidence suggests that he was probably educated at a Dissenting academy; his grandmother, who largely brought him up, had marked Presbyterian sympathies.[40]

What made him even more unlikely as a stern tribune of the churchmen was that he was, in fact, not even a Christian, but rather a freethinker, inclining to deism. Ironically, he himself took the Anglican sacrament purely in order to qualify for public office. He saw the Church of England as a useful political prop for maintaining public morality and order, and as an even more useful vehicle for his own political advancement, rather than the true apostolic church. He was, however, definitely a Tory of a sort: coming from an ancient landed family in Wiltshire, he certainly believed that the men of landed property were the natural leaders of the nation, possessed as they were of a permanent, fixed share in the kingdom; he heartily hated the nouveau riche stockjobbers and money men.

Contemporaries wondered at his abilities: his charm, intelligence and firm handle on business. Jonathan Swift, a friend and ally, described him as possessing a:

> . . . mind . . . adorned with the choicest gifts that God hath yet thought fit to bestow upon the children of men, a strong memory, a clear judgment, a vast range of wit and fancy, a thorough comprehension, an invincible eloquence, with a most agreeable elocution.[41]

Lord Chesterfield, remembering his boyhood later on in the eighteenth century, recalled:

> I am old enough to have heard him speak in parliament. And I remember that, though prejudiced against him by party, I felt all the force and charms of his eloquence. Like Belial in Milton, 'he made the worse appear the better cause'.[42]

The problem was that St John was known to be changeable and flighty, apt to betray his friends. His nickname was 'Mercury', which indicated agility and speed but also slipperiness and untrustworthiness. Like a shooting star, he was to blaze brilliantly in the political firmament for a while, but sustaining his success proved more difficult.

An even bigger problem – particularly, as it turned out, with the morally upstanding Anglican queen – was that he gave Wharton a run for his money in the 'rakehell' stakes. He could apply himself with enormous energy to political business, but he preferred to apply himself to debauchery. Later in his career, when he was in temporary forced retirement from politics, a 'gentleman' wrote the following verses in his voice:

> From business and the noisy world retired
> Nor vexed by love, nor ambition fired
> Gently I wait the call of Charon's boat
> Still drinking like a fish, and fucking like a stoat.[43]

His fondness for wine and women was legendary. According to Oliver Goldsmith's biography, he 'was noted for keeping Miss Gumley, the most expensive prostitute in the kingdom, and bearing the greatest quantity of wine without intoxication'.[44]

His treatment of his loyal (and beautiful) wife Frances became an open scandal. He barely bothered to conceal his many infidelities, and flaunted his mistress in public. Something of his attitude to women can be garnered from a letter he wrote to some fellow libertines:

> As to whores, dear friend, I am very unable to help thee. I have heard of a certain housemaid that is very handsome: if she can be got ready against your arrival, she shall serve for your first meal.[45]

On one occasion later in his career Jonathan Swift and a friend ran into him on the mall:

> [St John] met us and took a turn or two, and then stole away, and we both believed it was to pick up some wench; and tomorrow he will be at the cabinet with the queen: so goes the world.[46]

At one point, when he reached high office and was involved in negotiating the peace of Utrecht, the Whigs published a cartoon of him signing diplomatic papers using his mistress's arse as a writing desk. Unsurprisingly, his nickname 'Mercury' may also have implied that he had been treated for syphilis. He summed it up himself best when, years later, he reflected: 'Whilst

I loved much, I never loved long, but was inconstant to them all for the sake of all'.[47] Modern-day statesmen-lotharios are amateurs in comparison.

His drinking was also legendary: he quaffed his two favourite tipples, champagne and burgundy, with abandon, and would alternate nights of alcoholic oblivion with nights feverishly crouched over government papers (presumably not always using his sexual partners' buttocks as a desk). Jonathan Swift, an abstemious man, would years later spend a good deal of his time chiding a hungover St John for his binges:

> I was this morning with [St John], who was sick and out of humour; he would needs drink Champagne some days ago, on purpose to spite me, because I advised him against it, now he pays for it.[48]

Harley and St John had been acquainted since late 1701, and by September 1703 St John was writing to Harley offering him political intelligence; by October he was referring to him as his 'faithful unalterable friend'.[49] Seeing which way the wind was blowing, St John gradually began to extricate himself from his high-flying connections and seek Harley's favour, while making it clear that he wouldn't be bought off without due recompense.

On the resignation of Nottingham, when a government reshuffle was necessitated, St John received his reward: he was appointed Secretary at War, with the assumption that he would subsequently back the court on partisan measures. Many years later, in a probably apocryphal story, Voltaire (an acquaintance of St John in later life) was alleged to have joked that the prostitutes of London rejoiced at his appointment, given the augmentation of his income from the post and the likelihood that much of it would flow into their pockets.[50]

At the same time as St John was appointed, Harley replaced Nottingham as Secretary of State, marking his new pre-eminence in the ministry. St John wasn't his only new High Tory ally: Thomas Mansell replaced Seymour as Comptroller of the Household, and Sir Simon Harcourt, the Solicitor General, began to waver and pay his court to Harley too.

Harley even managed to buy off the most violent of the clerical High Tories, Francis Atterbury. Convocation had met again after the accession of Queen Anne, and Atterbury had every intention of using it as a platform for high-flying agitation. The same backbiting between the lower clergy and the bishops had ensued, with the same complete deadlock: when the representatives of the lower house marched to deliver a document outlining their high view of convocation's rights in February 1704, the bishops had simply packed up and gone home, leaving Atterbury and his allies to present their Protestation of Right to an empty room. Harley had been active as the Queen's ecclesiastical fixer in trying to placate Atterbury, but Atterbury was not happy at what he saw as his half-hearted support. However, in summer 1704, Harley conducted one of his classic charm offensives on Atterbury, and managed to persuade him to play the long game, act with more prudence, and wait for the opportunity to promote his High Church policies. The promise of a bit of ecclesiastical patronage – making him the Dean of Carlisle – helped grease the wheels. Another recruit to Harleian moderation – and a most unlikely one – had been secured.[51]

Harley had other tricks up his sleeve. He realised that it would be easier to peel off Tories from the high-fliers if he could convince them that the government was taking practical steps to help the Church. Harley was by no means hostile to the Church: indeed, he deplored the rise of freethinking and decline of congregations as much as anyone, and saw the health of the Church as a crucial test of the country's moral state. He merely thought – along with some Whigs and thoughtful Tories – that the Church should invest its energy in winning hearts and minds and evangelisation, rather than expending so much energy in political attacks upon the Dissenters. If the financial plight of the poor lower clergy could be relieved, he reasoned, more parish priests would have the resources and time to concentrate on their pastoral duties.

So he persuaded Anne – not that she needed much persuasion – to adopt a plan that became known as 'Queen Anne's bounty': the crown would give up its claim to the 'first fruits and tenths' – a clerical tax that had originally been sent to the Pope but which had been claimed by the monarch after the Reformation – and use the money to raise the stipends paid to the most needy clergymen. It proved popular and did something to spike Tory arguments that the government was indifferent to the Church.

Cracks were starting to appear between the high-fliers, determined to push the Occasional Conformity Bill through whatever the cost, and Harley's growing ranks of moderates. In the next session, those cracks were to become a gaping abyss.

The political situation, which was already sliding away from the High Tories, was further transformed by the tumultuous events in Europe in the summer of 1704. The war had not gone well for the allies in the previous year. By mid-1704 French armies were threatening Vienna, which would have overrun the Habsburg Empire and destroyed the Grand Alliance, leaving England and the Dutch to fight on alone against the mighty French. Marlborough knew that salvation could come only from the Anglo-Dutch armies, which would require a daring march down the Rhine, then across to the Danube. The cautious Dutch opposed such a risky move, so Marlborough had to organise his manoeuvre in semi-secret.

It worked. The decisive encounter came just outside a Bavarian village called Blindheim – better known to us as Blenheim. The allied forces crushed a larger French force in a bloody pitched battle: Marlborough described it a 'victory . . . greater then has been known in the memory of man'.[52] It seemed to set the Duke up for an invasion of France. Likely defeat in the war had been transformed into probable victory.

Overnight, bitter Tory critics who ranted about the futility of Marlborough's land campaign in Europe were silenced. The credit of the ministry and the duumvirs soared. The Tory arguments about the need for a 'blue water' strategy lost their currency. Moderate Tories were simply pleased that their land taxes had contributed to a tangible victory. The more implacable ones tried to promote Sir George Rooke, who had won a victory in August at Malaga, as an alternative High Tory military hero to rival Marlborough, which seemed churlish.

If anyone thought that this would deter the Tory ultras from a third attempt to pass the Occasional Conformity Bill, they were soon disappointed. The fact that the situation was slipping away from them only made them wilder: this time they were prepared to go nuclear.

Their big idea to finally force the bill through was 'the Tack'. Tacking was the procedure whereby the Commons would attach a desired bill to a crucial financial piece of legislation needed to raise taxes, so that the Lords, who by custom were not supposed to vote down money bills, and could hardly risk the nation's coffers by voting down supply, had little choice but to pass both. Tories had muttered darkly about resorting to this expedient before but had never followed through. Determined not to be humiliated again, this time they decided to screw their courage to the sticking place and dare the Lords to defy them: they would try to tack the Occasional Conformity Bill to the Land Tax Bill, which constituted the single largest contribution to government income. No government could fail to pass a Land Tax Bill without looking ruin in the face.[53]

Tacking was highly controversial. It was of dubious constitutional status – Wharton, canny as ever, had secured a Lords resolution against its constitutionality a few years before – and many felt that it was bad form to try to force the lords' hands in this way. More pertinently, playing chicken with the very basis of government finance in the middle of a major European war risked being seen as grossly irresponsible, and indicative of the weight placed on resisting French domination – and therefore Jacobite restoration – by the Tories, which is to say, not a great deal. The Tories were pinning their hopes on a very risky gambit.

Indeed, given that the Lords had passed Wharton's resolution against tacking comfortably a few years before, it is difficult to understand why the Tories thought they had any chance of succeeding. Many wavered: Bromley was undecided about introducing the bill at all, let alone tacking it, and rumours abounded that he had been offered a government place as the price of his inaction. The fact that a key group of influential figures in Oxford University told him that he had no chance of re-election unless he introduced the bill again probably focussed his mind, however. Even Rochester and Nottingham appeared to be doubtful. It was the arrival of diabetes-ridden and increasingly cranky Sir Edward Seymour that appeared to stiffen Church Party sinews; a meeting at the High Tory watering hole of the Fountain Tavern decided the issue. The Tack was on.

The third Occasional Conformity Bill was introduced on 15th November: this time, it only passed the Commons by twenty-six votes, a considerable drop in its majority. The omens for the bill, let alone the Tack, did not look good. Harley, although he had hoped to defeat the bill on its first reading in the Commons by appealing to wavering Tories, was heartened. He wrote to Marlborough saying that such a narrow majority meant that 'it will be impossible for them to tack it, if they be mad enough to attempt it'.[54]

They were precisely that mad. The virulence of the debate on the bill itself was shocking even by the tumultuous standards of the day. Seymour and Sir Simon Harcourt, a Tory defector to the court on the issue, had 'high words', and the bitterness of the resolute Tories against colleagues whom they now saw as turncoats panicked Harcourt, who wrote to Harley:

> Universal madness reigns. The more inquiry I make concerning the Occasional Bill, the more I am confirmed in my opinion, that if much more care than has been, be not taken, the Bill will be consolidated [i.e., tacked], I find the utmost endeavours have been used on one side, and little or none on the other.[55]

Harley, Godolphin and Harcourt conducted a thorough canvass of members, and found many wavering. It was becoming increasingly clear that the Tack threatened to throw the country's entire financial situation and war effort into complete chaos. The accusation that the Tories were intent on just that, in order to gift victory to France and bring in the Pretender, terrified many Tory backbenchers, even ones that supported the bill itself.

Harcourt need not have panicked. In the event, after an epic eight-hour debate, the Tack was pulverised in the Commons: the motion fell 251 to 134. The Tories had been split down the middle, with many – soon to be nicknamed 'Sneakers' by the hardliners – losing heart and abstaining, and still others actually voting against, including St John. The Bishop of Carlisle described the scene:

> This Defeat sat very uneasy upon many of our Highflyers; who were ventureing the Parliament and Nation's falling into any sort of Confusion, rather than not carry their point. When the Coaches began to move, I sent out my servant to enquire how matters went: And he presently return'd

with a lamentable story that The Church has lost it. This, he said, he had from several Clergymen; as well as others.[56]

The bill itself, untacked to the Land Tax, went forward, but its defeat in the Lords was a formality and the majority against this time was even higher: twenty-one. Even the Tories now got the message: 'old Occasional' was dead for the foreseeable. The extravagant ire of the Tories knew no bounds: one informed commentator wrote to a friend that 'their zeal is turned to rage, and they resolve to leve nothing undon to bring back their party to a Majority'.[57]

It would be a hard task.

The 1704–5 parliamentary session ended with the clash over Ashby and White coming to a head. Determined to stir the pot even more, Wharton encouraged five other men who had been deprived of their vote by Mayor White in Aylesbury to sue him in the law courts, in direct contravention of the Commons' resolution of January 1704. The Commons saw it as an intolerable provocation, had the men called to the bar of the House, declared them guilty of breach of privilege, and had them locked up in Newgate.[58]

Wharton proceeded to make a fine exhibition out of the whole affair. He lavished money, clothes and the finest foods on the five men in prison – several of whom were illiterate – and arranged for Whig notables to visit them in their fine carriages to fete them as martyrs for the noble cause of liberty. Another constitutional wrangle between the houses proceeded, with the Junto lords arranging for writs of habeas corpus to be moved in an effort to free the men. That failed, so they went to the Queen herself, petitioning for a 'writ of error', which would allow the case to be brought before the Lords as the highest judicial court: they were determined to free the men and gain a triumph in their epic struggle with the Commons.

The Commons was in uproar. It sent an address to the Queen calling on her not to allow such a writ, and resolved that the lawyers responsible for drafting it were also in breach of privilege, and therefore to suffer the same fate as the poor voters of Aylesbury. Wharton, anticipating this, tipped off the lawyers: when the serjeant-at-arms arrived to arrest them, they had escaped, one 'having shimmied down ropes and sheets out of his back window'.[59]

The Commons then determined to send the Speaker of the House – Harley himself of course, who had remained Speaker as well as becoming Secretary of State – into the Queen's Bench to order John Holt, the Lord Chief Justice himself, to attend the bar of the Commons. It seemed as if the Commons was actually going to try to cast the most senior lawyer in England into Newgate. Holt was not intimidated. He coolly answered: 'Mr Speaker, if you do not depart from this court, I will commit you, though you had the whole House of Commons in your belly.'[60]

The conflict between the Commons, the Lords and law courts was now so heated that open violence was anticipated by some. According to Burnet, by this point, 'the minds of all people were much alienated from the house of commons': certainly, their behaviour had been rather extraordinary, albeit under deliberate provocation.[61] The Queen had had enough. She knew that whatever she ruled on the writ of error would cause even greater strife, so she simply prorogued parliament, admonishing members for their 'unreasonable humour and animosity'.[62] Shortly after, she dissolved it and called a general election.

The bitter strife was to be taken to the country.

Given the wild political conflict in parliament over the previous three years, it was no surprise that the 1705 general election should have been the bitterest for some time.[63]

So far as the duumvirs, Harley and the court were concerned, the election was really a three-way contest, between Tackers, 'Sneakers' and Whigs. Their aim was to unseat as many Tackers as possible by using their patronage to sack Tackers from electorally sensitive positions such as Lord Lieutenancies and make it clear that voters who defied them could not expect their favour. They would do nothing against moderate Tories or Whigs, and in constituencies where there was no Tacker standing, they would largely leave events to their natural course.

Among the Tories there was some attempt to close ranks in the face of the common enemy: the whiff of Whig grapeshot tended to make them forget about their more bitter divisions over the Church, although the Tackers themselves stuck to their guns and implied that they, rather than the unmanly Sneakers, were the true lynchpins of queen and Church. Indeed, they appropriated the title of 'Tacker' as a badge of pride: in Northamptonshire, the high-fliers wore hats with 'Tacker' written on them, just so no one could be in any doubt as to their view. The Whigs, as united as they had been in some time, attempted to smear all Tories as essentially sympathetic to the Tack, and therefore little better than French stooges.

In many ways, the election turned on whether one thought the threat to the Church from the Dissenters, or the threat to England from France and the Jacobites, was the greater one. Harley's agents eloquently expounded the government view of the irresponsibility of the Tackers. Daniel Defoe, writing for Harleyite moderation in his periodical the *Review*, chided the Tackers for the mayhem they had tried to cause, claiming that if the Tackers had prevailed, the likely result would have been England 'Disabled from the War, the Confederacy broke, the Protestant Interest Abroad run down, the Dutch ruin'd, and the French victorious'.[64]

The Whigs went for the jugular. One pamphlet entitled *The Character of a Tacker* – which consisted of little more than none-too-literate, albeit lively, abuse – did not mince its words:

> Tackers in general are a sort of Animals spung from the Corruption of King James's evil government, and carrying two Shapes in one Body, like a Centaur, or the Irish Virgin with a Fish in her Tail, half Protestant half Papist.[65]

Playing on the Queen's 'a heart entirely English' speech from a few years ago, the pamphlet characterised a Tacker as 'an Englishman with a Heart ENTIRELY FRENCH'.[66]

One of the leading High Tory propagandists, nonjuring divine Charles Leslie, provided a vigorous defence of the Tackers and their cry of 'the Church in Danger' in his paper *The Rehearsal*. They were really the most sober and respectable element of the gentlemen of England, he argued, who were merely trying to save the Church from the republican and fanatical rabble:

'41 is here is again' was the subtext (or more often, simply the text). He also argued, in an attempt to counter Whig propaganda about the Tackers' supposed Jacobitism, that success in the war depended upon a national unity that could only be achieved by securing and uniting men around the Church of England, the true support of the state and bulwark of the Protestant interest. God would not reward a country that was indifferent to the fate of its true Church and conciliated the ungodly Dissenters.

Throughout the country candidates and supporters presented the election in highly polarised terms. In Middlesex, where two Tackers were turfed out, a Whig mob shouted 'No Jacobites', 'No French Government', 'No Wooden Shoes' (the latter was seen as a symbol of the poverty suffered by French peasants living under papist absolutism).[67] In Chester, a Whig mob cried 'down with the Church', and 'when about sixty of the clergy headed by the Dean came to poll, they said hell was broke loose and these were the devil's black guard!'[68] The mob then smashed the windows of the cathedral for good measure. Coventry saw a dramatic full-scale riot between rival Whig and Tory supporters.

In St Albans, the Duchess of Marlborough (whose family had an interest in the borough) attempted to intervene against a Tacker, John Gape. She canvassed the voters in person, telling one voter:

> . . . it was the Queen's desire that no such men should be chose, for such men would unhinge the government, and the Papists' horses stood saddled day and night, whipping and spurring.[69]

She did not enjoy a universally positive response, however, with one clergyman arguing with her openly in the street and various shopkeepers and townspeople treating her coldly. The Tacker scraped home by three votes, and the Tories had great fun mocking the 'Great Lady' for her dabbling in politics, although Gape was unseated on petition, so she had the last laugh.

As results trickled in, it was clear that the Whigs had made advances, particularly in the more populous constituencies, such as the City of London, where they swept the board. Government attempts to bring their patronage to bear against the Tackers bore some fruit: they unseated forty-four of the 134.

However, ninety held on, and the ministry encountered some notable setbacks, most obviously in relation to the Cambridge University seat, despite one of the Whig candidates being Godolphin's son and the other Isaac Newton. The government threw the kitchen sink at the seat, even persuading the Queen to intervene on behalf of the Whig candidates. However, the churchmen mobilised, Newton saw canvassing as beneath his dignity, and the Tackers held on. Godolphin was humiliated. He wrote to the Duchess of Marlborough: 'The loss of Mr. Godolphin's [i.e. his son's] election at Cambridg is no small mortification to mee, and I have now the same occasion to complain myself of the behaviour of the clergy, as some of my friends had before.'[70]

As the dust settled, the consensus was that the new parliament would be evenly balanced, although more Tackers had held their seats than the government would have liked. A modern estimate gives the final tally as being 260 Tories (which includes both Tackers and moderate men) to 233 Whigs, plus some twenty moderates of neither party. The duumvirs' mind began to turn to how the government could plot its way through the difficult situation it was likely to face when the new parliament met. Marlborough made his view clear to Godolphin:

> Upon my exsamaning the list you sent me of the new Parliament, I find so great a number of Tackers and their adherents, that I should have been very uneasy in my own mind, if I had not on this occasion beged of the Queen, as I have in my letter, that she would be pleased for her own sake, and the good of her kingdome, to advise early with you what incoragement might be proper to give the Whigs, that thay might look upon it as their own concern to beat down and oppose all such proposals as may prove uneasy to her Majesty or government.[71]

As the new parliamentary session approached, it was clear that tensions were emerging between Harley and the duumvirs about how to manage affairs. The duumvirs thought that some concessions had to be made to the Whigs, who had generally been more of a help to the government over the past few years than most of the High Tories. Harley disagreed. Hatred of the Junto and their tyrannising ways was one of the most consistent principles of his political career, and he feared turning to them. He believed that the Tackers and their ilk were an irresponsible minority in the Tories who could be detached from the more sensible body of the Church Party, a process he had already started. Combined with the government's placemen and the more independently minded Whigs, the government could manage parliament by isolating both the Junto men and the wild high-fliers: in essence, honest country members of both parties could unite to keep the Queen out of the clutches of party leaders. As he put it in a letter to Godolphin:

> If the gentlemen of England are made sensible that the Queen is the Head, and not a Party, everything will be easy, and the Queen will be courted and not a Party.[72]

Godolphin and Marlborough were a lot more sceptical about the Tory parliamentarians and thought they would inevitably need to lean more on the Whigs to get business in.

This is not to say that Godolphin and Marlborough relished the idea of giving more power to the Junto: both much preferred Harley's strategy by instinct, being moderate men who had no love for the Junto lords personally. Indeed, for a long time they had pursued such a 'mixed ministry' policy, which involved utilising, as much as possible, Whigs who were somewhat detached from the Junto: the so-called 'Lord Treasurer's Whigs', who were more interested in court places and preferment than partisanship and had been cultivated by Godolphin, and Whig nobles such as Lords Devonshire, Somerset and Newcastle, who had their own local power bases and liked to stay on good terms with the ministry and stay out of Junto scheming.

However, the behaviour of the Tories had by now thoroughly alienated the duumvirs. In any case, although the Junto did not hold complete sway over all Whigs, they exerted a degree of discipline over the majority of their party colleagues that was far in excess of anything any Tory leader could even dream of: making deals with them was accordingly easier and more effective, which was very appealing to busy and harassed men like the duumvirs who looked upon parliamentary manoeuvring with distaste.

Given this and the Whig gains in the election, a reluctant Harley had little choice but to acquiesce to the Lord Treasurer's views and make some concessions to the Whigs. A little-known young Whig MP from Norfolk called Robert Walpole was given a place on the Admiralty Board, and Whig Junto member Sunderland was made an official ambassador to Vienna. The biggest issue, however, was to find a new Speaker to replace Harley who would please the Whigs: the name fixed upon was a moderate Whig, John Smith. Harley was not happy but had to agree.

He was not going to have the government throw its lot in with the Whigs completely, however, and in this he had a valuable ally: the Queen. Anne was always suspicious of the Whig leaders, and, in any case, having escaped the presumptuous clutches of the High Tories, she was hardly in any mood to make herself the hostage of the Junto. Years of hectoring from the Duchess of Marlborough, who took every opportunity to pour poison into the Queen's ears about the Tories, had irritated her and if anything made her more determined not to throw her lot in with the Whigs any more than strictly necessary. Encouraged by Harley, she baulked at Godolphin's suggestion that Sir William Cowper, a relatively moderate Whig but a Whig nonetheless, be appointed to the position of Lord Keeper: she saw it as a step too far towards the Whigs. Harley wrote to Marlborough:

> The Queen hath wisely and happily delivered herself from a party, and I believe she will not easily put herself again into the power of any party whatsoever.[73]

The Queen agreed and entreated Godolphin:

> I can not help saying I wish very much that there may be a moderate Tory found for this employment, for I must own to you I dread ye falling into ye hands of ether party & ye Whigs have had soe many fayvours shewed them of late, that I feare a very few more will put me insensibly into theire power.[74]

Concerned not to offend her Lord Treasurer too much, she continued:

> There is no body I can rely upon but your self to bring me out of all my
> difficultys, & I do putt an intire confidence in you, not doubting but you
> will do all you can to keep me out of ye power of ye Mercyless men of
> both partys.[75]

By late September Godolphin had persuaded her that appointing Cowper
was the price of Whig support on key measures in the next session and she
gave in, but this wrangle was a sign of things to come.

The high-flying Tories reacted to this partial turn to the Whigs in their
usual measured and reasonable way: they suspected that Godolphin plotted
outright Whig government, and, with it, the destruction of the Church Party
and ultimately the Church itself. To counter this, they threw their weight
behind the Tory candidate for the Speakership, William Bromley (who had
been, amazingly, unanimously re-elected as the MP for Oxford University
in the general election, winning the vote of every qualified voter).[76] It was
seen as a key test of party strength, and in the press partisans busily went to
work for their respective candidates.

The most explosive result of this paper war was a pamphlet called
The Memorial of the Church of England, published on 9th July. It argued that
Godolphin and his allies had treacherously sold out the Church, thwarting
the High Tories' salutary efforts to defend it:

> All attempts to settle [the Church] on a perpetual foundation have been
> oppos'd, and rendred ineffectual, by Ministers who with a Prevarication
> as shameful as their Ingratitude, pretend to Vote and Speak for it
> themselves, while they solicit and bribe Others with Places and Pensions
> to be against it.[77]

Under the cover of 'moderation', the administration had not only refused
to take any measures to cure the 'Hectick Feavour lurking in the very Bowels
of [the Church of England]', but were now countenancing the 'old, seditious,
rebellious race of fanaticks and whigs'.[78]

These pretend churchmen were prepared to even turn to the Whigs, if Godolphin had his way, 'in Spite of Sodomy, Adultery, Pox or Prostitutes, Sunderland shall be a Saint: and Somers, Wharton and Halifax Prophets, Martyrs and Apostles'.[79] Harley was attacked as a 'Tricking Statesman, to whom Treachery was, thro' Habit, become almost as necessary as Breathing' and Godolphin was portrayed as guilty of 'premeditated Treachery'.[80]

It was, to say the least, spicy stuff. Godolphin, a sensitive man, was genuinely upset; Archbishop of York, John Sharp, reported that *The Memorial* left him 'in a great concern, and very near weeping'.[81] Marlborough was more angry than upset:

> In this camp I have had time to read the pamflet called the Memorial of the Church of England. I think itt the most impudent and scarolous thing I ever read. If the author can be found I do not doubt but he will be punished, for if such libertys may be taken of writting scandolous lyes, without being punished, no government can stand long. Notwithstanding what I have said, I can't forbear lafing, when I think thay would have you and I passe for phanaticks.[82]

Harley set about attempting to find its author to bring him to book for seditious libel, without success (the consensus now is that it was probably written by Tory hack James Drake, with possible assistance from Tory MPs Sir Humphrey Mackworth and Henry Poley). He also mobilised Defoe, and another recruit, old Whig John Toland, to reply to the pamphlet, but the tone had been set for the Tories' attitude to the government for the next session.

In the run up to the Speaker election, Harley and Godolphin worked like Trojans to canvass for Smith. Harley characteristically favoured some underhand methods: he found that an old book written by Bromley giving an account of his travels through Europe when a young man contained some passages that could be construed as implying Jacobite and even pro-papist sentiments. He added his own table of contents to draw attention to the most unfortunate parts – the subtlety of which one might be able to divine from such headings as 'The Author kissed the Pope's slipper, and his blessing though a Protestant. . .' – and then distributed the book among undecided MPs![83]

This industry was rewarded, but not handsomely. Smith triumphed by 248 votes to 205. This was a poor result for Harley, who hoped to recruit a lot of moderate Tories for Smith and demonstrate their responsibility and maturity. He was sorely disappointed: seventeen Tories in court employment voted for Bromley (most of them were later to be sacked for their pains), and only a small handful of other Tories voted for Smith. This was enough to secure victory, but not the stonking victory Harley needed to demonstrate the viability of his plan of appealing to moderate Tory sentiment. Godolphin felt it vindicated his view that the Tories were untrustworthy and hostile, and that a turn to the Whigs was inevitable.

If the Tories were on a mission to alienate themselves from the ministry, and indeed from the Queen herself, they could hardly have done a better job, and not long into the parliamentary session their behaviour became so provocative as to be politically suicidal.

For some time, the Queen had become increasingly irritated at the vehemence of the Tories' insistence that the Church was in danger. *The Memorial of the Church of England* had particularly riled her. She was, after all, the head of the Church of England, and suggesting that it was in mortal danger on her watch seemed to her to be an insulting reflection on her assiduity in its favour, and even her piety. She set down a pretty clear marker of her feelings in her opening speech to parliament in autumn 1705:

> there have not been wanting some so very malicious, as even in print to suggest the Church of England, as by law established, to be in danger at this time. I am willing to hope, not one of my subjects can really entertain a doubt of my affection to the Church, or so much as suspect, that it will not be my chief care to support it, and leave it secure after me; and therefore we may be certain, that they, who go about to insinuate things of this nature, must be mine and the kingdom's enemies, and can only mean to cover designs, which they dare not publicly own . . .[84]

This was a strong rebuke to the High Tories, implying that their cries about the Church were effectively cover for Jacobite sentiment.

At this point, one might assume that the Tories would have had the sense to back off and take pains not to offend the Queen further. One would assume wrongly. Shortly after her speech, Lord Rochester decided to support a motion in the Lords affirming that the Church was indeed in danger, in direct defiance of the Queen. Anne made sure to attend the debate to make her unhappiness with Rochester's temerity very clear. One can only imagine the look of contempt on her face as Rochester argued that her insistence that the Church was not in danger reminded him of 'the law in king Charles the second's time, to make it treason to call the king a papist; for which very reason, he said, he always thought him so'.[85] This amounted to an accusation that the Queen was lying. A more calculated insult could hardly be imagined. Wharton in response had great fun with Rochester, claiming that the danger to the Church appeared to boil down to him being out of office.[86]

The Tories did manage to land one notable blow on the Whigs during the debate. After a speech from the ageing Duke of Leeds (formerly the Earl of Danby) which implied that the Church was threatened by numerous enemies, external and internal, Wharton, in mocking tone, demanded that the Duke name 'who these rogues were that had got into the pale of the church'.[87] With great asperity, staring him down, the Duke replied, 'If there were any that had pissed against a communion table, or done his other occasions in a pulpit, he should not think the church safe in such hands'.[88] At this open reference to Wharton's youthful indiscretion, the Whig supremo was 'very silent for the rest of the day'.[89]

Gratifying as it doubtlessly was to humiliate Wharton, it didn't do the Tories much good. They were crushed in the vote on the motion sixty-one to thirty. The Whigs, no doubt wishing to please the Queen, passed a counter-motion:

> that the Church of England, Religion and divine worship, as also, on the
> as by law established . . . is now, by God's blessing, under the happy reign
> of her majesty, in a most safe and flourishing condition, and whosoever

goes about to suggest and insinuate, that the church is in danger under her majesty's administration, is an enemy to the queen, the church and the kingdom.[90]

The quarrel was nearly taken to violent blows: a row in the chamber between Rochester and Junto Lord Halifax almost ended in a duel (whether it occurred or not has been lost to history).

From a high point of jubilation and triumphant electoral success, the High Tories had, in three years, managed to completely throw away their predominance in the ministry; failed to pass the Occasional Conformity Bill; and made the naturally Tory-leaning and High Church Queen hate them with a white-hot fury. They had rendered themselves totally impotent.

The political battle for the next few years was to become a very different one: a contest between Godolphin, the unlikely champion of the Whigs, and Harley, the paladin of the moderate Tories.

The High Tory fox had been well and truly shot. For now.

6

The Battle in the Country

During the seventeenth and eighteenth centuries, upper-class ladies often used face patches – small scraps of silk, velvet or leather that would be stuck onto the face – either as a fashion statement, a coquettish symbol to send messages to potential amours, or to cover moles or smallpox scars.[1] This practice also had another potential significance during the reign of Queen Anne. If Joseph Addison is to be believed, face patching became a means of signifying one's party loyalties:

> About the Middle of last Winter I went to see an Opera at the Theatre in the Hay-Market, where I could not but take notice of two Parties of very fine Women, that had placed themselves in the opposite Side-Boxes, and seemed drawn up in a kind of Battle-Array one against another. After a short Survey of them, I found they were Patch'd differently; the Faces on one Hand, being spotted on the right Side of the Forehead, and those upon the other on the Left. I quickly perceived that they cast hostile Glances upon one another and that their Patches were placed in those different Situations, as Party-Signals to distinguish Friends from Foes . . . Upon Inquiry I found, that the Body of Amazons on my Right Hand, were Whigs, and those on my Left, Tories.[2]

This could become rather a problem if a lady had a mole on a politically uncongenial part of her face, leading to a choice between either leaving a blemish uncovered or risking being taken for a supporter of the wrong party.

This curious politicisation of ladies' fashion gives us some insight into just how all-pervasive partisan conflict became at its height. Among the elite, party feeling found its way into almost every crevice of cultural and social life: it wasn't just in hustings battles and election-day riots that the underlying political tensions of the day became manifest. Indeed, the battle was not confined simply to politicians and electors: women, who had no formal political rights, were involved, and, more broadly, non-voters too far down the social scale to be formally counted as part of the 'political nation' would also become embroiled in the struggle.

Of course, public life remained largely the preserve of a propertied male elite, and the explicit manifestations of political strife, on the electoral battleground and in parliamentary tussles, were the chief theatre for the great political drama of Whig versus Tory, and so are a good place to start. However, as will become clear, the confrontation was something much wider than a battle fought in the Commons or on the hustings: it was a vicious and sometimes highly irrational culture war too.

Conflict in the Constituencies

The electoral system of the early eighteenth century was bewilderingly complex. There were two basic types of constituency: boroughs and counties. During the medieval and early modern periods, many towns and cities had been incorporated as boroughs – that is, given charters by monarchs that assigned the right of self-government, the local corporation being akin to something like a modern local council. It was a marker of status as a 'significant' town. Each borough was entitled to elect two members of parliament (with a few exceptions: the City of London returned four members, for example). Simultaneously, each county was entitled to elect two MPs, 'knights of the shire', who typically enjoyed something of a higher status than borough MPs. [3]

County seats had a uniform national franchise qualification: to vote in a county election one needed to own freehold property of an annual rent of forty shillings or more per annum, thus ensuring that only voters who owned landed property could vote.

Boroughs, however, had no such uniform franchise and varied wildly, ranging from incredibly corrupt seats where hardly anybody had a vote to popular constituencies with a very large electorate.

In some boroughs, the right to vote was attached to the possession of 'burgages' (certain properties within the relevant town). The franchise in others was limited to members of the corporation – usually consisting of a mayor, twelve aldermen and twenty-four common councilmen. In still others, only 'freemen' could vote, a status that could be inherited, gained from membership of a company or issued by the corporation.

These were the narrow franchises. Other seats – based on inhabitant or householder franchises of some kind – tended to have wider electorates, although how much wider could vary hugely. Preston required nothing more than overnight residence in the borough before an election. In others – the 'potwalloper' boroughs – all inhabitants could vote who lived in a property containing a hearth. In others, only householders who paid rates ('scot and lot') possessed the franchise. Some constituencies had bizarre amalgams of these different franchises: the whole system was an enormously elaborate patchwork of divergent customs and rules.

There were other anomalies. The two universities sent two MPs each, elected by anyone who held an MA from either (wherever they happened to be living at the time). Some areas had a considerably disproportionate share of MPs: Cornwall, neither a very populous nor wealthy county, sent forty-four MPs (out a total of 513 seats in England). Some of the abuses that became notorious later in the eighteenth century – the famous 'rotten boroughs' – were already present. Old Sarum, a corrupt burgage borough, had as few as ten voters by 1705.

Despite these anomalies, overall the electorate had been growing throughout the seventeenth century and expanded even more dramatically in the early eighteenth. In the counties, the forty-shilling freehold condition declined in real value, meaning that people of relatively moderate property were increasingly able to vote. In the boroughs, electoral jiggery-pokery led to more freemen being appointed, as party electoral magnates and local corporations attempted to create more voters friendly to their cause.

The difficulties of assessing the evidence make it impossible to know the scale of the electorate in total, but one credible estimate suggests around 330,000–340,000 by the end of the Queen Anne period, which is 'not far short of one in four of the adult males in the country'.[4] The electorate at this time was, as a proportion of the overall population, higher than it was to be at any point until after the Great Reform Act of 1832 (the size of the electorate was to decline considerably in the mid-to-late eighteenth century).

Not only was the electorate surprisingly large, it had very frequent opportunities to exercise its right to vote, for the Triennial Act made elections more frequent than they would ever be at any other time in English history: there were ten general elections in twenty-two years after the Act was passed in 1694. Furthermore, there were far more contested elections than ever before, a product of the growing polarisation between Whig and Tory at the national level. Local elites, who previously had tended to divide up the parliamentary representation on the basis of gentlemen's agreements, often without a poll, found that the old consensual certainties broke down under the intensity of the party battle.

Nonetheless, elections were a very different business from anything we are used to in a modern democracy. The power of elites, particularly landed interests but also aristocrats and even the new 'monied men', to constrain and influence the choice of voters was considerable, and to a certain extent the electoral struggle was a process by which Tory and Whig factions of these elites went to war, using their interests to manipulate voters like chess pieces.

Elite manipulation of passive and powerless voters was, however, by no means the whole story: public opinion on the big issues of the day, informed by partisan campaigning, election propaganda and the newly flourishing political press, undoubtedly did swing voters. A significant floating vote, which local magnates often struggled in vain to bully or bribe into voting the 'right' way, existed, and was often decisive.

Let us examine how this process worked.

* * *

Neither Tories nor Whigs had national party machineries to co-ordinate election campaigns or influence the selection of parliamentary candidates: party organisation was usually a local, ad hoc process, although nationally important electoral magnates and leaders would use all of the resources and patronage in their possession to influence affairs wherever they could.

This localism is best understood within the framework of 'interest'. 'Interest' refers to the cumulative stake in and consequent influence over local areas possessed by property owners. This was an age in which property and political agency were widely seen as being intimately intertwined: public status and power were conceptualised as being attached far more to property, especially but not exclusively landed property, than to the individual personality, in contrast to our more democratic age.

However, property was not the only factor: historic loyalties and attachments, the deference widely felt to be owed to those of 'gentlemanly' or noble status, and specific institutional influences (of, for example, cathedral chapters or government employers) also weighed in the balance. Where an interest was overwhelmingly strong in favour of an elite who professed loyalty to either the Whig or Tory Party, there would be no meaningful electoral contest, but where that interest was divided, or weak, then party competition would come to the fore – and this became increasingly common.

In the county seats, the relevant 'interest' was landed property. The unwritten rule of county elections was that the candidates would be substantial county landowners, and that the process of selection would be decided by the local gentry and peers. They would usually gather to choose their candidate at the local assizes or quarter sessions. Traditionally, the process had been, at least in theory, a consensual one in which proceeding to an actual poll was seen as, ideally, unnecessary, and this serene reality continued where the key landowners were overwhelmingly of one party (usually Tory). Places where this continued, such as Warwickshire or Somerset, hardly ever saw a contested election.

In the vast majority of counties, however, the gentry and aristocracy were bitterly divided on Whig–Tory lines. A substantial minority of aristocrats were Tory, and a substantial minority of the landed gentlemen were Whigs, but often something of a Tory-dominated local squirearchy versus a

Whig-dominated local aristocracy dynamic emerged. Such divisions would mean that rival groups of Whig and Tory elites would hold meetings to select candidates in their own 'party interest' before proceeding to a contested campaign and a poll.

In the boroughs, the operation of 'interest' varied considerably. Sometimes, a local interest in a borough might be so dominant as to preclude any competitive elections. In the burgage borough of Heytesbury, William Ashe, a Whig, owned the vast majority of the burgages and nominated whomsoever he liked, usually a relative: between 1690 and 1713, at various times he nominated himself, his two sons, his brother-in-law and his son-in-law (all also Whigs).[5]

This, however, was rare, and even in seats with small burgage or corporation franchises, elites would engage in bitter (and very expensive) battles for control. For example, Thomas Tufton, the Tory 6th Earl of Thanet, fought, in alliance with his Tory ally James Grahme, a long, drawn-out battle for supremacy with Wharton in the Westmorland borough of Appleby. Both sides spent increasingly enormous sums of money to buy up burgages in the constituency: in 1704 Grahme spent £45, a colossal sum, buying just one burgage property; the next year Wharton, not to be outdone, retaliated by splurging £210 on just three burgages. In such constituencies, the price of burgages could spiral to immense heights as rival sides competed to buy them up.

The operations of electoral 'interest' were diverse. One crucial arena for its application was in the relationship between landlord and tenant, particularly in county elections. In an age where the secret ballot did not exist and votes had to be declared verbally and openly at the poll, the potential always existed to coerce direct economic dependents. A tenant who opposed the candidate favoured by their landlord risked eviction: Thomas Pelham (later to become a Whig prime minister) ejected three of his tenants after they refused to back the Whig candidates in the Yorkshire borough of Aldborough in the 1713 election. Often the voters of specific villages or towns would overwhelmingly back the candidates favoured by their local lord of the manor in county elections. When, for example, thirty-eight out of thirty-eight freeholders from the small Cheshire town of Stayley voted for the Whig candidates in the 1705 election, it is hard to believe that it was a coincidence that the entire settlement was owned outright by the partisan Whig George Booth, second Earl of Warrington.[6]

However, the 'interest' of landowners was not necessarily simply a matter of coercion or threats, but rather a mixture of implied or potential threat, customary deference based on an assumed paternalistic relationship, canny self-interest, and efforts by local elites to manage or treat their tenants to ensure that the wheels of deference were well oiled. In any case, the strength of landlord influence varied. The extent to which landlords might expect such deference depended on a whole range of factors: the nature of the local landlord–tenant relationships, the popularity and prestige of the local landowners, the sorts of land tenure involved (some offered considerably more security than others) and the whims of individuals. It differed from county to county and even village to village, and many tenants were by no means electoral pawns of their landlords, especially in hard economic times when many landowners often found it hard to attract tenants.[7]

Another important factor was patronage. Once one party or other had the ascendancy in a ministry, they gained the ability to reward their supporters by appointing them to plum jobs. The massive expansion of the scale of the state in the period meant that the number of government jobs to be handed out ballooned; places in government bureaucracies such as the customs and excise and the armed forces became excellent bargaining chips. The battle between Wharton and the Earl of Thanet in Appleby was not just a burgage auction: the rival parties battled to see who could best procure government patronage places (such as in the excise) for local worthies; Thanet's success in the 1701 and 1702 elections owed something to his ability to procure twenty-four government places, including twelve excise officer positions, for key voters and corporation officials.[8]

At a county level, local officers could be sacked and replaced for partisan motives. This was particularly the case with lord lieutenants, who were the leading local office holders, top of the tree of county society. Not only did incumbency in the lord lieutenancy give prestige and leadership to a county party, lord lieutenants also exercised considerable patronage themselves, appointing officers in the county militias and deputy lieutenants and exerting influence on the composition of the local commission of the peace. For example, with the Whigs ascendant after the Tack episode, in 1705 the government sacked the Tory Baron Guilford as Lord Lieutenant of Essex and replaced him with the Whig Earl Rivers, who purged many Tories as deputy lieutenants and replaced them with solid Whigs. In the subsequent general election, the Whigs won both county seats from the Tories.

When it came to influencing the wider electorate, the carrot was often more successful than the stick. One popular means of currying favour was to invest in local philanthropic enterprises to win repute and gratitude. Church towers would be repaired, free schools opened, new town halls constructed: all redounded to the prestige and popularity of the benefactors, which became useful political currency for those building or maintaining their 'interest' in a constituency. In Minehead, the local Tory patrons, the Luttrell family, pushed a bill authorising the repair of the local pier through parliament, then invested huge sums of their own money into the project.

Two closely related phenomena of more dubious morality were widely used in many constituencies: treating and outright bribery, the least subtle instances of electoral 'interest'. Technically, of course, both were illegal: an act of 1796 forbade making gifts to voters or 'treating' during elections. It had little effect.

Voters in many constituencies expected, as a matter of course, to be lavished with food and drink, the latter especially; many candidates were carried to victory on a flood of ale. A particularly notorious instance of this was the borough of Weobley in Herefordshire, nicknamed 'our liquid metropolis'.[9] One old hand advised a parliamentary candidate there that 'there is no going to Weobley for any agent without money in his pocket to set taps a running in the public house'.[10] Some candidates, however, were a little more canny, realising that indiscriminately putting huge amounts of cash behind the bars of local taverns wouldn't necessarily secure the loyalty of voters; some, such as Lord Brooke, when vying for supremacy in Warwick during the 1705 election, issued tickets that could be redeemed for ale later in exchange for a pledge to vote for the right candidates (in this case the Tories).

All sorts of direct and indirect methods of capturing votes were used. In 1708, in Shrewsbury, the two incumbent Tory members, John Kynaston and Richard Mytton, cornered the votes of one group of local tradesmen by ordering 2,000 pairs of shoes to be made by the local shoemakers. Such a huge boost to business endeared them to the cobblers, to the extent that:

> there was a general meeting of the said shoemakers at Ned's coffee-house; where it was proposed that, in consideration of their having made so many shoes upon the sitting Members' account, they should all vote for them.[11]

Richard Steele, the Whig journalist, came up with a novel strategy: when standing in Stockbridge, a notoriously venal constituency, in 1713, he offered a cash price for the baby born nearest to exactly nine months after the election, reasoning that giving wives a financial incentive to show affection to their spouses around election time could only improve his interest among the constituency's amorous husbands.[12]

Often votes were traded more brazenly, their price depending on the 'going rate' in the electoral market of a specific constituency, which might vary according to such factors as the size of the electorate, how hotly contested the seat was, and the poverty of the voters. One observer claimed that, in Ripon in the 1710 election, 'the candidates buy votes as publicly as if they were buying cattle in the market'.[13] Sometimes it was a clear cash transaction, with the price per vote varying from as little as 5 or 10 shillings (in Weobley and Ludgershall respectively), up to the princely sum of £20 at a by-election in Steyning in 1712. On other occasions bribery took place in alternative currencies: tin, sacks of wheat, coal, 'a load of straw' were all exchanged for votes during this period.[14]

Treating and bribery were widely used at all levels in elections of the period, although there were important distinctions. County elections were less susceptible to such practices, not least because they tended to have relatively large electorates, which made the cost prohibitive. Corrupt practices were more common in the boroughs, often used as one of many ways by which the long-established local interests attempted to 'seal the deal' during the election campaign. Occasionally, rich carpetbaggers might attempt to quickly build up support in a constituency without the bothersome long-term business of gradually constructing a more stable 'interest' via property ownership, social reputation and so forth.

This orgy of venality made elections a costly business. A vigorous attempt to secure a populous or particularly venal borough in the face of hot competition could cost a not-so-small fortune. In 1695, Sir Thomas Grosvenor, a Tory, spent £1,400 (around £250,000 in today's money) to secure his return in Chester in the face of a determined Whig campaign to use control of the corporation to stitch the borough up.[15] Lavish expenditure did not guarantee success: an attempt by a moderate Tory, John Chetwynd, to overcome a suspected Jacobite Tory in 1715 cost him £850: he came bottom of the poll. Electoral costs were so high that they were often cited alongside the economic impact of the war as factors contributing to the shaky financial position of the landed gentry of the time.

Corruption took other forms too. Returning officers in elections – sheriffs in county elections and usually mayors in borough elections – possessed many powers that could be flagrantly abused for partisan purposes. They typically decided who met the franchise qualifications as well as where and when the election would take place, which meant they could disqualify voters whom they suspected of supporting the opposite party– the issue at the heart of the famous Ashby versus White case at Aylesbury – or hold the poll in a location or at a time inconvenient for their opponents. For example, in 1705, the sheriff of Cumberland, conscious of a mooted attempt to put up a second pro-Tack Tory candidate to disturb an uneasy electoral arrangement between a Sneaker Tory and a Whig, moved the place of the poll to Salkeld Yeats, a tiny village located right next to the Whig candidate's estates and far from where the bulk of Tory support lived. This move made the election practically impossible to contest for the Tory wannabe and no poll was even held in the end. Even more outrageously, in 1708 in Hampshire, an unscrupulous sheriff used his power to adjourn the poll to the Isle of Wight, forcing disgruntled voters to set sail in order to exercise their franchise.

The prevalence of 'interest' in its various iterations may give the impression that elections were determined purely by elites. However, there were significant limitations to their power. Some seats were simply too large to consistently bribe or otherwise suborn voters on the required scale. Voters sometimes played off both sides to maximise their material advantage without letting the enjoyment of either parties' largesse affect their vote. If candidates hurt the amour propre of voters by taking them for granted or failing to court their votes or deliver in their interests, they might get a rude awakening.

Perhaps most pertinently of all, political circumstances might inflame voters with such passionate sentiments on the issues of the day that material considerations gave way to genuinely principled stances, with party fervour coming to the fore. Consequently, the parties had to fight hard to win votes by techniques that are recognisably the antecedents of the activities of the modern-day party activist, employing agents and canvassers to conduct the hard work of electioneering.

In the counties, election campaigns usually sprang up only in the immediate run up to general elections, but boroughs saw a more persistent state of organised party warfare. Because the make up of corporations often more-or-less determined the result of parliamentary elections, elections for the corporations (local elections, essentially) were crucial. Their frequency meant that many borough parties had to remain on a war footing permanently. As a result, partisan campaigning was almost continuous, as Bishop Burnet commented in 1708:

> The parties are now so stated and kept up, not only by the elections of parliament-men that return every third year, but even by the yearly elections of mayors and corporation-men, that they know their strength; and in every corner of the nation the two parties stand, as it were, listed against one another.[16]

Once an election had been called, county candidates would send a formal 'circular' letter to the electors, with usually some particular favour shown to the more substantial freeholders, who might receive a personal letter. In the case of the boroughs, a letter to the chief magistrate, usually the mayor, would do.

193

Such formal announcements tended to suggest that the candidate himself would hardly have *dreamed* of presuming to stand, but was merely responding to spontaneous demands on the part of local gentlemen, who thought that he might be able to serve the constituency. Magnanimous declarations of civic duty and promises to serve the constituency might dominate, but a partisan under (or over) tone was often present: many were vague, others were couched in general party terms (professing a 'steady zeal for the Church and Queen', if a Tory, or vigorous commitment to the Protestant succession and war with France if Whig), and some outlined a more detailed political programme, a sort of mini-manifesto.[17]

Once the battle lines were drawn, a candidate needed an efficient team to make sure they fought a vigorous campaign. They might seek the help of a local caucus, perhaps patronised by one of the major national party magnates, such as Wharton for the Whigs in his native Buckinghamshire, or a local semi-permanent party club. Many appointed paid agents to organise and carry out much of the donkey work, but the help of party allies drawn from among the chief local gentlemen would also be important. Local landowners and peers would work on appealing to their own tenants and servants on behalf of their favoured candidate. A county candidate might employ a team of clerks to churn out circular letters to be sent to freeholders (in Buckinghamshire during the 1713 election, the Tories paid clerks 2d per letter to copy 600 circulars to be sent to the county freeholders, for example).

However, personal application on the part of the candidate was almost always necessary. Most would be expected to canvass door-to-door. Treating and canvassing were in practice often more-or-less part of the same process: the voters liked to be flattered and entertained by their prospective member and his helpers, and such was the raucous nature of this type of electioneering that it could be physically taxing. John Chetwynd in his Preston campaign wrote to a friend about the course of his campaign, promising:

> more of this when we meet, if this d[amned] parliamenteering does not kill me. For I am half dead already what with drinking, smoking and walking the streets at all hours.[18]

In Appleby in 1700, one Tory agent, sozzled after a day of carousing and canvassing, became so intoxicated that he 'tumbled over the bridge ledge' into the River Eden and drowned.[19]

Some of the political elite clearly found grubbing for votes among the hoi polloi to be below their dignity. A friend of one energetic noble Tory canvasser wrote to him asking:

> how many hugs and squeezes have you had from brawny, greasy fists of belching freeholders; what toothless chops have you been forced athwart; for the sake of ancestors what compliances have you been obliged to, in the spirit of your popularity, against the grain?[20]

Others had much more fun. A candidate in Cambridgeshire in 1705 decided to make his electoral business his pleasure by riding through fen villages 'kissing the farmers' wives and begging their recommendation to their husbands' (perhaps unsurprisingly he was not successful).[21]

A large part of the point of canvassing, then as today, was, however, to identify and motivate one's supporters to ensure that they turned out to vote. Particularly organised candidates might divide a county into sections and employ agents to work the vote in each. If an early canvass showed the cause to be hopeless, a campaign might well end there; unlike in modern elections, parties would not bother with a poll unless they perceived a realistic chance of winning, as it simply wasn't worth spending a considerable sum on a lost cause. If, however, the canvass gave hope, it was crucial to keep a record of one's likely supporters and take steps to ensure they were able to make it to the poll.

A surviving set of canvassing notes by a Tory agent in Yorkshire during the 1710 election gives a good insight into this process. 'Parson Stapylton of Watlass' is described as a 'very kind and zealous friend' to the Tory interest, who would not only support Sir Arthur Kaye, one of the Tory candidates, but also pledged to work together with several other local allies to help coax '3 or 400' other sympathetic men to the poll.[22] Some voters would be evasive, refusing to pledge themselves either way: the agent lists them down as 'shufflers'. Others were openly hostile: one voter told the agent that he 'was come to the wrong place, for they were all Low Church men thereabouts and engaged to Strickland [a Whig candidate]'.[23]

Anyone who has ever canvassed in a modern election will hear distinct echoes of their own experiences here, although the risks facing canvassers in a more brutal age were somewhat greater. An agent working for the pro-Tack incumbent Tory MP in Queenborough during the 1705 election paid a soldier to beat up a fervent Whig canvasser 'for his sauciness' in daring to disturb the town's solid Tory denizens; unfortunately for the canvasser, the soldier got carried away and dashed his brains out.[24]

Any canvasser knew that the best indicator of likely party support was religion: a Tory might expect a warm reception from an impoverished parson, and any Whig would see a Dissenter as a vote almost certainly in the bag. The figures that are available suggest that around 70–80 per cent of clergymen typically voted Tory; in Essex in 1710 it was as high as 87.4 per cent.

However, typically the parson vote was too small to tip the balance; the bigger issue was the impact on public opinion of perceived near unanimity among the priesthood. The sight of troupes of parsons (attacked by Whigs in Chester in 1705 as 'the Devil's black guard') solidly marching to vote Tory gave a very clear demonstration of their political proclivities to their parishioners, which was influential in a society in which the traditional moral authority of the priest, although perhaps waning, was still powerful, especially in the countryside.

Anglican priests were usually far from reluctant to use their pulpits to drive the message home. In 1708 in Durham, a strong clerical supporter of the sitting Tory MP Thomas Conyers used his sermon to argue to the congregation that 'damnation would be their future lot if they did not repent of such a heinous sin, as the very attempting to reject so true and trusty a member of the Church [Conyers]'.[25] A clergyman in Scarborough was in the habit of carrying about *The Examiner*, a Tory periodical, 'to read to such as his parishioners as are weak in the faith . . . so that it is not doubted but he will in time make as many converts to the true interest of the State, as ever he did to the Church'.[26]

The intense partisanship of the lower clergy on behalf of the Tories is perhaps best summed up in an account (perhaps apocryphal, but still revealing) by Whig journalist John Tutchin, referring to the 1705 election:

> A certain parson in Hertfordshire not long since, being in the company of very creditable witnesses, and speaking of the Tackers, out of his passionate zeal for High Church said, 'The devil take me, if it be not a greater sin to poll against the Tackers than to murder my own father'.[27]

The Dissenters were no less solid for the Whigs, albeit in far smaller numbers. Where a substantial proportion of the population were Dissenters – particularly in the boroughs, Dissent being largely an urban phenomenon, but also in the counties in historically Puritan East Anglia – they were an important electoral consideration. Elections in places such as Norwich, Essex or Bristol were heavily influenced by a large bloc of Dissenting voters, and often devolved into heated bunfights between churchman and nonconformist.

However, their influence was weightier when seen in terms of their relative prominence in economic and civic life: many a Dissenting tradesman, merchant or financier was able to gain a place on a local corporation, or even, as in the case of London, reach the office of Lord Mayor. This disproportionate presence among the political elite gave them a role well beyond their numbers, particularly in London, where they were very well represented as both aldermen and common councilmen, and accordingly influential: as one disgruntled Tory put it,

> '. . . those Sycophants, who, tho' they dissent from and despise our Established Religion . . . fawn, and flatter and run up and down wheedling our Members by Awe, Interest , or Influence, to incline and dispose them to chuse such Persons as may most favour of their Faction'.[28]

It wasn't hard to understand why the Tories were so keen on outlawing occasional conformity.

When it came to motivating the voters, it wasn't just the pulpit that played a key role. Candidates would often attempt to stiffen their supporters' sinews and encourage fervent partisan identity by the means of banners, slogans and other symbolic appeals to party loyalty. In the 1705 election, at the height of the Tack controversy, Sir John Pakington marched to the polls in Worcester with a 'banner carried before him whereon was painted a church falling with this inscription *For the Queen and the Church, Pakington*'.[29]

Like the more enthusiastic loyalists at a modern US party convention, supporters would sometimes wear garish hats, cockades or other symbols proclaiming their partisan proclivities: in Suffolk during the 1710 election, cheerleaders for the Church Party 'wore gilded laurels inscribed with the initials of their favoured candidates'.[30] In Honiton in the 1705 election:

> The two parties were very nicely distinguished . . . buff was the symbol of the Whigs. These had box in their hats, doors and windows, the other had laurel leaves . . . the gentlemen who came in with Sir William Drake had a little knob of shoemaker's thread in their hats to show that they were Tackers.[31]

Appealing to emotive national issues for local purposes via propaganda was another key way of motivating one's supporters and attempting to sway undecided voters by blackening the reputation of party rivals. One common method was to distribute blacklists of MPs who had supported (or failed to support) some totemic measure, and using this to cast aspersions about the character, principles and loyalty of the local incumbent. This was a particularly common Whig stratagem: voting habits on symbolic Commons divisions – such as the Tack – were used to imply that the Tories were pro-French Jacobites. In 1705, efforts to distribute a blacklist of Tackers to the constituencies were strenuous: Bishop Burnet, doughty champion of ecclesiastical Whiggism, went so far as to arrange 'a publick entertainment' in Salisbury to distribute the blacklist, which contained the name of Salisbury's Tory MP Charles Fox.[32]

Poems, drinking songs and ballads were also popular means of smearing one's opponents and spurring on one's own side. One verse penned by the Whigs in Northamptonshire in 1705, attacking the Tackers and mocking the timorous 'Sneakers', ran as follows:

Here's a Health to the Knight
Who dares Vote and dares Fight
To maintain our Religion and Laws, Sir,
Against France and the Tack
And every mad Jack;
And never will Sneak from the Cause, Sir.[33]

Having identified and suitably geed up one's supporters, there was then the crucial business of ensuring that they voted. This was a particular problem in county elections: polling usually took place in the county town, which often meant a considerable journey for those living on the outskirts of a shire. It could also be a major problem in freemen boroughs, which often had no inhabitant restriction on the franchise, meaning that voters could live considerable distances away from the relevant constituency. Without considerable organisation, and sometimes incentives, electors could be reluctant give up an entire day's work and incur considerable transportation costs in order to cast their vote. 'Expenses' were therefore often paid, and sympathetic local landowners might arrange for coaches to be laid on to ferry their tenants to the poll on behalf of their favoured candidate. In 1710, the Surrey Tories organised a fleet of barges to convey voters up the Thames to Guildford to vote. In 1708, the Whigs managed to contrive the means to transport thirty-eight freeholders seventy-seven miles, from Sedbergh to York, to vote – a mighty distance in a pre-industrial age.

Once polling day arrived – in fact, polling days, as elections often stretched over two or three days – there would typically be a good deal of theatricality and crowd action. Although to vote at the poll one had to be sworn in as a properly qualified voter, non-voters had an important role to play. Candidates would encourage large crowds of supporters to attend to overawe their opponents, especially in county elections. The two Tory candidates in Northamptonshire in December 1701 were followed and whooped and cheered by a crowd as big as 10,000 strong (in a constituency with only 3,500 voters). To emphasise the respectability of their supporters, candidates arranged for large numbers of gentlemen to arrive on horseback, although they would generally be outnumbered by more socially modest participants on foot. Speeches by the candidates from the hustings would be heartily cheered (or theatrically booed), and crowds might carry banners and loudly shout their party slogans, or even play music and sing partisan songs, often set to the tune of traditional English ballads like 'Chevy Chase'. In Coventry in 1705, Tory supporters marched to the poll 'in a ritualistic procession carrying a maypole and a banner with a picture of a church on both sides'.[34]

An instructive account of the atmosphere of a poll, albeit one suffused with pro-Tory sentiment, was given in 1705 by Charles Leslie, High Church and nonjuror propagandist, in *The Rehearsal*. His description of the contest in the Suffolk county election between two Tackers, the Earl of Dysart and Sir Robert Davers, and the Whigs Sir Dudley Cullum and Sir Samuel Barnardiston, bears lengthy quotation:

> About ten in the Morning came the Lord DYSERT and Sir ROB. DAVERS, Usher'd into the Town by such a Body of all the Chief Gentry, and most Reputable Yeomanry of the County, as Enliven'd the Reputation of the Church party. When presently they were Succeeded, according to custom, by Sir SAMUEL BARNARDISTON and SIR DUDLY CULLUM. But to see what a Rabble had espous'd that Faction! You never beheld such a Scoundrel Medly. Excepting Sir THOMAS FELTON and two more, I do not think there were three Gentlemen to Head that Herd . . . the Earl of DYSERT &c Oppos'd that Rout of PRESBYTERIANS, INDEPENDENTS, ANABAPTISTS, QUAKERS who Appear'd in a Body, PAPISTS and MODERATION BROTHERS, who were all Covenanted against poor Church. And began such a Noise of NO TACKERS; NO FRENCH SHOOS; HEAR THE QUEEN &c. That you wou'd have Thought Hell had been broke loose. But when my Lord Dysert and Sir ROBERT DAVERS Appear'd (those Noble TACKERS) I was surpris'd to see how all that Glorious Appearance were Transported, and presently Entertain'd with the Gratefull Musick of NO FORTY EIGHT. NO PRESBYTERIAN REBELLION. SAVE THE QUEENS WHITE NECK. A TOWER. A TOWER. A DAVERS. SAVE YOUR COUNTRY BY MY LORD AND DAVERS[35]

Not surprisingly, such scenes sometimes gave way to intimidation and violence. A particularly notorious example was the Coventry election of 1705. On the night before the election, clashes between Whig and Tory mobs had ended up in a full-scale riot, including fighting with halberds (a sort of medieval weapon, a bit like a long axe).[36] The Tory mob prevailed, and 600–700 of them proceeded to occupy the guildhall, where the election was taking place. Over the three days of the election, they attempted to forcibly prevent anyone likely to vote for the Whig candidates from entering: 'things were quiet when they polled for the Sitting Members [the Tories]; but when any offered to poll for Sir Orlando Bridgman and Mr. Hopkins [the Whig candidates], they were ready to eat them'.[37]

Women too were drawn into the fight: the Tory mob contained a group of women, led by 'Captain Kate', who made a speech and 'urged the Tory candidates on with the cry "now, boys, or never, for the Church"'.[38] Tory tactics against Whig voters included beating them with sticks, imprisoning them on false pretences, and, in one case, attempted strangulation. Not surprisingly the Tory candidates won, but the election was deemed so 'tumultuous and partial' that the result was later declared null and void altogether by the Commons.[39]

Such a scene was an extreme example, but disorder was not uncommon, especially in and around London. Barely an election went by in Southwark without running battles between Tory and Whig mobs on the Tuttle (Tothill) Fields. In Westminster, voting was not for the faint-hearted. One account of the behaviour of the party mobs during the 1710 election there conveys well the atmosphere of intimidation:

> In front of the main door of the church . . . they had placed a table, on which lay two great books in which each man wrote his name. One book was for General Stanhope [a Whig candidate] and the other for Cross [a Tory candidate]. Now when it happened that two went up together, one writing in this, and the other in that book, they would be sure on their way down to fall together by the ears. In fact it rained blows right and left.[40]

201

Even the actual administration of the poll itself was a partisan matter. Lawyers would be appointed to challenge the right of opposition supporters to vote, or to defend their own supporters from similar challenges. Candidates could end up with large teams of workers desperately persuading their voters to get out to vote and defending their interests at the actual poll. Where running totals of the vote were given at the end of each day, as in some London constituencies, or where party workers kept their own tally, agents might hold back voters to lull the other side into a false sense of security, before flooding the poll last minute.

Once the vote had been declared and a victory speech made, the winning candidates would typically be hauled up into a chair and paraded around to cheers from supporters, the ringing of bells, and joyous musical celebrations. In Scarborough, the chairers would sometimes wade into the sea bearing the chaired member, allowing them to be 'admiral at sea'. Drunken celebrations would then ensue at a local tavern.[41]

This, however, was not necessarily the end of the matter. A winning candidate could always be the subject of an election petition, whereby his losing rival could bring a case to the House of Commons elections committee claiming that malpractice, corruption or other misdoings rendered the election void. However, a wronged candidate only had much chance of redress if they happened to be of the party with a majority in the House, as the elections committee was notoriously partisan, and a losing Whig seeking redress in a Tory-dominated Commons, or vice versa, was almost certainly doomed to failure.

Pugnacity in Parliament

Once the hundreds of individual battles were settled in any given general election, the composition of the House of Commons would, as the results filtered in over the course of a month or two (there was no standardised national polling day or days), be pored over by the political leadership of the Whigs and Tories. Often, the picture would be murky for some time, due to internal party splits and the fact that some members' exact party colours would not be immediately obvious. A number of seats would be dominated by government patronage – the Cinque Ports, for example – and would tend to return MPs complaisant to the incumbent ministry, although they typically numbered little more than twenty: it was not until later in the eighteenth century that governments would use their influence to turn elections decisively in their own favour.

Certain generalisations can be made, however. Over the course of the reigns of William III and Queen Anne, the 'natural' result, all other things being equal, favoured the Tories. The fact that the bulk – although by no means all – of the landed gentry tended to be Tory and the majority of the country was solidly Church of England weighed heavily. Tories usually dominated the county seats and, more often than not, held their own in the boroughs. No election in the entire period (until 1715) could be described as a 'Whig landslide', although they scraped a majority in 1695 and 1708 and came close to doing so in the second election of 1701. The Tories achieved three crushing landslides, in 1702, 1710 and 1713, and most of the other elections resulted in a small Tory advantage or something close to a dead heat.

Certain broad trends can also be detected in terms of political geography. The legacy of the Civil War still ran deep: it was no coincidence that the bastions of Toryism – Wales, the South-West, Oxfordshire, Warwickshire, Worcestershire and so on – had often been Royalist centres in the Civil War, whereas the Whigs tended to be strongest in London and the old Puritan strongholds of East Anglia. The North contained both patches of strong Tory support in old Royalist and Jacobite centres in Lancashire and Northumberland, but also important outposts of Whiggism, such as in much of Yorkshire and Dissenting pockets of Lancashire. However, the vagaries of the political predilections of local gentry and aristocrats meant that such regional or county trends were only rough: the political geography was highly variegated.

Individual electoral magnates could influence this picture. The paramount example was Wharton, who devoted much of his £16,000 annual income to nursing the Whig interest in multiple constituencies throughout the country, particularly in his home turf of Buckinghamshire, where he had an often decisive, although usually contested, interest in all the seats bar one, but also in Cumberland, Westmorland, Yorkshire, Northamptonshire and on occasion (often with less success) Oxfordshire.[42] Although he probably only directly controlled seven seats and had a (usually) decisive interest in twenty overall, his efforts were truly Stakhanovite, whether in terms of financing campaigns, canvassing, arm-twisting or pursuing election-related legal challenges; he would race all over the country at election time, devoting his entire energy and fortune to the Whig interest.[43]

No single Tory could quite match Wharton, but they possessed a number of influential national or regional brokers. Sir Edward Seymour possessed a substantial interest in the 'decayed' (i.e. often very corrupt) boroughs of Cornwall and Devon, and, when added to the enormous influence he exercised through a motley crew of relatives and cronies, it was not for nothing that his electoral sway was nicknamed 'Tsar Seymskie's Western Empire', although his suzerainty was far from unchallenged.[44]

Once the electorate had sobered up and the newly elected (or re-elected) MPs had gathered in Westminster, the parties faced the considerable problems of parliamentary organisation. Party discipline was a far harder task than in a modern age of formalised party whips and tight central control over candidate selection. MPs did not see themselves as beholden to national leaders and platforms in anything like the way they do now, and many had independent local power bases, or, if they were in government employment, divided loyalties between court and party. However, using a variety of methods, a surprising among of co-ordination and control was often exercised within parties.[45]

The difficulties started at the top. Without a unified leadership, it was obviously hard for any disciplined party line to be formulated, let alone imposed on the backbenchers. It was in this area that the Whigs had a crucial advantage. From the point at which the bulk of country MPs, many having previously been nominal Whigs, drifted into the Tory ranks, the Whigs were usually united firmly behind the leadership of the Junto lords. The Junto lords may have had occasional clashes of personality, but they generally demonstrated striking unanimity, and were extremely skilful at cajoling the Whig parliamentary party into line.

There were Whigs who defied the Junto on occasion. A small group of Country Whigs who had not followed Harley into co-operation with the Tories in the 1690s endured and occasionally made trouble, and for a while Godolphin cultivated a group of court-inclined Whigs who were more amenable to his leadership – the 'Lord Treasurer's Whigs'. Overall, however, a large majority of Whig parliamentarians fell behind the leadership of Wharton and his colleagues.

The Junto operated a brilliantly organised system of political management. The Junto lords would meet at big conclaves in the respective country houses of their members – or sometimes at Newmarket Racecourse or in London – to plan broad political strategy for a coming parliamentary session. Then, this strategy would be imparted to the most important parliamentary lieutenants, and then their immediate followers, at meetings in London, where at least two Junto lords would attend in order to ensure the line was absolutely clear, before being disseminated more widely to the parliamentary small fry at social gatherings and dinners organised by the Junto's henchmen: usually the dukes of Bolton, Devonshire or Kingston.[46]

The Tories had a far harder task. Not only were they usually more divided than the Whigs, they also lacked the sort of well-developed methods of co-ordination that the Whigs possessed. This was itself partially a product of their rivalries, both personal and political. The high-flying leaders, such as Rochester, Seymour and Nottingham, could often barely agree between themselves: concerted co-operation and harmony between them and Harley, whom they distrusted intensely, was usually only achieved sporadically and half-heartedly.

As a result their consultations were ad hoc and often characterised as much by bickering as co-operation. Although the High Tory chiefs in the Lords and leading commoners such as Seymour and later Bromley often managed some degree of co-ordination, harmony between the bulk of the Tories and the Harleyites was often elusive.

Overall, the Tory backbenchers were a force to be reckoned with, a tail that was very much prone to wagging the dog, in contrast to Whig backbenchers, who were much less rebellious. The Tories had a particular predilection for mass meetings of backbenchers in which leading Tory commoners would, at best, manage to persuade their rank and file to follow their lead, or if not then sit back and inform themselves about what their backbenchers intended to do in any case. Such meetings typically gathered at the Fountain Tavern in the Strand, where as many as 150–200 Tory MPs would meet to hammer out their line (or each other).

None of this meant that discipline was impossible, even for the Tories. Particularly on set-piece occasions relating to issues where the parties were mostly united, whips could have remarkable success. The Tories, conscious of the power of Tory solidarity on a local level, operated a relatively decentralised system of whipping in which particular influential MPs acted, effectively, as 'regional whips', chivvying along their colleagues from their county or area. William Bromley and Sir George Beaumont, for example, attended to MPs from the Midlands, Peter Shakerley, Tory MP for Chester, covered Cheshire and Lancashire, and so on. How precisely the Whig whipping system worked is not so clear, but their centralised system of leadership co-ordination meant that much of the work was already done before the nitty-gritty of individual parliamentary votes became pressing.[47]

The biggest issue facing the whips was not so much curtailing political rebellions as ensuring that their supporters actually showed up. At the start of a session, or when weighty partisan issues were at hand, and/or when a vote looked likely to be close, whips could ensure impressive turnouts. For example, the Speaker election of 1705 saw the Tories pull out all of the stops on behalf of William Bromley's (doomed) attempt to take the chair, resulting in an almost-full house, and in the tumult over war and peace of the 1710–13 period, packed houses were not uncommon. Whips would often send out plaintive messages to indolent country members begging them to return to the capital for an imminent knife-edge vote, which could result in a race against time across the country: the Tories even constructed a purpose built 'wyre cage' to ensure that members with gout could get to town quickly with minimum discomfort.[48]

However, the whips did not have an easy time. Being an MP was not a full-time job, and many MPs disliked the expense of staying in London and the tedium or confusion of parliamentary business: one Liverpool MP complained 'it will puzzle a more politick noddle than mine to find out wa[y]es and means to carry on the war'.[49] The country gentlemen were particularly notorious for their unreliability: many of them much preferred the pleasant bucolic diversions of their country seat to the undignified political bunfight of Westminster, and could only be chiselled out of their rural idylls with difficulty. Attendance tended to dwindle as a session went on, and getting members back to London after the Christmas festivities could be particularly hard. These fluctuations in attendance greatly affected political tactics. Smart operators could gain a handy advantage by springing a snap vote in the House at the right time. Often this benefited the Whigs, who would take advantage of the desultory attendance of sleepy Country Tories, particularly in the immediate post-Christmas period.

The Culture War

In London, party solidarity and organisation had a strong social aspect. Partisans liked to plot together over copious amounts of alcohol and food, and a surprisingly large amount of serious political business would take place in such gregarious contexts. The most famous example was the Kit-Cat Club, which acted as one of the Junto's key inner political sanctums and welded together the key Whig leaders around their shared political and cultural principles, as well as a common love of wine, attractive women and pies.[50]

The origins of the club lie in the relationship between Lord Somers and Jacob Tonson, a Whig publisher. These two drinking partners began, at some point in the mid-to-late 1690s, to frequent a London tavern called 'The Cat and Fiddle', partly due to their fondness for the pie-making skills of the proprietor, one Christopher Cat. Whether the origins of the club's name lie in the tavern's moniker or that of the pie-chef-cum-landlord ('Kit' being, of course, a common shortening of Christopher) is not entirely clear (probably the latter), but soon Tonson gathered around him a collection of young Whig poets, writers and politicians who met regularly and called themselves the Kit-Cat Club.

A select group – there were never more than forty-eight members at any one time – the Kit-Cat's membership included not only a galaxy of literary and cultural stars, such as playwright William Congreve, dramatist and architect John Vanburgh, writers Joseph Addison and Richard Steele, but practically the entire elite of the Junto and Whig Party, many of them peers or MPs: Wharton, Somers, Halifax and Sunderland (four of the five Junto lords) were members, as well as many Whig grandees, such as the Duke of Newcastle and the Duke of Somerset, and the Junto's key parliamentary allies and foot soldiers, such as the rising star Robert Walpole and military hero James Stanhope.

The club bonded these men together not only by eating pies and getting spectacularly drunk but also by their custom of drinking toasts to young ladies who met two crucial criteria: great physical beauty and staunch commitment to the Whig cause, such as Sunderland's wife Anne (the Duke of Marlborough's daughter) or Sarah Churchill. The club was a key organising forum for many acts of Whig artistic and cultural patronage, and brought together key Whig journalists, publishers and literary partisans (such as Arthur Maynwaring, who organised much of the Whig propaganda effort).

Increasingly, the club was also used as a means by which the key Whig leaders organised their parliamentary and political efforts, plotting and conferring when parliament was in session. The exact nature of the political transactions of the club remain obscure, but the Tories were in no doubt about its influence. William Shippen, poet and future Tory MP, satirised Tonson thus:

> I am the founder of your lov'd Kit-Kat,
> A Club that gave Direction to the State.
> 'Twas there we first instructed all our Youth,
> To talk Prophane, and Laugh at Sacred Truth,
> We taught them how to Tost, and Rhime and Bite,
> To Sleep away the Day, and drink away the Night[51]

The Tories could never quite match the Kit-Cat, but a similar dining society, the Society of Brothers, was founded in the final years of Anne's reign, as we shall see.

On a slightly less rarefied social level, a key social hub of party activity was the coffee-house, which reached its apogee during this era. Originating in Oxford, where a Jewish immigrant called Jacob had set up England's first coffee-house, the Angel, in 1650, they soon spread to London and by 1714 there were around 650 of them in the capital (some of them specialised in cocoa and were accordingly called 'Chocolate Houses').[52]

Hives of activity – 'some going, some coming, some scribbling, some talking, some drinking, others jangling . . . stinking of tobacco like a Dutch barge or a boatswain's cabin', in the words of Tory hack Ned Ward – coffeehouses were famous for gossip, debate, intrigue and political squabbling.[53] They retained something of an egalitarian atmosphere, in which anyone who paid a small nominal fee could sit, sip, read and tittle-tattle, an ethos conveyed well in this early description of 'The Character of a Coffee House':

> As you have a hodge-podge of Drinks, such too is your Company, for each man seems a Leveller, and ranks and files himself as he lists, without regard to degrees or order; so that oft you may see a silly Fop, and a worshipful Justice, a griping Rock, and a grave Citizen, a worthy Lawyer, and an errant Pickpocket, a Reverend Nonconformist, and a Canting Mountebank; all blended together, to compose an Oglio of Impertinence.[54]

In the coffee-houses political rumours would spread like wildfire, MPs would leak secrets to journalists, and gaggles of politicians would plot, gossip and scheme. Addison describes the hothouse atmosphere of the coffeehouse well, telling of how wild gossip – 'twilight visits paid and received by ministers of state . . . applications for places, with respective successes and repulses' and so on – would be published 'by eight o'clock in the morning at *Garaway's*, by twelve at *Will's*, and before two at the *Smyrna*.'[55] Partisan journalists might hover around in the haunts of political opponents to try to overhear enemy partisans making unguarded or unwise comments which could be used to attack their party.

Accordingly, many coffee-houses tended to become polarised by party. One contemporary reported that:

> I must not forget to tell you that the parties have their different places, where, however, a stranger is always well received; but a Whig will no more go to the Cocoatree than a Tory will be seen at the Coffee House, St James.[56]

The Tories would gather at Ozinda's Chocolate House in St James's Street and the Smyrna in Pall Mall, as well as the famous Cocoa Tree, and the Whigs numbered Button's near Covent Garden and Old Man's in the Tilt Yard, alongside the St James' Coffee House, as their chief haunts.

One of the chief activities that political hacks would engage in at these hubs of intrigue was leafing through the news: no self-respecting coffee-house would be without a full panoply of up-to-date political newspapers, pamphlets and periodicals. A contemporary estimated that it cost them 'four or five shillings per paper per week' to supply their patrons with the newspapers they wanted, the equivalent of £13 per year, a tidy sum.[57]

The press mushroomed during the 1690s and 1700s. Only three periodicals and newspapers were licensed during the first five years of the reign of William III, in addition to the government's official *Gazette*. After the lapsing of the Licensing Act in 1695, three more were set up, and by 1709 there were eighteen London newspapers and periodicals: in 1704, the government estimated a total circulation of the leading nine papers at 44,000 per week, amounting to 2.2 million over the year. Contemporaries suggested that each copy would be read by ten to twenty people, as they were often shared and passed around.[58]

So the newspaper and periodical reading public grew enormously, and the titles they were reading were, like everything else, divided on party lines. Whigs would devour George Ridpath's *Flying-Post*, John Tutchin's *Observator* or the *Post Man*. No Tory coffee-house that wished to keep its clientele would be without Abel Roper's *Post Boy*, or later, in 1710–11, Jonathan Swift's *Examiner* (which was vigorously attacked by John Oldmixon's Whig riposte *The Medley*).[59] The more extreme high-flying Tories would resort to Charles Leslie's *Rehearsal*, which backed the Tackers to the hilt in 1705 and had more than an undertone of nonjuring and Jacobite sympathy. Outside London papers also sprang up: by 1710 there were '13 provincial newspapers published in 9 towns', and many of them also gave a heavily party-slanted viewpoint.[60]

It wasn't just periodicals and newspapers that flooded the coffee-houses with partisan print. The publication of party political pamphlets, tracts and books spewed off the presses in enormous numbers. In the reigns of

William and Anne, between 5–6,000 such works were published, of which three million copies were sold (in a population of five-and-a-half million).[61] Many of these were hastily scrawled squibs and hatchet jobs, written and printed in a matter of days to respond to the issue of the hour before being sold on open-air stalls. Significant controversies would provoke a profusion of material: for example, there were around 150 books and pamphlets published relating to the debate on occasional conformity; later on, the brouhaha over Dr Sacheverell in 1710 attracted 600.[62]

Inevitably the publishing industry was riven by Whig–Tory rivalry; one commentator was able to assign a party label to every single member of the publishing trade.[63] Even the process of publishing a single volume sometimes became subsumed within the party battle: a Tory historian, Laurence Echard, was driven to distraction by the fact that one of his books was indexed by a Whig who used the index entries to provide a polemical redescription of the events described in the book, so a rebel in the Monmouth rebellion described as 'hanged for treason' in the text was listed as 'hanged without trial' in the index.[64]

So enormous was the outpouring of political papers, pamphlets and periodicals that one commentator suggested that it had become a serious drag on the British economy:

> The Manufacture of this Nation hath been of late Years hindred . . . by the misspending so much Time as the poorer Tradesmen do, in going about from one Coffee-House to another, poring upon Seditious, Heretical and Treasonable Papers.[65]

Whatever the truth of this, plenty of money was certainly made in Grub Street, which saw an extraordinary flourishing that was as much literary as financial; although much that was published was pure hackery or ephemeral scribbling, the era proved a magnificent showcase for the satirical genius of figures such as Daniel Defoe and Jonathan Swift.

Political writing was not confined to printed matter. Some manuscript publications also endured, most famously John Dyer's newsletter, which would be copied out by hand by a team of as many as fifty clerks before being distributed throughout the country by post.[66] Dyer was perhaps the most extreme and partisan Tory imaginable and his newsletter was eagerly devoured by high-flying churchmen and squires. He traded in a mixture of foreign and domestic news and scurrilous rumour. In early 1705, he reported that a mob of Bristol Whigs had, on 30th January (the anniversary of Charles I's execution and a sacred day in the Tory calendar), 'drest up a dog & led him out very formally & cut off his head in derision of ye Day' – he later retracted the story after being threatened with legal action.[67] On another occasion, after having described famously aggressive Whig peer Lord Mohun as 'one of the arrantest Rakes in town, and indeed a scandal to the peerage . . . generally a sharer in all riots', Mohun (not exactly disproving the accusation) hunted him down to a coffee-house and cudgelled him.[68]

For all his partisanship, Dyer was undoubtedly well informed, picking up gossip and genuine political intelligence designed to appeal to his rabidly Tory, and frankly often Jacobite, readers from his network of parliamentary and ecclesiastical informers. On at least one occasion, Whig ministers stopped entire postal deliveries to prevent his newsletter from being disseminated (indeed, appointing postmasters on partisan lines in order to tamper with the mail and disrupt the other side's lines of communication was by no means unknown at this time).[69]

Lurid and arresting propaganda such as Dyer's was far from unusual, and often found its way into longer pamphlet form. One particularly good example was Tory hack Ned Ward's *The Secret History of the Calves-Head Club, or the Republicans Unmask'd*, first published in 1703. Ward's pamphlet played on the Tory suspicion that the Whigs and Dissenters were, at heart, radical republicans. It purported to expose a secret club of Dissenters who allegedly met up every January 30th to toast Oliver Cromwell and the regicides and celebrate the anniversary of the beheading of Charles I by eating calves' heads. Having eaten the eponymous delicacy, quaffed wine from the calf's skull, and burnt a copy of the *Eikon Basilike*, the members would sing lurid songs about the decapitation of Charles I:

It was a pleasing wonder
Upon the Earth and under,
The Worms beneath
Rejoyc'd at his death,
And gladly seiz'd the plunder.[70]

Published as a slim volume of twenty-two quarto pages in 1703, by the time it reached its eighteenth edition in 1713 it had swelled to a hefty tome of over 200 pages, supplemented by ever more lurid details.

The alleged anthems sound like a crazed fabrication, representing the Whigs as what the Tories imagined them to be in their most paranoid nightmares: blaspheming, bloodthirsty, atheistical regicides. This is probably because that was what the pamphlet largely was: fabrication. There does appear to be some evidence that gatherings roughly along these lines did occur, but Ward's account was doubtlessly enormously exaggerated and sensationalised, and to a considerable degree completely fabricated, for party purposes, which probably accounts for its considerable popularity.[71] Fake news is not an exclusively modern phenomenon.

It wasn't just in newspapers, coffee-houses and clubs that partisanship took shape. The battle between Whig and Tory was a culture war at every level. The Whigs saw the Tories as backward insular chauvinists who would give absolute power to a motley crew of designing, quasi-papist priests, absolute monarchs (whether the Pretender or Louis XIV) and mad bigoted squires. The Tories saw the Whigs as fanatical seditious hypocrites who would happily destroy the monarchy and the Church and suck the entire country dry to enrich themselves and fund perpetual wars abroad. These passionate prejudices and violent hatreds found expression in every artistic and cultural medium, sometimes in the most unlikely places; the fissure was so intense that almost any means would be used to get one over on the other side or demonstrate one's party identity.

Lord Wharton, for example, a great maestro of the turf, used horse racing as an outlet for party passions. According to Thomas Macaulay,

He had the finest stud in England; and his delight was to win plates from Tories. Sometimes when, in a distant county, it was fully expected that the horse of a High Church squire would be first on the course, down came, on the very eve of the race, Wharton's Careless, who had ceased to run at Newmarket merely for want of competitors.[72]

Race meetings at Newmarket and in the county courses such as Brackley, York or Lincoln were often seen as proxies for party honour.[73] Much to the Tories' chagrin, the Whigs, led by Wharton, usually did have the best of it; one Tory gentleman, unable to attend the meet at Brackley in 1712, admitted that he was relieved to miss it because:

my spirits would have bin upon the fret to see King Tom runn away with the prize, and well may the Whigs have the best horses since they have all the money.[74]

Even medicine was not exempt: upper-crust doctors risked losing patients if they came out too warmly for one side. Dr Oliphant, one of the most fashionable doctors in London society, lost dozens of Whig patients when 'as M.P. for Ayr burghs after 1710, he went over to the Tories'.[75]

Perhaps the most spectacular example of a cultural partisan battleground was, aptly enough in an age of highly theatrical political machinations, the stage. From the Restoration until the Revolution, drama had been a Cavalier, then a Tory stronghold, not least because of the direct power that the Stuart monarchs had over the production of plays.[76] This all changed, however, after the Revolution, when the theatre increasingly became a cultural-political battleground in which Whig versus Tory was fought out in soliloquys and punchy dialogue – and indeed audience applause and barracking – as much as during elections and parliamentary votes.

In William's reign the theatre became increasingly a platform for the literal acting out of Revolution principles in the form of plays by leading Whigs such as John Vanbrugh, William Congreve and Nicholas Rowe. Rowe's *Tamerlane* (1701), for example, presented the historical story of the fourteenth-century Timurid emperor as an allegory of William III's battle with Louis XIV, presenting Tamerlane as a benign constitutional monarch who (somewhat implausibly) was a devotee of social contract theory and a believer in religious toleration.

By the beginning of Queen Anne's reign, critic and playwright John Dennis was complaining that 'the imaginative faculty of the Soul' was suffering 'in a Reign of Politicks'.[77] The Kit-Cat Club made it their business to patronise the theatre in service of the Whig cause, most notably by financing the construction of the Haymarket Theatre, the politics of which was made abundantly clear by the fact that its foundation stone was inscribed with a dedication to 'The little Whig' (a reference to Lady Sunderland).[78]

Soon London drama was dominated by Whigs. As well as having a commanding influence in the management of the theatres, almost all of the great contemporary playwrights tended to be friends of the Junto, and Halifax, under the auspices of the Kit-Cat, became a great patron of Whig stagecraft.[79] The Haymarket staged such works of Whig propaganda as *Liberty Asserted* (ironically by the very same John Dennis who had complained about the intrusion of politics onto the boards), which dramatized a Whiggish belief in contractual and limited monarchy and hostility to French absolutism. When events were running against the Whigs, Halifax would raise money 'for the encouragement of good comedies', one assumes to cheer up his own side.[80]

This was just as well, as Halifax and the Kit-Cat Whigs were not to hold the whip hand in the theatre for the entirety of Queen Anne's reign. Although the Tories produced few leading playwrights in the era, when they gained ascendancy between 1710 and 1714 they were able to use their power to cut off the stage as a site of Whig propaganda. Although pre-publication press censorship had been abolished, theatrical censorship had not, and the Tories were completely willing to use this power — wielded officially by the Lord Chamberlain, his Vice-Chamberlain and the magnificently entitled Master of the Revels, but in effect often by leading Tory politicians — to ban or censor any overtly pro-Whig productions. As a result — with one exception which we will cover later — the theatre for the rest of the Queen Anne era generally saw little political action.

Even the opera did not escape party strife. The Whigs attempted to exploit cultural suspicions of 'new-fangled' Italian operas – seen as foppish, possibly popish, and unEnglish – to attack the Tories.[81] In 1703, 'Dismal' Nottingham, belying his usual reputation for dreary asceticism, became entranced by Margarita de l'Epine, a leading Tuscan opera singer who had travelled to England to perform in the early 1700s. Taking time out of his duties as Secretary of State, he even invited her to join his family for a few weeks of musical diversion in September 1703. He attempted to raise money to fund a series of private musical performances to be given by Margarita for his Tory colleagues.

The Whigs pounced on this to suggest that Tory equivocations about the war, and the failures of the naval strategy that Nottingham was so fond of advocating, could be attributed to his sudden taste for Italian opera and susceptibility to the charms of Signora L'Epine. Both reflected his – and his Tory allies' – unmartial, womanly attitudes and dandified tastes, they argued.

Nicholas Rowe used this incident to savage Dismal, questioning even his dedication to the church:

> Did not base Grebers Pegg [Margarita] inflame
> The sober E[arl] of N[ottingham]
> Of sober sire descended,
> That Carless of his house and fame
> To Play-houses he nightly came
> And left Church undefended.[82]

The Whigs even claimed one of Margarita's rivals – English singer Catherine Tofts – as their own. Whig Lord Somerset set about promoting her concerts, presenting her as patriotic Whig musical alternative to the haughty Italian Tory. The rivalry reached an unseemly climax when Ann Barwick, a servant of Mrs Tofts, interrupted one of Margarita's performances by hissing and booing her and pelting her with oranges. Although Mrs Tofts disclaimed any knowledge and distanced herself from the incident (and in fairness doesn't seem to have been on bad terms with Margarita personally), the sense that party differences were being settled by an operatic rivalry was thereby deepened.

Even the refreshments one enjoyed in the interval had a political connotation. Traditionally, the Cavalier and then Tory drink had been claret. Claret, and French wine generally, dominated the wine market of the late seventeenth century, and the association of the Stuarts with France gave added impetus to Tory enthusiasm for French wine.[83] However, by the War of the Spanish Succession, French wines had been subject to an embargo, and the anti-French Methuen Treaty, signed between England and Portugal in 1703, committed England to offering a preferential duty on Portuguese wine. As a result, the most popular table wine soon became a sort of cheap red plonk from northern Portugal, which was known as 'porto-port', but soon became known simply as port (which was quite different from the fortified wine we now know as port); Portuguese wine went from accounting for under 1 per cent of English wine imports to 62 per cent during the War of the Spanish Succession.[84]

As a result, 'good solid Edifying port', as Whig writer Richard Steele described it, became the Whig drink: quaffing the Portuguese ambrosia was seen as a gesture of support for England's allies in the war against France, in contrast to the foppish and unpatriotic predilection of the Tories for claret.[85] The Whigs argued that upholding the embargo on French claret and drinking port prevented the French enemy from profiting from the duties English consumers would otherwise pay on importing claret. The Tories contended, in contrast, that the embargo had little effect, as claret continued to be smuggled in, but the restrictions resulted in much lost revenue and adulteration. They later repealed it.

Actually, the Whig predilection for port was, among the political elite, rather an affectation: most prominent Whigs continued to drink claret in private if possible. That did not stop them using the association between Toryism, claret and the French enemy as a political weapon, whatever their personal quaffing habits.

In this Tory versus Whig culture war, there was much knee-jerk tribalism on show. Such was the partisan hatred between the two sides that any means of displaying one's own colours and denigrating the other side was enthusiastically leapt on. Such all-encompassing and sometimes irrational polarisation was quite as in vogue then as in many subsequent eras of political division, including our own.

However, there were deeper trends underlying this culture war. The 'Rage of Party' provoked much discomfort and distaste among the contemporary elite, even among many who, paradoxically, enthusiastically participated in it. The passions it provoked and the whole phenomenon of 'party' itself – in contrast to disinterested promotion of the common good of the nation – were looked upon as worrying symbols of irrationality and prejudice. An older ideal of politics as wise management based on a reasonable broad elite consensus (however chimerical such an ideal had often proved, particularly in the seventeenth century) was being disturbed. This anxiety had a peculiarly powerful quality because it happened in the context of a newly prominent and reasonably broad electorate and a burgeoning political press. Although the electoral system of the era was far from democratic or egalitarian, there was no doubt that at this time a whole new factor was entering into the politics of the nation in a fairly regularised and routine way: the people.[86]

'The people' were not understood in a modern, egalitarian sense. The term was rarely used in a way inclusive of, say, the poor or women. However, 'the people' for political purposes in this new era did include a considerable portion of the country's broader population outside of its elite. Indeed, there is no doubt that a fair number of men who were of quite modest social and economic fortunes were incorporated into the political nation in this era: they read the papers and pamphlets, perhaps debated in coffee-houses, and quite possibly voted in elections.

The nub of this anxiety was that many elites suspected that the people were volatile, irrational and potentially dangerous. Many of them feared that the masses were easily swayed by rhetoric, bribery and the deluge of printed matter that became increasingly important factors in politics. Governments had to pay attention to the vicissitudes of public opinion in a way that they had never done before, and moralists, writers, politicians and gentlemen saw this as potentially making government a slave of the erratic and turbulent passions of a great mass of ignorant men who were simply not capable of exercising such agency responsibly or wisely, partly because they were poor and therefore economically dependent on others who could manipulate them for partisan ends. The intensity of party strife and divisions within the political and social elite had made some appeal to non-elites practically necessary, but neither Tories nor Whigs were terribly happy about the principle of opening up politics to the hoi polloi: it was something of a necessary evil *in extremis*.

However, although both parties were worried about 'the people', these anxieties mapped onto party politics in paradoxical, uneven and changing ways. At the birth of the Whig and Tory parties in the reign of Charles II, the great believers in hierarchy and deference were, of course, the Tories. Their elitism was very straightforward: the masses should know their place and stick to it, accepting the authority and direction of their betters, that is to say, the Church, the King, the aristocracy and the squirearchy. Those traditional authorities were constrained by the laws of God and accordingly had a duty to ensure the welfare of their subjects, parishioners and tenants, but any idea that 'the people' should have any autonomous political agency was completely taboo.

Although the early Whigs were ideologically heterogenous and many were quite conservative, their emphasis on consent, the right of the people to resist tyranny, and their scepticism towards the absolute authority of the pillars of the traditional order meant that they were far more aligned with at least some degree of 'popular' involvement in politics. That might vary between the more extreme and more conservative elements, but even the least radical Whig would struggle to deny some political recognition to the broader nation.

As such, in the earlier part of the period covered by this book, if any party were 'the populists', it was the Whigs. They struggled against what they saw as a repressive monarchical regime, backed by the traditional landed Anglican oligarchy, and were prepared to appeal to more 'popular' elements to support this struggle during the Exclusion Crisis and Glorious Revolution. The Whig 'popular' appeal was, no doubt, ambiguous and more implicit than explicit, conducted in large part in religious terms as

219

an anti-Catholic crusade, but it took very real forms. When Monmouth landed in 1685, his radical declaration was widely perceived as borderline republican and received much support from the lower orders. There was much popular rioting and mob action against 'papists' in 1688.

However, as we have seen, post-1688 the social and political character of Whiggism changed. It lost much of its 'populist' appeal, and Whiggery increasingly became the ideology of a new oligarchy, predominantly a financial one.

As time went on the Whigs became increasingly the *anti*-populist – and, more to the point, the broadly *unpopular* – party. This was exacerbated by various factors. Firstly, as the war dragged on, it became ever more unpopular, and not just among the landed gentlemen who paid the land tax. By 1710, the country had been at war for sixteen years out of twenty-one, and the burden of carrying on such a conflict had fallen heavily and widely: economic dislocation affected people of all social classes, the numbers relying on poor relief spiralled upwards, heavy taxation squeezed many of quite modest means, and men had to be recruited to go and fight and die in Flanders, Portugal, Spain and beyond. The only people who directly benefited from the war in a material sense were the financiers, bankers and contractors who made fat profits out of it, and they were mostly staunch Whigs.

Secondly, for all the outsized economic and social clout of the Dissenters, they were not necessarily particularly popular, not least because they were often associated with the financial and banking interests. England was indeed a Protestant nation that was quite prepared to rally against papism, but, for all the problems faced by the Church of England in the early eighteenth century, the fact remained that most Englishmen were Anglicans, not Dissenters, and the rallying cry of the 'Church in Danger' did, in the right context, have popular appeal in a way that Whig pro-Dissent sentiment did not. In 1710, when the High Church firebrand Sacheverell was prosecuted by a Whig ministry, there was (as we shall see) a massive outpouring of pro-Church sentiment among 'the masses', which found expression in, among other things, riots. For the majority, the bulwark of Protestantism was the Church of England, and Dissenters were seen to undermine or threaten rather than buttress it.

220

In short, as time went on, the sentiments of most of those who were part of the political nation, from the squire down to the poorest voters – and many of those who could not vote – became increasingly Tory. Of course, as is ever the case, a large proportion of the 'masses', particularly the poorest and most indigent, were too busy labouring for survival to care much about Whig versus Tory. However, among almost all strata of voters, from the socially lowest to the highest, the Whigs became ever less popular, and therefore ever less inclined to support the political pretensions of the populus. The Tories won thumping election victories in 1710 and 1713 for very good reason: in the country, the Whigs had a dwindling support base.

This dynamic meant that the Tories, traditionally the elitists, became a lot more equivocal in their fear of 'the people', many of whom appeared to actually be good Tories, and the Whigs, traditionally the populists, became ever more hostile to them; if before the Glorious Revolution the voice of the people was the voice of God (*'vox populi vox dei'*), then by the mid-1710s, according to one Whig propagandist, the *vox dei* had turned into the *'vox diaboli'* ('the voice of the devil').[87] Elite anxiety about the irrational, fickle masses became more pronounced among the Whigs, who increasingly suspected that the people were backwards and bigoted, irrationally attached to their traditional institutions – most notably the Church of England – and too stupid to understand the importance of continuing the war against France. They were, thought many Whigs, too easily swayed by Tory election propaganda and its appeals to emotion, and too poor and dependent to give their vote freely and rationally (i.e. to the Whig candidates).

This is not to say that the Tories abandoned their belief in traditional hierarchy: they also remained ideologically inclined to scepticism about appeals to the masses. However, the fact that the aforementioned masses seemed to be rallying to their side as the years wore on made them rather less inclined to complain about their irrationality. Indeed, in the practical sphere of electioneering, if not in theory, they were prepared to exploit this new situation to gain support as part of what might be termed 'Tory populism'.

These dynamics are brilliantly illustrated by the example of the politics of London.[88] During the Exclusion Crisis, London had been the political heartland of the radical Whigs, who, in the immediate, confused aftermath of the Glorious Revolution, seized control of the Corporation of London and put forward a radically populist programme of reform to its constitution. This entailed giving increased power to a common council elected by a wide franchise and also included provision for the direct election on a similarly broad franchise of aldermen and the Lord Mayor. This proposal was stymied in parliament, but it certainly gave the London Whigs the imprimatur of radical populism.

This was soon to change. By the mid-1690s, the wealthy Whig leadership of the corporation, composed largely of commercial and financial interests, wanted to entrench their own authority and limit popular participation, and in 1697 they actually passed a 'magisterial order' that drastically reduced the electorate of 'liverymen' (members of the traditional trade guilds who historically had the right to elect important positions such as the city's MPs, Lord Mayor and sheriff), limiting it to only the wealthiest among their number. The Whig oligarchy wanted no challenge to their established authority from anarchic plebs.

Gradually, the populist hole in London politics was filled by the Tories. Leading city Tories courted popularity among poorer Londoners by large-scale charitable benefactions and championing the electoral rights of the artisans and plebeian freemen. Increasingly, the Tories gained their support from the poorer wards in the city and the Tory common councilmen were more likely to be of lower social origins than their Whig rivals. By the mid-1700s, governance in the city had become fractured: the Tories dominated the common council (the more popular body) while the Whigs dominated the magistracy, particularly the oligarchic Court of Aldermen. The Whigs were the party of the wealthy inner-city wards, the Tories of the middling and poorer outlying areas. By 1710, when the Sacheverell affair and the war helped provoke a massive escalation of partisan politics, the London Tories were the populist anti-war, pro-Church party, attacking the wealthy Dissenting Whig elite for prolonging the war to fill their own pockets, and the Whigs were the unabashed oligarchic defenders of the war and the financial establishment.

This increasing chasm between the Whigs and their 'populist' heritage, and the phenomenon of plebeian Tory populism, shaped the 'culture war', including at the more rarefied literary and philosophical level. The increasing Whig anxiety about the irrationality of the masses needed to be finessed and made ideologically palatable for a party with their radical heritage. So, for leading Whig writers and philosophers – particularly Anthony Ashley Cooper, the third Earl of Shaftesbury (the grandson of the Whig leader during the Exclusion Crisis), and Richard Steele and Joseph Addison, who between them wrote the famous 'Spectator' essays – support for what they saw as the bigoted religious politics of the High Church Tories and the narrow-minded parochialism of popular Toryism needed to be countered by educating the people into a new culture of reason and politeness.[89]

For these thinkers, the mania for newspaper reading, the prominence of contested elections and the rise of coffee-house debate culture were highly ambiguous, even perhaps dangerous, phenomena. They were potential outlets for the propagation of Tory prejudice, because the discourse they produced was (in their view) often emotional and immoderate, appealing to prejudice more than reason. These new phenomena needed, therefore, to be disciplined according to a new model. The approved model for 'correct', polite discourse was that of a polished, free commercial society where rational bourgeois citizens aimed at mutual edification and delight through exchange, trade and credit. This view stressed artistic and cultural refinement, and a rational, temperate form of religion that emphasised moderation and private, individual piety free from the impostures of authoritarian priests and prelates and the claims of traditional, outmoded institutions like the sort of Church of England the High Churchmen wanted to revive.

This model was, unsurprisingly, predicated on the dominance of the social, economic and spiritual forces that had gained the ascendancy in the post-Glorious Revolution context: the financiers, tradesmen and latitudinarian bishops who formed the backbone of Whig social and political power. Indeed, to be a polite, reasonable citizen in this new moral and political vision was to be a Whig. To be irrational and partisan and prejudiced was presented as, almost by definition, to be a Tory.

This, was, of course, a classic attempt to promote a highly partisan political vision in a way that implied it was no more than objective, neutral and rational. It was an attempt to effectively delegitimise Toryism and make it anathema to the educated and civilised classes; one might say to cast it as the sort of view that was 'not worthy of respect in a commercial society'. Tories were 'deplorables', whereas polite Whiggery became high status: only backwoodsmen Tories and plebs clung onto low status opinions such as wanting peace and a dominant Church of England.

This was an extraordinary turnaround given that historically it was the Tories, with their ties to the court, literature and, indeed, most cultural production, who were seen as polished, sophisticated and high status, in contrast to the rude, ranting Puritans and their Whiggish allies. It was a highly effective strategy. The Tories had a huge amount of social and political support in the country, but an increasingly strong and assertive Whig cultural hegemony, the power of money and the contingencies of high politics were going to prove a hard combination for the Tories to defeat in the long run.

7

The Junto, the Union and the Battle with Harley

In the first years of Anne's reign, the issue of the succession to the throne had taken something of a back seat politically, although it lurked in the background and was often invoked by Whig propagandists. Ostensibly, the question of who was to succeed on Anne's demise had been solved by the passing of the Act of Succession in 1701: Sophia, Electress of Hanover, and her issue, were to inherit the crown of England.

However, merely passing a law was in itself no guarantee, especially with a Jacobite heir languishing in France, waiting for his moment. Unless some mechanism could be contrived to enforce this law, it was little more than some writing on a piece of paper. The Jacobites might seek to exploit any confusion that arose on the death of the Queen, and the Whigs were acutely conscious of this. In the autumn of 1705, however, it was the Tories who were to bring the issue to the fore.

Having comprehensively lost their influence and credit with the Queen over the Tack and the other events of the previous few years, the Tories stood on the edge of the abyss of complete political irrelevance. Nottingham, Rochester and the other leading Tories knew that they needed something spectacular to revive their fortunes.

The plan they came up with seemed to be a clever one. Conscious of the fact that they had seriously alienated the Queen, and were no more inclined to conciliate her than she was in a mood to be conciliated, they decided to divert their energy to courting the rising interest: that of the Hanoverians. The Queen's health was always poor: her mortality was never a very remote possibility, and if she died in the not-too-distant future her high dudgeon with the Tories would instantly become irrelevant. Sophia was old (seventy-five in 1705), but she had a son, George, who was likely to be the actual claimant of the throne. Securing the favour and good graces of Sophia and George could therefore secure for the Tories a happy political future. If this could be combined with some measure to help secure their succession, it would also quell Whig insinuations that they were at heart Jacobites.

In October 1705, Rochester corresponded with the Hanoverian court to sound out Sophia and George about a scheme that he had hatched to this end: an invitation to Sophia and George to reside in England. Rochester and Nottingham were both already friends with the old woman, who was by background and inclination a royalist and more inclined to a Tory view of the world, and they received an enthusiastic response: George gave gushing assurances of his conviction that Rochester had always been a champion of 'his Majesty's interests, of his religion, his homeland, and his family', and Sophia reassured Rochester that 'whenever the Queen and the Parliament call her, the next day she will go and wait on her Majesty in England'.[1]

The logic was that this would make their immediate accession to the throne far smoother; there were, argued the Tories, 'no means so sure to maintain [the Hanoverian succession], as to have the successor upon the place, ready to assume and maintain his right', as the first claimant always had an advantage in these situations.[2] If the Hanoverians were not in England, the Pretender would be in a far better position to get to England first, given the relative proximities of France and Hanover to England. Given that the Hanoverians were foreign, giving them some time to become familiar with the country whose throne they stood to inherit could also only do good, argued the Tories: they could become acculturated to English mores, religion and politics, and therefore seem less like an alien imposition when their time to rule came.

This was a strong argument. The obvious problem was that Anne detested it. She saw it as a gnawing reminder of her own mortality and did not relish the idea of having a 'reversionary interest' challenging her political authority on her home turf. So far as the Tories were concerned, this was, if anything, a further benefit to the plan. They had already alienated Anne so much that further insult could hardly make things worse, but Anne's attitude put the Whigs in a difficult position: they either had to oppose it, which would make them look like hypocrites, as they had previously suggested such a measure themselves, or they had to support it, and thereby alienate the Queen. So when Tory Lord Haversham moved this proposal on 15th November 1705, with the support of Rochester and Nottingham, the Tories were sure that they were laying a finely sprung trap for the Whigs.

It was a trap that was to ensnare no one other than themselves, for the Whigs, with their usual tactical flair, quickly turned the situation to their advantage. They had no intention of endangering their rising political credit with the ministry by supporting a measure that was so hateful to the Queen, but rather than allow the Tories to thereby 'steal their clothes' and pose as the true defenders of the Protestant succession, they immediately moved their own counter-proposal for ensuring the smooth accession of the Hanoverians to the throne.

The Whigs advocated a Regency Bill, an ingenious contrivance of Lord Somers, which would set up a regency council of leading ministers of state to rule in the interregnum period between the Queen dying and the Hanoverians arriving. This council would have powers to ensure the orderly transfer of sovereignty to the rightful heir and take any necessary measures to prevent Jacobite moves to regain the throne. The Act also ensured that neither the Privy Council nor parliament should be dissolved on the Queen's demise, but should continue to sit to ensure stability of government. In short, the proposal would ensure that there would be no vacuum of power or confusion during the crucial interregnum period for the Pretender to exploit.

So the Whigs were able to oppose and defeat the invitation proposal, and thereby please the Queen, but at the same time were able to maintain their position as true defenders of the Protestant succession and provide actual substantial legislation to solve a problem that they had been unhappily conscious of for some time. In the process, they were able to humiliate their opponents by highlighting the opportunism of the Tories. Wharton had great fun in his speech moving the Regency Bill, professing, in a masterpiece of parliamentary sarcasm, amazed delight at the Tories' apparent conversion to the cause of securing the Hanoverian succession. Burnet describes his speech:

> he rejoiced in their conversion, and confessed it was a miracle: he would not, he could not, he ought not to suspect the sincerity of those who moved for inviting the next successor over; yet he could not hinder himself from remembering what had passed in a course of many years, and how men had argued, voted, and protested all that while: this confirmed his opinion that a miracle was now wrought; and that might oblige some to shew their change by an excess of zeal, which he could not but commend, though he did not fully agree to it.[3]

The Tories predictably bungled their handling of the whole situation. They antagonised the Queen, who attended the debates, even more than was strictly necessary. The Tory Duke of Buckingham suggested that the invitation to Sophia was necessary in case the Queen should become senile 'and be like a child in the hands of others', which, given that the Electress was seventy-five and the Queen forty at the time, was not surprisingly taken as a great insult by Anne.[4] The Queen was further enraged by Nottingham's pompous advocacy of the invitation; he had previously told her, when opposing the same measure a few years before, that 'whoever proposed bringing over her successor in her lifetime, did it with a design to depose her'.[5] His hypocrisy disgusted her and she never forgave him for it.

The whole episode was disastrous for the Tories. They had gained nothing, especially since, in the wake of these events, the Whigs themselves sent emissaries to Hanover to persuade Sophia and George that their approach had been the more genuine move in their interests, with some success (though more so with George). They lost much, however, as the Queen was now as much inclined to call the Devil to lead her ministry as any High Tory leader, and the Whigs had used the incident to endear themselves to Godolphin and the Queen.

* * *

Another massive issue hanging over the country was brought into focus in the parliamentary session that began in autumn 1705. It too related to the succession question. That issue was the political status of Scotland.[6]

By the late 1690s, Scotland had been reduced to a desperate state. Terrible weather led to a series of appalling harvests in the mid-to-late 1690s, which caused a devastating famine. The population declined dramatically. This dire economic and humanitarian situation was exacerbated by the impact of the Nine Years' War, which hit Scottish trade badly and caused taxes to rise. To cap this run of disasters, a bold attempt to counter these problems and effect national economic revival – a scheme to establish a colony in Darien in Panama, called 'New Caledonia' – failed spectacularly due to disease, Spanish opposition and maladministration.

Perhaps as much as 20 per cent of the country's population was involved in investing in the scheme, directly or indirectly. When it failed, it was a disaster on an unimaginable scale: around 25 per cent of the entire nation's capital had been lost, but the blow to Scottish pride was perhaps even more calamitous. When added to the cost of famine relief, perhaps half of Scotland's resources had simply melted away.

Although clearly the Scottish disaster of the 1690s could hardly be blamed solely on England – even the pantomime villains south of the border could not control the weather – they were convenient scapegoats. To be fair, there was some justice in this. William III had deliberately hampered the Darien scheme, and Scottish trade was hindered by English duties and the monopoly given to English ships in large swathes of foreign markets by the navigation acts. William's war and his taxes were no more popular among many English people than they were among the Scots, but they were seen as English impositions.

William's approach to securing control in Scotland in the 1690s – symbolised in the minds of many by the massacre, in 1692, of a Highland clan from Glencoe who had been slow to pledge allegiance to him – was perceived as brutal. This exacerbated matters further, as did the high-handed and distant manner with which he treated Scottish complaints, which was seen by many in Scotland as indifference to their plight. In reaction to these apparent insults – focussed particularly around the national trauma of the Darien catastrophe – political opposition to the English court and the Scottish politicians who served it grew in the late 1690s and early 1700s.

Scotland also had problems of internal division, especially on religious and therefore political questions. The population was mainly Presbyterian, especially in the lowlands, but in the north-east and parts of the Borders there was a significant Episcopalian presence, and the Highlands and Western Isles were very different: there, remnants of Roman Catholicism remained, especially among the Highland clans, and Episcopalianism was common. After years of royalist persecution of the radical Presbyterian covenanters, one result of the Glorious Revolution in Scotland was that the Presbyterian 'Kirk' was made the established church. The royalist Episcopalians (roughly equivalent to Anglicans in England) were therefore politically reduced to the status that Dissenters endured in England. The majority of Episcopalian ministers were ejected from their livings. As such, they – along with the remaining Catholics – overwhelmingly became opponents of the Glorious Revolution settlement and were almost uniformly Jacobites. The Highland clans became particular hotbeds of Jacobitism. The lowland Presbyterians, on the other hand, tended to be the equivalent of Whigs, and they had a radical fringe, made up of the heirs to the old Presbyterian covenanters who had caused so much trouble for Charles I.

Paradoxically, therefore, Scotland became an epicentre of both hot Protestant dedication to Revolution principles and the exact opposite, rampant Jacobitism, and both sides were keen to flex their muscles and show the English that they were independent actors unwilling to be English puppets. Indeed, anti-English sentiment – or at the very least sturdy patriotic pride – was widespread across the political spectrum.

By the late 1690s, a number of parties – loose and complex, combining the febrile personal followings of various influential Scottish nobles, but recognisably parties of a sort – had formed in Scotland. There was the Court Party, led by the self-aggrandising Scottish magnate the Duke of Queensberry, which was essentially the Crown's vehicle in the Scottish parliament. It was a broadly pro-Revolution Party, not unlike the Junto Whigs in England, which combined pragmatic (and often self-seeking) courtiers and much of the mainstream Presbyterian interest. In opposition to it, there was the Country Party, which included quasi-Jacobites who were similar to English Country Tories, as well as people much closer to being effectively Scottish versions of pro-Revolution Country Whigs, suspicious of the English court establishment, while also wishing to gain their own share of the patronage and material advantages that official favour could bring. There was also a Jacobite party, the Cavaliers, who barely veiled their hatred for the revolutionary settlement and desire to bring back the Stuarts.

Anger with William and perceived English arrogance soon spilled over in the early 1700s into demands for limitations on monarchical power and the strict enforcement of the 'Claim of Right', the Scottish equivalent of the Bill of Rights, passed in 1689, which was a more radical document than its English counterpart, unequivocally based on the idea of the conditional and contractual nature of kingship. Such claims in effect amounted to demands for greater Scottish control over their own affairs and a corresponding diminution of the power of the Anglocentric monarchy over disconsolate Caledonia. The Country Party, led by the charismatic if quixotic Jacobite the Duke of Hamilton, became the leading outlet for these demands, fuelled by Scottish rage at their ill treatment and Anglophobia. The Cavaliers were quick to stir the pot further and exploit Scottish anger for their own ends.

Towards the end of his reign, William III had become increasingly anxious about the implications of these developments. Put simply, they had made Scotland an increasingly worrying security headache for England. As well as a hotbed of outright Jacobitism, Scotland was the obvious target for any French invasion within the context of a renewed war with Louis XIV. Although many of those who were angry with England due to the events of 1690s were by no means Jacobites, clearly sharing a land border with a highly discontented and febrile independent nation, a decent minority of whose inhabitants would welcome a French incursion as a means of putting the Stuarts back on the throne, was a huge concern. So at the end of his reign William announced his intention of finding a solution to this by pursuing a formal political union between England and Scotland, and it was a policy that Anne was keen to see through.

Unfortunately, however, the immediate effect of Anne coming to the throne was to provoke the Scottish opposition further. Although they accepted the accession of Anne to the Scottish throne, Scottish indignation against English arrogance was inflamed by the English government's blithe assumption that they would follow orders and agree to accept the Hanoverian succession after Anne's death in conformity with the English Act of Settlement. Accordingly, a Scottish general election in 1703 saw a greatly increased contingent of Country and Cavalier MPs elected. A consequently fractious Scottish parliament, stewarded ineptly by Queensberry as Lord High Commissioner, soon thereafter withheld supply and passed a series of explosive acts designed to assert Scottish autonomy, most notably the Act of Security.

This Act stipulated the conditions under which Anne's successor to the Scottish throne would be chosen, the aim being to ensure that the next monarch would be subject to a whole range of limitations designed to uphold Scotland's autonomy and pride. Its 'Communication of Trade' clause meant that England and Scotland would be fully separated on the death of Queen Anne unless, in the meantime, England had granted Scotland complete freedom of trade with England and its colonies. The obvious implication of the Act was that, in principle, the Scots might choose a different monarch to succeed Anne, and, since the only other likely candidate was the Pretender, the effect of passing the Act in English eyes was most alarming. Initially, Godolphin, who in practice, along with his Scottish fixer Lord Seafield, attempted to manage Scottish politics for the crown, ensured that Anne did not give royal assent to it.

The disastrous nature of the parliament that produced this Act was the death knell for a short-lived Tory policy towards Scotland. The accession of Anne had also brought rising Tory power in England, and they had decided to attempt to establish their own political bridgehead in Scotland by appealing to the Episcopalians and their supporters in the Country and Cavalier parties, whom they saw as effectively Scottish Tories. Nottingham was converted to a policy of courting the Episcopalians by pushing their claims to religious toleration and supporting (albeit briefly) union, envisaging a scenario whereby these 'Scottish Tories' could carry the policy and bring into a (hypothetical) newly unified British parliament a contingent of friendly Scottish parliamentarians who would ally themselves with the English

Tories. To this end, he had promoted a Cavalier–Court Party alliance in the 1703 parliament.

The policy was doomed to failure from the start. Nottingham was largely deluded about the nature of Scottish politics: the 'Scottish Tories' were in fact Jacobite Scottish nationalists who were both in a minority and highly unlikely ever to support union in any form. Queensberry, an opportunist always seeking to curry favour with whoever was in power, acquiesced in the doomed policy to try to appease the apparently all-conquering Tories, but the Cavalier–Court alliance quickly fell apart and in the chaos the Act of Security was passed.

These developments appeared to make the prospect of union more distant than ever, and halting negotiations to that end, begun in 1702, quickly petered out. However, the situation was rather more complex than this story of sturdy Scottish nationalist revolt may imply.

Firstly, the Scottish opposition was in reality very divided: different factions had very different objectives. The Cavaliers saw any question over the succession to be a way of advancing the Jacobite cause, but various other groups had sundry agendas. A small group of austere quasi-republican radicals, led by Fletcher of Saltoun, were not Jacobites but wished to use the whole situation to greatly reduce the power of the throne, whoever happened to hold it.

However, the majority, including much of the Country Party, which was itself an uneasy alliance between rather different groups, did not have such extreme aims in mind. One of their motives was self-interest: relatively impoverished Scottish nobles and lairds were ever conscious of the material rewards that could potentially be extracted from the court. Another was a rather nobler desire to secure concessions from the English, particularly on economic matters. Indeed, Scottish economic weakness meant that, however much many Scots might resent the English, they could hardly fail to engage with their southern neighbours, who were their biggest single export market.

Secondly, anti-English sentiment was not necessarily incompatible with a desire to protect the revolutionary settlement, which in the minds of many was synonymous with upholding Scotland's Protestant heritage and holding back the apparently rampant tide of Catholic absolutism in Europe.

233

For all the (relative) strength of Jacobitism in Scotland, and the willingness (however reluctantly) of some non-Jacobites to give succour to Jacobite hopes out of anti-English pique, the Presbyterian majority in Scotland was still predominant, and most of Lowland Scotland was not willing to countenance the risk of a papist king in the final analysis, however much brinksmanship they might indulge in. A section of the Country Party were really more like Whigs than anything else.

So in principle, a pool of Scottish political actors existed who, due to economic factors, self-interest and ultimate loyalty to the Glorious Revolution, might well be induced to co-operate with Godolphin to secure a union, or at least Scottish acceptance of the Hanoverian succession.

By the end of 1703, however, this prospect seemed dimmer than ever: the government's Scottish policy was in ruins, and the passing of the Act of Security and the political chaos that had accompanied it gave great encouragement to the Scottish Jacobites, and rumours of plots and 'ill practices and designs carried on in Scotland, by emissaries from France', as the Queen herself put it, flourished.[7] Queensberry wrote in secret to the Queen informing her of a massive Jacobite conspiracy – the Scotch Plot that discredited Nottingham – carried on, he alleged, by pretty much every other Scottish faction other than his own. This was actually based on very thin evidence provided by someone who turned out to be a French double agent, but it was very useful for Queensberry, who massively embroidered it and then used it to excuse his own failure in the 1703 parliament and smear his political rivals.

It was also useful to the Junto, who used it to imply that government policy, by encouraging the Cavaliers and bungling matters so as to make confirming the Hanoverian succession in Scotland further away than ever, had given encouragement to such Jacobite plotting. The Whigs made much political hay with the Scotch Plot, using it to discredit and smear Nottingham and the Tories and weaken Godolphin. The common interest of the Junto and Queensberry in fanning the flames of the Scotch Plot was to draw them into close alliance.

Queensberry, however, did himself no favours in the short term. It became obvious to most that the plot was largely a self-serving ploy on his part, and he ended up trying to exculpate himself by blaming the court. In any case, it had become obvious to Godolphin and Seafield that Queensberry and his Court Party were not well-adapted to gaining wide enough support to carry out the policy of the court. The Court Party essentially had too narrow a base of support to gain a majority in the Scottish parliament for just about anything, especially in the first few years of Anne's reign. Made ineffective by the recent election results, the self-serving grandeur of Queensberry himself, and their reputation of being England's lackeys, they were, nonetheless, still the biggest single party. Queensberry's enormous influence as a magnate, patron and political operator meant that, though he could not muster a majority, he could exercise enough influence to prevent anyone else getting the Crown's business through the Scottish parliament. So nothing could be done without Queensberry and the Court Party, but precious little could be done with them, either.

The solution that Godolphin adopted was to attempt to peel off the less wild elements of the Country Party and combine their votes with enough of the old Court Party to prevail. He and Lord Seafield, the court's man in Edinburgh, set about to use arm-twisting and persuasion, as well as the usual patronage, baubles and douceurs, to tack together a 'New Party', soon nicknamed the 'Flying Squadron' (or 'Squadrone Volonte'), composed of the more tractable elements of the Country Party. An attempt to sack Queensberry as Lord High Commissioner and rule through the Squadrone in 1704, led by the moderate but ineffectual Revolution man Lord Tweedale, failed miserably: Queensberry, his haughty nose put well and truly out of joint by this manoeuvre, sulked off into opposition along with a large chunk of the Court Party and sank attempts to settle the succession.

However, the formation of the Squadrone, unfruitful as it was in the short term, was to prove to be vital: the wilder Country men like the Duke of Hamilton, who notoriously flirted with Jacobitism, had been split off from the more reasonable ones, which in theory, if everything could be made to align and personal animosities and magnate pride soothed, could be the key to union.

Queensberry's obstructive behaviour in this parliament had had something to do with the position of the Whigs in England. Increasingly, the Junto had come to see Scotland as a pawn in the wider game of political chess they were playing with Godolphin. They wanted to ensure that they could keep the whip hand over Godolphin by frustrating his Scottish policy and keeping fears about the Hanoverian succession alive until they were in a position to solve the problem on their own terms.

As such, they had cooled on the policy of union. A full legislative union with the Scots would inevitably mean that a number of Scottish MPs and Lords would essentially join the English parliament to create a new, expanded British parliament. This infusion of Scottish parliamentarians obviously had the potential to substantially affect the political dynamics at Westminster. The Junto feared that, unless union was undertaken under their own political management, any resulting Scottish contingent of Westminster lawmakers would become clients of Godolphin and the ministry, not themselves, which might eliminate their effective majority in the Lords: and given that they were out of office, that seemed likely. Accordingly, they encouraged their ally Queensberry to wreck the Squadrone experiment: they would wait until they had the power to settle Scottish affairs from a position of strength, using their client Queensberry as the vehicle.

Meanwhile, the Jacobites were revelling in the chaos and a certain degree of panic set in among many Presbyterians: the Scotch Plot itself may have been largely a political hoax, but fears about Jacobite stirrings and possible French attempts to exploit Scottish instability were by no means without foundation. These worries were shared by Westminster, and English anxiety about the Scottish position towards the succession was further inflamed by one of the few things that the 1704 Scottish parliamentary session had been able to achieve. In that session, it had become clear that the only way to give some credibility to the Squadrone and gain supply was to allow a slightly watered-down version of the Act of Security to again pass, and this time be given royal assent. A very reluctant Godolphin agreed to this: he had little choice, as the alternative was to disband the Scottish army due to lack of funds, which would have been incredibly irresponsible in the heightened atmosphere of Jacobite plotting, and giving some concession to the Squadrone was the only way to bolster their very shaky credit in the Scottish parliament.

The passing of the Act of Security came shortly before the 1704–5 English parliamentary session, not long after the Tack fiasco. In this context, the increasingly discontented Tories saw it, in their pique, as a stick with which to beat Godolphin. The Act of Security was indeed an explosive piece of legislation: it essentially appeared to be an attempt by the Scots to dictate terms to England on pain of refusing to accept the Hanoverian succession, and was taken by many English politicians as, in effect, if not universally in intention, a Jacobite manoeuvre to exclude the Hanoverians from the succession. The Tories were aware of the general disquiet provoked by this reaction, and mounted an attack in the Lords on Godolphin to try to leverage those sentiments and embarrass the government, dubbing the legislation the 'Act of Exclusion'.

This put Godolphin in a very tricky position. It was hard for him to defend giving royal assent to the Act of Security without reference to the finer points of Scottish political horse-trading, most of which put no one in a good light, including Godolphin himself. The Tories were furious with Godolphin anyway in light of their discontent over occasional conformity and the Tack, and the Whigs were keen to flex their muscles and show how crucial they could be in making or breaking the ministry. In the key debate, Godolphin flailed and stalled: according to one observer, 'he talked nonsense very fast' and looked like a defeated man.[8]

The Whigs, however, preferred to make Godolphin dependent on them rather than humiliate him. During the course of the debate on the Act of Security, Godolphin scuttled over to Wharton, Somers and Halifax and openly conferred with them in hurried whispers. The Whigs decided to shield Godolphin in the debate, rather than join with the Tories to bury him. They would drive a bargain with the Lord Treasurer over Scottish affairs: this way, he could be made to continue his drift towards relying on the Whigs, with consequent rewards in terms of patronage, and the Whigs could also try to enforce their preferred Scottish policy on him. By now, their policy had swung towards trying to coerce the Scottish parliament into accepting the Hanoverian succession, therefore ensuring some degree of national security in the short term. The idea was to pause their advocacy of full union until they were in a position to pass it in such a way as to ensure that the resultant Scottish contingent in a post-union British parliament were their own clients: a Whig version of the policy that Nottingham had briefly pursued in 1703, albeit one with a far more realistic chance of success.

Their major condition for saving Godolphin's bacon was his acquiescence in their new legislative ploy, the Aliens Act. The most notorious provisions of this legislation – dubbed 'the menacing clauses' by its opponents – were that if the Scots failed to settle the succession by Christmas 1705, a devastating barrage of economic punishments were to be inflicted on them: all Scots would be treated as foreign nationals, making any property owned by Scots in England highly precarious, and a complete embargo on the importation of Scottish coal, cattle and linen would be imposed, a provision that would have been an unendurable blow on top of their already onerous economic burdens. Below the surface there lurked a hint of even more overt menace: the Act also forbade any export of arms to Scotland if the succession was not passed. The subtext was clear: English military action to force the Scots to accept the succession was not off the table. The Act also provided for a suspension of the Act if the Scots would enter into negotiations for a union, and made provision for appointing English commissioners to conduct such negotiations, but the Whigs saw this as a reserve policy if all else failed. Their main objective was to force Godolphin into working through the Court Party and reappointing their associate Queensberry, who could then proceed to pass the succession in Scotland.

There were several major problems with this policy. Firstly, the court was not prepared to re-appoint Queensberry, not least because the Queen was vehemently opposed to it, disgusted by his shenanigans in the previous parliamentary session. Secondly, and more importantly, the Whigs had believed the claims of Queensberry and other Court Party leaders that they had the ability to pass the succession under their own auspices, but in reality they did not have the numbers in the Scottish parliament to do so.

Godolphin's strategy for the 1705 Scottish parliament was to attempt to work through another Court Party magnate, the imperious Duke of Argyll. He hoped that he could thereby gain back a large part of the Court Party while also keeping some of the Squadrone in office: a Court–Squadrone alliance might then be able to, if not pass the succession, then at least agree

238

to open negotiations for a union treaty. Unfortunately, Argyll – on whom the Junto had also been working – was only prepared to accept office as Lord High Commissioner if he and his supporters were guaranteed a virtual monopoly of office and privilege. Argyll's haughtiness secured his pre-eminence in the new Scottish ministry, but it made his – and the Junto's – policy of attempting to pass the succession even more hopeless than it already was.

The 'menacing clauses' of the Aliens Act had caused predictable uproar in Scotland: unsurprisingly, the majority saw it as a case of English browbeating and bullying. However, the dire consequences of doing nothing in response did focus minds.

Unfortunately for the Junto and Argyll, it did not focus them in their preferred direction. It became obvious very quickly that passing the succession was out of the question: the Court Party had no majority for it without the votes of other parties, and it was obvious to the Squadrone and the Court Party that it would undermine the Scots' bargaining position, unlike the prospect of making provision for negotiating a treaty of union – a drawn-out process which could be loaded with all kinds of conditions.

The court was prepared to accept treaty negotiations, and a wide range of Scottish politicians were prepared to countenance it too: malcontents and Jacobites were confident that it would come to nothing and would buy them time, whereas others saw it as a useful way to put off the fateful provisions of the Aliens Act and attempt to extract some sort of bargain out of the English ministry.

Impelled by these varying logics, the Scottish parliament duly agreed to open union treaty negotiations, and, crucially, due to some truly bizarre behaviour by opposition leader the Duke of Hamilton – who was either suborned by the court or perhaps playing a too deep game by half – the court won a vote allowing the Queen herself to appoint the commissioners who would be tasked with negotiating for Scotland. This made it far more likely that negotiations might succeed, as the Queen would obviously nominate commissioners friendly to the notion of union.

Things had not worked out as the Whigs had hoped. They had overestimated the ability of their Court Party allies to pass the succession and had ended up with the possibility of a union that could undermine their grip on the Lords and reinforce Godolphin's ministry just at a point when they were making progress in making it dependent upon their support. The Aliens Act had given the Scots the option of opening union negotiations, and spurning their agreement to this and refusing to repeal the offensive legislation would have been inflammatory in the extreme. The blame for the inevitable ensuing breakdown in relations with Scotland, and the impetus to Jacobitism that would result from such an outcome, would have fallen on the Whigs.

So, in the immediate aftermath of the debacle of the invitation to Electress Sophia and the Regency Act, the Tories, desperately casting around for some way to win back a degree of popularity, decided to force the issue and give the Whigs a real dilemma. In late November 1705, they moved to repeal the Aliens Act, giving the Whigs the choice of either having to infuriate Godolphin and lose their growing influence over the ministry by opposing repeal, or pushing ahead with a policy that they clearly didn't support: clearing the way to union negotiations.

To their annoyance, Somers stood up to support repeal, suggesting that only the clauses allowing for appointment of English commissioners to negotiate a union might be retained. For the Whigs had decided to reverse policy, accept the repeal of the Aliens Act and support union, in the hope that they might be able to turn the situation to their advantage. If they could take over the negotiations – something that Godolphin, increasingly reliant on Whig support to avoid disaster in the Lords, might well be willing to agree to – it might be possible for them to use the process to gain maximum party advantage, perhaps ensuring that the new Scottish parliamentarians that would result from the Union could be made to adhere to the Junto interest.

The union negotiations were on.

At first glance, it may seem curious that, despite concerning such a contentious subject and having such momentous consequences, the actual negotiations between the English and Scottish commissioners over the terms of the proposed union, commenced in April 1706, ended up being so smooth and speedy. By July, agreement had been reached, and apparently with ease.

The reason for this dispatch was straightforward, however. The Queen had been given little choice but to appoint Scottish commissioners predominantly from among Queensberry's Court Party clients, as it had become clear that, for all of the Court Party's weaknesses, there was no stronger political basis on which to proceed: a disgruntled Queensberry had the power to sink the policy if discountenanced, and, although his support did not guarantee victory, his opposition certainly guaranteed defeat.

As importantly, the Whigs got what they wanted from a weakened Godolphin, who was in no position to refuse Junto demands: he appointed all five Junto lords to the English union commission and ensured that it would be Whig dominated. Furthermore, now that the Whigs had decided on a policy of union, they had every incentive to make it work. They also wanted to gain credit among the key players in Scottish politics – particularly Queensberry and the Court Party, but also the Squadrone men, whom they were also courting – in order to ensure their adherence to Junto aims in any resulting British parliament, so they had every incentive to offer the best terms that they felt were politically feasible in England, and to do everything they could to oblige Queensberry. Wharton and Somers set to work: Wharton flattered and charmed Queensberry and his acolytes, and Somers crafted the constitutional and financial framework of the proposed union.

The fundamental basis of the Union was essentially determined by the political realities. There were basically two possible models of union: a federal union and an 'incorporating' union. The former would have maintained a separate Scottish parliament with some varying degree of power over certain aspects of domestic Scottish affairs, the latter entailed a complete political merging of the two countries: one British parliament sovereign over all affairs in both England and Scotland.

Both the court and the Whigs were only prepared to conduct the negotiation on the basis of the latter, the former being seen as not addressing English security concerns. England needed, and wanted, extensive political control over Scottish military, financial and other matters to quash both Jacobitism and troubling grumbles of Scottish nationalism, and only an incorporating union would give them that. The Scottish commissioners had to accept this for any negotiations to take place at all. The quid pro quo was that, in return for Scottish acquiescence on this point, England would agree to complete freedom of trade within the new state, sweeping away all restrictive tariffs and duties on Scottish goods.

After a little bit of token resistance to placate Scottish public opinion, these interrelated points were quickly agreed. The trickier points related to the financial basis of the new state. Creating a completely unified state implied a common policy with regards to taxation and debt, which, given that Scotland was clearly a far poorer country, caused problems. Creating a uniform system of taxation implied higher taxes for Scotland, and the fact that England had a huge and growing national debt, required to pay for the war, whereas Scotland had practically none at all, meant that Scotland would become liable for a share of England's debts. The Scots were, unsurprisingly, unenthusiastic about both of these developments.

The solution to these difficulties represented a reasonably fair bargain. Although taxation would be levied on Scotland at the same rates with regards to the major taxes – the land tax and the customs and excise – exemptions on other taxes, many of which had been introduced in England to pay for the war, were negotiated. In order to address the debt issue, an attempt – imperfect but with some claim to a technical basis – was made to calculate what the Scottish share of the debt would amount to. The sum agreed was £398,085 10s. England agreed to pay this lump sum back to the Scots as a recognition of the injustice of forcing Scotland to cover debts racked up by the English state. The money – dubbed 'the Equivalent' – would be used, among other things, to compensate the investors of the Darien scheme and pay outstanding civil and military salary arrears, which had built up to huge levels since the Revolution. In reality, an awful lot of this money ended up flowing to the Scottish nobles and gentry, who had the biggest relevant liabilities, which led to accusations that the Equivalent was little more than a grand bribe. That political negotiations conducted in 1706 in whatever context should largely benefit elite interests was, however, hardly a great surprise.

Other matters were tied up with relative ease. Scotland was allowed to retain its separate legal system and the independence of the Presbyterian Kirk, which was to continue to be Scotland's established church, was guaranteed. A compromise over Scottish representation in the new parliament – amounting to forty-five MPs and sixteen peers – was reached relatively painlessly. Various proposals to create standards weights, measures and coinage and a new flag were agreed without much dispute.

The torturous and protracted process by which this proposed Treaty of Union was forced through the Scottish Parliament over the course of the autumn and winter of 1706–7 is too complex to recount here. The deciding factor in the end was the twenty-five Squadrone MPs, drawn to the Union by a mixture of self-interest (some of them had been heavy investors in the Darien scheme and therefore stood to gain handsomely from the Equivalent) and a feeling that there was no alternative plan for improving Scotland's perilous economic position other than to try the Union experiment. The political alliance that Seafield had correctly guessed was Godolphin's passport to success back in 1704 – Queensberry's Court Party allied with the Squadrone – had come up trumps.

Once the Squadrone declared for the Union, although the opposition tried every expedient to spin out proceedings and delay matters, passing the treaty was a foregone conclusion. The underlying political majority among the Scottish elites for union had gradually been unlocked over the past few years, and the Duke of Hamilton and his coadjutants could do little about it other than make fine speeches and appeal to public opinion – which was, at best, lukewarm towards and largely opposed to the Union – and the mob, which was prepared to make the lives of the Union's parliamentary supporters very unpleasant as they scuttled through the streets of Edinburgh to vote it through in Parliament House.

With the Union destined to pass, from the point of view of English politicians the issue became: who would the Scottish parliamentary contingent side with once they got to Westminster? The Tories had been so thoroughly outmanoeuvred and marginalised in English – and indeed Scottish – politics over the past few years that they had become an irrelevance in this arena. The Junto had done their best to ingratiate themselves with the magnates of the Court Party. Godolphin was, however, to have the last laugh.

Fundamentally, the Court Party are usually referred to as 'The Court Party' for very good reason. Although doubtless their leaders had some commitment to upholding the revolutionary settlement and were vaguely anti-Jacobite, their key priority was to retain their prestige and power in Scotland, and secure all available favour and patronage from the English government, once the Union was completed – and Godolphin and the court were in a far better position to do that than the Junto. Godolphin gave Queensberry £20,000 to cover his arrears of pay, which helped ease the passage of the Union and reminded Queensberry of where the real source of patronage lay. He also worked hard to keep the Squadrone (who were increasingly becoming friends of the Junto) onside, ensuring that they received 'financial encouragement' too. This was essentially an insurance policy: if the Court Party did drift towards the Junto post-union, then there was the option, with a broad base of support for the Union, to cultivate the Squadrone as an alternative court party at Westminster.

In the event, Godolphin got what he wanted: the adherence of the Court Party, who made up the bulk of the post-Union parliamentary delegation to the new British parliament, to himself and the English court. Indeed, the Scottish lords in particular became infamous for their slavish obedience to the court, whatever the balance of the ministry: when a later Tory-dominated government headed by Harley found itself in a tight parliamentary situation in the Lords in 1710–14, most of the Scottish Lords whom the Whigs had done so much to transplant to the Westminster parliament supported Harley.

The exception to this was the Squadrone. The Junto had wisely courted them as well as the Court Party, as a sort of insurance policy, and it was they who became the closest Scottish allies that the Junto had in parliament post-union. They tended to make up a minority of the Scottish parliamentary contingent, but provided useful backup for the Whigs, particularly in the Commons.

Obviously, the union between England and Scotland came about due to many complex factors, predominantly the security and foreign policy needs of England, the political calculations (and to some extent self-interest) of Scottish politicians and the dire economic straits of Scotland. However, the party battle – between the Whigs, the Godolphin ministry and to some extent the Tories – shaped when and in what form it happened.

The union negotiations and ratifications came about in 1706–7 because it had happened to coincide with the temporary political interests (or what they felt to be their interests) of the Whigs. The terms of the treaty owed more than a little to the political interest the Whigs had in attempting (vainly as it happened) to win over the Court Party. Indeed, it is possible that the Union would never have come about, or at least not until much later, if the Whigs had maintained the position they held between 1702 and 1705 for longer: a scenario in which the succession was secured but the Union postponed was not impossible.

The role of the Tories was, in the end, limited to a doomed attempt to oppose its ratification in the English parliament. Despite their ill-conceived attempts to manipulate the Scottish question to their advantage and their brief support for union, by the time the Union treaty came for ratification, the Tories faced the prospect of the passing of a measure which, in reality, they did not care for. If anything was certain about the Scottish delegation likely to arrive in Westminster post-union, it was that they were not going to be allies of the Tories. High Tories were naturally the allies of Episcopalians in Scotland for denominational reasons, but the reality confronting them was being part of a country in which the northern portion had as its established church not their own brand of Episcopal Anglicanism, but rather the sort of Presbyterianism that gave them nightmares, of both an ecclesiastical and political nature. There was nothing to the Tories' advantage in the Union, and so they had little choice but to oppose it, which in practice meant largely attempting to delay it and weigh the process down with unacceptable amendments.

It was futile. They had no chance against the combined forces of the ministry, the Whigs and the Harleyites. Sir John Pakington made a characteristically easy-tempered and moderate speech, comparing the Union on the part of England to 'marrying a woman against her consent' and claiming that it was 'carried on by corruption and bribery within doors, and by force and violence without'.[9] He was crying into the wilderness, however, and the only issue on which the Tories managed to gain any purchase was over the Church, where they gained some guarantees that the presence of a Presbyterian Scotland in the new unified country wouldn't be allowed to threaten the security of the Church of England. Ultimately, however, Tory quibbling about the union was futile: on 6th March 1707, the Queen gave royal assent to the Act of Union. It came into force on 1st May.

The irony of the whole business was that, politically, the Act of Union represented a failure for both Whigs and Tories. The Tories might have appeared to be the obvious losers, but in reality the Whigs failed to gain their main political prize, too; the only winners in the short term were the court and the ministers of the Godolphin–Marlborough regime. However, whatever the ugly partisan realities, the path had been cleared, within the maelstrom of English political intrigue and party manoeuvring, to a political and constitutional achievement of enduring importance.

The wranglings over the Scottish situation were part of a far wider struggle over the course of 1706 and 1707 between the Junto on one hand and Harley and the Queen on the other, with Godolphin and Marlborough playing the role of decidedly uncomfortable umpires, albeit ones leaning ever closer to the Whigs.

By early 1706, Godolphin was acutely aware that the government had been bailed out repeatedly by the Whigs over the previous parliamentary session: the Junto Lords had spared the Queen embarrassment over the invitation to Sophia by moving the Regency Act; they had defeated the Tories over the 'Church in Danger' motion, which also pleased the Queen; and they had acquiesced in the repeal of the Aliens Act, paving the way to union negotiations. The Junto – never ones to be shy about the rewards due to them for services rendered – felt that they deserved a return for such favours: although concessions had been made, not a single one of the Junto lords was yet in office.

The focus of their demands was their youngest rising star, the Earl of Sunderland, who they insisted be given one of the secretaryships of state, ideally that of Harley, but if not, that of Charles Hedges, a moderate Tory who had so far survived.

Sunderland – son of the notoriously unpopular turncoat and wire-puller who had worked for Charles II, James II and William III – was not a propitious choice. He embodied just about everything that the Queen hated about the Whigs. Educated in the Netherlands, as a youth he had become an extreme radical, reputedly (probably falsely) a republican.[10] He was notoriously hot-tempered and strident, to the extent that his own mother complained that his approach to politics was characterised by excessive 'heat and over earnestness'.[11] On one occasion, in the heat of a Commons debate, he had declared 'that he hoped to live to piss upon the House of Lords'.[12] The Queen made her opposition to his appointment immediately – and abundantly – clear.

This put Godolphin in a very difficult position. At first he supported the Queen and tried to make the Junto back off; he wrote plaintively to Marlborough in April 1706, reporting that he had 'had some conversations with [Somers] and his friends' in which they had been quite adamant about their demands: 'I am sorry to say they are not all so reasonable as is certainly very necessary, for their own sakes as well as for everybody else.'[13] He was stuck between the irresistible force of the Junto and the immovable object of the Queen.

He was also stuck in the middle of renewed feuding between the Queen and Sarah Churchill over the matter. For Sunderland was, crucially, the son-in-law of Sarah Churchill (and, of course, therefore Marlborough) having married her daughter, Anne, in 1700. Sunderland and Sarah shared a violently partisan Whiggish outlook and were close political cronies. By early 1706, relations between Sarah and the Queen had deteriorated considerably: years of impertinent badgering had alienated the monarch increasingly from her former favourite.

Sarah at first avoided entering the fray with the Queen directly, but kept in constant communication with Godolphin over the matter, and harassed her husband – who had his own doubts about Sunderland's suitability for the post – to intervene, which he was reluctant to do. Both Sarah and Godolphin began to suspect that the Queen was being encouraged in her defiance by someone else.

That someone else was Robert Harley, who was absolutely determined to fight a rearguard action against the encroachment of the Junto. In March, when Godolphin was still reluctant to attempt to force the issue with the Queen, he wrote to Harley outlining the problem as he saw it. Calculating that there were about 160 Whigs and 190 Tories, in addition to one hundred of the 'Queen's servants' (a figure which undoubtedly included many moderate court-inclined Whigs and Tories), he observed that in the last session, with one minor exception:

> the 160 voted always with the body of the Queen's servants. For every one we are likely to get from the 190 we shall lose two or three from the 160. And is it not more reasonable and more easy to preserve those who have served and helped us, than those who have basely and ungratefully done all that was in their power to ruin us?[14]

Harley, however, was not inclined to abandon his preference for a mixed ministry. To do otherwise was to destroy the Queen's prerogative and freedom of action and hand power to a small cabal of men whose priority was to promote their own interests, rather than those of their country. Godolphin felt that, whatever the merits of such sentiments (which at heart he agreed with), in practice running towards the Whigs was the only reliable way of passing the government's business.

By June, Godolphin managed to get Marlborough to write directly to the Queen to ask her to appoint Sunderland. The Queen, although full of pleasantries, was completely clear in her reply: 'you know very well it is not in my power at this time to Comply with your desire'.[15] Thereafter for several months she simply refused to discuss the matter with Godolphin until, on 20th August, he threatened to resign.

This rattled the Queen. Although she hated the idea of appointing Sunderland, she struggled to envisage a way of carrying on her administration without her trusty Lord Treasurer. She sought Harley's advice, and he attempted to strengthen her resolve, pointing out to her that 'Nothing wil satifie them' and that if she fails to make a stand now, 'it wil be too late hereafter' as 'Everybody wil worship the Idol party that is set up'.[16] Although glad of Harley's backing, she felt she needed to propose a compromise to stave off the threat of Godolphin's resignation. She proposed that Sunderland be given a position in the cabinet and a pension but no actual office – a sort of 'minister without portfolio' arrangement – for the time being.

This, however, did not satisfy the Junto, and nothing was settled. At this point Sarah decided to intervene, writing a typically spicy letter in which she implored 'God Allmighty' to make the Queen see her 'errors as to this notion before it is too late'.[17] Unfortunately, the Queen misread 'notion' as 'nation' and found the letter extremely offensive. Sarah had simply made the Queen's intransigence worse. In response, the Queen wrote to Godolphin underlining her refusal to appoint Sunderland and arguing that it was her constitutional duty to resist the bullying of political parties:

> All I desire is my liberty in encourageing & employing all those that Concur faithfully in my Service whether they are call'ed Whigs or Torys, not to be tyed to one, nor to ye other, for if I should be soe unfortunat as to fall into ye hands of ether, I shall look upon my self tho I have the name of Queen, to be in realety but theire slave, which as it will be my personal ruin, soe it will be ye destroying of all Government . . .[18]

Anne had no intention of being a Queen in name only.

Throughout September and October, the charade continued: Godolphin alternating between threats of resignation and Eeyorish complaining about his lot ('I cannot struggle against the difficulties of Your Majestie's business, and yourself at the same time'), Sarah fuming in the background and occasionally making things worse by writing a rude letter, the Queen alternating between stolid refusal to discuss the matter and almost hysterical self-pity, with Harley doing everything possible to encourage her in the background.[19]

As the next session of parliament neared, the situation was getting desperate: Godolphin envisaged disaster if the Whigs were not placated, but still the Queen refused to budge. Clearly without Junto support some other plan to put the ministry on a stable parliamentary footing was needed, so Harley put together a detailed plan for a reconstruction of the ministry on mixed lines, the idea being to cobble together a majority with Whigs weary with Junto arrogance and moderate Tories. He pinned his hopes on Marlborough, who throughout had been less keen on accepting the ominous embrace of the Junto, but it was to no avail: the duumvirs told him it was a non-starter in no uncertain terms.

Harley at this point realised that no other option existed if Marlborough stuck by Godolphin and both stuck firm to the Junto demands, and backed off. Finally, with parliament just about to meet, in December 1706, the Queen, isolated and miserable, gave in. Political reality had finally forced the Queen and Harley's hand. They may have lost the battle, but neither were resigned to losing the war, for both were certain that this would not be the last Junto demand.

By early 1707, Godolphin could survey the political scene with satisfaction. He had won his and the Junto's struggle with the Queen over Sunderland: as a result, the 1706–7 parliamentary session was the smoothest he had known for a long time. It culminated in the triumph of achieving the historic union between England and Scotland that he had been working towards for years.

In addition, 1706 had been a year of great military success for the allies: after relative stalemate in the campaign of 1705, Marlborough had made a decisive breakthrough in Flanders against the French at the Battle of Ramillies, which he followed up by capturing the entirety of the Spanish Netherlands. The French were reduced to a desperate defensive position. Furthermore, the Habsburgs had drummed the French out of Italy. Events in Spain were far more in the balance, but overall the allies had reached the high watermark of their military success. Godolphin hoped that one more push could completely break the French and secure an advantageous peace; he could count on the Junto to back him to the hilt in this strategy, making the domestic side of this war strategy apparently easy. To crown it all, the Queen had consented to bestow an earldom on him as a reward for his services.

Godolphin's satisfaction was to be short-lived.

He may have triumphed in the short term against the Queen and Harley, but their unhappiness about rising Junto power had not gone away: in fact, their disgruntlement and determination to resist had only been made stronger and more bitter. Anne soon found an issue on which to make her stand against the Junto and provoke another prolonged bout of anxious political wrangling.

Godolphin's resentments against the Tory clergy and High Churchmen had been smouldering for several years now. Their continual agitation against the government's ecclesiastical policy in convocation, and even more so their scurrilous attacks on the ministry and him personally, especially in *The Memorial of the Church of England*, had infuriated him. He thought that the Tack was the height of factious irresponsibility. His correspondence heaves with dark insinuations against 'the insolences of the clergy'.[20] His hatred for the black-coated clerical troops of High Toryism had become highly emotionally charged.

The defeat of the 'Church in Danger' motion in parliament in late 1705 marked a low point for the High Churchmen: their credit with the Queen and the ministry was exhausted and their overbearing aggression had cast them into the political wilderness. The Whigs sensed this, and their Low Church allies in convocation twisted the knife into the Tory clergy in autumn 1705 by demanding that the lower house endorse a motion concurring with the Lord's resolution that the Church under Anne was safe and secure, and anyone who suggested otherwise was 'an enemy to the queen, the church and the kingdom'.[21] The High Churchmen, led by Harley's now Lieutenant Atterbury, reacted with predictable outrage.

Godolphin heard of the lower clergy's reaction, and decided that the time was ripe to move against the Tories in the church. Previously, he had been content to leave questions of ecclesiastical patronage to the Queen and her chief advisers on such matters, Harley and the Archbishop of York, John Sharp (a moderate Tory), but now he decided to intervene on Church appointments: the Whigs were prepared to make the ministry's life easier on Church matters, so they should be obliged in this sphere as on more temporal matters. In early 1706 he and Marlborough did a deal with the Junto to give them the key say over future Church appointments: as bishops had a vote in the Lords, the potential rewards for the Whigs here were obvious. The Junto began to hold regular meetings with the chief Whig bishops to make recommendations on Church patronage.[22]

This state of affairs did not provoke any major confrontation until November 1706, when Peter Mews, the Bishop of Winchester, died. The Whigs saw this as the first major test of the 1706 deal: putting a Whig into the richest and one of the most powerful sees in England would be a great coup.

251

Godolphin, however, had a problem: some years before, he had promised the diocese to Jonathan Trelawny, Tory Bishop of Exeter, in exchange for helping the ministry against the Tackers in the 1705 election. He had no choice but to keep to this promise, and in doing so enraged the Junto, who were shocked at Godolphin's duplicity.

However, he soon had a chance to placate them. With Trelawny moved to Winchester, the bishopric of Exeter was free, and two other plumb church appointments had recently become vacant: the Bishop of Chester and the regius professor of divinity at Oxford had both recently died. Godolphin hoped that offering these posts to Whiggish clerics would make up for the Trelawny debacle.

The Queen, however, had quite other ideas. She had already promised the regius professorship to George Smallridge, a Tory ally of Atterbury and Harley, and she was not inclined to be bullied on Church appointments. She might have been angry with the Tories over the 'Church in Danger' outcry, but none of this changed the fact that she was a High Churchwoman in substance. Harley and Sharp, who had no intention of giving up their role in advising the Queen on Church patronage, stiffened her resolve and encouraged her to stand firm. In mid-April, she secretly offered the vacant bishoprics to two Tories, Dr Offspring Blackall and Sir William Dawes.

Word of this got out very quickly, and all hell broke loose. The Junto men were livid, and suspected treachery or double-dealing on the part of Godolphin and Marlborough, perhaps in collusion with Harley. Appointing fresh Tory bishops, on top of the accession of the Scottish Court Party lords, threatened their majority in the Lords, but, as importantly, the whole episode was a symbol of resistance to their march to ever greater power. Contemporary rumour had it that Wharton personally accosted Godolphin at his home 'and said in a very insolent manner that it was one of my Lord Marlborough's and his tricks, and that he'd make them both repent it'.[23] An enraged Marlborough went round to Wharton's house the next morning, found him in bed, and threatened him with a duel unless 'he would go along with him and beg my Lord Treasurer's and his pardon at my Lord Treasurer's house'.[24] A duel was avoided, so apparently Wharton climbed down.

Gradually the Junto's suspicion fell unequivocally on Harley, whom they (and Sarah Churchill, who was once again involved) suspected of manipulating the Queen on the bishoprics matters in order to cause a break between the Whigs and the ministry, which could create an opportunity for pursuing his scheme of a remodelled 'moderate' ministry. Sarah became increasingly convinced that a young servant in the Queen's bedchamber, Abigail Hill, who was becoming the Queen's closest personal confidante as the Duchess lost favour, was in league with Harley to encourage Anne's intransigence.

The substantive influence of Abigail is extremely doubtful – Sarah's jealousy and rage was becoming ever more unhinged – but there's little doubt that Harley did encourage the Queen in this way. However, the obsession of Sarah and the Junto with Harley's 'treachery' and scheming treated the Queen as if she was a helpless puppet being manipulated by a shadowy force behind the scenes. In fact, as the Queen insisted vehemently throughout, the decision on the episcopal appointments was her own: she was always a lot more stubborn than her opponents realised. She herself hated Whig domination and saw this as a means of resisting it and forcing the ministry into a 'mixed scheme': if Harley encouraged her, as he surely did, he was pushing at an open door.

On 25th June, the Junto issued a stark ultimatum: if they did not get their way on Church appointments, they would go into outright and open opposition to the ministry when parliament met in the autumn. An attack on the administration of the Admiralty – clearly designed to embarrass Prince George, the Queen's husband, still nominally in charge of the Admiralty, and thereby by extension the Queen herself – was hinted at in the event of continued defiance of their wishes. The Whigs arrogantly assumed that this would seal the deal. It might have terrified Godolphin, but the Queen didn't flinch. In response to this persistence on her part, Marlborough wrote to her in July warning her that anyone who might be going 'about to persuaide you that you can be served this time by the Torrys, considering the mallice of their chiefs, and the behavior of the greatest part of cleargy' will 'end in betraying your quiet' and should be made to openly avow their plan.[25] It was a transparent attack on Harley. It made no impact whatsoever.

The summer drifted on in a continued atmosphere of tension. On the one hand, the Junto knew that they could make the ministry's life very difficult indeed come autumn if the Queen held out. On the other, the nagging doubt that perhaps some sort of alternative administration on Harley's lines could be cobbled together, thus destroying the progress that they had made in forcing themselves on the government, persisted. They were reasonably confident that any such scheme would be scotched by Godolphin, and if not would fail anyway, but they couldn't be sure. They may have hated Harley, but they knew that he was a formidable operator. So they hedged, suggesting that they would be content if the Queen was allowed to appoint Blackall to the diocese of Exeter but allow them to have their way on the other church appointments. She remained unmoved.

The Junto lords were furious, and, gathering at one of their habitual 'councils of war' in August, they decided on a new strategy: an outright attack on Harley with the intention of driving him out of the ministry. Although he had been a thorn in their side for some time, their distrust of and hatred for him had now grown to leviathan proportions. They saw him – rightly – as their inveterate enemy, the man who encouraged the Queen to stand firm against them, the barrier to all their hopes. He was the worst of all things in their mind: a traitor, who had abandoned the Whig cause and drifted into a rascally semi-Toryism. William Cowper, who was a more moderate Whig than the Junto, nonetheless summed up the general Whig view of Harley when he wrote in his diary of Harley's tendency to:

> never . . . deal clearly or openly, but always with Reserve, if not Dissimulation, or rather Simulation; & to love Tricks even where not necessary, but from an inward Satisfaction he took in applauding his own Cunning. If any Man was ever born under a Necessity of being a Knave, he was.[26]

To the Junto, he would always be 'Robin the Trickster'. Although Harley was undoubtedly given to feint and misdirection, the truth was that he was the one person in English politics able to outfox them, and for that he could never be forgiven.

He had some tricks up his sleeve yet. He was working on the Whig magnates the Duke of Somerset and the Duke of Newcastle. Somerset was a notoriously proud man, far too convinced of his own importance to be controlled by the Junto, and Newcastle was a personal friend of Harley: they would be indispensable to any non-Junto ministry. Harley was also making overtures to some of the Tories, although they remained so suspicious of him that they kept their distance for now.

Nonetheless, however hard he caballed and plotted – and no one could cabal or plot harder than Harley – he was on an increasingly sticky wicket. The growing exasperation of Marlborough and Godolphin was isolating him inside the cabinet, and in September he made a bad mistake. He openly supported a petition from Francis Atterbury concerning a dispute over patronage within the diocese of Carlisle, a very rare open intervention on ecclesiastical matters from him, which confirmed suspicions that he was behind the bishoprics struggle and was formally outside his brief. It gave Godolphin and other unsympathetic cabinet figures – principally William Cowper – a chance to slap him down hard, and they took it. His position became very precarious. He professed his loyalty to Godolphin and tried to get his head down, but his imprudence had weakened his position. With Harley apparently quelled, Godolphin moved once again to try to persuade the Queen to give in on the church appointments. Once again she refused.

By October, Godolphin was besieged by troubles on all sides. With the Queen unmoveable, he could see no way to prevent the Whig onslaught on the government once parliament began, and they would have much to assail.

For if 1706 had been a military *annus mirabilis*, then 1707 was going from bad to worse. France's defeat in Italy was to prove a mixed blessing, as the retreating forces – allowed safe passage by the Habsburg Emperor under the Treaty of Milan – were used to reinforce their armies in Spain. Accordingly, the allies had been routed in April at Almanza, and the French had recaptured large swathes of Spain. The allied claimant to the throne, Charles III, now had only a foothold in Catalonia, and victory in Spain was looking increasingly impossible. An allied land raid on the French port of Toulon, designed to knock out the French navy and thereby make the resupply of their armies in Spain impossible, failed. The French might no longer be in a position to win the war, but it began to look far from certain that they would fall to utter defeat.

The result for Godolphin was that he was likely to face an inquest in parliament as to the allies' military setbacks at the same time as the Whigs were preparing to attack his ministry. It spelt potential disaster, and with the Queen holding firm on the bishoprics issue, his government drifted into the new parliamentary session divided and with no clear strategy. The nightmare of a ministry opposed by both parties simultaneously loomed.

The Whigs soon commenced their promised onslaught on the Admiralty. They justified this by reference to the loss of a number of convoys during the summer and the impact on trade, but it was really a political attack in revenge for the failure to oblige the Junto over the bishoprics. Initially, the Tories supported the Junto and the government faced an attack from both sides.

Gradually, however, the tide began to turn. The Junto overplayed their hand, their true objective too transparent. The Tories began to suspect that the real design was to force Lord Orford, the Junto's naval man, into the Admiralty. They realised that if the Whig attack on the naval mishaps were to fail, the government might begin to withdraw from its dependence on the Junto. So in a crucial motion of censure pressed by the Whigs, the Tories rallied to the court and helped defeat it. In any case, moderates on all sides were starting to suspect (rightly) that the Whig attack was not based on a reasonable concern with naval efficiency, but was being pressed for purely political reasons.

More importantly, the Whig attack caused Harley and the duumvirs to close ranks. The real subject of the Junto's reproaches over the Admiralty's mismanagement was George Churchill, Marlborough's Tory brother, who was the power behind Prince George, the nominal Lord High Admiral. Marlborough was irritated by this attack on his own kin. In any case, Godolphin and Marlborough, when under actual fire from the Whigs, had no choice but to seek some reconciliation with Harley and pursue his strategy.

On 5th December 1707, Harley presented his plan. The ministry would be reconstructed under the auspices of an alliance between the more reasonable Tories and the court-inclined Whigs, i.e. the 'Lord Treasurer's Whigs' and the Junto-sceptical Whig lords, who would declare 'that they would never come in to press the Queen and the ministry to measures so unreasonable in themselves'.[27] Cautiously, Godolphin and Marlborough, seeing little alternative option, allowed Harley to pursue this 'all party' plan, giving him permission to sound out relevant Tories.

The Queen was jubilant. The duumvirs at this juncture decided to give in to her over the bishoprics issue, although, in the spirit of the 'all party' reconstruction, some of the church posts, including the regius professorship at Oxford, were to be given to Whigs. The general tenor of events, however, appeared to be clear, at least in the Queen's mind. She reported to Archbishop Sharp that:

> she meant to change her measures, and give no countenance to the Whig Lords, but that all the Tories, if they would, should come in; and Whigs likewise, that would show themselves to be in her interests, should have favour.[28]

Harley seemed to be on the brink of victory.

It was not, however, to be. By 11th February, Harley had been forced out of office altogether, and the policy of an alliance between the ministry and the Junto had been cemented beyond all doubt.

Why? In essence, because Godolphin and Harley had different ideas about what the reconstructed ministry would look like. Very different ideas.

Godolphin was in favour of an all-party government in which the Junto would be given the bare minimum to ensure that they supported the ministry in parliament: this would entail concessions to them, but if at all possible the Junto lords themselves should be kept out of government.

Harley, on the other hand, favoured a mixed ministry which leaned more to the Tories, to the extent of giving the Tories more overt favouritism in the distribution of ministerial office, so long as the Tories so favoured were not the 'hot men', particularly Rochester. His reasoning was that the Tories were so divided that they would never be able to 'drive' the Queen and dictate affairs to the extent that the Junto could. The meeting of 5th December obscured this difference, as did another similar meeting to develop the plans on 14th January: Harley was given vague permission to put out feelers to the Tories, but that could mean different things to different people.

The other crucial issue was that the plan that Harley was concocting in his head did not have any place for Godolphin. Harley, not Godolphin, would lead such a reconstructed Tory-leaning ministry. This plan had the merit of getting rid of the man who had become the chief advocate of concessions to the Junto – and no doubt ambition on his own behalf was not entirely absent from Harley's mind. He calculated that Marlborough would swallow this, and it was not an unreasonable assumption. Marlborough had been more reluctant to cosy up to the Junto than Godolphin, for the Junto had persistently shown every sign of wishing to dictate war strategy and foreign policy to Marlborough, something he relished no more than being harassed by Rochester and Nottingham. Also, Marlborough was personally close to a number of the Harleyites, especially Henry St John, the Secretary at War, and might be amenable to an administration essentially run by that group.

So after the meeting of the 14th, Harley's scheming went underground. He appears to have touted the plan – his own version of it – to various important Tories, ones of political weight enough to be of real assistance but not of the sort of querulous humour that would lay any such ministry open to the problems of 1702–5: these seem to have included Sir Thomas Hanmer, a pragmatic High Tory, and Peter Shakerley, a Tory whip and general fixer.

Harley's move against Godolphin took place in the shadow of a whole new political front that was opening up regarding the conduct of the war in Spain, which was to prove something of a double-edged sword for Harley, as well as a momentous moment in the course of the politics of the era.

Not surprisingly, parliament was keen to investigate the disaster that had befallen the English–Portuguese army at Almanza, and discuss the import that the defeat had for the war in general. The Tories formed a curious alliance with Lord Peterborough (actually a Whig, albeit a mercurial one), overall commander of allied forces in Spain, in order to embarrass the ministry over the weakness of their Spanish war effort. They resorted to their old strategy of demanding that the government prioritise the war in Spain and divert resources away from the Flanders theatre, much to Marlborough's exasperation.

258

Both parties united to pass a fateful motion committing the allies to recovering Spain, in its entirety, for the Habsburg claimant as a major war aim. It stated that 'no peace can be honourable or safe for her majesty and her allies if Spain and the Spanish West Indies be suffered to continue in the power of the House of Bourbon'.[29] The Whigs claimed that the entire point of the war was to prevent the Bourbons from claiming the Spanish throne, but the motion – subsequently known as the 'No Peace without Spain' motion – seemed to imply that no compromise over Spain would be sufficient: it had to be recovered in its entirety. The problem was that this had become essentially militarily impossible, as the combined forces of the majority of the Spanish and the French now had established almost complete dominance over the peninsula. A few cool heads had already begun to wonder whether this resolution was wise, but it suited the purposes of Whig and Tory at the time to support it. It was to prove a deeply controversial and unfortunate commitment that over the next half decade would form the basis of an earth-shaking political struggle.

More important in the short term was the report that parliament requested over the details of the Almanza debacle. Henry St John laid the relevant papers before the House on 29th January. They revealed a shocking story of administrative incompetence. Despite the fact that parliament had voted supplies for 29,000 troops for the Spanish Peninsula the year before, only 8,000 had been actually present at the battle. As a result, the army had been woefully outnumbered by the Franco-Spanish forces, precipitating their heavy defeat. Corruption and peculation were widely suspected.

Harley had already got wind of this a few days before the debate, and the evidence suggests that he had used this to suggest to the Queen that she was right to support his plan to remove Godolphin. In essence, he blamed Godolphin for the debacle and used it as a weapon in his attempted political assassination of the Lord Treasurer. The likelihood was that she was already privy to Harley's plan for a reconstructed Godolphin-less ministry, and approved of it: she was sick of Godolphin attempting to cajole her to favour the Junto and was sore over the Sunderland incident.

Unfortunately for Harley, his denigration of Godolphin to the Queen somehow leaked out. Godolphin got wind of it and exploded with rage at what he saw as Harley's rank treachery. He sent a messenger to Harley to announce that their connexion was at an end, which was quickly followed by a note from Marlborough to Harley summoning him to his home, where he explained Godolphin's rage and the occasion for it. Harley hastily dashed off a letter to Godolphin denying everything, but Godolphin was no longer in any mood to believe a word that the Secretary of State said. He replied with passionate rage:

> I . . . am very sorry for what has happened to lose the good opinion I had so much inclination to have of you, but I cannot help seeing and hearing, nor believing my senses. I am very far from having deserved it from you. God forgive you![30]

At this point, not all was lost on Harley's part. Marlborough was still hedging his bets, but nonetheless Harley was under enormous pressure. Firstly, he was making only very limited progress in his approaches to the Tories, who remained suspicious of him. Secondly, the Junto were still out for his blood, putting huge pressure on the duumvirs to sack him. They had decided to relent towards Godolphin on 29th January by ensuring that their henchmen in the Commons adjourned the debate on the Almanza scandal until 3rd February, thus giving him a stay of execution from the Tory assault on the ministry's mismanagement. The message was clear: do a deal with us, sack Harley and we will continue to save your neck; refuse, and we will bury you.

So on 3rd February, Harley needed to give a sign to the Tories that he was on their side, and use it to try to peel Godolphin away from a deal with the Junto. He decided to refuse to intervene in the debate, pinning his hopes on the Junto trying to rescue the ministry by softening a harsh censure over the Almanza troop figures. He hoped that such an attempt would be defeated by a combination of the Tory Party and non-Junto backbenchers horrified at the mismanagement. Such an outcome would illustrate to Marlborough that the Junto would not always be able to save the government.

The Junto, however, failed to oblige: when the debate finally came on, their lieutenants in the Commons did nothing to defend the ministry, and the motion of censure was passed without a division. The Junto's point had been proven, and the fact that Harley did nothing to defend the ministry in the debate was not likely to endear him to Marlborough.

Harley had no recourse now other than to hope the Queen would stand firm. In the following days, Anne told Marlborough that she was prepared to part ways with Godolphin, and was determined to follow through with Harley's plan.

At this juncture, Marlborough had a fateful choice to make. Would he side with Harley and seek a path forward free of the Junto, but free also of his faithful servant Godolphin? Or would he stick to his friend, albeit at the cost of potentially being dictated to by haughty Whig Lords? The fact that Godolphin's son Francis was Marlborough's son-in-law must have entered his calculations.

It is, however, probably a mistake to see his choice mainly in terms of any personal friendship, either with Godolphin or the Harleyites. His chief consideration was the war, and two things tipped the balance for him in favour of Godolphin and against Harley. Firstly, Godolphin had a proven track record of financial competence: why take a leap in the dark now? Secondly, the Tories had just supported an address viciously attacking the ministry's management of the war, and were attempting to dictate a strategy to him (focusing on Spain) that he did not like. He was just as likely to be harassed by the Tories regarding war strategy as he was by the Junto. So on the night of Friday 6th February, Marlborough wrote to the Queen informing her that unless she sacked Harley, both he and the Lord Treasurer would be forced to resign. They gave her three days to decide.

The Queen might be able to do without Godolphin, but she could not do without Marlborough, whose military leadership and prestige was the lynchpin of the entire Anglo-Habsburg-Dutch alliance. That did not stop her attempting to stand firm and assert her own right to appoint whomsoever she liked as her ministers.

The dramatic showdown came on Sunday 8th February at Kensington, where a cabinet meeting was due to take place. She met Godolphin, the Duchess of Marlborough and the Duke in an apartment adjoining the cabinet room, with the cabinet about to begin its deliberations. She held firm, telling Godolphin that 'in respect of his long service she would give him til tomorrow to consider. Then he should do as he pleased, with all she could find glad enough of that staff [the white staff, the symbol of the Lord Treasurer's authority]'.[31] She gave Sarah short shrift, telling her, in essence, to sling her hook and go back to St Albans. Then came a very tense exchange with the Duke:

> He told her he had ever served her with obedience and fidelity, that [he] had used that sword he must now resign to her to her honour and advantage; that he must lament he came in competition with so vile a creature as H(arley); that his fidelity and duty should continue so long as his breath; that it was his duty to be speedy in resigning his commands that she might put the sword into some other hand immediately, and it was also his duty to tell her he feared the Dutch would immediately on that news make a peace very ruinous for England. 'And then, my Lord', says (she), 'will you resign me your sword. Let me tell you', says (she), 'your service I have regarded to the utmost of my power, and if you do, my lord, resign your sword, let me tell you, you run it through my head'. She went to the council [cabinet], begging him to follow; he refusing, so the scene ended.[32]

Anne walked through to find that the cabinet meeting had already started. After an initial discussion about Admiralty business, Harley began to speak, at which point the Duke of Somerset 'rose, and said, if her Majesty suffered that fellow (pointing to Harley) to treat affairs of the war without the advice of the General [i.e. Marlborough], he could not serve her', at which point he stormed out.[33] Several of his like-minded Whig colleagues followed suit, and although the meeting stuttered on, it was clear that unless Harley was dismissed, business would be almost impossible to continue.

Fundamentally, although the Queen had the guts to try to soldier on without Marlborough, hardly anyone else did. The Whig lords who had been prepared to enter into Harley's scheme would only do so if he carried Marlborough with him. Amazingly, the Queen did not give in, but went about trying to canvass Tory support for a new ministry the next morning, despite the extraordinary scene at the cabinet meeting.

Later in the day, however, she realised that the game was up. Word went around that she had broken with Godolphin and Marlborough and thrown her weight behind Harley, and as a result, that afternoon the Commons let a 'bill of supply lie on the table, though it was ordered for that day'.[34] The implication was clear: reconcile to Marlborough or else. At the same time, the Junto lords moved on to another matter.

On 2nd January, a clerk in Harley's office, William Greg, had been arrested, and all his papers seized. There had been suspicion for some time about leaks to the enemy relating to shipping movements, and one of the avenues of enquiry had been messages sent from French prisoners of war back to their homeland, which Greg had been in charge of censoring. A search of the prisoners' post revealed that Greg had offered the French war minister information about British shipping in exchange for a pass for a British merchant ship which would allow it to move unmolested by French privateers: Greg had been offered 200 guineas by the merchant if he could secure such a pass. The temptation proved too much for Greg and he succumbed.[35]

There was no evidence of any wrongdoing on Harley's part, but the Junto were not likely to let that get in the way of a politically convenient smear: there had been treachery in Harley's office, and the Whigs suspected that they would be able to find some way of connecting Harley to it. On the same afternoon as the Commons signalled their reluctance to vote on supply unless Marlborough was reconciled, Wharton moved for a committee of enquiry into the affair with the obvious intention of moving against Harley. There was talk of an impeachment or even an attainder if he did not resign immediately.

At this point, even operators as tenacious and determined as the Queen and Harley realised that they were beaten. The Queen summoned Marlborough and informed him she would comply with his demands, then she had an emotional final interview with Harley. Ultimately, no amount of rearguard fighting on their part had been able to resist the inexorable force of the Lord Treasurer, the captain-general and the Junto lords. The Queen, weeping, accepted Harley's resignation. She faced a future of growing Junto domination and political isolation, and Harley faced his first return to the backbenches since the 1690s.

Harley was down. But, as the Junto were about to find out, he was by no means out.

8

The Junto Ascendant

The Scottish mindset in the aftermath of the passing of the Act of Union was summed up by a story gleefully related by Scottish Jacobite George Lockhart in his memoirs. Shortly after the Union passed, a Scottish merchant was travelling on business in England:

> shewing some apprehensions of being Robbed, his Landlady told him he was in no hazard, for all the Highwaymen were gone, and upon his enquiring how that came about; why truly, replied she, they are all gone to your Country to get Places.[1]

The bureaucratic machinery introduced quickly after the Union to enforce the payment of customs and excise in Scotland was, it is fair to say, not popular. Many Scots were convinced that their fears that England would simply use the Union to exploit and plunder their country were rapidly being proved right.

Lockhart was an unabashed Jacobite, and he clearly exaggerated when he claimed that Scottish people 'of all Ranks and Persuasions . . . were daily more and more persuaded that nothing but the Restoration [of the Stuarts] . . . could restore them to their Rights'.[2] He did not, however, exaggerate that much. The majority of Scots were furious, and the 'King Across the Water' gave a clear political focus for their bitter discontent.

As a result, the Jacobite court was keen to act quickly to exploit these sentiments. They were not alone: the French king, under whose protection the Pretender lived, had his own sound, albeit more cynical, reasons for encouraging a fresh attempt to reclaim the throne of Scotland, and perhaps even England, for his Stuart dependents. Whether James had any realistic chance of success or not, anything that might tie up some of Marlborough's troops for a while as campaign season began to draw near would be a boon for Louis XIV. So the decision was made to attempt an invasion of Scotland, which, it was hoped, would be accompanied by widespread pro-James uprisings in Scotland – and perhaps in England too.

As it turned out, the whole thing ended, like so many Jacobite plots, in shambolic farce, caused by the usual mixture of cock-up and bad luck. A by no means negligible Franco-Jacobite force, consisting of twenty-four frigates, five warships and 6,000 troops, was assembled. James himself – who only just recovered from an attack of the measles in time – joined the expedition, which set off on 9th March 1708.

However, it was commanded by a world-weary French sea-dog, the Chevalier de Forbin, who was utterly convinced that he'd been sent on a pointless mission that was doomed to failure: he accordingly treated the whole affair as a cross between a dangerous folly and a vaguely absurd joke. As importantly, the Jacobite agents made a total hash of it, failing to give the prearranged signal to land in the Firth of Forth. Pursued by Admiral Byng's fleet, prevented from making an improvised later landing near Inverness by bad weather, the invasion flotilla withdrew and about two-thirds of the troops died of exposure.

However, there was no doubt that it was a credible invasion attempt, and if it had close to zero military impact, its political consequences were seismic, and in precisely the opposite direction to that intended by James and Louis. There was nothing quite like an actual Jacobite military threat to bring the Whigs' routine warnings about the threat of popish tyranny and French invasion vividly to life in the minds of the bulk of the political nation. Nothing could have strengthened the credibility of the muscular pro-war Whiggery of the Junto, and the Junto's credit with Marlborough and Godolphin, more than the abortive invasion.

* * *

While the French forces were being gathered in Dunkirk, Robert Harley had faced a rather more personal attack. The Junto had no intention of easing off just because they had won the battle – at least for the time being – to force him out of office. No one was in any doubt that the Queen harboured fond hopes of resurrecting the idea of a moderate government under Harley in more propitious circumstances. Harley still presented the single biggest threat to Junto predominance in the government, and they knew it. The arrest and investigation of one of Harley's clerks, William Greg, for treasonable correspondence with the French was a chance to extinguish Harley's political career – and indeed his life – for good. So far as the Junto were concerned, if they could find no evidence of Harley's involvement in the scandal, then they would just have to invent some.

Their chief means of implicating Harley was to apply enormous pressure on Greg, dangling in front of him the possibility that, if he were to incriminate Harley, there was a hope of reprieve. A committee of investigation was appointed, stuffed full of the most partisan Whigs, including Wharton, Somers and Halifax, and sent to interrogate Greg in the Tower of London.[3] Edward Harley, Robert's brother, later alleged (on the basis, or so he claimed, of the testimony of Greg himself) that this delegation had offered Greg his life, plus a pension of £200 per year, to accuse Harley.[4] Whether or not that is true, Greg must have known that accusing Harley was his best – indeed, his only – chance of escaping a last, grim trudge to Tyburn. If such an accusation were extracted, there was every chance that Harley would accompany him.

As the investigation proceeded in February 1708, Westminster held its breath. An attempted political assassination was underway which could transform the entire balance of power: no one could imagine the Tory Party without Harley's wiles to aid them in challenging the Junto. Robert's son, Ned, studying at Oxford, was so nervous that he struggled to concentrate on his studies.[5] Francis Atterbury put it bluntly in conversation with Edward: 'your brother's head is upon the block'.[6]

Yet Harley was completely serene. Ever at his best in the most trying circumstances, he maintained a remarkable sang-froid. Edward observed that, during the whole affair, he 'never observed the least discomposure' in his brother.[7] Atterbury, on visiting him, was astonished to find that he 'seems to have no concern about it'.[8] His deep confidence in his own innocence and the just designs of providence helped him remain totally calm.

Amazingly, his confidence was proven to be completely justified. Despite the fact that Greg was a character with a shady past – he had a criminal record and had only escaped conviction for forgery in 1697 by passing the blame off on his wife – he maintained that he had acted alone, due to his sore need for money (he was in debt).[9] No matter what inducements were put before him, to everyone's astonishment, he simply would not implicate Harley. He maintained to the very scaffold that his only prompters were 'the Devil and his necessities'.[10] Indeed, he appears to have been genuinely remorseful, and died, although a traitor, a true Christian penitent. Even a last attempt to suborn him as he was on his way to his execution failed: on the gallows themselves he insisted, in a loud voice, that 'Mr Harley is perfectly innocent as to any knowledge of the correspondence I was engaged in, neither he nor anybody [else] had any hand in it'.[11]

The Whig plot to judicially murder Robert Harley had failed.

The Junto were not, however, unduly downcast. Their petty and anticlimactic report on the Greg affair duly appeared, and managed to prove nothing more damning against Harley than the fact that he was sometimes a bit careless with his paperwork. However, the whole incident was quickly overshadowed by the French invasion plot, which soon decisively turned events in their favour.

With Harley gone and his friends having resigned en masse from the ministry, the government was completely dependent on Whig support. Godolphin and Marlborough were, therefore, at the Junto's mercy: complete capitulation to their demands for high office could only be a matter of time. Furthermore, a general election was due later that year. Harley may have been found innocent of actual treason, but the Junto was quick to use the Jacobite menace to tar him, his moderate friends and the bulk of the Church Party as unpatriotic tools of the popish designs of the Pretender and his Gallic myrmidons. A Lords' address congratulating the Queen on the invasion's failure put the boot in:

We hope Your Majesty will always have a just Detestation of those Persons, who, at a Time when this hellish Attempt was a-foot, and so near breaking out, were using their Endeavours to misrepresent the Actions of Your best Subjects, and create Jealousies in Your Majesty of those who had always served You most eminently and faithfully. And we beseech Your Majesty not to give so just a Cause of Uneasiness to Your People, as to suffer any such hereafter to have Access to Your Royal Person.[12]

The Queen, genuinely shocked at the Jacobite invasion attempt, seemed also to be moving in their direction. In her response to one of the Lords' addresses of support, she appeared to give what amounted to her blessing to the Whigs, saying:

I must always place my chief dependence upon those who have given such repeated proofs of the greatest warmth and concern for the support of the Revolution, the security of my person, and of the Protestant Succession.[13]

This was highly unusual: the Queen had never used such explicitly pro-Revolution language, and even referred to her half-brother as 'the Pretender'. In this favourable political climate, with even the Queen apparently onside, the Junto had every reason to expect an unusually favourable election result.

Parliament was dissolved on 15th April, and the election that ensured was relatively low key, with fewer contested seats and less propaganda published than normal.

It did not, however, lack partisan heat. The Whig case was put in a fiery pamphlet, conceived by Sarah Churchill and jointly written by her and chief Whig propagandist Arthur Maynwaring, entitled *Advice to the Electors of Great Britain*. It was a crudely effective attempt to exploit the French invasion and the Queen's apparently pro-Whig response to it. It argued that

There can be nothing more certain, than that the French would never have undertaken their late dangerous Expedition for Scotland, if they had not receiv'd great Encouragement . . . and very large Promises of Assistance.[14]

This assistance must have come from either the Tories or Whigs – which was more likely? Given that the pamphlet characterised the Tories' goals as having ever been 'to set up an Establishment opposite to Liberty, void of Property, and destructive of all the Ends of human society', the reader was not left in much doubt as to the 'correct' answer.[15]

The main problem for the Tories was that the French invasion scare had made the election close to a single-issue affair, and that issue was their weakest one. Tory propagandists of various hues tried to either plead innocence of any complicity in the invasion or move the election onto more comfortable territory. Charles Leslie in the *Rehearsal* tried to show how the principles of Whig ecclesiastical firebrand Benjamin Hoadly would inexorably lead to the downfall of the Church and revolutionary tumult on the scale of the 1640s, but this tired battle-cry cut little ice in a context where the main threat to internal stability clearly appeared to be from the Jacobites and the French.

Sarah and Maynwaring also made great play of the apparently pro-Whig attitude of the Queen: although they misleadingly attempted to imply that Anne would have agreed with the dark aspersions they cast on the Tory leaders, the fact that she had undoubtedly seemed to utter pro-Whig sentiment must have weighed heavily in the minds of many voters. Surely the Queen, the bulwark of the Church, would not back anyone who was a threat to the Church? Surely the safest option this time was to vote in the Whig interest?

The other problem faced by the Church Party was a certain listlessness and lack of focus. Those who could broadly be described as Tories were still bedevilled by a marked lack of mutual trust between the Harleyites and the High Tories, and on occasion there was even active hostility between the two demoralised factions. As Arthur Maynwaring put it in a letter to Sarah Churchill:

> The natural reason [for lack of Tory energy] seems to be their being broken in their fortunes, & hopeless of succeeding in the projects, which are recommended to them by men that they do not believe. For your Grace may be assured that there is not a word said to them by their new Allies, Harley, St. John . . . that they have more faith in, than your Grace would have.[16]

The Tory campaign lacked energy, and all that most of their candidates managed was the standard 'rally to the Church' cry, which was not uppermost in the mind of many voters.

And so a demoralised and underpowered Tory Party sputtered to defeat in the face of a real, albeit low—key, upswing in Whig sentiment. In some parts of the country, the Tory vote held up better than expected, but overall the tide ran in the favour of the Whigs. Wharton was champing at the bit to press home his party's advantage, and when the election was called he 'departed London as if on a crusade, or on a grand campaign tour of his vast electoral network, which after thirty-five years of construction had reached its absolute peak'.[17] He consolidated his grip over his Buckinghamshire empire and helped to contrive multiple Whig gains, especially in Westmorland and Cumberland. Even Cornwall, traditionally part of Seymour's Tory western empire, saw Whig advances.

As the dust settled, it was clear that, as Sunderland put it, the net result of the election was to be 'the most Wig Parliament has been seen since the revolution'.[18] Estimates for the Whig majority vary between twenty and sixty, but for them to get any overall majority in the House was very unusual in the period. Ominously for the Whigs, however, it was not clear that their victory was based on a large swing in public opinion so much as their superior motivation and organisation in the smaller borough seats; in larger boroughs and county seats the Tories made only minor losses. Even the Whigs' strongest election showing since 1688 represented only a somewhat anaemic victory.

However, the advantages that the Whigs gained from the election were not limited to their victories at the polls. On heading back to his family home when parliament was dissolved in April, Harley's ally St John had found his father, Henry Sr — a vicious old rake— determined to turn him out of the family pocket borough, Wootton Bassett, and stand himself.[19] Whether this was the result of a personal dispute over money or a political disagreement — Henry Sr was, nominally at least, a Whig, and was alleged to have objected to his son resigning with Harley from the government — is unclear.[20] Henry Jr was deeply mortified but shied away from challenging his own father, who managed to contrive to lose the seat (partly because of uproar at his treatment of his son).[21]

Unfortunately for St John, frantic attempts by various allies to find him an alternative parliamentary berth failed: various other possible seats had been stitched up already for others, and he could find no way of getting returned to the new parliament. So Harley would have to face the arduous job of co-ordinating opposition to the Junto in the new parliament without one of his most capable and trusted lieutenants.

With their hand strengthened by the election result, the Junto now intensified their campaign to force their members – particularly Somers and Wharton – into the ministry. When Harley and his allies had resigned in February, they had been replaced by men who, although Whigs, were by no means the Junto's top choices: Henry Boyle had replaced Harley as Secretary of State, and Robert Walpole had stepped into St John's shoes as Secretary at War.

Both men were Lord Treasurer's Whigs: moderate men allied to Godolphin and the court more than the Junto. These men had for some time been the one major factor standing between the Junto and their complete monopoly of political leadership over the Whigs, and for now they gave the Queen an invaluable buffer: she could appoint them and claim she was favouring Whigs, but without thereby handing over excessive power to the Junto.

Even before the election, the Junto had begun to importune the Queen for richer pickings. Their first objective was to force Somers into the cabinet as Lord President, but once the strong Whig showing at the polls became clear, they upped their requests, demanding that Wharton be brought in as Lord Lieutenant of Ireland.

They might have hoped that after the invasion scare – which seemed to have frightened Anne into voicing unusually pro-Whig sentiments – the Queen would be more co-operative than she had been in the past over such Junto demands. However, as the drama died down, the Queen quickly returned to her usual hostility to the Junto. Somers was bad enough – appointing him was, she complained to Marlborough 'utter destruction to me' – but Wharton, the atheistical old sinner, was beyond the pale.[22] She was strengthened in her resolve by her husband, who deeply resented the way that the Junto had used attacks on the Admiralty – and thereby him – as their chief political battering ram in the last parliamentary session, although many suspected that he was being egged on by Marlborough's brother, George Churchill, the man who really ran the Admiralty on the Prince's behalf, who was an unabashed Tory.

The usual pattern – Junto fury, desperation and threats to resign on the part of Godolphin, a spate of letters imploring Anne's co-operation pouring in from Marlborough abroad, all resulting in utter intransigence on the part of the Queen – ensued over the summer of 1708.

Her intransigence turned to anger when Godolphin and the Junto seized upon the old canard of an invitation to the Hanoverians to reside in England in order to pressure her: if she did not submit to the Junto demands, they sketched plans to force a vote on the issue in the next session of parliament. The Queen got wind of this – always a wounding and distressing proposal to her – and immediately wrote to Marlborough, who, although desperate for the Queen to give in, wasn't prepared to go against her personally on such a matter, and the idea died a death, although not without further inflaming the wrath of Anne against the Junto.

The Queen held out over the summer but the question was: how long could she resist the combined pressure of her Lord Treasurer, Marlborough and the Junto?

The Junto were not the only ones busy scheming over the summer of 1708. Harley spent his dog days thinking and plotting at his ancestral home of Brampton Bryan in Herefordshire. His fall from office may have been painful, but it clarified things wonderfully. His relations with Godolphin and his court supporters now totally broken, Harley and his supporters, St John chief among them, quickly realised that they had to find new allies. Their own little gang of 'Harleyites' had held up fairly well in the 1708 election, with the exception of the departure of St John, but they were no more than a handful of MPs.

St John, who now had much leisure to contemplate these things, set out his political thinking in a letter to Harley. There is, he argued, only one thing that 'can redeem us from more than Egyptian bondage':

> There is no hope I am fully convinced but in the Church of England
> party, nor in that neither on the foot it now stands, and without more
> confidence than is yet re-established between them and us. Why do you
> not gain Bromley entirely? The task is not difficult, and by governing him
> without seeming to do so, you will influence them.[23]

St John's view made a lot of sense. The bulk of the Church Party,
who Harley had so effectively divided four years before, were the only
obvious and obtainable source of parliamentary numbers to underpin a
Harleyite anti-Junto strategy. The problem was, of course, that suspicions
still ran deep: many Tories still heartily despised Harley for how he
had undermined them during the epic confrontations over occasional
conformity in 1704.

However, the task was by no means impossible. Bromley, still the key
High Tory figure in the Commons, was a genuinely honest and able man,
and though one with strong convictions, he wasn't adverse to a pragmatic
course. Most Tories knew that Harley had something they desperately
needed, but had lost so calamitously in 1705: the trust and good opinion
of the Queen, who still looked with great disfavour on Rochester and
Nottingham. St John's basic advice was shrewd:

> You broke the party, unite it again, their sufferings have made them wise,
> and whatever piques or jealousies they may entertain at present, as they
> feel the success of better conduct these will wear off, and you will have
> it in your power.[24]

Harley accepted the obvious logic of this argument and that summer
began putting out feelers to the Tory leaders, particularly Bromley.

At first, his overtures were received politely but icily. Bromley complained
in June that Harley 'continues very Mysterious & unintelligible'.[25] Harley
tried to make himself rather clearer in a letter to Bromley in August, talking
darkly of the many outrages that 'the gentlemen of England and the Clergy
have to fear' from the Junto. The Whigs, he wrote:

have taken advantage of the mistakes of others, and tho' they hate one another, yet they unite together to carry on their designs. Why may not the same thing be done to preserve the whole and for good purposes which they do to destroy and overturn everything?[26]

In his reply, Bromley rather acidly remarked that Harley's complaints about lack of Tory unity brought to mind a prayer he had lately heard uttered by a 'blasphemous fellow': 'O God, many are the hands that are lift up against us, but there is one God, it is Thou thyself O Father, who hath done us more mischief than they all.' [27] He wasn't about to easily forgive the man who had broken the Tories in recent memory.

However, this dig notwithstanding, Bromley knew that he probably had little choice but to cautiously ally himself to Harley: the High Tories had no other obvious alternative leader of his skills or statesmanship. Accordingly, he made it clear to Harley that he was 'determined, notwithstanding anything past, to join with you'.[28] The problem was that Harley was being frustratingly vague about the basis of any such co-operation: Bromley and the High Churchmen would need more than woolly platitudes about the clergy and the gentlemen of England to unite them.

The simple fact was that the basis of Harleyite–High Tory co-operation was by no means clear. Though both heartily despised the Junto, the same differences on Church matters that had rent them apart in 1704–5 were still a major barrier to reunification. There was, however, one issue that might just unite them, albeit one that Harley was reluctant to raise directly, at least yet.

By the summer of 1708, the country had been at war for six years continuously, not to mention eight years of conflict under William. Since 1689, it had enjoyed a mere five years of peace out of nineteen. The issue that had originally bound together the renegade Whig Harley and the Tories in the first place had been, of course, 'Country' weariness with the endless continental war of the 1690s, and particularly the taxes needed to sustain it. Many Tories had never been very enthusiastic about the renewed war that began in 1702, but a combination of Louis XIV's outrageous behaviour in 1702 and Marlborough's sparkling string of victories had generally kept

Tory grumblings to a minimum. Even the debate about a blue water versus a land strategy had receded since Blenheim. Both sides used perceived military incompetence or maladministration of the war effort as a political tool, but that had become about the limit of serious political debate about the war.

By 1708, Harley's antennae began to tell him that the tide was close to turning. The British state's ability to revolutionise its fiscal base had allowed it to sustain an extraordinarily long war remarkably well, but even though the squirearchy still hated and detested the four-shilling land tax, it was inadequate to fund the war. The result – as well as an ever-growing national debt – was that the burden fell increasingly on forms of indirect taxation, such as the customs and excise, which made life ever harder for the great mass of common people, who were already afflicted by the bitterly unpopular methods required to raise recruits for the army and navy, such as the infamous press-gang. The situation was not yet unmanageable, but it would only take an end to Marlborough's run of victories, or a bad harvest or two, to tip the country into outright anti-war sentiment.

Harley had never been enthusiastic for war as an end it itself, but had loyally accepted its patriotic necessity since 1702, and indeed had ably served Godolphin and Marlborough in their efforts to wage it for nearly six years. It seems, however, that he had begun to take a more sceptical view by the time he took to his country residence to contemplate affairs in the spring and summer of 1708. Around this time, he drafted a pamphlet setting out his thoughts snappily entitled *Plain English to all who are Honest, or would be so if they knew how.*

In this pamphlet, his bitterness and exasperation with Marlborough and Godolphin combined with his old Country anti-war sentiments to produce a potent new line of argument. It was an attack on 'the Family', by which he meant the Marlboroughs and the Godolphins, who were related by marriage since Godolphin's son Francis had married the Churchills' daughter Henrietta. 'The Family' had come to dominate, with the assistance of the Junto, the entire patronage and administrative system of the state, reducing the Queen to a mere cipher and manipulating parliament so as to effectively undermine its independence. They did this, he argued, at least in part for their own advantage. He wrote:

It is plain that everything they do is calculated to support either the power or profit of one family . . . Thus we see what is to be our lot. As long as these rule, victories obtained are employed for their private advantage and profit, and not to the end of designed for obtaining a safe and honourable peace, but to aggrandise themselves and to prolong that war by which they get such vast wealth, and secure to themselves so much power.[29]

Whatever the truth of this – and it certainly contains at least a kernel of veracity in relation particularly to the Marlboroughs – he had fixed upon a potentially very powerful political argument, and one that could unite him with the High Tories. For now, with the Whigs rampant and the parliamentary situation hopeless, such sentiments had limited appeal. He put his pamphlet away in a drawer and did not publish it. But Harley knew that it would not take much for such arguments to become political gold dust. The country would not tolerate a 'forever war'. He simply had to bide his time and wait for his opportunity.

Harley did not, however, begin the process of reunification with the Tories around about this time in isolation. He never stopped believing in moderate government, in which the Queen would be freed from the tyranny of the parties, and this required more than just Tory support. Any future Harley-led administration would have to find some allies on the Whig side: if he were to become the prisoner of the Tories, he risked subjecting the Queen – and himself – to another bout of 'Egyptian bondage', this time to the Tories. Counterweights – and considerable ones – from the other party were essential. On the face of it, this seemed very difficult. The Junto were his sworn enemies, there were few Country Whigs, and the Lord Treasurer's Whigs were Godolphin's men.

Harley, however, had several aces up his sleeve, the most important of which was the charming Charles Talbot, the Duke of Shrewsbury, nicknamed the 'King of Hearts' for his easy address, good looks and winning way with the ladies. Shrewsbury was a curious figure. Of impeccable Whig credentials – he was one of the signatories to the invitation to William III in 1688 – he was by nature independent-minded. Furthermore, he had effectively retired from politics in 1700 due to (genuine and persistent) ill health: from then until 1706 he lived in Italy, free from the cares of the life of a statesman. This absence cooled his relations with the Junto, who were chagrined at the fact that he had, in their eyes, abandoned his post just as the fierce battle over the impeachments of Somers, Orford and Halifax was looming in 1701.[30]

His absence from the hurly-burly of domestic English politics gave him a different, more detached perspective: he had lost that sense of day-to-day *esprit de corps* that drives much clannish partisanship and which the Junto markedly retained. Furthermore, Harley had taken care to retain a cordial relationship with him throughout his years abroad, doing him little favours and writing to him in warm terms. Arriving in England with an outside perspective, Shrewsbury was shocked at the deleterious impact of the war on everyday life, and was much more inclined to sue for peace as early as possible than most other Whigs.

By May 1708, Harley was arranging to meet Shrewsbury. They shared a preference for moderation and political temperance, as well as antiquarian passions for book collecting and manuscripts, and Harley quickly gained him as an ally. Given that his pro-Revolution credentials were beyond question and he was well-liked by the Queen, Shrewsbury was a very useful asset for Harley. Harley also put out renewed feelers to the Whigs who had almost come over to him in his attempt to oust Godolphin earlier that year — the Duke of Newcastle and the Earl of Somerset — and they were not entirely unreceptive.

The first building blocks of Harley's — and with him, the Tories' — political recovery had been laid.

Events in the short term, however, only made Harley's job more difficult.

Firstly, Marlborough proved himself once again to be apparently invincible on the battlefield. On 11th July, he routed the French at the battle of Oudenarde, a victory on the scale of Blenheim. It opened up an advance on heavily fortified Lille, the last key obstacle to a march into the heart of France and thenceforth onto Paris. By October, Lille had fallen, and the path to total victory seemed open, even if it would have to wait for the next campaigning season. France, Europe's only superpower, whom most had assumed when the war began in 1702 to be unbeatable, seemed to be at the allies' mercy. While the 'Family' kept on delivering such triumphs, Harley could do little but bide his time.

Nonetheless, as yet the Junto had not yet successfully 'forced the chamber': most of their leading figures remained out of office due to the obstinate opposition of the Queen.

So over the course of the summer and autumn of 1708, the Junto applied pressure with every means at their disposal. They threatened to run their own Speaker candidate against Godolphin's choice, which risked letting Bromley, the Tory choice, in. They then decided to use the issue of supposed Admiralty underperformance as their main pretext, telling Godolphin that it was 'impossible for them . . . to go any longer with the court upon the foot things are at present', because the state of the government, particularly the management of the navy, 'are all of a piece, as much tory, and as wrong if Lord Rochester and Lord Nottingham were at the head of everything'.[31] Unless Prince George was replaced at the Admiralty with their preferred choice, the Earl of Pembroke (a cipher who could hold the position until they could force Orford, the Junto naval expert, into office), and Somers and Wharton admitted to the ministry, they would go into outright opposition. They were tired of Godolphin's 'promises and words' which came to nothing, 'and . . . therefore they must take their measures, till this thing was actually done'.[32]

There is even a hint that Wharton resorted to out-and-out blackmail. Godolphin had, like many key political figures looking for an insurance policy, corresponded in friendly terms with the Jacobite court in the 1690s, an accusation that had been raised in parliament in 1705 by an outspoken Tory MP, Charles Caesar. One account suggests that Wharton had acquired one of Godolphin's letters to James II around this time and threatened to make it public unless Godolphin overcame the resistance of the Queen and secured agreement to their ultimatum.[33] It is impossible to know whether this is true, but if so it must have made Godolphin, who was already at his wit's end, frantic.

In October, the dam began to crack. The Queen was stubborn, but even she couldn't ignore the reality that her government would not enjoy the confidence of parliament when it met in November. She made her first step – a typically reluctant concession – on 22nd October when she bowed to Junto demands and agreed to appoint the Whig candidate as attorney general. The Whigs, who had hitherto resisted the Junto's leadership and co-operated with Godolphin and most prominently Robert Walpole, began to conclude that it was better to court the rising interest and made their peace with the Junto. Godolphin no longer had the political cover to resist the Whig advance.

It was, however, a personal tragedy that finally broke the Queen's resistance. The very day after she agreed to give in to the Whigs over the attorney generalship, her husband Prince George fell seriously ill. The Queen personally nursed him, but it was to no avail. He declined rapidly and died on the 28th.

In a life marked by innumerable tragedies, this one was perhaps the most devastating. Everyone else might have thought of her husband as an affable but empty-headed old duffer, but Anne adored him, and he had been her constant and immovable confidante and comforter. Separated from Harley, bullied by the Junto, constantly harassed by Godolphin and Sarah, and without her faithful companion, she felt almost totally alone and was inconsolable with grief. Her resolve vanished.

The Whigs were gleeful: 'You will hear by this post the news of the Prince's death', wrote Sunderland to a Whig Admiral, '. . . it opens an easy way to have everything put upon a right foot'.[34] They weren't wrong. Although she had enough spirit to delay the changes formally until late November, the Junto got everything they wanted: Pembroke got the Admiralty, Wharton became Lord Lieutenant of Ireland and Somers became Lord President of the Council.

The Junto had taken their biggest single step so far to forcing single-party government on a reluctant Queen: the chamber had well and truly been 'forced' and their ascendancy was, for the time being, unquestioned.

A whole other story had been going on under the surface as the Junto fought and won the battle for dominance of the ministry over the course of 1708.[35]

The fall of Harley had made it clear that, while Britain remained at war, any permutation of party strength and personnel in a ministry depended, in

'The Committee or Popery in Masquerade', Tory satirical print from a pamphlet by Roger L'Estrange.
Bridgeman Images)

'The Prospect of a Popish Successor', a Whig satirical print depicting the supposed consequences of ames II becoming King, published during the Exclusion Crisis. (© *The Trustees of the British Museum*)

(above left) Thomas Osborne, the Earl of Danby (later the Marquess of Carmarthen and Duke of Leeds): 'the First Tory'. (Wikipedia)

(above right) Anthony Ashley Cooper, 1st Earl of Shaftesbury, Whig leader during the Exclusion Crisis. (Print Collector / Getty Images)

(left) King James II, shortly after his 'abdication' in 1688. (Bridgeman Images)

Willem Hendrik van Oranje,
Stadtholder of the Dutch Republic,
latterly King William III.
(Fine Art / Getty Images)

Laurence Hyde, 1st Earl of
Rochester, High Tory Leader.
(Wikipedia)

Daniel Finch, 2nd Earl of Nottingham, High Tory Leader.
(Wikipedia)

Thomas Wharton, 1st Earl (later Marquess) of Wharton, Junto Lord.
(Prisma Archivo / Alamy Stock Images)

John Somers, 1st Baron Somers, Junto Lord.
(The Print Collector / Getty Images)

Queen Anne.
(Robert Aledxander / Getty Images)

(above) John Churchill, 1st Duke of Marlborough and Sarah Churchill, Duchess of Marlborough.

(The Print Collector / Getty Images)

(left) Robert Harley, Earl of Oxford and Mortimer, Lord Treasurer 1711–1714.

(Wikipedia)

Henry St. John, Viscount Bolingbroke, Tory Secretary of State 1710–1714.
(Universal History Archive / Getty Images)

(left) A scene from the trial of Dr Henry Sacheverell. *(Ken Welsh / Design Pics / Universal Images Group via Getty Images)*

(below) Commemorative earthenware dish of Dr Henry Sacheverell.
(Fitzwilliam Museum / Bridgeman Images)

Jonathan Swift, chief Tory propagandist, 1710–11.
(The Print Collector / Getty Images)

Satirical Print of Viscount Bolingbroke signing papers related to the Treaty of Utrecht using his mistress' arse as a writing desk.
(© The Trustees of the British Museum)

the final analysis, on the consent of Marlborough. He remained the lynchpin of the entire military and political strength of the government. Godolphin was by no means indispensable – if Marlborough had backed Harley at the fatal point in January–February 1708, Harley would have won the day and Godolphin would have had to accept his defenestration as a fait accompli. But a ministry without Marlborough's backing was doomed.

Marlborough had in effect – albeit very reluctantly – made his choice: he had thrown his lot in with the Junto. As he put it in a letter to his wife, 'the principles of the whigs are for the good of England, and . . . if the tories had the power, they would not only destroy England, but also the liberties of Europe'.[36] Any lingering idea that he was in some sense a Tory, or 'above party politics', had been dispelled, even though, conscious of the Queen's hatred of the Junto, he judged it unwise to drive her too hard. This, combined with his own distaste for party politics, left him in a ticklish position: backing the Junto in reality, but feeling far from comfortable about it. However, at least in the short term, his and the Junto's position seemed to be consolidated by Oudenarde, despite Tory attempts to denigrate him and to give the credit for recent military success to one of their own supporters, Major-General Webb.[37] Marlborough appeared militarily and politically secure.

However, there was another battlefield that was steadily undermining Marlborough, even as the general course of public events appeared to still be going his way: the home front. Marlborough might be able to master his Dutch allies and humble the French, but reining in his increasingly intemperate wife was quite beyond him.

Over the course of 1708, relations between Anne and Sarah, which had deteriorated steadily since Anne's accession to the throne, reached new lows.

Some of the problem stemmed from the perceived influence of Abigail Hill, lady of the bedchamber, on the Queen. Abigail had, ironically, been appointed back in 1697 on the basis of Sarah's patronage, as she was actually her poor cousin, and for a while she was Sarah's loyal lieutenant. However, as the Queen became disenchanted with Sarah, who was increasingly absent from court, she became more dependent on Abigail and started to show some signs of personal favour to her – helping her brother John and then suitor, Samuel Masham, to gain army appointments, and then gifting her a generous dowry when she married and became Abigail Masham in 1707.

Sarah was madly jealous of such a rival and became paranoid that Abigail was replacing her in the Queen's affections, but the salient political factor was that Abigail was also a distant cousin of none other than Robert Harley. Sarah became ever more convinced that Abigail was Harley's mole at court, pulling strings in the Harleyite and Tory interest in Machiavellian style: as she wrote when she later heard about the favours that the Queen lavished on Abigail, 'I . . . discovered then beyond all dispute Mr. Harley's correspondence and interest at Court by means of this woman'.[38]

In reality, Sarah grossly exaggerated. Mrs Masham did correspond with Harley and was undoubtedly his informer of goings on at court, and an intermediary between Harley and Anne. The truth was, however, that Abigail was of too lowly a social status to be a major political player at court, and Harley had already independently established himself as a favourite of the Queen. There is no doubt that the Queen valued Abigail's personal company more and more: Abigail gave her quiet, easy companionship rather than the incessant drama offered by Sarah. None of this made her politically significant, however.

Sarah was convinced otherwise. In March 1708, she discovered that the Queen had allowed Abigail to move into some rooms that were technically part of one of Sarah's lodgings at Kensington. Sarah hardly ever used this accommodation, but she took this as a terrible insult and a furious argument ensued. This incident heightened her suspicions that, with Harley now out of office, Abigail must be worming her way further into the Queen's affections as a Tory agent of Harley. It made her more determined than ever to bully the Queen into favouring the Junto, break Anne's connections to Harley (including through Abigail) and to make her husband support her in this endeavour.

She was accompanied in this mission by her closest political crony, Arthur Maynwaring, who shamelessly egged Sarah on to ever greater excesses of temper and recklessness. As well as jointly writing *Advice to the Electors of Great Britain* to put forward the Whig case in the 1708 election, they began to cabal together to persuade the Queen to dismiss Abigail and to intimidate Abigail herself. They began to send anonymous threatening letters to Abigail, making it clear what her likely fate was if she continued to defy them:

> You cannot but have heard your master Harley often talk of the Greeks and Romans because he is always showing his small learning out of season and [he will] tell you how those great and wise nations proceeded against persons that they thought endangered their state. Death was always the reward of such people . . . and if you and your oracle H are not traitors to this state 'tis certain there never were any.[39]

They even drafted a long anonymous letter to the Queen attacking her for allowing Harley and Abigail, the latter of whom they described as 'a little shuffling wretch, whose character is too bad to be describ'd', to retain influence, although even they thought better of sending it.[40] Instead Sarah assailed Marlborough with letters pressuring him to move against them too, and lectured the Queen on the impropriety of chambermaids being royal confidantes.

Things came to a bitter head in July. As the Queen still refused to buckle to the Junto, Sarah showed her a letter she had received from Marlborough just after the battle of Oudenarde, in which he had said 'you must give thankes to God for his goodness in protecting and making me the instrument of so much happyness to the Queen and nation, if she will please to make use of itt'.[41] His meaning was clear: unless the Queen gave into Junto demands, it would be impossible to capitalise on his victory and push the war to a triumphant conclusion.

This provoked an exchange of letters between the Queen and Marlborough in which the latter lectured the Queen on her Christian duty to forgive the Junto men, and darkly warned her against the influence of advisers other than him and Godolphin, by which he obviously meant Harley and Masham (Marlborough had also become convinced of Masham's baleful influence). The Queen was not impressed and insisted that she would not give in to 'the five tyrannizing Lords'.[42] Her relationship with Sarah may have been in freefall, but she was scarcely in better humour with her husband.

Sarah's anger against the Queen reached an extraordinary pitch, and in late July she crossed the line in an extraordinary way. Arthur Maynwaring had, shortly before, published a libellous squib, entitled 'A New Ballad to the tune of Fair Rosamond', strongly implying that the Queen's relationship with Masham went beyond the boundaries of propriety:

When as Queen Anne of great renown
Great Britain's sceptre swayed
Beside the Church she dearly loved
A dirty chambermaid

O Abigail that was her name
She starched and stitched full well
But how she pierced this royal heart
No mortal man can tell

However for sweet service done
And causes of great weight
Her royal mistress made her, Oh!
 A minister of state

Her secretary she was not
Because she could not write
But had the conduct and the care
Of some dark deeds at night.[43]

Not only did Sarah show these verses to the Queen, for good measure she then proceeded to directly accuse the Queen of lesbianism herself. Having 'so great a passion for such a woman' must, she argued in a letter to Anne, besmirch her good name, as 'there can bee no great reputation in a thing so strange & unaccountable . . . nor can I think the having noe inclination for any but of one's own sex is enough to maintain such a character as I wish may still bee yours'.[44] She also threatened her, writing that any second attempt to sack Marlborough and Godolphin 'will certainly cost you dearer than the last'.[45]

The Queen, unsurprisingly, did not reply to this extraordinary outburst, and never forgave Sarah for it. Communication between them ceased until they had to interact in August to attend the thanksgiving service for the victory at Oudenarde: the Queen refused to wear the jewels that Sarah had suggested (she was still formally Mistress of the Robes and responsible for the Queen's attire), and they had another blistering row in the carriage on the way to St Paul's.

An even worse act of spite and scorn came in the aftermath of Prince George's death, when Sarah went out of her way to mock the Queen in her mourning and imply that her sorrow was fake. She jeered that the Queen was eating a bit too heartily for someone supposedly inconsolable with grief. She hinted that Anne merely 'fancied she loved him' and was so 'very hard' that she didn't even cry.[46] She even removed a portrait of the Prince that was hanging in the Queen's bedchamber.

The idea that the Queen's grief was insincere was ludicrous. No other contemporary doubted her misery and deep mourning. Sarah had simply decided, in her frustration and bitterness that Anne had *dared* to defy her tyrannical whims, to wound and insult her at her most sensitive point, and to torture a woman whom everyone knew had loved her husband sincerely and dearly.

It was one of many acts of gross folly on her part, acts that cumulatively destroyed her relationship with the Queen. Anne could not dismiss her, because that would be seen as a decisive move against her husband, and it was as yet unthinkable to sack him. But when Sarah left the court in December 1708, 'Mrs Morley and Mrs Freeman' were completely and finally estranged.

This was far more than a soul-destroying personal feud between two old friends. Every word of contempt, every insult, every nasty little dig fed the Queen's quiet but absolute determination that, sooner or later, she would rid herself not only of Sarah, but of the entire Marlborough—Godolphin connexion, 'the Family', and with them the hated Whigs who mercilessly bullied her and drove Sarah on in her folly and her vituperation. Anne knew that she would have to wait for her chance, but she would not tolerate her bondage for ever.

* * *

The chill that settled on the Queen's heart as she mourned George and had to endure being dictated to by men like Wharton was more than matched by the teeth-chattering winter of 1708–9. The coldest snap in living memory, it became known as the 'Great Frost'. On Christmas Eve 1708 it began to freeze: snow fell continually for a fortnight, and then early in January the Thames froze over so comprehensively that a frost fair was held on the ice. The arctic conditions continued well into March. One aristocrat wrote the following to her brother:

> If I might tell you all the stories are daily brought in of accidents accationed by the Great Frost I might fill sheets, as children drown upon the Thames, post-boys being brought in by their horses to their stages frose to their horses stone dead. . .[47]

The ordinary people, already squeezed by years of high taxes and economic dislocation, suffered worst. Many simply froze to death in their homes. Travel became nigh on impossible. It was a winter that no one who endured it would ever forget.[48]

Tory prospects in the parliamentary session of 1708–9 were a little warmer – but not much. The Speaker election was a damp squib after the Junto, satisfied by the Queen's concessions to them, dropped their mooted spoiler candidate. The Tories didn't even take it to a vote. However, Harley had offered to back the Tory candidate Bromley, and irrelevant as it was, it signalled that Tory reunification was proceeding, albeit slowly.[49]

It was a reunification that was to be handicapped, however, by the fact that in a piece of partisan kneecapping seen as dubious even by many at the time, one of Harley's key parliamentary lieutenants – star lawyer Sir Simon Harcourt – was removed on petition. Harley would face the new Whig-dominated parliament with neither Harcourt nor St John to assist him.

However, Harley did make some moderate progress in the course of the session, helping to give the Whigs more discomfit than might have been expected. When the government attempted to bring Scottish treason laws into line with harsher English ones, in response to the ease with which some Jacobites involved with the invasion attempt had escaped prosecution, it quickly found itself opposed by angry Scottish parliamentarians, who saw it as against the spirit of the Union. They were backed by the Tories and even some Country Whigs. Although the bill was eventually passed, the government/Junto majority was very narrow. Harley skilfully played on the sympathies of Tories and Country backbenchers to advance an amendment to make the legislation less repressive, and succeeded in making the Whigs sweat. He was still a formidable parliamentary operator.

In January, he began to pull on a crucial thread that would eventually help to unravel the entire Whig fabric. Marlborough was apparently on the verge of victory against France – but that was not the whole story. The war in Spain was a running sore, and the question of mismanagement in that theatre had not gone away. Harley again raised these thorny questions in a knowledgeable speech, and appealed to backbench sentiment by implying that vast sums of taxpayers' money were being wasted on fighting a war that largely redounded to the benefit of the Habsburgs. Although he didn't openly question the 'No Peace without Spain' policy that had been adopted with Tory support in December 1707, he certainly began to sow the seeds of doubt – and with very good reason, as events were about to prove.

Harley's manoeuvring could not hide the fact that the Whigs, for the first time in many years, held a comfortable numerical advantage in the Commons, to add to their existing strength in the Lords. This gave them the opportunity to advance several longstanding political priorities. One of these was a bill to allow for the naturalisation of foreign Protestants who came to England, introduced in January 1709. This was no abstract issue, for war, economic distress and in some cases religious persecution created a considerable impetus for many Protestants in continental Europe to attempt to flee.[50]

The Whigs, who had advocated a similar measure in the 1704–5 parliamentary session, saw the measure as a no-brainer. Their major argument was that immigration was good for the economy: as they put it, 'the increase of people is a means of advancing the wealth and strength of a nation'.[51] Previous influxes of French Huguenot refugees, prompted particularly by French state persecution in the 1680s, had, they argued, been a real boon:

'by the industry of the said refugees, new manufactures had been set up, and others improved, to the great advancement of trade, and the total turning the balance thereof, to the prejudice of France, and benefit of this nation'.[52] They had also invested heavily in government debt, subscribing to the tune of £500,000 to the Bank of England. Why not reward and encourage immigration if it contributed so much to national wealth? One could combine such practical advantages with the warm glow that comes from providing humanitarian assistance to those fleeing persecution. The fact that they were brave Protestants fleeing devilish papists did no harm to their cause either.

It wasn't long before these arguments were put to the test. In early May, 852 refugees from the Palatinate, a western German principality near the Rhine, arrived, and they kept coming: over the summer of 1709, somewhere around 10,000–13,000 of the 'Poor Palatines', as sympathetic observers dubbed them, poured into England.

It was by no means only the passing of the Naturalisation Act that precipitated this influx. Nor was it primarily religious persecution: the Protestants of the Palatinate were generally tolerated, to at least a minimal extent, by their Catholic ruler. The biggest factor was the simple fact of suffering and disruption caused by living in a war zone: the Palatinate was the victim of frequent French incursions and pillaging, and their situation was brought to a pitch of particular misery by the devastating winter of 1708–9. It also seems that some of them were given encouragement by various land speculators and co-religionists on the basis that coming to England was the first step on a journey to set up new lives in the American colonies. The fact that a small group of Palatines had been given generous charitable assistance by Queen Anne personally when they had arrived in 1708 may also have been a factor.

As the waves of Palatines arrived over the summer it quickly became clear that England in general, and London in particular (where most of them came initially), was not in a great state to be supporting the refugees, most of whom were completely destitute. This was partly because provision for even the native poor was so rudimentary and the state machinery to provide accommodation and subsistence for thousands of newcomers basically non-existent, and partly because economic distress and shortages had battered

England itself as a result of the terrible winter and poor harvest, rendering it even less able to absorb the newcomers than usual. The simple fact was that in the context of 1709, the arrival of over 10,000 people who had little more than the rags they stood up in was a massive social problem: given the population of London then, it was the equivalent of 150,000 penniless refugees descending on London over the course of one summer today.

In the short term, the Queen personally stepped in again to support the Palatines, gifting 40 shillings per day per hundred refugees for subsistence, and giving them permission to stay in various naval dockyards and warehouses around the River Thames. An appeal for funds was organised through the churches and chapels and the Queen appointed commissioners to distribute the funds thereby raised, which were considerable. Nonetheless, this hastily improvised system was little better than a temporary stopgap.

The Tories, who had opposed the Naturalisation Bill, were not slow to exploit the obvious difficulties raised by expecting London, and subsequently perhaps the whole country, to accommodate the Palatines. They had predicted from the first that the economic consequences of sudden mass immigration would not be as positive as the Whigs assumed. A paper circulated during the original parliamentary debate had opined:

> That it was more than probable, that the greatest number that would come over, would be of poor people, which would be of fatal consequence with respect to the many poor industrious families, who would thereby be reduced to the uttermost straits; it being evident, that no hands were wanted to carry on our manufactures, from the great quantities that lay on hand, their cheapness, and the lowness of wages now given.[53]

They would therefore, the paper argued, be likely to fall as a charge on the parishes, which scarcely needed the extra expense in a time of general dearth and want. Although this may have been obviated in the short term by private and regal charity, this would not last for long.

When the Palatines actually started to arrive, the Tory anti-immigration argument started to gain serious traction among the poorer classes of London. Tory candidates in elections (particularly the heated general election held in the ensuing year, 1710) were not above exploiting xenophobic sentiments, but the basic moral intuition of the Tory campaign was not unreasonable, and they were merely reflecting the reality of what many poor Londoners already thought. One pamphlet summed it up pithily:

> I think our Charity ought to begin at Home, both in Peace and War, before we extend it to our Neighbours. I confess we are commanded to love them as ourselves, but to love them better, will be counted Madness: The Palatines may be Poor enough, but their coming hither can never make us Rich (as has too often been learnedly worded) when we had so many before, we could not tell what to do with them.[54]

It simply seemed perverse to many to accept a large number of refugees when plenty of poor Londoners were close to starving themselves; the author of the same pamphlet asked, how does it 'consist with our Negligence for many Year last past, in not providing for our own Poor?'[55]

The main principled thrust of the Tory argument was, however – unsurprisingly – religious in character. So far as the Church Party were concerned, the Palatine influx amounted to the importation of a fresh load of Dissenters, Palatine Protestants being mainly Calvinists and Lutherans. Pan-Protestant solidarity did not cut much ice with the Church Party, and when it transpired that a not inconsiderable number of them were, in fact, not even Protestants – perhaps as many as 2,000 were Roman Catholics – it gave their arguments a force that it was hard for the Whigs to dismiss entirely.

As it transpired, this was a moot point, because the Palatine exodus to England ended in farce. The government decided instead to try to settle them piecemeal across the country, offering parishes 'a bounty of £5 for every Palatine they would receive'.[56] Very few took them up on the offer, although the Queen, as usual, did her bit, giving them several hundred jobs, including as royal gardeners. The rest ended up either being shipped to Ireland, or more distant colonies. These schemes were chaotic, and most of the Palatines who had been sent to Ireland eventually decided to take their chances and actually returned to their homeland. Many of those who had temporarily settled in England had followed their lead by 1712.

The whole episode ended so shambolically for various reasons, but one of them related to the weakness of the economic argument made by the Whigs when advocating the Naturalisation Act. Most of the Palatines were agricultural workers, and a large percentage of them had been employed on vineyards.[57] They were not skilled silk weavers or wealthy merchants, as many of the Huguenots had been. There wasn't much call for experts in the production of wine in England. They simply added to the ranks of unskilled labour when there wasn't much demand for it. Furthermore, being unable to speak English, it was very hard for them to integrate. This was interpreted by many – including some increasingly disillusioned Whigs – as mere perversity and presumption on their part. One staunch Whig reflected bitterly:

> The Palatines, I fear, will not come up to ye expectations ye charitable had of ym; of ye number sent me I am sorry to say how very few are likely to answer. The men lazy, very expecting, unthinking, & without ye least tollerable concern for ye good of those who are willing to employ 'em.[58]

This was probably an unfair reflection on some very disorientated and weary refugees stuck in a strange land, but nothing could alter the reality that the Palatine episode had been a poorly thought through Whig-sponsored fiasco. Its immediate political impact would be muffled, but they had done themselves no favours so far as public opinion was concerned. It would come back to haunt them.

Nonetheless, in the short term the Whigs were united and confident on the issue that underpinned their entire overall strategy: foreign policy. By March 1709, the French war effort seemed to be in the process of total collapse. The 'Great Freeze' had affected them too: their crops failed and the strain of such meteorological rigours contributed to their reaching a point of social and financial catastrophe. Mighty a state as they were, fighting a four-front war for year upon year against a surprisingly effective militarily coalition had taken its toll. Bankruptcy loomed: Louis XIV even resorted to melting down his silver furniture to stave off insolvency, while peasants starved to death in the fields. Feelers were put out for peace by a chastened France.[59]

In parliament in March, the minimum British terms for such a peace were spelled out, terms soon enshrined in the 'preliminary articles' of peace agreed between Britain and its allies in May. They included complete French surrender over Spain, with no compensation at all for the Bourbon claimant Philip V (who was, we should recall, at the time firmly in control of the majority of Spain), as well as vast territorial, trading and commercial concessions for the allies, recognition of the Hanoverian succession and expulsion of the Pretender by France, and the demolition of the fortifications at Dunkirk. Given that Marlborough seemed to be poised to invade France and capture Paris, such harsh terms were hardly surprising. It looked like Louis had no choice but to accept them.[60]

Marlborough was convinced that total victory was just around the corner, but at the same time he was worried that his prestige, particularly with the Queen, chipped away by his support for the Junto's demands for office and his wife's antics, was on the wane. If Anne ever did find a way to turf out the Whigs and seek political solace in the tempting embraces of Harley, it seemed increasingly likely that his position would be very shaky. Peace looked likely to reduce his prestige and power anyway. So, to secure both his short-term and long-term position, he sought from the Queen a fresh sign of her confidence: in around March 1709, he requested that she make him captain-general for life.[61]

This was a terrible mistake, as several advisers (Cowper and his own secretary James Craggs) advised him it would be. Anne, hardly slow to heap accolades on him in the past, was in no mood to do so now: the very reasons that made Marlborough anxious about his standing with Anne made her unlikely to grant his request. In any case, there were more solid reasons for her to be not only reluctant, but outright disturbed.

England's distaste for and distrust of a standing army had not gone away overnight: in fact, the enormous expansion of military bureaucracy and spending that had taken place during the course of the long war with France had sharpened it. Englishmen saw a successful soldier as, at best, a distasteful necessity, and they were apt to detest one who forgot his place. Oliver Cromwell cast a long shadow: any hint of an army leader yearning for excessive power was seen with extreme suspicion. If Marlborough was to be made what was in effect the supreme commander of the army for life, then he would be beyond the constitutional control of the Crown or parliament. The request might be seen in a charitable light as misguided, but a less sympathetic observer might see it in rather more sinister terms.

The Queen temporised and asked for advice from Somers, her new Lord President and perhaps England's greatest legal mind. He – a man of considerably more integrity than a partisan cynic such as Wharton – advised her against such an unprecedented step. She delayed giving Marlborough any definite answer, but soon after intervened in several cases of military discipline against the wishes of the Duke (including to ensure that a convicted rapist was stripped of his commission). The message was clear: she, not a mere upstart called John Churchill, was the ultimate authority, including on military matters.

Marlborough was on ice considerably thinner than that which, at that very moment, was making the Thames into England's biggest skating rink. Before long it would start to creak.

The Duke was soon proved wrong on another matter: the inevitability of French submission and a favourable peace.

The shift in the balance of power of the government in favour of the Junto meant that they were in a position to effectively dictate British foreign policy to a cowed and increasingly passive Godolphin. The 'five tyrannising lords' were in no mood for anything other than total victory. They feared the Dutch, wearied by war and desperate for peace, would abandon the allies' united front and seek for peace on separate (and less harsh) terms. So they decided to tie the Dutch into a hardline set of peace terms by promising them a Barrier Treaty. This stipulated which towns and fortresses on the French-Dutch border – a 'barrier' against future French aggression – the Dutch could hope to claim once peace was signed. The barrier offered was very generous to the Dutch, promising them a whole range of territorial gains that went well beyond what was needed for a military barrier.

The general peace terms were designed to utterly smash French power, and with it even the tiniest sliver of a chance of a Stuart Restoration. The sticking point was Spain: the Junto would not accept anything short of the total withdrawal of the Bourbon claimant from Spain. The Junto, in co-operation with their diplomatic representative Lord Townshend, who joined Marlborough to negotiate the peace in The Hague, ruthlessly enforced their unyieldingly harsh policy, at which even Marlborough had begun to baulk.

The problem was that Louis XIV was, in fact, in no position to guarantee what was being demanded of him. His grandson, Philip V, was in firm control of most of Spain, the one scene of recent allied military failure, and had no intention of giving up his kingdom, whether his grandfather asked nicely or not.

The allied solution to this problem was the notorious Article 37 of the proposed peace conditions. It asked Louis to agree that, if Philip V had not unilaterally withdrawn from Spain within two months of any peace treaty being passed, he would join with the allies to force Philip out. In effect, it asked him to wage war on his own grandson.

Louis, desperate indeed, was prepared to swallow the other onerous and humiliating peace terms – but not, never, that. He saw it as so dishonourable, so contrary to natural and familial affections, that, no matter how terrible his situation, it must be rejected. The Junto and the duumvirs calculated that, no matter how hard it may be to swallow, Louis would have no choice but to agree to it. They were wrong.

The French sovereign decided that he had nothing to lose: so ludicrous were the terms that even in his hour of desperate weakness he could not accept them. In early June, he publicly rejected the proposed peace and made a rousing plea to his countrymen in a declaration distributed across his kingdom. He declared that:

> I have considered proposals for peace and no one has done more than I to secure it . . . I can no longer see any alternative to take, other than to prepare to defend ourselves. To make [the allies] see that a united France is greater than all the powers assembled by force and artifice to overwhelm it.[62]

As his countrymen might have put it some eighty-odd years later: *aux armes, citoyens!*

The Junto and Godolphin looked upon this with equanimity. The French were starving to death, unable to feed their armies and in total disarray. These, they concluded, were empty words. One last shattering blow inflicted on the wounded Gallic beast would put them in a position to impose whatever terms they liked on a bloodied and beaten foe.

They were wrong again.

Louis appointed the only man who could save France: Marshal Claude Louis Hector de Villars. Villars mixed extraordinary, swaggering energy and confidence, even in the face of apparently insurmountable odds, with organisational genius and the confidence of his men. Somehow, he accomplished a miracle: he cobbled together a serviceable army out of a ragtag band of starving peasants; begged, stole and borrowed bread to feed them; and gave France a fighting, if remote, chance of defending itself against Marlborough's amassed ranks.[63]

When the autumn campaign began, after a hard and bloody siege of the fortress of Tournai, Marlborough spotted his chance to engage Villars in what he hoped would be one last definitive victory. With only one major army left, the French could not afford another Blenheim or Ramillies; they were down to their last line of defence. Marlborough's plan was to launch a massive and definitive attack against Villars's force, which was entrenched in a gap between two woods not far south of Mons, near a tiny hamlet called Malplaquet. By 10th September, Marlborough's army was strong enough to strike. However, more troops were on their way, and the decision was taken to wait for them. The battle was delayed by a day.

It was a catastrophic decision. Every hour gave the French more time to fortify their position. Not only had the Gallic battalions been roused by Villars, but the legendary French commander Louis-François de Boufflers, whose heroics had galvanised Louis's forces many times before, arrived and agreed to serve under Villars. French morale was boosted further.

The result was a tremendously bloody and hard-fought stalemate. This time, there was to be no rout. After eight hours of brutal fighting, Boufflers (Villars having been injured) ordered a general retreat. The French army came close to collapse under intense pressure, but it held firm and withdrew in an orderly fashion, its formations intact.

Marlborough claimed victory and not completely unreasonably. He had driven the French out of a strong position, and not long after the allied armies took Mons. He wrote to Sarah: 'God almighty be praised, it is now in our powers to have what peace wee please'.[64]

He was, however, deluding himself. The allies had lost something in the order of 20,000–25,000 troops, the French around 12,000–15,000, but far more important was the simple fact that the French had demonstrated that they were not defeated: their will to resist had been tried and not found wanting. Pride and fighting spirit, and, more importantly, morale had been restored. If the allies wanted to take Paris, it was now abundantly clear that it would not happen without more bloody, and possibly protracted, fighting.

And bloody was the word. Malplaquet quickly became a byword for slaughter. One witness – an experienced officer named Major Blackader – claimed that 'in all my life, I have not seen the dead bodies lie so thick as they were in some places among the retrenchments'.[65] A senior British commander remarked that 'As to the dead and wounded . . . no two battles this war could furnish the like number . . . [the dead] lie as thick as ever you saw a flock of sheep'.[66] On hearing the news, Queen Anne is supposed to have reacted by asking, in anguished tones, 'When will this bloodshed ever cease?'[67]

This last story may well be apocryphal, but it captured the political feeling of the moment as news of the massacre filtered through to England. A very advantageous peace had been on the table months earlier, and yet – or so many felt – the Junto and the duumvirs had contemptuously scorned it on the basis of the arrogant – and, as it turned out, false – assumption that the French had no more resistance left to muster. Tens of thousands had died as a result, and, what was psychologically more important, an imminent peace had suddenly been snatched away, at least for the moment.

A lengthy war began to seem, in the minds of many Englishmen who had never been that keen on the whole business in the first place, like a forever war. Furthermore, the Duke's run of extraordinary martial successes had been halted. The battle was in fact, in military terms, no disaster, but after the extravagant and unambiguous triumphs of Blenheim, Ramillies and Oudenarde, the score draw at Malplaquet seemed almost like a defeat. Marlborough was no longer an invincible conqueror.

In fact, he would never lead his armies into a major battle again.

While Marlborough contended with French forces in the Spanish Netherlands, relations between the Queen and Sarah had once again taken a turn for the worse.[68]

The Queen, incensed at Sarah's behaviour the previous year, could not sack her chief commander's wife, so she instead chose to largely ignore her and override the traditional authority that Sarah as Mistress of the Robes (among other titles) would usually have held, particularly over appointments to the royal household. This came to a head in July, when the Queen appointed a bedchamber woman of her own, ignoring Sarah's candidate. Predictably, Sarah reacted by firing off a series of highly disrespectful epistolary tirades to her sovereign, culminating in an extraordinary self-justifying narrative of relations between the two women in October, which, among other things, lectured the Queen on her spiritual discipline and implied that Mrs Masham, as well as dominating her, was perhaps also something more ('such things can proceed from nothing byt extravagant passion').[69]

Marlborough, only semi-conscious of the increasingly outrageous nature of Sarah's behaviour, waded into this undignified row with several letters to the Queen decrying 'the several indignitys' that Mrs Masham had (supposedly) inflicted on his wife with Anne's blessing; accusing Anne of being a puppet of Harley and Mrs Masham; and, for good measure, making a rather whiny reference to her refusal to offer him the captain-generalcy for life.[70] He finished by threatening to resign as soon as the war was over.[71]

The imprudence (and impudence) of Sarah's behaviour hardly requires comment: such impetuosity was too inherent to her character to ever be surprising. Why Marlborough felt that such a high-handed tone was wise shortly after Malplaquet is harder to say. Possibly he was driven by Sarah and her mad fury; he was probably not fully aware of the depths of her mistreatment of Anne. Whatever the reason, it was a terrible misjudgement.

Anne's reply made it abundantly clear that she would tolerate Sarah's 'teasing & tormenting' no longer.[72] Although the letter made some rather unconvincing noises about being sorry for Marlborough's resolution to resign, its tone was very different to their previous correspondence. Whereas any hint of his resignation would have evoked desperate-sounding attempts to soothe and compliment him not so long ago, her tone in this letter lost its semi-pleading and laudatory tone. It is clearly the letter of a woman who was increasingly indifferent about whether Marlborough stayed or not.

The thin ice that Marlborough had been dancing on for some time was starting to crack.

It perhaps partly explains Marlborough's behaviour that the psychological and political impact of Malplaquet, obvious in hindsight, was not immediately apparent. It certainly did not change the political situation immediately. Indeed, the good ship Junto had not yet reached top speed: its momentum was to take it forward for a while yet.

After the appointment of Somers and Wharton to the cabinet in the autumn of 1708, one-party Whig ascendancy in the government had been clearly established. This did not stop the Junto lords continuing to obsess about any area where even a shadow of real non-Whig power might linger – hence their neurotic preoccupation with the supposed influence of Harley through Abigail. Indeed, they would not be satisfied until any meaningful resistance to their power within the government was crushed.

This was demonstrated by their final push to cement their dominance over the government: to install Orford at the Admiralty over the course of autumn 1709. A familiar game of insistence and refusal ensued: once again, the Whigs threatened to resign en masse if their demands were not fulfilled, and a desperate Godolphin – not helped by the prickly and particular behaviour of Orford himself – plotted, pleaded and prevaricated with the Junto men (in between races at Newmarket) while battling to persuade the Queen. The Whigs, never satisfied, bullied the Lord Treasurer, implying once again that he was double-dealing them. In fact, he had nowhere else to go and protested, not unfairly, that he was 'labour[ing] like a slave in the Galley' to achieve their ends.[73] Sarah piled pressure on Marlborough to exert his influence in Orford's favour again – despite the fact that Marlborough personally disliked Orford, a difficult and irascible man.[74]

With the political tide yet to turn over the war in the aftermath of Malplaquet, and Harley as yet just still too weak to assist her, over the course of October and November 1709 the Queen gave in again. There was no viable political alternative to another Whig 'forcing of the closet'. Orford was in. The Junto had undoubtedly reached the acme of their power under Anne. The Whig flagship appeared to rule the waves.

Unfortunately for Wharton and his cronies, this was a highly misleading impression. They hadn't just lost momentum due to events on the battlefield of Malplaquet. They already been holed below the waterline. They just hadn't realised it yet.

9

The Political Consequences of

Dr Sacheverell

At around noon on 5th November 1709, the great and the good of the corporation of London gathered at St Paul's Cathedral for one of the set-piece services of the year. The leading Whig metropolitan grandees, from the serried ranks of the 'monied interest' to the aldermen, MPs and councilmen who bore the banner of the Whig interest on the battlements of their historic citadel, crowded in for the commemoration of the Fifth of November.

This date was the holiest one in the Whig liturgical calendar: the anniversary not only of the Gunpowder Plot but also William III's landing at Torbay in 1688. When coupled with the fact that, with the ascent of Orford to head of the Admiralty days away, the Whigs were just reaching the summit of their political power in the state, it was all set up to be a day of Whig pomp and celebration. St Paul's rapidly filled up with an enormous congregation: a happy throng, perhaps, to commemorate such a providential date.

The more eagle-eyed among the Whig attendees might, however, have noticed some rather more unwelcome attendees: a gaggle of notorious high-fliers, nonjurors and even Jacobites. Some would doubtlessly have already started to realise just who was due to give the sermon. The thought must have considerably dampened their ardour for the proceedings.

At first, however, the service proceeded much as one might expect, with the customary set prayers and hymns performed as usual. No doubt among some members of the congregation, obliged to attend many such church services every year, concentration failed, attention began to wander and perhaps a few started to feel drowsy.

But seated at the front there waited a staring, intense, goggle-eyed man, tall and powerful, who was 'locked away in a private world, working himself up into [a] mood of frenzied anger and near-hysteria'.[1]

At the appropriate point, this striking-looking man arose and strode intently up to the pulpit.

And then the storm broke.

The preacher that day was none other than 'the bloody flag officer', the man who had gained national notoriety in 1702 for his incendiary High Church sermon 'The Political Union': Dr Henry Sacheverell. The sermon he was about to preach was to take him to unimagined new heights of fame and break the world of British politics wide open.

The man on the cusp of catapulting himself to the centre stage of national life was no ordinary clergyman. In an age of rambunctious and highly coloured individuals, Sacheverell stands out. His presumption, spleen and shamelessness are apt to take the breath away even at three hundred years' distance. 'Full of himself' does not seem to do the man justice: 'overflowing with himself' might be more accurate.

Sacheverell was an unlikely High Church champion. Born in Marlborough, Wiltshire, his family history was largely a Presbyterian one, and his maternal grandfather, Henry Smith, appears to have been one of the regicides who signed Charles I's death warrant. It was only in his father's generation that the Sacheverells became churchmen. Henry, sent up to Oxford in 1689, was clearly keen to make up for such a shameful ancestry by going very much to the opposite extreme, and, despite initially being refused ordination for inadequate Latin, he was appointed a fellow of Magdalen College in 1701 before being awarded a doctorate in divinity in 1708. During the typhoon of controversy about to engulf him, the Whigs delighted in digging up every piece of dirt about him that they could find, and his behaviour at Magdalene meant that there was an awful lot to uncover.

The most vicious example was a pamphlet entitled *The Modern Fanatick* by William Bisset. A short extract of Bisset's account of Sacheverell's reputation at Oxford gives a fairly good flavour of the doctor's character:

> It is well known how imperiously he carried himself in Maudlin-Colledge, how disrespectfully to the President . . . How rude to the Fellows, and how he laid violent Hands upon one or two of the Members: How many Stories are there in that Place, of his insulting the Vice Chancellor, and his quarelling with whole Houses?[2]

His tirades were not restricted to his social superiors and equals. On one occasion an Oxford glover named Ryley, whom Sacheverell had repeatedly failed to pay, sought him at his rooms and asked him for his money to feed his children. When Sacheverell refused, Ryley threatened to take him to court: 'then the Doctor fell a cursing and swearing, that if he sued him to Eternity, he would not pay him'.[3] According to Bisset, Sacheverell used 'near twenty' oaths against the poor glover.[4]

Bisset was, of course, a Whig opponent of Sacheverell, but it seems likely that the bulk of his testimony was true, for political allies who had every incentive to defend him held strikingly similar opinions about the Doctor's general character. Oxford antiquarian Thomas Hearne, a man who was if anything more openly extreme in his Tory opinions than Sacheverell, was particularly unsparing, describing him thus (in Latin):

> This Sacheverell, an ignorant, wine-soaked, loquacious and rash individual, frequently gave sermons in the Church of the Blessed Virgin Mary before the scholars; on these occasions everyone knows that his face was full of fury, his eyes of criminality, his speech of arrogance. Stirred up doubtless by a frenzy he blurted out words that were abusive and utterly inappropriate to the holy pulpit; at times also he assailed zealots and rebels [i.e. Dissenters and republicans] with insults, as if an honourable man. Even so, he was an utterly wicked mountebank, as is evident from his numerous misdeeds, which men of decency deplore and execrate.[5]

It rarely speaks well of your character if this is the best your political allies have to say about you.

Among Sacheverell's many faults, mentioned in passing by Hearne, was his habitual inebriation, for which he was notorious even at Oxford. On one occasion, a particularly boisterous revel ended up with him and his drinking partner Lord Henry Somerset drunkenly tumbling into a saw pit, 'from whence they were delivered in a very nasty pickle after much struggle'.[6] Sacheverell in his cups was as familiar a sight to the seasoned Oxford scholar as the Bodleian Library or Christ Church.

Unsavoury a character as he was, Sacheverell was also burningly ambitious. As a scholar he had but little distinction, and he was not likely to achieve fame and fortune by charming his superiors or subtle academic politicking. He did, however, espy another route to glory.

He was, by all accounts, an astonishingly powerful preacher, and willing to use this ability to advance the High Church cause in the most emphatic manner possible. In an age of churchgoing, when hearing sermons was not only a pious duty but a form of popular entertainment, this skill was a considerable boon, and his unabashed partisanship meant that he was almost guaranteed a certain popularity among the less restrained partisans of the High Church cause and the High Tories. He hoped that such men, awed by his rhetorical fireworks, could secure him preferment and patronage.

As historian Geoffrey Holmes remarked, his sermons in cold print seem extraordinarily over the top: his phraseology was 'garish, exaggerated, even grotesque'.[7] He piled up intemperate extravagance upon intemperate extravagance; histrionic is often the only suitable way of describing his style. Nonetheless, contemporary observers, even those who despised him, almost uniformly attest to the magnetic power that his pulpit oratory had over many a congregation. A mixture of intense personal magnetism, an extraordinarily rich and well-modulated voice, and sheer theatrical power seemed to carry him through.

He was about to give the performance of his life.

Sacheverell had initially come to prominence with his 'The Political Union' sermon in the context of the Tory campaign to outlaw occasional conformity, which appeared, with the accession of Anne and the ascendancy of leading Tories in the government, to be on strong ground in 1702. By the time Dr Sacheverell stood up to harangue the civic luminaries of London in November 1709, High Church anger had not diminished, but the political situation had increasingly rendered it both more ineffectual and more vociferous.[8]

The Tory bungling of 1704–5, which culminated with the disastrous 'Tack', had wrecked the political hopes of the High Churchmen. They had been faced with a choice: take their chances with Harley, who promised them rewards if they were prepared to wait, show restraint and trust him, or howl into the wilderness.

Most Tory high-fliers had chosen the latter course. In the case of the lay High Churchmen in parliament, this had, in practice, largely meant a retreat into grumbling passivity as the political situation rendered them increasingly irrelevant. In the case of clerical high-fliers, it meant continuing to wage the war through an unceasing round of sermons, pamphlets and plotting within the structures of the Church.

One Tory who had decided to throw his lot in with Harley was Francis Atterbury. Atterbury was nearly as vehement in his High Church views as Dr Sacheverell, but possessed a great deal more learning and acumen. Having become the intellectual leader of the High Churchmen in the late 1690s, he had also become their leader in Church politics, skilfully marshalling the forces of the lower clergy against the Whig bishops in convocation. But he soon came to realise that the high-fliers could not storm the barricades of the state in the direct and artless way that many Tories in both church and parliament appeared to assume they could. He concluded that they would need the deft feints and political skills of Harley to assist them.

As such, between 1704 and 1708, Atterbury occupied a very uncomfortable, if politically shrewd, position, generally attempting to restrain his High Church allies in convocation in line with Harley's advice, all while retaining their trust. This was a difficult tightrope to walk. Many simply didn't trust Harley and what they saw as his pie-crust promises. In addition, from the Tack incident onwards Godolphin became increasingly hostile to the High Churchmen and worked on behalf of the Junto and their desire to gain power and patronage within the Church. Harley, who did what he dared on behalf of Atterbury and the Tories on ecclesiastical appointments, most notably by encouraging the Queen's resistance during the bishoprics crisis of 1707, was increasingly working against the tide. He could do little to restrain Whig Archbishop Tenison from wreaking vengeance on Atterbury and his allies in convocation, and before long he was out of office himself.

However, the ejection of Harley and his allies from office created promising new vistas of effective opposition. Atterbury was no longer tied to Harley's ambiguous political movements within the Godolphin ministry. He, like Harley himself, had more room for manoeuvre. The trick was to harness the energies and appeal of the High Church movement while keeping enough of a rein on its adherents to ensure that something of a viable Tory ecclesiastical programme could be carried through politically: the old 'Church in Danger' campaign had to be recast in more cautious and appealing terms in order, as historian G. V. Bennett puts it, to 'appeal to the minds of conservative men . . . and speak to that religious view of authority and society in which so many implicitly believed'.[9]

This strategy was greatly assisted by the fact that, from 1708, a heavily Whig-dominated ministry quickly began to rattle the sabre against the Church — or were certainly perceived to do so. Once installed as Lord Lieutenant of Ireland, Wharton began to sound out Irish opinion on his pet scheme: to repeal the sacramental test for public office. Although this was only intended to apply within the Emerald Isle, it was seen as a test balloon for doing the same in England. Atterbury was certainly sufficiently convinced that this was the case as to draft a short pamphlet caustically attacking the Whigs for considering such a measure. Rumours spread that a bill was also being prepared to break the hold of the Church on Oxford and Cambridge. The correspondence of Tory MPs and the squirearchy buzzed with alarm.

Although Wharton certainly wanted to repeal the test opened up in Ireland, it seems unlikely that there were any immediate plans to repeal or weaken the Test Act in England, not least because of the likely opposition of the Queen. However, it is probable that some Whigs — most notably perhaps Sunderland — were only held back from doing so by political realities. There had always been a section of the Whig Party, including at its most senior levels, that opposed the privileges of the Church, and years of High Church agitation had hardened this antipathy. Some Low Churchmen themselves, though not freethinkers like some Whigs, were sceptical of the high claims of authority made for the Church by many Tories.

This Whig–Tory conflict on the nature of the Church and its relationship to the state had become neatly personified by a long-running debate, which was wrapped up in much personal hostility, between Atterbury and a hot-headed Low Churchman called Benjamin Hoadly.

The dispute went back to the dilemmas created for High Churchmen and Tories by the Glorious Revolution. In centred on the question of the extent to which the old principle of both the Tories and the Church of England – non-resistance – was still applicable in the aftermath of the Glorious Revolution. How could non-resistance – the idea that active rebellion against the sovereign could never be justified – be said to still be valid given that the entire basis of the post-1688 political settlement was the forcible removal of an ordained monarch, James II?

Although, as described in chapter three, prominent Tories had been reconciling their traditional commitment to non-resistance with the facts of the Glorious Revolution to their own satisfaction since the 1690s, it remained hotly controversial. While the Tories insisted that non-resistance was still a valid principle, many Whig writers assailed it as a 'slavish' tenet that went hand-in-glove with tyranny (and, it was implied, popery).

One of the key contributors to this debate was Francis Atterbury. As early as 1701, he outlined his version of the 'new' Tory doctrine of non-resistance. He argued that God intervened by an act of special providence in certain situations to remove governments that were actively oppressive. 'No people can be reduced to such a wretched and forlorn condition, but that the good Providence of God may and will, if it sees fit, come to their rescue and deliver them'.[10] The governance of God can be manifested in such sudden and extraordinary events as those of 1688, as well as the normal operation of settled government, to which subjects are obliged to submit quietly. Exceptional, providential deliverances from tyranny did not sanction any general or settled right of resistance.

Hoadly, rector of St Peter-le-Poer and darling of the more trenchant Whigs, thought that this was nonsense. However modified, such an argument appeared to him to still be a slavish one that legitimated the idea that men should passively accept the depredations of evil rulers. Government, he argued, is intended by God in general terms to serve its broad purpose, namely 'the Public Happiness of Mankind'.[11] Any government that fails to uphold the ends which it was instituted to serve can be resisted and replaced according to man's needs. To argue to the contrary was 'against the Laws of Nature and Reason'.[12]

Whatever the strength or otherwise of his arguments, Hoadly was an unattractive figure, and quickly became the pantomime villain of Church Whiggery. His desiccated, logic-chopping sermons, delivered in a harsh monotone, were guaranteed to empty the pews; he was widely seen as a 'thin, meagre, sour fellow', and rude and unpleasant.[13] His enemies were also only too willing to exploit his unprepossessing appearances and physical disability: extremely short and fantastically ugly, an illness had left him able to walk only with crutches and he could only preach while kneeling down on a cushion. He was loathed far beyond the ranks of High Churchmen, but admired by many Whig ideologues for his fanatical devotion to the most rationalistic and 'low' views of the authority of Church and State.

Atterbury heartily detested him, and they conducted unseemly public warfare throughout the 1700s. Atterbury got convocation to condemn one of Hoadly's sermons as a 'scandal' and 'grave dishonour' to the Church; Hoadly struck back by implying (entirely falsely) that Atterbury had publicly endorsed a life of vice over virtue.[14] Then in autumn 1708 Atterbury gave a virtuoso sermon that slapped Hoadly down very hard. He accused him of wanting to 'destroy all Government, and reduce everything to its first Chaos and Confusion'.[15] The spiral of increasingly heated sermons on both sides attacking or defending non-resistance continued, and had reached boiling point by summer 1709.

It was in this febrile context that Dr Sacheverell stood up to deliver his sermon on that fateful afternoon in November 1709, entitled 'In Perils Among False Brethren'.

After making the most laughably perfunctory references to the Gunpowder Plot – the ostensible subject of the sermon – he turned to his main theme. Ever since the betrayal of Christ and the dissensions levelled against St Paul in Corinth, the Church, he argued, has struggled with those who would subvert it from within. Such was the sad fate of the Church of England in 1709:

> Her holy communion has been rent and divided by factions and schismatical impostors; her pure doctrine has been corrupted and defiled; her primitive worship and discipline profaned and abused; her sacred orders denied and vilified; her priests and professors calumniated, misrepresented, and ridiculed; her altars and sacraments prostituted to hypocrites, Deists, Socinians, and Atheists; and all this done, not only by our professed enemies, but, which is worse, by our pretended friends and false brethren.[16]

These false brethren fell into two broad categories: those within the Church and those within the state.

Within the Church, he railed against doctrinal heretics who called into question the established doctrines of the Church of England and attempted 'blasphemously to corrupt that inviolable Fountain of Truth with Erroneous Conjectures and vain Philosophical Systems' and thereby 'Make the house of God not only a Den of Thieves, but a Receptacle of Legions of Devils'.[17] He also attacked those who would undermine the Church's discipline and worship, by demolishing 'the exterior Fences to guard the Internals of religion, without which they are left naked, without Beauty, Order or Defence'.[18] Such men would make the catholic, apostolic Church of England into a 'Latitudinarian, Heterogenous Mixture of all Persons of what different Faith soever', thereby rendering it 'the most Absurd, Contradictory and Self-inconsistent Body in the World'.[19] The Church would lose its distinct identity and become a laughing stock, which would encourage the masses towards outright atheism and infidelity.

Even greater obloquy was heaped on the political doctrines of 'false brethren'. He began by expounding his favourite theme, the idea that 'Our

Constitutions both in Church and State has [sic] been . . . Modell'd to the Mutual Support, and the Assistance of one another', such that 'tis almost impossible to offer a Violation, to the One, without Breaking in upon the Body of the Other'.[20] The chief demonstration of this, he claimed, was the importance of two fundamental historic Church of England doctrines to political order:

> . . . the steady Belief of the Subjects Obligation to an Absolute, and Unconditional Obedience to the Supreame Power, in all Things Lawful, and the utter Illegality of Resistance upon any Pretence whatsoever[21]

Alas, what did he find but that these doctrines were now 'Exploded, and Redicul'd out of Countenance' by 'our New Preachers, and Politicians'.[22] These evil men, he argued, upheld 'Villanous and Seditious Principles' such as granting a power to 'the People to judge and dethrone their Sovereigns, for any Cause they think fit'.[23] The result would be complete anarchy. He didn't mention Hoadly by name, but few could have doubted who he had in mind.

Even Sacheverell realised that he could hardly ignore the elephant in the room: the Glorious Revolution, surely a textbook example of 'resistance'. He argued that to claim that the events of 1688 constituted resistance was, in fact, to cast 'Black and Odious' colours upon William III.[24] His claim to the throne was purely based on its vacancy after James II had fled. The Convention Parliament itself had, he argued, 'unanimously condemn[ed] to the Flames . . . that infamous Libel, that would have pleaded the Title on Conquest by which Resistance was suppos'd'.[25] Only secret republicans and exponents of the principles of Forty-One would impugn the Revolution by implying it was an act of resistance.

As one might expect, when it came to the chief exponents of such sedition, his fire turned onto the Dissenters, who were busy infiltrating the state via occasional conformity. They were still rebels and anarchists like the ones who had waged war on Charles I and executed him in 1649: 'the old Leaven of their Fore-fathers is still working in their present Generation, and . . . this traditional Poyson still remains in this Brood of Vipers'.[26]

Enabled by nominally Anglican internal traitors – the 'false brethren' of the title – within the government, who hid their true face of treachery and sacrilege behind a mask of moderation, the Dissenters would not rest until they had destroyed the traditional constitution and established a republican tyranny. He went so far as to accuse the 'false brethren' of 'Fall[ing] Down and Worship[ping] the very Devil himself, for the Riches and Honours of this World'.[27]

Even in worldly terms, the falseness and baseness of these men, their utter lack of principles and honesty, was disastrous: he railed with great vigour against the 'Crafty Insidiousness of such Wily Volpones'.[28] 'Volpone' had been a widely used nickname for Godolphin for some years now, and this passage was seen as a thinly veiled attack on the Lord Treasurer. The message was clear: the current government was infiltrated by men who would destroy the Church and ruin the State, whether openly as Whigs or whether more insidiously as false servants of the court, to line their own pockets.

Sacheverell ended his sermon with a rousing call to action. Traitors and enemies must be 'treated like growing Mischiefs, or Infectious Plagues, kept at a distance, lest their deadly Conttagion Spreads' and neutralised by priests 'Thundering out their Ecclesiastical Anathemas': a true Church Militant would be needed to defeat them.[29] As he reached his dramatic peroration, he resorted to scripture, and in particular Ephesians 6.10–13:

> My brethren, be strong in the Lord, and in the power of his might. Put on the whole armour of God, that ye may be able to stand against the wiles of the devil. For we wrestle not against flesh and blood, but against principalities, against powers, against the rulers of the darkness of this world, against spiritual wickedness in high places. Wherefore take unto you the whole armour of God, that ye may be able to withstand in the evil day, and having done all, to stand.

In many ways Sacheverell's sermon was nothing new. It rehashed many of his favourite themes. Hyperbole from High Church firebrands was hardly unheard of.

This time, however, was different. Firstly, Sacheverell had preached it at the heart of the Whig establishment in London, on an occasion supposed to be dedicated to celebrating England's deliverance from popish tyranny. It was a calculated and provocative insult to the government and the Whigs, designed to openly challenge their authority. Secondly, he had clearly gone further than he had ever gone before. Not only had he defended the old doctrines of passive obedience and non-resistance openly and with little qualification, his view of the Glorious Revolution was also extremely controversial.

The only reason why the throne was vacant in 1688 was because there obviously had been resistance, in the form of uprisings in the country and, of course, William's invasion, which had been supported by many English subjects. James II would hardly have fled the country otherwise. Sacheverell's trenchant restatement of the absolute illegitimacy of any resistance *at all* seemed to render the Revolution illegitimate: his claim that it was justified because it wasn't really resistance could only logically be seen as a fig leaf covering his real position.

Even if one accepted what he said at face value, it could easily be taken to imply Jacobitism: if William only became king because James II's throne was vacant, why couldn't the Stuarts reclaim their throne when they wanted? Was only their presence in the country required to resume their right? As the leading historian of the Sacheverell affair, Geoffrey Holmes, put it, the High Church champion's words 'meant that the Revolution had implied nothing revolutionary, that it was an unfortunate and regrettable accident which had established no new principle of government'.[30] If this were the case, why would Anne be the heir to the throne instead of her half-brother?

Sacheverell's sermon spoke to those Tories who had little time for the attempts of their more moderate colleagues to establish the congruence of old Tory values with the Revolution. Although he added some qualifications in order to give himself plausible deniability, there was little of the subtlety of Atterbury's efforts in it. It was widely seen as a barely coded appeal to the nonjurors and Jacobites who argued that 1688 amounted to armed resistance to the divinely ordained monarch, and was therefore simply wrong by the Church's own well-established principles. Arguments about providence could not wish away the simple reality that resistance had clearly occurred, and a monarch had clearly been deposed. This was, curiously, something that the most hardened Jacobite and the most thoroughgoing Whig could agree on. They merely disagreed on whether such resistance – and therefore the entire Revolution and post-1688 political settlement – was right or wrong.

Although the circumstances and the content of Sacheverell's sermon clearly marked it out as unusual, the factor that ultimately transformed it from one of many sermons delivered at civic occasions across the country into a national political convulsion was that it was *printed*. In fact, we do not know whether Sacheverell had ever gone so far before, as many of his sermons, delivered once and then forgotten, are unknown to us. But what was certain was that he had never before made quite such incendiary remarks in printed and published form.

Not only did he print the sermon – apparently with the approval of the Lord Mayor – but it became an overnight publishing sensation. Within a few months, eleven official editions and four pirated editions had been produced. Around 40,000 copies of the cheaper octavo version of the second edition were printed, and by the end of the affair around 100,000 copies were in circulation, an extraordinary number at any time, but a mind-boggling figure for that age.[31] It was soon being eagerly devoured in coffee-houses and taverns throughout London, and then the entire country.

Soon the sermon had come to the attention of Godolphin and the senior Whig ministers, and they had to decide what – if anything – to do about it. It seemed difficult to ignore such a deliberate and gratuitous challenge to their authority. Some – chiefly Sunderland and Wharton – sensed a great opportunity: a chance to prosecute not just Sacheverell the man, but his ideas, and thereby vindicate the Whigs' Revolution principles once and for all, deliver a crushing public blow to the Tories and High Churchmen, and harshly punish Sacheverell, *pour encourager les autres*.

Godolphin, smarting from the personal attack on him, agreed to such a strategy; only Somers and Marlborough seem to have had doubts. Wharton and Sunderland argued that the whole exercise could underline the Whigs' political dominance, and lure the Tories onto the 'Church in Danger' territory that had proved so damaging for them four years before. For good measure, it was a perfect opportunity for tarring them all as Jacobites as well, always the Whig's go-to ploy.

Such a dramatic proposition needed an appropriately grand stage. So the fateful decision was taken that the Whigs would soon bitterly come to regret. Sacheverell would be impeached for high crimes and misdemeanours before the highest court in the land: the House of Lords.

The die was cast.

At first, every indication was that the Whig strategy was sound. Even many Tories who had time for Sacheverell's arguments sounded a fearful note. A High Church crony of Thomas Hearne's, who had actually witnessed the sermon, wrote to him about it:

> I could not have imagined if I had not actually heard it my self, that so much Heat, Passion, Violence, & scurrilous Language, to say no worse of it, could have come from a Protestant Pulpit, much less from one that pretends to be a Member of the Church of England . . . I'm sure such Discourses will never convert anyone, but I'm afrayd will rather give the Enemies of our Church great advantage over her; since the best that her true Sons can say of it, is that the Man is mad.[32]

Many High Churchmen thought that Sacheverell had gone too far, and the Whigs were merciless. A pamphlet war soon started up, and initially it consisted of a flood of vicious attacks on the Doctor and his sermon, which savaged his argument and the 'brazen-faced banter' it was couched in.[33] The Queen remarked at the early stages of the whole affair that 'it was a bad sermon, and that he deserved well to be punished for it'.[34] Atterbury's fears that an incautious or headlong 'Church in Danger' campaign could rebound heavily on the Tories looked set to be amply fulfilled.

This mood was reflected when a motion to officially consider the sermon was moved in the Commons on the 13th December by John Dolben, a lieutenant of the Junto. Tory defence of the Doctor was sparse indeed. The very next day the official motion to impeach Sacheverell was moved, and the Whigs were on fighting form: one, Sir Stephen Lennard, was heard to shout, with great enthusiasm, that they were going 'to roast a parson' (Lennard had a stroke and died the next day, which 'seemed to many offended Tories a particularly speedy manifestation of divine retribution').[35] The motion passed without even a division.

The underlying situation was not, however, altogether rosy for the Whigs. In the country, the unpopularity of both the Whigs and the other leading government figures was rising rapidly. Poor weather and harvests over the past few years had caused bread prices to rise considerably. The failure of the peace negotiations and the stalemate at Malplaquet demoralised a people weary of constant warfare and high taxes; dashed hope was worse than none at all. In London especially, the spectacle of large numbers of Palatinate immigrants arriving to compete for jobs and gain the lion's share of private charity rankled hard with the poorer labouring classes. The gap between their plight and the lavish bounty heaped upon Marlborough, who was continuing to build his enormous pile at Blenheim Palace, was obvious.

This unpopularity was reflected even before Sacheverell stood up at St Paul's to deliver his sermon by a book, by turns titillating and coruscating, published in two volumes in March and October 1709 entitled *The New Atalantis*. The author was Mrs Delarivier Manley, a cheerful, buxom Tory lady, who described herself as 'a perfect Bigot from a long untainted Descent of Loyal Ancestors and consequently immovable'.[36]

A truly bizarre narrative, the book largely consists of the most scurrilous gossip and rumour about the leading Whigs and the Marlboroughs – and indeed many other totally obscure figures – that she could either find out or else make up. Genuinely true stories were blended with total fiction, in the context of a curious half-dystopian fantasy world that clearly allegorised real events going back to before the Glorious Revolution, to present a picture of a morally depraved, self-serving Whig elite mostly interested in sexual intrigue and siphoning off as much cash as possible.

She related old tales of Marlborough's affair with the Duchess of Cleveland (waxing in a slightly coy way, for example, about the 'amiable Disorders, and transporting Joys, that attend the possession of [their] early Love'), painting a picture of him as ungrateful, disloyal and avaricious, both for money and power.[37] She dragged up old rumours about William Cowper seducing a poor orphan girl and embroidered them, suggesting he had staged a mock marriage using a false priest to seduce her. She related Somers's amorous tendencies, Halifax's vanity and overall left almost no prominent Whig or courtier untouched. Rather more outrageously, she described 'a lesbian cabal' involving various leading Whig ladies, and implied that Godolphin and Sarah Churchill had had an amorous liaison.[38]

Leading Whigs, half outraged and half grimly fascinated by where she got her information from (they knew that at least some of her stories were true), were (wrongly) convinced that she was a hired pen of Robert Harley. *The New Atalantis*, with its mixture of Tory propaganda, outrageous rumour concerning political 'celebrities' and Mills and Boon-style soft porn, was soon a succès de scandale, selling in droves as everyone with a prurient interest in 'sexual wickedness in high places' rushed to acquire their copy. The book might have been scandalous, but it was also intended as a serious satirical attack on Whig corruption and arrogance, and its success suggests that this message, as much as the *Carry On*-style antics, struck home. Whig attempts to suppress the book and prosecute the author simply increased its notoriety and failed anyway.

However, the senior Whigs and ministers who gathered to decide the nature of the impeachment charges against Sacheverell still thought themselves in a strong position. They had time: under the Triennial Act, there was no obligation to hold a general election until mid-1711. Their calculations were not strongly informed by public opinion so far away from an election. If they could successfully roast their parson and with it the credibility of the Tory cause, the whole affair might redound to their advantage.

Some wanted to keep the charges – technically the 'articles of impeachment' – focussed and simple. Sacheverell could be charged with sedition, as his incendiary rhetoric at the conclusion of his sermon did seem (rather ironically for someone whose political watchword was 'obedience') to veer rather close to inciting some sort of rebellion against the authorities. He could also be charged with preaching the 'Church in Danger' against parliament's express condemnation of such sentiments back in 1705. For Marlborough and Godolphin, these focussed charges would suffice: raising bigger questions about the political and religious justifications for the Glorious Revolution and right of resistance seemed to them to be opening up a very awkward can of worms; how would the Queen react to her own government justifying resistance against any government, including her own?

However, opening up such questions was just what some of the senior Whigs wanted to do, and accordingly the charges, when published, threw the kitchen sink at Sacheverell. They took in not only the 'Church in Danger' and sedition charges but also his interpretation of the Revolution, his denial of a right of resistance and his extremely jaundiced view of the Toleration Act. In the wide-ranging preamble to the impeachment articles, Sacheverell was charged with:

> a wicked, malicious and seditious intention to undermine and subvert her Majesty's government and the Protestant succession as by law established, to defame her Majesty's administration, to asperse the memory of his late Majesty, to traduce and condemn the late happy Revolution, to contradict and arraign the resolutions of both Houses of Parliament, to create jealousies and divisions amongst her Majesty's subjects, and to incite them to sedition and rebellion.[39]

The general sentiments of the Junto were summarised by Wharton who, when asked by the vacillating and politically cautious Marlborough what the government should do, answered: 'Do with him, my Lord? Quash him and damn him.'[40]

By the time the articles came to be debated in parliament in January, the more perceptive Whigs might have found the odd doubt creeping into their calculations, however. The Tories began to flood into Westminster in unusually large numbers, headed by Harley, who gave a speech that, although somewhat hedging and equivocal in its attitude towards Sacheverell, clearly signalled that he would not support the impeachment.

Harley was no supporter of the unvarnished high-flying principles of the Doctor, and his famous political antennae would have recommended a non-committal response or tactical absence from parliament on the occasion if he sensed that it represented a dangerous trap that would retard the efforts of him and his Tory allies to bring down the Junto. The fact that he clearly didn't meant that he had something up his sleeve.

Two things were persuading him that the Sacheverell case presented more opportunity than peril for his prospects.

Firstly, he sensed the stirrings of a reaction in the Doctor's favour. Days after the impeachment motion had passed, High Church clergy took to their pulpits all over London to deliver highly pointed discourses on the sorrows of suffering for Christ's sake and of the vengeance that the Lord would wreak on those who persecute the godly. Clergymen across the country began to wonder whether the prosecution of Sacheverell presaged a general assault on them and the Church, and concluded that the Doctor's cause was their own: as one put it, 'in this one man the House of Lords must encounter with a legion'.[41]

Sacheverell had started to receive a steady stream of lavish presents and visits from the great and the good of the Church Party, who showed signs of reviving from their long lethargy. Tory and High Church ranks – even among those who privately had little time for Sacheverell – began to close behind him. However distasteful the man might be, they concluded (not altogether wrongly) that the attack on him was part of a wider attack on Toryism in general. They would have to hang together, or they might end up hanging separately.

There were also signs that the Doctor's case might attract wider support and make him something of a popular figure, even a demagogue. On the day of the infamous sermon itself, crowds had cheered and applauded him as he left St Paul's, and during the next few weeks his fame had spread. He preached at St Margaret Lothbury a few weeks later, and his presence attracted a huge, adulatory crowd desperate to hear the Doctor's sermon: when space ran out and the doors had to be closed, the High Church throng 'threaten[ed] to pull down the doors and break the windows' to get in.[42]

In short, it looked like Sacheverell might prove a formidable focal point for discontent against the government. Pro-Church popular sentiment could, given the right circumstances, be stoked to great effect, and it was easy to present the prosecution as a David and Goliath fight between a doughty and unjustly maligned champion for Mother Church and an arrogant and vindictive Whig government. In the context of wider Whig unpopularity, a charismatic – albeit monstrously egotistical – figure like Sacheverell might be well placed to exploit a broad sense of resentment towards the government.

Secondly, something was afoot at court. Behind the scenes, Harley's position was strengthening. He had started visiting the Queen in secret, probably for the first time since his dismissal, and used his audiences to fan the flames of her resentment against the Marlboroughs and the Whigs. He was pushing on an open door given the infamous treatment she had received at their hands: she knew that Harley was her ticket out of this captivity and was prepared to listen to any scheme he might have for rescuing her. Aware that the keystone in the Whig–Godolphin–Marlborough arch was the Duke and his domination of military affairs, Harley decided to encourage the Queen to strike at just this point.

On the very day that the articles of impeachment were debated in the Commons, the Earl of Essex, who was colonel of the 4th Dragoons and Constable of the Tower of London, died. Marlborough assumed that, as normal, his recommendations to fill these posts would prevail. The Queen, however, had other ideas. An ally of Harley's, Earl Rivers, immediately visited Marlborough to solicit him for the Tower of London post. Marlborough had no intention of offering it to Rivers – he had his own clients to satisfy – but he politely, if disingenuously, told Rivers that he would have no objections to his appointment. The Queen, however, quickly forced his hand by offering it to Rivers immediately. Since Marlborough had said he had no objections, what was his problem?[43]

Soon after, the Queen decided to make a bid to re-establish her authority by ordering Marlborough to appoint Captain John Hill as captain of the 4th Dragoons. Since Hill was the younger brother of none other than Abigail Masham, the challenge to Marlborough could hardly have been more obvious. Not only was he being overruled, but someone connected to the Harley–Masham connexion was being favoured.

Marlborough, egged on as ever by Sarah, was furious. He decided to respond in a similar way as he had done to the crisis over Harley's removal in February 1708: he refused to attend cabinet and was willing to threaten to resign if he didn't get his way. He and some of the senior Whigs, driven on by Sarah's ally Maynwaring, decided to widen the battle by demanding not only satisfaction over the army appointments, but also the dismissal of Mrs Masham from the Queen's household. A threat to bring a parliamentary motion to the Commons to that effect was mooted. Marlborough made it clear that, unless the Queen gave in to him completely on all these points, he would resign.

At this point the Queen went to war. The Commons attempting to dictate who she appointed to her own household was almost without precedent and an extraordinary interference in her affairs: she would *not* stand for it. White-hot fury alternated with tearful reproaches as she embarked on a series of interviews with all the key political figures in which she emotionally implored them not to personally insult their sovereign against all tradition. Support for the idea ebbed away even among the Whigs, who realised that they had overplayed their hand and that such a motion would be hard to publicly justify. The Junto lords hesitated and decided not to back Marlborough's ultimatum.

In short, the Junto had hung Marlborough out to dry: he had no option but to withdraw his threat of resignation and any idea of the Queen dismissing Mrs Masham. The Queen and her ministers had gone head-to-head, and the ministers had blinked first. Although a compromise was agreed whereby Marlborough would get his way on the 4th Dragoons appointment – the Queen had to retain his services for as long as the war went on and so couldn't completely humiliate him – his authority had been dented and the unity between him and the Junto exposed as weak. He skulked off to the continent in high dudgeon; the government had suffered a major blow to its credibility; and Tory morale began to soar. Perhaps the Queen's anger towards – and victory over – her Junto ministers gave them a chance to recover favour?

In sum, the whole incident made people believe that the Marlborough–Junto relationship that had made the government apparently unassailable was breakable. This was highly significant in another direction.

Since May 1708, as we have seen, Harley had been putting out feelers to a group of Whigs whom he felt he might be able to peel away from the Junto, most notably Shrewsbury and the Duke of Somerset, but also including Argyle, the Duke of Newcastle and others. They would be essential to any scheme to throw out the Junto and institute a Harley-led pro-peace 'moderate' ministry, as the Tories were simply not strong enough to prop up such a government on their own. Gradually, over the course of 1709, he had made major inroads, slowly but surely winning them over. But it was hard to see how any alternative government was possible, even if they supported the idea, while the Junto–Marlborough–Godolphin alliance held so firm.

The Queen's victory during what became known as the 'Regiments Crisis' started to make them believe that such a plan had a chance of success. Furthermore, the Sacheverell trial, which the Junto lords had decided to treat as a grand political set piece to illustrate their political dominance, might give them and Harley a chance to turn it to quite the opposite purpose. After all, most of Harley's Whig recruits were members of the Lords, who would ultimately vote on the impeachment. What if the vote on the impeachment didn't turn out to be quite the crushing blow against Sacheverell and the Tories that the Junto hoped for? What for their authority then?

As signs of Sacheverell's popularity became clearer on the streets – when he presented his official written answer to the impeachment charges to parliament in January, he was mobbed by yet another huge crowd who loudly huzzaed him – two things became clear.

Firstly, the more the trial could be delayed, the more steam could build up behind the Doctor's cause. Secondly, the more it could be made into a huge public spectacle, the more opportunity there would be for exploiting these bubbling sentiments and for making use of Sacheverell's greatest assets: his brilliant sense of theatricality and sheer cock-snooking chutzpah.

The Tories got lucky on both counts. Firstly, the legal niceties of organising an impeachment trial took rather longer than the Whigs expected. Weeks passed as the legislative wheels creaked slowly towards finalising arrangements for the trial. Secondly, the Tories achieved an extraordinary political coup in the Commons on 4th February. The Whigs wanted the trial to take place in the House of Lords itself, at its bar. This would mean that only a handful of spectators would be able to witness proceedings and almost no MPs. The Harleyites and the High Tory chiefs, however, co-operated to concoct a plan to hold the trial at Westminster Hall, with special arrangements to be made to accommodate as large an audience as possible, including all MPs and other onlookers. Amazingly, due to bad luck and poor whipping, the Whigs lost the vote on this proposal. The scene was set for the trial being a huge public spectacle.

As the trial was increasingly becoming the hottest political show in town, anyone who was anyone in London society wanted a ticket. Sir Christopher Wren was accordingly asked to construct a huge set of public stands to accommodate as many spectators as possible, and requests to put in even more seating meant that his job kept getting bigger. Although his workmen laboured furiously, all of this had the effect of delaying the trial even further. But after delay upon delay, the date was finally set. The great clash between High Church and Low, Tory and Whig, Dr Sacheverell and the Junto, was set for 27th February 1710.

The nation waited with baited breath for battle to commence.

As the trial approached, the ideological temper of London reached boiling point. Whereas in the early stages the propaganda war had been almost monopolised by the Whigs, in January and February the tide turned. On 30th January, the anniversary of Charles I's execution, a fusillade of clerical loyalism thundered forth from the pulpits of London, strongly implying that the consequences of the Doctor's defeat and the vindication of Whiggish doctrines of resistance and rebellion would lead to '41 come again'. All loyal churchmen were called to 'take up their cross and follow him': whether 'him' was meant to be Jesus Christ or Dr Sacheverell was deliberately left unclear.[44]

At the same time a stream of emotionally charged pro-Sacheverell pamphlets was pumped onto the market. It became common to depict the Doctor as a suffering Christian martyr of unblemished moral character, cruelly persecuted by hard-hearted Whig miscreants. Many a Whig rebuttal of the Doctor's case followed, but momentum was building in his favour. A slew of prints came onto the market, many comparing the Doctor to Charles I, the prototypical High Church martyr, who had been tried at Westminster Hall himself.

Indeed, prints became crucial to the pro-Sacheverell campaign. Somehow Sacheverell found time before the trial to sit for his portrait, and a copy of the painting was quickly mass produced using the innovative new technique of mezzotinto, which gave the impression of 'paint-like shadows and texture'.[45] Portraits of the Doctor soon became both objects of private religious devotion, as well as devotion of quite a different kind.

For, extraordinarily, Sacheverell had become something of an unlikely sex-symbol. Portraits of the Doctor were quickly pirated in large numbers, and they became pin-ups for many a Tory lady: as one commentator put it, the portraits were used to heighten 'concern both for the Church and the afflicted assertor of its rights' among 'the fair and tender-hearted sex'.[46] Non-resistance seemed to take on a very different meaning in this context: as Whig Sarah Cowper observed in her diary, the Doctor had

> become the Toast of Such Ladys as Strenuously adhere to the Doctrine of Non:Resistance. To accomadate their Full Petticoats 24 Inches of Seat is allow'd to Each Non:Resisting Female as Comes to this Audience and 'tis Thought there will be no Small Appearance, for the Criminal 'tis said, is a Hansome Bonny priest.[47]

Never before or since have High Church doctrines been such an aphrodisiac: as one pamphlet put it, 'Strange! How the women love a High-flyer'.[48]

This outpouring of tender feelings among the ladies no doubt contributed to the feverish scramble for tickets that ensued among the quality of London as soon as the date of the trial was announced. There was a flourishing black market in which many peers of the realm (who had been allocated most of the tickets) played the role of shameless ticket touts. Before long 'all the ladies' were 'making advances to the lords to get tickets from them to see and be seen at the trial'.[49]

As swooning ladies and the political world desperately fought for tickets, the two sides prepared for the judicial battle of the century. The government assembled a legal team full of glittering talent – numbering twenty in total – including, most notably, two of the most admired Whig rhetoricians in the land: Robert Walpole and dashing military hero Lieutenant-General

James Stanhope, who had scrambled home from the front line in Spain to be there.

Meanwhile, it became clear that Sacheverell's case was to be managed by agents of Harley. Atterbury was brought in as the key adviser, and in terms of chief counsel, the Doctor had a tremendous stroke of luck. As he had been thrown out of the Commons on petition due to the highly partisan Whig manoeuvre against him in the aftermath of the 1708 election, Sir Simon Harcourt, former attorney general, was available to act for Sacheverell (as the impeachment case had been bought by the Commons, no MP could act for the defence). Harcourt was renowned as a majestic, Ciceronian orator and easily the greatest legal mind in the Tory Party. The rest of the legal team – including the magnificently named Humphrey Henchman – was less impressive, but in Harcourt the Doctor had a formidable weapon.

As the trial loomed and Harley surveyed the scene, his plan had become clear. Harcourt and Atterbury were to try to rein in the Doctor and put up the most plausible legal defence they could. It was key to present Sacheverell in the most moderate and respectable terms possible, introducing enough doubt surrounding his alleged Jacobitism and attack on the Glorious Revolution to make it hard for the Whigs to smear the Tories – who had undoubtedly thrown their lot in with the Doctor – as seditious partisans of the 'King Across the Water'. Meanwhile, Harley would seek to cabal behind the scenes with his disgruntled Whig allies to ensure that, when the key votes on the case in the Lords occurred, the result would be equivocal enough to humiliate the Whigs and deny them the resounding victory that they expected. If all of this could be pulled off, then confidence might drain away from the Whigs and the Queen might feel strong enough to move against them and reconstruct the ministry.

It was a narrow path to victory, but if anyone could pull off such a coup, it was Robert Harley.

At 9 a.m. on 27th February, an extraordinary vehicle pulled up in the Temple area of London: an elaborate and ostentatious carriage made almost solely out of glass. Shortly after, Dr Henry Sacheverell emerged from his lodgings and climbed in. This 'tawdry chariot', as some mockingly described it, proceeded to convey the Doctor to his destiny.[50]

The transparent nature of the carriage meant that the Doctor could be seen as he was conveyed to Westminster Hall by the mob which 'attended him thither . . . with loud Huzza's and Acclamations'.[51] He lapped up the attention, waving to the enthusiastic throng. Along the route he was cheered by a heterogenous crowd, ranging from footmen to well-to-do Tory ladies, who bellowed encouragement: cries of 'God bless you' and 'They shall not hurt a hair on your head' rung out.[52] Large amounts of cash were tossed to the crowd (donated no doubt by wealthy Tory benefactors) to maintain the spirits of the Doctor's admirers.

Meanwhile, the clamour was building in Westminster Hall, where the enormous stands, forming something like an amphitheatre, were bristling with London society, who had been staking out the best seats since well before 7 a.m.: in all 2,000 people, including the Lords, Commons and the Queen, crammed in to watch. Keener partisans awoke as early as 4 a.m. to ensure that they could claim an advantageous perch. Crammed cheek to jowl onto the scaffolding, the crowds periodically broke out into party bickering (and worse). Lady Rooke, a Tory grande dame, offered a peckish gentleman seated beside her a chicken wing on the first day of the trial. Before handing over the grub, she recollected herself and asked the man what side he was on. He made it clear that he was against the Doctor, to which the outraged Lady replied, 'Then, by God, sir, I'll have my wing again', before snatching the greasy morsel from his mitts.[53] On other occasions, young Whig and Tory ladies had to be physically separated from prosecuting politically inflected catfights by their parents.

Indeed, some young women in the stands had their own agendas. Many saw this extraordinary gathering, which was as much a social occasion as a political and legal battle royale, as a good opportunity to acquire a husband. They dressed up in their finest clothes, worked out who among the gentlemen were on the 'right' political side, and fluttered their eyelashes keenly. How many matches were made is not recorded, but it certainly became a notorious marriage mart for the young and unattached.

But such affairs of the heart were nothing compared to the seismic political significance of the gladiatorial combat about to play itself out on the biggest stage.

* * *

The articles of impeachment drawn up against the Doctor covered numerous issues, but the political pith of the case centred in article one, which concerned the justifiability of resistance in general, and the Glorious Revolution in particular.

On 28th February and 1st March, the Whig big guns presented the guts of their case, which constituted in effect a grand defence of their party's basic political principles.

One of the great set piece speeches was delivered by Robert Walpole. His case was overall fairly straightforward, albeit (according to one Tory source) washed down with rhetorical lashings of 'Billings-Gate Barbarity'.[54] He argued that 'when an utter Subversion of the Laws of the Realm threaten', as was clearly the case during the reign of James II, resistance is justified.[55] The idea that there was no resistance during the Revolution, as Sacheverell had claimed, was clearly false:

> surely, my Lords, it cannot be necessary to prove Resistance in the Revolution. I should as well expect that your Lordships would desire me, for Form's sake, to prove the Sun shines at Noon Day.[56]

Another Whig advocate, Sir John Holland, pressed the point home:

> That there was Resistance, is most plain, if taking up Arms in Yorkshire, Nottinghamshire, Chesire, and almost all the Counties of England; if the Desertion of a Prince's own Troops to an Invading Prince, and turning their Arms against their Sovereign, be Resistance.[57]

The reference to Yorkshire was an obvious reference to the fact that one of the most famous Tories of the age, the Earl of Danby himself, had spearheaded armed resistance in God's own county. The fact that Danby (now the Duke of Leeds) had visited the doctor to offer support seemed to the Whigs to illustrate Tory hypocrisy.

Walpole admitted that arguments in favour of resistance could be used for more radical purposes, 'as maintaining antimonarchical schemes', but without the sort of 'necessary and commendable Resistance used at the Revolution', he contended, the entire fabric of the post-revolutionary state, including Anne's title to the throne and the entire concept of a Protestant succession, fell down.[58] Sir John Holland spelled out the issue in no uncertain terms:

> My Lords, the present consideration is of the greatest importance; no less than whether so many of your Lordships and the Commons of Great Britain who took up arms at the Revolution, and were then thought patriots of your country, were really rebels; whether our late Deliverer was an usurper; and whether the Protestant Succession is legal and valid. All these considerations depend upon the lawfulness of the Resistance at the Revolution.[59]

The Whig speakers tried to draw out from this the wider political implications. If Sacheverell was implicitly stating that the Glorious Revolution was invalid, and if he railed heartily against the entire governmental edifice that upheld the Revolution settlement, and yet chose to take his stand on the religious duty of total non-resistance and obedience, then the question was: to whom was this obedience due, in his eyes? It could hardly be to the Queen and the state that he had more-or-less stated was illegitimate. It could only be to the Pretender. In short, the only logical interpretation of his argument was a Jacobite one, which made the Doctor a seditious opponent of the Queen and her title to the throne.

This was a line of argument that was taken up with aplomb by James Stanhope. The dashing military man made one of the most widely admired and brilliant speeches of the trial: even a staunch Tory conceded that it was 'inspired' (although another accused of him 'Indecent Passon').[60] He argued that if the Tories were — as they appeared to be — so keen to align themselves with the seditious, Jacobite principles of Sacheverell, surely it was they who were the real agents of chaos and anarchy, the real Puritans and 'fanaticks'? When they courted public office and preferment, wasn't it they who were the real creeping hypocrites?

He turned their own language against them to brilliant effect:

My Lords, if these Puritans . . . would confine themselves to their own Conventicles, to get Mony from a few deluded Women; it may perhaps be consistent with the Indulgence of the mildest of Governments . . . But when they shall come and vent their Treasons abroad; when they shall occasionally conform, and take the Oaths to the Government, in order the better to destroy it; when they shall abjure the pretended Prince of Wales, but not forget him; when they shall invade the Pulpits of the true Church of England . . . When (I say) that Pulpit shall be prostituted and polluted by venting Sedition against the best of Queens; it is high Time for your Lordships to animadvert upon it . . .[61]

At this point, you might think that the Whig speakers were succeeding in fulfilling the worst nightmares of Harley, of tainting the whole Tory Party as factious Jacobites.

However, brilliant as Stanhope or Walpole were as speakers, the Whig case had its weaknesses.

Firstly, there were underlying inconsistencies in the theoretical basis of the arguments put forward by the Whig speakers. Was government the result of a contract or compact between ruler and ruled, which allowed the ruled to rebel if its terms – such as protection of 'natural' rights – were broken? Was there, in short, a right of resistance of quite broad application, of which the 1688 Revolution was an example? Or was 1688 a one-off – an exceptional case from which a general, wide-ranging doctrine of resistance could not be extrapolated?

The Whig advocates did not concur on this. Stanhope, the most radical, seemed to endorse a general right of resistance to defend the rights secured by the social contract. It was easy for the Tories to claim that this gave rise to anarchy: if the people were able to unilaterally rebel whenever they felt that their fundamental rights were being abrogated by government, wasn't it a recipe for chaos? Surely, *somewhere at least*, there must be a supreme power in the state that is owed absolute obedience.

Other Whig spokesmen were, accordingly, more cautious than Stanhope. Walpole hedged around this question, concentrating on the exceptional case of necessity facing the country in 1688 and ignoring the broader issue. But one of the Whig speakers – the most cautious, Sir John Hawles – argued something rather more conservative. He claimed that there was, in fact, a supreme power against which resistance was illegitimate: he simply claimed that such a power was claimed, not by the monarch personally, but rather all three parts of the constitution – monarch, Lords and Commons – as a whole: 'the Crown in Parliament'.

If one accepted this claim, then one could argue that the Revolution of 1688 was a case of one part of the co-ordinate sovereign power – the monarch – rebelling against the other parts to destroy the very laws jointly approved by those three bodies in their collective role as sovereign power. 'Resistance' was construed only very narrowly as an effort by Commons and Lords to stop the monarch usurping the supreme power exclusively for itself. No 'right of resistance' on the part of the people at large could therefore be said to exist: and therefore one could maintain that the traditional Anglican doctrines of non-resistance and passive obedience were consistent with the Glorious Revolution. Such a view seemed hardly that different from the 'moderate' brand of Toryism being advocated by Atterbury against Hoadly.

The problem for the Whigs was, therefore, that their argument could be taken to have implications so radical as to potentially sanction an unruly general right of resistance that might apply, at least theoretically, even against the current queen; or it could be interpreted in terms so conservative as to be amenable to a Tory interpretation. On this fatal ambiguity the Whig case was soon to falter.

The problems of unruliness, anarchy and chaos were very soon to become far more than abstract points of theoretical debate.

Mass gatherings in favour of Sacheverell in the capital had been building up steam for some time: even up until the first day of the trial, they had been lively but not particularly ominous. However, on the 28th, the day the Whigs' opened their prosecution, events on the streets started to grow more serious.

The crowds began to swell noticeably and become far more assertive. Some presented themselves as providing the Doctor with personal protection against his enemies, including a gang of butchers. Others started to arm themselves with 'staves and clubs'.[62] The Doctor revelled in the attention from his supporters and admirers, sometimes regally stretching his hand out of his coach to be kissed, but to most it was clear that the masses were starting to get dangerously aggressive. One of the Whig lawyers, Spencer Cowper, warned that 'the fruit to be expected' of Sacheverell's seditious principles and rabble-rousing 'was civil discord and confusion, unless some Remedy was apply'd to prevent it'.[63]

He wasn't wrong. By the next day, it was clear that the crowds were getting more and more tumultuous. Having escorted the Doctor into court that day, they did not disperse, but hung around into the evening. When the proceedings for the day finished, many of the Whig trial managers were roundly abused. Mostly, the mob swore insults at them, but a group caught Dolben, the original mover of the impeachment, 'and were going to hang him upon a tree' until he swore that he was not Dolben at all and managed to scramble free.[64]

Things were escalating quickly. Large mobs of men, numbering 3,000 in total, had gathered round the Temple area armed to the teeth with crowbars, axes and, ominously, a whole range of carpenters' implements. They were literally tooled up for disorder, and soon it became very clear where their ire was to be directed: against the Dissenters' chapels and conventicles. They proceeded to a large Presbyterian meeting house, near Fleet Street, which was presided over by leading light of London Dissent, Daniel Burgess, and forced their way in. But their aim was not just some desultory and chaotic vandalism: they quickly proceeded to systematically and comprehensively dismantle the entire building, stone by stone and floorboard by floorboard. Every single piece of wood in the building, from the pulpit and pews to the doors and the panelling, was wrenched out and piled up into an enormous combustible mound, which was then set alight. For three hours, a colossal bonfire raged.

An orgy of destruction, accompanied by incessant, stentorian shouts of 'High Church and Sacheverell!', started to rage more widely. Soon, other Dissenting meeting houses were targeted in similar fashion to Burgess's, in New Street and Drury Lane. Passers-by began to be stopped and threatened; only hearty cheers for the Doctor and a few shillings to fund liberal toasts to his health guaranteed safe passage. It soon became clear that the private houses of various prominent Whigs – including those of Wharton, Hoadly and Cowper – were next in the mob's sights. There was even talk of marching on Mercer's Lane and making short work of the Bank of England, the nerve centre of London Whiggery.

The response of the authorities was very slow. Initially, the routine watches in the various localities were simply overwhelmed. It wasn't until about 9 p.m. that a very shaken William Cowper, accompanied by the Duke of Newcastle, panicked and fled to the office of Sunderland, the Junto Secretary of State, who was at work in Whitehall. Realising the scale of the disorder, Sunderland made haste to St James's Palace and sought an emergency audience with the Queen. There was no time to call out the militia: the only option was to deploy the Queen's personal guard. Sunderland was in a funk: if he ordered out her guards to suppress the mob, there was a risk that the crowds might find their way to the defenceless palace and threaten the person of the monarch. If he didn't, there might be no end to the violence.

The Queen, acting in her characteristically calm and courageous manner, took control. She ordered Sunderland to suppress the riots with her guards, exclaiming that 'God would be her guard'.[65] Mercifully, the professional soldiers suppressed the disorders with great calmness and efficiency, dispersing the crowds with few casualties and no gunfire. It took some hours, but by 3 a.m. an uneasy quiet had descended on the streets of London.

Amazingly, in total there were only around two deaths and fifty rioters wounded. The destruction to Dissenting property was considerable, but the chief result was the sheer panic and alarm caused. The next day, the guards, reinforced by troops from several other regiments, patrolled the streets from dawn until dusk. The authorities were deeply unnerved by the riots, and from the start the leading Whigs suspected that they were far from simply a spontaneous uprising.

They speculated that the disorder was carefully planned and incited, perhaps by some senior Tories, an impression reinforced by the fact that the crowd's actions appeared to be very well-planned and specifically targeted. Strangely, many of the mob appeared to have precisely the right tools for the dismantling of the Dissenting chapels, and the mob – although no doubt swelled by the usual hoodlums who enjoy destruction for the sake of it – seemed to contain an unusual number of 'white-collar' professionals. Rumours abounded of shadowy 'gentlemen' apparently present during the riots to direct proceedings while taking great pains to conceal their identity. Had senior Tories been involved in planning the disorder?

Perhaps, but ultimately it is not possible to make people riot and risk their liberty unless they are already well-motivated to do so. The underlying causes of the riot must at least partially have been genuine conviction, perhaps mixed with general discontent with an increasingly unpopular Whig ministry. When the rioters said that they were protesting in defence of the Church, and attacking its Dissenting 'enemies', they meant it. Religious prejudice was a very powerful thing in the early eighteenth century, and the wave of High Church propaganda that had been unleashed from the pulpit and printing press had, it seems, had its effect.

The irony of a mob rampaging and rioting in favour of non-resistance and obedience was not lost on observers. One Tory bemusedly commented:

> We are now come to fresh paradoxical circumstances, that while the rabble are pulling down houses out of zeal for passive obedience the vile tools of the most arbitrary ministry that ever the nation groaned under are rending their throats in defence of forcible resistance.[66]

From the other side of the partisan divide, Sarah Cowper dryly asked of the riots: 'are these ye Effects of Passive Obedience?'[67] The hypocrisy of the mob disgusted her.

Indeed, the entire spectacle, whipped up by Sacheverell's sermons, full as they were of 'Malice, Bitterness, Reviling, Insolence' and designed 'to raise in his Auditors the Passions [he] himself put on', were widely seen by Whigs as a telling demonstration of how Toryism had become a form of vulgar bigotry appealing chiefly to lower class 'deplorables'.[68] The implied contrast with polite, urbane Whiggery was not hard to discern.

Whatever the truth or otherwise of such a patrician Whig response, the main effect of the riots was to instil fear into the Doctor's opponents and make everyone weary of the consequences that a harsh sentence for him might provoke.

As such, the mood as the trial moved towards the case for the defence was an ominous one for the Whigs.

Nonetheless, Sir Simon Harcourt had a formidable task ahead of him as he prepared to open the case for the Doctor's defence. Not only did he have the delicate task of trying to extricate Sacheverell from the legal case mounted against him, but the task of vindicating the legitimacy of the entire edifice of post-revolution Toryism also fell upon his shoulders. Furthermore, he had fallen so ill with flu that he had to have a doctor at his side throughout his entire speech.

To cap it all, he was also engaged in a furious battle against time. Since being ejected from the Commons on petition, he had made concerted efforts to find a new parliamentary seat, and had duly won a by-election for Cardigan a few days *before* the trial had opened. It was only because the Tory sheriff had delayed the election and then sat on the official writ returning Harcourt as the member that he was allowed to act at all: the moment the return reached London, he would be a member of the Commons and disqualified from acting for Sacheverell.

It is therefore little short of a miracle that he rose to the occasion as brilliantly as he did. Contemporary commentators united in their wondering notices of his performance. He was widely regarded as the supreme advocate of his generation, but his defence of Sacheverell was his finest moment. A Tory diarist recorded that it could 'with modesty be said that it at least equalled anything we yet know of the Grecian or Roman oratory'.[69]

The heart of his case was an attempt to show that Sacheverell's argument concerning resistance was very much in line with the sort of reasoning that the Whig Sir John Hawles had himself used.

His first main argument was that Sacheverell had argued that what was totally unjustifiable was resistance to 'the Supreme Power'. 'Supreme Power' was an ambiguous term: it could mean resistance to the monarch – and therefore in the case of 1688, James II – but it could mean the entire legislative power, as invested in the King (or Queen)-in-Parliament. In that case, what had happened in 1688 was not 'resistance', as the 'Supreme Power', in that sense, had not been resisted: indeed, it was parliament that had been the prime actor against the King. As he put it:

> [Sacheverell] has indeed affirm'd the utter Illegality of Resistance on any Pretence whatsoever to the Supreme Power; but it can't be pretended, there was any such Resistance used at the Revolution; the Supreme Power in this Kingdom is the Legislative Power, and the Revolution took effect by the Lords and Commons concurring and assisting in it. Whatever therefore the Doctor has asserted of the utter Illegality of Resistance, his Assertion being applied to the Supreme Power, can't relate to any Resistance used at the Revolution, and consequently, can't be an Affirmance, that such Resistance [was] Odious and Unjustifiable.[70]

In short, he attempted to compass Sacheverell's sermon within the mainstream of the 'new school' of moderate post-revolutionary Toryism.

This, however, was only the first part of his defence. Aware that this all relied on a somewhat debatable interpretation of Sacheverell's argument, and particularly what he had intended by the phrase 'Supreme Power', he then sought to argue that even if Sacheverell had referred only to the monarch and not the legislature, he was still innocent.

He did this by a rather clever sleight of hand. He argued that, when a general rule – such as non-resistance – was proposed, any possible exceptions that might arise in 'extraordinary cases . . . of necessity' were not necessarily to be expressed explicitly, but rather 'understood or implied'. In short, one could maintain a *general* principle of non-resistance while still accommodating the idea that there might be extreme circumstances where the requirements of self-preservation interposed and necessitated a one-off act of resistance. As the Revolution clearly was such an exceptional case, why would Sacheverell have needed to have mentioned that explicitly?

This argument had an obvious weakness and a clear strength. The obvious weakness was that it was hard to credit that Sacheverell had taken it for granted that 1688 *was* an exceptional case, given that he had explicitly denied that any resistance had taken place during the Revolution at all.

The strength was that arguments of this kind, from exceptional necessity, were the stock-in-trade of more conservative Whig – and some moderate Tory – arguments for the Revolution, and therefore familiar to his audience. When added to his argument about 'the Supreme Power', Harcourt could argue with some plausibility that there was reasonable doubt about whether Sacheverell's words had impugned the Revolution. In short, Harcourt had used his brilliance as a lawyer to cast enough doubt on the Whig case to give everyone who had ulterior motives a reasonable cover for what they wanted to do anyway: deliver a sufficiently equivocal verdict on the Doctor so as to weaken the Junto, perhaps fatally.

Much of the rest of the defence case was taken up with enumerating the venerable pedigree of non-resistance and passive obedience as the official doctrines of the Church, and demonstrating the virulent – and, to most, genuinely shocking – strains of atheism, deism and free-thinking that Sacheverell's tirades against 'false brethren' could be argued to have been chiefly directed against.

On many of the other charges, the defence were on a sticky wicket, and overall the Whigs, who delivered a rigorous and brilliantly detailed summing up, had the best of much of the legal argument. Unfortunately for them, this was not, in the end, to count for very much, for the dry proceedings of the second half of the trial were completely overshadowed by Doctor Sacheverell's contribution. On 7 March, he personally replied to the charges against him.

Sacheverell was bright enough to realise that a furious rant along the lines of his usual performances was not the ideal tone to strike in his own trial. He had been persuaded to let his cabal of advisers – most prominently, Atterbury – draft a speech for him. They went for a very different tone – martyred and suffering innocent – and he performed the role magnificently.

The fact was that his original sermon had always been couched in terms *just* about ambiguous enough to bear a less incendiary reading, and in the speech the Doctor played on this fact shamelessly, insisting that any more sinister reading of his words was an unfair attack on a pious and unassuming minister of the Almighty. He theatrically declared, in response to the accusations of Jacobitism, that, with God as his witness, he repudiated the Pretender and pledged undying and unlimited loyalty to the Queen.

Playing on the fact that the Whigs had had to put their own interpretation on his words and motivations, constructions that, while often quite reasonable, were not certain given the equivocations of his original sermon, he insisted that only God alone could know his true, loyal, honest thoughts:

> I call on the Searcher of Hearts to witness in the most solemn and religious manner, as I expect to be acquitted before God and his Holy Angels at that dreadful tribunal before which not only I but all the world . . . must appear . . . that I had no such wicked, seditious or malicious intentions; that there is nothing on earth I more detest and abhor; that my designs were in every respect directly contrary.[71]

He ended with an extraordinary attempt to play on the Christian instincts of his audience, presenting himself as a man heinously wronged by the extraordinary allegations brought against him, attacked merely for defending the traditional doctrines of Christ's Holy Church – truly 'the man of sorrows'. The public manner and publicity of his trial having made him:

> a Gazing-Stock, both by Reproaches, and Afflictions, and a Spectacle to the whole World, I have stood in this Place Day after Day, to hear my self Accus'd of the Blackest Crimes, and openly revil'd.[72]

He veered remarkably close to comparing himself to Christ himself, ready to forgive those enemies who had so unfairly wronged him.

By the time he ended his peroration with a lengthy quotation from the Litany (the penitential service from the Book of Common Prayer), he had his audience spellbound. He had needed to give the speech of his life, and he hadn't come up short. Swathes of the female portion of the audience had begun to weep into their handkerchiefs; some were sobbing hysterically; even old warhorses like Rochester and Nottingham were seen to shed a tear. He had pulled at the heartstrings brilliantly: those who knew what he was really like no doubt found it hard to credit, but many bought his virtuoso performance wholesale.

The trial ran on for a few more days, but none of it made much difference. Harcourt and the doctor had achieved everything that Harley needed them to: they had, by mastery of legal argument, political dexterity and shameless heartstring tugging, done enough to take the worst of the sting out of Whig accusations of sedition and Jacobitism that were potentially so damaging to Harley's delicate manoeuvrings. The rest was up to him.

At first, it looked as if the efforts of Harcourt had been in vain. Many of the lords were most interested, not in what had happened in Westminster Hall, but what the Queen wanted: courtiers, whether nominally Tory or Whig, did not want to displease their sovereign. The first indications were favourable to the Whigs: on 5th March, the Lord Chief Justice of the Queen's Bench, Sir John Holt, died, and by the 9th the Queen had appointed one of the Whig managers of the case against Sacheverell, Sir Thomas Parker. She then offered two recently vacant bishoprics to two Low Church Whigs. This was widely seen as an indication that the Queen was against Sacheverell and wished to see him convicted and harshly punished.

As the lords geared up to deliver their verdict, could Harley engineer an acquittal despite the Queen's apparent attitude? The problem was that even the Whig lords who were doubtful about the Junto's dominance and wished to join Harley's 'moderate scheme' were reluctant to go so far as to actually let Sacheverell off: the trial was too clearly a straight partisan fight that went to the heart of the basic philosophical differences between the two parties. Harley managed to get Somerset to absent himself and so miss the vote, and various moderate Tory courtiers who usually voted with the government were persuaded to acquit the Doctor. Shrewsbury, who was by now thick as thieves with Harley, also voted with the Tories.

But it wasn't enough. As the lords individually announced their decisions of guilty or not guilty, it became gradually clear that the Whigs were edging ahead. Cowper, as Lord Chancellor, carefully tallied the vote. Given the pro-Whig political composition of the Lords, it was closer than might have been expected, but not that close. By sixty-nine votes to fifty-two, the Lords had adjudged Henry Sacheverell to be guilty of the charges laid against him.

A weary but relieved Godolphin wrote to Marlborough announcing the government's victory. Marlborough was a little surprised at how close the vote was – he assumed a wider margin of victory – and was surprised that Shrewsbury was reckless enough to range himself against the government. But a cautious note of satisfaction prevailed.

What they didn't realise was that Harley had another ace up his sleeve and Shrewsbury good reasons for his boldness.

Realising that he couldn't win on the vote on the Doctor's guilt, Harley shrewdly changed tack. The wavering Whig lords might not want to vote to *acquit* Sacheverell, but there was still the vote on the *verdict* to come, and that was essential. The original point of the conviction was not only to convict the Doctor, but to punish him harshly: indeed, the harsh penalties afforded by an impeachment hearing were part of the point of taking the case to the Lords. Perhaps the waverers could salve their Whig consciences by voting to convict, but then play Harley's game by voting for a light sentence? A mild enough sentence might be a sufficient blow to Junto credit to persuade the Queen to move against them.

Just at this point, the Queen played beautifully into Harley's hands (perhaps not altogether coincidentally). She started to indicate her desire for a light sentence. She told the Lord Chamberlain that she 'thought the Commons had reason to be satisfied that they had made their allegations good, and the mildest punishment inflicted upon the Doctor she thought the best'.[73] It seems likely that she feared a harsh sentence might give rise to further public riots and disorder. This helped Harley win over a number of wavering Scottish lords, such as Argyll, and various other flaky Whigs; gradually he bartered them down over the punishment until he could feel victory within his grasp.

Originally, the Junto were hellbent on a harsh sentence for the doctor: a lengthy term of imprisonment, a stiff fine and a lifetime ban on preaching and all further ecclesiastical preferment. However, by the time the lords packed into the chamber on 21st March 1710 to vote on the sentence, the course of the trial and the indications coming from the palace meant that they had been forced to settle on proposing a mere three-month prison sentence, a ban on preaching and further preferment for seven years, and the burning of his sermons by the common hangman.

And then they watched with horror and astonishment as even these relatively mild terms were hacked away, piece by piece. They managed to hold onto a ban on preaching for a mere three years and the burning of the sermons, but that was it. The proposal to bar him from all preferment within the Church for the course of his preaching suspension was, amazingly, lost by one vote, and any idea of a prison sentence or a fine was dropped without even a vote. The moderate Whigs and Scottish opportunists whom Harley had been courting abandoned the Junto and the ministry in droves. 'Robin the Trickster' had utterly routed them.

Their humiliation was immense. A bitter and frustrated Godolphin summed up his feelings to Marlborough:

> So all this bustle and fatigue ends in no more but a suspension of three years from the pulpit, and burning his sermon at the Old Exchange.[74]

The Tories could hardly believe their luck. They immediately went on the offensive in the Commons over a motion to thank the Whig organisers of the impeachment 'for their faithful management in charge of the trust reposed in them'.[75] A gale of Tory sarcasm and mockery engulfed the chamber: the attacks on Dolben were so harsh that he fled the chamber almost in tears, and one Tory got a hearty laugh when he suggested that the strongest argument in favour of the motion was that if the Commons didn't thank the Whig managers, no one else would. Much salt was rubbed into some very raw wounds.

Most worryingly for the Whigs, they sensed (rightly) that it was an ominous straw in the political wind. Clearly a floating party of Scots and moderate Whigs in the Lords had abandoned the Junto – and they would only have dared to do so if they had good reasons to believe that the Queen was inclined the same way, and the temper of the country was against the ministry. And behind it all was one man, using every ounce of his political acumen to tease and manipulate the situation behind the scenes and eject the Junto from office.

The revenge of Harley was nigh.

* * *

The seismic shocks of the Sacheverell trial soon started to shake the whole nation. The derisory sentence was widely seen as tantamount to an acquittal. The sentiments that the case had stirred – of sympathy for an innocent man of God persecuted by a wicked ministry and of panic over the danger allegedly facing the Church from Dissenters and the Junto – were truly formidable.

Edition after edition of Sacheverell's emotive trial speech poured from the presses, as did a stream of pamphlets presenting him as a holy man persecuted by a set of godless heathens.[76] These productions – the fact that one prominent example was entitled *The Pious Life and Sufferings of the Reverend Dr Henry Sacheverell* gives a good idea of the tone – were akin to the lives of early Church saints and martyrs, dramatising his plight with extraordinary pathos and, some might say, chutzpah. The fact that Sacheverell was about as far away from being a meek innocent victim as it is possible to imagine was totally engulfed by a wave of emotion that appealed to deep seams of raw pro-Church sentiment in the nation's psyche.

The boisterous celebrations began in London but soon spread across the country. Between 21st and 23rd March, the capital was lit up with bonfires and illuminated windows to honour the Doctor's triumph. Church bells rang out everywhere in cacophonous jubilation. Beer flowed freely and toasts to the Doctor filled the air in almost every street in London. Then the news reached Oxford, that bastion of High Church influence, and was greeted with an enormous procession accompanied by a ceremonial burning of an effigy of Burgess (the Dissenting minister whose meeting house had been burnt down in the riots) and some copies of Hoadly's works.

This was predictable, but what was less so was how the celebrations spread like wildfire to the whole country: towns, sleepy villages and tiny hamlets across England were convulsed with wild pro-Sacheverell sentiment and exuberant celebrations of his sentence. From Barnstaple to Cirencester, from Shrewsbury to Sherborne, the nation lit up in an orgy of toasts, bonfires, and wild celebrations. In many places events turned rather nastier, with Dissenting chapels and meeting houses targeted: in Gainsborough, for example, a mob broke down the door of the local conventicle and ransacked the place.

Perhaps the most remarkable manifestation of 'Sacheverell-mania' was the enormous tide of loyal addresses that started to flow in from the country. The Tory gentry and clergy of county after county flocked to their assizes and archdeaconry meetings to propose extravagant statements of support for the Church and the Queen. Sacheverell was rarely mentioned by name, but the ultra-loyalism that he had stirred up was very much in evidence in the vast majority of the addresses. The clergy of Coventry, for example, expressed their 'most hearty Concern and Sorrow' that:

> there should any Men be found so daringly Wicked and Ungrateful, as openly to Espouse and Maintain the same Detestable Principles, which gave Rise to the unnatural Rebellion, which involved this Nation in all the Miseries of a Long and Intestine War, the Overthrow of this Primitive Establish'd Church, and the Barbarous Murder of your Royal Grandfather, the meekest of Kings, and the best of Men.[77]

As ever with the Tories, memories of the Great Rebellion were never far away.

Sacheverell himself did everything he could to personally help sustain this outpouring of Church-and-king Tory sentiment. On 14th May he travelled to Oxford in the company of hundreds of well-wishers. He received a rapturous reception when he reached his destination. A delegation of Oxford politicians and all the leading academics in the university welcomed him and gave him a lavish celebratory meal before he settled into Magdalen College to receive a stampede of congratulatory visitors.

Having been wined and dined and extravagantly toasted for just over a fortnight in Oxford, the Doctor set off on an extraordinary tour of the country, a sort of emulation of a royal 'progress'. He had been offered a lavish new living (the rectory of Selattyn in Shropshire) to celebrate his victory by a Tory patron, and so he travelled very slowly to claim it before turning back to Oxford, taking care to visit as many towns and villages as he possibly could. His 'progress' took in Oxfordshire, Warwickshire, Staffordshire, Cheshire, Denbighshire, Flintshire, Shropshire, Worcestershire and Gloucestershire.

On his route, he was honoured and feted with extraordinary lavishness. Most boroughs put on civic receptions, banquets, celebratory breakfasts and 'treats' in his honour. He dined and usually stayed with baronets, bishops, earls, Tory MPs: at each stop the local gentry and clergy flocked to see the great man and give their regards. During the course of this whirlwind social tour, he drank enough wine to float one of the Royal Navy's prize fighting ships and consumed over fifty vast feasts. The persecuted 'man of sorrows' presumably encountered enough liquid hospitality to drown even his considerable woes.

Everywhere he went he was met with extravagant displays of adulation and support. In Coventry the civic band trumpeted his arrival with music and fanfare, and then the town gave him the honour of a triple artillery barrage accompanied with a raucous toast; in Wrexham, the inhabitants 'strew[ed] their streets with flowers and decorat[ed] their houses with boughs', before burning effigies of Hoadly in a bonfire for good measure.[78] His entry into Shrewsbury was accompanied by a 'huge cavalcade of mounted gentry and yeomen, headed by the two prospective Tory [parliamentary] candidates and numbered by most observers at 5000, by some at 7000'.[79] Church bells clamoured the length and breadth of the shires to herald the great Christian hero of England.

In short, Sacheverell became little short of a political and ecclesiastical rock star, stirring up loyalist and Tory sentiment throughout the country. Parents started to christen their babies 'Sacheverell' and Tory cockfighters changed their fighting birds' names to that of the Doctor. A wave of Sacheverell-themed merchandise was produced, which included ceramic dishes, statuettes, letter seals, coat buttons, tobacco stoppers, playing cards and ladies' fans.[80] Engravings of him sold in enormous quantities.

The Whigs made some efforts to respond to Sacheverell fever with their own counter-symbols. They marketed similar engraved portraits of Hoadly so that those of a Low Church, Whiggish bent could display their loyalties too. Tory Thomas Hearne describes how 'some honest gentlemen' bought up a load of copies and vandalised them, 'putting on him Asses Ears and Two Horns, with a Couple of Wings' and a Latin tag implying that Hoadly's wife 'cuckol'd [him] every day', so this stratagem seems to have only been

341

a limited success.[81] More commercially rewarding was a range of chamber pots that a Whig ceramics manufacturer produced with a portrayal of the Doctor on the bottom, so that hearty Whigs could defecate on an image of their their bête noire's face. Overall, however, there was no doubt who won the merchandise war.

While this whirlwind was raging, the leading Tory politicians held their breath to see if the shenanigans over Sacheverell's nugatory sentence presaged promising developments within the Queen's court and government.[82]

The Queen and Harley had to move very cautiously. On the one hand, the simple fact was that however much the political situation in the country was turning decisively against the Whigs, they had a solid majority in the Commons. On the other, the pro-Tory wind that was blowing so vigorously throughout the country meant that an early election could result in an enormous Tory landslide. Neither Harley nor the Queen wanted a government in hock to newly emboldened high-flying Tories any more than one dominated by the Junto. Harley's aim was for a moderate, mixed ministry, led by him rather than Godolphin, that would, as he put it, 'graft the Whigs on the bulk of the Church Party'.[83] The broader objective that united them both was to deliver the Queen from being driven by the overbearing chiefs of any political party – and the 'Family'. The Tories were an invaluable counterweight, but the danger was that they could become the drivers themselves.

Key to this plan was coaxing enough Whigs into such a mixed scheme. Some Whigs, like Shrewsbury, had been won over to Harley's side due to war-weariness, others due to gripes with the Junto and personal ambition (Somerset), but many Whigs – including even some members of the Junto – were prepared to countenance doing a deal with Harley largely because they were petrified of a general election, which, given the ferment in the country, seemed likely, if held in the short term, to deliver a massive Tory majority. If Harley could delay a dissolution, and if the changes to the government were piecemeal and managed carefully, then he could perhaps amputate the most offensive parts of the current ministry piece by piece, dividing and ruling the Whigs while keeping the High Tories in check.

In April – spurred on by another outburst from Sarah – the Queen made her first delicate tactical incision. On 13th April, she wrote to Godolphin, who was relaxing at the races in Newmarket, to inform him of her decision to remove the Marquis of Kent as Lord Chamberlain and appoint key Harley ally Shrewsbury as his replacement. Kent – nicknamed 'the Bug' because of his unpleasant bodily stink – was a Whig, as was Shrewsbury. Such a like-for-like replacement, especially given Shrewsbury's reputation as one of the 'Immortal Seven' during the Glorious Revolution, meant that it was a very hard appointment for the Junto Whigs to oppose openly. Shrewsbury was appointed on the 14th.

Whatever problems Harley faced, the travails of the Junto were far worse. They could resign en masse and take down Harley's whole operation, but they all knew that the almost certain result of that would be a general election in which they would be massacred. In any case, their united front had broken down. Harley had put out feelers to several of the Junto men, including Somers, Sunderland and Halifax, implying in his usual gnomic way that perhaps terms could be reached that would allow them to stay on in a reconstructed ministry. How sincere Harley was is hard to say, but each clung on to the possibility of their own political survival: caught between the risks of a Harley-led reconstruction of the government and the unappetising option of going to the country, it seemed like the least unfavourable option.

The Queen's next projected move was a clean, tactical amputation: she planned to sack Sunderland, the rude quasi-republican Junto lord whom she had always hated. The fact that he was Sarah's son-in-law no doubt played a role too. His ejection would nicely clip the wings not only of the Junto, but of the 'Family'.

Godolphin feverishly attempted to prevent this step. His fear related to foreign policy. In February, the Dutch had reopened negotiations for peace with France, and stuck, at the behest of the British government, to the harshest terms possible. He feared that any sign of cracks in the Junto hold on the ministry would encourage the French to break off negotiations and await a less hardline ministry who might give them better terms. He attempted to use this argument to persuade the Queen to retain Sunderland, but to no avail.

When the blow fell against Sunderland, on 14th June, it proved once again to be a clever move. The fact that everyone knew that the Queen despised him personally made him a tricky person to go in to bat for, and he was replaced by a figure sufficiently colourless – a moderate and competent Tory, the Earl of Dartmouth – as to defang violent Whig reaction. None of the Junto lords felt that this was worth resigning over, especially with the prospect of a general election hanging over them.

Instead, they and Godolphin attempted to stop the rot: they made one last effort to prevent changes to the ministry.

On 15th June, a delegation from the Bank of England, led by the staunchly Whig governor Sir Gilbert Heathcote, visited Anne and gave her an ultimatum: either she promise to delay a dissolution and make no further changes in the ministry, or she would see the loans that kept the government's head above water dry up. The next day they fired a warning shot by temporarily refusing a routine request from the government for a loan. The financiers were Whig in their politics and supported the hardest line possible against France, and they had confidence in Godolphin, with whom they had worked for years.

At this point, Harley had reached something of an impasse. He was determined to replace Godolphin and come to some sort of agreement over a mixed ministry that would retain enough Whigs to give it credibility while placating the Tories. The Tories were getting restless: conscious of their soaring popularity in the country, given hope of preferment by the drip-drip of ministerial changes, and desperate for an election, they wanted their reward. One frustrated Tory wrote to Harley's brother:

> We think your proceedings too slow, and are afraid you are terrified by the Bank. But should the power of the Bank come down to Kensington, we must call up Dr. Sacheverell and his posse to encounter them.[84]

St John agreed and did nothing to discourage such Tory discontent.

Harley, who was caballing with the Tories as much as with the Whigs, could hardly ignore such sentiments altogether. However, the threat of a strike of capital on the part of the Bank of England was a major obstacle to more radical steps, as was the fact that the Queen was still reluctant to lose the services of Godolphin, who was, after all, her oldest and most loyal retainer.

Indeed, it is by no means clear what the Queen and even Harley really wanted at this juncture. With the hated Sunderland out, Anne may have been content with no further changes. Harley definitely wanted Godolphin out and himself in, but he would probably have been content with retaining Marlborough as a politically neutered military figurehead, and replacing only the most recalcitrant allies of the Junto—Marlborough connexion with his own nominees, largely moderate Tories. He wanted peace, but not at any price, and so such a scheme was attractive insofar as it might avoid a dissolution, allow the government to continue with a military and foreign policy only moderately different from the existing one, all while allowing the Tory storm in the country to settle down.

The first objective – removing Godolphin – Harley managed to achieve largely by virtue of the Lord Treasurer's own behaviour. It became clear that he, the Junto and Marlborough had been manoeuvring behind the scenes to get the Dutch to communicate to the Queen their desire for no further changes in the ministry. Unfortunately for Godolphin, this simply enraged the Queen, who did not appreciate being ordered around by foreign governments and told them to mind their own business in no uncertain terms. In cabinet, Godolphin became ever sharper with the Queen on this point, which offended her. The Queen also wanted to wield the threat of a dissolution and election in order to exercise leverage over her Whig ministers, but Godolphin was absolutely convinced of the need to rule out such a move. By late summer, the Lord Treasurer teetered on the edge of dismissal.

Meanwhile, Harley was formulating a new plan. Over the course of the tumultuous summer of 1710, as Sacheverell-fever raged and the Tories became ever more bullish about their chances, it became increasingly clear to him that the plan he had until recently favoured, of indefinitely delaying a dissolution and trying to reconstitute a mixed ministry without an election, was impossible. If he adopted the strategy, he would very quickly lose the support of the entire Tory Party. His whole mixed ministry plan depended on the support of the bulk of the Church Party in parliament, and much as he wanted to retain as many Whigs as possible, he could not afford a rupture with the Tories.

Tory suspicion had been building throughout the summer. Why was he spending so much time trying to persuade Whigs to stay on in his new ministry? Why was he keeping his Tory allies in the dark? Why did he delay a dissolution? Senior Tories suspected that Harley was preparing to betray them. St John feared that Harley was going to exclude him, and he and Harcourt seriously considered breaking with him altogether. Instead, they sent Atterbury – always a man of bold and direct methods – to have it out with him. Atterbury acquainted Harley with 'how very uneasy' his Tory friends were 'at his conduct'. [85] A snappish Harley rebuked Atterbury, but he knew that Tory patience was close to breaking point. [86]

So, he concocted a scheme to sack Godolphin, but rather than replace him directly, put the Treasury into commission, headed by himself as Chancellor of the Exchequer, and stuff it with his personal adherents. Effective control of the Treasury gained, he could improvise some short-term financial expedients to keep the government solvent even if the Bank of England went to war against it. Then, he could use the patronage of the Treasury – which had potentially a lot of influence over elections if it wished to use it – to limit the Tory landslide threatened by a dissolution. If he could do all this while also persuading at least some 'big-hitter' Whigs to remain in the government, he could keep his moderate ministry scheme on track, get rid of Godolphin, and retain the support of the Tories, some of whom would have to be given office.

The first part of this plan worked. At cabinet on 30th July Godolphin pushed the Queen too far: he rebuked her in harsh terms in front of her own ministers. Harley could see victory within his reach: '[Godolphin] every day grows sower and indeed ruder to the Queen, which is unaccountable, & will hear of no accomodation, so that it is impossible he continue many days'.[87] Despite much dithering, on 8th August, she finally sent him a letter of dismissal:

> The uneasiness which you have showed for some time has given me very
> much trouble, though I have borne it; and had your behaviour continued
> the same it was for a few years after my coming to the crown, I could
> have no dispute with myself what to do. But the many unkind returns

346

> I have received since, especially what you said to me personally before the Lords, makes it impossible for me to continue you any longer in my service.[88]

So ended the political career of the man who had acted as the political and financial lynchpin of the Queen's government for eight years. He broke his white staff, sent the pieces back to the Queen and calmly advised Marlborough not to resign.

Harley's difficulties were not over. The government's finances were already in an extremely shaky state: in order to fund Britain's military and diplomatic obligations, Godolphin had been forced into some desperate expedients. Although taxes had gone up, poor weather and the strain of war had hit the economy hard, and tax yields had remained static or even fallen. The result was a hotchpotch of short-term and often unfunded government debts. The situation was so dire that, when Harley became Chancellor of the Exchequer in August 1710, the government had over £8 million in unfunded debts, and a mere £5,000 in cash in its coffers.

The situation was only about to get worse. On the news that Godolphin had fallen, the Whig bankers, suspicious that a full-scale Tory reconstruction of the ministry was on the cards, pulled the plug, stopping loans and making it impossible for the British army in Flanders to pay its bills. It was only by a superhuman whirl of financial wizardry that Harley was able to save the situation. He succeeded in finding other private bankers willing to lend to the government, and even persuaded the Bank of England to ease up: they loaned him much less than he wanted on very stiff terms, but overall he managed to find the money, at least for the time being, and calm the markets.

By 12th September, with the financial situation temporarily eased, the next part of the plan could be put into action: dissolution and a general election. However, this was where Harley's plan partially came unstuck. Once they realised that a dissolution was certain, the remaining Whigs in the Cabinet decided that there was nothing left to keep them there. They decided that their best course of action was to let Harley and the Tories run the show, wait for them to fail, either through financial or diplomatic crisis, and then ride to the rescue in a year or two.

So the entire Junto, and even more moderate Whigs like Cowper, resigned in unison despite (somewhat unconvincing) claims by Harley that 'a Whig game [was] intended at bottom'.[89] Cowper's response to Harley's blandishments was recorded in his private diary:

> I have reason to believe . . . that things were plainly put into Tories' hands; a Whig game, either in whole or part, impracticable; that to keep in, when all my friends were out, would be infamous.[90]

Harley was only able to retain the Whigs he had already peeled off by the time of the Sacheverell sentencing – semi-independent ones like Shrewsbury, Newcastle and Somerset. Harley and the Queen had no choice but to turn to the Tories.

The Church Party was back.

Harley now faced another, entirely different problem: to prevent his and the Queen's desire for moderation from being overwhelmed by a re-energised and rampant Tory Party. In the short term, they had no choice but to appoint a predominantly Tory ministry.

Rochester had been convinced all along that the only solution was – funnily enough – a Tory-dominated ministry led by none other than himself. He deeply distrusted Harley. Shortly before the Whigs resigned, he had told the Queen in no uncertain terms that:

> the plan to form a government independent of the parties was unworkable. Neither he, nor any other member of the High Church Party was inclined to serve with men who did not agree with them in principle. On the other hand, if the Queen trusted the High Church Party, it would serve her as one body.[91]

The High Tories were completely right to be worried, of course: it was only the impossibility of managing affairs in such a way as to avoid a dissolution that led Harley to the expedient of a Tory-dominated ministry.

The fact that this occurred did, in the short term, reconcile the Tories to Harley. Rochester was appointed Lord President of the Council, but he had no choice but to resign himself to the fact that the Queen would lean on Harley as her chief minister, not him. Further appointments over the course of mid-to-late September followed: Harcourt came in as Attorney General, St John as Secretary of State for the Northern Department (with the able, well-respected Tory moderate Dartmouth remaining as the other Secretary of State), and a whole range of other Tories filled up the government. Harley did his best to maintain as many Whigs in office as possible, refusing to clear out the lower offices for Tory claimants en masse, but the general tenor of the new ministry was unmistakable: the leading men of the Church Party were in.

The major exception to this was Nottingham. The Queen still detested him and Nottingham despised and distrusted Harley. The feeling was mutual: Harley felt that the prickly, lowering figure of Nottingham represented the most reckless instincts of the Tories that had sunk them back during the furore over occasional conformity and the Tack. As one ally of Harley put it:

> Nottingham has undone [the Tories] once, and you have saved them; and if anything ever disturbs your government, it must be the taint of old courtiers.[92]

Furthermore, Nottingham's views on foreign policy put as much weight on the importance of 'No Peace without Spain' as did the Whigs. Harley knew that such a position was madness and that Nottingham was likely to be a thorn in his side over future peace negotiations. Accordingly, Nottingham did not solicit a position, and he certainly wasn't offered one.

Although the new ministry was Tory enough to quieten Tory discontent, the whole episode had reminded them of what they saw as Harley's slipperiness. They trusted Harley little more than the Whigs did and frankly hoped to be able to exploit Harley to serve their own purposes. Through his scheming they had, eventually, got the dissolution and the new ministry they hoped for; once they had swept all before them in a general election, they could, they reasoned, use him for as long as he was convenient to them, and then toss him aside and govern uncompromisingly according to the principles of High Church Toryism.

Much would depend on the result of the upcoming general election.

It soon became clear, as the election campaign began, that the fires lit by Dr Sacheverell were very far from having burnt out. This was hardly a surprise. In addition to the tremendous momentum gained by Sacheverell's 'progress', which gave the Tory election campaign a power that had not been known since the beginning of Anne's reign, one group in particular – the clergy – did everything they could to pour fuel on the fire. As Bishop Burnet noted:

> besides a course, for some months, of inflaming sermons, they went about from house to house, pressing their people to shew, on this great occasion, their zeal for the church, and now or never to save it: they also told them in what ill hands the queen had been kept, as in captivity, and that it was a charity, as well as their duty, to free her from the power the late ministry exercised over her.[93]

A particularly piquant example gives, perhaps, a good indication of the mindset of the lower clergy as the election campaign burst into action. In Whitechapel, the Tory rector commissioned and installed an altarpiece depicting the Last Supper. White Kennett, a leading Low Church Whig dean who had written one of the most impressive and high-profile attacks on Sacheverell, was depicted on it as Judas, and in case anyone failed to get the point, the words 'The Dean, Traitor' were written underneath.[94]

The election was unusually violent even by contemporary standards, especially in London, where mobs intimidated anyone who dared to try to vote Whig. One eye-witness account gives a sense of the disorder:

> Honest men have been afraid to come to the Poll, for fear of being abus'd, and many that have attempt'd to come, have been so beaten and bruised, kick'd, thrusted, and otherwise abus'd, that they have thought it a happiness to get safe back again, and . . . so have not poll'd at all.[95]

Stanhope, who had been one of the Whig 'managers' of Sacheverell's trial, was routed in Westminster, where he was 'called a sodomite, and other scandalous names, and charged with having profaned and defiled the altar'.[96] The fury of the Tory crowd was such that it seemed 'rather to be a Combat than an Election'.[97] There were similar scenes – sometimes perpetrated by the desperate Whigs rather than the Tories – at Northampton, Chester, Coventry, Nottingham and Newark.[98]

The Whig 'managers' of the Doctor's trial had a torrid time indeed. Robert Walpole fell victim to the outrages of a Tory mob in Norwich:

> [The Tories] had Dr Sacheverell's picture carried before them and the cry was 'no manager', 'no scaffolder', but that was not all for they pelted Mr Walpole with dirt and stones and drove him out of his tent, spoiling his fine laced coat which they told him came out of the Treasury.[99]

He was routed in Norwich and only managed to get back into the Commons via one of his family's pocket boroughs, King's Lynn.

It wasn't just the managers who suffered. The Tories produced 'division lists', inventories of every MP who had voted to take forward Sacheverell's impeachment, and circulated them in huge numbers in the constituencies. Except in the safest Whig close boroughs and areas of strong Dissenting or Low Church tendencies, being thought to be 'against the Doctor and the Church' was the political kiss of death. Even in the relatively quiet pastures of Wensleydale, Yorkshire, a Whig canvasser noticed the sensational effect on the voters of the Doctor: 'all the town are Sacheverellians and value themselves mightily upon it'.[100]

All over the country, Tory candidates ranged themselves under the banner of the Doctor, parading enormous portraits of him as they marched to the polls. At the poll for the Cambridgeshire county election, one defiant Whig managed to take a knife to one such portrait, which proved to be an unwise move: 'he was subjected to various indignities involving the "powdering" of his wig with dirt, and the loss of his trousers'.[101] This swift mob justice was an accurate reflection of the sentiments of the voters: the Tories 'carried it gloriously . . . by a majority of almost 700 voices'.[102]

Although the Sacheverell factor and the 'Church in Danger' cry undoubtedly did most for the Tory cause, there was another issue: the desire for peace.

St John played cleverly on this theme in an election pamphlet, *A Letter to the Examiner*. He did not, as yet, come out openly for abandoning 'No Peace without Spain', but, getting in a little dig at Sarah Churchill as well as the Whigs, he did present the war as prolonged by the 'Will of an Arbitrary Junto, and . . . the Caprice of an Insolent Woman', to the benefit of the Whig financiers and the Dutch, at the expense of much British 'blood and treasure'.[103] Until the Whigs were ejected, he argued:

> Britain may expect to remain exhausted of Men and Money, to see her Trade divided amongst her Neighbours, her Revenues anticipated even to future Generations, and to have this only Glory left Her, that She had proved a Farm to the Bank, a Province to Holland, and a Jest to the Whole World.[104]

Overall, the Tories, perhaps cautious not to lay themselves open to the charge of being 'soft on France', did not make as much of this issue as they might have done, but it was clear that a war-weary nation saw little hope for peace from a Whig parliament, and this certainly did the Tory cause no harm.

Some Whig commentators presented the election as an orgy of High Church intimidation, corruption and violence orchestrated by the ministry to bully a reluctant people into voting for the Tories. Although there was violence, they were deluding themselves. The unsettling truth for the Whigs was that public opinion – and crucially the views of those who were eligible to vote – had turned decisively against them. As one of the more clear-eyed Whigs wrote to Marlborough during the campaign, 'there never was so prevalent a fury as the people of England shew against the Whigs and for the High Church'.[105]

Furthermore, of course, it was absolutely false that the ministry used its influence on behalf of the Tories: Harley did everything he could to use Treasury patronage to achieve the opposite. The last thing he wanted was a colossal High Tory majority, which might soon overwhelm his schemes for moderation. Indeed, Harley engaged Defoe to write 'moderating' propaganda designed to support him while pouring cold water on High Church extremism. None of it, however, had much effect. The forces unleashed by Sacheverell and pent-up frustration at the Whigs were too strong for anyone to restrain.

Accordingly, as the results began to trickle in during October and November 1710, the scale of the Whig bloodbath became clear. It was a Tory landslide beyond even the most partisan High Churchman's wildest dreams.

The Tories swept the board in London, and in the counties that Sacheverell had toured, Whig after Whig fell to defeat. Both in county elections and the boroughs with relatively wide electorates, the Tories triumphed, often by huge majorities. They gained 132 seats in England, leaving them with 329 MPs to the Whigs' 168, a position that was improved even further by similarly good results in Scotland. Estimating their majority with any precision is hard given the difficulties of classification, but it was probably around 130–155.[106]

As Harley surveyed the likely composition of the new parliament, he knew that the challenge of a lifetime awaited him. Could he secure a lasting peace and stave off government bankruptcy, all while avoiding being overwhelmed by his rampant Tory allies, resisting the fury of the Whigs and keeping the good offices of the Queen?

The nation was about to find out.

10

The Conduct of the Allies

On 7th September 1710, just as Harley was hurriedly throwing together a Tory-dominated ministry and awaiting the dissolution, a weary middle-aged Irish clergyman reached London after a tedious journey of nearly a week's duration. His name was Jonathan Swift, and he was a man on a mission.

Restless and intellectually brilliant, Swift's literary reputation was already considerable. He had made his name with *The Tale of a Tub*, a pessimistic satire on the failings of various branches of Christianity since the Reformation. By turns playful and gloomy, wittily charming and misanthropic, Swift was an intense personality, roiled both by a complicated and mysterious love life and a tortured relationship with his own faith. Conscious of the dangerous potentialities of his own inner conflicts, he was fired his whole life by an intense hatred for hypocrisy. This sentiment contributed to his intense polemical power: he was, without a doubt, the most effective, lacerating satirist of his age, his pen feared throughout the land by any politician who knew what was good for him.

He had been sent to London on behalf of the Anglican Church of Ireland to right a wrong. When 'Queen Anne's Bounty', the scheme to supplement the miserly stipends of the clergy by redirecting the 'First Fruits' (a sort of clerical tax) into their pockets, had been announced in 1704, there had been no explicit mention of whether it would apply to the Church of Ireland.

Vague promises had been made, but there had been no action. In 1707–8, William King, Archbishop of Dublin, had sent Swift on a mission to persuade the ministry to honour this promise. He had been vaguely fobbed off by Somers and Sunderland, before finally being allowed an audience with Godolphin. A brusque Godolphin implied that a deal might be done if the Irish Church would acquiesce in the repeal of the Irish Test Act, which was completely unacceptable to the Irish Church (and Swift).

Subsequently, Swift had also attempted to persuade Wharton, in his capacity as Lord Lieutenant of Ireland, to act on the First Fruits question, but Wharton had no interest whatsoever in helping out the Irish Anglican clergy. Wharton was far more interested in assisting Ireland's Dissenters and repealing the Test. He rudely rebuffed Swift's entreaties. It was to be an action he would soon regret.

Until his brush with Wharton, Swift's politics were highly ambiguous. He was perhaps best described as that unusual hybrid, a High Church Whig with some Country leanings. A firm churchman, he was deeply hostile to Dissent and believed strongly in Anglican hegemony, but he had also keenly supported the Glorious Revolution and detested the papists as much as the Dissenters. He was undoubtedly a strong supporter of the Protestant succession and saw himself in constitutional terms as a 'friend to liberty'. Nonetheless, he was strongly small 'c' conservative, and was deeply suspicious of the 'new men' of the City of London and their usurpation of the authority of the landed gentlemen. This paradoxical – but broadly coherent – collection of political opinions was typical of Swift's complex personality.

Not long after Swift's arrival in England, Robert Harley picked up gossip that Swift was in town and none too pleased with the Whigs, who continued to ignore him. One of Harley's agents reported to him that Swift had been heard 'talking treason' against the Whigs.[1] Harley's ears pricked up: he knew that in the battle to come he would need the cream of polemical talent to put his case to the country. He summoned Swift into his office and treated him with 'the greatest respect and kindness imaginable'.[2] By 19th October he announced to Swift that it was done: the Queen had agreed to grant the First Fruits to Ireland. Swift was delighted:

> I believe never any thing was compassed so soon, and purely done by
> my personal credit with Mr. Harley who is so excessively obliging, that I
> know not what to make of it, unless to shew the rascals of the other party
> that they used a man unworthy, who had deserved better.[3]

Before long, Swift was apprised of precisely why Harley was so 'excessively
obliging'. In August, a new journal had appeared called *The Examiner*. The
brainchild of Harley, St John and a few of their cronies, it was to be the voice
of the more reasonable churchmen: it would be written in fluent Tory, but
attempt to persuade the Church Party to act reasonably while also lashing
the administration's Whig enemies. Harley's plan was to recruit Swift as
the chief polemicist of *The Examiner* – and his obliging behaviour over the
First Fruits greased the wheels nicely. Swift agreed to help Harley, and
before long had become a key personal confidante of Harley and St John. He
recorded his impressions and meetings over the next few years in a journal,
which he sent as a series of letters to his close friend (and probable lover)
Esther Johnson, aka 'Stella'.

The ministry had recruited their top propagandist, and historians
acquired thereby an intimate, day-by-day account of many of the internal
workings of Harley and his ministers as they battled to keep their political
heads above water.

It soon became clear that Harley would need all of the support he could
recruit. The problems that he faced as the dust from the general election
settled were immense. The Junto lords and their Whig adherents, mauled
in the general election and out of office, slunk away to lick their wounds, but
other problems and enemies crowded in upon him on every side.

First and foremost was the dire financial situation. Put simply, the
government was weeks away from bankruptcy. Its creditors – chiefly the
Bank of England – had been severely spooked by the results of the general
election. Would a parliament dominated by Tory backwoodsmen, many of
whom hated the 'monied interest' almost as much as they hated taxes, be
prepared to cough up the revenue needed to finance the government's debts?
In any case, pondered the bank, might a bit of financial politicking help

destroy the Harley ministry and quickly restore the political standing of those reliable friends of the City, the Junto? The Bank of England was in no hurry to help Harley.

As a result, Harley struggled to find funding to pay the allied army in Spain – ironically, given that the Whigs were about to take their stand on the need to gain victory on the Iberian front – with the result that the allied forces had fallen to defeat in November and December 1710.

Gradually, however, he began to get a handle on the financial situation. Early in 1711, by a mixture of fiscal reassurance and veiled threats, he managed to persuade the Bank of England to back a scheme to restore confidence in the financial instruments – 'exchequer-bills' – upon which short-term government borrowing depended. He then instituted a series of enormously successful state lotteries to help take care of pressing short-term debts to the bank. A longer-term scheme to provide for Britain's underlying – and worryingly large – unfunded debts would be needed, but in the short term public credit was restored. Harley, widely regarded as the foremost parliamentary wizard of the age, was quickly proving himself adept at pulling financial rabbits out of hats too.

If the Bank of England and the financial interest represented one potent source of external anxiety for Harley and his ministry, then the figure of the Duke of Marlborough loomed even larger. Marlborough looked upon the formation of the new ministry and the results of the general election with horror. He feared that the new ministry would seek an unsatisfactory and premature peace, potentially in the process dividing the grand continental alliance that he had done so much to piece together. This in turn, he feared, could only benefit France, and anything that benefited France bolstered the interests of the Pretender.

Although these considerations were no doubt genuinely part of the Duke's thinking, there was a rather less charitable interpretation of his hostility to Harley available. War was the means by which Marlborough maintained his power and reputation. His dazzling victories had made him the most famous man in Europe, Louis XIV excepted. With power had come wealth, status and many other rewards. Every fresh campaigning season brought an enormous load of taxation and military impressment down on the heads of

England's landed and labouring interests; but it brought Marlborough ever greater status, and, until Malplaquet at least, continued glory.

His critics also pointed out that much of his current predicament was of his own – or his wife's – making. Sarah's outrageous behaviour had thoroughly alienated the Queen, and as she and Marlborough came as a package deal, it had inevitably made Anne less and less willing to reconcile with the pair. When added to his misjudged and alarmingly self-aggrandising requests to the Queen for his captain-generalcy for life, he could hardly claim that he hadn't given a good deal of credence to the less charitable interpretation of his motivations, or a considerable amount of disquiet to the Queen. And it showed: whereas Marlborough had been able to scotch Harley's plan to reconstruct the ministry on a more Tory footing in 1708, in 1710 his attempt to do the same had failed. He was no longer indispensable.

However, as much as they despised and distrusted each other, Harley and Marlborough still needed each other, at least for now.

Marlborough was quite right to suspect that Harley was keen for peace sooner rather than later, but Harley realised that it was essential to keep Marlborough's armies in the field for one more campaign so that he could negotiate from a position of strength. If Harley had any doubts about the lunacy of 'No Peace without Spain', the allied defeats there in late 1710 had comprehensively dispelled them. In his mind, the Junto/Marlborough attitude was frankly unrealistic and irresponsible. Peace would have to be negotiated on terms that conceded Spain sooner or later, and better to do it as quickly as possible rather than drag the war out, to little or no purpose, for years to come. However, within these constraints he still had every desire – and political incentive – to extract the best terms possible from the French. So Marlborough had to stay – for the time being.

On the other hand, Marlborough – despite his persistent threats to resign – had no real intention of giving up his supreme military command before he had to. He hoped, given his personal reputation, relationships with the leaders of the other major allied powers, and immense diplomatic experience, to be able to hold together the alliance through force of personality and persuasion, and thwart or at least modify any plans Harley might have for an overly hasty or dishonourable peace. Even when the Queen finally bit the bullet and officially dismissed Sarah, in January 1711, pressure from the Whigs and allies meant that a thoroughly gloomy Duke stayed in post: the fact that the scale of Sarah's disrespect to the Queen had finally become clear to him made him only too suppliant.

So, until Harley showed his hand on the peace question, the two were locked into a very uneasy mutual co-dependency.

In addition to these two major sources of anxieties from without his administration, Harley also had reason to worry about risks closer to hand. The ministry was only months old, but even at this early stage the first signs of another problem were apparent, one which would eventually metastasize in a way that would threaten the very vitals of the government.

Henry St John had been one of Harley's key lieutenants since 1704, and his appointment as Secretary of State marked him out as one of the most important props of the new ministry: he quickly became one of their most important and eloquent speakers in the Commons. However, the simple fact was that, whereas Harley saw himself as a man of no party but rather a moderate servant of the Crown, St John was unequivocally a Tory, and in the main one of true-blue instincts.

It is true that his attitude to the Church was one of cynical opportunism: although he would play the Church card very freely to win favour with Tory backbenchers, he was not really even a Christian, let alone a churchman, but rather a sort of free-thinking deist. However, in his belief in the natural authority of the landed interest, his detestation of the 'monied men', and his desire for peace and lower taxes, he was a natural ally of the Tory firebrands who had just been elected to parliament in great numbers.

Beyond this latent ideological divide, there were personal sources of mutual distrust. Harley suspected that St John, an old friend of Marlborough's, might leak crucial information to the Duke. Additionally, Harley had apparently been quite reluctant to appoint St John to so senior position as Secretary of State in the first place, partly because at that stage he was still hoping to retain senior Whigs; he offered St John, at first, a more minor role, which irritated the former. St John was ambitious and didn't relish being merely a junior partner to the older and more politically experienced man.

If St John was prepared to exploit it, the means to further his ambitions were there. At any point, he could resume his earliest parliamentary role: that of fiery leader of High Tory sentiment in the Commons. He was aware of this, and not adverse to signalling the possibility to his Tory contacts. Earlier in 1710, while Tory frustration at Harley's apparent reluctance to support a full-blooded Tory ministry had been growing, St John had been making it very clear to his Tory allies that, whatever the tergiversations of Harley in relation to the Church Party, he would 'neglect nothing in my power wch may contribute towards making ye Church interest the prevailing one in our Country'.[4]

And if St John chose to go down such a path, he would not be short of parliamentary foot soldiers. For one of the major issues that Harley had to contend with almost immediately after the general election was that a large number of the new Tory MPs were in no mood for compromise. After having endured five years in the wilderness, they were greedy for power. They hadn't cheered and toasted Dr Sacheverell, shouted 'The Church in danger!' on the hustings, and then stormed to a landslide victory only to be fobbed off with Mr Harley's usual policy of fudge and delay. They wanted measures to strengthen the Church against its canting 'fanatick' enemies; they wanted peace and a good whack off the land tax; they wanted all of the government's sweet patronage for themselves; and they wanted it yesterday. In addition, repeating the tactics of a decade earlier, they wanted revenge on the Whigs who had lorded it over them for so long, which meant impeachments.

This agenda posed real difficulties for Harley. He needed Tory votes in the Commons to prop up his government, but much of what the High Tories demanded he thought impossible or undesirable. A cut to the land tax in the context of the government's parlous finances was impossible in the short term. He did want peace, but he was conscious that it would take time to achieve. He wanted to ensure that his government kept as broad a base of support as possible, and so was keen on keeping as many Whigs in government positions as he could: a policy of prosecuting the last ministry would only create much bitterness and cut off any back channels he might maintain with the leading Whigs. He was a friend to the Church of England, but he was no fan of what he considered to be a policy of intolerance or persecution and was therefore reluctant to open up, for example, the question of occasional conformity. Some of the Tory agenda he could accommodate but, even on those points, he needed time.

For a while, the High Tories gave Harley the benefit of the doubt. After all, he had removed the Junto from office and installed a largely Tory administration, which to some extent made up for the betrayal of 1705. Furthermore, the desperation of the financial situation and the need for emergency measures to stave off government bankruptcy bought him some time. By Christmas, however, it was clear to Jonathan Swift that the headstrong backbenchers of the Church Party were 'very eager to have some Enquiries made into past Managements, and are a little angry with the Slackness of the Ministry'.[5]

By the beginning of 1711, these Tory malcontents had formed themselves into a sort of parliamentary pressure group: 'The October Club'. Named either after the type of (very potent) ale that they enjoyed putting away in large quantities or possibly after the month in which they had achieved their great landslide election victory, this club soon began to meet every Wednesday evening when parliament was in session, usually at the Bell Tavern in King Street, Westminster. One observer summarised their activities:

> This loyal country club is a great disturbance to Mr. Harley, who finds they are past his governing; their Number is increased to a 150. They are most of them young gentlemen of estates that has never been in Parliament before, and are not very close, but declare to everybody what they designe, to have every Whig turn'd out, and not to suffer that the new Ministry shou'd shake hands as they see they do with the old.[6]

Although many of the October Club members were new faces who had been carried for the first time into parliament on the coat-tails of Dr Sacheverell, they also included a good number of old hands – experienced men like Peter Shakerley and Sir Thomas Hanmer. More pertinently, they had numbers: 150 backbenchers were sufficient to cause Harley considerable headaches in the Commons. It wasn't to be long before they materialised.

* * *

Problems he might have, but like the wily old grandmaster he was, Harley was already plotting his next move on the political chessboard.

Firstly, his thoughts turned to the need to set the terms of the debate that he knew was coming. He was well aware that, when the time came to make his first open moves towards a peace settlement, the combined forces of Marlborough and the Junto would bitterly resist it. So what better than to begin the process of setting up his own political narrative early, and discredit his chief enemies now?

And of course he had at hand a potent weapon: the sharpest pen in Christendom. The first fruits of Jonathan Swift's great journalistic campaign on behalf of the Harley ministry were at hand.

One element of his campaign combined business with pleasure on Swift's part. *The Examiner* of 9th November 1710 was ostensibly about the art of political lying, but to anybody with any familiarity with British politics, it was obviously a none-too-coded attack on the man who had so rudely slighted him in Dublin, Lord Wharton.

In it, he obliquely compares Wharton to the Devil, 'the Father of Lyes'.[7] After all, Satan's

> first Essay of [lying] was purely political, employed in undermining the authority of his prince, and seducing a third part of the subjects from their obedience; for which he was driven down from Heaven, where (as Milton expresses it) he had been viceroy of a great western province . . .[8]

The allusion to Wharton's recent administration over Ireland ('a great western province') made clear his intention of painting Wharton as the evil archetype of Whiggery, his party's shadowy answer to Old Nick himself. Indeed, Swift implied that Wharton had perfected his master's tricks:

> But although the devil be the father of lies, he seems, like other great inventors, to have lost much of his reputation, by the continual improvements that have been made upon him.[9]

His mendacious spirit had inspired the wicked arts of the Whig Party for a generation. Political lying, he argues, has

> been the guardian spirit of a prevailing party, for almost twenty years. It can conquer kingdoms without fighting, and sometimes with the loss of a battle. It gives and resumes employments; can sink a mountain to a mole-hill, and raise a mole-hill to a mountain: has presided for many years at committees of elections; can wash a blackmoor white; make a saint of an atheist, and a patriot of a profligate . . .[10]

The purpose of Swift's volley of attacks on Wharton was to drum into the public mind the clear message: don't trust a word this man says. If he tells you, in the coming years, that the ministry is in the pay of the French and the Jacobites, don't believe him.

Swift's approach to Marlborough was more subtle. What Harley needed was not a full-frontal character assassination, as the Duke was too important to his plans – and too publicly venerated – to attack in such a direct way. The political objective in his case was to puncture the standard line of the Whigs and the 'Family': that Marlborough was not given his due by an insufficiently adulatory nation and ministry, that he was in some sense *hard done by*. What else, argued his partisans, could be concluded from the fact that the new ministry had been formed in defiance of the great man's wishes? If this picture could be undermined, then Marlborough's achievements could be acknowledged while attacking his right to dictate political terms.

Swift's subject was, accordingly, that of ingratitude. Mocking the Whig line, he asked:

> If a stranger should hear these serious outcries of ingratitude against our general without knowing the particulars, he would be apt to inquire, where was his tomb, or whether he was allowed Christian burial? not doubting but we had put him to some ignominious death. Or has he been tried for his life, and very narrowly escaped? has he been accused of high crimes and misdemeanors? has the prince seized on his estate, and left him to starve? has he been hooted at, as he passed the streets,

by an ungrateful rabble? have neither honours, offices, nor grants been conferred on him or his family?[11]

The answer, of course, was that none of these genuine indignities was his lot: rather, the country had feted him for years, loading him with garlands, grants and gifts galore, most notably that of Blenheim Palace. Wisely, Harley had agreed to allow monies to continue to go forward towards finishing that grand mansion, to allay any sense that the ministry was inclined to be vindictive towards the Duke, and this gave extra piquancy to Swift's attack.

Swift's *coup de grâce* was to compare the rewards lavished upon Marlborough with the relatively moderate recompense that a successful Roman general could expect as marks of the Senate's gratitude. He drew up 'to fair Accounts, the one of Roman Gratitude, and the other of British Ingratitude': the former amounted to the equivalent of just under £1,000, the latter to £540,000.[12]

The message to Marlborough was spelled out in restrained but unmistakable terms:

> We find many ungrateful Persons in the World, but we make more, by setting too high a Rate upon our Pretensions, and under valuing the Rewards we receive.[13]

Swift's fusillade was so wounding because it struck at what everyone knew to be Marlborough's genuine weakness: his seemingly endless appetite for money and status. No one could ever quite look upon his complaints about the ministry in the same way again.

The power of Swift's writing in *The Examiner* was not, however, based simply on his mastery of the arts of ironic deflation and outright vituperation. He outlined an overarching Tory narrative of contemporary politics in such a way as to appeal to the deepest instincts of the October Club men while managing to hew to a line of pragmatism and moderation.

It was, at heart, the gospel of Country Toryism judiciously pruned to discountenance the old Whig parrot cries: that the Tories were merely handmaidens of the King Across the Water, imbued with a mixture of French absolutism and Anglican bigotry.

In this narrative, the beating heart of England was at grave risk of being torn out by an unholy alliance between a corrupt standing army and a new class of nouveaux riche financiers who 'find their Profit in prolonging the War'.[14] To Swift, this was as clear as day:

> But yet there is no great mystery in the matter. Let any man observe the equipages in this town; he shall find the greater number of those who make a figure, to be a species of men quite different from any that were ever known before the Revolution, consisting either of generals and colonels, or of such whose whole fortunes lie in funds and stocks: so that power, which according to the old maxim, was used to follow land, is now gone over to money.[15]

The only way to stop the rot was to secure a peace as quickly as possible: 'if the war continues some years longer, a landed man will be little better than a farmer at a rack rent, to the army, and to the public funds'.[16] This would be disastrous. Whereas the landed gentlemen had the interests of the broad sweep of the nation at heart, the stockjobbers and 'monied men' cared not one jot either way: their only concern was for the best rate of return.

To add insult to injury, the war that underpinned so much of this process was being fought largely for the benefit of foreigners – principally the Dutch – despite the costs falling hardest on Britain. Indeed, the Whigs, 'with the Spirit of Shop-Keepers', would even compromise the religious and cultural integrity of the country by making it 'a common receptacle for all nations, religions and languages' under the (spurious) guise of boosting the nation's wealth.[17] Hence the Whigs had 'invited over a great Number of Foreigners of all Religions, under the Name of Palatines'.[18] But the reality was that they:

> understood no trade or handicraft, yet rather chose to beg than labour; who, beside infesting our streets, bred contagious diseases, by which we lost in natives thrice the number of what we gained in foreigners.[19]

In drawing this picture, Swift cleverly (and somewhat disingenuously) tried to redraw the political map. He disclaimed any love for party and instead claimed to draw a distinction between patriotic, disinterested men who wished to uphold the traditional institutions of the country – the constitution and Church – and wild, self-serving factious men who would sacrifice the country to their ambitions. The latter, in order to further their sinister designs, had to find ways of smearing the true patriots. They did this by casting anyone who ever showed any scepticism towards never-ending war, debt and taxes as an agent of the Pretender:

> But at present, the word Pretender, is a term of art in their profession. A secretary of state cannot desire leave to resign, but the Pretender is at bottom; the queen cannot dissolve a parliament, but it is a plot to dethrone herself and bring in the Pretender; half a score stock-jobbers are playing the knave in Exchange-alley, and there goes the Pretender with a sponge.[20]

This was, according to Swift, a desperate lie. Patriots and good church-men had largely supported the Revolution: they were good Protestants, after all, who had no desire to install a papist king. Yes, there were a few extremists, nonjurors like Charles Leslie and his *Rehearsal*, who were friends of the Pretender, but the bulk of the honest men opposed both the knavish tricks of Whiggery and the tiny fringe of Jacobites. It was the Whigs, and not the Tories, who really depended on the Pretender, as the political bogeyman 'to whom their whole Party is in a high Measure indebted for all their Greatness'.[21]

Swift's narrative was potent and cleverly framed. Although it exaggerated and sometimes veered close to a conspiracy theory, its main thrust was rooted in a good deal of truth. The financial establishment, the 'new men' of the funds and stocks, *were* largely Whigs, and they clearly had made a lot of money out of a very expensive war. Their party had prolonged the war already by not agreeing to peace on extremely good terms in 1709. Heathcote and the Bank of England clearly were highly partisan, and they had used their muscle to attempt to keep in the Junto and undermine Harley's new administration.

Of course, the Whigs – who had their own organs which vigorously responded to Swift, such as Arthur Maynwaring's *The Medley* – would argue that the fortunes of the Pretender were closely tied to the fate of the French state and Louis XIV, who shielded him and had assisted him in his abortive invasion attempt in 1708. Only a comprehensive trouncing of the French and a peace on ruinous terms could make the Protestant succession absolutely secure and tame the papist threat in Europe. Such a war had to be funded, and a national debt was made necessary by the simple fact that the country – including, very prominently, the landed interest – would not countenance taxes high enough to fund the entire war effort without resorting to borrowing. Only a nation prepared to embrace new financial methods and a new spirit of religious and commercial openness would be prosperous enough to defend liberty. These were realities that the squire and the parson would have to accept, like them or not.

Swift's rhetoric was designed, among other things, to enlist the regiments of October Club Toryism behind Harley's leadership. It went further than anything Harley would have privately been comfortable with in order to lure such men in, but then attempted to show them how their ends could only be served by the patient, grown-up methods of Harley and his ministry.

Unfortunately for Harley, the October Club men were not in the mood for patience. As Swift observed in his journal, the October men would not be satisfied unless they could 'drive things on to extreams against the Whigs . . . call the old ministry to account, and get off five or six heads'.[22]

Their first beef was that so many Whigs continued to hold office at the lower levels of government. What was the point of power if they couldn't turn out all of their political enemies and monopolise places for themselves? They declared openly that 'they design to have every Whig turn'd out, and not to suffer that the new Ministry should shake hands as they see they do with the old'.[23] St John and Rochester were not unsympathetic to this line, and so Harley realised that he had to throw them a bone. He decided to sack Robert Walpole, who had hung onto one of his posts (Treasurer of the Navy) despite clearly opposing the ministry; Harley had hoped to perhaps tempt him from his Junto allegiances, but it clearly hadn't worked and his dismissal might sate the Tory thirst for Whig blood for a while.

This was accompanied by various other concessions calculated to be just sufficient enough to satisfy the Tory backbenchers' predilections, but not enough to rock the boat. To allay their concerns about the 'monied men' usurping the landed interest, the ministry allowed a Property Qualification Bill to pass. The aim of this legislation was to tighten the property qualification for members of the House of Commons: it meant that only men in possession of land of a certain minimum value would be allowed to sit as an MP. In theory, it excluded men whose only property was in stocks or cash to enter the Commons (although in practice it was easily evaded).

Ominously for Harley, the debate on this bill was used by St John to play shamelessly to the Tory backbenchers, claiming that, without the legislation, 'we might see a time when the mony'd men might bid fair to keep out of that house all the landed men', with disastrous results.[24] Bashing the 'money'd men' and standing up for the landed interest was music to the ears of the October Club. Increasingly, they were to see St John as the man to throw off Harleyian caution and lead them onto the barricades against the Whigs.

The October Club next turned its sights to vengeance on the last ministry. The new Commons, which had elected High Tory chieftain William Bromley as its Speaker, wanted blood, and in early 1711 it started to turn up the temperature. Its aim was to inquire into what they assumed would be the mass of corruption and peculation undertaken under the last ministry. Harley tried to head them off by offering them an investigation into alleged abuses in victualling in the navy and a series of inquisitions into the conduct of the war in Spain. He even offered them a sacrificial victim to 'squeeze . . . heartily' – a hapless Whig victualling officer.[25]

If Harley thought this would satisfy them, he was dead wrong. The October Club wanted to expand their investigations and delve into the entire financial record of the previous government. They soon latched onto the idea of reviving an old Country tactic from the 1690s and early 1700s: setting up a Commission of Accounts to investigate every pound, shilling and pence spent by the government. Sir Simeon Stewart, a twenty-five-year-old Tory firebrand, made the October Club's agenda very clear. The parlous state of the public credit was the consequence of the mismanagements of the former ministry who had exhausted all the funds, and squandered the money away. The only thing that was left to this honest Parliament was to inquire into these mismanagements and rectify them as far as possible, and punish the offenders to the terror of others.[26]

The October men clearly had impeachments in mind: Wharton was talked of as an obvious target, but Marlborough and others were in their sights too. Stewart gave a very clear warning to Harley: if he 'would not let them into these secrets' then it could only be because 'a certain great man of the late ministry had compounded matters with another great man in this ministry'.[27] In other words, Harley was doing grubby deals to let the Junto off the hook, and the October Club – who had actually adopted as their motto 'we will not be Harl'd' – would not be fooled by the machinations of 'Robin the Trickster'.[28]

Various other embarrassments crowded in upon Harley. The Tory backwoodsmen pushed for that old Country canard, a Place Bill. They also demanded the repeal of the Protestant Naturalization Act and an investigation into 'upon what invitations or encouragement the Palatines came over'.[29] Although Harley did support one of their very clear (and very characteristic) priorities – lifting the restriction on the importation of French wines – the fact that most of these measures fell in the Lords, often with Harley's tacit connivance, enraged the October men. A measure to raise funds to build fifty new churches in London, promoted by Atterbury, did pass with Harley's support, but it didn't buy him the good will of the High Church Tories for very long.[30]

Meanwhile, St John had been careful to do as much as he could to help them without openly declaring himself. He had surreptitiously smoothed the way for a bill appointing the Commission of Accounts to pass the Lords against Harley's wishes. Harley suspected that St John was preparing to strike against him and install himself at the head of the ministry.

By February 1711, things were getting desperate for Harley. The key business of getting financial estimates and supply through parliament had screeched to a halt as the October Club dug its heels in. Without supply, the government's parlous financial situation threatened once again to collapse. Harley's ministry was only surviving vote-to-vote, sometimes by appealing for Whig support, but he knew that he could only rely on them when it was in their interests (when, for example, it came to avoiding investigations into their own alleged misconduct). Jonathan Swift observed in his journal that:

> The ministry is upon a very narrow bottom, and stands like an isthmus between the whigs on one side, and violent tories on the other. They are able seamen, but the tempest is too great, the ship too rotten, and the crew all against them.[31]

Harley's dextrous parliamentary management was near the end of its capacity to stave off disaster, and he was near the end of his tether, sick and feverish from the nervous strain of it all.

But everything was about to be transformed and in the most dramatic of ways.

The 8th March 1711 was the anniversary of the accession of Queen Anne. In honour of the occasion, Harley decided to dress to impress: he put on a 'think embroidered waist-coat, richly decorated with gold brocade flowers on a background of silver and blue'.[32] Because he was still feeling the after-effects of his illness and it was a chilly day, he also put on a flannel waistcoat and a heavy, stiff buff coat.

On his way to the palace he spotted a dissolute-looking man with a bruised face walking in the Mall. Harley recognised him and hurried to see the Queen with a great deal more urgency. Having congratulated Anne, he advised her to have the man arrested, immediately.

For the man in question was the Marquis de Guiscard, and Harley had good reason to suspect him of being a dastardly French spy.

Guiscard was a shadowy individual: he went nowhere without a bottle of poison and a dagger. He had good reason for these precautions, for he had turned his coat twice, betraying first his own and then his adopted country.

His career of perfidy began when he defected to England and was involved in a plot to land Huguenot refugees near Bordeaux, who were to be tasked with inciting a Protestant rebellion against the French king. This plan was shelved, but he was offered a pension of £500 by the British government and took refuge in London. A rake and debauchee, naturally Guiscard soon fell in with Henry St John's social circle (for a time they shared a mistress). Soon enough, he realised that even his generous pension was insufficient to fund his wild lifestyle, particularly after an economising Robert Harley cut it to a mere £400 per annum. In order to rectify this unsatisfactory situation, Guiscard crawled back to Louis XIV and offered to spy for him.

A few days before spotting him on the Mall, Harley had received intercepted packages that revealed that Guiscard was sending secret messages across the Channel. It appeared that St John, unaware that Guiscard was a French agent, had been indiscreet and mentioned several pieces of secret information to Guiscard, which Guiscard had passed on. St John was furious with himself for his indiscretion.

Then, before Harley could take further action, he fell ill and was in bed for a few days – and so Guiscard remained at large. But now, on 8th March, Harley took decisive action, and Guiscard was arrested. Guiscard was doubly incensed when he saw St John's signature on the arrest warrant: they had recently fallen out, squabbling about which of the two men bore responsibility for their joint mistress's recent pregnancy, and this was the final straw. His anger mounted further when he realised that he had forgotten to transfer his dagger and poison over to the suit he put on that morning.

Harley hastily summoned the cabinet: they would interrogate Guiscard, who was held on a charge of high treason. Harley and St John gathered with Rochester, Harcourt and various other senior ministers in the Secretary of State's quarters in the Cockpit. As they prepared their interrogation, Guiscard was allowed some lunch in a side room as he awaited his fate. Finding a penknife in this room, he snuck it into his pocket.

The prisoner was summoned in, and the interrogation began. Guiscard, arrogant as ever, laconically denied everything and grinned impishly at his captors. At one point Harley noticed that he seemed to be fiddling around with something in his pocket, but ignored it. After a while, Rochester suggested that the interrogation was futile and best adjourned. Harley reluctantly agreed. Guiscard was ordered to leave the room.

It was at this moment that the Gallic spy struck. He leapt towards Harley suddenly and stabbed him as hard as he could in the chest. Harley fell back into his chair, stunned by the blow of the impact. All hell broke loose as his cabinet colleagues struggled to prevent Guiscard striking a second blow. St John was bawling at the top of his voice, 'The villain has killed Mr Harley!'[33] Harley temporarily fell into unconsciousness, but awoke in time to inspect his wound and smell 'whether his guts were pierced'.[34] Seconds later, a frantic Guiscard made another run at Harley, who managed to fend him off with a chair.

At this point, St John and Ormonde, High Tory Lord Lieutenant of Ireland, chased Guiscard, drew their swords and managed to catch and wound him: in fact St John stabbed him so hard in the back that he broke his sword, before haring off to fetch a doctor. After various cabinet members had given the Frenchman, who was still alive, a good thrashing, they tied him up and sent him, carried like a trussed turkey, to Newgate.

As Guiscard was taken away, Harley remained so unperturbed that his colleagues were astonished. He calmly pulled the penknife out of his flannel waistcoat, asked Rochester to break the news to the Queen, and ordered that Guiscard should receive the best medical attention possible.

Mercifully, the thick clothes that Harley was wearing, combined with the fact that Guiscard had forgotten his normal dagger that morning and had to make do with a penknife, had severely reduced the severity of the injury. The knife had entered, according to Swift, 'just under the Breast, a little to the Right side; but, it pleased God, that the Point stopped at one of the Ribs, and broke short half an Inch'.[35] A doctor dressed the wound and Harley was taken home in a hackney chair.

The wound was painful and incapacitated Harley for several weeks. At one point it seemed like it might do for him: he had several bad nights and a fever – even gangrene was suspected. But slowly he recovered. He would live.

Being stabbed was just about the best thing that could have happened to Harley at that moment. A wave of sympathy was aroused. His calmness and bravery in the course of hunting down a French traitor became the talk of the town. The Commons passed a resolution decrying Guiscard's 'villanous

Attempt' on the Chancellor of the Exchequer's life.[36] The Queen was beside herself with worry: on hearing the news, she 'wept uncontrollably for two hours', passed a restless night and even contracted a fever.[37]

St John had mixed feelings, to put it mildly. Had Harley been assassinated, his assent to the top of the ministry was very probable. Now, with Harley's popularity skyrocketing, any chances he had of displacing his rival had diminished appreciably. In response, he tried to spread a rumour that the real target of the attack was himself, and Harley had been struck down as second choice. This transparent attempt to gain a share of the sympathy fooled no one, and merely aroused Harley's mistrust. The breach between the two men grew wider.

Furthermore, St John had no compunctions about using Harley's convalescence period to further his own ends. For some time, he had been pushing the idea of mounting a naval expedition against French Quebec. It was a classic blue water Tory alternative to Marlborough's land campaigns: the idea was that it would provide a quick success, which could strengthen Britain's hands in any peace negotiations. By suggesting that Captain Hill, Abigail Masham's brother, should command the Quebec expedition, St John hoped to curry favour with the Queen and her favourite. Harley was at first undecided, but by the time of his stabbing had turned against it, as had Rochester. St John, however, used the opportunity provided by Harley's incapacity to drive the plan through cabinet.

The real effect of Harley's absence was, however, to prove how rudderless the government was without him. Although silenced for a week or two by the shock of the assassination attempt, the October Club men soon started to run amok. St John took charge of the attempt to fill the gap between supplies voted and taxes so far levied, which, despite Harley's gargantuan efforts, remained substantial. St John's answer was to increase the leather tax, but the Tory backbenchers outmanoeuvred him and voted the measure down. Business in the Commons ground to a halt: as Swift observed, 'all things are at a stop in parliament for want of Mr. Harley; they cannot stir an inch without him'.[38] Harley may have struggled; St John bungled his management of the Commons completely.

The whole experience made him morose. A naive Swift, not yet aware of St John's designs against Harley, rebuked him for being 'out of temper'.[39] A chastened St John insisted that 'nothing ailed him but sitting up whole nights at business, and one night at drinking', but the real reason was that his political stock was falling rapidly.[40]

In fact, St John's fortunes were about to reach a new low. For Harley had used his weeks of recuperation to put the finishing touches to his grand plan to restore public credit and solve the problem of Britain's biggest economic problem: the enormous sum of unfunded debt contracted by the government in recent years to pay for the war effort.

In May, Harley's scheme was unveiled to the Commons. The idea was to consolidate all the government's outstanding unfunded debt and assign it to a new entity, the South Sea Company. All who held the debt were to become the company's shareholders, and were guaranteed a 6 per cent return on their shares. The company would hold a monopoly on all income from future trade in South America. As South America was held by Spain at that moment in time, this was speculative, but it was assumed that a considerable portion of this trade would be coming Britain's way when the peace was negotiated. The trade in question would be largely the Assiento: the South American slave trade.

The scheme was (at least at this stage) a success: it provided something of a Tory rival to the Bank of England, without significantly affecting the latter's business. Quickly, confidence in public credit was greatly restored. The momentum provided by this success and his greatly increased popularity allowed Harley to get the final supply bills through the House. The war would carry on for one more year to allow Britain to negotiate the peace from a position of strength.

At practically the same moment that Harley was unveiling the South Sea scheme in the Commons, Rochester died. The old Tory warhorse, who had effectively been the ministry's chief representative in the upper house, had actually gradually thawed in his relations with Harley over the past six months, and had proved surprisingly co-operative. In response, in order to give the ministry leadership of due stature in the Lords, and in recognition of Harley's services, the Queen decided to elevate him to the peerage as the Earl of Oxford and Mortimer and promote him to the position of Lord Treasurer (Godolphin's old position).

It was an elevation to the highest pinnacle of prestige in the British state. Harley (henceforth referred to as 'Oxford') had gone from the verge of destruction to triumph in the space of a few months.

Now it was time to turn his shoulder to the biggest wheel yet: securing the peace.

In fact, unbeknownst to all but a tiny group of confidantes, the peace negotiations had already begun.

The key reality underlying Oxford's approach was the recognition that any hope for a Habsburg accession to the throne of Spain was moonshine. Spain was the one theatre of war the allies had lost, and this had to be accepted. Harley's attitude was reinforced in April 1711 when the Habsburg emperor, Joseph, died, and his son Charles acceded to all the Habsburg dominions as Charles VI. If he were to acquire the throne of Spain and its dominions, he would be scarcely any less of a threat to the balance of power in Europe than Spain under the rule of the Bourbon claimant Philip V. 'No Peace without Spain' meant, in effect, no peace at all, and there was no longer any clear strategic reason to insist on it, unless one's agenda was to perpetuate war with France indefinitely.

Oxford's peace would have to recognise this reality while also grappling with the problem of the Dutch. In 1709, the Whigs had, as part of the Barrier Treaty, made a whole series of extravagant promises to the Dutch to keep them in the war. These promises included giving the Dutch equal access to trading privileges within the Spanish Empire once a general peace was concluded, and effective control of the Spanish Netherlands in order to provide a 'barrier' of fortresses against the French. This 'barrier' conceded various important trading ports which competed with British commercial interests. In sum, the Barrier Treaty was directly against British interests: it was such a poor deal for Britain that even Marlborough had wanted nothing to do with it when it was being negotiated.

The Barrier Treaty left Oxford with an invidious choice. Either he tried to continue to negotiate a joint Anglo-Dutch peace, which meant respecting the Dutch claims to the detriment of Britain's national interest; or he accepted the need to secretly negotiate a peace with the French and then present it as a fait accompli to the Dutch. This latter course would inevitably be presented by the Junto as a 'betrayal' of Britain's allies to the benefit of France.

Oxford faced numerous domestic limitations relevant to the peace negotiations. His own ministry was split between figures like St John, who was vehemently anti-Dutch and a strong supporter of a separate peace with France, and Shrewsbury, who, although pragmatic, was much more sympathetic to Dutch claims. The Commons was strongly in favour of a speedy peace, but the Lords presented a massive problem for Oxford: it still had a Whig majority, which might well unite to block a peace deal.

Once defeat in Spain was clear by December 1710, Oxford decided that the time was ripe to start sounding out the French. Spain was lost, and any peace negotiations had to be conducted on the basis of that assumption. Oxford couldn't admit that to the Habsburgs, so he needed to talk to the French secretly. Back channels were opened, and Oxford and Shrewsbury made broad suggestions to the French on possible draft terms. By April 1711 the French had drawn up draft preliminary peace articles along these lines

During these early stages, Oxford kept the Dutch informed of the progress of the negotiations. After having informed the cabinet of the draft articles, he communicated them to the Dutch. They responded to the effect that they wanted to become full signatories of any articles, acting in lockstep with the British.

It was at this point that Oxford decided to negotiate separately with the French and cut the Dutch out of the loop. The main reason related to the South Sea Company. The entire basis of this was future British trading rights in South America: this would be undermined if the Dutch were to insist on dividing such rights between Britain and themselves in the peace articles. In any case, reasoned Oxford, it wasn't the job of the British government to serve Dutch commercial interests at the expense of their own.

So in June, Oxford employed a personal friend of his – poet Matthew Prior – to go on a secret mission to Paris to thrash out more details of the peace deal. These draft terms prioritised British, not Dutch, interests, giving them significant territorial gains from both France and Spain and plum trading rights in Spanish America, including the Assiento contract.

Additional terms included a French promise not to unify the crowns of Spain and France (they might both be held by Bourbons, but under this stipulation both countries had to maintain separate monarchs); recognition by France of the Hanoverian succession; and the existence of a barrier to protect the Dutch (albeit a less generous one than that conceded under the 1709 Barrier Treaty). Oxford tried to placate the Dutch with soothing reassurances, but they were fast becoming very suspicious.

In September, despite Shrewsbury's misgivings, the preliminary articles were signed. Oxford knew that once they were made public, all hell would break loose: the Whigs would go berserk and the Dutch would be indignant in the extreme. But the reality was that Oxford had good reasons to be confident that once 'official' negotiations including all parties began, the combined forces of British and French diplomatic might would be able to force them through, no matter how much the allies squealed. He had the support of the Queen, who was increasingly frantic for peace, and he knew that the Tory high-fliers would (for once) be squarely on his side. More broadly, the country wanted peace, and the vast majority couldn't give a fig for Habsburg claims to the throne of Spain or Dutch trading rights.

Oxford's big external headache was the attitude of George, the Elector of Hanover. He would, on the death of his octogenarian mother Sophia, become heir to the throne of Great Britain, and with Anne in such poor health he could soon thereafter accede to the throne.

George's overwhelming concern was to ensure that he, not the Pretender, became King of England and Scotland. So long as the war between Britain and France continued, a Jacobite restoration was (except in the now remote eventuality of a crushing French victory and invasion) impossible. George's other concern was to raise the status of his own German principality, the electorate of Hanover. He had designs on it being designated a kingdom, and for that he needed the support of the Holy Roman Emperor, who (nominally at least) ruled over all these statelets: in other words, Charles VI, the Habsburg monarch. Charles bitterly opposed a peace in which he lost Spain, and so it was in George's interests to ingratiate himself with Charles VI over the issue.

So Oxford was faced with an tricksome dilemma. He desperately needed a settlement as quickly as possible: the Tories in the Commons continued to back Oxford's ministry almost solely because they were united by their common desire for peace. But the only viable basis for a peace was a set of terms that were guaranteed to alienate George. So peace could only be achieved at the cost of making it overwhelmingly likely that, once Queen Anne died, Oxford and the Tories would be cast into the political outer darkness. A Whig king, which is what George would almost certainly be, could throw the entirety of government largesse behind the Whigs and entrench them in power indefinitely.

Oxford had no choice but to plough on with the peace and hope that something would turn up before Anne's demise. As the clock ticked down on the Queen's fragile health, the knowledge of impending political doom was to make for an ever more febrile political and personal atmosphere among the leading ministers.

And in the meantime, as he waited for the controversy over the peace preliminaries to break back in Britain, Oxford contemplated what was to be the political fight of his life.

At the beginning of August 1711, Matthew Prior, having made significant progress in his clandestine negotiations with the French, prepared to slip home, accompanied by the two chief French negotiators, Gaultier and Mesnager, who wanted to have final talks with the ministers in London to finesse the details of the peace negotiations. It was essential that his mission remain secret, so Prior adopted a false name and attempted to drift anonymously back to London.

Unfortunately, he had no luck: by chance he was recognised by a customs official who was suspicious that he was travelling under a false name. Soon, the coffee-houses of London were ablaze with the news. Everyone was convinced that Prior had been on a secret peace mission, and the very fact that it had been done in the shadows raised Whig suspicions: what reason, other than a betrayal of the allies, could have occasioned such furtiveness? The rumours soon leaked out to the Habsburg ambassador and the Dutch.

The rumours weren't wrong: at that very moment, Oxford was closeted away with the French plenipotentiaries in London putting the final touches to the peace preliminaries.

Before long, the storm must break. St John was convinced that the ministry should be prepared to boldly defend itself and go on the offensive. Rumours that Somerset and his wife, the chief rival to Mrs Masham in the Queen's bedchamber nowadays, were pouring poison into Anne's ears infuriated him. In his view, Somerset – who, being a Whig, would, St John judged, do everything to try to undermine the peace – must be sacked. Oxford baulked at such a bold move: he wanted to keep some semblance that the ministry was a cross-party enterprise.

St John despaired at Oxford's attitude. So far as he was concerned, it was no use pretending that their strategy was anything other than what it was: a bold attempt to deceive the allies, then coerce them into accepting a peace that was far more in Britain's interests than theirs. Oxford seemed to think that, by his usual tactics of prevarication, he could put off the evil day indefinitely. Perhaps, somehow, he could even persuade the allies to accept the peace preliminaries: his faith in the power of his torturous ruses to achieve his ends was immense.

St John argued instead for more boldness: embrace the strategy, ruthlessly force it through, and defend it to the hilt. He anticipated much criticism about the 'betrayal' of the allies, but to his mind, this was so much empty moralising. Diplomacy was a hard game: the ministry was acting in the national interest, and if the allies didn't like it, tough. In the words of Swift – who stayed up drinking long in the night with St John and the French ambassadors chewing the fat – 'there will be the devil and all to pay; but we'll make them swallow it with a pox'.[41]

Relations between Oxford and St John began to deteriorate further. The fact that Oxford had kept St John in the dark in the early stages of the peace negotiations had already infuriated him. Swift despaired at worsening relations between the two men, rumours of which had started to leak out:

> The Whigs whisper that our new Ministry differ among themselves, and they begin to talk out Mr. Secretary: they have some reasons for their whispers, although I thought it was a greater secret. I do not much like the posture of things; I always apprehended that any falling out would ruin them, and so I have told them several times.[42]

As he anticipated the impending hullaballoo over the peace preliminaries, St John also held his breath over the Quebec expedition, which was in progress. The tension was clearly too much for him. His whoring was becoming more shameless. His marriage was increasingly a notorious sham. He relieved the tension, when not haunting houses of ill repute and seducing other men's mistresses, by necking ever greater quantities of champagne and burgundy. An associate of the Harley family, who had visited him at home over the summer, summarised St John's domestic peccadilloes:

> I met there nothing but sorrow and disorder. That unfortunate gentle-man is more irregular, if possible, in his private than [his public] capacities. A sad instance to all young gentlemen of quality, how the greatest parts and expectations may be made useless and disappointed by the folly of vice.[43]

His other source of distraction over the tense summer of 1711 was the founding of a new Tory literary-social club, 'The Brothers' Club'. The aim was to allow some of the leading lights of the Tory Party – mainly St John's friends – to socialise, organise and cabal with important Tory-sympathising wits and writers. These included Swift himself and a Scottish doctor-cum-satirist called John Arbuthnot.

At first, the club purported to be an orderly and sober one: St John wrote to a friend that 'None of the extravagance of the kit-cat, none of the drunkenness of the beef-stake is to be endured', but rather the aim of the society was to be 'the improvement of friendship and the encouragement of letters'.[44] It was notable that the person whose friendship St John could have done with improving most urgently – Oxford – was excluded, and it seems that sobriety did not remain the club's watchword for long.[45]

In any case, St John's time for bibulous literary distractions was soon to be severely restricted. As autumn dawned, events started to move quickly. Firstly, news of the Quebec expedition – which St John saw as his ticket to glory, the bold masterstroke which would allow the ministry to screw more concessions out of the French – came back on 6th October. It was a disaster. The naval force had been wrecked before even engaging the enemy by a terrible storm. St John's gambit had failed.

Then, the peace storm broke. The ministry decided to bite the bullet, inform the Habsburgs of (at least some of) the peace preliminaries and begin their attempt to woo them to accept them; or, if that failed, bully them into it. The Habsburg ambassador, Gallas, leaked it to a Whig newspaper, the *Daily Courant*, who made an enormous splash on 13th October by printing the peace articles.

This was a major headache to the ministry. Leaking the terms at all was less than ideal, but the big problem at this stage was that Gallas had not, in fact, revealed all of the preliminaries. He was only cognisant of the articles outlining the general terms on which the official negotiations were to be based. A whole secret set of other terms, which outlined all of the special privileges that the French were to concede to Britain in terms of trading rights and territorial gains, were necessarily withheld from the allies, who naturally would have been furious that Britain conducted separate negotiations with the French to their own advantage.

The public peace articles did not seem impressive. They were considerably less advantageous to the allies in general than the terms that had almost been agreed in 1709. Abel Boyer, a Whig-inclined journalist, was not neutral, but he was right when he noted that 'the Generality of People, of both Parties' looked upon the preliminaries as 'Captious, Insidious and Insufficient to ground a Treaty upon', in contrast to the 'Glorious and Advantageous Terms' they had been led to expect.[46]

The Whigs smelt blood and went on the offensive. Arthur Maynwaring published a blistering attack on the articles. The 'Chief End of the War' he argued, was to stop Spain and its empire falling into the hands of the Bourbons, and 'No Peace without Spain' had been a policy agreed on several times in parliament, by both the bulk of the Whigs and Tories.[47] Therefore:

whoever are for entring into any such Treaty as leaves Spain and the Indies to France, have neither a due Regard for Her Majesty's Great Character, nor for the Publick Declarations of her Allies, nor the Resolutions and Dignity of our Parliaments.[48]

Indeed, entering into separate negotiations that would concede Spain against our allies' wishes 'must certainly dissolve all Trust and Agreement among the Allies; and sure[ly] nothing that weakens the Alliance can tend to secure our own Dominions, or to reduce France'.[49] Once the solidarity of the Grand Alliance had been undermined, then France would be able, he argued, to divide and rule. The inevitable result would be the retention of territory and economic advantages far beyond anything the French could achieve if the allies stuck together, which would preserve them as the ruling force in Europe and keep alive their dreams of a 'Universal Monarchy'.[50]

The implications of the virulent Whig press campaign against the peace preliminaries were clear. The ministry could only countenance a peace so bad if it were part of a deliberate policy of preserving French power to the end of using it to install the Pretender. Hence, Maynwaring strongly hinted, why the negotiations had been done in cloak and dagger fashion: otherwise, why wouldn't they have negotiated in an open and public manner, including their allies in the process?

The simple answer was: Spain. The only way the allies could hope to be in a position to force the French to give up the Bourbon claim to Spain and its empire was to fight on indefinitely. It was impossible to say how long such an objective would take to be achieved militarily. The country, the bulk of the Tory Party and now the Queen herself were extremely war-weary. Fighting on with no end in sight would have been completely politically impossible for Oxford, but the allies would not countenance a peace without recovering Spain for the Habsburgs, and therefore they had to be kept in the dark. It did not require a conspiracy theory about the supposed Jacobitism of the ministry to explain the tortuous path of the peace negotiations.

Oxford hoped to muddle on through, somehow persuade the allies to go along with his policy and wait until the formal peace negotiations could be convened, at which point it would prove a fait accompli. The key was to get the peace preliminaries through parliament. But he knew that he would have a job to persuade the Lords. Various court Whigs, who had been largely supportive of his ministry so far, made clear that they would not back the peace. It was difficult to see how he could avoid defeat in the upper house.

Oxford retreated into his usual habit: intrigue. Astonishingly, even at this point he wondered if a deal could be done with some of the more moderate Whigs to winkle the deal through the Lords. It might presage a reconciliation, which could end his dependence on the Tories and St John. His hopes were buoyed by the fact that in mid-November, the Dutch had, after much tormented soul-searching, reluctantly acceded to participate in a peace congress in Utrecht. They feared that the alternative – fighting on without British support – would be worse. Perhaps this might be used as the bait, with the help of Somers or Halifax, to coax just enough Whigs to vote with him in the Lords.

Oxford had made a major error of judgement. The Whigs, who had been rendered ineffective since their election drubbing in autumn 1710, had sprung back into life. They might be prepared to nibble with Harley to play divide and rule, but such negotiations were going nowhere. The Junto were up for the fight, and none more so than Lord Wharton.

As well as scheming with the Habsburg ambassador to embarrass the Tories, he and his Junto allies hoped to put the fear of God into the Tories by stirring up an outpouring of Francophobia and resorting to that old tried and tested method, rampant anti-popery. In Wharton's mind, the issue was simple: anyone who supported the peace was clearly a dirty papist Jacobite who wanted to deliver England over to the Pretender and the forces of absolutism. All of the old prejudices aroused during the Exclusion Crisis campaign and the Popish Plot could be dusted down and wielded against the ministry. Inspired by his zeal, the morale of the Whigs started to skyrocket.

He decided to resurrect some old-school, tried-and-tested methods: anti-Catholic demonstrations, timed, as was traditional, to coincide with Elizabeth I's birthday. 'Effigies of the Devil, the Pope, and the Pretender' – with the Devil designed to bear an uncanny resemblance to Oxford – 'were to be carry'd in Procession' and burnt, with the usual trimmings of music, costumes and revelry.[51] It was all timed to coincide with the Duke of Marlborough's return to London for the start of the new parliamentary session.

Much to Whig outrage, the ministry decided to crack down. They raided the house where the effigies where kept, confiscated them and banned the demonstration. They called out the trained bands to keep order. Wharton's great demonstration would not go ahead. The Tory press speculated that it amounted to a coup attempt: Mrs Manley, a leading Church Party propagandist and notorious author of *The New Atalantis,* even claimed that the intention was to storm St James's Palace and install Marlborough as king. The Whigs fumed at this abrogation of their rights. If they wanted to burn an effigy of the Pope, then what could be more becoming for stout Protestant Englishmen? They were determined to give the ministry an almighty bloody nose.

They soon found a way to do so.

While Oxford had been tilting at Whig windmills, Wharton had been scheming to achieve an extraordinary coup.[52]

Nottingham, who had never trusted Oxford, was a disgruntled man by mid-1711. He saw little evidence that any of his principles had been forwarded by the new ministry. Nothing was done for the Church. He skulked in the Lords, muttering darkly about Harley's treachery.

However, unlike many of his High Church allies, Nottingham's views on the peace were by no means standard issue Tory ones. From his time as Secretary of State early on in Anne's reign, he had been in favour of a 'Spain first' policy: after all, wasn't the whole point of the war to prevent the Bourbons taking the Spanish throne?

Something else made him uneasy too. The truth was that, despite having endured years of being accused of being a Jacobite, Nottingham's hostility to popery meant that he really did support the Protestant succession. The Whigs had misjudged him: sour and dour he may have been, but he was also absolutely sincere. What's more, his distrust and contempt for Oxford was so strong, and (in his judgment) the peace preliminaries so poor, that he began to suspect that a Jacobite game was indeed afoot.

So, by the time he reached London for the new parliamentary session in November 1711, he had made up his mind. Under no circumstances would he support Oxford's rotten, underhand peace.

However, if he was going to vote with the Whigs on the peace, he was determined to extract his price. Rumours had reached both ministry and the Whigs by the time he arrived in Westminster that he was unhappy about the preliminaries. Representatives of both assailed him with blandishments and flummery. He met them with a poker face. He would make them sweat.

But before long, he was prepared to make his proposal clear to Wharton. If the Whigs were prepared to give him – and some of his personal allies in the Lords – 'some real security' as to their good will, then he could assure them of his support.[53] The 'real security' was to be the prize he had coveted for years: finally passing the Occasional Conformity Bill.

It was a bitter pill for the Junto to swallow. It would mean selling their oldest political allies – the Dissenters – down the river in spectacular fashion. They assured their Dissenting allies that it was only a temporary measure, a necessary price to pay to prevent a 'French peace' that they would reverse once they had won the battle. It was embarrassing, but anything that might bring down Oxford was too tempting to resist.

Politics makes for the most curious of alliances, and so it was that Wharton and Nottingham – sworn enemies for well over twenty years – did their deal. To Nottingham, it must have felt like making a pact with the Devil himself. The greatest objective of the High Churchmen, the prize that their wizened old leader had strived for in vain for years, was to be passed at the behest of their oldest and most bitter foe, the atheist rake whom they saw as the political anti-Christ. Wharton could barely hide the mixture of astonishment and bemusement in his voice as he exclaimed to his cronies: 'Tis Dismal will save England at last'.[54]

The penny finally dropped with Oxford: the Whig Lords were not serious about a deal. He realised that his only hope was to stick to his alliance with the Church Party. At a meeting with Bromley, Hanmer and other High Church Tories, he hammered out a deal to reassure the October men (or at least the more reasonable ones). If they would support him over the peace preliminaries, he promised them an early peace, a cut to the land tax and a purge of the Whigs still in office. He would give them freer rein to investigate and possibly impeach leading Whigs. He hinted at possible support for an Occasional Bill as well, 'when the time is right', but this was too little, too late to gain him much credit overall, given that Nottingham could, after his deal with Wharton, promise the more hot-headed Tories its immediate passage.[55] Overall, Oxford did manage to ensure that the Tories would back him solidly – if unenthusiastically – in the Commons, but it did him no good in the Lords, where it was increasingly apparent events were slipping away from him.

He had dithered too long, and as the parliamentary session loomed, he knew he was in deep trouble. St John, meanwhile, had been pursuing quite a different approach. He decided that the ministry had to aggressively attack its enemies and put its case, and to this end he called upon the ministry's chief pen, Jonathan Swift.

On 27th November a new pamphlet hit the newsstands. Entitled *The Conduct of the Allies*, it was soon being furiously read – and variously lauded or cursed, according to whether its purchaser was a pacific Tory or a bellicose Whig – in every coffee-house and tavern from Westminster to Change Alley, and very soon throughout the country.

Swift's scintillating text went for the Whigs' jugular. Its aim was to show that Britain's involvement in the war had, from the very beginning, scarcely been in its own interests. Despite this, due to the 'the Folly, the Temerity, the Corruption, the Ambition of its domestick Enemies' and the 'Insolence, Injustice and Ingratitude' of its 'foreign Friends', it had ended up bearing the brunt of the conflict.[56] In essence, Britain had been played for a fool: gulled into footing the bill for a war that largely benefited, not its own countrymen, but the Dutch and Britain's other allies, not to mention Whig financiers, military parasites and political mountebanks.

The pamphlet retailed a shocking list of instances when Britain's allies had failed to meet their financial and military obligations. He reflected with great indignation on the extraordinary concessions made to the Dutch in the 1709 Barrier Treaty, arguing with force that they were directly contrary to British commercial interests (which was undoubtedly true). Swift had been carefully primed by St John with a wealth of detail on these matters, many of which were previously unknown to his readers, all of which gave the pamphlet the shock of novelty.

He also made the point that, for a war supposedly fought to prevent Spain falling into Bourbon hands, remarkably little attention had been given to the Iberian front. Why pour millions into a ruinously expensive land war in Flanders while neglecting the very theatre of combat at the heart of the alliance's purported war aims? Was it, perhaps, because a land war gave far more scope to Marlborough to indulge his taste for military glory and self-enrichment? Why couldn't Britain have focussed on a naval war, which would have been cheaper and allowed us to harry the French in the Spanish West Indies, and thereby strengthen our own claims to territorial and trading gains in that sphere once peace came? In a sly dig at Marlborough, he observed that:

> It was the kingdom's misfortune, that the sea was not the duke of Marlborough's element; otherwise, the whole force of the war would infallibly have been bestowed there, infinitely to the advantage of his country, which would then have gone hand in hand with his own.[57]

Swift put over the old Tory arguments about the war with biting eloquence and spiced them with insider information to great effect.

How could all of this come to pass? To answer this question, Swift wheeled out exactly the same arguments that Oxford had contemplated in 1709: in short, the drivers of the process were 'the Family'. The Marlboroughs and Godolphin, their families linked by marriage, had gained prodigiously from forcing the honest Tory gentlemen to pay for these enormous land wars. The gold had poured into their pockets, the glory accrued to their names, and yet still, after 'ten glorious campaigns', the country was half bankrupt and very little of advantage had accrued to it.[58] It was clear that 'whether this war were prudently begun or not . . . the true spring or motive of it, was the aggrandising a particular family'.[59]

This aggrandisement was not just a matter of money. 'The Family' had allied themselves with the bankers and the Whigs to put power into their own hands and thereby to ensure that the war continued indefinitely: a vicious circle of war and domination by 'The Family' had been initiated. The danger flowing from this was that 'a general during pleasure might have grown into a general for life, and a general for life, into a king'.[60] This frightening prospect could only be prevented by Oxford and the Queen putting a stop to the mechanism that kept the whole tawdry swindle in motion: the war. Otherwise, Britain would continue to be the 'the dupes and bubbles of Europe' indefinitely.[61]

The source of the pamphlet's power was the fact that it wove a compelling narrative that appeared neatly to explain many apparently mysterious events of the previous decade. It did this by using reasonable arguments, as often as not based on undeniable facts – but the ultimate conclusions were often no better than half-truths. No doubt Marlborough's greed had found much to feed it over the past decade, but to claim that the entire war was a grand deception that had come about purely for his aggrandisement was clearly unfair. Had Marlborough been ill-advised and acted unconstitutionally in demanding to be made captain-general for life? Yes, but the idea that he seriously countenanced becoming king was highly implausible. No doubt the Barrier Treaty and the failure to make peace in 1709 were great errors; and no doubt England had borne a heavy burden, plausibly disproportionate to that endured by its allies; but to claim that there were not compelling reasons to have undertaken it on some scale at the beginning was a distortion of the facts.

The fact was, however, that its coherence and chutzpah gave *The Conduct of the Allies* a potency that no Whig equivalent possessed. Its effect was electrifying. After weeks of drift, finally a clear and trenchant Tory position, rooted in a persuasive if perhaps selective interpretation of recent history, had been put forward. Copies poured off the presses and were distributed to stiffen the backbone of the Church Party in the country. Swift, immodestly but not inaccurately, observed that 'the Tory Lords and Commons in Parliament argue all from it; and all agree that never anything of that kind was of so great consequence, or made so many converts'.[62] Finally, the ministry had showed some fight, rather than allowing itself to get lost in a fog of drift and delay.

However, this did not change the fact that the administration's efforts to pass the peace had been severely hamstrung by a lack of unity. They had no coherent approach: while Oxford made a futile effort to bring over Whig moderates, St John had pursued a more 'Tory first' policy. This certainly hindered the government's efforts to rally their parliamentary troops. Swift fretted:

The Parliament will certainly meet on Friday next: the Whigs will have a great majority in the House of Lords, no care is taken to prevent it; there is too much neglect; they are warned of it, and that signifies nothing: it was feared there would be some peevish address from the Lords against a peace.[63]

In fact, much care was taken. Oxford was, belatedly, trying every expedient he could to shore up the government's position in the Lords, but he had little luck. A number of Scottish peers, all pledged to vote for the ministry, were holed up in Scotland, delayed by floods. Efforts to induce the Bishops of Durham and Exeter to make the journey to London in time failed: the former pleaded the effects of 'old age and the depths of winter'.[64]

On 5th December, two days before the vote, the Tories suffered another blow. The *Daily Courant* had another exclusive: they printed an extraordinary protest by Baron von Bothmar, the Hanoverian envoy to London, which made the Elector's opposition to the ministry's peace terms very clear. The knowledge that the next king of England looked askance at the terms focussed minds in the Whigs' favour, and gave countenance to warnings about Jacobite designs.

Swift was on tenterhooks, waiting for the fateful day. To pass the time, he decided to vent his spleen on old turncoat Dismal. He penned a vicious squib:

> How I always pretended to be for the tories:
> I answer; the tories were in my good graces,
> Till all my relations were put into places.
> But still I'm in principle ever the same,
> And will quit my best friends, while I'm Not-in-game.
> . . .
>
> Since the tories have thus disappointed my hopes,
> And will neither regard my figures nor tropes;
> I'll speech against peace while Dismal's my name,
> And be a true whig, while I'm Not-in-game.[65]

389

It was, in truth, a harsh and unfair bit of doggerel. It alluded to the fact that several of Nottingham's relations had been given minor government offices over the previous summer, implying that his deal with the Whigs was a product of his discontent at not being given government office himself. Whatever the wisdom or otherwise of his deal, the idea that he was motivated by self-interest was very wide of the mark.

Parliament finally met on 7th December. In the Lords, Nottingham moved an amendment to the Queen's Speech that 'no Peace can be safe or honourable to Great Britain or Europe, if Spain and The West-Indies are to be allotted to any Branch of the House of Bourbon', with the backing of the Junto lords, Godolphin and Marlborough.[66] Nottingham made a fiery speech in its favour, declaring dramatically, according to one observer, 'that though he had fourteen children, he would submit to live upon five hundred pounds a year, rather than consent to those dark and unknown conditions of peace' proposed by the government.[67] Marlborough, who was of course a member of the Lords, followed up with an eloquent and heartfelt speech against the peace in which he emotionally defended his own integrity, which weighed heavily: he was, after all, still the great hero of the war effort.

In response, the government speakers gave a distinctly lacklustre performance – Shrewsbury, embarrassed, stayed silent, and others, including Oxford, spent more time trying to defer the debate by procedural tactics than defending their policy. A motion to defer the amendment (on the basis that the peace terms were a separate issue best debated apart from the Queen's Speech debate) was lost by one vote. Soon after, the vote on the actual amendment was carried easily.

Ironically, Nottingham's defection had made little difference: he failed to bring any of his Tory colleagues in the Lords over with him. What was decisive was, in fact, the success of the Junto in persuading a number of court Whigs – including Somerset – to abandon Oxford: ultimately, the call of partisanship had proven too great for them. The Whig bishops – who made up a majority of the episcopal contingent – stood firm, despite considerable pressure from the ministry, and Oxford must have despaired when several Tories failed to turn up, due to a not-unheard-of combination of incompetence and indolence.

The government won the vote by a large majority in the Commons – despite a small rebellion of 'Hanoverian Tories' who shared some of Nottingham's dark suspicions of Oxford's motives – but the defeat in the Lords was a tremendous blow. The constitutional convention, in an age when the Lords was generally seen as the chamber with the greater honour and weight, was that no proposal could go forward if defeated in the Lords (with the exception of money bills, on which the Lords did not vote).

All appeared to be lost. The whole world seemed ranged against Oxford: the Habsburgs, Hanoverians and Marlborough were all more-or-less openly scheming with the Whigs to destroy him. As he walked dejectedly away from the Lords chamber after the vote, Wharton (it was rumoured) had 'clapped his hand upon the Lord Treasurer's shoulder, and said, by God, my lord, if you bear this you are the strongest man in England'.[68]

In the febrile political atmosphere of those grim days, no doubt another thought had more than once crossed Oxford's mind. Now Hanover had made their stance very clear indeed, what if, after Anne's death, the new king decided to listen to Whig claims that Harley was a Jacobite traitor? Impeachments after changes of governments were not uncommon, and the penalty for high treason was beheading, if you were lucky.

During the Lords debate, Sunderland had given a heavy hint that impeachment might be on the agenda in the future, and Wharton gave 'fair notice . . . that if any of them [the ministers] should concern themselves in a peace without Spain and the Indies he might answer it to the house with his head', a point he backed up emphatically by means of some vigorous and gruesome throat-cutting gestures directed at Oxford.[69] If things continued to go this badly, it wasn't just Oxford's ministry or reputation at stake. His neck was on the line.

And yet. There was a chink of light still. If the Queen chose to stamp her considerable authority on the situation then all could be saved. She could sack individuals in the pay of the Crown who had voted with the Junto – and even, if need be, create new peers. The vote could be reversed.

The problem was that the Queen's view was unclear. She had held private audiences with the Hanoverian envoy, Marlborough, various Whig lords and others. All had told her the same thing: her ministers were in a conspiracy against her to secure a bad peace, raise up France and bring in the Pretender.

And some feared the worst. Swift was rattled. According to reports from Mrs Masham, it seemed that 'the Queen is false, or at least very much wavering'.[70] Previously she had seemed to back Oxford completely, but had her sentiments changed? Had Marlborough or the Junto nobbled her? Oxford himself, affecting his usual stoical attitude, gnomically resorted to a biblical quotation: 'The hearts of Kings are unsearchable'.[71] He appeared far from certain of the Queen's support. It boded, thought Swift, ill. He feared that the game was up.

Lord Oxford, however, had not lost the wiles of Mr Robert Harley on his elevation to the peerage. He held his cards very close to his chest, and speculation mounted. What was going on in the Queen's bedchamber? Could Oxford pull something out of the bag?

Meanwhile, the unedifying business of Whigs voting through an Occasional Conformity Bill was in full flow. One can only imagine how much the ranks of the Whig Party, the friends of the Dissenting interest, must have squirmed as Nottingham passed his bill almost without opposition. Oxford – still in his heart a friend to the Dissenters – reluctantly acquiesced in its passing to avoid irritating Tory backbench opinion. Thus, in an atmosphere of distinct anticlimax, was 'Old Occasional' finally passed.

Swift spent a miserable, freezing Christmas contemplating the likely doom of his friends. The tone of his journal took on a despondent tone: on 20th December, after a meeting with St John, he concluded that a 'languishing death' awaited them all.[72] 'God knows what will become of us' was his grim ejaculation a few days later.[73]

And then, just on the stroke of the New Year, everything changed.

Oxford, although he had remained tight-lipped, had finally decided that enough was enough: fudge had not worked. He must strike back with vigour. His demands to the Queen were brutal: sack every last office-holder who had defied her ministry over the peace, including Somerset and Marlborough, and create twelve new Tory peers to force the preliminaries through the Lords. He worked every atom of his persuasive ability as hard as possible, cajoling and begging her to take the bold, necessary steps.

It soon became clear that the Queen was *not* false. She wanted peace and would not flinch from pushing it through. Indeed, she had already privately decided to sack Marlborough: she could hardly have her military supremo directly defy her policy. But now, much to Oxford and St John's relief and amazement, she announced her intention to do so, replacing him as captain-general with a staunch Tory, James Butler, Duke of Ormonde. Not only that, she agreed to dismiss Somerset and create the new Lords too. Swift was ecstatic: 'we are all safe . . . She is awaked at last . . . We are all extremely happy. Give me joy, sirrahs!'[74]

The new Lords – quickly dubbed 'Harley's Dozen' – were swiftly appointed: they were mainly personal friends, followers and relations of Oxford, including Samuel Masham, Mrs Masham's husband. The Whigs were furious and muttered darkly about unprecedented and possibly unconstitutional methods. One could easily see why: at a stroke their greatest source of political strength, their inbuilt majority in the Lords, was broken. With this precedent set, what limits were there to the monarch's ability to appoint peers and undermine the independence of the upper house according to the partisan political exigencies of the day?

However, there was precious little the Whigs could do about it. Wharton quipped that Oxford 'played well at whist', for 'what he could not make by tricks, he made up by knaves'.[75] When 'Harley's Dozen' assembled in the Lords chamber on 2nd January, Wharton dryly enquired 'whether they voted by their foreman'.[76] Bon mots such as this did not hide the fact that the Whig assault had been broken. The Tories were exuberant as the new peers were introduced, but 'the sober whigs cast their eyes to the ground, as if they had been invited to the funeral of the peerage'.[77] Their sombre mood was not improved when the ministry successfully carried their adjournment motion – which effectively neutralised the vote against the peace preliminaries carried on 7th December – by a comfortable majority of thirteen.

The great Whig offensive had, finally, been broken. The peace was alive.

11

Winning the Peace

On New Year's Day 1712, the Queen had sent the Duke of Marlborough a short note informing him that his services as captain-general of her army were no longer required. The first Englishman since Henry V to comprehensively rout the mighty armies of France, his stunning series of victories – Blenheim, Ramillies, Oudenarde – had made him into a military hero on the scale of Nelson or Wellington a hundred years later. Now he was dismissed in a few terse paragraphs.

The Duke, consumed by indignation and fury, hurled it into the fire immediately on having read it. The icily polite prose of his reply barely conceals his rage:

> I am very sensible of the honour your majesty does me, in dismissing me from your service, by a letter of your own hand, though I find by it that my enemies have been able to prevail with your majesty, to do it in the manner that is most injurious to me. And if their malice and inveteracy against me had not been more powerful with them than the consideration of your majesty's honour and justice, they would not have influenced you to impute the occasion of my dismission, to a false and malicious insinuation contrived by themselves, and made public, when there was no opportunity for me to give in my answer . . .[1]

The 'false and malicious insinuation' he mentions is a reference to the fact that the ministry had, in December, let the October Club backbench attack dogs well and truly off the leash. The Commission of Accounts that had been formed earlier in 1711 had been allowed to report and make a series of accusations of corruption against the Duke, the means of political assassination much in vogue among partisans of both parties in an era not renowned for financial probity.

Given that Marlborough had so publicly come out against the peace preliminaries and made his alignment with the Whigs as plain as day, the ministry now had no compunction about attempting to destroy him totally and utterly. They had hinted that if he went along with the peace and kept quiet, he would be safe from any such actions – but he had made his choice and now came the inevitable political consequences.

Given that he had been the most lauded and admired man in the country for years, and his prestige was potentially a powerful weapon against the peace and the ministry, his reputation needed to be obliterated all the more thoroughly. Swift had begun the work in earnest a year earlier, but now there was to be no mercy. Prosecuting Marlborough for corruption not only legitimised sacking him but also gave credence to the Tory narrative that the war had been fought chiefly to burnish his ego and cram his pockets – and those of his allies – with gold.

The accusations themselves were typical: an attempt to politicise practices that were (by modern standards) questionable but widely accepted at the time. Marlborough was accused of peculating money from the wages earmarked for the payment of foreign troops, and for receiving a 'premium' from the contractor who supplied the army with bread.

These charges were combined with a similar attack on Robert Walpole, who had proved himself the most eloquent and wily Whig lieutenant in the Commons over the past few years. His former position as Secretary at War – in charge of managing military supplies and contracts, which gave immense scope for dodgy dealing – made him a prime target for accusations of peculation and mismanagement, in this case relating to irregularities in the contract to provide forage for the army's horses.

Part of Oxford's motivations in allowing the attack on Walpole to proceed was to sate the Tory backbenchers' appetite for revenge and encourage
the impression that the Whigs had enriched themselves by prolonging the
war. A simple motion of censure and slap on the wrists would have sufficed
for that. Oxford, however, had another, more important, motive: political
assassination. By tabling motions branding Walpole as guilty of 'notorious
corruption' and expelling him altogether from the Commons, he could
remove the man most likely to obstruct the government's business in the
lower chamber.[2]

The charge against Walpole came on first, and in fact nearly backfired.
Some Tories felt that the whole exercise was too nakedly partisan to be
strictly honourable, particularly when it came to the motions to expel
him from the House and actually imprison him in the Tower of London.
Swift's Tory MP contacts 'talked dubiously' of the whole proceeding.[3] Some
opposed the government and so many decided to absent themselves that
the vote to commit Walpole to the Tower only passed by twelve votes.
Walpole – gratified no doubt by managing to run a government that usually
commanded a majority of over a hundred so close – remained in the Tower
for five months, but his hardships were not great: regularly visited by the
great and the good and lavished with provisions, 'his room in the Tower was
more like the scene of a levée than a prison'.[4]

The ministry had been curiously limp during the whole affair: Oxford
and St John had made little attempt to prime the court's rhetorical big guns
to speak against Walpole, assuming that they could simply let the Tory
backbenchers off the leash. Their whipping operation was unusually lax,
largely due to complacency. This desultory effort produced an embarrassingly
slim majority of the kind apt to dent confidence in any ministry.

Oxford was absolutely determined that no such thing was to occur when
the charges against Marlborough came up a week later. He pulled together a
crack team of personally approved whips who drew up a list of 200 MPs to
beg or browbeat into turning up. Every lazy, wine-bibbing and perennially
absent Tory MP was rounded up from whatever tavern, country estate or
knocking-shop they customarily preferred to parliamentary business and
dragged to the House.

It had its effect. The truth (or at least some of it) came out in the parliamentary debate: the monies in question had been paid to Marlborough for him to use to engage secret service agents to gather military intelligence and had been approved a decade ago by no less than a former Tory Secretary of State, Sir Charles Hedges.[5] It is questionable whether such large sums were required for intelligence purposes and quite plausible that some of the monies were diverted to less noble ends, but it was certainly true that such perquisites were seen as standard practice until it was politically convenient to pretend otherwise (exactly the same monies were paid to Marlborough's Tory successor, Ormonde). However, such trifling matters as the truth counted for little in such a cold-blooded partisan affair: motions censuring his conduct as 'unwarrantable and illegal' and calling on him to account for the sums involved were passed mostly by majorities of over one hundred.[6]

However, the affair went no further. The obvious next step was an impeachment: it did not come. Oxford realised that his chances of actually passing an impeachment in the Lords, given the flimsy nature of the charges, were far from certain, 'Harley's Dozen' notwithstanding. Better to play the role of magnanimous statesman and not pursue the matter. Oxford was never averse to keeping open the option of intriguing with the Whigs – or, perhaps, in extremis, even Marlborough himself – if all else failed.

Instead, the assault against Marlborough came elsewhere: in the press. The Tory section of Grub Street launched a merciless campaign of character assassination against the Duke, presenting him as a corrupt, faithless and overmighty would-be tyrant. William Oldisworth in *The Examiner* was particularly vicious, focusing particularly on the issue of the money skimmed off from the contract to supply the army with bread:

> Amongst all the founding Names of Greek and Roman Heroes, to which they have parallelled our late General, can they find one who condescended to rob the Soldiers of their Bread? or who suffered the Brave Men, wounded in the Field, to perish there, because their Leader pocketed the Money, allotted for those Contingencies, that were to preserve them.[7]

Given that Marlborough's troops were unusually well looked after by the standards of contemporary warfare, this was a cruel smear. Whatever his faults were, this was not among them. Even Swift – who was no longer editing or writing for *The Examiner* – thought that 'Lord Marlborough is used too hardly'.[8]

Perhaps the most effective attack on Marlborough came in the form of a pamphlet entitled *Oliver's Pocket Looking-Glass*. This scurrilous production painted Marlborough as a scheming traitor who had used any and every contrivance – including sleeping with Charles II's mistress and effectively prostituting his own sister out to James II – to gain the trust of and then betray successive monarchs, all with the eventual goal of supplanting good Queen Anne and becoming the new Oliver Cromwell. The problem for Marlborough was that although its central charge was deeply unfair, many of the details of the pamphlet were true. He *had* slept with Charles II's mistress, his sister *had* been James II's mistress, he *had* gone over to William III in 1688 and then had possibly treasonable correspondence with the Jacobite court once he fell out of favour with the new king. Marlborough's eventful career gave superficial plausibility to these sorts of wild attacks, which did his reputation no favours.

Ultimately, however, Marlborough's fall was the result of his grave political misjudgements. From around 1709 onwards he had totally and openly aligned himself with the Whig policy of continuing the war indefinitely, and thereby not only made himself the implacable enemy of the Oxford ministry, and therefore fair game in the partisan hurly-burly, but also set himself against the nation's (and the Queen's) desperate desire for peace. In short, no amount of gratitude for his martial valour was enough to outweigh a widespread desire to end a bitter and bloody conflict, and his enthusiasm for fighting on and on was easily presented by his enemies as a desire to prolong the circumstances that had proved the precondition of his rise to riches and greatness. Although these charges were largely exaggerated and sometimes completely untrue, his very real lust for wealth and power gave credence to them and sealed the downfall of a very great, and very flawed, man.

* * *

While the Tories undertook the grim, but in their view necessary, task of destroying Marlborough to clear the path to peace, the official peace congress had been officially convened in Utrecht in late January 1712. The preliminaries may have been agreed, but there were many unsettled issues to resolve before a decade of warfare could formally draw to an end.

Britain's allies came to the negotiating table at Utrecht with extreme misgivings. The Dutch had essentially been strong-armed into participation by the Oxford ministry. They were not terribly bothered about abandoning Spain to the Bourbons if their own interests were served, but they knew that any new defensive arrangements to protect their border from the French were almost certainly going to be considerably less generous than the 1709 Barrier Treaty. They suspected that their trading interests were in severe danger from any deal cut behind closed doors between the French and the British.

They weren't wrong, but in late 1711 the British ambassador to the Hague had given them a brutal ultimatum: engage in the peace congress, or Britain would leave them to fight on for the Habsburg claim over Spain with only nominal support. This terrified them, and they caved. The prospect of being abandoned by both the Dutch and the British also brought the Habsburg Empire – extremely reluctantly – to Utrecht too.

In essence, the formal negotiations at Utrecht were little more than a grand charade for public consumption. Neither Oxford nor St John had any intention of treating the Dutch or the Empire as equal partners in the negotiations. They were resolved to come to an agreement with France and then force it on the allies.

There was, however, a key difference between the two men. Oxford saw the political necessity of this strategy – it was the only way to get a peace quickly and advantageously enough to placate the Tory Party – but felt uneasy about selling out the allies, especially the Dutch, too brutally. He accordingly wished to protect the interests of the other allies – especially the Dutch – at least to some extent in the secret negotiations with the French, in the hope that they might accept them without too much bad grace. St John, on the other hand, was much more cynical. He was quite happy to cut a quick and dirty deal with the French with more-or-less zero regard to the interests of the Dutch.

The issues facing the ministry as the negotiations began were complex. Probably the biggest sticking point was that the French wished to retain various important fortresses on their border with the Spanish Netherlands, most notably the strategically vital one at Tournai, which would clearly be very detrimental to Dutch security and undermine their barrier. St John cared little about this, but Oxford was adamant that the Dutch barrier must at least be protected to this extent, and he was very much in the driving seat of the British side of the negotiations (much to St John's irritation).

The other major issues concerned Britain's trading and commercial rights in the Spanish Empire relative to the claims of the Dutch, including the potentially lucrative Assiento contract to supply African slaves to South America. On this Oxford and St John were as one: Oxford's South Sea Company was financially dependent on securing the Assiento for Britain, and both knew that massively beneficial commercial concessions for Britain would almost certainly outweigh any pious lamentations for unjustly selling out the Dutch within the domestic political arena, particularly in Tory eyes. To calm Dutch nerves in the short term, Oxford made vague promises of some financial package to compensate them for losing the Assiento, but his intentions of fulfilling them were precisely zero.

The means by which the ministry were prepared to force the Dutch into accepting such a peace deal were potent, albeit not pretty.

The first was essentially the threat of being militarily abandoned. Oxford had no intention of fighting another campaign when spring 1712 came around. The reason was simple: either it would be unsuccessful and therefore futile, or it would be successful, in which case it might leave the French in such a weak state that the very beneficial terms they were prepared to grant Britain in separate negotiations would be undermined. In short, total French defeat meant that the spoils of victory would have to be shared far more equally between the allies. Either way, Tory rage at another summer of war would be unmanageable.

This fact meant that, one way or another, the Dutch and Austrians were about to be militarily abandoned in the field, left to shoulder the cost and military effort without Britain's subsidies and armies. Such a fact was inevitably likely to concentrate minds, especially Dutch ones: it held out the possibility of an even less advantageous peace than the one that Britain was prepared to secure for them.

The other trump card held by Oxford and St John was the (hitherto not publicly disclosed) terms of the 1709 Barrier Treaty negotiated between the Whigs and the Dutch. These terms were so extremely generous to the Dutch – and contrary to British commercial interests in the Low Countries – that disclosing them in detail would prove enormously embarrassing to the Whigs and discredit their complaints about 'selling out' the Dutch.

So in February 1712, the ministry decided to stage a parliamentary set piece in order to publicise and condemn not only the terms of the Barrier Treaty, but also the entire conduct of the allies – particularly the Dutch – over the course of the war. It gave Tory backbenchers a tremendous opportunity to give vent to years of frustration with alleged Dutch perfidy and self-seeking, and work up some patriotic (or, according to one's view, xenophobic) fervour, all to the congenial end of advancing the peace and dishing the Whigs.

In essence, the Tory case was that the alliance had always been a one-sided affair, in which Britain had borne the burden and heat of the day to serve predominantly Dutch ends, often to the detriment of British interests, all while the Dutch welched on their agreements and even attempted to interfere with British politics.

There was no doubt that there was a large dollop of truth in all this. The failure of the Dutch (and indeed also the Austrians) to honour their commitments when it came to financial and military contributions to the war effort was conspicuous and irritated British ministers of all political colours throughout the war: again and again they failed to supply subsidies and troops as promised, expecting (rightly) that Britain would pick up the slack. The Dutch, despite briefly agreeing to stop trading with the French back in 1703, had quietly recommenced doing so not long after. A long paper detailing these failures was placed before the House of Commons, and a motion condemning the Dutch for not fulfilling their side of the bargain passed by a swinging majority.

The Tory press had a field day. One pamphlet calculated that, when taking into account everything, the Dutch had made the (suspiciously precise) profit of £12,235,857.5.5d out of the war.[9] *The Examiner* declared that:

> No Nation, no, not a petty Conquer'd Province, was ever treated with more Contempt, or more infamously Bubbl'd and Amus'd, than Great-Britain has been by its Allies, especially the Dutch.[10]

These scribblers were obviously exaggerating – indeed, the Dutch people tottered under a heavy load of taxes themselves – but the Tory propaganda had more than a scintilla of truth to it.

It was, however, the Barrier Treaty of 1709 that represented the most outrageous betrayal of the national interest in Tory eyes. In their desperate desire to keep the Dutch in the war in 1709, the Whig ministry had given them more or less whatever they wanted – most notoriously, an equal share in all trading concessions to be extracted from the Spanish Empire, and control of the towns of Ostend and Dendermonde as part of their barrier against the French, despite those towns being essential ports for British traders.

In the Commons, St John led the charge, making a wittily effective speech in which he argued that although it *was* Britain's 'business to provide a Barrier for the Dutch against France' it was nonetheless 'amasing that any Englishman shou'd think of giving them one against England'.[11] He pointed out that, in previous negotiations, even William III – who was, of course, Dutch – had rejected the idea of giving his own country commercially sensitive cities such as Ostend as 'prejudicial to England'.[12]

This was music to backbench Tory ears, and they duly piled in to lash the Dutch and the Whig lords who had negotiated such a disastrous treaty. Harsh motions condemning the treaty as 'destructive to the trade and interest of Great-Britain' and impugning those responsible for it as 'enemies to the queen and kingdom' were duly passed by thumping majorities of over 150.[13] The Whigs were powerless to prevent the reputation of both themselves and the allies being ground into the dust in front of their eyes.

* * *

This anti-Whig public mood was perfectly expressed by a satire which began to appear in March 1712, penned by John Arbuthnot, an amiable and modest man nonetheless possessed of a considerable fund of dry wit, who was, as well as being one of the Queen's personal doctors, a friend of Swift and St John and member of the Brothers' Club. The first instalment of this work, entitled *Law is a Bottomless Pit*, gained much of its impact through its use of a homely allegory that could be easily grasped by any stout squire.[14]

In it, Arbuthnot recasts the entire war as a long-running lawsuit over the inheritance of a country estate, in which tradesman John Bull (representing Britain) is tricked by a slick lawyer named Humphrey Hocus (Marlborough) and fellow tradesman Nicholas Frog (curiously representing the Dutch) into recovering debts owed to him from the estate by Lewis and Philip Baboon (that is, Louis XIV and Philip of Anjou, the Bourbon claimant to the throne of Spain). The case becomes ever more protracted and complicated, and the costs (borne by John Bull) mount. It soon becomes clear that 'nobody got much by the matter but the men of law'.[15]

Eventually, John Bull is alerted to the fact that he is being swindled and hires honest old country attorney Sir Roger Bold (Oxford) to compound the lawsuit and come to a compromise (i.e. secure peace) before he runs out of money and is completely ruined by the whole affair, much to the irritation of both Frog, who has avoided paying the costs of the lawsuit and still hopes to gain from it, and Hocus and his friends, the many lawyers and hangers-on who have made a fortune out of swindling John (the Whigs and their financier allies).

Law is a Bottomless Pit and its sequels, later collected into a book entitled *The History of John Bull*, are chiefly remembered now as the first appearance of John Bull, who was to live on as among the most memorable national personifications of Britain. John Bull's origin, however, is inextricable from the rhetorical purposes of Arbuthnot as he attempted to put the Tory case in the circumstances of 1712.

Arbuthnot needed to both flatter Bull – for to cast him as a completely gullible idiot would hardly be compatible with a robust Tory patriotism – while also giving a plausible explanation of how he could have been so badly conned. His answer was to characterise Bull as 'an honest plain-dealing

403

fellow' who is also good natured, impulsive and liberal to his friends – a 'boon companion, loving his bottle and his diversion', adverse to bean-counting and penny-pinching.[16] In other words, Bull's failures are the products of an excess of his admirable qualities: his honesty, lack of suspicion, impulsive generosity and fondness for a good time.

Ultimately, however, no matter how unsuspicious and generous he is, he has his limits: as he puts it, 'Look ye gentlemen, John Bull is but a plain man; but John Bull knows when he is ill used'.[17] In other words, Britain has been imposed on for too long, and enough is enough. In short, Arbuthnot made skilful use of national self-flattery to immunise his readership against Whig defences of the allies, as well as invoking a whole host of other powerful prejudices, such as hatred of lawyers and suspicion of nefarious foreigners.

The Whigs pumped out much of their own propaganda attacking the Tory position on the war in spring 1712, much of it full of solid, sterile argument and vigorous logic: but none of it had half of the impact or was a quarter as memorable as Arbuthnot's homely tale of stolid old John Bull and cunning old Humphrey Hocus.

Despite the fact that public and parliamentary opinion was uncompromisingly pro-peace – and increasingly so – the Tory ministry was not to find it all plain sailing in spring 1712.

Not long after it had started, the Utrecht Peace Congress was thrown into confusion by a rapid succession of deaths in the French royal family. Although the Oxford ministry had accepted the reality that the Spanish throne would remain in the hands of Philip, and therefore a Bourbon, it was still imperative to ensure that the thrones of Spain and France would not literally be united in the hands of one man. A Bourbon megapower that would combine both the entire Spanish empire and the French kingdom had to be avoided.

This did not seem to be much of an issue while there were still three living heirs above Philip in the French line of succession, as there were when the peace congress at Utrecht opened. However, in February and March two of the three died, and the third (the future Louis XV) was a two-year-old child of persistently poor health. The ultimate nightmare – Philip becoming both the Spanish and French king – seemed perilously close.

This suddenly became the absolutely key diplomatic issue: Oxford knew that without a solution to this problem the whole peace might collapse. Initially, he proposed that Philip simply renounce his claim to the French throne, but the French claimed that this was technically impossible under French law.

So Oxford came up with a clever solution. Philip must be made to choose straightaway: either he retain Spain and a legal way be found for him to renounce his claim to the French throne, *or* he must retain his claim to the French throne, but immediately hand over the bulk of the Spanish Empire to another European prince (the Duke of Savoy), ruling in the meantime over a small but not negligible chunk of Spain's possessions, mainly in modern-day Italy (Savoy-Piedmont, Mantua, Montferrat and Sicily). Oxford's plan would have achieved peace 'with Spain' (more or less) while giving the French the consolation of acquiring parts of Italy once Philip inherited the French throne: a brilliant compromise. The French accepted this plan.

Oxford's assumption was that Philip would prefer to retain his claim to the French throne. If he did, then any qualms about 'No Peace without Spain' would instantly fall away: Spain and Spanish America would no longer even be in possession of a Bourbon, let alone the heir to the French throne. The balance of power would be thoroughly secured and Habsburg and Hanoverian objections to the peace either severely weakened or destroyed altogether. Oxford became optimistic that he was on the verge of securing 'the best peace that has been made these 200 years'.[18] A French envoy was despatched to Spain to put the stark choice, upon which the terms of the peace of Europe depended, to Philip. Oxford held his breath.

It was in this context that Oxford, St John and the Queen decided to take the ministry's policy to its logical conclusion. They concluded that the time to make it absolutely clear that no further military campaign would be fought by British troops had been reached. It would give the allies, especially the Dutch, the rude jolt they needed to accept peace on whatever terms the British and French agreed as inevitable, and cement the (nearly) complete peace deal with the French. So it was that on 10th May the so-called 'restraining orders' were communicated to Marlborough's replacement as British supreme commander, the Duke of Ormonde. They ordered him to 'avoid engaging in any siege, or hazarding a battle, till you have farther orders from her majesty', and to conceal the fact from the other allied generals (although Ormonde's subsequent inactivity soon made the upshot of the order very clear).[19] Even more controversially, St John (probably but not certainly with Oxford's endorsement) then communicated this order to the French.

The restraining orders have long been almost universally condemned by even the least moralistic of historians as shocking and treacherous: communicating one's military orders to one's enemies but not one's allies is hardly the height of political morality, to say the least. However, the strategy that Oxford and St John had already agreed on made something like the restraining orders inevitable, and their assumption was that the imminent announcement of Philip giving up most of the Spanish Empire would overshadow the whole episode. Gaining credit with the French by communicating the orders to them would simply grease the wheels of the imminent peace, which everyone either knew or suspected was being stitched up between Britain and France anyway.

What scotched these calculations was the simple fact that Philip did not play ball. He had become too attached to his Spanish kingdom to give it up – and remained hopeful that he might manage to acquire the French throne anyway, no matter what 'renunciation' he made. He chose to stay in Madrid and renounce his claim to the French throne.

Oxford's mistake, then, was to be excessively sanguine about the prospects of Philip renouncing Spain, although it is also true that it was premature to show the ministry's hand to France in the context of the negotiations at that stage, as other major points of the peace – the nature of the barrier and the status of the Spanish Netherlands, for example – had not yet been agreed. The restraining orders were, then, arguably mistimed. The degree to which any further moral obloquy deserves to be heaped upon Oxford and St John's heads depends upon the extent to which one thinks that considerations of strict morality are aptly applied to the cut and thrust of diplomatic negotiations designed to further the national interest.

London was thrown into a great flutter when, on 27th May, the Whig paper *The Flying Post* announced in a late postscript that 'one of the Generals' had announced to the allies that he had orders not to attack the French.[20] Daniel Defoe hastily wrote to Oxford to stress that the news was being 'told in such a manner and received with such a temper as raises a mighty popular clamour and does much mischief through the nation'.[21] 'Great murmerings' were abroad, and Halifax, torn between great emotion and great pomposity, made a dramatic announcement to the upper chamber that he had 'a matter of the greatest importance to impart to them', one 'which concerned the interest, honour and security of the Queen, themselves, the whole nation, and the constitution of both Church and State'.[22] He moved that all peers be summoned to the Lords to hear his news.

As the Junto gathered its forces to confront the ministry in the Lords the next day, the Whigs were convinced that the tide was turning. Here, at last, was surely evidence that Oxford and St John were in cahoots with the French to end the war in the most dishonourable way possible. If the ministry were betraying the allies on the field of battle, who knew what other dark traffic was passing between the Tory leaders and the enemy? It all smelt very funny indeed and appeared to give great credence to suspicions about covert Jacobite manoeuvrings. The Junto leaders were 'so sanguine, as to whisper about their fond Hopes, that . . . the Lord Treasurer would be sent to the Tower'.[23]

Amazingly, however, the Whigs fluffed it. The next day, Halifax and Marlborough went on the offensive, making great play of the travails of 'the allys who had relyed upon the aid and friendship of the British nation' only to be 'expos'd to the revenge of that power against whom they had been so active'.[24] Halifax proposed an address to the Queen asking for the restraining orders to be brought before the House and exhorting her to instruct Ormonde to ignore any such orders.

Oxford produced a bland speech in which he said that it would inappropriate to reveal military orders given by the Queen to one of her generals without her agreement, and that, in any case, 'it was Prudence not to hazard a Battel, upon the Point of concluding a good Peace'.[25] He then directly lied and claimed that the orders had allowed Ormonde to join in a siege, if not outright offensive action. He was followed by his (temporary) ally Argyll, who turned the course of the debate in a canny speech in which, among other things, he simply pointed out the obvious: 'a Battel, won or lost, might intirely break off a Negotiation of Peace which, in all Probability, was near being concluded'.[26] Why rock the boat and waste lives unnecessarily at this stage?

One Harleyite Tory, Lord Powlet, unfavourably contrasted Ormonde's restraint with the Duke of Marlborough's alleged willingness to lead 'Troops to the Slaughter, to cause a great Number of Officers to be knock'd on the Head in a Battel . . . to fill his Pocket by disposing of their Commissions'.[27] Shortly after the debate, a furious Marlborough sent notoriously pugnacious Whig bruiser Lord Mohun to challenge Powlett to a duel on his behalf, which was only prevented when a nervous Powlett, no doubt regretting his words and not fancying his chances in a duel against the greatest soldier in Europe, revealed his predicament to his wife, who managed to secure the intervention of the Queen and the Earl of Dartmouth to prevent the inevitable bloodbath.[28] Feelings were, safe to say, running high.

As the bad-tempered debate wore on, despite salty contributions from Wharton and Nottingham, it became clear that the Whigs had bungled it. The only evidence at this stage for the existence of the orders was rumour and private correspondence. Court moderates and anti-Jacobite Tories were not inclined to take whatever the Whigs claimed on trust. Furthermore, it was impossible for anyone to prove that Oxford was lying, and the argument that waging another battle with peace imminent was at best futile and at worst could delay a settlement weighed heavily. Halifax was routed in the vote on his motion.

At this stage it was imperative for Oxford to move fast. So long as a peace could be announced quickly, the momentum would stay with him, the logic of Argyll's speech would win out and any difficulties over the restraining orders, particularly if any further awkward truths about them were to come out, would be overshadowed.

The problem was, of course, that many points of a peace in fact had *not* yet been agreed. However, one point had been quickly settled: the French dropped their legalistic quibbles about the difficulties of Philip giving up his claim to the French throne and Philip indicated his willingness to renounce his claim. This was certainly not Oxford's preferred option, but it would suffice. By announcing this, outlining various other terms that had been secretly agreed with the French and were very much to British advantage, and vaguely passing over the as yet unresolved sticking points, the ministers were able to present a statement of the bulk of the peace terms, which the Queen duly announced on 6th June.

Finally, the ministry could announce some of the fruits of their secret negotiations with the French. Britain was to acquire a monopoly of the Assiento. Large territorial gains, including significant swathes of Canada (the Hudson Bay colony, Nova Scotia and Newfoundland) as well as Minorca, Gibraltar, Port Mahon and St Kitts were announced. Crucially, the French offered to allow Britain to occupy the strategically important French fort of Dunkirk and destroy its harbour and fortifications as an assurance of French good faith and security for British military interests. Vaguer and less certain assurances were made about the Spanish Netherlands, various trading issues and the nature of the Dutch barrier, but overall the package was an attractive one.

Once this announcement was made, the current of popular and parliamentary opinion began to run so strongly with the Tories that Whig unity crumbled. Many of the opposition could see that the simple political reality was that the country was so desperate for peace, and the terms announced sufficiently advantageous, that the game was up. Pious lamentations about breaking faith with the allies buttered few parsnips at this stage, particularly given the remarkably effective anti-Dutch propaganda campaign that Swift, Arbuthnot and their understrappers had conducted. The usual Whig suspects bitterly made the usual complaints in the ensuing debate, but even their own side was abandoning them. In a Lords vote on a motion to endorse the terms, twelve Whig peers – all of whom had voted in favour of the 'No peace without Spain' motion just seven months earlier – defected to the ministry, which won by eighty-one votes to thirty-six. Whig opposition to the peace had taken a mortal blow.

The Dutch were no happier about the Queen's announcement than the Whigs, but they were in no better position to do anything about it. In July, a temporary armistice was announced between France and Britain. British troops marched away from the frontline and even occupied Ghent and Bruges to concentrate Dutch minds. The Dutch and Austrians decided to continue the war, and were assisted by British-employed German mercenaries, who decided to give up their pay, leave British service and fight on with the allies. It did the allies no good: in late July, the French won a great victory at the Battle of Denain, shattering any remaining Dutch desire to continue military action. They had no choice but to throw themselves on the mercy of Britain and accept what peace terms Oxford and St John chose to give them. The Austrians vowed to fight on, but they were scarcely in a stronger position.

The parliamentary session had ended on 21st June with the Tories triumphant. All that was required now was for a last burst of diplomatic activity to tie up the peace. Parliament would not sit again until the Treaty of Utrecht was finalised.

To a casual observer, the Oxford ministry's position may have seemed close to unassailable by mid-1712. The Tories had recovered amazingly well from the apparent disaster of the Lords vote on 'No Peace without Spain': to go from losing a key division in the Lords on one of the most basic principles of the peace by eight votes in December to winning a division on the entire peace settlement by forty-five in June seemed to indicate a tremendous strengthening in the government's overall position. The October Club Tories in the Commons had proved remarkably tractable in the 1711–12 session relative to their sabre-rattling during the previous winter, and a combination of 'Harley's Dozen', careful management and the rapidly changing politics of the peace had seemingly broken the Junto stranglehold over the Lords.[29]

In reality, however, there were deep fissures in the Tory Party that were only being temporarily pasted over by the grand unifying factor of support for the peace. If one looked carefully, they were already visible.

The great open secret of the Tory Party by summer 1712 was the existence within their parliamentary ranks of an increasingly bold Jacobite wing. There had always been Jacobite sentiment among post-1689 Tory MPs, but until recently unguarded Jacobite sentiment had been rare, and the overall numbers of discreet but unambiguously Jacobite Tory MPs probably small (although no doubt there were many equivocal Hanoverians among them). The deep well of old loyalist emotion stirred up by Sacheverell had changed this.

This was partly because some Tories had never really embraced the 'new' school of Toryism, which had attempted to ideologically square the old Tory doctrines of non-resistance and passive obedience with the Glorious Revolution. They were distinctly sceptical of Harcourt's defence speech during Sacheverell's trial, which had accepted the idea that in extreme circumstances resistance might be justified. Although Harcourt held that this did not contradict the general principle of non-resistance, many Tories – who had made their less moderate views known in the press debate that raged in the aftermath of the Sacheverell trial – disagreed.

Their view was simple: resistance was never justified in any circumstances, including 1688. Although it was possible to try to square this view with acceptance of the Glorious Revolution and the deposition of James II by claiming that no resistance had taken place in 1688 because James had 'abdicated', this argument – never very convincing – was running out of road. This was because of another core Tory principle: hereditary succession. One might just about be able to justify the accession of Anne, James II's daughter, on such grounds, but the prospect of a family of Germans, with a very tenuous hereditary claim to the throne, acceding made a mockery of old-fashioned Tory scruples. Furthermore, these Tories had gradually come to the view (perhaps over-optimistically) that the only alternative to the country's broader post-1688 social and spiritual slide into rule by financiers and 'false brethren' was to restore the Stuarts.

It was in this context that the wave of staunch pro-Sacheverell feeling that had played such a huge role in giving the Tories their landslide in the 1710 election had in the process carried a sizeable number of Jacobites into the Commons: there were almost certainly forty to fifty staunch supporters of the Pretender elected, as well as around twenty or so Jacobite peers in the Lords. These numbers gradually grew as time went on and the Hanoverian hostility to the Tory Party became clearer. This latter factor was crucial in persuading a sizeable number of Tories who had previously been unenthusiastic supporters of the Hanoverian succession to change allegiance: if the accession of the Elector of Hanover was to mean permanent Tory exclusion from office, as increasingly seemed possible, self-interest as much as any ideological proclivities proved decisive.

The English Jacobite MPs had many contradictions to contend with. The most obvious one was the fact that the Glorious Revolution had been, as much as anything, a revolt of the Church of England against a Roman Catholic monarch, and the basic dynamics behind this had not really changed. This made the position of Jacobite Tories – who were, after all, members of the Church Party – delicate, for the Pretender was as staunch a Roman Catholic as his father. While the Jacobite court, unable to believe that anyone could be a Protestant except out of 'ignorance or self-interest', deluded itself that the loyal English population in general, and the Church of England in particular, would welcome a Roman Catholic monarch with open arms, English Jacobites knew better.[30] This led to a persistent dynamic whereby the English Jacobite MPs desperately – and in vain – attempted to persuade James to turn Anglican, or at least promise a practical pro-Church of England policy were he to regain the throne.

Other misunderstandings and ambiguities plagued the English Jacobite Tories. The Jacobite court failed to comprehend that the Tory Party of 1710 had altered its ideological position. Even Jacobite Tories took a 'constitutionalist' position in which obedience was owed to the King-in-Parliament. Although the Jacobite constitutionalist Tories saw the Stuart line as possessing indefeasible hereditary right, they did not endorse the sort of absolutism that the Pretender had inherited from his father. The English Jacobites were – somewhat paradoxically for loyal supporters of the Stuart family – enthusiastic Country Tories, suspicious of the corruption of courts, be they Stuart, Williamite or Hanoverian. James paid lip service to such views when politically necessary but in reality despised them.

The Pretender's high-handedness also extended to the belief that the best means of securing a Restoration was military invasion, assisted by France, as this would entail as few concessions to such constitutionalist or country sentiments as possible. In contrast, the English Jacobites showed themselves as susceptible to delusional wishful thinking as the Pretender: unable to stomach the unpatriotic idea of a Jacobite restoration by means of French invasion, they convinced themselves that Queen Anne was at heart a Jacobite and that her endorsement of the succession of the Pretender (her half-brother), plus deft politicking, could effect a peaceful Stuart Restoration on her death.

Immediately after the 1710 election, however, these ambiguities were moot points. The natural locus for the fiercely Anglican, Country Tory Jacobites was the October Club, which attracted both Jacobite old stagers like Sir John Pakington and new blood, younger firebrands such as Simeon Stewart, Charles Eversfield and William Shippen. As they could hardly openly declare themselves as Jacobites, they concentrated on manoeuvring their own men into leading positions and co-operating with non-Jacobite Tory Country MPs (many of whom were also October Club members) to harass Oxford. Practically speaking, they were, at first, indistinguishable from the general ranks of angry backbench Tory MPs determined to dish the Whigs and save the Church – but their underlying agenda was different, and this was to become increasingly important.

Oxford was far from unaware of the existence of the Jacobite parliamentarians. He himself was unequivocally not a Jacobite – originally a Whig, he always remained a friend to the Dissenters, and firm supporter of the Glorious Revolution, no matter how sceptical he may have been of some of its consequences. However, he was not averse to using any tool at hand to achieve his political objectives. Like many politicians of all sides in the era, he kept various back channels open with the Jacobite court, partly for purposes of insurance in case a Jacobite Restoration were to happen, but mainly to serve his own immediate ends.

Firstly, he wanted to prevent any attempt at a French-assisted Jacobite invasion. If anything could revive Whig fortunes and endanger his own position and the peace, it was an invasion scare. Making the Pretender (and indeed the French court) believe that he secretly supported a Stuart restoration and had some intricate (but never disclosed) political scheme for achieving it, if only James would be patient, was a good way of discouraging any such attempt, and in general inducing the Jacobites to adopt a policy of inactivity.

Secondly, he saw his contacts with St Germain as a means of exercising some indirect control over the unruly Tory Jacobite backbenchers. The fact that many of the rowdiest October Club MPs had become much less troublesome in the parliamentary session of 1711–12 was not a product simply of more careful whipping. In mid-1711, Oxford told the Jacobite court that his entire 'secret strategy' for achieving a peaceful Jacobite restoration through political means was dependent on the peace being achieved first, something most easily achieved if the October Club stopped rocking the boat in general.

Accordingly, in November 1711 a formal directive from St Germain came through to the Jacobite parliamentarians to 'do [Oxford] what service they can'.[31] Although many of them were not happy about it, they automatically deferred to the person who, after all, they considered to be their true monarch. When combined with general Tory support for the peace anyway, this proved sufficient to give the ministry a much easier ride in the Commons from autumn 1711 onwards. Indeed, some Jacobite October Club men became vocal supporters of the ministry.

To some, this smelt suspicious. The sight of avowed Jacobites suddenly becoming the poodles of the ministry made a substantial group of Tories – loyal Country Tories who were nonetheless firm supporters of the Hanoverian succession – uneasy. For some time, it had been clear that overt statements of support for the Pretender were no longer taboo among at least a few of the Jacobites within the October Club. Even in parliamentary debates, some of the more gung-ho Jacobites had flown close to the wind: William Shippen had described James II at one point as being 'too good and too well tempered to be king of England' in a Commons debate, and it wasn't hard to see through the wafer-thin veil of irony that the notorious Jacobite had draped this statement in.[32]

Pro-Hanoverian Tories had, in this context, become increasingly anxious about the nature of the peace that the ministry was pursuing. At first, Tory opponents of the peace had been very few: Nottingham, then his son Daniel and a few other of his associates. Gradually, however, during the course of the parliamentary barrages aimed against Marlborough, Walpole and the Barrier Treaty, disquiet among committed anti-Jacobite Tory MPs had begun to grow. Why were these measures being loudly heralded by notorious Jacobites in the House? Was the ground being laid for a dishonourable peace designed to let France off the hook?

While few were prepared to go as far as Nottingham and openly suggest that the ministry was playing a Jacobite game, they began to entertain genuine suspicions along those lines. Accordingly, a still small but growing group of disaffected Tory MPs began to vote, at least some of the time, with the Whigs on issues related to the peace. This group was not enough to threaten the huge Tory majorities in the Commons, but it was the first serious hint of something that would become increasingly troublesome for the ministry.

By March 1712, this group decided to break away from the October Club and form their own Tory splinter group, which they claimed embodied the true founding spirit of the original club. These 'Primative October men' soon came to call their group the 'March Club' and began to meet every Monday.[33] Their numbers soon grew, from thirty-five initially to fifty by April and perhaps even more. They distinguished themselves by stressing their absolute commitment to the Hanoverian succession, their support for a vigorous last push in the war effort to secure the best peace possible, and their disdain for the close relations they perceived developing between the court and the October Club, which reflected either corruption (contrary to their stout Country principles) or perhaps something more sinister.

Most of the March Club, unsure about the true nature of the leading ministers' loyalties, were prepared to give Oxford the benefit of the doubt for now, and indeed over the course of the controversy over the restraining orders and the announcement of the interim peace terms in early June, they generally towed the ministry's line. However, the existence of a group of suspicious, organised pro-Hanoverian Tory backbenchers would, from now on, have to be factored into Oxford's ever more murky calculations. It was a glimmer of hope for the Whigs throughout most of 1712.

After the announcement about the shape of the impending peace agreement made by the Queen in June, the bulk of parliamentarians and other keen political observers could have been forgiven for assuming that the announcement of the final treaty was imminent. In fact, there was still much hard negotiating to do: the June announcement had been little more than an interim announcement that jumbled together firmly agreed terms with pious generalities.

Increasingly over the summer St John became a more prominent player in the peace negotiations, much to the distaste of an exasperated Oxford, who was growing ever more wary of St John's impetuosity and determination to come to a quick peace with France that frankly ignored the interests of the allies. Oxford, however, could not dispense with St John: on the contrary, he needed him more than ever.

St John's brilliant French, unmatched grasp of diplomatic detail and his determination to elbow his way into the peace negotiations at any cost made his involvement both practically necessary and politic. Furthermore, St John's political stock domestically was rising: he had led the Tory assault on the Barrier Treaty with aplomb, and had successfully ingratiated himself with the October Club men, who increasingly looked to him as their real leader. Indeed, he had even been elected as the president of the October Club, which was, in fact, the immediate trigger for the formation of the March Club. These successes meant that – at least in his own estimation – he deserved reward.

He wasn't the only one during the summer of 1712 who wanted rewards. By the end of the parliamentary session of 1712, Oxford, against all his instincts, had moved perilously close to one-party Tory government. The Whigs had fought so hard against the peace that he'd had no choice. The loyal support for the peace demonstrated by the Tory parliamentary party meant that there was a huge host of MPs, lords and hangers-on demanding recognition. Government places and douceurs were the currency of political loyalty and deal-making in this era, and in order to keep his parliamentary support united enough to force through the final peace treaty during the next session, Oxford had no choice but to dole out the rewards accordingly, which, of course, created a self-reinforcing loop that committed him more and more overtly to the Tory Party. Many of the remaining Whigs left in office were purged, and Tories from all over the spectrum – many Oxford's clients, but some prominent supporters of St John too – were given office.

Ironically, St John's reward was greatly to deepen the rift between him and Oxford. St John had long craved a peerage, and saw it as only a due recompense for his recent political services. Specifically, he was convinced that only the earldom of Bolingbroke (previously a title belonging to a branch of the St John family) would represent a fitting tribute to his honour and worth. Unfortunately for him, the Queen point-blank refused to offer him an earldom, largely because she did not see cavorting with a not inconsiderable proportion of London's prostitute population as being consistent with that dignity; he would have to do with a viscountcy instead (a rung down in status from an earldom, and presumably therefore tolerably consistent with St John's erotic peccadilloes).

St John (henceforth Bolingbroke) was furious and blamed Oxford. It was, so far as he was concerned, an outrageous affront not only to him personally, but to his entire family – but mainly, judging from his extraordinarily whiny correspondence, the former:

> Thus far, there seems to be nothing done for my sake, or as a mark of favour to me in particular . . . I own to you that I felt more indignation than ever in my life I had done; and the only consideration which kept me from running to extremities, was that which should have inclined somebody [Oxford] to use me better.[34]

In reality, there is no evidence that Oxford had any hand in the appalling affront of merely raising Bolingbroke to a 'lowly' viscountcy; the Queen's longstanding doubts about his dubious private life more than adequately explain it, and Oxford had no desire for an unnecessary row. Bolingbroke remained convinced to his dying day, however, that the insult was due to Oxford's malignant offices, and never forgave him.

Later that summer, in August, Oxford hoped that he could salvage some goodwill from Bolingbroke by offering him an alternative ego boost. The French had requested that the British government send a suitably senior minister to Paris to speed up and complete the more delicate parts of the outstanding peace negotiations. Despite heavy misgivings, Oxford agreed to send Bolingbroke in the hope that it might placate him. It would prove no more conducive to harmony between the two men than his elevation to the peerage.

It did, however, give Bolingbroke a chance to cut a tremendous dash in the French capital, where, as a natural Francophile, he was in his element. He was, according to Swift, 'received at Court with particular Marks of

Distinction and Respect' and experienced every honour that Parisian society had to offer, which no doubt helped soothe his bruised ego.[35] One night a theatrical performance was even paused as he entered so that the audience could give him a standing ovation. A French populace desperate for peace treated him like a hero, with crowds following him around and cheering wherever he went.

His actual business – which Oxford had strictly limited to a few well-defined points – was all settled in two days. But the French saw Bolingbroke's trip as an opportunity privately to sound him out about the prospects for a more rapid, separate peace that would forsake the interests of the Dutch totally. The French minister Torcy, knowing Bolingbroke's amorous reputation, recruited a beautiful ex-nun turned glamorous socialite of great charm but questionable morals, Claudine de Tencin, to put feelers out (of, it was widely rumoured, every kind) to this effect (and almost certainly spy on him to boot).[36]

Bolingbroke was very receptive. As well as spending some no doubt pleasing hours with Mademoiselle Tencin, he gave every indication to Torcy that the British government would be prepared to consider making an almost instant peace in which Britain would make no effort to secure Dutch demands. His trip dragged on far longer than Oxford had expected. Rumours began to filter through to London that he'd had a secret meeting with the Pretender. This was, in fact, probably not true, although he undoubtedly did attend the opera at the same time as James, sitting mere yards away from him.[37] None of this was calculated to ease the concerns of the March Club men, or indeed Oxford.

When Bolingbroke eventually did tear himself away from the pleasures of Paris and returned to London, tension between him and Oxford became unbearable. He had clearly exceeded his instructions, and Oxford was furious. One of the official plenipotentiaries representing the British at Utrecht, Lord Strafford, made it clear that if the Dutch acquired Tournai, they would probably grit their teeth and swallow the entire peace deal, and Oxford knew that Dutch acceptance (however grudging) of the final Utrecht agreement would defang some of the Whig attacks and satisfy his own sense of honour.

Furthermore, Oxford had recently sent his own cousin on a special diplomatic mission to try to woo the Hanoverian court: nothing was calculated to ruin such a mission more neatly than Bolingbroke attempting to conduct his own private pro-French foreign policy. So Oxford spent much energy attempting to undo the damage Bolingbroke's diplomacy had, in his eyes, done: he even went so far as to transfer responsibility for the negotiations to the other Secretary of State, Dartmouth (who technically should have been overseeing them all along). This was seen as another humiliation by Bolingbroke, whose resentment towards Oxford, whom he regarded as intolerably wet and vacillating, soon reached boiling point.

At a cabinet meeting on 28th September, these tensions spilled over into a furious row. Bolingbroke proposed a bold strategy to his ministerial colleagues: agree a peace with the French now, selling out the Dutch while acquiring excellent terms for Britain, and go straight to the country with a snap general election. That way, the Tories could reap the electoral 'peace dividend' and increase their majority still further. The cabinet split. Harcourt, Buckingham and, bizarrely, Shrewsbury backed Bolingbroke; Dartmouth and old Harleyite ally Poulett supported Oxford.

Unusually, Oxford, who felt that his carefully planned strategy was being compromised by Bolingbroke's rashness, exploded, angrily upbraiding Bolingbroke for exceeding his diplomatic remit in Paris. Bolingbroke responded in kind: the two were practically at each other's throats in full cabinet, in the presence of the Queen, who was reported to have been so upset at the altercation that she wept all night. She came down on Oxford's side. Soon after, Oxford retired to his sickbed with rheumatism and Bolingbroke stormed off to the country to sulk. Swift was at his wit's end, writing with intense frustration of his increasingly vain attempts to 'keep People from breaking to pieces, upon a hundred misunderstandings'.[38]

It was, in short, increasingly hard to see how Bolingbroke and Oxford could continue to work together without the personal venom between the two men slowly dripping into the bloodstream of the body politic.

Paradoxically, while the process of negotiating the peace was driving Oxford and Bolingbroke apart, it was also the only thing still keeping them tied, however dysfunctionally, into a common enterprise. Until a final treaty was signed, they had no choice but to soldier on in pursuit of peace.

As summer drifted into autumn, and the usual time for the meeting of parliament came and went, the negotiations – despite Bolingbroke's best efforts in Paris – dragged interminably on. Progress was real: in October, the French finally agreed that Tournai would be ceded to the Dutch. The terms of Philip's renunciation of his right to the French throne were finally agreed soon after. The Byzantine world of early eighteenth-century diplomacy was, however, famously complex, tortuous and slow, and the endless backroom parleys, negotiations over detail and formal fripperies at Utrecht itself appeared to have no end.

The June announcement had been presented as the prelude to an imminent peace. Given this, Oxford felt constrained not to recall parliament until the treaties were agreed. The result of this was a tense political hiatus in which parliamentary formalities were suspended and everyone waited anxiously for news of the diplomatic negotiations. As the delay lengthened, the atmosphere became ever more feverish. Political nature abhors a vacuum, and the lack of concrete news meant that any tiny modicum of information became the subject of intense speculation. In a context of already rabid political partisanship thick with suspicions of conspiracy and subterranean rumblings of Jacobite treason, the pens and imaginations of many an idle Grub Street partisan found less than innocent exercises to occupy their time.

Many Whigs suspected that the delay was the product of some intricate Franco-Tory plot to bring in the Pretender. Fuel was poured on these fires when, in late summer, the Duke of Hamilton – widely considered to be a Jacobite – was appointed as an ambassador extraordinary to France to disentangle one of the knottier parts of the outstanding negotiations: territorial and trading agreements related to North America. The Whigs became convinced that Hamilton was, in fact, being sent to negotiate the terms on which the Pretender would be restored.

Hamilton was certainly an eccentric choice. He was probably chosen for domestic political reasons. Although in 1710 he had thrown in his lot with the Harley/Oxford ministry, he had, throughout much of the previous year, been in high dudgeon with the ministry (largely over a dispute concerning the validity of his recently awarded British peerage). Hamilton had contemplated going into opposition and even agitating for a repeal of the Act of Union, so Oxford had good reasons for attempting to placate him. However, it was hardly surprising that, as Jacobite memoirist Lockhart put it, his appointment 'did afford abundance of pleasure and discontent, as people stood severally affected towards the Kings [i.e. the Pretender's] interest'.[39]

It would not be long before this rising sense of menace and barely suppressed partisan loathing, heightened further by the sensational appointment of Hamilton, would break out into actual violence.

The Duke of Hamilton had, for over ten years, been involved in a bitter lawsuit against Charles, Lord Mohun, over rival claims to the sizeable estates of the Earl of Macclesfield. Both had claims to it via their respective wives, and the complex case had dragged on through the Court of Chancery in typically tortuous fashion. Both men were spendthrift rakes deep in debt: neither could afford to lose the case.[40]

Mohun was not only a common-or-garden rake: he was among the most notorious aristocrats of his age. Wharton seems by comparison to be little more disreputable than a maiden aunt with a heavy picquet habit.

Mohun was addicted to drinking and whoring only slightly less than his real passion in life: violence. He fought his first duel aged fifteen, and by the age of twenty-one had achieved the extraordinary distinction of having been tried for murder in front of the entire House of Lords twice (peers could claim the privilege of a trial before their equals). Indeed, it was only a personal pardon from William III that prevented a third such trial. The number of duels he fought over a similar period is hard to tally.

As well as being a notorious hellraiser, Mohun was a committed Whig, and would occasionally interrupt his standard routine of stabbings and booze-sodden punch-ups to make partisan speeches in Lords debates. Gradually throughout the first decade of the eighteenth century his life became (somewhat) more regular, and he developed into a fairly significant political player and close associate of the Junto, being admitted to the Kit-Cat Club in 1707. He also climbed the ranks of preferment in the army and became a client and supporter of Marlborough.

By 1712, however, Mohun faced disaster. He desperately needed the Macclesfield lawsuit to be resolved in his favour due to his mounting debts, but Hamilton's rise to favour in the eyes of the court and ministry in mid-1712 boded ill, as the legal battle between them was fought in the Lords as well as in Chancery (over Mohun's immunity from being pursued in the courts by Hamilton by virtue of his parliamentary privilege). The case appeared to be heading for resolution in Hamilton's favour. Mohun teetered on the edge of losing the estate and falling into utter bankruptcy. The appointment of Hamilton – a political opponent as well as legal adversary – as ambassador extraordinary also seemed to presage the ultimate disaster for a Whig as partisan as Mohun: a Jacobite restoration. His world seemed to be falling apart.

It so happened that the crucial Chancery hearings, upon which the whole lawsuit might turn, had been scheduled for November. Hamilton delayed his departure to France so that he could look after his legal interests, much to the annoyance of Oxford and the Queen. On 13th November, Mohun and Hamilton met at the offices of the master of the Court of Chancery to discuss elements of the case. In the course of the conversation, Hamilton remarked that the evidence of one of Mohun's key witnesses, Richard Whitworth, 'had neither truth nor justice in it'.[41] Mohun brusquely replied that Whitworth 'was an honest man and had as much honour and justice in him as his Grace'.[42] The two parties retired without further conflict, and Mohun went off to brood over a bottle or ten in the company of his close friend General George MacCartney, a fellow Whig and former close associate of Marlborough.

But at about 8 a.m. on 15th November, Lord Mohun and the Duke of Hamilton, with respectively MacCartney and Colonel Hamilton (a relative of the Duke's) as their seconds, arrived at Hyde Park to fight what would become one of the most notorious duels in British political history.

It is impossible to know the precise course of events on the 14th that led to the duel. Supposedly, Mohun had taken Hamilton's derogatory remark about the honesty of his witness as a personal aspersion on his own probity, and sent MacCartney as his second to challenge him. They later met at the

Rose Tavern, Covent Garden, presumably to either try to prevent the duel or agree the details of the combat (or both). It seems a very thin pretext for a duel, even by Mohun's standards. This – and the fact that Mohun conducted a mysterious meeting with Marlborough on the morning before the duel – was to give rise to a swirl of political rumour before long.

What is clear is that the two men went at each other with extraordinary ferocity. The Duke of Hamilton may have been the rather more civilised of the two – albeit quite the louche man about town – but he gave no more quarter than the vicious Mohun. Neither of the assailants made much effort at defensive swordsmanship: they set about trying to slash each other to pieces mercilessly.

Hamilton was twenty years older than Mohun, but the decades of carousing and feasting had made Mohun fat and cumbersome. Hamilton got the upper hand as the two men desperately grappled, stabbing Mohun through his belly, thigh and left side before delivering a mortal blow through his groin. As Mohun tried to parry the final blow, Hamilton cut three of his fingers to 'bloody ribbons'.[43] Mohun died in a matter of minutes. His shredded corpse was taken back to his London house, where his long-suffering wife had little comment to make other than to complain that the blood was ruining her 'magnificent counterpane'.[44]

Hamilton, however, was not to last much longer than Mohun himself. It is essentially impossible to say who wounded him and when, but it is certain that his right leg had been slashed, an artery in his arm had been severed and his left side had been run through. These wounds proved fatal. Both men were dead. Colonel Hamilton grimly remarked to MacCartney: 'We've made a fine morning's work on it.'[45]

Afterwards, some (largely Whigs) claimed that the Duke had simply been wounded by Mohun in the course of the duel. Others (largely Tories) claimed that, after Colonel Hamilton had dropped his weapon to help the Duke, who lay injured on the floor, MacCartney had approached the two unarmed men and run the Duke through his left side. This, at least, was the testimony of Colonel Hamilton. Other witnesses do not support his account, but neither do they contradict it.

If the Colonel's account were true, then Hamilton's death was not the result of a fair fight. It was cowardly murder; the brutal stabbing of an unarmed man, against all the rules of honour.

The political implications of this were obvious. Was the whole duel concocted by Mohun and MacCartney, premeditated in order to give them an opportunity to, one way or another, kill Hamilton and prevent him taking up his ambassadorial role in France? Was this at the suggestion of Marlborough, with whom Mohun had met on the morning before the duel? Was it (asked Tories), in short, a dastardly Whig plot to murder one of the Queen's Tory ministers and endanger an advantageous peace? Or perhaps it was nothing more than hot-blooded aristocratic pugnacity, in which case, Colonel Hamilton's accusation was false, and perhaps it was part of a Tory plot to discredit the Whigs? Had the Colonel been persuaded to tell such a lie by a political higher-up, perhaps Oxford?

This was the debate that was to rage in the partisan press for weeks, driving political animosity between Whig and Tory to new heights of passion and outrage.

The Whigs could, with some justice, question Colonel Hamilton's testimony. Why, if MacCartney had just killed the Duke in the way that the Colonel had suggested, had the latter let the alleged murderer wander off without anything more than a jocular remark? Some evidence in favour of the idea that the incident was premeditated has subsequently emerged, and it is possible that Colonel Hamilton was simply in too great a state of shock to respond as one might have expected. What really happened is lost to history.

The Tories, however, gleefully exploited the situation. Thomas Hearne's reaction to the affair was fairly representative of the general Tory view: it was, he declared, 'Willfull Murder' committed by 'ye great Debauchee and Bully of ye Age'.[46] Given Mohun's reputation and the fact that MacCartney had, back in 1709, been personally dismissed from his army commission by the Queen herself for raping a clergyman's widow, it was not hard for the Tories to paint the pair in a dark light.

Accordingly, the Tory press pushed the argument home in a bid for full party advantage. Oldisworth in *The Examiner* was brutal:

I cannot but observe that the Whig-party are now resuming their Old Way of Management, wherein We never can pretend to be their Match. They have try'd all other Methods in vain, and return with fresh Vigour to their last Expedient of Murder.[47]

He even went so far as to strongly imply the involvement of Marlborough, pointedly observing that it was Marlborough who had used Mohun as his means of challenging Powlett to a duel earlier the same year.

Whatever the truth of the Tory accusations over the duel, one can understand their paranoia, for the duel had occurred a mere ten days after another sensational incident.

On the morning of 4th November, Oxford was sitting in his bedchamber, deep in conversation with Swift, when his servant brought up to him a smallish, non-descript parcel. Oxford unwrapped it to find inside a bandbox (a lightweight box often used for clothes or hats). He began to open the package, and, having only prised it open a sliver, stopped dead.[48]

He remarked, more puzzled than afraid, that he could see inside it a pistol.

At this point Swift, who was considerably less nonchalant about the Lord Treasurer's personal safety than Oxford was himself, grabbed the box and took it over to the window. Pointing the box away from him, he cut the threads used to tie the box and examined it. The box was an elaborate booby trap, using two inkhorns, some nails and thread, designed to pull the trigger and shoot whoever opened the box. Swift managed to disarm it without it going off – but it was a close-run thing.

Someone had tried to assassinate Oxford for the second time.

A detailed report of this incident reached the pages of the next edition of the Tory paper *The Post Boy*, but even before that the Whigs, catching wind of the incident, had poured scorn on it. They claimed that it was entirely fabricated by Oxford and Swift to blacken the reputation of the Whigs. This would form a staple of Whig propaganda for many weeks. *The Flying Post* imagined:

> a Raree-Show of the Ban-box-Plot, wherein should be seen the Doctor [Swift], first, letting off the Quills and Inkhorn, and the Pistol; and, in the next Apartment, using those very Quills and Inkhorn, to write A Full and True Account of that Black Design.[49]

It seems hard to credit that the incident was simply fabricated, however. Swift was clearly genuinely shaken by it.[50]

Who, then, was responsible? It hardly seems a coincidence that the mysterious package was delivered on 4th November, the eve of the great Whig feast day, 5th November. This year, as in 1711, the Whigs organised a traditional extravaganza to mark the commemorations. The usual mob revels, toasts and bonfires were held: dark aspersions were cast about the Jacobite tendencies of the government and effigies of the Pope and Pretender were burnt.[51]

Attempting to assassinate Oxford on this day, using gunpowder, would seem peculiarly apt for some extreme Whig with an eye for symbolism who was convinced that Oxford was planning a Jacobite restoration. Doing it using inkhorns may have been a coincidence, but given Oxford's brilliant use of hired pens, most famously Swift, to excoriate Marlborough and put the ministry's case, one cannot rule out that being a further deliberate, darkly humorous, twist.

The Whig attempt to suggest that it was a fabrication played on the fact that the perpetrator was not found – there were dark suggestions that little effort had been made to find him.[52] This, however, makes little sense. If Oxford had fabricated the incident for party purposes, it would hardly have been in his interest to downplay it, but (characteristically) that is exactly what he did. That the culprit was never found is not in itself indicative of much: tracing such a thing would not have been easy, and Oxford had more pressing matters at hand.

What is striking is that this incident emerged from an atmosphere of menace and barely submerged violence that had stalked the land – and particularly London – for most of the year.

As early as March 1712 Swift had noticed the appearance of a 'race of Rakes' called the Mohocks who allegedly played 'the devil about this Town every Night . . . Slitt[ing] peoples noses, & beat[ing] them'.[53] This roving band of aristocratic hooligans were, he alleged, all Whigs who 'had malicious Intentions agst te Ministers & their Friends'.[54] A stream of Tory ballads and pamphlets appeared attributing the violence to a Whig attempt to 'o'erturn the Government' and possibly murder the leading ministers.[55] Oxford and Shrewsbury were even given special lodgings at St James to protect them against Mohock outrages.[56]

The truth of the matter is hard to discern. The violence was certainly greatly exaggerated by the press. Dark tales of brutal outrages, often with something of an undertone of sexual violence, spread like wildfire. According to one paper, 'women were so frightened that they locked themselves in their houses before eight o'clock in the evening'.[57] It was said that the Mohocks mutilated their victims, which, in light of the well-publicised visit of some Iroquois chiefs for an audience with Queen Anne in 1710 and the contemporary reputation of Native Americans for such violence, probably explains the 'Mohock' nickname.[58]

However, these lurid stories were based on a solid core of truth. A number of men were arrested for such attacks, and among them were some high-born men, including Edward Montagu, Viscount Hinchingbroke.[59] Hinchingbroke was undoubtedly a Whig – and curiously enough, it appears that some months later he was overheard, shortly before the Hamilton–Mohun duel, remarking to some acquaintances that 'they might depend upon it His Grace [the Duke of Hamilton] wou'd not see France at this time'.[60]

It is far from impossible that some of the cruder Whigs dabbled with genuine plots of violence – whether the Mohock panic, a premeditated plot to kill Hamilton, or the Bandbox Plot, or all three. The Junto and their supporters were certainly increasingly convinced of the desperation of the situation: in their eyes, there was a grave threat to the Hanoverian succession, and therefore probably their own lives to boot. One can quite imagine Wharton or Mohun seriously considering such measures. The Whigs had resorted to such plots before in the febrile circumstances of the 1680s – indeed, there is some evidence that Wharton had himself been peripherally involved in the Rye House Plot, although he escaped prosecution.[61]

We cannot know for sure whether such Whig plots existed – the evidence is mixed and many of the rumours were outright lies driven by partisan sentiment – but what is certain is that the political temperature had risen to such a degree that wild ideas like these were widely considered plausible.

The stakes were only going to get higher.

The net result of the sensation caused by the Hamilton duel was that pro-Hanover Shrewsbury was appointed as ambassador extraordinary to France. A little of the tension of the preceding months was defused.

The peace negotiations, however, dragged on interminably. The general assumption by November 1712 was that a deal would be signed, and therefore parliament recalled, at any moment, and so hundreds of MPs began to drift into London even before Christmas. Prorogation followed prorogation, and many backwoodsmen Tory politicians began to grumble; many couldn't afford to stay in town indefinitely.

This delay could not, however, mask the fact that it had begun to dawn on the Whigs that the game was up insofar as the peace was concerned. Even Wharton was beginning to realise that the Whigs would have to change tack: there was simply no point in concentrating their energy on opposing a peace that was popular in the country and by this point unstoppable. By Boxing Day 1712, Halifax was conceding defeat on this to Oxford; he even went so far as to welcome a speedy peace:

> God make it soon, and lasting! I must own, I think your Lordship and I differed in the way of obtaining that blessing, but the scene is quite changed, my schemes are at an end, and I am neither so obstinate or romantic, to pursue things made impracticable.[62]

The Junto's thoughts turned instead to convincing everyone, once the peace was inevitably concluded, of the profound threat to the Hanoverian succession posed by the Tory ministry.

To this end, the Junto gave their backing to a concentrated propaganda campaign, spearheaded by one of their chief pensmiths George Ridpath. Ridpath set out, in his virulently Whig paper *The Flying Post*, to terrify the populace with, as Defoe put it to Oxford, 'terrible dismal apprehensions of Popery and the Pretender'.[63] It was crude – and familiar – stuff:

> they are now spreading it over the countries that the papists are arming and preparing for a general massacre; that innumerable numbers of priests and Irish papists are come over, and the like . . .[64]

Just as during the Exclusion Crisis and Glorious Revolution, the Whigs turned to their most enduring themes: virulent anti-Catholic and anti-Irish demagoguery.

However, the peace was rolling on to its inexorable conclusion. Between 17th February and 26th March there were no fewer than five further prorogations of parliament as last-minute hitches emerged in the course of the negotiations, and Swift was, like most of the ministry, finding the wait interminable:

> We have lived almost these two Months past, by the Week, expecting that Parliament would meet, and the Queen tell them that the Peace was signed.[65]

Finally, however, the logjam was broken and the terms finally agreed. On 31st March, the British plenipotentiaries at Utrecht signed the treaties of peace and commerce with France. The general peace included the Dutch, and so, in some formal sense at least, Oxford could claim that a separate peace between Britain and France had been avoided. The Austrians held out against the treaty, only finally agreeing to a peace a year later.

Nonetheless, it was hard to argue that the peace was not greatly advantageous to Britain's power, wealth and status: great trading and territorial concessions had been wrung out of the French. Britain, not the Dutch Republic, would be the chief beneficiary on the allied side.

The Queen ratified the treaties on 7th April and announced her 'great pleasure' at the happy news to parliament on the 9th. Little more than a token effort was made in parliament to oppose the ratification.

Europe would finally have peace.

Church bells rang out across the country. In London, the *Evening Post* reported 'Bonfires, Illuminations, and other Demonstrations of Joy, in all Parts of this City, on Account of the Peace'.[66] Swift claimed that the news was met with 'louder Acclamations, and more Extraordinary Rejoicings of the People, than had ever been Remembered on like Occasions'.[67] Mobs of revellers even smashed windows that were not suitably illuminated in celebration of peace at last.

The battle for the peace was won.

The battle for the Protestant succession had barely begun.

12

The Perils of Victory

On 13th April 1713, a mere matter of days after the announcement of the peace, the great and good of political London, in all their finery, had flocked to Drury Lane theatre for the first night of a much-hyped new play by Joseph Addison, entitled *Cato*. Oxford and Bolingbroke and other leading lights of the ministry were there, as were most of the Junto. As the two sides stared across the stalls at each other, the tension between them was palpable. The play on stage was soon to provide them with new ammunition.[1]

Addison was a Whig, albeit a personally amiable one who maintained friends across the party divide, and his new play was a glorification of the life of Cato the Younger, the stern Roman defender of republican liberty and virtue against the rising tyranny of Julius Caesar. The message of the play – it is better to die free than live ignobly as a slave under a despot like Caesar – was latched onto by the Whigs in the audience. In their eyes, Oxford (or perhaps more plausibly Bolingbroke), plotting as they believed he was to hand the nation over to popish absolutism and Stuart tyranny, was the latter-day equivalent of Caesar, being bravely opposed by courageous Cato-like spirits such as Wharton.

During the prologue (actually written, ironically enough, by Addison's friend Alexander Pope, himself a Roman Catholic Tory), the Whigs began to ostentatiously clap and cheer certain lines that they felt had particular contemporary relevance, such as:

> Here tears shall flow for a more generous cause,
> Such tears as Patriots shed for dying laws[2]

Indeed, one line led to such thunderous Whig applause that the theatre literally shook:

> When vice prevails and impious men bear sway,
> The post of honour is a private station[3]

The Whig interpretation of these lines was obvious: only their party, out of office and struggling manfully against the administration's dastardly plot, retained their honour and virtue, as opposed to the vile, corrupt Tory ministers.

The Tories, however, decided to claim the play as their own. To their mind, Caesar, an overmighty soldier who threatened to become an oppressive king, was a portrait of Marlborough. Cato was, in fact, either Oxford or Bolingbroke, resisting the corruption of the leading Whigs and their would-be military overlord. So they began to loudly clap the play at significant points too – indeed, future bishop and philosopher George Berkeley, who was in the audience, observed that 'My Lord Harley, who sat in the next box to us, was observed to clap as loud as any in the house all the time of the play'.[4]

And so the play was enacted in the bizarre circumstances of Whig and Tory partisans competing to see who could clap the loudest, much to the discomfit of both the Whig author of the play (Addison) and the Tory author of the prologue (Pope):

> The numerous and violent claps of the Whig party on the one side the theatre, were echoed back by the Tories on the other, while the author sweated behind the scenes with concern to find their applause proceeded more [from] the hand than the head. This was the case too of the prologue-writer, who was clapped into a stanch Whig sore against his will, at almost every two lines.[5]

At the end of the performance, Bolingbroke – a man of theatrical gifts – played a masterstroke:

after all the applauses of the opposite faction, my Lord Bolingbroke sent for Booth who played Cato, into the box, between one of the acts and presented him with 50 guineas; in acknowledgment (as he expressed it) for [his] defending the cause of liberty so well against a *perpetual dictator*.[6]

The gesture infuriated the Whigs, but pleased the actor, Barton Booth, who was a High Tory himself.

The play went on for twenty performances, and each night crowds of Tory and Whig supporters turned up to cheer on the play like crowds of well-spoken football supporters. It was clear that, if anything, the peace had escalated tensions even further, as arguments about Utrecht started to give way to accusations and suspicions about the ministry's intentions on the succession.

The hard reality facing the Tories once the peace had been signed was that the struggle to achieve it had been the one thing binding them together. It had crowded out almost all other issues since late 1711, and had thereby temporarily papered over a mighty array of cracks. All the problems liable to now come to the fore — especially the question of the Hanoverian succession and perennial Tory grievances about the Church — were likely to split the ministry and its supporters down the middle. As Bolingbroke was later to put it:

> Instead of gathering strength either as a ministry or as a party, we grew weaker every day. The peace had been judged with reason to be the only solid foundation whereupon we could erect a Tory system; and yet when it was made, we found ourselves at a full stand. Nay, the very work, which ought to have been the basis of our strength, was in part demolished before our eyes and we were stoned with the ruins of it.[7]

Almost as soon as the peace was signed Swift was alarmed by rumours that Oxford was caballing with the Whigs. The rumours were true: in late March he had met with senior Whigs and assured them that measures to make the Queen and ministry's allegiance to Hanover very clear would be forthcoming.

The Whigs were distinctly sceptical, and immediate rapprochement between them and Oxford was stymied anyway, as the Junto was committed to fighting the various elements of the peace – including the complex commercial treaties, the terms of which had not yet been revealed – that were due to be considered by parliament over the next few months. Oxford had no choice but to stick with the Tories for now. But the possibility that Oxford would abandon them was planted in Tory minds almost immediately.

Swift also feared that the tensions between Oxford and Bolingbroke that had been both aggravated and temporarily restrained by the peace negotiations would now become ungovernable. With the peace done, the October Club had little incentive to show the uncharacteristic moderation that they had demonstrated during 1712, and the temptation on the part of Bolingbroke to put himself at the head of the High Tory majority in parliament and wrest control of the ministry from Oxford was ever present. The only thing restraining him was the fact that Oxford retained the favour of the Queen, a situation that Bolingbroke was constantly seeking to undo.

It was, ultimately, the Queen who provided the key to the increasingly perilous situation facing the Tories. So long as she lived, the Tories were assured of political predominance. The life of the Queen was, however, a very precarious thread on which to hang the hopes of an entire political party. She had been an invalid for a very long time and was plagued constantly by a grim array of health problems. Every passing minute was one small step closer to her demise and with it a moment of great peril for the Tories.

For over the winter of 1712–3 the Whigs had been, slowly but surely, cementing their links with George and the Hanoverian court. George was already thoroughly ill-disposed towards Oxford and the Tory Party, but he had been hitherto somewhat reluctant to enter too wholeheartedly or openly into intrigues with the Junto. The arrival in December 1712 of a new Hanoverian envoy to London, Baron de Grote, marked a move towards more wholehearted co-operation: de Grote had instructions to consult with Somers and Halifax regularly, and George even began to make payments to impoverished Whig lords to ensure that they would maintain the economic independence needed to continue voting against the government. He even bunged George Ridpath £50 towards the costs of keeping the stream of Whig invective characteristic of his *Flying Post* newspaper pouring out.

The Whig strategy was to put maximum pressure on the ministry to openly take steps to smooth the way to a Hanoverian succession. This would either succeed, and gain them credit with Hanover, thereby securing the favour of their future monarch; or fail, thereby helping them to convince the nation (and perhaps suspicious Hanoverian Tories) of the government's secret Jacobite tendencies, which would strengthen them immensely.

Here again the Queen was key to Tory fortunes. Both Oxford and Bolingbroke, however much they dabbled with the Jacobite court, knew that the restoration of a papist king would never be politically acceptable to the bulk of the nation. Both men were, whatever their faults, realists. However, neither found it straightforward to wholeheartedly and publicly embrace the Hanoverian cause. The most important barrier was to be the Queen, who detested any talk of her successors or any measures that involved them coming into the country so much as to render them politically impracticable.

The other barrier was the numerically significant and growing Jacobite wing of the parliamentary Tory Party, whom Bolingbroke in particular had to keep stringing along in order to ensure they would back him when the key moment came for him to try to seize the leadership of the ministry. The fact that Hanoverian hostility to the Tories became ever clearer made this element of Tory opinion more and more important: if a Hanoverian succession meant that the Tories were doomed to political Siberia whether they backed George's succession or not, a Jacobite succession became more attractive to a significant minority of Tories, and the dilemma of Bolingbroke and Oxford became more and more acute. Tory Jacobitism became an increasingly self-fulfilling prophecy in many quarters.

So increasingly the ministry was pushed into a position neither substantively pro-Jacobite nor anywhere near as full-throatedly pro-Hanover as the Whigs – and many Tories – would have liked. Within this fateful morass of political ambiguity sprouted a lush profusion of political innuendo, rumour and fear that was to plunge the government into ever greater crisis. A ministry that was not, in fact, in favour of a Jacobite succession found itself struggling to dispel the idea that it was indeed secretly in the interest of the

Pretender, even among many of its own supporters. Whether they could extricate themselves from such a quagmire was to determine the fate of British politics.

The Whigs enjoyed little success initially as parliament began its business again after the long peacemaking hiatus. The Queen's speech announcing the peace was unambiguously pro-Hanoverian. The treaty itself involved France recognising Anne's right to the throne and the Protestant succession, agreeing to cease all support for the Pretender and his heirs, and expelling the Pretender from French territory. Anne emphasised these points, declaring that:

> What I have done for securing the Protestant Succession, and the perfect friendship there is between me and the House of Hanover, may convince such who wish well to both, and desire the quiet and safety of their country, how vain all attempts are to divide us . . .[8]

This reassured many pro-Hanoverian Tories and the debates on the political aspects of the treaty were a damp squib: the Whigs found it impossible to get any real purchase. The Tories, promised the fruits of a 'peace dividend' – chiefly a substantial cut to the land tax – were in a cheery mood (by their standards) and any fractiousness in their ranks was not obvious. They had yearned for peace for years, and would not spurn the opportunity to revel in the bounties of Utrecht, at least for the time being.

In any case, Oxford had taken steps to forestall any potential October Club antics by his usual method: patronage, places and promises. He induced Country Tories to turn up and vote for his ministry in large numbers – and agree to avoid embarrassing initiatives – by promising to discuss their grievances. He then promised many of them an endless succession of future goodies, mainly jobs and other perks. This certainly worked in the short term, although was obviously storing up problems: as the Hanoverian envoy observed, 'he promises the same thing to five different persons, which, at least, will procure him four enemies for one friend'.[9] He also sacked a few remaining Whig office holders, which placated the October men while making his exit strategy of seeking a deal with the Whigs rather more fraught. These measures eased the initial stages of the parliamentary session, although they did not stop the Tory backbenchers ambushing the ministry to cut the land tax by more than Oxford thought prudent.

Furthermore, the Whigs were in a bind. They simply could not agree a strategy with the Hanoverian court for attacking the ministry over the succession issue. The Junto was convinced that the best strategy was for the Elector to send his son, also called George, the Duke of Cambridge (the future King George II), to reside in England and take up his place in the House of Lords. It was thought that his presence would rally the Whig opposition and make it far easier to secure the Hanoverian succession. The ever-rash Sunderland pushed this policy hard, and indeed got most of the Junto and even Marlborough to agree to support it. The Elector, however, knew how provocative it would be to the Queen and was reluctant to pursue it. He preferred the idea of introducing a bill into parliament disqualifying the Pretender irrespective of his religion, which the Junto saw as a waste of time. As a result, the Whigs struggled to find a convenient way of broaching the issue. They were to regain the initiative through some rather less direct means.

The main peace treaties were not the only diplomatic business that had preoccupied the ministry over the previous few years. Alongside the main peace treaty, Bolingbroke had taken the lead in the negotiations of a new treaty of commerce with France. The terms of this treaty had not been announced when the main peace was signed, but at some point parliament would have to repeal the old anti-French trade laws and ratify various clauses of this treaty.[10]

Bolingbroke had largely seen this treaty as a political one, designed to cement peace and amicable relations with France (or, in the view of his critics, to help ease the path to a French-assisted Jacobite restoration). His vision was of Britain coming to terms with France in order to concentrate on swatting its main commercial rival: the Dutch.[11] He had, however, delegated the negotiation of many of the technical details of the commercial terms to his longstanding, and extremely disreputable, factotum, Arthur Moore.

Among the terms of the treaty were two articles – eight and nine – that were wide open to criticism. Article eight established that France and Britain would give each other 'most favoured nation' trading status, and article nine reduced the tariff on French goods. The major underlying issue with these terms was that they risked upending the close trading relationship that Britain had established with Portugal under the Methuen treaties, which – as many MPs quickly realised – had worrying implications for various British commercial interests.

Shortly before this treaty came before parliament, the Portuguese ambassador to Britain had issued a statement threatening an embargo on all British woollen goods if Portuguese wines lost their preferential trading advantages, as the Commercial Treaty implied they would. Whigs seized on this, arguing that any advantages that might accrue from free trade with the French would be undermined by the loss of the lucrative Portuguese woollen export market, with knock-on effects for clothiers and weavers. Furthermore, many feared that the treaty would result in an influx of cheap French silks, which would undermine the domestic silk industry. Those who had a vested interest in the Portuguese wine trade also feared being commercially destroyed by renewed French competition.

In short, those who had an existing established interest in trade with Portugal, or feared French competition, had every reason to be suspicious and mobilise. On the principle that those who have something to lose are more tenacious than those who may have something to gain in the future, the political impetus lay behind those who wished to retain the solid current benefits of Portuguese trade rather than hypothetical future beneficiaries of a renewed commerce with France.

This fact gave the Whigs an excellent opportunity to split the Tories in the Commons, because such commercial questions had an impact that depended more on questions of economic geography than party politics: many Tories represented seats the prosperity of which depended substantially on the wool trade. At first, most Tories had seen the Commercial Treaty purely as a party political question, inextricably linked to the question of the main peace deal. However, the Whigs realised that if they could whip up opposition in the country from areas likely to be negatively affected by the treaty, Tory MPs – alive as MPs generally are to discontent among key interests in their constituencies – might come to see it less as a Whig vs

Tory question and more as a 'do you want to keep your seat?' question. Representations from commercial interests in the wool, silk, cloth and Portuguese wine trade flooded in – in total there were thirty-eight petitions addressed to the Commons and a further ten to the Lords – and many Tories found themselves in the firing line.

Peter Shakerley, veteran Tory MP for Chester, is one such example. Chester had become a centre for the importation of Portuguese wines, and reducing the duties on French wines and brandy had the potential to gravely injure the city's business. The corporation and merchants of Chester petitioned the Commons against any reductions in duties on French wines and wrote anguished letters to Shakerley demanding his support for their cause.[12] This was not an isolated case.

At first, the votes on the Commercial Treaty went well for the ministry in the Commons. However, as every day went on, more and more representations were received and the trickle of petitions became a flood. Anguished lobbyists for the silk and cloth industry thronged Westminster and lambasted wavering MPs. There were strong rumours that the silk workers of London, stirred up by Whig propaganda suggesting that the treaty would ruin them, would riot; the militia was called to quell any disturbance, leading to loud accusations from Tory hacks that the Whigs were stirring up 'the mob' to intimidate parliament.

MPs like Peter Shakerley knew that a general election was due later in the year, and it began to dawn on them that voting for the Commercial Treaty might be signing their own political death warrant. Even more ominously for the government, the whole situation had awoken fears among the March Club men that the ministry's desire to forge such close economic links with France reflected something more sinister than simply a desire to boost Britain's trade. Why had Bolingbroke agreed to terms that seemed to many as if they were excessively favourable to the French? Was this all part of some Jacobite design? Tory unity began to look very shaky.

In the Commons, a leading spokesman for the government, William Wyndham, High Tory Secretary of War, taunted the Whigs, arguing that it was not the decline of trade, but rather the 'decline of their own exhausted faction' that was irking them.[13] Wyndham's comment, however, merely reflected the government's failure to realise the growing discontent over the Commercial Treaty on the Tory (as well as Whig) benches.

There was some belated recognition of the problem on the part of the ministers. Swift – who had recently departed back to Ireland – was not on hand to write a *Conduct of the Allies*-style defence of the treaty, so the ministry had to look elsewhere. A new newspaper specifically devoted to defending the Commercial Treaty – the *Mercator* – was set up, to be written – at Oxford's behest – by Daniel Defoe. The *Mercator* pointed out that the Whigs were mobilising traders with narrow vested interests, whereas free trade with France would, in the long run, be in the broader national interest.

It wasn't enough. The complacent attitude of ministers like Wyndham cost the ministry dearly. Tory momentum against the bill reached the point where the government's colossal Commons majority began to look shaky in the extreme. Several senior Tories, whose opinions carried significant weight among the parliamentary party, began to waver. This was far more serious than a little unfocussed backbench anxiety.

The *coup de grâce* was delivered by Sir Thomas Hanmer. Hanmer had a lot of credibility in Tory eyes. His credentials as a stalwart of the Church Party were unshakeable – he had been a Tacker in 1704, he had refused office under the Oxford administration in order to burnish his credentials as an incorruptible Country Tory, he was a High Churchman to his fingertips, and he had been a founder member of the October Club. He nonetheless had a reputation for being on the more pragmatic and reasonable wing of the High Tories. So far, he had been a loyal supporter of the Oxford ministry, and even voted for the Commercial Treaty Bill in its initial stages – but that was changing. He was just about to lay a landmine under the bill that would rock the ministry to its foundations.

The key debate was on the third reading of the bill, on 18th June. The debate dragged on, in total, for eight hours. The Whigs held back in the hope that the Tories would dominate the debate and thereby show up the divisions in their ranks. The debate ebbed and flowed quite evenly for some time: the general view was that the ministry would still manage to sneak it through, albeit by a small majority. Then Thomas Hanmer stood up and delivered a speech that stunned the House:

> Having . . . maturely weighed and considered the allegations of the
> traders and manufacturers . . . he was convinced that the passing of it
> would be of great prejudice to the woollen and silk manufacturers of this
> kingdom, consequently increase the number of the poor, and so, in the
> end, affect the land.[14]

His speech was couched in high-minded terms. He implied that the
Whig side of the argument was, in this instance, the truly patriotic one,
and he would not put party before country. The fact that he represented the
county seat of Suffolk, which had a substantial woollen industry, suggests
that other, less noble, considerations were not absent from his deliberations.
More significantly, however, it seems that he had also begun to have doubts
– not openly voiced on this occasion but known to some of his political
associates – about whether the treaty had a darker Jacobite subtext.

Whatever the reasons, Hanmer's contribution turned the tide of the
debate. It emboldened scores of wavering Tory MPs to vote against the treaty.
In total seventy-six – including other Tory old stagers like Peter Shakerley –
rebelled, and dozens more abstained. Out of the four MPs for London – all
Tories since 1710 – only one stuck with the ministry: intense representations
on behalf of city wine and textile interests had put the wind up them.
The Commercial Treaty Bill fell by nine votes, 194 to 185. For the first time,
the Oxford ministry had been defeated in the Commons on a major bill.

The drapers and weavers of London celebrated wildly on the news that
the bill had been defeated, 'expres[sing] their Satisfaction by Bonefires and
Illuminations'.[15] The Whigs were elated, believing that they had finally found
a breach in the hitherto formidable fortifications of the ministry. Bolingbroke
was apoplectic: he took the defeat as a personal blow, and suspected foul play on
the part of Oxford, who was known to be close to Hanmer. He wrote passive-
aggressively to his rival complaining of the Dutch reaction to the defeat:

> The news was public at the Hague on Monday, and the packet did
> not arrive till Tuesday, they are overjoyed at it, and laugh openly at
> us . . . Indeed, my Lord, we make a despicable figure in the world. You
> have retrieved many a bad game in your time; for God's sake make one
> push for government.[16]

Oxford, calm as ever, reacted stoically and began to do what he always did in times of political trouble: plot and scheme.

The defeat over the Commercial Treaty Bill appeared to be a moment of considerable peril for the ministry. An ominous alliance between backbench 'Whimsical' Tories and the Whigs had destroyed a major plank of their entire diplomatic and economic policy. From riding high at the start of the session, Oxford's government appeared to have lost a good deal of its credibility. If the Whigs could find a way of pulling further on this string of Tory disunity, the whole government might collapse. Tory morale began to drop.

The Whigs followed up their success with another stratagem: the Lorraine motions. Louis XIV having made good on his promise to expel the Pretender from French territory, James had fled to Lorraine, where the Duke who ruled it had received him cordially. The Whigs laid a careful ambush on the ministry to attempt to highlight possible Tory divisions over the succession. With the help of Nottingham, they proposed an apparently innocuous debate related to the privileges of the Lords on matters concerning the civil list, and summoned all lords to attend. With a near full House, they then revealed their real purpose: a motion calling on the Queen to use all her influence with the Duke of Lorraine to expel the Pretender from his territory, and to ensure that no other friendly ruler in Europe harboured him either.

A long silence followed Wharton's speech, before a curious game of Whig attack and Tory feint ensued. The whole point of the motion was to tempt Jacobites on the Tory benches to out themselves by some imprudent comment or speech. Oxford – rightly – saw the whole business as a purely factious bit of party politicking, and decided that simply agreeing to the motion – while suggesting that it was unnecessary, as the ministry was already making such representations – was the easiest way to defuse it.

The damage was limited. Only one Jacobite in the Commons – William Whitlock – openly opposed the motion, making a speech widely seen as a veiled threat. He observed that:

in Oliver Cromwell's time, when he [Cromwell] obliged France to banish the person Charles Stuart, it hastened on his glorious restoration which followed in a year and a half afterward.[17]

Generally, however, a lot of immensely irritated Jacobites held their tongues, and allowed the motions to go through without a division.

Nonetheless, the Lorraine motions were an ominous straw in the breeze for the Tories. It was well-known that Anglesey, a respected Tory peer, had been involved in planning the ambush in the Lords, which served to widen the gap between an increasingly organised group of Hanoverian Tories and the ministry. The motions brought home to the Jacobite Tory MPs that Oxford was no friend to them, whatever the Pretender (who was still ordering them to back the ministry) thought. They began to contemplate outright opposition to the ministry.

Despite this, Oxford had actually done a surprisingly successful job of damage limitation in the last few weeks of the 1713 parliament. He quashed an attempt by the Whigs to use discontent over a new malt tax to peel away Scottish lords from the ministry, and even threaten the union with Scotland. Then, in the aftermath of Hanmer's speech, Oxford scrambled to do everything in his power to assure him of the ministry's sincere support for the Hanoverian succession. He persuaded Hanmer to move a conciliatory motion conveying to the Queen

> the humble Thanks of this House, for the great care she has taken of the security and honour of her kingdoms in the Treaty of Peace; and also for what she has done in the Treaty of Commerce with France, by laying so good a foundation for the interests of her people in trade.[18]

The same motion called for new trade commissioners to be appointed to negotiate with the French to the end of ensuring that the commercial treaty might be 'explained and perfected'.[19] It was a tactful and partially unifying way of trying to put the issue to bed. Oxford followed this up with various announcements designed to reassure the country that, on issues ranging from the Assiento slave contract through to the protection of the woollen industry, the ministry was on the side of British manufacturers and would not be mere lapdogs of the French.

As the session ended and thoughts turned to the general election that was due in autumn, there was no doubt that the Whigs had made progress. The Tories no longer looked as invincible as they had a mere six months earlier, and the seeds of some very fruitful divisions within the Tory ranks had been sown. Nonetheless, Oxford's skilful manoeuvres had limited the damage and generally held together the parliamentary situation with calmness under some not inconsiderable fire – albeit with immense difficulty.

But Oxford's problems were only just beginning.

The 1713 parliamentary session had gradually turned into an increasingly ad hoc rearguard action on the part of Oxford, and although it had (just) succeeded, many troubles had been building up. The prestige of finally passing the peace had boosted them initially, but Oxford's flimsy promises to the Country Tories increasingly appeared to be only delaying the day when they would become ungovernable. Meanwhile, behind the scenes Bolingbroke was plotting to manoeuvre himself into a position to exploit these Tory discontents.

The view of most Tories – ranging both from Jacobites to many Hanoverian High Tories – was that now the peace was done, it was time to carry through a thoroughgoing Tory programme. As Bolingbroke put it later:

> Things which we pressed were put off upon every occasion, till the Peace: the Peace was to be the date of a new Administration, and the period at which the millenary year of Toryism should begin.[20]

The key to such a 'millenary year' was the Church. For years Oxford had placated his High Church allies – men such as Atterbury – by telling them to be patient. If only they would follow him and wait, eventually something would be done. This had worked for some time, because most High Churchmen had remembered how disastrous the Tack had been and decided that taking the Harleyite course was prudent. After the convulsions of 1710,

Oxford had (largely) managed to put off this reckoning by the argument that nothing could be done until the peace was secured.

By spring 1713, however, High Church Tories were restless.[21] Since 1710, Oxford had essentially done nothing to further the interests of the Church, except the welcome but hardly revolutionary act of building new churches in London. The most successful pro-Church legislative effort – 'Old Occasional' finally being passed – had ironically been carried by a curious alliance of Whiggery and Nottingham. Wharton had done more for the Church than Oxford in recent years. The Tories grew impatient.

The man who symbolised this growing irritation was Atterbury. He had been a loyal lieutenant of Oxford for years, but the years between 1710 and 1713 had been a bitter disappointment to him. For years he had tried to rein in his supporters to help Oxford, and it had got his cause nowhere. Ecclesiastical appointments under the Oxford ministry had largely gone to moderate Tories who were chosen specifically not to rock the boat. Convocation had become hopelessly bogged down in sniping between the Whig Bishops and the Tory lower clergy, who were rallied ceaselessly – but to little effect – by Atterbury. Oxford had done nothing to help him.

So increasingly Bolingbroke courted Atterbury, who was warmly receptive: if Oxford would not advance the interests of the Church, the High Church attack dog would find someone who would. Soon, Bolingbroke and his ally Harcourt acted on his behalf. Back in summer 1711, Oxford, under pressure from the two men, had realised that he had to make some concessions to ease High Church Tory discontent, and agreed – very reluctantly – to give Atterbury the prestigious appointment of the Deanery at Christ Church, Oxford. Having helped Atterbury in this way, Bolingbroke now expected Atterbury to build a powerful political connexion in Oxford to advance his interest in the intellectual and social powerhouse of High Toryism, Oxford University. Atterbury assumed that in due course Bolingbroke would lead the High Church assault he yearned for.

It soon became apparent that this was a pyrrhic victory for Atterbury, largely due to his own incredibly intemperate behaviour. He decided to assert his total control over Christ Church so that he could wrest the college's – and in due course the university's – enormous resources of patronage and use them to advance supporters of Bolingbroke. He set about doing this by a campaign of relentless, high-handed bullying, terrorising the more placid dons and using very dubious bureaucratic tactics to outmanoeuvre them. Among other outrages, he accused the Chapter of Christ Church (for Christ Church is a cathedral as well as an Oxford college) of embezzling trust funds. Outright war between the two factions at Christ Church ensued, with shouting matches in chapter meetings. It created a scandal nationwide, and Atterbury soon realised that he had not gained total control of Christ Church, but rather reduced it to a complete standstill and consolidated his reputation as a remorseless bully. He had done his cause no good at all.

However, he still had the good offices of Bolingbroke. In April 1713, the two men, in alliance with other angry High Tories — most prominently Sir Simon Harcourt — began to cabal against Oxford. Now peace was here, the Tories must seize total control in Church and State and restore the Church of England to its dominant position. Oxford's brother described the scene:

> About this time Lord Bolingbroke, Lord Harcourt, and [Atterbury] fell into a strict alliance, and endeavoured to raise a great prejudice in the Church party against the Treasurer, upbraiding him for not being a sincere churchman, as they called it; and to make this pass got lists out of every office of the names of such persons as they called Whigs, who were continued in their employments. Then Lord Bolingbroke told me, if your brother will not set himself at the head of the Church Party, somebody must.[22]

Atterbury was to be Bolingbroke's ecclesiastical agent, tasked with promoting Bolingbroke's leadership of the party and helping to push through a thoroughgoing Tory revolution in the Church and among High Churchmen in parliament. He was a more credible voice to this wing of the party than whoremongering deist rake Bolingbroke.

He got to work quickly. While the chaos over the Commercial Treaty had been going on, Atterbury had worked behind the scenes to promote several bills designed to galvanise Tory pro-Church sentiment, one to give ecclesiastical courts more teeth and another to deprive Quakers of their vote in parliamentary elections. Neither had passed, but only by the skin of Oxford's teeth. A shot had been fired across Oxford's increasingly shaky bows.

So it was already clear by the end of the 1713 session that the forces of High Church Toryism were rising fast, and that Bolingbroke and Harcourt could not be ignored without the government losing its control of the Commons in the next session. It was at this point that the Bishop of Rochester, Thomas Sprat, died, leaving both that bishopric and the deanery of Westminster free. These positions by custom went together, as the bishopric of Rochester had a meagre income and the lucrative Deanery of Westminster was used to supplement it.

Harcourt – by now Lord Chancellor – and Bolingbroke decided that this was the moment to push for Atterbury's promotion to the bishop's bench and thereby reward their new lieutenant. Oxford – and indeed the Queen – were desperate to avoid this, knowing of Atterbury's fiery reputation. However, Oxford's position was so weak that, despite lengthy attempts to block the appointment, it became clear that there was no other way of placating his High Tory enemies. The appointment would, at least, end the undignified squabbling at Christ Church. Dartmouth, the moderate Tory minister, had desperately attempted to prevent the appointment, and reported that he 'never knew the Queen do anything with so much reluctancy' as signing off on his appointment: Atterbury was, she knew, 'meddling and troublesome'.[23] But Harcourt had threatened to resign unless Atterbury was obliged. Atterbury finally got his reward and became Bishop of Rochester and Dean of Westminster.

After this success, Bolingbroke smelt blood. His fundamental weakness – aside from the fact that the smash over the commercial treaty had not done his reputation much good – was that, despite many attempts to do so, he still could not displace Oxford in the affections and regard of the Queen. By this point, Oxford's position as the Queen's stay and support was his major remaining political trump card. Bolingbroke, however, felt that he could overcome this by the sheer logic of the fact that he increasingly had the support, at least implicitly, of many Tory backbenchers.

So, in July 1713, he pushed a new scheme, which he outlined in a trench-ant letter to Oxford. It was imperative to 'separate, in the name of God, the chaff from wheat', sack all remaining Whig office holders and milquetoast Tories like Dartmouth, and promote trenchant High Churchmen to carry the fight to the Whigs.[24] Behind his back, Bolingbroke was boasting to his allies that Oxford was 'to have terms put upon him, and a junto' (i.e. his personal ascendancy was to be ended by a Tory administration run by a small cabal).[25]

Towards the end of the 1713 parliamentary session and for a few weeks after, Oxford had once again fallen ill and became disconsolate. He wondered whether he could resist the forces bearing down upon him, and allegedly remarked to a Quaker friend that he was on the verge of 'giving up the game in his hands'.[26] He longed for a quiet retirement to spend time with his family, and, more importantly, his books and manuscripts. However, gradually his lethargy dissipated and he decided that he owed it to the Queen to rouse himself once more and protect her from being ruled by a Tory Junto as high-handed and bullying as the old Whig one.

In this context, in August 1713 he pulled off his last unquestionably successful bit of political legerdemain. He managed to convince the Queen to reshuffle the government, but very much not in the direction that Bolingbroke had had in mind. He knew that he still had resources of support among the Tories – such as William Bromley – and the Queen still didn't trust Bolingbroke. He decided to exploit these points of strength by clipping his old rival's wings. He shuffled Dartmouth sideways from the secretaryship of state to being Lord Privy Seal, and strengthened his hand in cabinet by appointing Bromley as Secretary of State. This left the Speakership of the Commons open: he planned to use this vacancy to reassure the Hanoverian Tories by attempting to persuade Sir Thomas Hanmer to fill it. He threw Bolingbroke only a few crumbs of consolation by giving a couple of ministerial positions outside of the cabinet to Bolingbroke allies, most notably William Wyndham, who became Secretary at War.

Bolingbroke was furious and skulked off to his country seat to sulk. He considered resigning but knew that he had no chance of pulling off the coup he longed for unless he could win over the Queen, something that he could hardly do from the backbenches. He also knew that, for all Oxford's clever tricks, once parliament met again things might look very different.

Nonetheless, Oxford seemed, once again, to have pulled off a stunning bit of political alchemy, turning the base metal of Tory rebellion into the gold of his renewed political hegemony.

And then he made the biggest mistake of his political career.

Robert Harley, the Earl of Oxford, had maintained his high standing in the eyes of the Queen over the years for various reasons. Chief among them was the fact he had been the only man with the will and ability to protect her from being ruled by high-handed party magnates. He had never abandoned his ideal of disinterested men of all parties serving her in the national interest, although in recent years circumstances had made it an increasingly hard task. Still, he had performed the role as well as anyone could.

However, the Queen also admired Oxford's personal virtues. She disliked the partisans not only because they tried to bully her into immoderate courses, but also because she suspected (rightly in many cases) that they were selfish opportunists using party slogans to gain office and preferment. Oxford was undoubtedly a slippery political character, but he was not personally corrupt. He might make promises he couldn't keep and show a distinct willingness to be economical with the truth, but he did these things for what he considered noble ends.

However, he had a weakness: his family. One of the reasons the Queen liked him was that he was a good family man. He was overfond of a drink when stressed – and he was always stressed – but there were no mistresses or debauches to his discredit, no Bolingbroke-style scandal. It was, however, his desire to promote the interests of his beloved children that undid him with the Queen.

For some years, he had been negotiating a marriage pact with the family of the Duke of Newcastle. Oxford's son Edward was to be married to Lady Henrietta Holles, the Duke's daughter and a fantastically rich heiress. In 1711 the old Duke died, and as he had no sons the dukedom of Newcastle became extinct. The Dowager Duchess, taking over the negotiations after her husband's death, was desperate to extract everything out of the marriage for her family's honour. One of her conditions was that the dukedom should be revived and bestowed upon Edward. Oxford assured the Dowager Duchess (with what truth it is impossible to say) that the Queen had agreed to do so once the couple were married. On the eve of the marriage, in August 1713, he broached the question of reviving the dukedom and giving it to his own son.

The Queen was deeply unimpressed. Part of the marriage deal had actually involved the bulk of the Newcastle estate being inherited not by Henrietta but the late Duke's nephew, Thomas Pelham. Being presented a dukedom – the most prestigious rank in the English aristocracy – without a commensurate level of wealth to support its dignity was seen by the Queen as being quite inappropriate. She also deeply resented Oxford's presumption in presenting it to her as a fait accompli, and was disillusioned by the apparently self-interested nature of the request. Even Oxford was just another corrupt seeker of royal favours.

So she refused, and not only that, the incident – what Oxford himself called 'my never enough to be lamented folly' – fundamentally wrecked her relationship with her long-standing servant.[27] The trust would never be there again, and he made it worse by his response to this humiliating rebuke. He relapsed into depression, self-pity and apathy, and began, for the first time, to neglect his duties, missing cabinet meetings.

At this point, Bolingbroke swooped. Even while Oxford had been away celebrating his son's marriage, he had begun to work on the royal household in an attempt to sully Oxford's reputation and suborn various courtiers. Oxford had been very tardy at paying salaries to the royal household, which meant that he was not in good odour among those who daily attended on the Queen. In typically cynical fashion, Bolingbroke exploited this situation. He offered Mrs (by now Lady) Masham a share in the profits of the Assiento slave contract and other shady revenues in exchange for her allegiance. A deal was struck: Masham would whisper poison into the Queen's ears about Oxford if Bolingbroke would fill her pockets with gold.

Bolingbroke attended the court assiduously that summer, turning the full force of his charm on Masham and the Queen. He ruthlessly exploited

Oxford's neglect of public affairs and laziness, continually alluding to the contrast between his devotion to his beloved sovereign and Oxford's slipshod negligence. Oxford, weary in body and mind and close to what we would now call a nervous breakdown, seriously contemplated resignation – the evidence is unclear, but it appears that he may actually have even offered his resignation to the Queen in late October. The Queen did not yet trust Bolingbroke sufficiently to go so far as getting rid of him, and so affairs drifted, with neither Oxford out nor Bolingbroke fully in.

Soon after this, another blow put even these matters out of Oxford's mind. In November, his beloved daughter Betty (the Marquess of Carmarthen) suddenly died. Tragedy piled upon misfortune, and Oxford could not bear it. He had been very close to Betty, and the grief floored him. He stayed away from court even longer, prostrate with misery, thereby giving Bolingbroke even more time to ingratiate himself with the Queen. However, as Christmas approached, his loss gave Oxford some relief with the Queen, as she had suffered too many bereavements herself to be insensible of what a bitter blow it was.

The question remained, however – was Oxford down and out? In the face of such blows, could he find the energy and willpower required to fight back against Bolingbroke?

While these momentous personal dramas were playing themselves out in the summer and autumn of 1713, the small matter of a general election, compulsory under the Triennial Act, was underway.[28]

On the face of it, one might have expected the Whigs to be able to exploit Tory divisions and opposition to the Commercial Treaty in the election. They certainly made a valiant attempt to paint themselves as the defenders of England's wool and textile trade against treacherous Tory attempts to sell the nation's commercial interests out to their French allies. In Southwark, Guildford, Wiltshire and Buckinghamshire, Whig partisans wore bits of wool in their hats to bring the message home. Lady Wharton even handmade some of the wool cockades for the Buckinghamshire election. In Liverpool, Whigs varied the theme somewhat by using tobacco as their symbol of Tory trading betrayals.[29] Such a theme was typically tied to accusations that the

Tories were Jacobites cosying up to the French in order to facilitate a Jacobite restoration. One earthy Whig squib gives a good sense of this:

> Oh! The wretched damn'd sham peace
> That must our rents and stock decrease,
> Must starve our poor,
> And open the door
> To let in a Popish Son of a Whore[30]

In reality, these two core Whig messages – on trade and the usual theme of accusing the Tories of being Jacobites – got them close to nowhere. The latter was discounted by an electorate that had heard it all before. One Whig rector summed it up:

> [many] are utter infidels as to any present danger from the pretender, reckoning that an useful Election cry, but an attempt soe dangerous and soe pernicious that noe men in their wits could make it: not considering what a desperate Ministry will doe . . .[31]

The trade issue contributed to them making some minor gains in relevant boroughs, but many textile areas were simply not enfranchised and so couldn't elect any MPs. The Whig vote tended to go up modestly in the more 'popular' boroughs, but not enough to make much difference. The Tories mocked the Whigs' efforts, claiming that Whig 'wits were gone a wool-gathering, and that they looked very sheepish'.[32]

Indeed, the underlying factor behind the Whigs' lacklustre performance was straightforward. The issues made precious little difference in many seats because all over the country the key local offices that could manipulate elections – lords lieutenants of counties, mayors of corporations and suchlike – were, after three years of Crown patronage running in their favour, overwhelmingly Tories, who happily rigged the election in their own favour. It seems likely that the Occasional Conformity Act had hit Whig strength in key corporations as well. The whole electoral landscape had been tilted in favour of the Tories.

Nonetheless, insofar as issues of substance played a role in the election, the Tories had strong cards to play. Most fundamentally, they had brought peace and lower taxes, which was very popular. Whig attempts to complain about the Commercial Treaty or the supposedly unpatriotic nature of the peace simply drew attention to the fact that the Tories had ended a decade of punishing warfare, while the Whigs would still be waging it, had they been in power.

The result in England and Wales was almost exactly the same as in 1710, in terms of numbers, although Whig success in Scotland boosted their parliamentary representation overall. There was nonetheless still a colossal Tory majority.

This, however, masked the reality that in many ways the election was at least as much an intra-Tory fight as a Tory–Whig contest.[33] Hanoverian Tories vied with the Tories who supported the ministry. A not inconsiderable minority of the 'ministerial' Tories were, sometimes more-or-less openly, Jacobites. Where there was a Whig candidate, the Tories generally put their differences aside to avoid splitting the vote, although in a few seats – Rutland and Wiltshire, for example – Hanoverian Tories openly allied with Whigs against ministerial Tory candidates. In some seats, however, there was no Whig candidate and the election became a straight fight between a Hanoverian and a ministerial Tory, such as in Salisbury and Canterbury: these contests usually devolved into an argument about the Commercial Treaty, which was sometimes something of a proxy for 'Hanover vs Jacobitism'. In most such cases the ministerial Tory won, but overall most of the Hanoverian Tories from the last parliament were re-elected, not least because in many cases the Whigs did not put up candidates against them.

The result of this confused mess was a Commons that, although containing a large majority of Tories, was really split more ways than can easily be distinguished. On the one hand, there was a united and slightly augmented force of Whigs, numbering around 150 in England and Wales, reinforced by various segments of pro-Whig Scottish MPs. Then there were the outright Hanoverian Tories, who looked to Sir Thomas Hanmer for leadership. Hanmer had forty convinced supporters, but could command the support of around seventy Tory MPs if there were genuine fears that the Protestant succession was at stake. In opposition to them were the outright Jacobite Tories. Only forty to fifty of those were prepared to operate as a self-conscious group, but there were, in addition, perhaps another thirty to fifty more cautious Jacobites, making something like eighty to one hundred in total.

There was also the split between supporters of Bolingbroke and supporters of Oxford, a split that to some extent overlapped with the previous two categories. Bolingbroke's allies, made up largely of high-flying Tories who wished to establish a complete Tory domination in Church and State, contained many (but by no means exclusively) Jacobites. Oxford's supporters formed a smaller phalanx of outright Tory moderates and non-party figures who were sceptical of the High Churchmen. All of this was complicated by the fact that the Hanoverian Tories were mostly staunch High Church Country Tories themselves, albeit ones who had no truck with Jacobitism, and the fact that some didn't fit easily into any category. Similar divisions existed in the Lords, although Oxford was much stronger there, able as he was to call upon many court-orientated lords who generally voted consistently with the government.

What on earth this parliament, enormously complicated by such a bewildering mass of Tory factions and the rivalry of Oxford and Bolingbroke, would do in practice was anybody's guess.

It was a question that was soon to be electrified by a festive crisis.

The Queen's health in 1713 had not, in the context of her overall lamentable physical condition, been so bad. But on Christmas Eve, she was suddenly convulsed by a terrible illness. She:

> complained of a pain in her thigh, and was seized with violent shivering, which lasted above two hours. Extreme heat followed, with intense thirst, great anxiety, restlessness and inquietude.[34]

The consensus of her closest attendants was that she nearly died. By 28th December she had rallied and her condition had improved. She was able to receive a few visitors by New Year's Eve, but she continued to be sick throughout January. Her body, battered by endless failed pregnancies, multiple ailments and a heavy burden of duties, was close to giving up the ghost.

The succession issue instantly rocketed to the top of the agenda, and the Tories could no longer ignore it or pretend that the Queen was immortal. Many Whigs struggled to hide their glee as Anne lay stricken over Christmas; like vultures the Junto lay in wait. A bitter Jonathan Swift later reflected:

> It was confidently reported in town, that she was dead; and the heads of the expecting party were said to have various meetings thereupon, and a great hurrying of chairs and coaches to and from the earl of Wharton's house. Whether this were true or not, yet thus much is certain, that the expressions of joy appeared very frequent and loud among many of that party; which proceeding, men of form did not allow to be altogether decent.[35]

It was clear that the final crisis of her life – and by extension, of the Tory Party – was close at hand. Perhaps she had months, at a stretch a year, but the great axe hanging over the ministry could not be stayed for very much longer. The chaos in the ministry and the Queen's illness allowed a series of prorogations to delay the beginning of the new parliament, but neither that nor Anne's mortality could be delayed indefinitely.

It is hard to overstate the extent of the Tory predicament over the succession. That they had alienated Hanover over the peace and their failure to do anything concrete to settle George's nerves over the succession was undeniable. The death of Anne and accession of George seemed almost certain to herald a new age of exclusive Whig rule, and with it possibly impeachment and even execution for Oxford and Bolingbroke. Should they make some desperate ploy to win over the Hanoverians? Or else throw their lot in with the Jacobites and seek a Stuart restoration?

It has usually been assumed by historians that Oxford, despite his dabbling with the Pretender's court, was always a Hanoverian, no matter how much it became directly contrary to his political interests, but that Bolingbroke was far more sympathetic to the Jacobites and willing, if necessary, to install the Pretender. Certainly many – most notably Oxford himself – believed this at the time. There is no doubt that Oxford was no Jacobite, but Bolingbroke's attitude is much harder to discern. What is true about the traditional view is that Bolingbroke was sufficiently cynical to support a Jacobite restoration if he had ever believed that it was a realistic option; Bolingbroke cared not a straw for either the Church of England or the Roman Catholic Church, but he did certainly care a great deal for his own political prospects.

The reality is, however, that Bolingbroke was such a totally ruthless pragmatist that he knew that the only game in town was a Hanoverian one: a Jacobite restoration would simply not be accepted, other than at the point of a sword, and a successful Jacobite military invasion was highly unlikely, and at best likely to trigger civil war.[36] He also knew that his real strength lay in the Commons, among the high-flying Tories, and that a sizeable proportion of them were Jacobites. He therefore had to attempt to pursue a pro-Hanoverian policy of some kind in secret while also appealing to the Jacobites.

His strategy for doing this was a bold carrot-and-stick one. On the one hand, via ruthless exploitation of patronage, he would entrench a totally united Tory Party so thoroughly in every crevice of both Church and State that an incoming Hanoverian monarch would face a lengthy and possibly extremely troublesome process of rooting them out. On the other, he would, sensationally, promise to restore the now exiled Marlborough – a former personal friend with whom he had always attempted to maintain links – as captain-general, and offer to support the Hanoverians in their current war against Sweden once the Queen died.[37] It's not clear whether this plan would ever have worked – Marlborough had no reason to throw his lot in with Bolingbroke unless something dramatic changed, the Jacobites were apt to get suspicious and smell his double game, and it seemed doubtful whether the Elector would ever accept such a scheme. But in the dire circumstances of early 1714, it was the best he could come up with.

Oxford, on the other hand, hoped to somehow muddle through by using promises to the Pretender to prevent the Jacobites from going into outright opposition, while keeping a door open to an alliance with the Whigs – his old trick – and the Hanoverian Tories. If he could persuade the Queen to agree to practical moves to reconcile Hanover while also placating George via diplomatic means, he might, in due course, be able to ditch the High

Tories altogether and move his ministry into an overt pro-Hanover stance. He might even be able to remain Lord Treasurer in alliance with Whigs and Hanoverian Tories once George became king.

The problem was that both men were still, as 1714 begun, ostensibly at least, the leading ministers in the same government, which they had to attempt to prevent from collapsing while both pursued their own very different – and in some ways contradictory – agendas. Furthermore, because Whig discipline and unity in parliament were high, and the backbench Tories of whatever stripe were liable to get bored and return to their country estates, the ministry was in a situation where a mere rebellion of fifty backbench Tories could bring them down. At the same time, both men needed to try to placate both Hanoverian and Jacobite Tory MPs, despite the fact that each of those two sides wanted mutually contradictory things, and neither side was really sure of either Oxford or Bolingbroke's agenda.

Could either man prevail, straighten out the hopeless factional tangle of their own party and win over Hanover, all while fending off the political assaults of the Junto?

At first, the Queen's illness scared the leading Tories into a show of unity: the prospect of an impending Hanoverian succession focussed the mind wonderfully. Even before Christmas, Bolingbroke hoped that he might be able to persuade Oxford to join in his scheme; he even wrote to one associate with genuine hope: 'I begin to reckon upon a clear Tory scheme, more concert, and better method'.[38] If Oxford would throw his weight behind a plan of purging all public offices in Church and State of all but die-hard Tories, then so much the better. If Oxford dragged his feet, the only way of achieving this was to continue his attempt to discredit Oxford with the Queen in the hope that he could get Oxford sacked and take over himself. That might take time, and time was something he could run out of at any moment.

He wrote a letter to Oxford talking grandly of 'an opportunity of giving new strength, new spirit to your administration, and of cementing a firmer union between us'.[39] By January, he was even informing the Queen that her ministers were making excellent preparations to take the fight to the

Whigs. Bolingbroke realised that the only Tory hope now was complete and unflinching unity and resolution. In his words, the Queen:

> has but one life, and whenever that drops, if the Church interest is broke, without concert, without confidence, without order, we are of all men the most miserable.[40]

The idea that Oxford might agree to Bolingbroke's approach was largely an illusion, however. The Trickster was still deeply committed to hedging his bets and, even while they were plotting to destroy him, to keeping backchannels to the Whigs open. The days of Robin and Harry as harmonious master and apprentice had in reality been over for some time: events were now rapidly heading to a position where even the semblance of co-operation between the two would become impossible.

Around about the time of the Queen's Christmas illness, Oxford strained every sinew to rally himself and defeat the forces of despair and apathy assailing his weary mind. As rumours spread around town that the Queen was actually dead, he refused to scurry to Windsor (fearing that that might give credence to the rumour), but rather made an effort to be seen, calm and collected, in public.[41] He began to return to his usual caballing with parliamentary associates in London. Although not the man he was – mourning and illness were etched all over his face – he was not quite out yet. What was he planning?

The first part of his strategy had been brewing since the end of the previous parliamentary session. He had been working on Hanmer. At first he was rebuffed. Hanmer did not want to tie himself to the ministry or compromise his independence: he was a loyal Tory and *wanted* to believe that the succession was safe under Oxford, but reserved his right to do anything necessary to ensure it if he needed to. But gradually it became clear that he would be prepared to become Speaker of the House, a position that gave him more freedom for manoeuvre than becoming a minister. He was still being courted by the Whigs as well, but Oxford hoped that he could reconcile Hanmer, assure him over the succession, and thereby placate the Tory Hanoverians in the House. To further this end, he even promoted Sir William Dawes, an outspoken Hanoverian Tory, to be Archbishop of York.

Meanwhile, Oxford was doing everything he could through diplomatic channels to calm Hanover. He sent his brother, Thomas, as his secret ambassador, to inform them that the Queen would agree to any proposal that would assure the security of the Hanoverian succession 'if consistent with her safety and the laws of the realm'.[42] However, the same old problem endured: the only security that the Elector wanted – an invitation to a member of his family (probably his son) to reside in England – was the one thing the Queen would not agree to. Although Hanover made noises about not doing anything to distress the Queen, it was obvious that nothing short of this would make the Elector trust the ministry (if that).

The other part of his strategy was also not new: make representations to the Jacobite court reassuring them – while promising nothing – in order to try to ensure that the Jacobite MPs and lords would not bring down his ministry. The offer was the same one as ever: eventual restoration of the Pretender *if* he would convert to Anglicanism and agree to withdraw from Lorraine. It was a manifestly insincere offer, as no one believed that James would convert, but Oxford hoped it might buy him some parliamentary breathing space.

Here he was hindered by the fact that Bolingbroke was doing the same thing, with the difference that he was hoping that he could win over the Jacobite MPs to back him personally, if necessary against Oxford. They engaged in a sort of bidding war to convince the Pretender of their sincerity. The difference was that Bolingbroke was also prepared to directly appeal to the Jacobite MPs, continually hinting that, once his ironclad Tory regime in Church and State had been installed, he would restore the Pretender. This Oxford would and could not do.

The fundamental problem Oxford had was that his reserves of credibility were simply running out. He had promised too many things to too many people that he had never delivered. His vagueness, his endless 'wheels within wheels' machinations, his attempting to play every side at the same time: it all had begun to wear thin with everybody.

The French envoy to London remarked that 'there is almost no one who does not say that the man is a double-dealer'.[43] He had lied to the Country Tories too many times; the Jacobites (rightly) didn't believe that he was on their side; and the Hanoverians (and indeed the Whigs) never really knew whether they could trust him (understandably, but, as it turned out, wrongly). No one really trusted Bolingbroke either, but he still had credibility in High Tory and Jacobite circles, and at least he didn't dither and fudge in Oxford's infuriating way.

As the 1714 parliamentary session finally opened and elected Hanmer Speaker on 16th February, a very fragile peace between Bolingbroke and Oxford was still holding.

It wouldn't take long for this forced, unnatural sense of consensus to break down in the most spectacular fashion.

13

Tory Apocalypse

On the eve of the meeting of the new parliament, a charismatic Whig writer – and now MP – had published a sensational pamphlet which rocked Westminster to the core.

Richard Steele was an Anglo-Irish Protestant. A roister-doistering, high-spirited carouser, always in debt and very often drunk, Macaulay described him as 'a rake among scholars and a scholar among rakes'.[1] His sparkling essays in *The Idler* and *The Spectator*, written with his rather staider friend Joseph Addison, had made him a literary sensation by 1714.

In the aftermath of the 1710 election, he had managed to retain one of his government jobs thanks to the intercession of his friend, fellow Anglo-Irish Protestant Jonathan Swift. However, as the 1713 general election loomed, Steele decided that he could no longer hold a place, however minor, under Oxford's government; the time had come for all good Whigs to nail their colours to the mast and come out fighting for the Protestant succession. He resigned and threw himself into a journalistic campaign against the Oxford ministry, while also using his Whig connexions to find him a seat, Stockbridge, where he was duly returned.[2]

Steele's literary assault on the Oxford ministry was relentless. In his papers – the *Guardian*, and later the *Englishman*, as well as various pamphlets encouraged by Wharton – he excoriated the Commercial Treaty and strongly implied that a monstrous Tory conspiracy to install a popish Jacobite tyranny was afoot. He fell out with Jonathan Swift: a personal friendship made across party lines dramatically blew up as the political atmosphere became ever more poisoned by partisan rancour.

Steele's campaign reached its zenith with the publication of *The Crisis*, a work that gave full voice to the Whig argument concerning the risks to the Protestant succession under Oxford.

In many ways, to twenty-first-century eyes the pamphlet seems something of a curiosity. Much of it is an extremely tedious rehearsal of the various laws passed, from the Glorious Revolution onwards, to secure rights to liberty and property and to ensure the Protestant succession. It forms a crude, triumphalist Whig account of the events of 1689 and after, from the Bill of Rights up to the union with Scotland, larded with plenty of alarmist references to the tyranny and barbarism of popery.

The rest is simply a garbled and portentous account of the supposed almighty nature of French power in the aftermath of what he paints as a dishonourable and ruinous peace, and a series of innuendos about the ministry and its supporters in which the utterances of fringe Jacobites and nonjurors are presented as sure proof that, unless the country wakes up and 'struggle[s] to the last Drop of Our Blood for its Religion and Liberty', it faces the ruin of a Stuart restoration and the destruction of true religion, liberty and property.[3] The warning to the ministers is pretty clear:

> those who by their Practices, whatever their Professions are, have discover'd themselves Enemies to the Constitution, and Friends to the Pretender, cannot make a Step farther without being guilty of Treason, without standing in broad Daylight, confessed Criminals against their injured Queen and Country.[4]

Whatever the flaws of *The Crisis*, it clearly made an impression on the MPs gathered for the new parliamentary session and the wider political world of London. Many believed that Steele was right, and the country teetered on the edge of a renewed age of Stuart absolutism.

One person who didn't was Daniel Defoe. Defoe had briefly fallen out of the political ambit of Oxford, but had been re-recruited as one of his chief client journalists by mid-1710. By the time of Steele's pamphlet, he had spent four years doggedly defending the ministry of his benefactor whom he (rightly) saw as a moderate supporter of the Protestant succession. He was deeply unimpressed by what he saw as Steele's antics, and still smarted from a Whig attempt, a year before, to have him prosecuted for an ironical pamphlet intended to satirise the Jacobites by suggesting some 'advantages' of a restoration: the Whigs pretended to take it at face value and almost had Defoe imprisoned for his trouble. Unsurprisingly therefore, Defoe's hatred for the Whigs, of whom Steele was a prominent literary example, had grown to majestic heights – despite, in many ways, being a natural Whig himself.

Defoe's ire spilled over when, in the new parliament, Steele made a very ill-advised maiden speech congratulating Hanmer on being elected Speaker. Oleaginous and wordy, his speech was poorly received. Tory MPs heckled him by shouting, 'Tatler! Tatler! Tatler!' When he made an ill-advised sexual innuendo about 'rising up to do [Hanmer] honour', the House collapsed into gales of laughter.[5] Defoe, unimpressed by this rhetorical failure and outraged at Steele's alarmism, wrote to Oxford urging him to expel Steele from the House for his outrageous slurs on the ministry:

> The new champion of the party, Mr Steele, is now to try an experiment upon the ministry, and shall set up to make speeches in the House and print them, that the malice of the party may be gratified and the ministry be bullied in as public a manner as possible. If, my lord, the virulent writings of this man may not be voted seditious none ever may, and if thereupon he may be expelled it would suppress and discourage the party and break all their new measures.[6]

Swift – temporarily back in London – also saw an opportunity to stick the knife in. Within a few weeks he had published an (anonymous) response to *The Crisis* entitled *The Public Spirit of the Whigs*. It eviscerated Steele's pamphlet, and mocked him roundly in the process: 'He hath a confused remembrance of words since he left the university, but hath lost half their meaning'.[7] It heaped scorn on the hypocrisies and lies of the Whigs.

Unfortunately for Swift, he made one mistake in this production. In an aside, he had made a barbed comment about the poverty of the Scottish lords. They were outraged, and at this point, Wharton (who was sure that the author was Swift) saw his chance for vengeance on his old enemy. Seizing on a comment in the Queen's Speech about the need to tackle the growing menace of seditious libels, he rose in one of the first sittings of the Lords in the new parliamentary session to draw the ministry's attention to Swift's supposed smear on the Scottish lords. He demanded that they 'find out the villain, who was the author of that false and scandalous libel', and even forced the Queen to offer a reward of £300 to anyone who could reveal the author.[8] Oxford, who feigned ignorance, had no intention of allowing Swift to be arrested: he stymied the investigation and even managed to get a volunteer 'that will own [having] written it which will save the Doctor's bacon'.[9]

Steele, on the other hand, was not so lucky. Oxford was not impressed by *The Crisis* and the attempts to smear him as a Jacobite, particularly given that he had allowed Steele to continue at the stamp office for several years despite knowing that he was a Whig. He quickly pounced and decided to get his lieutenants in the Commons to press for Steele's immediate expulsion from the House. William Wyndham accused the newly elected Whig MP of making 'insolent and injurious reflections' on the Queen and encouraging a 'spirit of rebellion', and soon a hearing was called to determine whether *The Crisis* and several inflammatory editions of the *Englishman* were seditious.[10]

The dissolute Steele managed to buy a week to prepare his defence by claiming, not altogether convincingly, that, since he could not be expected to profane the Sabbath by work, a weekend would not be sufficient. When his hearing was convened, the House was full to the brim, and the Whigs had prepared carefully. Steele, assisted by Addison, who sat by him with a sheaf of notes, made a marathon three-hour speech in his own defence. Walpole followed this up with an impassioned and explosive oration in which he painted the attack on Steele as an 'extraordinary and violent prosecution' prompted merely by a brave patriot daring to expose the ministry's 'notorious mismanagements'.[11] He managed to broaden the speech out in a way that caused some of the Hanoverian Tories distinct unease: he raised the issue of payments that the government had allegedly made to notoriously Jacobite Highland clans.

None of this changed the outcome: most of the Hanoverian Tories, including Hanmer, were not yet quite convinced that the ministry had Jacobite intentions, and the House voted, by 245 votes to 152, that Steele's writings constituted 'scandalous and seditious libels', falsely suggesting that the Hanoverian succession was in danger under Her Majesty's government. He was duly expelled from the House.

In some ways this was a unifying boost to the government. However, the whole episode surrounding Steele and *The Crisis* had brought the succession question centre stage, and unnerved many. Twenty-two Hanoverian Tories voted in favour of Steele. The issue about the Highland clans – and the fact that one of the government's tellers in the Steele debate was a notorious Jacobite – provoked a rising sense of suspicion, even among generally loyal Tories. All over London, politicians and hacks began to ask themselves: was it possible that there was no Jacobite fire behind the billowing clouds of suspicion that the Whigs were wafting everywhere?

The scene was set for what would turn out to be some of the most dramatic and chaotic months that parliament – and the court – would ever see.

Even while Steele's ordeal in the Commons was going on, the truce between Oxford and Bolingbroke was disintegrating.

In early March, the Pretender finally gave his answer to Oxford and Bolingbroke: he would not convert to Anglicanism, and he would not remove from Lorraine. This surprised no one, but it meant that the attempts of both men to win over Jacobite support by going over the heads of the Jacobite MPs to the Pretender were over. From now on, the Pretender would not give his supporters in parliament instructions on how to proceed. This benefited Bolingbroke, as he could blame the delay in acting to secure the Pretender's interests on Oxford and go directly to the Jacobite MPs to win them over to his personal allegiance.

Indeed, this course was forced upon him. The Jacobite MPs were incensed at Hanmer's election to the Speakership and alarmed by the Queen's dwindling health, and were sure that unless action was taken soon, the chance for a restoration would be missed. So in early March, they deputed Sir John Pakington and George Lockhart, the most senior Jacobite MPs, to tell Bolingbroke that 'as their patience cou'd last no longer, something to purpose must be quickly done'.[12] They particularly insisted that the army should be purged of all non-Tories and 'sound men' put in control – by which they meant, presumably, Jacobites, or at the very least 'officers known to be well affected to the Crown and Church'.[13]

Bolingbroke saw here an opportunity. He blamed the failure to act to secure the Pretender's interest on Oxford. The Jacobites laboured under the delusion that the Queen was at heart a Jacobite: Bolingbroke encouraged them in this, and claimed that, if only they would back him and give a little time, he would be able to remove Oxford and secure the succession for James, with Anne's approval, by entrenching the Tories so deeply into all offices of state and church that he could use this powerbase to repeal the Protestant succession. Although Lockhart and Pakington were (rightly) suspicious, and loath to wait longer, many of the Jacobite parliamentary rank and file decided to back Bolingbroke. Even they had little patience, though.

So Bolingbroke had to move fast to try to remove Oxford, whom he suspected would be likely to now move towards a Whig alliance to secure the Hanoverian succession. In mid-March he began an open attempt at court to destroy Oxford's remaining credit with the Queen and win over senior Tories like Bromley to his side. He persuaded Lady Masham to intensify pressure on the Queen to come out openly for Bolingbroke. He successfully got the cabinet to agree to a purge of army officers that would have removed any remaining Whigs and most Hanoverians from their commissions. It seemed that the momentum was with him.

But it wasn't. The Queen had relied on Oxford for so long that, for all his faults, she was still reluctant to part with him. She and other senior Tories still didn't trust a man of such dubious personal morality as Bolingbroke. Churchmen were reluctant to back a known deist; the only senior clergyman that Bolingbroke had on his side was Atterbury, whose reputation for bullying had only been deepened by the Christ Church imbroglio. Bolingbroke relied too much on the support of various rakish scapegraces and Jacobites. Oxford called his bluff and threatened to resign, which panicked the Queen: she refused the resignation, and told Bolingbroke and Oxford to get their act together and reunite. A charade of a reconciliation was affected, but no one except the Queen believed it. It was unclear how the ministry could function in the face of the obvious division between two men: as Lord Peterborough put it, 'betwixt two stools the arse goeth to the ground'.[14]

While the Bolingbroke–Harley row was going on behind closed doors, the Whigs had begun an all-out assault on the ministry during a series of debates on the state of the nation, asking to be provided with a whole range of papers related to various commercial and diplomatic negotiations and governmental attempts to get the Pretender removed from Lorraine. They hoped that they would be able to dig up enough dirt to deepen Hanoverian Tory suspicions and weaken the ministry fatally. Oxford dug in to defend the government in the public glare of the Lords against the Whig big guns, all while conscious that he was being strafed by friendly fire behind the scenes.

By this point, various developments – including a quixotic proposal by Oxford to make it high treason to bring foreign troops into Britain, which some thought was an attempt to preclude Dutch troops being brought in to secure the Hanoverian succession, as they were bound to under the new Barrier Treaty – had started to cause rising panic among the Hanoverian Tories. News of Bolingbroke's intrigues and attempted coup at court and the changes in the army convinced many that there was indeed a plot against the Protestant succession in train. Strange rumours that army officers were being asked whether they would follow orders 'no questions asked' began to buzz around the coffee-houses. Frantic efforts were made by senior Whigs (and Nottingham) to persuade the two most senior 'Whimsical' Tories, Hanmer and Anglesey, to wake up and take action before it was too late. They were reluctant and agonised for days over it.

Then the dam broke. Both Hanmer and Anglesey were finally won over by the Whigs. At a meeting on 1st April, the senior Hanoverian Tories and the Whigs thrashed out an understanding. Although the Hanoverian Tories reserved the right to continue to advance solidly Tory policies in general, they agreed to work hand in glove with the Whigs to preserve the Protestant succession. They would divide with the Whigs on issues such as the need to remove the Pretender from Lorraine and pressure the government to ensure the Dunkirk fortifications were destroyed (the delay of which had also caused suspicions). Most importantly, they agreed to work for the removal of Oxford and his replacement with something like a Whig–Hanoverian Tory coalition.

The intensity of the subsequent attack on the government, particularly in the Lords, forced Oxford and Bolingbroke to cease hostilities. On 5th April, the Whigs and Hanoverian Tories, during a general debate on the state of the nation, hammered away on a number of issues. The Junto's best speakers were wheeled out for the occasion, and fired salvo after salvo: the administration had employed known Jacobites; they had made no effort to try to remove the Pretender from Lorraine; all Europe and the Protestant succession lay exposed to the will and pleasure of the French in light of the government's abysmal treaties and unsatisfactory peace. Wharton, not known for his sentimentality, even struck a personal (albeit also truculent) note, ending his speech thus:

> For my part, my lords, I am an old man, and cannot expect to live long; but I have a son, and he, I hope will live to see his country revenged upon these wicked ministers.[15]

The Tories, however, rallied. Bromley forced the leading ministers, including both Oxford and Bolingbroke, to meet and plan: the two hated rivals 'proposed that we should exert ourselves and not let a majority in Parliament slip through our hands'.[16] Bolingbroke even defiantly claimed that the Queen was with them, and she 'would not leave a Whig in employ' before long.[17]

Simply passively watching and waiting for the blows would not work. So Oxford sprang a trap. Rather than face death by a thousand innuendos and minor attacks, he would take the Whigs by surprise and force one grand debate on the succession issue. He got an ally to propose the motion in the Lords that 'the Protestant Succession in the House of Hanover was not in danger'.[18] One straight up-and-down vote would settle the hue and cry for the immediate future.

The Whigs were alarmed, because Oxford had whipped his lords furiously and was able to rely on the votes of two new High Tory bishops to strengthen his forces in the upper house. Then, the government changed the motion to add at the end 'under her Majesty's government': if the motion fell, then the implication would be that the Queen herself was hostile to the Hanoverian succession. This was not something that any lord, wary of alienating the Queen unnecessarily, would do lightly.

Then, sensationally, Anglesey, the true-blue Tory who had been caballing with the Whigs, stunned the Lords with a blistering attack on the government. He claimed that the debate had altered his mind: the poor response of the government to the Whig accusations had convinced him that the Protestant succession *was* in danger from the current ministers. As recently as a fortnight earlier, Anglesey had been openly attacking the Whigs in the House; now he was claiming that the ministry were traitors. He followed it up with an emotional mea culpa over his own support for the peace:

> I own I gave my assent to the cessation of arms, for which I take shame to myself, and ask God, my country, and my conscience pardon. However I did not commit until that noble lord [at this point he turned to Oxford] had assured the Council that the Peace would be glorious and advantageous, both to her Majesty and her allies.[19]

The implication was clear: all along he had been fooled by a wily crypto-Jacobite ministry.

Oxford appealed to the House to believe his own innocence. No doubt genuinely outraged, 'laying his Hand upon his Breast', he decried the imputations and, in anguished tones, declared that he had 'on so many Occasions, given such signal Proofs of his Affection to the Protestant Succession, that he was sure no Member of that August Assembly, did call it into Question'.[20]

There was no doubt that Anglesey's defection was a blow to the government, but Oxford had whipped his forces well. The House divided: the ministry won by fourteen votes. The Protestant succession was not, according to the Lords, in danger: but winning a vote by a far from crushing majority on a motion where losing would have amounted to an accusation

469

of high treason was not *altogether* a comfort. Wharton cheerfully bellowed across the chamber: 'Lord Treasurer, you were saved by your dozen!'[21] A chastened ministry let two Whig motions pass: one calling for further action on the Lorraine question, and another for an address to the Queen asking for a royal proclamation that would offer a cash reward to anyone who apprehended the Pretender 'dead or alive'.

The Queen was deeply disturbed by the latter proposal. James was, after all, her flesh and blood, and she found the idea of offering a reward for his dead body distasteful in the extreme. She called in wavering lords for personal interviews, expressing her disquiet. A few days later the ministry managed to get amendments passed leaving the timing of such a proclamation to the Queen, and limiting the reward to apprehending the Pretender alive. Even Anglesey voted for these amendments after a personal appeal from the Queen. Oxford then scored a victory by showing that the monies paid to the Jacobite Highland clans were to keep them quiet, not to ensure they were armed: it was, he pointed out, a practice begun by, of all people, Godolphin.

Momentum seemed to be slipping away from the Whigs, when another game-changing event threw everything back into the air. Senior Whigs met at Lord Halifax's where they were told that the Hanoverian court had been persuaded to ask their envoy to make a formal request to the Queen to move the writ calling the Electoral Prince, George's son, to take up his place in the Lords.

The government was in the most dreadful position. The Queen was livid: her intense and emotional opposition to any member of the Elector's family being invited to take up such a position, or even live in the country, while she was still alive, was proverbial. Oxford wrote to his brother next day:

> I never saw her Majesty so much moved in my life. She looked upon it as that she is treated with scorn and contempt, and she will not believe that he [the Hanoverian envoy] could have any orders for it.[22]

If, however, the government refused to move the writ, then it would give enormous currency to the idea that they opposed the Hanoverian succession and bolster their Whig and 'Whimsical' opponents hugely. They had no choice but to either mortify the Queen or alienate Hanover.

Bolingbroke decided to curry favour with the Queen, and indeed the Jacobite backbenchers whose support he was courting, by suggesting that she flatly refuse to move the writ. Most of the rest of the cabinet saw that this was very unwise politically and possibly illegal. Instead, a compromise was agreed on, whereby the Hanoverian envoy would be told he could collect the writ if he wished, but that if he did, the icy displeasure of the Queen would be incurred and a diplomatic brouhaha risked.

The political impact of the writ incident was instant. It convinced many Hanoverian Tories that, if Hanover were sufficiently worried to risk such a row, then the succession *must* be in peril. In the Lords, Wharton moved a motion for a new address to the Queen re-asserting the reasons for their deep apprehension about the succession. Court supporters began to shuffle uncomfortably. Support leaked away from the government. Several bishops defected. Even a necessitous Scottish lord went over. When the House divided, the vote was exactly even, sixty-one to sixty-one. It was only when the proxy votes were opened that the government squeaked home by two votes.

Meanwhile in the Commons, the writ incident had a similarly explosive effect. The Whigs, led by Walpole, were seeking to use the Hanoverian Tories' ebbing faith in the government to bring the entire government programme, including supply, to a standstill. A government that could not pay its creditors or pass basic financial bills would soon fall.

The government knew that it would have to stem the bleeding and try to restore confidence in the lower chamber. A similar motion, that the Hanoverian succession was not in danger, was moved in the Commons. It achieved the greatest turnout of any vote in Anne's reign: Tories had been whipped and rounded up from every obscure bucolic spot that graced England. The House heaved.

Walpole fired an opening shot, but then left the Tories to tear each other to pieces. Hanmer, in a 'more in sorrow than in anger' speech, darkly intimated that 'a great deal of Pains were taken to screen some Persons, and, in order to that, to make them overlook the Dangers that threaten'd the Queen, the Nation, and the Protestant Succession'.[23] It was a signal to his supporters to oppose the ministry, which they duly did. Jacobites and ministerialists bitterly returned fire upon their 'Whimsical' Tory brethren: the debate devolved into internecine Tory warfare. Ultimately, the government held on to win the debate by forty-eight votes, but a quarter of Tory MPs voted with the Whigs.

Many more victories like this, and the government would be ruined.

The Whigs appeared to have the government on the run. Chaos reigned as the government tried to shove through supply with both Houses volatile in the extreme. A tobacco tax bill was lost when a Tory MP went to the toilet at the wrong moment: the division was called as he relieved himself, and despite running through the corridors of parliament to vote, 'breeches in his hand', he didn't make it in time.[24] The vote was a dead heat, meaning the measure fell. A Place Bill fell in the Lords by one vote. The government grimly dug deep to eke out even a skeletal legislative haul.

However, the Whig momentum gradually dissipated, for several main reasons. Firstly, they simply began to run out of parliamentary road. They had tried everything, and the obvious issues had now been debated to death. The agenda moved on to less polarising, more banal topics. It was hard to sustain Hanoverian Tory anger on more routine matters. Gradually, the parliamentary logjam began to ease and the government, bit by bit, started to force through its financial business. Bolingbroke began to gain back some confidence. On 20th April he wrote to Matthew Prior:

> The Whigs have affronted the Queen, and teased her servants almost a month without control; at last a spirit has been exerted which should, in my poor opinion, have been sooner shown, and they have been defeated in all their attacks, though fortified by a considerable detachment from our own party.[25]

The second reason was that it gradually transpired that Oxford, by some neat diplomatic footwork, had persuaded Schütz, the Hanoverian envoy, not to activate the writ summoning the Prince Elector. Then the Queen forbade Schütz from court, and Oxford inveigled the Elector into recalling him altogether. An imperious letter from the Queen to Hanover made her white-hot fury clear. Hanover backed off and decided not to press the matter further – for now, at least. The Prince Elector, George, Duke of Cambridge, would not take his place in the Lords and provide the massive rallying point and morale booster that the Whigs wanted.

Oxford seemed for a while to reassert his control. It was not to last.

Although the Queen had stuck by Oxford in the cabinet row of mid-March, this had obscured some fundamental changes in her thinking. When she had nearly died at Christmas, some Whigs had made their jubilation fairly clear. Doubtless many were genuinely concerned for her health, but a minority at least had been positively gleeful. Lady Masham and Bolingbroke made great pains to impress this fact upon her, probably exaggerating it in the process. According to Jonathan Swift, this had affected a change in the Queen's political attitude:

> The result was, that the queen immediately laid aside all her schemes and visions of reconciling the two opposite interests; and entered upon a firm resolution of adhering to the old English principles, from an opinion that the adverse party waited impatiently for her death.[26]

In other words, an ailing Queen had become, more or less, a thorough-going Tory. This moved her rather closer to Bolingbroke. She still found him personally distasteful, but Oxford could no longer rely on her looking upon him as her faithful shield, protecting her from the 'merciless men of both parties'.[27]

The straw that broke the camel's back was, in fact, the question of Oxford's relations with Hanover. Around about the time of the writ incident, Bolingbroke dropped hints to the Queen that it was Oxford, in an attempt to gain favour with the Elector, who was responsible for persuading Hanover to demand the writ be moved. He spread rumours to this effect more widely, to galvanise his support among Jacobite MPs.

It was completely untrue – indeed it was Oxford who had done more than anyone to prevent the Prince Elector from entering the country. Whether the Queen took any notice immediately or not is unclear. Oxford attempted to counter the accusation and retain his hold on the Queen by insisting that, by virtue of his and his brother Thomas's exceptional influence at Hanover, only he could prevent any further attempts by the Elector to insult her by sending members of his family to England. For a while, this worked: it was practically the last hold Oxford had on the Queen.

Unfortunately for Oxford, although the Elector had agreed to drop the writ, he hadn't given up on the idea of sending one of his family members over to London in order to safeguard 'the security of her royal person, and for that of her kingdoms, and of the Protestant religion'.[28] As April ran into May, the Elector and Electress wrote a formal 'memorial', to be delivered to the Queen, demanding this, and a whole range of other 'securities' for their succession. Oxford did everything he could to prevent it being delivered, but it was in vain.

Whether or not she believed in Bolingbroke's insinuations about the original writ, the reception of the memorial shattered the whole basis for her continuing to depend on Oxford. He could not protect her from these Hanoverian insults. An extraordinarily hostile reply was sent back by Oxford on behalf of the Queen to Hanover telling them in no uncertain terms that no member of their family would be welcome in the Queen's lifetime. Shortly after, the ailing, ancient Electress, Sophia, deeply perturbed by this, died. In the niceties following this, the Elector – now the immediate heir – had the temerity to repeat his request. It sealed Oxford's fate. He would not yet be removed as Lord Treasurer, but his substantial influence with the Queen was at an end. His claims that he could tame Hanover had been exposed as empty bravado.

The Queen turned – slowly and haltingly – to Bolingbroke.

From now on, it was a fight to the political death between Harry and Robin. No more reconciliations, however insincere, were possible. As the Queen's health ebbed and flowed, both were in a race against time to implement their last, desperate gambits. The cost of failure was, potentially, their lives.

Oxford became increasingly convinced that Bolingbroke's scheme was, at bottom, a Jacobite one. He feared that his old rival, aided by Lady Masham's tender ministrations, might succeed in talking a very ailing Anne into favouring her half-brother. He did what he could to encourage the Queen to make some gesture to reassure those who feared for the Hanoverian succession, but it did him little good: as he remarked to Swift in mid-May, 'he found his credit [with the Queen] wholly at an end'.[29]

He could see only one option left. For the last time, he reverted to his oldest tactic: a turn to the Whigs. If he could convince them of his sincerity and come to a working arrangement with them and the Hanoverian Tories, he might be able to bring down Bolingbroke, or at least save his own neck once the Elector became king. He had always kept lines of communication open with Halifax, and had been trying to thaw relations with Cowper for some time. By early May he was reported to be meeting with the Whig big-wigs nightly. The question is: would they trust him any more than anyone else? Did the old political magician have any rabbits left to pull out of his parliamentary hat?

Bolingbroke could hardly complain that Oxford – and as May went on, just about everyone – was convinced that he had comprehensively turned Jacobite. His strategy had not changed: he would go all out to win over the Country Tories in parliament and attempt to use his growing influence with the Queen to appoint High Tories to every position in the army, government and Church. Given how many Jacobites there were on the Tory backbenches, to win control of the Commons he had to convince them of his sincerity, and in so doing he became indiscreet. One Tory MP observed that:

> In his private cabals, he gave hints and innuendos that the Kings [James's] restauration was much at this heart and wou'd be accomplisht, frequently diverting himself and others with jests and comical stories concerning the Elector of Hanover and his family.[30]

One imagines that, possibly after the consumption of too much burgundy, Bolingbroke got carried away with his Jacobite act, to the delight of the vehement backbench partisans of the Pretender. The problem is that these conversations were leaked. Everyone was convinced that he was in earnest.

Bolingbroke was in a bind. To gain control of the Commons, he had to play up to these Jacobites. In doing so, he was taking a great risk. If his strategy of entrenching Tories in total control of the state and accepting the Elector on his terms did not work, then his future looked dark. As dark as the gallows.

For his strategy to succeed, winning control in the Commons was not enough. Bolingbroke *had* to win over the Queen and remove Oxford as Lord Treasurer. Day by day he made halting progress. The Queen began to favour Bolingbroke's suggestions on patronage over Oxford's, and was clearly barely listening to an increasingly incoherent and sometimes tipsy Oxford. Lady Masham poured poison in her ear. But still the Queen hesitated about sacking Oxford altogether.

While Bolingbroke worked on the Queen, the division between him and Oxford began to spill out into parliament. The first test would be the question of arrears of pay still owed to Hanoverian mercenaries in British employ, who had refused to obey Ormonde in 1712 when they had been ordered to cease fighting. This was seen as an indirect test of loyalty to the Hanoverian succession. It was to be the first challenge to the new Oxford–Whig alliance.

The problem for Oxford was that the Whigs, led by Walpole, jumped the gun and called for a vote on the question before he had properly rallied his parliamentary supporters, a mixture of his personal and family friends and court placemen. Bolingbroke and his supporters had already agreed to block any attempt to pay the arrears. When pushed to a vote, although Oxford personally supported the motion, his own supporters had not been properly briefed and did not know what to do. They split, and the Hanoverian Tories – and indeed even some Whigs – were caught on the hop, many not present in the chamber. Bolingbroke won the vote by thirteen votes: it later transpired that thirteen members of the Whig 'Hanover Club' (a group convened especially to defend the Hanoverian succession) were absent.

The Whigs blamed Oxford for the failure and suspected that he was double-dealing them. It was not a good start, and an ominous speech by a Tory MP accusing the Elector of preferring 'his German interest and dominions to the interest and honour of Brittain' was seen as a sign that the Jacobites were growing in confidence.[31]

Soon, Bolingbroke decided to go on the offensive. His idea of uniting the Tories might have seemed an optimistic one, to put it mildly, but there was a solid basis for Tory unity on Church questions. If he could put himself at the head of an uncompromising pro-Church agenda, he might be able to draw the parliamentary Tory Party behind him. Even most of the Hanoverian Tories were good High Churchmen who were quite content to sock it to the Dissenters. He just needed to find the right rallying point.

The idea came from Atterbury. What vexed many churchmen as much as anything was the growth in Dissenting schools and academies. They were, claimed High Tories, 'nurseries of sedition', breeding and spreading Dissenting principles to the next generation, and they had begun to rise steeply in numbers since the Toleration Act. Only if a total Anglican monopoly on education were established could the menace be stopped. So Atterbury suggested what became the Schism Act. It meant that all teachers, at all levels, would have to be licensed by a diocesan bishop, and would have to have a certificate confirming that they were a regular communicant of the Church of England and would always conform to the Anglican liturgy. Any teacher with such a certificate who then attended a Dissenting service would be liable for imprisonment for three months. In essence, it would make it impossible for Dissenters to educate their children in anything but a Church of England school or academy. The idea was that, in the long term, as education is so important to the formation of young minds and souls, it would help to destroy Dissent altogether.[32]

This bill put Oxford in a terrible fix. He came from a Dissenting background himself and hated any idea of persecuting Dissenters. On the other hand, it gradually emerged that the Queen supported the Schism Bill, and so if he openly opposed it, it would alienate him further from Anne. It would also antagonise the Tory backbenchers, who were always suspicious of his links with Dissenters. It was, as Defoe remarked, intended as a 'mine to blow up the White Staff'.[33] Bolingbroke knew that it would not only unite the Tories behind him, but also dramatically embarrass Oxford.

The bill could hardly have been better calculated to serve Bolingbroke's interests. Hanoverian Tories who had been caballing with the Whigs over the succession wanted to prove their true-blue Tory principles. William

Bromley, who was still broadly aligned with Oxford, supported it: how could the leading lay churchman in the House of Commons and MP for Oxford University not? It was a master stroke.

There was little question of successful opposition to the bill in the Commons, dominated as it was by a huge Tory majority that on this question would barely be divided. It passed its third reading by 236 votes to 127, with Bromley making an impassioned harangue about the dangers of Dissent to Church and State. Whig pleas for tolerance were heard in stony silence by the vast mass of Tory squires. The real battle would be in the Lords, where Bolingbroke had less support and Oxford and the Whigs were stronger.

Wharton had tremendous fun in opposing this particular measure. Bolingbroke was not only as notoriously irreligious as Wharton himself, but he himself had actually been educated by Dissenters. Wharton played on this obvious weakness relentlessly. Whig journalist Abel Boyer recounted his bitingly ironic speech in some detail:

> He was agreeably surprized to see, that some Men of Pleasure [meaning Bolingbroke and his supporters] were, on a sudden, become so Religious, as to set up for Patrons of the Church: But he could not but wonder, that Persons who had been educated in Dissenting Academies, whom he could point at, and whose Tutors he could name, should appear the most forward in suppressing them. That this was but an indifferent Return for the Benefit the Publick had receiv'd from those Schools, which had bred those Great Men, who had made so glorious a Peace, and Treaties that executed themselves; who had obtain'd fo great Advantages for our Commerce, and who had paid the Publick Debts, without any further Charge to the Nation: So that he could see no Reason there was to suppress those Academies; unless it were an Apprehension that they might still produce greater Genius's, that should drown the Merits and Abilities of those Great Men.[34]

His wit did not, however, prevent the vast majority of Tory Lords — relieved at finally having a traditional party political issue to get their teeth into — from voting for it. It passed.

Nonetheless, Oxford was not completely beaten yet. The Whigs put down a series of amendments designed to take some of the sting out of the measure, and, in his usual secretive backstairs way, Oxford strained every nerve and sinew, in co-operation with the Whigs, to win over those Tories with whom he still retained some influence. The old master of parliamentary management wasn't beaten yet. He managed to winkle out just enough Tory votes on the amendments to help the Whigs win most of them. The bill was still formidable, but Oxford had eased it appreciably. He was then able to vote *for* the bill as amended, so as not to lose credit with the Queen.

Just for a time, the Trickster rolled back the years and showed a little of the old genius.

Oxford's rearguard action did not hide the fact that the passage of the Schism Act appeared to show that Bolingbroke was gaining ascendancy in parliament. However, Bolingbroke continued to face major problems. The Hanoverian Tories still suspected him of Jacobite tendencies and certainly did not trust him. The Queen herself, who was – contrary to what many Whigs and Jacobites had come to believe – no Jacobite, did not trust him on the succession issue either. Bolingbroke desperately needed to convince them that he was *really* a Hanoverian – which, in fact, he almost certainly was, albeit not out of any real principle. It would be hard task, given how hard he had courted the Jacobites only weeks before.

The means he chose to attempt this was to revive the question of the proposed royal proclamation offering a reward for the apprehension of the Pretender. Parliament had voted for it, but the Queen had reserved the question of its timing for her own judgement. Bolingbroke realised that he could now gain credit with both the Queen and the Hanoverian Tories by raising the issue and suggesting that it be enacted, with a reward attached of £5,000. He risked the wrath of the Jacobites, but he reasoned that he could have it both ways: tell the Jacobites that it was Oxford's idea, tell the Hanoverians that it was his, and gain credit with the Queen whatever the rest of them believed. Oxford would be unlikely to deny that it was his work, because it would help gain him credit with the Whigs.[35]

When this was announced, the Hanoverian Tories were delighted and, in concert with the Whigs, proposed to increase the reward to the enormous sum of £100,000, which was, despite some grumbling about extravagance, carried without a division. Bolingbroke followed this up by exploiting dark rumours that French officers had been discovered recruiting British subjects, presumably to serve in a Jacobite army (or so it was suspected). He proposed – successfully – to ban 'raising any forces in her Majesty's dominions for the Service of any Foreign Prince without her Majesty's own seal'.[36] His efforts to quash the idea that he was a Jacobite began to be noticed. He even appeared to have the support of Shrewsbury, the old Whig grandee, who had returned to England after a stint as Lord Lieutenant of Ireland.

The downside of this was that the Jacobite MPs suspected foul play on his part and decided to go rogue. There was certainly doubt about these pro-Hanover measures – many attributed the whole manoeuvre to Oxford, who eagerly attempted to gain credit for them – but at the very least, they reasoned, Bolingbroke must have failed to prevent them. Possibly he was scheming with Hanover. They canvassed various wild schemes of revenge, such as actually instituting a parliamentary invitation to the Elector *themselves*, just to spite Bolingbroke, but settled on a rather simple scheme: they would do everything they could to gum up parliament's financial business and throw the House into total confusion and stalemate; a task the Whigs would surely help them with. This would undermine Bolingbroke's control of the House.

So it was that a truly bizarre coalition of Whigs and Jacobites set the stage for Oxford's last throw of the parliamentary dice. By now, he had little object in mind but to destroy Bolingbroke and therefore prevent his rival from ousting him as Lord Treasurer. Day by day his stock was falling with the Queen, but he had one last ace up his sleeve, if only parliament could be spun out as long as possible to give him time to work his magic. As Dr Arbuthnot observed in a letter to Swift, 'the Dragon dy's hard. He is now kicking & cuffing about him like the divill. & you know parliamentary manaagement is his forte' (another longstanding nickname for Oxford was 'the Dragon').[37]

His plan centred around Bolingbroke's involvement in another treaty. When the main peace had been agreed, it had entailed not only a commercial treaty to agree terms of trade with France, but also one with Spain. This treaty settled all kinds of matters, not least the details of Britain's new role in monopolising the Assiento slave trade with South America. Oxford had suspected for some time that Bolingbroke and his friends had manipulated the treaty in some very shady ways.

A quarter of the profits of the Assiento trade were to go to the Queen directly, and Bolingbroke had then arranged that these funds would go, in part, to both himself and Lady Masham. This was one of the chief ways he had persuaded Masham to use her powers of persuasion with the Queen in his, not Oxford's, favour: in short, bribery. This had been bitterly resisted by the directors of the South Sea Company, who were relying on the profits of the Assiento to fund their operations. The issue was further clouded by suggestions that Bolingbroke's notoriously dodgy trade envoy, Arthur Moore, had attempted to manipulate the treaty to line his own pockets.

The Whig assault had begun in June, when they had managed to find a witness who testified that he had been offered a bribe by Moore to allow ships sailing under the official British concession to carry unauthorised goods, out of which Moore stood to make a personal profit. At this point, Bolingbroke decided to try to secure the Queen's agreement to surrender her quarter share of the Assiento profits: the hope was that such a concession would draw a line under the enquiries and prevent any further damage to his (and Masham's) reputation. She agreed, and Bolingbroke pinned his hope on this disarming his pursuers.

It was a vain hope. The Whigs smelt blood, and now Oxford agreed to pass them private documents and give them advice on where Bolingbroke's weak spots were. On 30th June, the Lords called for a full-scale enquiry. Evidence from trade commissioners, who could testify to Moore's corrupt dealings, was brought forward. On 2nd July, Oxford sought an audience with the Queen, where he told her that the damage likely to be done to Bolingbroke's reputation by continued investigation was so serious that she should sack him now. She refused.

Bolingbroke now became desperate. His only course was to try to end the parliamentary session as soon as humanly possible. The main thing holding this up was the passing of supply, and particularly a Lottery Bill. He begged the Jacobite MPs to stop their obstinate obstruction of the bill. He managed to convince them (or at least half convince them) that if parliament were prorogued, the Queen would be in a better position to secure the restoration of the Pretender. It was a complete lie, but the Lottery Bill began to move again. Time was running out for Oxford and the Whigs: once the Lottery Bill passed, the key business of the session would be over. There would be no time to pursue the Spanish trade enquiries.

Bolingbroke then managed to slow the momentum of the Whigs by making a strong case that the evidence against Moore was weak. Some of it was rather confused and contradictory. The smoking gun was not present. He began to win the votes against the Whigs in the Lords, but then spoiled it all with a stupid mistake. His arrogance got the better of him, and he drafted a reply on behalf of the Queen to a Lords address on Spanish trade that was needlessly dismissive and provocative. The mood turned against him and it looked like the gruesome details of the Spanish trade treaty might come out yet.

And then he breathed a sigh of relief. The Lottery Bill passed. His angel of deliverance came in the form of Black Rod knocking on the door. The Queen immediately prorogued. The parliamentary session was over. Just in time, he had been saved from possible censure or impeachment.

Bolingbroke had survived. For now.

The Whigs were convinced that, having ridden out this attack, Bolingbroke must now usurp Oxford, become Lord Treasurer, and establish a full-blown pro-Jacobite ministry. As parliament was prorogued, Stanhope cried in despair, 'I look upon our liberties as good as gone.'[38] Panic started to take over, and the idea that a civil war over the succession might be in the offing was taken seriously by many.

If there were a civil war, the Whigs hoped and assumed that Marlborough, who had been mouldering away on the continent in self-exile for the past few years, would return from the wilderness to deliver his country with the help of Dutch troops. This had been Marlborough's own plan for a while – he had cooked up several outlandish schemes earlier to destroy the Tory ministry and prevent the peace by means of invasion.[39] None of this had stopped him also negotiating with the Jacobite court for the purposes of reinsurance in case of a restoration – as Bolingbroke put it, 'It is hard for so old a gamester to leave off playing' (and he would know).[40]

As the tension built throughout 1714 and the Whigs became more and more convinced that a Jacobite restoration was on the cards, Marlborough desperately pushed the Dutch, Hanoverians and indeed the Habsburg Empire to help him prepare an invasion to drive out the Tory ministry and protect the Protestant succession by force. They would not agree to such a plan unless there was an actual Jacobite invasion on the death of the Queen. He also feverishly tried to persuade the Elector to send a member of his family to England to secure the succession: although George pushed the issue several times, he was not prepared to do anything unilaterally without Anne's permission, for fear of looking precipitous and provoking anti-Hanover sentiment.

So Marlborough decided that the best he could do was return to England to rally the Whigs politically. Oxford and Bolingbroke both concluded that their best bet was to try to cut a deal with their old adversary, whereby in exchange for securing the Hanoverian succession and restoring Marlborough to all his senior military offices, he would work with one of them to destroy the other.

Astonishing as it may seem given his recent campaign to destroy Marlborough, Oxford had been keeping this option in his locker for some time, forbearing to take impeachment proceedings against Marlborough any further and opening secret negotiations with Marlborough in April. But when Oxford claimed to the Whigs, in an attempt to ingratiate himself with them, that he had instigated the writ move, he little realised that Marlborough, through his own intelligence sources, knew that this was a lie.

Realising that Oxford was still as duplicitous as ever, on 1st July Marlborough dealt a mortal blow to Oxford's credit with the Whigs. Through Hanoverian contacts, he acquired copies of the letters that had been sent by Oxford (albeit on behalf of the Queen) that had made it absolutely clear that no member of George's family would be welcome in England in the Queen's lifetime. In early July, he arranged for them to be published in London. It became even clearer that Oxford had no influence at Hanover and had lied to the Whigs. Despite Oxford's attempts to help the Whigs over the Spanish trade treaty, the Whigs had learned, finally and totally, not to even contemplate trusting Oxford.[41]

Bolingbroke, on the other hand, had a lot more success with Marlborough. They had always had a personal rapport – indeed, Bolingbroke had been something of a protégé of Marlborough's when he was Secretary at War. Furthermore, Marlborough heartily detested Oxford, and when Oxford was discredited in early July, the choice became easy. So in mid-July, via Marlborough's 'man of business' James Craggs, Bolingbroke had concluded a deal whereby, on the death of the Queen, Marlborough would be restored to all of his previous offices, the Anglo-French Commercial Treaty would be ditched, and Bolingbroke would be reconciled to Hanover. A Hanover–Bolingbroke–Marlborough alliance would rule. Shrewsbury, who had unexpectedly defended Bolingbroke over the Spanish trade allegations and whom Bolingbroke had been cultivating for a long time, seemed to at least wink at the plan, if it became necessary.

This plan still depended on Bolingbroke being sufficiently well entrenched in office when the Queen died and the agreement of the Elector. If a Bolingbrokean Tory Party was sufficiently in control of the entirety of the state, it might become the path of least resistance for the Elector to simply rule through it. So it became a race for Bolingbroke to finally persuade the Queen to install him as Lord Treasurer and come up with some viable, united Tory ministry that might be acceptable to Hanover.

However, this was not to prove straightforward. The problems of a Bolingbroke regime were obvious. He just could not win over enough of the big-hitting Tories who would give a ministry run by him credibility. He had won over Tory military supremo Ormonde, and Harcourt, the leading lawyer of the Church Party, was his most consistent ally, but most of his other supporters were largely minor figures or wild backbenchers. He had tried to win over Hanmer: unsurprisingly, he had no luck. Bromley, Dartmouth, Buckingham: all were too suspicious of him. His support among the Church was nugatory: only two bishops, Atterbury and (possibly) John Robinson, the Bishop of London, supported him. His appeal was too narrow: it was hard for the man who had courted the hardcore Tory partisans and flirted with the Jacobites to present himself as the responsible statesman now. As one observer put it, 'the man of mercury's bottom is too narrow, his faults of the first magnitude'.[42]

It was, ultimately, a credibility problem. Bolingbroke had struggled to manage parliament in its last days: financial business had almost broken down in shambolic scenes. His ministry would be full of junior nobodies with no experience of government. The whiff of scandal over the Spanish trade treaty only compounded general fears that he was a man of highly questionable character. Could a solid Church Party administration *really* be based on a womanising free-thinker who constantly had his hand in the till?

The Queen, always reluctant to make any drastic decision, still couldn't bring herself to trust Bolingbroke. She hummed and hawed. The days of July slipped by, each one a bitter blow to Bolingbroke's chances. Oxford made desperate attempts in personal audiences to stave off a Bolingbroke ministry, and rumours started to fly about that the Queen was shifting back to him. At one point, frustrated and tense, Lady Masham lost her temper completely, screaming, 'you never did the Queen any service, nor are you capable of doing her any!' in Oxford's face.[43] The Queen appeared to be heartily sick of both the rivals for power, complaining to her doctor that 'they had neither regarded her Health, her Life, nor her Peace'.[44]

But then something snapped. On 19th July, Bolingbroke desperately called his chief supporter Harcourt back from the country, as the time was apparently very close. What finally caused Anne to take the plunge was not clear. It may have been that Bolingbroke started to push a plan where the Treasury would be put into commission, meaning that he would not be Lord Treasurer, but instead sort of de facto political leader of the administration in parliament. The Queen – probably not hugely keen on trusting Bolingbroke with the financial affairs of the nation after recent revelations – may have been more amenable to that. There was a rumour that some detail of Oxford's apparent negligence with regard to Irish affairs had come to light. The Queen made it clear that Oxford's days were numbered: on Friday 23rd July, he went into the Treasury to sort out any last matters of business.

On Saturday 24th, the (rather lacklustre) names of Bolingbroke's proposed Treasury commission were openly being discussed in the coffee-houses. Oxford, who, amazingly, had been still working with Bolingbroke and his allies on official business with apparent calm up until that moment, finally lost his nerve. His friend Erasmus Lewis wrote to Swift:

> I had intelligence that the Dragon has broke out into a fiery passion with my Lord Ch. [Harcourt]—sworn a thousand oaths that he w'd be reveng'd, &c. this impotent womanish behaviour vexes me more than his being out.[45]

Up until the end, Oxford did everything he could to find excuses not to have to travel to Kensington Palace to bear the inevitable blow, but on the morning of 27th July, he received a direct order to attend the palace. At 2 p.m., he held a short audience with the Queen, who told him of his dismissal, and asked him to return that evening to give up the white staff in person. In the meantime, a cabinet was held without Oxford there, at which the Queen gave her reasons for dismissing him:

> the Q. has told all the Lords the reasons of her parting with him, viz. that he neglected all business, that he was seldom to be understood, that when he did explain himself, she could not depend upon the truth of what he said; that he never came to her at the time she appointed, that he often came drunk, that lastly to crown all he behav'd himself towards her with ill manner indecency & disrespect.[46]

At somewhere between 8 and 9 p.m., he arrived back at the royal palaces, having composed a brief epitaph on his ministry 'in imitation of Dryden' in the carriage there. It read:

> To serve with love
> And shed your Blood
> Approved is above
>
> But heer Below
> The Examples shew
> tis fatal to be Good[47]

He gave up the white staff, and stayed in conference with the Queen for forty-five minutes while he did so. On his way out, he ran into Lady Masham and Harcourt and saw red. He broke into an angry rant about how their 'lies and misrepresentations' had bought him down, before rounding on Harcourt, his old protégé turned follower of Bolingbroke:

> My Lord, I found you a poor rascall, and by my means you became rich and great, but by God, I'll never leave you till I make you again what you was at first. I go out an honest man, but you stay in a rogue.[48]

By the time all of this happened, the Queen had already become increasingly sick and mentally agitated. Another cabinet was held after her audience with Oxford. There was no agreement on Bolingbroke's proposed Treasury commission, a curious hodge-podge of Jacobites and Hanoverian Tories. The Queen would definitely not make Bolingbroke Lord Treasurer. The meeting broke up inconclusively at 2 a.m. A bitterly depressed Queen spent the night weeping to herself.

The next day saw no agreement on a new government. Marlborough was known to be waiting to cross to England from Ostend (winds delayed him). In his last audience with the Queen, Oxford is reported to have warned her *against* Marlborough, telling her not to trust him. Was it possible that the Queen, unable to stomach Bolingbroke, was stalling so as to appoint a government under the leadership of her old stay and support Marlborough?[49]

Any new government seemed increasingly unlikely to be under the meaningful leadership of Bolingbroke. The reality was that the Tories were as divided as ever and Bolingbroke had no viable alternative ministry to offer. In desperation he arranged dinner with leading Whigs and Whig-inclined generals, who were flabbergasted to be invited but accepted. As his guests sat in a mixture of embarrassment and incredulity, Bolingbroke professed his undying loyalty to the Hanoverian succession. It seems likely that Bolingbroke realised that his only hope now was a deal between himself, the Whigs and Marlborough, and hoped to at least offer feelers for this.

James Stanhope, the young Whig military hero and rising parliamentary hope, was having none of it. His words were blunt:

> Harry! You have only two ways of escaping the gallows. The first is to join the honest party of the Whigs, the other to give yourself up entirely to the French King and seek his help for the Pretender. If you do not choose the first course, we can only imagine that you have decided for the second.[50]

Bolingbroke's real preference — an alliance between the Elector, Marlborough and a unified and dug-in Tory Party — was a busted flush. Neither Hanover nor Marlborough would have the slightest need for him as it stood, and coming out openly for the Whigs, as Stanhope suggested, would destroy him within his own Tory powerbase. The Jacobite option was totally futile. He had nowhere to turn.

And time was running out. On Friday 30th July, he had plans to suggest another Treasury commission, but that morning, as the lords of the committee (what the cabinet was called when the Queen wasn't present) were just about to meet, dire reports were received of the Queen's health. The strain of recent tumults had broken her. She had had a fit, and lay 'speechless, motionless, and unsensible'.[51] They all rushed to Kensington to attend to her.[52]

They instantly realised that she was dying. The doctors were unequivocal. She did recover consciousness, sporadically, not long after, but she could barely speak much more than to say the odd word. One account suggests that she did ask for the Duke of Marlborough, but mostly all she said was 'yes' and 'no'.[53]

The ministers realised that they must appoint a new Lord Treasurer, as if they didn't, under the Regency Act, which determined what should happen on her death in order to protect the Hanoverian succession, Oxford would still be deemed to be the Lord Treasurer and would be one of the regents appointed to oversee the process. Everyone knew that the Privy Council, the constitutionally correct body to proclaim Anne's successor, must be convened almost immediately. This wider body, which by now had little day-to-day function, contained many Whigs. Given this, there was no point picking someone unacceptable to the Whigs at this point, and Bolingbroke and his allies did not want Oxford involved any more than strictly necessary. The best that Harcourt could suggest was Shrewsbury, a moderate Whig of impeccable Hanoverian credentials. Everyone agreed to this, and the Queen, in her last official act, her hand steadied by Harcourt, handed the white staff to Shrewsbury.

Soon Whigs – the dukes of Somerset and Argyll prominent among them – streamed in to take their place on the Privy Council. Power was visibly slipping away from the Tories and to the Whigs. Bolingbroke could do nothing except tamely go along with making preparations to secure the Hanoverian succession under what were, in practice if not yet officially, Whig auspices: the fleet was put on a war footing; the London militia raised; the ports closed; orders issued to lord lieutenants to disarm any known Roman Catholics; a messenger was sent to the Elector of Hanover to prepare him to make haste to claim his throne.

As it happened, these furious preparations and elaborate precautions were unnecessary. The Pretender, having been promised so many times that his restoration would be secured by waiting and trusting to various Tory leaders, had made no military preparations. His trust had been misplaced, as neither Oxford nor Bolingbroke had been sincere in their promises. The accession of George, Elector of Hanover, was a total certainty, and as Oxford and Bolingbroke had spent far more time destroying each other than entrenching the Tories' civil, ecclesiastical and military power, he would come to power with no earthly need to trust in a political party that had thoroughly alienated him, was broken and disunited, and contained a significant number of backbenchers pledged to his rival, the Pretender. These grim truths must surely have crowded in upon the thoughts of Henry St John, Viscount Bolingbroke, as he watched the starting gun being fired on his political, and possibly bodily, doom.

And meanwhile, a woman lay dying.

She gradually lost consciousness completely. Her doctors asked members of the Privy Council to come and pray at her bedside. Whigs and Tories temporarily paused hostilities as they knelt together in supplication on behalf of the stubborn, dutiful, pious sovereign under whom they had served for so many years.

At 7.45 a.m. on the morning of Sunday 1st August, Queen Anne was finally released from her mortal troubles and went to meet her maker. She was forty-nine years old.

Bolingbroke tried to strike a note of detached stoicism in the face of the ironies of his downfall. A few days later he wrote to his old friend Jonathan Swift:

> The earl of Oxford was removed on Tuesday; the queen died on Sunday. What a world is this! and how does fortune banter us.[54]

This attempt at philosophy could not hide the reality. For though he might clutch at straws and hope for redemption for a while, in his heart of hearts Bolingbroke knew the truth.

The battle was over.

The Whigs had won.

Conclusion

On the night of Saturday 26th March 1715, Viscount Bolingbroke went to see a play at the Drury Lane theatre. Despite rumours that the new Whig ministry was preparing evidence against him for an impeachment, to all observers he appeared calm, even unconcerned. He affected total sangfroid. He occupied a box and booked the same box for the next evening's performance. He even gave money towards a subscription for a new opera that was being planned. It was a characteristically nonchalant show of public defiance.[1]

Early next morning, he hurriedly dressed in a 'plain surtout and black bob-wig'.[2] He and one of the French government's messengers – Monsieur La Vigne – then rode as fast as a carriage could take them to Dover. Everyone assumed that Bolingbroke was La Vigne's valet. The pair met an old acquaintance of Bolingbroke's from the army, Captain Morgan, at the Dolphin Inn. 'Affecting a clownish air', the three men then embarked on a boat previously chartered by Morgan. Bolingbroke made sure to cover his face as he clambered aboard.[3]

By 6 p.m. on Sunday evening, Bolingbroke was at Calais. By July of that year, the Pretender had given him an 'earldom' and made him the Secretary of State in his government in exile. The Whigs rejoiced in this confirmation of his perfidy: of course, they said, he had been a Jacobite all along.

What had happened?

* * *

When the Elector of Hanover acceded to the throne and became George I, it was obvious that he would favour the Whigs. Although at first he expressed his desire – not unlike his two predecessors – to choose the best men regardless of party, it is highly likely that he always intended to lean heavily to the Whigs, for he had obvious reasons to be suspicious of the Tory Party. They had seriously displeased him over their support for a peace which, in his eyes, had betrayed the allies and undermined his own interests. As a Lutheran, he was no friend to what he saw as extremist Anglican intolerance towards Dissenters. He feared their Jacobite wing. The Whigs were his obvious natural preference given their unambiguous support for his accession and opposition to the peace.[4]

However, like William III, he wasn't keen to be a mere cat's paw of hubristic and domineering Whig lords, and he was aware that he could hardly ignore the Church interest that the Tories represented altogether. In the short term, George knew that a good chunk of the Church Party had backed the interests of Hanover with vigour and there were some capable, moderate Tories. He hoped to include some of them in a new ministry.

Oxford and Bolingbroke, the personal authors of the objectionable peace, whom he suspected had both been agitating for a Jacobite restoration, were a different matter. George particularly distrusted the double-talk and bluster of Oxford. Neither had any chance of office; indeed, both would be lucky to live for much longer.

Men like Sir Thomas Hanmer and William Bromley, however, were well-known to be loyal to Hanover, experienced and widely respected in the House. George did indeed offer them government positions. They refused, saying that they would only serve in a properly balanced administration in which the Tories got 50 per cent of the places. This was, in the circumstances, clearly unrealistic, a futile gesture of party loyalty. The only Tory who accepted office was Nottingham, who was now thoroughly alienated from his party, so heartily did most Tories despise him for what they saw as his treachery.

At this point, the Tories were down, but all was not necessarily lost. Perhaps George would find the Whigs too imperious and mighty and, in due course, wish to balance them out or even replace them altogether. Bad as things looked, the Tories were not *necessarily* doomed to be indefinitely in the wilderness at this point.

However, various factors soon conspired to destroy the Tories' chances of ever being realistic competitors for actual power with the Whigs in the era of Hanover.

One obvious problem was a hopeless lack of leadership. They had long since been a fissiparous party with seemingly infinite capacity to fall out and fragment. The only two men who had gone any way (albeit very imperfectly) to solving this problem in the reign of Queen Anne were Oxford and Bolingbroke, who were both out of the equation.

One obvious candidate – Hanmer – had little chance of uniting the party. His co-operation with the Whigs over the succession issue had made him and his supporters very unpopular in many quarters of the Tory Party, and not just among open Jacobites. The obvious man for the job was Bromley, who was able to retain credibility both with most of his party and George I, and he was as close as the Tories got to an effective leader in the aftermath of the Queen's death. Bromley, however, had, over the past four years, increasingly become an agent of Oxford, and struggled to assert himself without Oxford's presence. He was liked and respected, but not the forceful leader required.

Whoever had led them would have been fatally encumbered, however, by two other, related factors.

First was the simple fact that the Tories were a disunited party easily tarred as Jacobites, and events made this an ever greater problem. The second was the brutal determination of the Whigs to monopolise power and ensure that George I ruled through them.

These facts were soon to become very clear.

The refusal of the Hanoverian Tories to serve in the new ministry made things simple for the new king. Soon a predominantly Whig ministry was formed, albeit under no clear single leader.[5]

This new government heralded a changing of the guard for the Whigs. The old Junto lords – particularly Wharton, Halifax and Somers – were on their way out. Somers had been in poor health for a long time, but the others soon followed: all three were dead by 1716, worn out by the struggles of the previous decades. New men were rising through the ranks to dominate the Whig leadership – eloquent and dashing James Stanhope; wily and forceful Robert Walpole and his fellow Norfolk landowner Charles Townshend; and the youngest, most vigorous member of the Junto, Sunderland.

Fissures of disunity were soon to emerge among these men, but in the short term, they were all heartily agreed on the need to wreak vengeance on Oxford and Bolingbroke. Wharton had not been joking when he mimed cutting their throats during the peace preliminaries debate in 1711. Walpole remembered having been locked in the Tower of London not so long ago. No one had forgotten Tory cries for blood when the boot had been on the other foot.

First, they needed a general election to secure a more sympathetic parliament for such prosecutions. Tories placed high hopes on these elections as a way of halting the Whig juggernaut, but this was wildly overoptimistic: George I and the Whigs threw the kitchen sink at the election. Every resource of state patronage was mobilised to purge every Tory office holder: barely a Tory sheriff, lord lieutenant, military officer, revenue office holder or any other official was left standing. The resources of the Treasury were fully mobilised on behalf of Whig candidates. Whereas Godolphin and Oxford had always restrained such efforts to some degree, now there were no compunctions: the government would win this election, come what may. By December 1714, one observer claimed that 'hardly one Tory is left in any place, though never so mean a one'.[6]

Unsurprisingly, these machinations had their predictable effect. It says something about the lingering popularity of the Tories in the country that they did as well as they did: they won 217 seats to the Whigs' 341, but after petitions were decided in their usual madly partisan style, the numbers were 186 to 372. For the first time ever, the Tories were at the receiving end of an unambiguous Whig landslide.

Now the Whigs went on the offensive. The papers of Lord Strafford, one of the Tory diplomats who negotiated the Treaty of Utrecht, were seized. The aim was to comb through every last scrap of paper to find evidence that leading Tories – especially Oxford, Bolingbroke, Ormonde and Strafford – had conducted treasonable correspondence with the French and/or the Jacobites.

When Bolingbroke heard that the papers of Matthew Prior, who had conducted the early, secret part of the negotiations with France over the peace, had been seized, he started to panic. Was there a smoking gun? There had been so many furtive negotiations and correspondences, so many papers that could at least be construed in a sinister sense, that he could not be sure. He sensed the mood in Westminster among the Whigs, who were acting like a pack of hungry hounds, led by Walpole, the master of the hunt. He decided he had no option but to flee.

This was a colossal mistake. The fury of the Whigs and George was actually more concentrated on Oxford, and all sorts of political manoeuvrings and deals might have been done. More importantly, everyone took his flight as evidence of his guilt. He wrote to a friend from Paris to try to defend his conduct:

> You will excuse me, when you know that I had certain and repeated informations, from some who are in the secret of affairs, that a resolution was taken by those who have power to execute it, to pursue me to the scaffold.[7]

He went on to claim that he could not 'hope for a fair and open trial' for political reasons, and resoundingly claimed that he 'served her majesty faithfully and dutifully' and was 'too much an Englishman, to sacrifice the interest of my country to any foreign ally'.[8] He was no Jacobite.

If this steadied Tory nerves, then Bolingbroke was soon to make an even bigger error that shook the Church Party to its foundations.

In June, Walpole had announced that Bolingbroke was to be impeached on charges of high treason. It was clear that members of the previous Tory administration were going to be proscribed from office indefinitely under the new king. Bolingbroke was ambitious and impatient, and decided that his only hope for ever returning to political office was a Jacobite restoration. He therefore made a decision he would come to regret for the rest of his long life. He defected to the Pretender. He was not alone: the Duke of Ormonde, also impeached and vulnerable because of his role in the restraining orders incident, followed suit.

Meanwhile, Oxford had stayed, calm and stoical as ever, to face his accusers. He faced sixteen articles of impeachment, mostly relating to supposed maladministration or treachery relating to the peace deal, although later six further ones were brought forward that accused him of working in secret for the Pretender. He defended himself ably and with dignity, despite being confined to the Tower of London while the impeachment proceedings dragged on, where he fell severely ill, wracked by arthritis, rheumatism and flu, and was treated harshly by his jailer. His brother remarked:

> I must say that, notwithstanding the great pains and indisposition my Lord was under during the greatest part of his imprisonment, I never observed that either his pains or imprisonment deprived him of the sereneness and composure of his mind.[9]

When he started to recover from his illness, he consoled himself by reading Cassius Dio's Greek history of Rome, no doubt finding solace in the trials suffered by many a beleaguered ancient patriot.[10]

While in prison, Oxford heard news of the 1715 Jacobite uprising, which in fact delayed the completion of impeachment proceedings. It was this, combined with the defections of Bolingbroke and Ormonde to the Jacobite camp, that really destroyed the Tories as a governing political force.

There was no doubt that George I was not popular on his accession. It was widely rumoured that, when the news of Queen Anne's death was announced, he was hoeing turnips, and he was continually mocked thereafter for being a turnip-like bucolic mediocrity.[11] He was also ridiculed for his supposed mistress (actually his half-sister) being so enormous that she was nicknamed 'the Elephant and Castle'. Jacobites made bitter jokes about beds collapsing under their combined weight.[12] His actual mistress was scrawny and mocked as 'the Maypole'.[13] George was also widely (and correctly) supposed to be a cuckold.

However, the bigger problem was that he was German, and many suspected that, just as William III had, in their view, favoured his Dutch homeland over England, George would use his new country to advance Hanoverian interests over British ones – indeed, even some of the Whigs were wary about this. Although he communicated to his own ministers perfectly well (in French), he neither liked nor was very proficient at speaking English, which did not endear him to his new nation. His Lutheranism hardly fitted obviously into the English religious divide, but he was widely seen as effectively a Dissenter. Even many of those who were strongly for the Hanoverian succession saw him as being merely the best of two unattractive options.

Accordingly, on his accession there was considerable unrest. The same crowds that had cheered on Sacheverell and cried 'the Church in danger' in 1710 showed similar signs of fury at George's accession, and, particularly, his coronation. On the day he was crowned, there were riots in around twenty-two provincial towns protesting against his accession. The wilder elements of Tory England made their feelings known.[14] A crowd in Bristol bellowed 'Sacheverell and Ormonde, and damn all foreigners!', and in Birmingham they shouted 'Kill the old Rogue [George], Kill them all, Sacheverell forever'.[15] A few Dissenting chapels were attacked, and in Bedford 'the maypole was put in mourning on coronation day, and remained so for almost a month'.[16] Many members of the Tory gentry made their lack of enthusiasm for the coronation celebrations clear, and even supported the rioters. They feared an authoritarian anti-Church administration ruled by Dissenters and even mad 'Roundheads': the anti-Tory purges that had recently begun inspired fear in many. The Whigs quickly proved that their concern for the liberties of the subject went only so far: they passed the Riot Act, soon to be followed by the suspension of habeas corpus.

These signs of discontent were eagerly seized upon by the Jacobite court as evidence that the time was ripe for an uprising. Ormonde had in fact been arranging one in the west of England before he fled to France. It was decided that, with the new king not securely settled and signs of disaffection in the country, the time was ripe: as the Pretender himself famously put it, 'now more than ever, Now or Never!'

'The Fifteen' was a fiasco. The Highland clans rose up in arms and the Pretender landed in person to rally the cause, but the death of Louis XIV meant that no French help was forthcoming. Most of England did not rise, as the Jacobites had mistaken widespread disaffection with the government with something rather different: widespread willingness to risk life and limb for the Stuart cause. The Scots fought bravely, but there was hardly any question about the outcome.

All of these events had left the Tories indelibly marked with the brand of Jacobitism. The extent to which many leading Tories were actively involved in 'the Fifteen' is not really clear, but William Wyndham, a leading ex-minister and supporter of Bolingbroke, was clearly implicated and arrested, as were various other Tory peers and MPs.[17] A series of further botched plots over the next six years, including the 1722 plot led by Francis Atterbury, which led to him fleeing to the court of the Pretender, merely confirmed the impression, and the Whigs ruthlessly exploited the connection between Jacobitism and Toryism to utterly cement their power. They passed the Septennial Act in 1716, which extended the period between elections from three to seven years: it was designed to give stability and breathing space to the new Whig regime. Even Nottingham was dismissed in February 1716. The Whigs couldn't even be bothered to move forward with the impeachment against Oxford, who mouldered away in the Tower for two years.

It is true that in the years between 1715 and 1722, the Whigs were not free from divisions themselves, and this did give the Tories some minor room to exert influence. Ambitious young Whigs starved of office for years were greedy for power and prepared to fight to get it. They were also conscious that they no longer faced any serious challenge for power from the Tories, and so had the luxury of engaging in such quarrels. In addition, for years matters of Whig principle had hardly been canvassed: the need to unite to oppose the peace and support the Protestant succession was so obvious that any underlying disagreements were subsumed in the struggle.[18]

Soon, however, splits emerged. George I's desire to ally with France and drag Britain into the Great Northern War in order to support Hanoverian military action against Sweden in the Baltic was bitterly opposed by Walpole and Townshend, who argued that it was in effect a Tory pro-French foreign policy. They darkly muttered about the baleful influence of the King's German favourites. Stanhope and Sunderland supported the King's foreign policy. The Whigs broke into factions, Walpole and Townshend were sacked, and the two factions started to fight each other in parliament. The dissident Whigs made a bid for the support of the King's son, the Prince of Wales, who set up something of an opposition court.

This had the slightly unexpected result of saving Oxford's bacon. Both Whig factions started to bid for Tory support against the other, and ironically, Walpole – the man whom Oxford's administration had locked in the Tower in 1712 – did a deal by which he would drop the impeachment of Oxford in exchange for Tory support in parliament. Oxford's plight was over. His neck was safe.

Oxford was to play no more significant part in politics. He occasionally dabbled, but he'd had more than his fill of public life. He spent most of his retirement augmenting his immense library by collecting more books and manuscripts, idling with his literary friends Swift and Pope, and sorting his family affairs. His health slowly declined and he died in 1724.

By 1714, Oxford was widely despised. The great tactician, the man who had made an intricate form of late Stuart 3D political chess into something of an art form, had, in the end, run out of road. His reputation for untrustworthiness and double-dealing finally undid him.

However, the simple fact was that the forces that assailed him were so great, his position so difficult, that probably no one else could have held things together for as long as he did. That he managed the Tory Party as deftly as he did, and held them together long enough to pass a peace which, although much assailed by the Whigs, in fact proved both enduring and manifestly in Britain's geopolitical interests, was something of a miracle. There was no doubt that by the end he had become almost addicted to intrigue and subterfuge, but his sense of duty to the public good can hardly be questioned, and although politically duplicitous, paradoxically he was, by the standards of his age, remarkably incorrupt: his trickery was never (except perhaps in the case of his son's marriage) to the end of his personal enrichment. His friends could say to him with some conviction, as he reached the end of his long and winding career: 'Well done, thou good and faithful servant.'

The Whig schism that saved Oxford was not to last. The two Whig factions both made bids for Tory support, and, from 1717 until 1720, it did give the Tories some limited influence. They sided with Walpole to limit Whig attacks on the privileges of the Church, staving off an attempt by Sunderland to effectively nullify the Test and Corporation Acts (although both the Occasional Conformity and Schism Acts were repealed). They also combined with Walpole to defeat the Peerage Bill, which would have limited the creation of new peers. It was seen as a dangerous bit of constitutional tinkering that was really intended to cement Sunderland and Stanhope's control of the upper house. After this defeat, Sunderland even put out feelers to the Tories to come into government, to neutralise the Walpole–Tory coalition in parliament. Once again no Tory would agree to come individually, only as a bloc in a truly mixed ministry. It was probably never a realistic outcome.

If the Tories thought that this period presaged a new era of Tory influence, they were soon disabused of the notion. In 1720, the Whigs healed their divisions and Walpole and Townshend were reconciled to the ministry. And then Walpole used multiple crises to cement a grip on power that would last for twenty years.

In 1720, the South Sea Bubble stunned the political world. The original purpose of the South Sea Company, as set up by Oxford, had been gradually altered. The Spanish trade on which it was predicated had not emerged on any scale, and had been halted in 1718 by a short war with Spain. In response, it changed direction, and an ambitious plan to effectively 'privatise' and deregulate the company and then let it take over much of the national debt emerged. This led to a splurge of speculation as the directors made extravagant claims about the opportunities for new trade in the Americas and investors, including many politicians (from both sides), hurriedly bought up shares. But it was an empty promise, and in autumn 1720 the bubble burst, with dire consequence for private investors and public finances.

Walpole, who had been developing a reputation for being something of a financial wizard for some time and had been critical of aspects of the company reform plan, was brought in to save the situation. He steadied the ship, came up with a scheme to restructure the national debt and restored confidence in the public finances. His (and the country's) stock rose, while Sunderland and Stanhope bore the brunt of the frenzy of public ire over the fiasco. Walpole's vigorous action to check the Atterbury Plot also helped secure a reputation as a competent, steadying figure. By 1722, he had become the unquestionable head of the government and the Whig Party.

Walpole brought a political stability that the country had not seen for a very long time. His methods were not pretty. He systematised and expanded the judicious use of patronage, bribery and corruption in order to cement the dominance of himself and his party. He was a brilliant political manager, conscious always of his need to heed the complaints of the landed country gentlemen who made up the bulk of the Commons and manipulate and placate them carefully. His canny financial management and determination to avoid, if at all possible, British involvement in war helped him to maintain (mostly) a moderate agenda of peace and low taxes that proved popular with the political nation.

In 1723, Bolingbroke, who had abandoned the Jacobites in disgust at their incompetence and hopelessness, was allowed, through machinations involving the King's mistress, to return and eventually recover his estates. Walpole would never allow him to take his place in parliament, but that didn't stop him becoming a major rallying point for opposition. He was one of the powers behind the throne of the Tory Party, spending much of his time attempting to forge various alliances between the Tories and 'Patriot' Country Whigs who were also suspicious of Walpole's corrupt methods (or at least claimed to be while in opposition).

He agitated against Walpole in his *Craftsman* journal, but neither he nor the Tory–Patriot Whig alliance ever got very far. They raged and moaned about what became known as 'Robinocracy', decrying the decline of public spirit, the corruption of the constitution and the rule of stockjobbers and boroughmongers. The closest they ever got to bringing down Walpole was during the Excise Crisis in 1733, when Walpole made a rare misstep in his political judgement – but they failed. Bolingbroke, still brilliant, still deeply flawed, became a European man of letters, but never got near power again, his ambitions fatally damaged by that fateful trip to Dover in March 1715.

Fundamentally, the Tory Party had become a party of perpetual opposition. There has been much debate between historians about the extent to which they were infiltrated by Jacobites and thereby reduced to a no-hope scrag end of a party.[19] It is true that they remained a not inconsiderable social and political force until at least the 1740s, at a stretch the 1750s. Some of the more ambitious Tories defected to the Whig Party, but by no means all. The Tory Party continued to return MPs, retained a variable but sometimes impressive parliamentary and constituency organisation, and clearly still represented an important segment of the population. The extent of Jacobite infiltration will, in light of the paucity of the evidence, always remain uncertain, but it seems fair to say that they were not *simply* the parliamentary wing of the Jacobites. Nonetheless, while the Pretender, and then Bonnie Prince Charlie, were still around to press the Stuart claim (however forlornly), the taint of Jacobitism remained radioactive for their chances of ever being a major governing party again. Gradually, almost imperceptibly at first, they withered. By the mid-1740s, a new generation of Whig magnates were in charge, and the Forty-five Jacobite rebellion put the last nails into the coffin of whatever remained of the Tory Party. Gradually, the Tory Party ceased to function as anything like a meaningful political force at any level.

By the time that George III became king in 1760, the Tories were, to all intents and purposes, finally dead.

Politics from then on was simply a question of what flavour of Whig one happened to be.

What, then, was the meaning of the fierce party battle that was conceived in the aftermath of the feverish fantasies of Titus Oates, came into existence during the struggles of the Exclusion Crisis, was transformed by the Glorious Revolution and the reign of William III, and came to a rambunctious, scintillating climax during the reign of Queen Anne? What long-term effects did it have? Why did the Whigs win, and was it inevitable that they would do? What was the afterglow of those fiery years? What lasting difference did it make?

One might wonder whether it all meant very much at all, except insofar as a fight for patronage and preferment among elites means anything of consequence. It is easy to forget that Whigs and Tories had, for all the partisan fireworks, much in common. They were both part of a landed elite who had, in many respects, similar political attitudes: they all wanted property to be safe, to be governed by a constitutional system balancing the rights of monarchy, Lords and Commons, and to retain some limited, albeit meaningful, rights and liberties for the subject. Even when it came to religion, for all that the Whigs were seen as the party of the Dissenters and the Whigs jibed that the Tories were 'Church papists', in fact the mainstream of both parties was fundamentally Anglican. Both accepted, except on their fringes and with varying degrees of enthusiasm, a significant if incomplete level of religious toleration.

When it comes to the leaders of the parties, one might argue that the differences were even smaller. Between 1702 and 1712, Britain funded and organised an almighty war effort that necessitated big increases in taxation and debt, the maintenance of a huge army and the continued development of an increasingly complex financial system. For much of that time, this was achieved by governments containing both Whigs and Tories. The two men who principally sustained this effort in terms of domestic politics were Godolphin (a Tory turned nominal Tory turned de facto Whig) and Oxford (a Whig turned Country Whig turned reluctant and highly ambiguous 'Tory'). Political leaders of both sides participated in what was often, at the underlying level of material and 'practical' politics, something of a policy consensus.

This case is not without merit. It is not, however, the whole story. The Tories only really had one leader after the Glorious Revolution who was able to manage (at least to some extent) the new realities of massive government debt, war and religious diversity. That was Oxford, and in some sense he always remained, at heart, an eccentric sort of Whig. Excepting the court Tories, who were usually little more than government placemen, the vast majority of the Tory Party, particularly in the country but also to a large extent in parliament, remained ill at ease with the transformations that had been ushered in by the Glorious Revolution, and were often frankly ill-disposed towards the task of managing them.

The Tories had supported the Glorious Revolution for one reason and one reason only: the threat that a papist king posed to the Church of England. They had been comfortable with the latter years of Charles II, when he ruled without parliament but firmly in the Church interest. The majority of Tories in the country – the bulk of the gentry, elements of the aristocracy who had remained loyal to the Cavalier cause during the Civil War, a large majority of the clergy – stood, fundamentally, for the old ways: a social and economic hierarchy based upon the prestige and authority of the Church, the monarchy and the landed gentlemen. There is no reason to think they would have countenanced any change in that status quo were it not for the fact that a Roman Catholic monarch made it impossible to maintain.

The importance of the Glorious Revolution was not mainly a question of its direct constitutional implications. It was, fundamentally and in a formal sense, a constitutionally conservative event that merely settled some legitimately contested points in favour of parliament and against any idea of overweening monarchical power. In general, the Tories adapted their constitutional theories to the 1689 settlement surprisingly adroitly. It was really important for two reasons. Firstly, it ended, albeit gradually and with many caveats, the Anglican religious, social and political monopoly. Secondly, by elevating the status and power of parliament, it laid down the conditions for a financial revolution that ended in the creation of a national debt, mediated by the Bank of England, and a newly powerful City of London. It was a truly momentous extension of the power of both the state and those who lent it money.

The other catalyst that drove this process was war, Britain's involvement in which was itself mainly a product of the Glorious Revolution. There is no doubt that the bulk of the Tories in the country were at best deeply unenthusiastic about, and often viscerally opposed to, the long series of European wars that the country was first dragged into by William III, and then brought into again by Anne and her ministers.

For war made the new gigantic system of debt, stock-jobbers, fundholders and money men absolutely indispensable, and it also radically transformed the state.[20] A vast new army of public servants was created in the course of this revolution to collect the taxes that were needed to make the debt viable, and to create the bureaucracy and army needed to fight the war itself. From customs and excise officers and land tax commissioners and the new civil servants in the Treasury through to the men who supplied, transported and commanded the vastly expanded army, the state expanded in ways that seemed extraordinary to many contemporaries. New expertise to manage the colossal and incredibly complicated new machinery of debt, tax and war was in short supply, and managing it was a business far more congenial to the Whigs.

One should not let this picture create the impression that the Tories were simply or only the party of reactionary squires and a static economic and social system. Indeed, many manufacturers and even some bankers were Tories. Both Tories and Whigs accepted the need to encourage trade and investment, seen as a crucial motor of the country's underlying prosperity. Indeed, both parties were more-or-less mercantilists, supporting strong state intervention to bolster British exports: as the debate over the 1713 Commercial Treaty showed, if anything it was the Tories who were in support of what might somewhat anachronistically be called 'proto-free trade' policies.

What the Tories *were* more sceptical about was the *financial* revolution, inextricably linked to its main driver: war. Once one accepted the need for war, one accepted the need for a hugely expanded national debt and massive tax increases. Once one accepted these requirements, it became increasingly impractical to achieve a complete Anglican monopoly of social, religious and political power. Too many of the financiers who kept the system running were Dissenters, jealous of the limited freedoms they had won by virtue of the Toleration Act and wanting more. A market for government bonds and securities was transnational and involved gaining investment from the Dutch, a country that was essentially Protestant Dissent in national form. A more modern, financial country implied a more European, outward looking one, tied to its Protestant neighbours ideologically by bonds of financial expansion and cosmopolitan religious tolerance. All of this ran against deep Tory instincts.

Tory and Whig were not static categories, and the fundamental fact is that, over the course of William III's reign particularly, the Whigs went from being the 'Country' Party to, essentially, the 'Court' Party, and the

Tories did the opposite. The Whigs were the Country men of oppositionist virtue when central government had been one based on Anglican hegemony (and suspected popery), a relatively ramshackle and underdeveloped fiscal-financial state, powerful monarchical authority and relative isolation from foreign military entanglements, just as the Tories were the courtiers under these circumstances.

The 1690s changed all that: slowly at first but then very definitely, the Tories became the Country Party, opposed to the new 'court order', based as it was on religious toleration, war, taxes and debt, and indeed on a more European pan-Protestant perspective (hence later Tory opposition to the immigration of the 'Poor Palatines'). The Tories neither wanted nor could adjust to this new order: with the heroic exception of Oxford, practically all of the people who understood and could manage this brave new world were Whigs, or, like Godolphin, effectively became Whigs – and even Oxford himself was in many respects a Whig. A few Country Whigs bravely continued to argue for the old Whiggish principles, just as some Tories tried to adjust themselves to the new court order, but the logic of both these changes and their own parties was against it, particularly in the country and among their backbenchers.

So the Tories were on a losing wicket from the moment they accepted the governmental, economic and political revolution ushered in by the Glorious Revolution. Once a party accepts a hegemonic framework that cannot be reconciled to their basic instincts and principles, they are doomed to division and decay. The Tories' divisions and ambiguities over the Jacobite question simply posed these dilemmas in their starkest, most unvarnished form, and in a way designed – due to the rogue factor of the Stuart claimants to the Protestant throne of England being Roman Catholics – to destroy them by setting their basic instincts at war with all religious and practical realities.

The Oxford administration was a heroic – and in some ways amazingly successful – attempt to defy this logic, which succeeded to the extent it did because Oxford was a man able to 'speak Whig' sufficiently well to stave off financial disaster in the post-1689 context, and because the Whigs massively overplayed their hand, and strained the patience of a war-weary nation by not ending the war in 1709. Once, however, the war issue faded, the raw fact was that behind Oxford sat a Tory Party that wasn't prepared to accept the realities – harsh, impious and unromantic ones in their eyes, civilised, commercial and tolerant ones in the eye of their Whig opponents – of the post-Glorious Revolution order.

The choice between Hanover and the Pretender increasingly became a proxy for maintaining the entire political and economic order that had been entrenched since 1688, or overturning it altogether and – perhaps in imagination more than reality, given the upheaval any attempt to turn back the clock would have entailed – restoring the status quo ante. Although in 1714–15 – and indeed even since the Sacheverell case – a rising number of Tories were prepared to contemplate that broad restoration of the old order, the religious wildcard factor of popery made it a bridge too far for the majority of them, and certainly was seen by the men who really mattered – Bolingbroke and Oxford – as a practical impossibility.

For many years – indeed, several hundred years – the standard story of the Tory apocalypse of 1714 was told in terms of Hanoverian Oxford battling Jacobite Bolingbroke. Modern work by historians has shown that this was not, in fact, true. Both were, certainly by March 1714 and probably earlier as well, committed to Hanover. The only difference was that this was a matter of principle for Oxford and merely a pragmatic reality (like most things) for Bolingbroke.

This was obscured for a long time for many good reasons incubated in the whirl of political double-dealing that became necessary, if not edifying, in the heady drama of that year. Both men had to woo the Jacobite MPs in the Tory Party, often by appealing over their head to the court of the Pretender, to maintain their ministry in power and promote their own personal supremacy in the Commons, whether they liked it or not (they did not). The sorts of obvious public gestures and measures to defend the Hanoverian succession that could have been made by either man were rendered either impossible or fiendishly difficult by the foibles and insecurities of Queen Anne. Bolingbroke's desire to preserve his life, and then the move to an outright Whig state monopoly, lead him, out of fear and ambition, to flee to the Pretender, giving everyone a false impression that he had been a Jacobite all along. Whigs had every partisan reason to smear him and Oxford as traitors, and most of the history for a long time was written by Whigs.

Actually, however, the dramatic events of 1714 illustrated the extent to which any Tory who wanted to actually govern without enormous upheavals, including probable financial collapse and possible civil war, had no choice but to accept a Whig monarch, and with it, fundamentally, a Whig social, political and financial order. The entire 'crisis' over the Protestant succession was, ultimately, rather like the Exclusion Crisis, re-run as an insubstantial farce, this time with the result practically pre-ordained in favour of the Whigs. By 1714, a Jacobite restoration was simply not on the cards, short of military intervention from outside that was obviously not forthcoming. The scare was the result of Whig paranoia, a series of unfortunate political accidents created in the heat of a chaotic moment, and the more substantial fact that a lot of Tories who did not have to actually try to govern the country, but who were well-represented on the backbenches, *were* committed to either a Jacobite restoration come what may, or would have preferred one if the Pretender had converted to the Church of England. These men found the consequences of Tory acquiescence to the Glorious Revolution much harder to stomach once they had to face the long-term consequences of deposing James II: that is, the accession of a family of unattractive Germans with a very tenuous claim to the throne. These men, however, simply did not have the political power to prevent it.

This is not to say that the Tories could not have won had they been utterly united and ruthless in their determination to crush the new order created by the Glorious Revolution and war from at least the mid-1690s. In reality, events made this very unlikely, and they would always have been hobbled by the fact that, in terms of monarch, they faced a choice between a hopelessly inept and unpopular Roman Catholic exile, or two monarchs who, although very different, both basically endorsed the post Glorious Revolution order, albeit with greatly varying levels of enthusiasm and consistency.

None of this meant that the vast bulk of Tories who voted, protested, opined, wrote, fought and sometimes rioted during this era realised that they were always probably fighting a lost cause against unstoppable forces of encroaching financial modernity. Theirs was a cause that to many modern people may seem distasteful or antediluvian, but to them it seemed a necessary and noble rearguard action to preserve a society that, if less polite, commercial and (possibly) civilised, was more cohesive, rooted and stable than the likely alternative.

There is, however, a counterpoint to all this. The basic structural forces that prevailed were, ultimately, Whig. However, the Whig victory was not, in fact, complete.

One reason was that much of the Whig Party was more than a little bit Tory itself. Although the Whigs were more at ease with some degree of religious toleration and engagement with Protestant Europe, and more accepting of the financial revolution of the 1690s and the need to use that revolution to fight a war against the French, their acceptance of these trends can be exaggerated, and the man who eventually led the Whig hegemony — Walpole — was among the most cautious of the Whigs.

Walpole understood that, although the Tories had been defeated and their old order could not be restored fully, the social forces of Toryism were by no means dead in 1714, or in 1722. The financial revolution of the 1690s and the years of war may have weakened the landed gentry, but it hadn't broken them. Indeed, many of them proved more adaptable than one might think, and economic forces did not destroy them, they merely set them into something of a different framework. The Church certainly had not been destroyed or fatally weakened: it may have proven impossible to maintain its religious monopoly, but it remained potent, and indeed supported not only by the Tories but also by most Whigs, albeit in a slightly less militant form than the one favoured by the High Churchman of the 1700s and 1710s. The *ancien régime* of hierarchy, Church and landed property had undoubtedly been reordered by the events of the era of party. New forces had been unleashed. But that regime still persisted in modified form, and to govern it, Walpole had to compromise with it.[21]

Walpole therefore engineered a settlement that was actually something of a middle ground, which absorbed some of the most widespread and deeply entrenched social and religious elements of Toryism, and thereby made his and the Whig Party's grip on power all the stronger. Broadly speaking, he gave the gentry (and indeed the mass of the unenfranchised people) something that they wanted and that the Tories had given them in 1712: peace and lower taxes. He was very cautious on religious questions, giving surprisingly little of substance to the Dissenters, who were the 'progressive' outriders of the Whig Party. He did soften the harder edges of a still fundamentally Anglican religious and political order for them, but he basically refused to touch the religious legislative framework of the Church of England as it stood in 1722. He did not repeal the Test and Corporation Acts or take any other actions to weaken the dominance of the Church, as Sunderland and Stanhope had tried to do in the late 1710s. The memories of the Sacheverell riots and the havoc they wreaked on the Whigs in 1710 died hard: Walpole never wanted to risk lighting the touchpaper of popular pro-Church sentiment ever again.

It is for this reason that the Whig settlement of the era of Robert Walpole became the status quo that, a hundred years later, another set of people, again calling themselves Tories, defended – at least for a while.

We still live, in some important respects, in the world shaped by the battle between Whigs and Tories that this book has outlined.

The War of the Spanish Succession – waged mainly with Whig enthusiasm, and ended by Tory efforts – and the new order created to sustain it helped to give Britain a material and geopolitical foundation for what was to become the British Empire. The Treaty of Utrecht was a watershed in the history of both British power and European politics. By its terms, French ascendancy was (whatever Whigs may have claimed at the time) seriously checked, and Britain gained new territories, new strategic resources and new economic opportunities that marked the coming of a great European power. It laid the basis not only for future British naval predominance in the western Mediterranean, but also for victory in the Seven Years War, which truly did create a powerful and global British Empire. After Utrecht, it was merely a matter of time before the old mantle of European supremacy passed across the English Channel, from France to Britain. Even the old Tory blue-water strategy, never very successful during the War of the Spanish Succession, was later adopted with extraordinary results by Pitt the Elder as Britain finally gained supremacy in India, Canada and the West Indies. The world created by that empire – for good or ill – was forged, in an important sense, both by the victories of Marlborough and the intrigues of Oxford and Bolingbroke at Utrecht.

The union between England and Scotland is another extraordinary legacy of the great battle between Whig and Tory. Fundamentally, whatever ambiguities there were over the Union among Tory leaders, it was a Whig gambit, passed by Whig politicians to achieve Whig ends. The fact it took the form it did was partly a matter of political happenstance, but the truth of the Union was that it was an English initiative undertaken to safeguard the post-Glorious Revolution settlement, particularly the Protestant succession. The benefits (or disadvantages, according to taste) that have subsequently accrued to Scotland from the Union were, ultimately, incidental to its original, highly English and political, purpose. No doubt some of the Scottish advocates of the Union were quite sincere – 'bought and sold for English gold' is a misleading oversimplification of what actually happened – but this should not blind us to the fact that it was most basically a product of English political exigencies, and ones that were fundamentally shaped by the rage of partisanship between Whigs and Tories.

Although our financial sector has altered immensely over the past 325 years, the basic innovation that changed everything – of a massive national debt made viable by the political fact that a powerful parliament would be there to consistently underwrite it and the Bank of England was there to manage it – was forged in the 1690s by the Whig Party. Quite soon many Tories had to adapt to that, and many did quite successfully: we should not pretend that the Tory Party and those who supported it were naïfs committed purely to some sort of totally insular agrarian economy. However, there is no doubt that, to the landed gentlemen that lined the Tory backbenches, to many of those who scribbled for Tory newspapers or cheered on Sacheverell in 1710, the brave new world of 'Big Finance' and debt was alien and disturbing. They struggled ineffectually against it. They lost. Their defeat, for good or ill, made the British Empire and the rise of capitalist modernity in Britain possible.

The cultural divide that defined so much of the Whig–Tory divide – Tory High Churchmanship versus Whig Dissent and Low Churchmanship – continued, in a very direct way, to form a crucial basis for the underlying framework of political division in British politics until the early twentieth century. Many of the debates that dominated politics in the age of Peel, Wellington, Melbourne and John Russell – and even Salisbury, Disraeli and Gladstone – were still, at root, the same basically politico-religious debates that pitted Benjamin Hoadly against Francis Atterbury, Rochester against Wharton. The original fuel of the Whig Party – anti-Catholic bigotry – was still a real force in British politics as late as 1850, when John Russell opposed the formation of the Roman Catholic hierarchy in Britain.

It is true that this divide really originates in the seventeenth century, during the upheavals of the 1640s, but it is significant that the 'Rage of Party' was the era when a politics recognisable to modern sensibilities started to form out of the outright violence, sectarian savagery and chaos that characterised much of early modern England. It was a politics that seems sometimes very familiar – Wharton canvassing shopkeepers is a scene that any modern-day political activist can recognise, and some of the partisan squibs of the day are not very different to the unhinged political rants one finds on contemporary social media. Under the surface, however, lurked a religiosity and a menace that are less familiar (although perhaps decreasingly alien in a divided contemporary world). This uncanny sense of being both recognisable and strange at the same time makes the 'Rage of Party' era a particularly clear example of the transition between a dim and distant past and something beginning to look an awful lot like modernity.

Indeed, the era reminds us that we are not, perhaps, as modern as we like to think. The extraordinary changes of the past 300 years, from the industrial revolution and the rise of democracy to the development of the railways, the car and the internet, cannot excise some of the temperamental and cultural instincts – often not terribly rational ones – that lie behind contemporary political partisanship in Britain, and perhaps beyond.

When Tories in the 1700s and 1710s complained about being drawn into a European alliance to fight a war on behalf of foreigners that caused them nothing but trouble and expense, when they bitterly protested against taking in foreign refugees, and when they did a controversial deal with a longstanding and much vilified European power who had been cast as an enemy for generations to secure peace, the echoes seem loud indeed. Equally, when Whigs argued in favour of a deep involvement with the political affairs of Europe, supported vigorous international military intervention, cast by their enemies as 'forever wars', and decried Tory indifference to the plight of the 'poor Palatines', only the details reveal that one is writing about the eighteenth rather than the twenty-first century.

The affinities go still deeper. Tories venerated established institutions and forms of authority, such as the Church, land and monarchy; Whigs tended to be far more sceptical of those institutions, embracing the rising forces of a more mobile, more commercial and more 'polite' society, casting their opponents, in effect if not in quite the same terms, as backwards, as clinging to outmoded old identities: as 'deplorables'. Old parties realigned as questions of international co-operation versus national self-determination became the key political dividing lines. The past is never only the past.

In a sense – although it may not easily fit onto modern party political distinctions – we are all still, in our heart of hearts, either Whig or Tory.

Which are you?

Acknowledgements

I suspect that this book will not be to the taste of all academic historians. Nonetheless, whatever their misgivings about my frivolity, without them this book would be impossible. Although I do have a PhD in history from Cambridge, this was not the exact subject of my scholarly research and I approached this book keen to enjoy a certain freedom from the shackles of the academic style and approach. Despite this, my aim is to make more accessible reams of research conducted by some brilliant and extraordinary historians whose work in many (but not all) cases languishes in undeserved obscurity.

Beyond my assembly of the material, construction of the narrative and occasional raids into archival material and the mass of newspapers and pamphlets published in the era, I claim no great originality in writing this book. It is a synthetic work heavily based on the work of the many historians who have researched this area over the past century or so (mostly since the 1960s, some of them no longer with us). Without the work of – to name only the most obvious – Geoffrey Holmes, Bill Speck, Tim Harris, Mark Knights, J. P. Kenyon, David Hayton (and more broadly the work of all of the contributors to *The History of Parliament* project and particularly its volume on the 1690–1715 period), Mark Goldie, Henry Horwitz, Edward Gregg, Harry Dickinson, G. V. Bennett, Brian Hill, Henry Snyder, Keith Feiling, Daniel Szechi and John Miller (the list could go on . . .) – I could not have written this book. I suggest that anyone who wishes to follow up on this book consults the endnotes.

I fell in love with this era partly as a result of reading Michael Foot's brilliant account of Jonathan Swift's role in the battle over the peace of Utrecht, *The Pen and the Sword*. I do not suppose for a second that this book is as good as Foot's, but I do have in common with Foot the fact that I am not a professional historian, or indeed in my case a professional writer. I wrote this book while working a full-time job, in the midst of being a father to a lively toddler, in evenings and holidays. That has only proven possible due to the extraordinary forbearance, love and support of my wife, Clare, who has not only put up with me wittering on about Robert Harley and occasional conformity for the past two years, but went out of her way to give me the time and space I needed to write it. She has also been my best reader. I love her very much. Thanks also to my sons, Charles and James. When Charles was a baby, I sometimes put him to sleep by giving him an account of the political battle over the Peace of Utrecht. James has been spared this, but his turn will come.

I would also like to thank my mother, Johanna Hastings, and my father, Michael Owers, for their love and support. My in-laws, Mark Gore and Pauline Walker, were also a big help. Many thanks also to Ashley Walsh: this book emerged partly out of an online quiz we co-wrote as a lockdown distraction during the Covid pandemic, and his conversation, assistance and friendship have been invaluable over many years. Thank you to friends such as Alastair Curry, Andrew Howarth, Dan Ratcliffe, Dave Doherty, Richard Johnson, Matt Bird, Jim Robinson, Dan Jones and others for keeping me sane when writing the book. My gratitude to those scholars who have helped me out at various points – Mark Goldie, Max Skjönsberg, Robin Eagles, Joseph Hone, David Hayton and doubtless others I have forgotten – is immense. Thanks also to my agent, Matthew Hamilton, and my editor, Andreas Campomar, both of whom have given me invaluable assistance, and taken a frankly inexplicable risk in supporting this project – but I am glad they did. Thanks also to James Nightingale for his excellent copy-editing.

All errors in this book are mine: most of what is good in it is courtesy of others.

Endnotes

Note on sources and referencing

In most chapters, I have based the overall shape and basic facts of the narrative on a number of secondary works that are listed at the start of the endnotes for each chapter. Where specific sections have been chiefly based on particular secondary works, I have noted this at the beginning of that section. I have only referenced these secondary works in the endnotes where I have quoted from them directly. I have attempted to supplement the secondary works by consulting various contemporary diaries, memoirs, pamphlets, journals, letters (etc), and where possible archival sources, which are referenced in the main endnotes.

Introduction

1   General Election: "You're joking – not another one!", BBC News (https://www.youtube.com/watch?v=H6-IQAdFU3w)
2   Jeremy Fradkin, 'Who was a refugee in early modern England? The "Poor Palatines" of 1709' (https://www.folger.edu/blogs/collation/the-poor-palatines-of-1709/)
3   Ibid.
4   *A Brief History of the Poor Palatine Refugees, Lately Arriv'd in England* (London, 1709), p. 3.
5   *Cobbett's Parliamentary History of England: From the Norman Conquest, in 1066 to the Year 1803*, vol. VI (London, 1810), pp. 780.
6   *Remarks and Collections of Thomas Hearne*, ed. C. E. Doble, vol. II, (Oxford, 1886) pp. 239–40.

Chapter 1

The secondary sources upon which the narrative of this chapter is chiefly based are as follows:

Richard Ashcraft, *Revolutionary Politics and Locke's Two Treatises of Government* (Princeton, 1986)
K. H. D. Haley, *The First Earl of Shaftesbury* (Oxford, 1968)
Tim Harris, *Restoration: Charles II and his Kingdoms* (London, 2005)
Tim Harris, *London Crowds in the Reign of Charles II: Propaganda and Politics from the Restoration until the Exclusion Crisis* (Cambridge, 1987)

Ronald Hutton, *Charles II: King of England, Scotland and Ireland* (Oxford, 1989)
J. R. Jones, *The First Whigs: The Politics of the Exclusion Crisis, 1678–1683* (London, 1961)
John Kenyon, *The Popish Plot* (London, 1972)
Mark Knights, *Politics and Opinion in Crisis, 1678–81* (Cambridge, 1994)
John Miller, *Popery and Politics in England 1660–1688* (Cambridge, 1973)
David Ogg, *England in the Reign of Charles II* (Oxford, 1984 [1934])
Specifics and other references are in the following notes.

1 This section is chiefly based on Kenyon, *The Popish Plot*.
2 Alan Marshall, 'Oates, Titus (1649–1705), informer.' *Oxford Dictionary of National Biography*, 23rd September 2004. https://www.oxforddnb.com/view/10.1093/ref:odnb/9780198614128.001.0001/odnb-9780198614128-e-20437
3 Kenyon, *The Popish Plot*, p. 45.
4 Ibid., p. 54.
5 Marshall, 'Oates, Titus'. *ODNB*.
6 Ibid.
7 Ibid.
8 This section is chiefly based on Miller, *Popery and Politics in England 1660–1688*.
9 Miller, *Popery and Politics*, p. 69.
10 Ibid., p. 11.
11 This section is chiefly based on Hutton, *Charles II* and Ashcraft, *Revolutionary Politics*, ch. 1.
12 Miller, *Popery and Politics*, p. 133.
13 Ibid.
14 Quoted in M. Knights, 'Osborne, Thomas, first duke of Leeds (1632–1712), politician.' *Oxford Dictionary of National Biography*, 4th October 2008. https://www.oxforddnb.com/view/10.1093/ref:odnb/9780198614128.001.0001/odnb-9780198614128-e-20884
15 Robert S. Bosher, *The Making of the Restoration Settlement: The Influence of the Laudians 1649–1662* (London, 1951), chs. 1–2.
16 This section, and the three following, are chiefly based on Kenyon, *The Popish Plot*; Miller, *Popery and Politics*; Haley, *The First Earl of Shaftesbury*; Jones, *The First Whigs*; Knights, *Politics and Opinion in Crisis, 1678–81*; Harris, *London Crowds in the Reign of Charles II*; and Harris, *Restoration: Charles II and his Kingdoms*.
17 Haley, *The First Earl of Shaftesbury*, p. 455.
18 Tim Harris, 'Green Ribbon Club (act. c. 1674–c. 1683).' *Oxford Dictionary of National Biography*, 24th May 2008. https://www.oxforddnb.com/view/10.1093/ref:odnb/9780198614128.001.0001/odnb-9780198614128-e-92786
19 Roger North, *Examen: or, an enquiry into the credit and veracity of a pretended complete history. . .* (London, 1740), p. 573. *Eighteenth Century Collections Online*, link.gale.com/apps/doc/CW0101669329/ECCO?u=cambuni&sid=bookmark-ECCO&xid=4fb559f8&pg=1.
20 Cited in Haley, *The First Earl of Shaftesbury*, p. 220.
21 Ibid., p. 27.
22 Anthony Ashley Cooper, First Earl of Shaftesbury, *A Letter from a Person of Quality to his friend in the country against the Test Act* (London, 1675), pp. 1–2.
23 *Cobbett's Parliamentary History of England*, vol. IV, p. 1025.
24 Cited in Ashcraft, *Revolutionary Politics*, p. 174.
25 Jones, *The First Whigs*, p. 109.
26 Hutton, *Charles II*, p. 396.
27 Ibid., p. 400.
28 This section is chiefly based on Ashcraft, *Revolutionary Politics;* Harris, *Politics under the Later Stuarts: Party Conflict in a Divided Society, 1660–1715* (London, 1993); and Harris, *Restoration*; Harris, *London Crowds*.

29   See Ashcraft, *Revolutionary Politics*, pp. 190–1.

30   *A Scheme of Popish Cruelties* (London, 1681).

31   Cited in Harris, *London Crowds*, p. 101.

32   Harris, *London Crowds*, pp. 103–4.

33   Harris, *Politics under the Later Stuarts*, p. 104.

34   S. Taylor, ed., *The Entring Book of Roger Morrice: The Reign of James II, 1687–1689*, vol. IV (Martlesham, 2007), p. 476; M. Knights, ed., *The Entring Book of Roger Morrice: The Reign of William III, 1689–1691*, vol. V (Martlesham, 2007), p. 200.

35   This section is chiefly based on G. Kitchin, *Sir Roger L'Estrange: a contribution to the history of the press in the seventeenth century* (London, 1913); H. T. Dickinson, *Liberty and Property: Political Ideology in Eighteenth-Century Britain* (London, 1977); Harris, *London Crowds*; Harris, *Restoration*, ch. 4.

36   Pepys cited in Harold Love, 'L'Estrange, Sir Roger (1616–1704), author and press censor.' *Oxford Dictionary of National Biography*. 23rd September 2004.https://www.oxforddnb.com/view/10.1093/ref:odnb/9780198614128.001.0001/odnb-9780198614128-e-16514

37   Harris, *London Crowds*, p. 139.

38   Love, 'L'Estrange, Sir Roger'. *ODNB*.

39   Cited in Kitchin, *Sir Roger L'Estrange*, p. 257.

40   Brian Cowan, *The Social Life of Coffee* (New Haven, 2005), p. 170.

41   Harris, *Restoration*, p. 245.

42   Ibid., p. 246.

43   Cited in *Poems on Affairs of State: 1678–1681*, ed. E. F. Mengel (New Haven, 1965), p. 412.

44   Dickinson, *Liberty and Property*, p. 23.

45   Cited in Dickinson, *Liberty and Property*, pp. 20–21.

46   Ibid.

47   *The Character of a Tory* (London, 1681).

48   *The Entring Book of Roger Morrice*, various volumes.

49   Cited in Ogg, *England in the Reign of Charles II*, p. 610.

50   Harris, *London Crowds*, p. 147.

51   Roger L'Estrange, *The Observator*, 2nd July 1681, no. 29.

52   Haley, *The First Earl of Shaftesbury*, pp. 202–205.

53   Cited in ibid., p. 212.

54   Cited in ibid., p. 735.

55   John Dryden, *The Works of John Dryden*, ed. Walter Scott, revised Saintsbury (Edinburgh, 1884), vol. IX, pp. 209–10.

56   Ibid., p. 239.

57   Ibid., p. 241.

58   This section is chiefly based on R. Willman, 'The Origins of "Whig" and "Tory" in English Political Language', *The Historical Journal*, 1974, 17(2), 247–264. http://www.jstor.org/stable/2638297

59   Knights, *Politics and Opinion in Crisis*, p. 109.

60   Ibid.

61   Cited in Willman, 'The Origins...', p. 248.

62   This section is based chiefly on Hutton, *Charles II*; Haley, *The First Earl of Shaftesbury*; Jones, *The First Whigs*; Knights, *Politics and Opinion in Crisis, 1678–81*; Harris, *Restoration*; Harris, 'Cooper, Anthony Ashley, first earl of Shaftesbury (1621–1683), politician.' *Oxford Dictionary of National Biography*. 23rd September 2004; and Alan Marshall, 'Rye House plotters (act. 1683).' *Oxford Dictionary of National Biography*, 22nd September 2005. https://www.oxforddnb.com/view/10.1093/ref:odnb/9780198614128.001.0001/odnb-9780198614128-e-93794

63   Haley, *The First Earl of Shaftesbury*, p. 664.

64   Ibid., p. 681.
65   Ibid.
66   Harris, *Restoration*, p. 295.
67   Ibid., p. 281–2.
68   Ibid., p. 283.
69   Algernon Sidney, *Speech on the Scaffold* (1683) https://www.originalsources.com/ Document.aspx?DocID=J7EPQEUAMX37II5

Chapter 2

The secondary sources upon which the narrative of this chapter is chiefly based are as follows:

Stephen Baxter, *William III* (London, 1966)
Tim Harris, *Revolution: The Great Crisis of the British Monarchy, 1685–1720* (London, 2006)
B. W. Hill, *The Growth of Parliamentary Parties, 1689–1742* (London, 1976)
Henry Horwitz, *Parliament, Policy and Politics in the Reign of William III* (Manchester, 1977)
John Miller, *James II* (New Haven, 2000 [1978])
Christopher Robbins, *The Earl of Wharton and Whig Party Politics, 1679–1715* (Lampeter, 1992)
Craig Rose, *England in the 1690s: Revolution, Religion and War* (Oxford, 1999)
Bill Speck, *Reluctant Revolutionaries: Englishmen and the Revolution of 1688* (Oxford, 1988)

1   Miller, *James II*, p. 206.
2   *Life of James II*, ed. J. S. Clarke (London, 1816), vol. II, p.252.
3   Harris, *Revolution*, p. 303.
4   *Life of James II*, vol. II, p. 253.
5   Ibid.
6   This and the next few sections are chiefly based on Harris, *Revolution*; Speck, *Reluctant Revolutionaries*; and Miller, *James II*.
7   Harris, *Revolution*, p. 46.
8   Ibid., p. 9.
9   Cited in ibid., p. 71.
10   Cited in Miller, *James II*, p. 120.
11   John Evelyn, *The Diary of John Evelyn* (London, 2006), p. 750.
12   *Cobbett's Parliamentary History of England*, vol. IV, pp. 1373–4.
13   Ibid.
14   Cited in Harris, *Revolution*, p. 239.
15   Cited in Speck, *Reluctant Revolutionaries*, p. 67.
16   Harris, *Revolution*, p. 267.
17   Ibid., p. 253.
18   This section is chiefly based on Baxter, *William III*; Harris, *Revolution*; Speck, *Reluctant Revolutionaries*; and Miller, *James II*.
19   Cited in Speck, *Reluctant Revolutionaries*, p. 75.
20   Cited in John Childs, *The Army, James II, and the Glorious Revolution* (Manchester, 1980), p. 176.
21   Gilbert Burnet, *Bishop Burnet's History of His Own Time: With Notes by the Earls of Dartmouth and Hardwicke, Speaker Onslow and Dean Swift,* vol. III (2nd ed., Oxford, 1833), p. 333.
22   Harris, *Revolution*, p. 293.
23   Andrew Browning, *Thomas Osborne, Earl of Danby and Duke of Leeds, 1632–1712, vol. I* (Glasgow, 1951), p. 401.

24 This section is chiefly based on Harris, *Revolution*; Speck, *Reluctant Revolutionaries*; J. P. Kenyon, *Revolution Principles* (Cambridge, 1977); and Henry Horwitz, *Revolution Politicks: The career of Daniel Finch, Second Earl of Nottingham, 1647–1730* (Cambridge, 1968).

25 *The Entring Book of Roger Morrice*, vol. IV, p. 489.

26 Cited in Kenyon, *Revolution Principles*, p. 10.

27 *Cobbett's Parliamentary History of England*, vol. V, p. 50.

28 *The Entring Book of Roger Morrice*, vol. IV, p. 401.

29 *Cobbett's Parliamentary History of England*, vol. V, pp. 39–40.

30 Cited in Horwitz, *Revolution Politicks*, pp. 81–2.

31 *Cobbett's Parliamentary History of England*, vol. V, pp. 58.

32 This section is chiefly based on Rose, *England in the 1690s,* chs. 2–3 and Hill, *The Growth of Parliamentary Parties*, ch. 1.

33 *A Supplement to Burnet's History of My Own Time*, ed. H. C. Foxcroft (Oxford, 1902), p. 192.

34 Cited in Baxter, *William III*, p. 255.

35 Cited in Hill, *The Growth of Parliamentary Parties*, p. 29.

36 Cited in Mark Goldie, 'The Roots of True Whiggism 1688–94.' *History of Political Thought*, vol. 1, no. 2 (1980): 195–236, p. 197. http://www.jstor.org/stable/26211778

37 J. P. Kenyon, *Robert Spencer, Earl of Sunderland, 1641–1702* (London, 1958), p. 251.

38 This section is chiefly based on Daniel Szechi, *The Jacobites: Britain and Europe, 1688–1788*, 2nd edition (Manchester, 2019), chs. 4–5 and Mark Goldie, *Tory Political Thought, 1689–1714* (Unpublished PhD thesis, University of Cambridge, 1977), ch. 3.

39 This section is chiefly based on G. V. Bennett, *The Tory Crisis in Church and State, 1688–1730: The Career of Francis Atterbury, Bishop of Rochester* (Oxford, 1975), ch. 1; Rose, *England in the 1690s*, ch. 5; John Spurr, 'The Church of England, Comprehension and the Toleration Act of 1689', *The English Historical Review*, vol. CIV, issue 413, October 1989, pp. 927–46. https://doi.org/10.1093/ehr/CIV.413.927

40 Cited in Rose, *England in the 1690s*, p. 165.

41 Cited in ibid.

42 Cited in ibid., p. 164.

43 Spurr, 'The Church of England. . .', pp. 941–2.

44 This section is chiefly based on Hill, *The Growth of Parliamentary Parties*, ch. 1; Rose, *England in the 1690s*, chs. 2, 3 & 5; Horwitz, *Parliament, Policy and Politics*, ch. 2.

45 Evelyn, *The Diary of John Evelyn*, p. 807.

46 Cited in William L. Sachse, *Lord Somers: A political portrait* (Manchester, 1975), p. 49.

47 Cited in Rose, *England in the 1690s*, p. 76.

48 Ibid., p. 155.

49 Cited in Horwitz, *Parliament, Policy and Politics*, p. 35.

50 'A Letter Concerning the Disabling Clauses Lately Offered to the House of Commons, for Regulating Corporations' (London, 1690), p. 19.

51 Henry Horwitz, 'The General Election of 1690', *Journal of British Studies 11*, no. 1 (1971): 77–91. http://www.jstor.org/stable/175038, p. 85. This section is chiefly based on this article.

52 Cited in ibid., p. 86.

53 Ibid., p. 83.

54 Cited in ibid.

55 This section is chiefly based on Robbins, *The Earl of Wharton and Whig Party Politics* and Eveline Cruickshanks and Stuart Handley, 'WHARTON, Hon. Thomas (1648–1715), of Winchendon, nr. Aylesbury and Wooburn, nr. Chipping Wycombe, Bucks' in: *The History of Parliament: The House of Commons 1690–1715*, eds. D. Hayton, E. Cruickshanks, S. Handley (Martlesham, 2002). History of Parliament Online, https://www.historyofparliamentonline.org/volume/1690-1715/member/wharton-hon-thomas-1648-1715

56   Cited in Robbins, *The Earl of Wharton and Whig Party Politics, 1679–1715*, p. 299.
57   Ibid., p. 305.
58   Robbins, *The Earl of Wharton and Whig Party Politics*, p. 2.
59   Cited in ibid., pp. 41–2.
60   Robin Eagles, 'WHARTON, Thomas (c. 1648-1715)', https://dev. historyofparliamentonline.org/lord-biography/wharton-thomas-c-1648-1715
61   *The Life of Robert Frampton, Bishop of Gloucester*, ed. T. Simpson Evans (London, 1876), p. 165.
62   Jonathan Swift, *The Examiner, and Other Pieces Written in 1710–11*, ed. Herbert Davis (Oxford, 1966), p. 57.
63   Burnet, *History of His Own Time*, vol. V, p. 228.
64   Richard Steele, *Memoirs of the Life of the Most Noble Thomas Late Marquess of Wharton* (London, 1715), p. 34.
65   Robbins, *The Earl of Wharton and Whig Party Politics*, p. 67.
66   David Hayton, 'FOLEY, Paul I (c. 1645–99), of Stoke Edith, Herefs.' in: *The History of Parliament: The House of Commons 1690–1715*, eds. D. Hayton, E. Cruickshanks, S. Handley (Martlesham, 2002). History of Parliament Online, https://www.historyofparliamentonline. org/volume/1690-1715/member/foley-paul-i-1645-99
67   Cited in Robbins, *The Earl of Wharton and Whig Party Politics*, p. 108.
68   Horwitz, *Revolution Politicks*, p. 144.
69   J. H. Plumb, *The Growth of Political Stability in England 1675–1725* (London, 1977), p. 134.
70   Cited in Rose, *England in the 1690s*, p. 87.

Chapter 3

The secondary sources upon which the narrative of this chapter is chiefly based are as follows:

B. W. Hill, *The Growth of Parliamentary Parties, 1689–1742* (London, 1976)
Henry Horwitz, *Parliament, Policy and Politics in the Reign of William III* (Manchester, 1977)
Henry Horwitz, *Revolution Politicks: The career of Daniel Finch, Second Earl of Nottingham, 1647–1730* (Cambridge, 1968)
Christopher Robbins, *The Earl of Wharton and Whig Party Politics, 1679–1715* (Lampeter, 1992)
Craig Rose, *England in the 1690s: Revolution, Religion and War* (Oxford, 1999)

1   Horwitz, *Parliament, Policy and Politics*, p. 254.
2   *The House of Lords, 1660–1715*, ed. Ruth Paley, vol. III (Cambridge, 2016), p. 830.
3   This section is based chiefly on Rose, *England in the 1690s*, ch. 4 and P. G. M. Dickson, *The Financial Revolution in England: A study in the development of public credit* (London, 1967), ch. 1.
4   Cited in Dickson, *The Financial Revolution*, p. 18.
5   Gary Stuart de Krey, *A Fractured Society: The Politics of London in the First Age of Party, 1688–1715* (Oxford, 1985), pp. 109–10.
6   Cited in Rose, *England in the 1690s*, p. 40.
7   Cited in Robbins, *The Earl of Wharton and Whig Party Politics*, p. 124.
8   Horwitz, *Parliament, Policy and Politics*, p. 150.
9   Ibid., p. 155.
10   Ibid., p. 215.
11   Burnet, *History of His Own Time*, vol. IV, p. 288.
12   This section is chiefly based on Brian W. Hill, *Robert Harley: Speaker, Secretary of State and Premier Minister* (New Haven, 1988); Angus McInnes, *Robert Harley: Puritan Politician* (London, 1970); Elizabeth Hamilton, *The Backstairs Dragon* (New York, 1969); and Sheila Biddle, *Bolingbroke and Harley* (New York, 1974).

13 Cited in Hill, *Robert Harley*, p. 7.
14 Cited in Mark Knights, *The Devil in Disguise: Deception, Delusion, and Fanaticism in the Early English Enlightenment* (Oxford, 2011), p. 163.
15 Jonathan Swift, *The History of the Four Last Years of the Queen*, ed. Herbert Davis (Oxford, 1951) p. 75.
16 *Cobbett's Parliamentary History of England*, vol. V, p. 987.
17 Ibid., p. 991.
18 John Toland, *An Argument shewing, that a Standing Army is inconsistent with a Free Government* (London, 1698), p. 7.
19 Cited in Hill, *The Growth of Parliamentary Parties*, p. 74.
20 Cited in Kenyon, *Robert Spencer, Earl of Sunderland*, p. 304.
21 Cited in Hill, *The Growth of Parliamentary Parties*, p. 75.
22 Cited in Horwitz, *Parliament, Policy and Politics*, p. 238.
23 Ibid.
24 Horwitz, *Revolution Politicks*, p. 158.
25 *The Parliamentary Diary of Sir Richards Cocks, 1698–1702*, ed. D. W. Hayton (Oxford, 1996), p. 14.
26 *Cobbett's Parliamentary History of England*, vol. V, p. 1215.
27 Hill, *Robert Harley*, p. 60.
28 Sachse, *Lord Somers*, p. 163.
29 Horwitz, *Parliament, Policy and Politics*, p. 263.
30 This section is chiefly based on Rose, *England in the 1690s*, ch. 4.
31 Dryden, *The Works of John Dryden*, vol. XI, p. 81.
32 Cited in Rose, *England in the 1690s*, p. 147.
33 *Cobbett's Parliamentary History of England*, vol. V, p. 1251.
34 Ibid.
35 Ibid., p. 1253–4.
36 Ibid., p. 1253.
37 Ibid., p. 1256.
38 Ibid., p. 1295.
39 Baxter, *William III*, p. 397.
40 John Somers, *Jura populi Anglicani: or The subject's right of petitioning set forth* (London, 1701), p. vii.
41 Ibid.
42 Ibid., p. ix.
43 Ibid., p. x.
44 Charles Davenant, *The True Picture of a Modern Whig. . .* (London, 1701), p. 33.
45 Cited in Kenyon, *Revolution Principles*, p. 53.
46 Ibid.

Chapter 4

The secondary sources upon which the narrative of this chapter is chiefly based are as follows:

Winston Churchill, *Marlborough: His Life and Times* (vols. 1 & 2) (London, 1967 [1933])
Edward Gregg, *Queen Anne* (New Haven, 2001 [1980])
Geoffrey Holmes, *British Politics in the Age of Anne* (London, 1967)
J. R. Jones, *Marlborough* (Cambridge, 1993)
W. A. Speck, *The Birth of Britain: A New Nation, 1700–1710* (Oxford, 1994)
Roy A. Sundstrom, *Sidney Godolphin: Servant of State* (London, 1992)

1   Cited in Joseph Hone, *Literature and Party Politics at the Accession of Queen Anne* (Oxford, 2017), p. 53.

2   Cited in ibid., p. 51. Other details in this paragraph and the next based on Hone, *Literature and Party Politics*, pp. 48–54.

3   'The English Muse: or, a congratulatory poem upon Her Majesty's accession to the throne of England' (London, 1702), p. 11.

4   Cited in Gregg, *Queen Anne*, p. 152.

5   Ibid., p. 129.

6   This section and the next are chiefly based on Jones, *Marlborough* and Churchill; *Marlborough: His Life and Times* (vols. 1 & 2); and Frances Harris, *A Passion for Government: The Life of Sarah, Duchess of Marlborough* (Oxford, 1991).

7   Cited in ibid., p. 35.

8   Burnet cited in Churchill, *Marlborough*, vol. I, p. 52.

9   Churchill, *Marlborough*, vol. I, p. 58.

10 Cited in ibid., p. 403.

11 Cited in ibid.

12 Cited in Harris, *A Passion for Government*, p. 4.

13 Ibid., p. 5.

14 Ibid.

15 Cited in Gregg, *Queen Anne*, p. 138.

16 This section is chiefly based on Holmes, *British Politics in the Age of Anne*, chs. 6 & 11.

17 Holmes, *British Politics in the Age of Anne*, p. 189.

18 Lord Macaulay, *The History of England from the Accession of James II*, vol. I (London, 1858), p. 256.

19 This section is chiefly based on Sundstrom, *Sidney Godolphin*, chs. 1 & 5.

20 *Cobbett's Parliamentary History of England*, vol. VI, p. 23.

21 James Drake, 'Some Necessary Considerations relating to all future Elections. . .' (Originally London, 1702) in: *A Collection of Scarce and Valuable Tracts. . .*, ed. Walter Scott, vol. XII [subsequently 'Somers Tracts'] (London, 1814), p. 203.

22 Mark Knights, 'SEYMOUR, Sir Edward, 4th Bt. (1633–1708), of Maiden Bradley, Wilts. and Berry Pomeroy, Devon' in: *The History of Parliament: The House of Commons 1690–1715*, eds. D. Hayton, E. Cruickshanks, S. Handley (Martlesham, 2002). History of Parliament Online, https://www.historyofparliamentonline.org/volume/1690-1715/member/seymour-sir-edward-1633-1708

23 Macaulay, *The History of England...*, vol. I, p. 472.

24 Roger North, *The Lives of the Right Hon. Francis North, Baron Guilford...*, eds. Henry Roscoe, Montagu North, (London, 1826), vol. II, p. 57.

25 *Memoirs of Sir John Reresby*, ed. A. Browning (Glasgow, 1936), p. 411.

26 Edward Hyde, Earl of Clarendon, *The History of the Rebellion and Civil Wars in England begun in the year 1641* (Oxford, 1958 [1702]), vol. I, p. xxxii.

27 Ibid., p. xxvii.

28 Ibid., p. xxv.

29 Burnet, *History of His Own Time*, vol. V, p. 45.

30 D. W. Hayton, 'Constituencies and Elections', in: *The History of Parliament: The House of Commons 1690–1715*, eds. D. Hayton, E. Cruickshanks, S. Handley (Martlesham, 2002). History of Parliament Online, https://www.historyofparliamentonline.org/volume/1690-1715/survey/constituencies-and-elections

31 This section is chiefly based on T. J. Denman, *The political debate over war strategy, 1689–1712* (Unpublished PhD thesis, 1985). [Apollo, University of Cambridge Repository]. https://doi.org/10.17863/CAM.11484, part III, ch. 1; and Speck, *The Birth of Britain*, ch. 2.

32 This section is chiefly based on Bennett, *The Tory Crisis*, chs. 1–3; Kenyon, *Revolution Principles*, ch. 6; Geoffrey Holmes, 'Religion and Party in Late Stuart England' in Geoffrey Holmes,

Politics, Religion and Society in England, 1679–1742 (London, 1986), pp. 181–215; and M. Goldie, 'The nonjurors, episcopacy, and the origins of the convocation controversy', in E. Cruickshanks, ed., *Ideology and Conspiracy: Aspects of Jacobitism, 1689–1759* (Edinburgh: Edinburgh University Press, 1982).

33 Bennett, *The Tory Crisis*, pp. 15–16.

34 Cited in Kenyon, *Revolution Principles*, p. 86.

35 Bennett, *The Tory Crisis*, p. 49.

36 Holmes, 'Religion and Party', p. 195.

37 Daniel Defoe, *The opinion of a known Dissenter on the bill for preventing occasional conformity* (London, 1702).

38 Henry Sacheverell, *The political union. A discourse shewing the dependance of government on religion in general: and of the English monarchy on the Church of England in particular* (Oxford, 1702), p. 48.

39 Ibid., p. 49.

40 Ibid., p. 59.

41 Cited in Holmes, 'Religion and Party', p. 190.

42 Cited in W. A. Speck, *Tory & Whig: The Struggle in the Constituencies, 1701–1715* (London, 1970), p. 89.

43 *The evidence given at the bar of the House of Commons, upon the complaint of Sir John Pakington, against Wiliam [sic] Lord Bishop of Worcester and Mr. Lloyd, his son. Together With the proceedings of the House of Commons thereupon* (London, 1702), p. 8.

44 Ibid., p. 17.

45 *Cobbett's Parliamentary History of England*, vol. VI, p. 53.

Chapter 5

The secondary sources upon which the narrative of this chapter is chiefly based are as follows:

Edward Gregg, *Queen Anne* (New Haven, 2001 [1980])

Geoffrey Holmes, *British Politics in the Age of Anne* (London, 1967)

J. R. Jones, *Marlborough* (Cambridge, 1993)

Roy A. Sundstrom, *Sidney Godolphin: Servant of State* (London, 1992)

W. A. Speck, *The Birth of Britain: A New Nation, 1700–1710* (Oxford, 1994)

George Macaulay Trevelyan, *England Under Queen Anne: Blenheim* (London 1948 [1930])

1 Andrew A. Hanham, 'BROMLEY, William II (1663–1732), of Baginton, Warws. and St. James's, Westminster' in: *The History of Parliament: The House of Commons 1690–1715*, eds. D. Hayton, E. Cruickshanks, S. Handley (Martlesham, 2002). History of Parliament Online, https://www.historyofparliamentonline.org/volume/1690-1715/member/bromley-william-ii-1663-1732

2 *Cobbett's Parliamentary History of England*, vol. VI, p. 169.

3 Alexander Cunningham, *The History of Great Britain: From the Revolution in 1688 to the Accession of George I* (London, 1787), vol. I, p. 318.

4 *A Letter to a Peer, Concerning the Bill Against Occasional Conformity: Wherein Among Several Others, a Late Pamphlet, Entitul'd, The Case of Toleration Recogniz'd, is More Distinctly Consider'd* (London, 1702), p. 18.

5 *Cobbett's Parliamentary History of England*, vol. VI, p. 80.

6 Ibid., p. 73.

7 Defoe, *The shortest-Way with the dissenters: or proposals for the establishment of the church* (London, 1702), p. 20.

8 Ibid.

9   Ibid., p. 18.

10 This and subsequent paragraph based on Richard West, *The Life & Strange Surprising Adventures of Daniel Defoe* (London, 1997), pp. 72–5.

11 Cited in Speck, *The Birth of Britain*, p. 46.

12 Cited in Sundstrom, *Sidney Godolphin*, p. 99.

13 Cited in Speck, *The Birth of Britain*, p. 53.

14 Cited in Horwitz, *Revolution Politicks*, p. 177.

15 This paragraph is based on Mark Knights, *Representation and Misrepresentation in Later Stuart Britain: Partisanship and Print Culture* (Oxford, 2005), ch. 5.

16 This and the next paragraph are based on J. A. Downie, *Robert Harley and the Press: Propaganda and public opinion in the age of Swift and Defoe* (Cambridge, 1979), pp. 60–3.

17 Gregg, *Queen Anne*, p. 177.

18 Ibid.

19 *Cobbett's Parliamentary History of England*, vol. VI, p. 151.

20 Ibid., p. 155.

21 Marlborough to the Duchess, 10th December 1703(?) in H. L. Snyder, ed., *The Marlborough–Godolphin correspondence*, vol. 1 (Oxford, 1975; Oxford Scholarly Editions Online, 2013). doi:10.1093/actrade/9780199670185.book.1

22 Charles Davenant, *Essays upon peace at home, and war abroad. In two parts. Part I.* (London, 1704), p. 240.

23 D. W. Hayton, 'DAVENANT, Charles (1656–1714), of Red Lion Square, Mdx.' in *The History of Parliament: The House of Commons 1690–1715*, eds. D. Hayton, E. Cruickshanks, S. Handley (Martlesham, 2002). History of Parliament Online, https://www.historyofparliamentonline. org/volume/1690-1715/member/davenant-charles-1656-1714

24 Swift to the Rev. William Tisdall, London, 16th December 1703, in *The Correspondence of Jonathan Swift*, vol. 1, ed. H. Williams (Oxford, 1963; Oxford Scholarly Editions Online, 2014). Doi:10.1093/actrade/9780199670093.book.1

25 'A history of great British storms', the *Guardian*, 10th March 2008 (https://www.the guardian. com/ world/2008/mar/10/weather)

26 Trevelyan, *England Under Queen Anne: Blenheim*, p. 310.

27 Daniel Defoe, *The Storm Or, a Collection of the Most Remarkable Casualties and Disasters which Happen'd in the Late Dreadful Tempest, Both by Sea and Land* (London, 1704), p. 68.

28 Cited in Maximillian E. Novak, *Daniel Defoe: Master of Fictions: His Life and Ideas* (Oxford, 2001), p. 219.

29 Burnet, *History of His Own Time*, vol. V, p. 109.

30 Cited in Trevelyan, *England Under Queen Anne: Blenheim,* p. 331.

31 The account of Ashby versus White is based on Eveline Cruickshanks, 'Ashby v. White: the case of the men of Aylesbury, 1701–4' in Clyve Jones, ed., *Party Management in Parliament, 1660–1784* (Leicester, 1984), pp. 87–106; Trevelyan, *England Under Queen Anne: Ramillies and the Union with Scotland* (London, 1932), ch. 1.

32 *Cobbett's Parliamentary History of England*, vol. VI, p. 255.

33 Ibid., p. 300.

34 Marlborough to the Duchess, 3rd/14th June 1703, in H. L. Snyder, ed., *The Marlborough–Godolphin correspondence*, vol. 1.

35 Horwitz, *Revolution Politicks,* p. 198.

36 Cited in Sundstrom, *Sidney Godolphin*, p. 94.

37 Marlborough to the Duchess, 10th/21st June 1703, in H. L. Snyder, ed. *The Marlborough–Godolphin correspondence*, vol. 1.

38 Ibid., 9th/20th October 1704.

39 Defoe to Harley, 2nd November 1704, in Historical Manuscripts Commission. *Manuscripts of His Grace the Duke of Portland* [Hereafter Portland MSS], vol. 4 (London, 1897), p. 147.

40   The following sketch of St John is based chiefly on: H. T. Dickinson, *Bolingbroke* (London, 1970) and Stuart Handley, 'ST. JOHN, Henry II (1678–1752), of Bucklebury, Berks' in *The History of Parliament: The House of Commons 1690–1715*, eds. D. Hayton, E. Cruickshanks, S. Handley (Martlesham, 2002). History of Parliament Online, https://www.historyofparliamentonline.org/volume/1690-1715/member/st-john-henry-ii-1678-1752

41   Cited in Handley, 'ST. JOHN, Henry II'.

42   *The Letters of Philip Dormer Stanhope, Fourth Earl of Chesterfield*, ed. Bonamy Dobree (London, 1932), vol. IV, p. 1463.

43   Jonathan Swift, *Journal to Stella* (London, 1937), p. 96.

44   *The Miscellaneous Works of Oliver Goldsmith with an Account of His Life and Writings*, ed. Washington Irving (Paris, 1825), vol. IV, p. 36.

45   Cited in Dickinson, *Bolingbroke*, p. 6.

46   Swift, *Journal to Stella*, p. 216.

47   Cited in Dickinson, *Bolingbroke*, p. 6.

48   Swift, *Journal to Stella*, p. 312.

49   St John to R. Harley, 16th October 1703, Portland MSS, vol. IV, p. 73.

50   Cited in Dickinson, *Bolingbroke*, p. 316 (note 26).

51   This paragraph is based on Bennett, *Tory Crisis*, ch. 5.

52   Marlborough to Godolphin, 3rd/14th August 1704, in H. L. Snyder, ed., *The Marlborough–Godolphin correspondence*, vol. 1.

53   The rest of this section is chiefly based on, H. L. Snyder, 'The Defeat of the Occasional Conformity Bill and the Tack: A Study in the Techniques of Parliamentary Management in the Reign of Queen Anne'. *Historical Research*, 41, 1968: 172–186. https://doi.org/10.1111/j.1468-2281.1968.tb01247.x

54   Cited in Speck, *The Birth of Britain*, p. 77.

55   Cited in ibid.

56   *The London Diaries of William Nicolson Bishop of Carlisle, 1702–1718*, eds. Clyve Jones and Geoffrey Holmes (Oxford, 1985), p. 238.

57   Cited in Snyder, 'The Defeat of the Occasional Conformity Bill. . .', p. 185.

58   This second part of the account of Ashby versus White is based on Eveline Cruickshanks; Trevelyan, *England Under Queen Anne: Ramillies and the Union with Scotland*, ch. 1; and Robbins, *The Earl of Wharton and Whig Party Politics*, ch. 8.

59   Robbins, *The Earl of Wharton and Whig Party Politics*, p. 190.

60   Ibid.

61   Burnet, *History of His Own Time*, vol. V, p. 194.

62   *Cobbett's Parliamentary History of England*, vol. VI, p. 437.

63   The account of the 1705 election is based chiefly on Speck, *Tory & Whig*, ch. 7; D. W. Hayton, 'Constituencies and Elections'; James O. Richards, *Party Propaganda Under Queen Anne: The General Elections of 1702–1713* (Athens, Georgia, 1972), ch. 2; Trevelyan, *England Under Queen Anne: Ramillies and the Union with Scotland*, pp. 25–32.

64   Cited in Richards, *Party Propaganda*, p. 60.

65   *The Character of a Tacker* (1705?), p. 1.

66   Ibid., p. 2.

67   Trevelyan, *England Under Queen Anne: Ramillies and the Union with Scotland*, pp. 27–8.

68   Ibid., p. 27.

69   Cited in Geoffrey Holmes and W. A. Speck, eds., *The Divided Society: Party Conflict in England, 1694–1716* (London, 1970 [1967]), p. 85.

70   Cited in Sundstrom, *Sidney Godolphin*, p. 147.

71   Marlborough to Godolphin, 25th June/6th July 1705, in H. L. Snyder, ed., *The Marlborough–Godolphin correspondence*, vol. 1.

72   Cited in Gregg, *Queen Anne*, p. 208.

73   Cited in Hill, *The Growth of Parliamentary Parties,* p. 104.

74   Cited in Gregg, *Queen Anne*, p. 204.

75   Ibid.

76   Andrew A. Hanham, 'Oxford University' in *The History of Parliament: The House of Commons 1690–1715*, eds. D. Hayton, E. Cruickshanks, S. Handley (Martlesham, 2002). History of Parliament Online, https://www.historyofparliamentonline.org/volume/1690-1715/constituencies/oxford-university

77   Memorial of the Church of England (London, 1705), p. 6. This account of the controversy over the Memorial of the Church of England draws on Downie, *Robert Harley and the Press,* ch. 4 and Joseph Hone, *The Paper Chase: The Printer, the Spymaster, & the Hunt for the Rebel Pamphleteers* (London, 2022 [2020]).

78   Ibid., p. 3.

79   Ibid., p. 20.

80   Ibid., p. 8.

81   *The Life of John Sharp, D.D. Lord Archbishop of York*, ed. Thomas Newcome (London, 1825), vol. I, p. 366.

82   Marlborough to Godolphin, 13rd/24th August 1705 in H. L. Snyder, ed., *The Marlborough–Godolphin correspondence*, vol. 1.

83   Cited in Trevelyan, *England Under Queen Anne: Ramillies and the Union with Scotland*, p. 86n.

84   *Cobbett's Parliamentary History of England*, vol. VI, p. 452.

85   Ibid., p. 481

86   *The House of Lords, 1660–1715*, ed. Ruth Paley, vol. III (Cambridge, 2016), p. 567.

87   See the footnote in Burnet, *History of His Own Time*, vol. V, p. 242.

88   Ibid.

89   Ibid.

90   *Cobbett's Parliamentary History of England*, vol. VI, p. 509.

Chapter 6

1   John Ashton, *Social Life in the Reign of Queen Anne* (London, 1882), vol. I, pp. 169–172.

2   Addison and Swift, *The Spectator,* vol. I (London, 1950 [1907]), no. 81, p. 253.

3   This section and subsequent other electoral sections of this chapter are heavily based on W. A. Speck, *Tory & Whig*; D. W. Hayton, 'Constituencies and Elections'; and Geoffrey Holmes, 'The Electorate and the National Will in the First Age of Party', in Geoffrey Holmes, *Politics, Religion and Society in England, 1679–1742* (London, 1986), pp. 1–33. They are particularly heavily based on David Hayton's majestic survey of the electoral scene of this era.

4   Holmes, 'The Electorate and the National Will', p. 23.

5   D. W. Hayton, 'Heytesbury' in *The History of Parliament: The House of Commons 1690–1715*, eds. D. Hayton, E. Cruickshanks, S. Handley (Martlesham, 2002). History of Parliament Online, https://www.historyofparliamentonline.org/volume/1690-1715/constituencies/heytesbury

6   S. W. Baskerville, P. Adman and K. F. Beedham, 'The Dynamics of Landlord Influence in English County Elections, 1701–1734: The Evidence from Cheshire' in *Parliamentary History*, 12: 126–142. https://doi.org/10.1111/j.1750-0206.1993.tb00194.x, p. 130.

7   This paragraph is based on ibid.

8   Eveline Cruickshanks and Richard Harrison, 'Appleby' in *The History of Parliament: The House of Commons 1690–1715*, eds. D. Hayton, E. Cruickshanks, S. Handley (Martlesham, 2002). History of Parliament Online, https://www.historyofparliamentonline.org/volume/1690-1715/constituencies/appleby

9   D. W. Hayton, 'Weobley', in *The History of Parliament: The House of Commons 1690–1715*, eds. D. Hayton, E. Cruickshanks, S. Handley (Martlesham, 2002). History of Parliament Online, https://www.historyofparliamentonline.org/volume/1690-1715/constituencies/weobley

10   Hayton, 'Constituencies and Elections'.
11   Cited in D. W. Hayton, 'Shrewsbury' in *The History of Parliament: The House of Commons 1690–1715*, eds. D. Hayton, E. Cruickshanks, S. Handley (Martlesham, 2002). History of Parliament Online, https://www.historyofparliamentonline.org/volume/1690-1715/constituencies/shrewsbury
12   T. H. B. Oldfield, *The Representative History of Great Britain and Ireland* (London, 1816), vol. III, p. 515.
13   Hayton, 'Constituencies and Elections'.
14   Ibid.
15   Eveline Cruickshanks and Richard Harrison, 'Chester' in *The History of Parliament: The House of Commons 1690–1715*, eds. D. Hayton, E. Cruickshanks, S. Handley (Martlesham, 2002). History of Parliament Online, https://www.historyofparliamentonline.org/volume/1690-1715/constituencies/chester
16   Burnet, *History of His Own Time*, vol. VI, p. 224.
17   Hayton, 'Constituencies and Elections'.
18   Cited in Speck, *Tory & Whig*, pp. 58–9.
19   Eveline Cruickshanks and Richard Harrison, 'Appleby'.
20   Hayton, 'Constituencies and Elections'.
21   D. W. Hayton, 'Cambridgeshire' in *The History of Parliament: The House of Commons 1690–1715*, eds. D. Hayton, E. Cruickshanks, S. Handley (Martlesham, 2002). History of Parliament Online, https://www.historyofparliamentonline.org/volume/1690-1715/constituencies/cambridgeshire
22   Holmes and Speck, eds., *The Divided Society*, p. 158.
23   Ibid., pp. 159–60.
24   Speck, *Tory & Whig*, p. 61.
25   Hayton, 'Constituencies and Elections'.
26   Portland MSS, vol. IV, p. 641.
27   Hayton, 'Constituencies and Elections'.
28   Cited in de Krey, *A Fractured Society*, p. 114.
29   Trevelyan, *England Under Queen Anne: Ramillies and the Union with Scotland*, p. 27.
30   Hayton, 'Constituencies and Elections'.
31   Ibid.
32   Mark Knights, *Representation and Misrepresentation*, p. 193.
33   Cited in Speck, *Tory & Whig*, p. 99.
34   Harris, *Politics under the Later Stuarts*, p. 191.
35   Charles Leslie, *The Rehearsal*, no. 42, 12th May 1705.
36   This account is mainly based on Andrew A. Hanham, 'Coventry' in *The History of Parliament: The House of Commons 1690–1715*, eds. D. Hayton, E. Cruickshanks, S. Handley (Martlesham, 2002). History of Parliament Online, https://www.historyofparliamentonline.org/volume/1690-1715/constituencies/coventry
37   *Journals of the House of Commons* (London, 1803), vol. 15, p. 277.
38   Hayton, 'Constituencies and Elections'.
39   Hanham, 'Coventry'.
40   Perry Gauci, 'Westminster' in *The History of Parliament: The House of Commons 1690–1715*, eds. D. Hayton, E. Cruickshanks, S. Handley (Martlesham, 2002). History of Parliament Online, https://www.historyofparliamentonline.org/volume/1690-1715/constituencies/westminster
41   Eveline Cruickshanks/Ivar McGrath, 'Scarborough', in *The History of Parliament: The House of Commons 1690–1715*, eds. D. Hayton, E. Cruickshanks, S. Handley (Martlesham, 2002). History of Parliament Online, https://www.historyofparliamentonline.org/volume/1690-1715/constituencies/scarborough

42 Robbins, *The Earl of Wharton and Whig Party Politics*, chs. 4 & 7.

43 Ibid.

44 Speck, *Tory & Whig*, p. 11.

45 The rest of this section is based on Holmes, *British Politics*, chs. 7, 8 & 9 and D. W. Hayton, 'The Politics of the House' in *The History of Parliament: The House of Commons 1690–1715*, eds. D. Hayton, E. Cruickshanks, S. Handley (Martlesham, 2002). History of Parliament Online, https://www.historyofparliamentonline.org/volume/1690-1715/survey/politics-house

46 Hayton, 'The Politics of the House'.

47 Ibid.

48 Holmes, *British Politics*, p. 307.

49 Ibid., p. 304.

50 This section on the Kit-Cat Club is chiefly based on Ophelia Field, *The Kit-Cat Club* (London, 2009 [2008]).

51 William Shippen, *Faction Display'd* (London, 1704), p. 15.

52 Aytoun Ellis, *The Penny Universities: A History of the Coffee-Houses* (London, 1956), chs. 3 & 4; W. A. Speck, *Society and Literature in England, 1700–60* (London, 1983), p. 194.

53 Cited in Howard William Troyer, *Ned Ward of Grubstreet: A Study of Sub-Literary London in the Eighteenth Century* (Cambridge, Mass., 1946), p. 43.

54 *Character of a Coffee-House* (London, 1673), https://www.digitens.org/en/anthologies/character-coffee-house-1673.html

55 Addison and Swift, *The Spectator*, vol. 3, no. 457, pp. 222–3.

56 Cited in Bryant Lillywhite, *London Coffee Houses: A Reference Book of Coffee Houses of the Seventeenth, Eighteenth and Nineteenth Centuries* (London, 1973), p. 502.

57 Cowan, *The Social Life of Coffee*, p. 173.

58 Knights, *Representation and Misrepresentation*, pp. 226–7.

59 Holmes, *British Politics*, p. 30.

60 Knights, *Representation and Misrepresentation*, p. 227.

61 Goldie, *Tory Political Thought*, p. 39.

62 Ibid., p. 38.

63 Ibid., p. 44.

64 Ibid., p. 188.

65 Cited in ibid., p. 43.

66 Henry L. Snyder, 'Newsletters in England, 1689–1715: with Special Reference to John Dyer – A Byway in the History of England' in *Newsletters to Newspapers: Eighteenth-Century Journalism*, eds. Donovan H. Bond and W. Reynolds McLeod (Morgantown: School of Journalism, W. Va., 1977), pp. 3–19, p. 9.

67 *Remarks and Collections of Thomas Hearne*, vol. II, p. 31.

68 Snyder, 'Newsletters in England', p. 5.

69 Holmes, *British Politics*, pp. 25–6.

70 Ned Ward, *The Secret History of the Calves-Head Club, Complt*, 6th edition (London, 1706), p. 66.

71 Troyer, *Ned Ward of Grubstreet*, pp. 115–118.

72 Lord Macaulay, *The History of England from the Accession of James II*, vol. IV (London, 1861), p. 459.

73 Holmes, *British Politics*, p. 26.

74 Ibid.

75 Ibid., p. 23.

76 The following section on the theatre is based on John Loftis, *The Politics of Drama in Augustan England* (Oxford, 1963), chs. 2 & 3.

77 Ibid., p. 3.

78   Ibid., p. 41
79   Speck, *Tory & Whig,* p. 93.
80   Ibid.
81   The following section on the opera is based on Thomas McGeary, *Opera and Politics in Queen Anne's Britain, 1705–1714* (Martlesham, 2022), ch. 3.
82   Cited in ibid., p. 121.
83   This section on the politics of wine is chiefly based on Charles Ludington, '"Be sometimes to your country true": The politics of wine in England, 1660–1714' in: Adam Smyth, ed., *A Pleasing Sinne: Drink and Conviviality in Early Modern England* (Woodbridge, 2004), pp. 89–106.
84   Ibid., p. 91.
85   Addison and Swift, *The Spectator,* vol. I, no. 43, p. 129.
86   The rest of this section is chiefly based on Knights, *Representation and Misrepresentation* and de Krey, *A Fractured Society.*
87   Knights, *Representation and Misrepresentation,* p. 371.
88   This and the next two paragraphs are chiefly based on de Krey, *A Fractured Society.*
89   This paragraph and the rest of this section is based on chiefly on Lawrence Klein, *Shaftesbury and the Culture of Politeness: Moral Discourse and Cultural Politics in Early Eighteenth-Century England* (Cambridge, 1994), especially part II.

Chapter 7

The secondary sources upon which the narrative of this chapter is chiefly based are as follows:

Edward Gregg, *Queen Anne* (New Haven, 2001 [1980])

Geoffrey Holmes, *British Politics in the Age of Anne* (London, 1967)

W. A. Speck, *The Birth of Britain: A New Nation, 1700–1710* (Oxford, 1994)

Christopher A. Robbins, *The Earl of Wharton and Whig Party Politics* (Lampeter, 1992)

P. W. J. Riley, *The Union of England and Scotland: A Study in Anglo-Scottish Politics of the Eighteenth Century* (Manchester, 1978)

P. W. J. Riley, 'The Union of 1707 as an Episode in English Politics', *The English Historical Review* LXXXIV.CCCXXXII (1969): 498–527.

Roy A. Sundstrom, *Sidney Godolphin: Servant of State* (London, 1992)

George Macaulay Trevelyan, *England Under Queen Anne: Ramillies and the Union with Scotland* (London, 1932)

1   *The Correspondence of Henry Hyde, Earl of Clarendon and of his Brother, Laurence Hyde, Earl of Rochester,* ed. Samuel Weller Singer (London, 1828), vol. II, pp. 459–60.
2   Burnet, *History of His Own Time,* vol. V, p. 231.
3   Ibid., p. 234.
4   Cited in Gregg, *Queen Anne,* p. 211.
5   Ibid.
6   This section and the following two are based heavily on P. W. J. Riley, *The Union of England and Scotland;* P. W. J. Riley, 'The Union of 1707 as an Episode in English Politics'; and Speck, *The Birth of Britain;* consulting also Michael Fry, *The Union: England, Scotland and the Treaty of 1707* (Edinburgh, 2006); and Allan I. Macinnes, *Union and Empire: The Making of the United Kingdom in 1707* (Cambridge, 2007).
7   *Cobbett's Parliamentary History of England,* vol. VI, pp. 172–3.
8   See note c, Burnet, *History of His Own Time,* vol. V, p. 182.
9   *Cobbett's Parliamentary History of England,* vol. VI, p. 560.
10   Robin Eagles, 'SPENCER, Charles (1675-1722)' (https://dev.historyofparliamentonline.org/lord-biography/spencer-charles-1675-1722)

11 Cited in Harris, *A Passion for Government*, p. 82.
12 Ibid.
13 Godolphin to Marlborough, 16th April 1706, in H. L. Snyder, ed., *The Marlborough–Godolphin correspondence*, vol. 1.
14 Cited in Trevelyan, *England Under Queen Anne: Ramillies and the Union with Scotland*, p. 82.
15 Cited in Gregg, *Queen Anne*, p. 221.
16 Cited in ibid., p. 222.
17 Cited in ibid., p. 223.
18 Cited in ibid.
19 Cited in ibid., p. 224.
20 Godolphin to Harley, September 1705, in Commission on Historical Manuscripts, *Calendar of the manuscripts of the Marquis of Bath, preserved at Longleat, Wiltshire, Royal* [Subsequently Bath MSS] (London, 1904), vol. I, p.76.
21 Op. cit.
22 The rest of this section, and the next, is chiefly based on Gregg, *Queen Anne*, chs. 9 & 10; G. V. Bennett, 'Robert Harley, the Godolphin Ministry, and the Bishoprics Crisis of 1707', *The English Historical Review* 82, no. 325 (1967): 726–46. http://www.jstor.org/stable/561098; and Geoffrey Holmes and W. A. Speck, 'The Fall of Harley in 1708 Reconsidered', in *The English Historical Review* 80, no. 317 (1965): 673–98. http://www.jstor.org/stable/559307
23 Cited in Bennett, 'Robert Harley, the Godolphin Ministry, and the Bishoprics Crisis of 1707', p. 737.
24 Cited in Robbins, *The Earl of Wharton and Whig Party Politics*, p. 219.
25 Marlborough to the Queen, 7th/18th July 1707, H. L. Snyder, ed., *The Marlborough–Godolphin correspondence*, vol. 2.
26 *The Private Diary of William, First Earl Cowper, Lord Chancellor of England* (Eton, 1833), p. 33.
27 Cited in Bennett, 'Robert Harley, the Godolphin Ministry, and the Bishoprics Crisis of 1707', p. 744.
28 Cited in ibid., p. 745.
29 *Cobbett's Parliamentary History of England*, vol. VI, p. 608.
30 The Earl of Godolphin to Robert Harley, 1707–8, 30th January, Bath MSS, p. 190.
31 Holmes and Speck, 'The Fall of Harley in 1708 Reconsidered', p. 695.
32 Cited in ibid.
33 Cited in ibid., p. 696.
34 Ibid., p. 697.
35 This paragraph is based on Hamilton, *The Backstairs Dragon*, pp. 104–6.

Chapter 8

The secondary sources upon which the narrative of this chapter is chiefly based are as follows:

Edward Gregg, *Queen Anne* (New Haven, 2001 [1980])
Elizabeth Hamilton, *The Backstairs Dragon* (New York, 1969)
Brian W. Hill, *Robert Harley: Speaker, Secretary of State and Premier Minister* (New Haven, 1988)
Christopher Robbins, *The Earl of Wharton and Whig Party Politics* (Lampeter, 1992)
W. A. Speck, *The Birth of Britain: A New Nation, 1700–1710* (Oxford, 1994)
Roy A. Sundstrom, *Sidney Godolphin: Servant of State* (London, 1992)
George Macaulay Trevelyan, *England Under Queen Anne: Ramillies and the Union with Scotland* (London, 1932)

1 *The Lockhart Papers* (London, 1817), vol. I, p. 224.
2 Ibid.

3   *Letters Illustrative of the Reign of William III. From 1696 to 1708. Addressed to the Duke of Shrewsbury, by James Vernon,* [Henceforward The Vernon Letters] ed. G. P. R. James (London 1841), vol. III, p. 344.

4   Edward Harley, *Memoirs of the Harley Family, especially of Robert Harley, first Earl of Oxford, by Edward Harley, Auditor of the Exchequer* in Portland MS, vol. V, p. 648.

5   Hamilton, *Backstairs Dragon*, p. 115.

6   Harley, *Memoirs of the Harley Family,* p. 648.

7   Ibid.

8   Ibid.

9   Hamilton, *Backstairs Dragon*, pp. 105–6.

10 *The Vernon Letters*, vol. III, p. 362.

11 Hamilton, *Backstairs Dragon*, p. 119.

12 Cited in Speck, *The Birth of Britain*, p. 140.

13 Quoted in Gregg, p. 262.

14 *Advice to the Electors of Great Britain; occasioned by the intended Invasion from France* (London, 1708), p. 1.

15 Ibid., p. 2.

16 Cited in H. T. Dickinson, *Henry St. John and the Struggle for the Leadership of the Tory Party, 1702–14* (Unpublished PhD thesis, Newcastle, 1967), p. 366.

17 Robbins, *The Earl of Wharton and Whig Party Politics,* p. 223.

18 Holmes, *British Politics*, p. 353.

19 Handley, 'ST. JOHN, Henry II'.

20 Dickinson, *Bolingbroke,* pp. 63–4.

21 Handley, 'ST. JOHN, Henry II'.

22 Gregg, *Queen Anne*, p. 2264.

23 Henry St. John to Robert Harley, 11th October 1708, in Bath MSS, vol. I, p. 191.

24 Ibid., p. 192.

25 H. T. Dickinson, *Henry St. John and the Struggle for the Leadership of the Tory Party, 1702–14,* p. 377.

26 Cited in Calyton Roberts, *The Growth of Responsible Government in Stuart England* (Cambridge, 1966), p. 298.

27 William Bromley to Robert Harley, 18th September 1708 in Portland MSS, vol. IV, pp. 504–5.

28 Ibid.

29 Downie, *Robert Harley and the Press*, p. 105.

30 This paragraph and the next two are chiefly based on Hamilton, *Backstairs Dragon*, p. 123 and Hill, *Robert Harley*, p. 120.

31 Lord Sunderland to the Duke of Newcastle, undated letter, *Original Letters Illustrative of English History*, ed. Henry Ellis (London, 1827), 2nd series, vol. IV, p. 252.

32 Ibid., p. 253.

33 Burnet, *History of His Own Time*, vol. V, p. 393, footnote h.

34 Cited in Speck, *The Birth of Britain,* p. 151.

35 This section is chiefly based on Gregg, *Queen Anne*, ch. 10.

36 William Coxe, *Memoirs of John Duke of Marlborough with his Original Correspondence* (London, 1820), vol. iv, p. 363.

37 Henry L. Snyder, 'The Duke of Marlborough's Request Of His Captain-Generalcy For Life: A Re-Examination', *Journal of the Society for Army Historical Research*, vol. 45, no. 182, 1967, pp. 67–83. http://www.jstor.org/stable/44229151, p. 70.

38 Cited in Gregg, *Queen Anne*, p. 237.

39 Cited in Hamilton, *Backstairs Dragon*, p. 126.

40 Cited in Harris, *A Passion for Government*, p. 141.

41   Cited in Gregg, *Queen Anne*, p. 274.

42   Cited in ibid., p. 272.

43   Cited in ibid., p. 275.

44   Ibid., p. 277.

45   Ibid., p. 278.

46   Ibid., p. 282.

47   Cited in Trevelyan, *England Under Queen Anne: Ramillies and the Union with Scotland*, p. 394.

48   This paragraph is based on ibid., pp. 394–5.

49   The rest of this section is chiefly based on Hill, *Robert Harley*, pp. 122–3.

50   This section is based chiefly on H. T. Dickinson, 'The Poor Palatines and the Parties', *The English Historical Review* 82, no. 324 (1967): 464–85. http://www.jstor.org/stable/559423

51   *Cobbett's Parliamentary History of England*, vol. VI, pp. 782.

52   Ibid.

53   Ibid., p. 781.

54   Cited in Dickinson, 'The Poor Palatines', p. 473.

55   *The Palatines Catechism, Or, A True Description of their Camps at Black-Heath and Camberwell* (London, 1709), p. 4.

56   Dickinson, 'The Poor Palatines', p. 476.

57   Robin Eagles, 'The "Poor Palatines" – political ramifications of eighteenth century migration', https://thehistoryofparliament.wordpress.com/2015/09/03/the-poor-palatines-political-ramifications-of-eighteenth-century-migration/

58   Cited in Dickinson, 'The Poor Palatines', p. 477.

59   Richard Holmes, *Marlborough: England's Fragile Genius* (London, 2008), pp.409–10.

60   Trevelyan, *England Under Queen Anne: Ramillies and the Union with Scotland*, p. 39.

61   The rest of this section is based chiefly on Henry L. Snyder, 'The Duke of Marlborough's Request of His Captain-Generalcy For Life: A Re-Examination', *Journal of the Society for Army Historical Research*, vol. 45, no. 182 (Summer, 1967), pp. 67–83 and Gregg, *Queen Anne*, pp. 286–7.

62   Cited in Holmes, *Marlborough*, p. 411.

63   This section is chiefly based on Trevelyan, *England Under Queen Anne: The Peace and the Protestant Succession*, ch. 1.

64   Marlborough to the Duchess, 11th September 1709, in H. L. Snyder, ed., *The Marlborough–Godolphin correspondence*, vol. 3 (Oxford, 1975).

65   Cited in Holmes, *Marlborough*, p. 433.

66   Cited in ibid.

67   Cited in Gregg, *Queen Anne*, p. 289.

68   This section is chiefly based on Gregg, *Queen Anne*, pp. 289–296.

69   Cited in ibid., p. 295.

70   Ibid., pp. 292–3.

71   Ibid., p. 292.

72   Ibid., p. 293.

73   Cited in Henry L. Snyder, 'Queen Anne versus the Junto: The Effort to Place Orford at the Head of the Admiralty in 1709', *Huntington Library Quarterly*, vol. 35, no. 4, 1972, pp. 323–42, p. 337.

74   This paragraph and the next are chiefly based on Henry L. Snyder, 'Queen Anne versus the Junto'.

Chapter 9

The secondary sources upon which the narrative of this chapter is chiefly based are as follows:

G. V. Bennett, *The Tory Crisis in Church and State, 1688–1730: The Career of Francis Atterbury, Bishop of Rochester*, ch. 6 (Oxford, 1975)

Clayton Roberts, 'The Fall of the Godolphin Ministry', *Journal of British Studies* 22, no. 1 (1982): 71–93. http://www.jstor.org/stable/175657

Edward Gregg, *Queen Anne* (New Haven, 2001)

Hill, *Robert Harley: Speaker, Secretary of State and Premier Minister* (New Haven, 1988)

Geoffrey Holmes, *The Trial of Doctor Sacheverell* (London, 1973) (The account of the man and the trial is based heavily on this book)

J. P. Kenyon, *Revolution Principles,* ch. 8 (Cambridge, 1977)

The Tryal of Dr Henry Sacheverell before the House of Peers for High Crimes and Misdemeanours (London, 1710) [Hereafter '*The Tryal*']

1   Cited in Holmes, *The Trial*, p. 63.

2   William Bisset, *The Modern Fanatick* (London, 1710), p. 18.

3   Ibid., p. 63.

4   Ibid.

5   *Remarks and Collections of Thomas Hearne,* vol. II, p. 229 – I am indebted to the translation of this passage from the Latin into English to a gentleman on Twitter whose account has now disappeared and whose name I cannot recall.

6   Cited in Holmes, *The Trial*, p. 14.

7   Ibid., p. 49.

8   This section is chiefly based on Bennett, *Tory Crisis*, ch. 9.

9   Bennett, *Tory Crisis*, p. 99.

10 Cited in Bennett, *Tory Crisis*, p. 104.

11 Benjamin Hoadly, *The Measures of Submission to the Civil Magistrate Consider'd* (London, 1710), p. 24.

12 Cited in Bennett, *Tory Crisis*, p. 106.

13 Cited in Holmes, *The Trial*, p. 31; Bennett, *Tory Crisis*, p. 105.

14 Cited in Bennett, *Tory Crisis*, pp. 106–7.

15 Ibid., p. 108.

16 Henry Sacheverell, *The Perils of False Brethren, both in Church, and State, set forth in a sermon* ... (London, 1709), p. 7.

17 Ibid., p. 9.

18 Ibid., p. 10.

19 Ibid., p. 16.

20 Ibid., p. 12.

21 Ibid.

22 Ibid.

23 Ibid., p. 13.

24 Ibid., p. 12.

25 Ibid., p. 13.

26 Ibid., p. 18.

27 Ibid., p. 20.

28 Ibid., p. 21.

29 Ibid., p. 23.

30 Kenyon, *Revolution Principles,* p. 130.

31 Holmes, *The Trial,* pp. 74–5.

32 J. Bennett to Hearne, 1st December 1709, in *Remarks and Collections of Thomas Hearnl,* vol. II, p. 317.

33 Cited in Holmes, *The Trial*, p. 78.

34 Cited in Gregg, *Queen Anne*, p. 297.

35 Holmes, *The Trial*, p. 93.

36   Cited in Rachel Carnell. *A Political Biography of Delarivier Manley.* (London, 2008), p. 13 – the rest of this section is partly based on Carnell, especially ch. 7.
37   Delarivier Manley, *Secret Memoirs and Manners of Several Persons of Quality of Both Sexes from the New Atalantis, an Island in the Mediteranean* (London, 1709), p. 22.
38   Carnell, *A Political Biography of Delarivier Manley*, p. 183.
39   Cited in Holmes, *The Trial*, p. 280.
40   Cited in ibid., p. 97.
41   Cited in Ibid., p. 96.
42   Cited in Ibid., p. 79.
43   The following account of the Regiments Crisis is based on Gregg, *Queen Anne*, pp. 300–4.
44   Cited in Holmes, *The Trial*, p. 119.
45   Mark Knights, *The Devil in Disguise: Deception, Delusion, and Fanaticism in the Early English Enlightenment* (Oxford, 2011), pp. 149–150.
46   Cited in Holmes, *The Trial*, p. 119.
47   Cited in Knights, *The Devil*, p. 150.
48   Cited in Holmes, *The Trial*, p. 119.
49   Holmes, *The Trial*, p. 120.
50   Cited in ibid., p. 128.
51   Abel Boyer, *The History of the Life & Reign of Queen Anne* (London, 1722), p. 416.
52   Cited in Holmes, *The Trial*, p. 128.
53   Cited in Holmes, *The Trial*, p. 126.
54   'The Osborn 'Account': Beinecke Library, MS S 13043', *Parliamentary History*, 31: 42–79. https://doi.org/10.1111/j.1750-0206.2012.00291.x, p. 50.
55   *The Tryal*, p. 62.
56   Ibid., p. 63.
57   Ibid., p. 58.
58   Ibid., p. 61.
59   Ibid., p. 58.
60   Cited in Holmes, *The Trial*, p. 137; 'The Osborn Account', p. 51.
61   *The Tryal*, p. 75.
62   Holmes, *The Trial*, p. 156.
63   Cited in Knights, *The Devil*, p. 152.
64   Cited in Holmes, *The Trial*, p. 161.
65   Cited in ibid., p. 170.
66   Speck, *Tory & Whig*, p. 94.
67   Cited in Knights, *The Devil*, p. 161.
68   Mark Knights, 'Introduction: The View from 1710', *Parliamentary History*, 31, 2012: 1–15, p. 6. https://doi.org/10.1111/j.1750-0206.2011.00284.x
69   Cited in Holmes, *The Trial*, p. 181.
70   *The Tryal*, p. 118.
71   Ibid., p. 246.
72   Ibid., pp. 248–9.
73   Gregg, *Queen Anne*, p. 306.
74   Cited in Holmes, *The Trial*, p. 229.
75   Ibid., p. 230.
76   For the scale of this press avalanche, see F. Madan, *A Bibliography of Dr. Henry Sacheverell* (Oxford, 1884).
77   *A collection of the addresses which have been presented to the Queen, since the impeachment of the Reverend Dr. Henry Sacheverell* (London, 1711), part II, p. 1.
78   Holmes, *The Trial*, p. 247.

79   Ibid.

80   Brian Cowan, 'Doctor Sacheverell and the Politics of Celebrity in Post-Revolutionary Britain', in Emrys D. Jones and Victoria Joule, eds., *Intimacy and Celebrity in Eighteenth-Century Culture Intimacy* (Basingstoke, 2018), pp. 111–137, p. 117.

81   *Remarks and Collections of Thomas Hearne*, vol. III, p. 20.

82   This section and the next are chiefly based on Hill, *Robert Harley*, pp.124–32; Clayton Roberts, 'The Fall of the Godolphin Ministry'; and Gregg, *Queen Anne*, ch. 12.

83   Cited in Roberts, 'The Fall of the Godolphin Ministry', p. 79.

84   Cited in ibid., p. 83.

85   Cited in Bennett, *Tory Crisis*, p. 124.

86   Ibid.

87   Cited in Gregg, *Queen Anne*, p. 319.

88   Ibid.

89   Cited in ibid., p. 321.

90   Cited in Roberts, 'The Fall of the Godolphin Ministry', p. 89.

91   Cited in ibid., p. 87.

92   Horwitz, *Revolution Politicks*, p. 222.

93   Burnet, *History of His Own Time*, vol. V, p. 16.

94   Trevelyan, *England Under Queen Anne: The Peace and the Protestant Succession*, p. 93.

95   Cited in Mary Ransome, *The General Election of 1710* (Unpublished MA thesis, London, 1938), p. 142.

96   Stuart Handley, 'STANHOPE, James (1673–1721), of London' in *The History of Parliament: The House of Commons 1690–1715*, eds. D. Hayton, E. Cruickshanks, S. Handley (Martlesham, 2002). History of Parliament Online, https://www.historyofparliamentonline.org/volume/1690-1715/member/stanhope-james-1673-1721

97   Cited in Ransome, *The General Election*, p. 141.

98   Ibid., pp. 143–4.

99   Cited in Hayton, 'Constituencies and Elections'.

100 Speck, *The Birth of Britain*, p. 191.

101 D. W. Hayton, 'Cambridgeshire' in *The History of Parliament: The House of Commons 1690–1715*, eds. D. Hayton, E. Cruickshanks, S. Handley (Martlesham, 2002). History of Parliament, https://www.historyofparliamentonline.org/volume/1690-1715/constituencies/cambridgeshire

102 Ibid.

103 Somers Tracts, vol XIII, p. 74.

104 Ibid., p. 73.

105 Ransome, *The General Election*, p. 141.

106 Hayton, 'Constituencies and Elections'.

Chapter 10

The secondary sources upon which the narrative of this chapter is chiefly based are as follows:

Sheila Biddle, *Bolingbroke and Harley* (New York, 1974)

H. T. Dickinson, *Bolingbroke* (London, 1970)

Michael Foot, *The Pen and the Sword: Jonathan Swift and the Power of the Press* (London, 1984 [1957])

Elizabeth Hamilton, *The Backstairs Dragon* (New York, 1969)

Brian W. Hill, *Robert Harley: Speaker, Secretary of State and Premier Minister* (New Haven, 1988)

Geoffrey Holmes, *The Great Ministry* (Privately printed, 2005: available at the Institute for

Historical Research)
David Noakes, *Jonathan Swift: A Hypocrite Reversed* (Oxford, 1985)
Daniel Szechi, *Jacobitism and Tory Politics, 1710–1714* (Edinburgh, 1984)

1   Downie, *Robert Harley and the Press*, p. 127.
2   Swift, *Journal to Stella*, 4th October 1710, p. 20.
3   Ibid., 21st October 1710, p. 35.
4   Cited in Dickinson, *Bolingbroke*, p. 22.
5   Swift to Archbishop King, London, 30th December 1710, in *The correspondence of Jonathan Swift*, vol. I.
6   H.T. Dickinson, 'The October Club' in *Huntington Library Quarterly*, Feb. 1970, vol. 33, no. 2, pp. 155–173, pp. 155–6 – this paragraph is based on this article.
7   Swift, *The Examiner, and Other Pieces, The Examiner* no. 14, p. 8.
8   Ibid.
9   Ibid., pp. 8–9.
10 Ibid., p. 10.
11 Ibid., *The Examiner*, no. 16, p. 19.
12 Ibid., pp. 22–3.
13 Ibid., p. 23.
14 Ibid., *The Examiner*, no. 13, p. 5.
15 Ibid.
16 Ibid.
17 Ibid., *The Examiner*, no. 21, p. 48.
18 Ibid., *The Examiner*, no. 44, p. 169.
19 Ibid.
20 Ibid., *The Examiner*, no. 15, p. 17.
21 Ibid.
22 Swift, *Journal to Stella*, 18th February 1711, p. 117.
23 Cited in Dickinson, 'The October Club', p. 156.
24 Cited in Dickinson, *Bolingbroke*, p. 78.
25 Szechi, *Jacobitism and Tory Politics*, p. 72.
26 Paula Watson and Ivar McGrathin, 'STEWART, Simeon (1685–1761), of Hartley Mauditt, Hants', in *The History of Parliament: The House of Commons 1690–1715*, eds. D. Hayton, E. Cruickshanks, S. Handley (Martlesham, 2002). History of Parliament Online, https://www.historyofparliamentonline.org/volume/1690-1715/member/stewart-simeon-1685-1761
27 Ibid.
28 Cited in Dickinson, 'The October Club', p. 159.
29 *Cobbett's Parliamentary History of England*, vol. VI, p. 1000.
30 Holmes, 'Religion and Party', p. 210.
31 Swift, *Journal to Stella*, 4th March 1711, p. 125.
32 Hamilton, *The Backstairs Dragon*, p. 178. This section is chiefly based on ibid., pp. 176–186.
33 Cited in Hamilton, *The Backstairs Dragon*, p. 181.
34 Ibid.
35 Swift to Archbishop King, London, 8th March 1711, in *The correspondence of Jonathan Swift*, vol. I.
36 *Cobbett's Parliamentary History of England*, vol. VI, p. 1007.
37 Gregg, *Queen Anne*, p. 337.
38 Swift, *Journal to Stella*, 26th March 1711, p. 137.
39 Ibid., 3rd April 1711, p. 141.
40 Ibid.

41 Ibid., 28th September 1711, p. 239.
42 Ibid., 27th August 1711, p. 221.
43 Cited in Dickinson, *Bolingbroke*, pp. 84–5.
44 Bolingbroke to the Earl of Orrery, 12th June 1711, *Letters and Correspondence, Public and Private, of the Right Honourable Henry St. John, Lord Visc. Bolingbroke . . .* , ed. Gilbert Parke, vol. I (London, 1798), p. 246.
45 Swift, *Journal to Stella*, 7th February 1712, p. 316.
46 Boyer, *The History of the Life & Reign of Queen Anne*, p. 521.
47 Arthur Maynwaring, *Remarks upon the present negotiations of peace begun between Britain and France* (London, 1711), p. 6.
48 Ibid., p. 9.
49 Ibid., p. 10.
50 Ibid., p. 9.
51 Abel Boyer, *The history of the reign of Queen Anne, digested into annals. Year the tenth* (London, 1712), p. 278.
52 This section is based on Horwitz, *Revolution Politicks*, pp. 229–233; Robbins, *The Earl of Wharton*, pp. 263–5.
53 Horwitz, *Revolution Politicks*, p. 231.
54 Cited in Robbins, *The Earl of Wharton*, p. 263.
55 Szechi, *Jacobitism and Tory Politics*, p. 106.
56 Swift, 'The Conduct of the Allies' in *Political Tracts, 1711–1713*, ed. Herbert Davis (Oxford, 1964), p. 15.
57 Ibid., p. 23.
58 Ibid., p. 20.
59 Ibid., p. 41.
60 Ibid., pp. 44–5.
61 Ibid., p. 40.
62 Swift, *Journal to Stella*, 18th December 1711, p. 288.
63 Ibid., 1st December 1711, p. 277.
64 Portland MSS, vol. 5, p. 121.
65 Cited in Foot, *The Pen and the Sword*, pp. 320–1.
66 *Cobbett's Parliamentary History of England*, vol. VI, p. 1036.
67 Horwitz, *Revolution Politicks*, p. 232.
68 Cited in Biddle, *Bolingbroke and Harley*, p. 231.
69 Robbins, *The Earl of Wharton*, p. 265.
70 Swift, *Journal to Stella*, 8 December 1711, p. 282.
71 Ibid., p. 283.
72 Ibid., 20th December 1711, p. 289.
73 Ibid., 27th December 1711, p. 292.
74 Ibid., 29th December 1711, p. 294.
75 Cited in Robbins, *The Earl of Wharton*, p. 266.
76 Cited in *Cobbett's Parliamentary History of England*, vol. VI, p. 1062.
77 Coxe, *Memoirs*, vol. VI, p. 155.

Chapter 11

The secondary sources upon which the narrative of this chapter is chiefly based are as follows:

Sheila Biddle, *Bolingbroke and Harley* (New York, 1974)

H. T. Dickinson, *Bolingbroke* (London, 1970)

Elizabeth Hamilton, *The Backstairs Dragon* (New York, 1969)

Brian W. Hill, *Robert Harley: Speaker, Secretary of State and Premier Minister* (New Haven, 1988)

Geoffrey Holmes, *The Great Ministry* (Privately printed, 2005: available at the Institute for Historical Research)

Daniel Szechi, *Jacobitism and Tory Politics, 1710–1714* (Edinburgh, 1984)

1   Coxe, *Memoirs*, vol. vi, p. 153.

2   *Cobbett's Parliamentary History of England*, vol. VI, p. 1068.

3   Swift, *Journal to Stella*, 17th January 1712, p. 305.

4   Churchill, *Marlborough*, vol. 4, p. 435.

5   Ibid., pp. 440–1.

6   *Cobbett's Parliamentary History of England*, vol. VI, p. 1077.

7   *The Examiner*, 17th January 1712, in *The Second Volume of the Examiners* (London, 1714), p. 34.

8   Cited in Downie, *Robert Harley and the Press*, p. 165.

9   Douglas Coombs, *The Conduct of the Dutch: British Opinion and the Dutch Alliance during the War of the Spanish Succession* (The Hague, 1958), p. 292.

10 Cited in ibid.

11 Peter Wentworth to Lord Berkeley of Stratton, 19th February 1712, *The Wentworth Papers*, ed. James J. Cartwright (London 1883), p. 268.

12 Ibid.

13 *Cobbett's Parliamentary History of England*, vol. VI, p. 1093.

14 This section is based on George A. Aitken, 'The Life of Dr. Arbuthnot' in *The Life and Works of John Arbuthnot*, ed. George A. Aitken (Oxford, 1892), plus 'The History of John Bull' in the same volume.

15 'The History of John Bull', p. 205.

16 Ibid., p. 203.

17 Ibid., p. 229.

18 Cited in Hill, *Robert Harley*, p. 182.

19 Cited in Gregg, *Queen Anne*, p. 356.

20 *Flying Post*, 24th May 1712–27th May 1712, *17th and 18th Century Burney Collection*. link-gale-com.ezp.lib.cam.ac.uk/apps/doc/Z2001377471/BBCN?u=cambuni&sid=bookmark-BBCN&xid=3dbaf3c0

21 Defoe to Oxford, 27th May 1712, in Portland MSS, vol. 5, p. 178.

22 *Lockhart Papers*, vol. I, p. 387.

23 Boyer, *The History of the Life & Reign of Queen Anne*, p. 570.

24 Coxe, *Memoirs*, vol. VI, p. 190.

25 Boyer, *The History of the Life & Reign of Queen Anne*, p. 570.

26 Ibid.

27 Ibid., p. 571.

28 Ibid.

29 This section is heavily based on Szechi, *Jacobitism and Tory Politics,* especially chs. 2–5 & 9.

30 Ibid., p. 47.

31 Cited in ibid., p. 93.

32 Paula Watson and Sonya Wynne, 'SHIPPEN, William (1673–1743), of Norfolk Street, London', in *The History of Parliament: The House of Commons 1690–1715*, eds. D. Hayton, E. Cruickshanks, S. Handley (Martlesham, 2002). History of Parliament Online, https://www.historyofparliamentonline.org/volume/1690-1715/member/shippen-william-1673-1743

33 Szechi, *Jacobitism and Tory Politics*, p. 98.

34   Cited in Dickinson, *Bolingbroke*, p. 100.
35   Swift, *The History of the Four Last Years of the Queen*, p. 149.
36   Thomas MacKnight, *The Life of Henry St. John, Viscount Bolingbroke* (London, 1863), p. 301.
37   Ibid., p. 305.
38   Swift, *Journal to Stella*, 15th September 1712, p. 363.
39   *Lockhart Papers*, vol. I, p. 387, p. 401.
40   This section and the next are chiefly based on Victor Stater, *High Life, Low Morals; The Duel that Shook Stuart Society* (London, 1999), especially chs. 5 & 6, and H. T. Dickinson, 'The Mohun-Hamilton Duel: Whig Conspiracy or Sham Plot?', Durham University Journal, lvii, June 1967, pp. 159–165.
41   Cited in Stater, *High Life*, p. 216.
42   Cited in ibid.
43   Ibid., p. 235.
44   Ibid., p. 241.
45   Ibid., p. 236.
46   Cited in ibid., p. 253.
47   *The Examiner*, Thursday 20th November 1712, in *The Second Volume of the Examiners* (London, 1714), p. 254.
48   The account of the Bandbox Plot is based on the account in the *Postboy*, 13th November 1712.
49   *Flying Post*, 9th December 1712–11th December 1712, *17th and 18th Century Burney Collection*. link.gale.com/apps/doc/Z2001377635/BBCN?u=cambuni&sid=bookmark-BBCN&xid=cb18f3b6
50   See Swift, *Journal to Stella*, 15th November 1712, pp. 374–5.
51   *Flying Post*, 4th November 1712–6th November 1712, *17th and 18th Century Burney Collection*. link.gale.com/apps/doc/Z2001377600/BBCN?u=cambuni&sid=bookmark-BBCN&xid=1eabee83
52   Abel Boyer, *The history of the reign of Queen Anne, digested into annals. Year the eleventh* (London, 1713), p. 295.
53   Swift, *Journal to Stella*, 8th March 1712, p. 334.
54   Ibid., 9th March 1712, p. 335.
55   'Plot upon Plot' in *Political Ballads of the Seventeenth and Eighteenth Centuries*, ed. W. Walker Wilkins (London, 1860), p. 121.
56   Gregg, *Queen Anne*, p. 354.
57   Cited in Daniel Statt, 'The Case of the Mohocks: Rake Violence in Augustan London', *Social History*, vol. 20, no. 2, 1995, pp. 179–99. http://www.jstor.org/stable/4286266, p. 194.
58   David Walther, 'Mohock scare', *The Digital Encyclopedia of British Sociability in the Long Eighteenth Century* [online], ISSN 2803–2845. https://www.digitens.org/en/notices/mohock-scare.html
59   Ibid.
60   Statt, 'The Case of the Mohocks', p. 188; Lockhart, *Memoirs*, vol. I, p. 403.
61   Robbins, *The Earl of Wharton*, p. 43.
62   Halifax to Oxford, 26th December 1712, Portland MSS, vol. V, p. 254.
63   Defoe to Oxford, 14th February 1713, Portland MSS, vol. V, p. 266.
64   Ibid.
65   Swift to Archbishop King, 28th March 1713, in *The Correspondence of Jonathan Swift*, vol. I.
66   *Evening Post*, 2nd April 1713–4th April 1713, *17th and 18th Century Burney Collection*. link.gale.com/apps/doc/Z2001368650/BBCN?u=cambuni&sid=bookmark-BBCN&xid=d53a6113
67   Swift, *The History of the Four Last Years of the Queen*, p. 167.

Endnotes

Chapter 12

The secondary sources upon which the narrative of this chapter is chiefly based are as follows:

Sheila Biddle, *Bolingbroke and Harley* (New York, 1974)
H. T. Dickinson, *Bolingbroke* (London, 1970)
Brian W. Hill, *Robert Harley: Speaker, Secretary of State and Premier Minister* (New Haven, 1988)
Geoffrey Holmes, *The Great Ministry* (Privately printed, 2005: available at the Institute for Historical Research)
Daniel Szechi, *Jacobitism and Tory Politics, 1710–1714* (Edinburgh, 1984)

1   This section is based on Trevelyan, *England Under Queen Anne: The Peace and the Protestant Succession*, pp. 270–2 and Loftis, *The Politics of Drama*, pp. 57–8.
2   Cited in ibid., Trevelyan, p. 271.
3   Ibid.
4   George Berkeley to Sir John Percival, 16th April 1713, in *Berkeley and Percival*, ed. Benjamin Rand (Cambridge, 1914), p. 114.
5   Alexander Pope to John Caryll, 30th April 1713, in *The Works of Alexander Pope*, ed. Whitwell Elwin (London, 1871), vol. VI, p. 184.
6   Ibid.
7   Viscount Bolingbroke, 'Letter to Sir William Windham', in *The Works of Lord Bolingbroke* (London, 1967 [1844]), vol. I, p. 121.
8   *Cobbett's Parliamentary History of England*, vol. VI, p. 1172.
9   Cited in Szechi, *Jacobitism and Tory Politics*, p. 121.
10 This section and the next are chiefly based – in addition to Holmes, *The Great Ministry*, ch. 6 and Dickinson, *Bolingbroke*, ch. 6 – on Perry Gauci, *The Politics of Trade: The Overseas Merchant in State and Society, 1660–1720* (Oxford, 2001), ch. 6.
11 Doohwan Ahn, 'The Anglo-French Treaty of Commerce of 1713: Tory Trade Politics and the Question of Dutch Decline', *History of European Ideas* 36.2 (2010): 167–180.
12 Trevelyan, *England Under Queen Anne: The Peace and the Protestant Succession*, p. 276.
13 Cited in Holmes, *The Great Ministry*, p. 260.
14 D. W. Hayton, 'HANMER, Thomas II (1677–1746), of Pall Mall, Westminster; Bettisfield Park, Flints.; and Mildenhall, Suff.' in *The History of Parliament: The House of Commons 1690–1715*, eds. D. Hayton, E. Cruickshanks, S. Handley (Martlesham, 2002). History of Parliament Online, https://www.historyofparliamentonline.org/volume/1690-1715/member/hanmer-thomas-ii-1677-1746.
15 Boyer, *The History of the Life & Reign of Queen Anne,* p. 638.
16 Bolingbroke to Oxford, June 1713, Portland MSS, vol. V, pp. 299–300.
17 Cited in Szechi, *Jacobitism and Tory Politics*, p. 139.
18 *Cobbett's Parliamentary History of England*, vol. VI, p. 1224.
19 Ibid.
20 Bolingbroke, 'Letter to William Windham', p. 123.
21 The following account of Atterbury's role in the events of 1713 is based upon Bennett, *Tory Crisis*, pp. 140–171.
22 Cited in Bennett, *Tory Crisis*, p. 165.
23 Cited in Gregg, *Queen Anne*, p. 370.
24 Bolingbroke to Oxford, 27th July 1713, Portland MSS, vol. V, p. 311.
25 'The Earl of Oxford's Account of Public Affairs', Portland MSS, vol. V, p. 467.
26 Cited in Holmes, *The Great Ministry*, p. 280, n. 18.
27 Cited in Gregg, *Queen Anne*, p. 373.

28   This account of the 1713 is chiefly based on Holmes, *The Great Ministry,* pp. 286–307.
29   Speck, *Tory &Whig*, p. 61.
30   Cited in Richards, *Party Propaganda*, p. 134.
31   Cited in Holmes, *The Great Ministry*, p. 301.
32   Cited in Hayton, 'Constituencies and Elections'.
33   The rest of this section is chiefly based on Szechi, *Jacobitism and Tory Politics*, ch. 7.
34   Cited in Gregg, *Queen Anne*, p. 374.
35   Swift, 'An Inquiry into the Behaviour of the Queen's Last Ministry', in *The Works of the Rev. Jonathan Swift, D.D.*, ed. John Nichols (London, 1801), vol. IV, p. 337.
36   On Bolingbroke's attitudes towards the succession and its relevance to his political strategy, see Szechi, *Jacobitism and Tory Politics*, pp. 161–4, p. 190 – these paragraphs and the rest of this book assumes Szechi's convincing account to be sound.
37   Ibid., p. 163; see also G. V. Bennett, 'English Jacobitism, 1710–1715; Myth and Reality', *Transactions of the Royal Historical Society*, 1982, vol. 32 (1982), pp. 137–151; Edward Gregg, 'Marlborough in Exile, 1712–1714', *The Historical Journal* 15, no. 4 (1972): 593–618, p. 614.
38   Cited in Dickinson, *Bolingbroke*, p. 116.
39   Cited in ibid.
40   Cited in ibid., p. 117.
41   Hamilton, *The Backstairs Dragon*, pp. 243–4.
42   Cited in D. W. Hayton, 'HARLEY, Thomas (c.1667–1738), of Kinsham Court, Herefs.' in *The History of Parliament: The House of Commons 1690–1715*, eds. D. Hayton, E. Cruickshanks, S. Handley (Martlesham, 2002). History of Parliament Online, https://www.historyofparliamentonline.org/volume/1690-1715/member/harley-thomas-1667-1738
43   Cited in Gregg, *Queen Anne*, p. 379.

Chapter 13

The secondary sources upon which the narrative of this chapter is chiefly based are as follows:

Sheila Biddle, *Bolingbroke and Harley* (New York, 1974)
H. T. Dickinson, *Bolingbroke* (London, 1970)
Brian W. Hill, *Robert Harley: Speaker, Secretary of State and Premier Minister* (New Haven, 1988)
Geoffrey Holmes, *The Great Ministry* (Privately printed, 2005: available at the Institute for Historical Research)
Daniel Szechi, *Jacobitism and Tory Politics, 1710–1714* (Edinburgh, 1984)

1   Cited in Leo Damrosch, *Jonathan Swift: His Life and His World* (New Haven, 2013), p. 181.
2   This paragraph and the next are based on Andrew A. Hanham, 'STEELE, Richard (1672–1729), of Bloomsbury Square, London, and Llangunnor, Carm.' in *The History of Parliament: The House of Commons 1690–1715*, eds. D. Hayton, E. Cruickshanks, S. Handley (Martlesham, 2002). History of Parliament Online, https://www.historyofparliamentonline.org/volume/1690-1715/member/steele-richard-1672-1729
3   Richard Steele, 'The Crisis' in *The Political Writings of Sir Richard Steele* (London, 1715), p. 179.
4   Ibid., p. 178.
5   Hanham, 'STEELE, Richard'.
6   Defoe to Oxford, 19th February 1714, in *The Correspondence of Richard Steele*, ed. Rae Blanchard (Oxford, 1968 [1941]), p. 86.
7   Cited in Nokes, *Jonathan Swift*, p. 196.
8   *Cobbett's Parliamentary History of England*, vol. VI, p. 1263.
9   Peter Wentworth to Lord Berkeley of Stratton, 5th March 1714, The *Wentworth Papers*, p. 359.

10   *Cobbett's Parliamentary History of England*, vol. VI, p. 1266.
11   Ibid., p. 1269.
12   *Lockhart Papers*, vol. I, p. 441.
13   Ibid.
14   Cited in Damrosch, *Jonathan Swift*, p. 263.
15   Cited in *The Great Ministry*, p. 360.
16   Hanham, 'BROMLEY, William II'.
17   Cited in Dickinson, *Bolingbroke*, p. 121.
18   Ibid.
19   Cited in ibid., p. 362.
20   Ibid., pp. 362–3.
21   Ibid., p. 363.
22   Cited in ibid., p. 368.
23   Hayton, 'HANMER, Thomas II'.
24   Cited in Holmes, *The Great Ministry*, p. 377.
25   Ibid.
26   Swift, 'An Inquiry into the Behaviour of the Queen's Last Ministry', p. 338.
27   Op. cit.
28   Cited in Gregg, *Queen Anne*, p. 383.
29   Swift, 'An Inquiry into the Behaviour of the Queen's Last Ministry', p. 343.
30   *Lockhart Papers*, vol. I, p. 460.
31   Ibid., p. 469.
32   This paragraph is based on Bennett, *Tory Crisis*, p. 13, p. 177.
33   Cited in ibid., p. 177.
34   Boyer, *The History of the Life & Reign of Queen Anne*, p. 704.
35   It has sometimes been thought that the proposal to revive the proclamation was Oxford's idea – this is Holmes' view in *The Great Ministry*. But see Gregg, *Queen Anne*, p. 286.
36   'Newsletter' in the *Wentworth Papers*, p. 393.
37   John Arbuthnot to Swift, 26th June 1714, in *The Correspondence of Jonathan Swift*, vol. II.
38   Handley, 'STANHOPE, James'.
39   Gregg, 'Marlborough in Exile, 1712–1714'. This and the ensuing section on negotiations between Marlborough and Harley and Bolingbroke are based on this article.
40   Cited in ibid., p. 606.
41   This paragraph is based on Gregg, *Queen Anne*, p. 387.
42   Erasmus Lewis to Swift, 6th July 1714, in *The Correspondence of Jonathan Swift*, vol. II.
43   Ibid., Erasmus Lewis to Swift, 17th July 1714.
44   Cited in Gregg, *Queen Anne*, p. 389.
45   Erasmus Lewis to Swift, 24th July 1714, in *The Correspondence of Jonathan Swift*, vol. II.
46   Cited in Gregg, *Queen Anne*, p. 391.
47   The Earl of Oxford to Swift, 27th July 1714, in *The correspondence of Jonathan Swift*, vol. II.
48   Cited in Holmes, *The Great Ministry*, p. 430.
49   Gregg, 'Marlborough in Exile, 1712–1714', pp. 615–6.
50   Cited in Dickinson, *Bolingbroke*, p. 130.
51   Gregg, *Queen Anne*, p. 392.
52   The rest of this chapter is chiefly based on Gregg, *Queen Anne*; Henry L. Snyder, 'The Last Days of Queen Anne: The Account of Sir John Evelyn Examined', *Huntington Library Quarterly* 34, no. 3 (1971): 261–76.
53   Gregg, 'Marlborough in Exile, 1712–1714', pp. 615–6; Snyder, 'The Last Days', p. 271.
54   Bolingbroke to Swift, 3rd August 1714, in *The Correspondence of Jonathan Swift*, vol. II.

Conclusion

1   Walter Sichel, *Bolingbroke and His Times* (New York, 1968), vol. I, p. 525–6.

2   Ibid., p. 525.

3   Ibid., p. 526.

4   This section is based on Geoffrey Holmes, 'Harley, St. John and the Death of the Tory Party' in Geoffrey Holmes, *Politics, Religion and Society in England, 1679–1742* and Ragnhild Hatton, *George I* (New Haven, 2001 [1978]), inc. Jeremy Black's 'Foreword to the Yale Edition'.

5   This section is based on Hill, *The Growth of Parliamentary Parties*, ch. 9; Romney R. Sedgwick, 'The General Election of 1715 and the First Whig Opposition, 1717–20' and 'The Tories', both in *The History of Parliament: The House of Commons 1715–1754*, ed. R. Sedgwick, 1970. https://www.historyofparliamentonline.org/volume/1715-1754/survey/ii-general-election-1715-and-first-whig-opposition-1717–20 & https://www.historyofparliamentonline.org/volume/1715-1754/survey/v-tories; Dickinson, *Bolingbroke*, ch. 8; and Hill, *Robert Harley*, ch. 16.

6   Sedgwick, 'The Tories'.

7   *The Miscellaneous Works of Oliver Goldsmith with an Account of His Life and Writings*, vol. IV, p. 45.

8   Ibid., p. 46.

9   Harley, *Memoirs of the Harley Family*, p. 666.

10   'Lord Oxford in the Tower' in Portland MSS, vol. V, p. 530.

11   Monod, *Jacobitism and the English People, 1688–1788* (Cambridge, 1989), p. 57.

12   Ibid., p. 58.

13   Hatton, *George I*, p. 50.

14   This paragraph is based on Monod, *Jacobitism and the English People*, pp. 173–9.

15   Ibid., p. 174.

16   Ibid., p. 176.

17   Sedgwick, 'The Tories'.

18   This section is chiefly based on Hill, *The Growth of Parliamentary Parties*, ch. 9; Romney R. Sedgwick, 'The General Election of 1715 and the First Whig Opposition, 1717–20'; Hill, *Robert Harley*, ch. 16; and Dickinson, *Bolingbroke*, ch. 8.

19   See the debate best summarised by Linda Colley, *In Defiance of Oligarchy* (Cambridge, 1982) versus Eveline Cruickshanks, *Political Untouchables: The Tories and the 45* (New York, 1979). This paragraph draws chiefly on Colley.

20   This paragraph is based on J. H. Plumb, *The Growth of Political Stability in England, 1675–1725* (London, 1967), ch. 4.

21   This section is informed by J. C. D. Clark, *English Society 1660–1832* (Cambridge, 2000 [1985]).

Index